Walras's Market Models describes and evaluates Léon Walras's models of competitive markets. The book differs from previous examinations of his work by identifying his career phases and the associated general equilibrium models, which are shown to be very different in character.

During his mature phase of theoretical activity, Walras was concerned with a competitive economy that passes through a stage of disequilibrium in the production and sales of commodities. His work on this topic was rich with theoretical innovations and provided realistic insights into economic behavior. In his last phase of theoretical activity, he tried to construct a model in which there is no hiring, production, sales, consuming, or saving in disequilibrium. The defective structure of that model and its fragmentary nature prevented it from becoming a functioning system.

Until now, the models of the two phases of Walras's theoretical work have not been subjected to an accurate analysis and evaluation. *Walras's Market Models* fills this gap.

T0312128

Walras's market models

Walras's market models

Donald A. Walker

Indiana University of Pennsylvania

CAMBRIDGE
UNIVERSITY PRESS

CAMBRIDGE UNIVERSITY PRESS
Cambridge, New York, Melbourne, Madrid, Cape Town, Singapore, São Paulo

Cambridge University Press
The Edinburgh Building, Cambridge CB2 2RU, UK

Published in the United States of America by Cambridge University Press, New York

www.cambridge.org
Information on this title: www.cambridge.org/9780521562683

First published 1996
This digitally printed first paperback version 2005

A catalogue record for this publication is available from the British Library

Library of Congress Cataloguing in Publication data

Walker, Donald A. (Donald Anthony), 1934–
Walras's market models / Donald A. Walker.

p.   cm.

Includes bibliographical references and index.

ISBN 0-521-56268-6

1. Commodity exchanges – Mathematical models.   2. Commercial
products – Mathematical models.   3. Equilibrium (Economics) –
Mathematical models.   4. Walras, Léon, 1834–1910.   I. Title.
HG6046.W28   1996
332.63′28–dc20   96-12024
                                                           CIP

ISBN-13 978-0-521-56268-3 hardback
ISBN-10 0-521-56268-6 hardback

ISBN-13 978-0-521-02295-8 paperback
ISBN-10 0-521-02295-9 paperback

To Patricia and Valerie

Contents

Part II. The models of the phase of decline

Section I. The written pledges models

Section II. Other models and conclusion

Figures

Preface

This is a new book and not simply a collection of essays. Although based on some essays, it differs from them in various ways. I have changed all of them to some degree, and I have extensively rewritten many of them so as to present the material as effectively as possible and to reflect the limited number of ways in which my views have changed since the essays were written. Moreover, I have devised titles of parts, sections, and chapters that are intended to guide the reader through the complexities of the subject matter, and I have organized the material in a way that displays clearly the phases and sequence of Léon Walras's modeling of markets. In most cases, the chapters have titles that differ from those of the essays. I have eliminated most of the repetitions that are to be found in the essays, but I found that preserving some of the repetitions is desirable.

In a general way, the book accomplishes three major tasks. First, by emphasizing the concept of models in relation to Walras's work, it becomes possible to identify many of his constructions that have until now been passed over as comments on the real economy or as brief speculations about economic relationships, or that have escaped notice altogether. The word "model" rather than "theory" will ordinarily be used in reference to Walras's work because in many instances he defined special situations not found in reality and created a variety of different hypothetical constructions relating to the same general subject matter. Second, the book reveals in broad outlines and great detail that Walras had a mature phase of theoretical activity followed by a phase of decline of his analytical powers. Recognition of this circumstance is enormously liberating and energizing for the historian of Walrasian economic thought. Everything falls into place. It becomes clear that Walras put the models of his mature phase and the models of his last phase, despite their incompatibility, into the same edition of the *Eléments d'économie politique pure*. It then becomes clear, for example, why it has been possible to have such divergent interpretations of his work on tatonnement, and how scrutiny of one and the same text – the 1926 edition of the *Eléments d'économie politique pure* – can lead one scholar to argue that Walras was interested in the dynamics of market processes and another to argue that he was exclusively interested in statics. The reader will see that

students of Walras's work have been laboring in the dark because they have
tried to understand it on the basis of their scrutiny of the fourth and fifth
editions of his *Eléments d'économie politique pure*. They have not been
furnished with the information that would enable them to have a true understanding of what is on the page in front of them. The plight of readers of
William Jaffé's translation of the fifth edition is even worse, because in
addition to presenting the admixture of conflicting models, it does not correctly convey Walras's meaning in a number of respects that are crucially
important for an understanding of his entire body of work.

Third, the book analyzes and evaluates Walras's models. There is no point
in studying the history of economic thought, except as an antiquarian pursuit,
unless lessons can be learned from it. That entails revealing its structure and
implications, knowing whether or not it is nonsense, showing its insights and
suggestive ideas – in short, indicating why some of it is worth studying and
why some of it does not merit much attention. Accordingly, this book reveals
the character of the models that Walras constructed during his mature phase,
showing that he made his finest contributions during that phase and that he
produced inferior work during his last phase. Unfortunately, the latter was
used as the basis of modern general-equilibrium theory. Scholars have unwittingly filled in some of the blanks in Walras's last comprehensive model,
have supposed that his equations make sense in relation to it, and have
imputed their own beliefs about the workings of competitive markets to it.
For example, Walras's written pledges model was regarded by Oskar Lange,
Don Patinkin, Michio Morishima, and other writers as being the true expression of Walras's thought on tatonnement, so they neglected his earlier writings. Jaffé represented them only as constructions that Walras discarded on
the way to the definitive formulation that Jaffé considered the written pledges
model to be, or believed that those earlier writings should be interpreted as
having the same intent as the written pledges model but as being imperfect
expressions of its characteristics. An appreciation of the fact that Walras had
a mature phase of theoretical activity followed by a phase of decline provides
a corrective to that situation. The student of his work is able to approach the
material that he introduced in his last phase without the supposition that it
presents his best thoughts.

This is not a work of polemics, controversion, or argumentation with the
opinions of other interpreters of Walras, with a few exceptions. I have
examined the views of some economists with whom Walras had disagree-
ments and the opinions of some modern economists on his model of tatonnement. I have on occasion discussed Jaffé's writings because of the prominent
position that has been accorded them and because I wrote many of my
articles on Walras during a period in which Jaffé was the only author who
had expressed an opinion on some of the subjects covered. I have not drawn

on or built on Jaffé's analyses to achieve my own, and my references in this book to his work are mainly critical. I therefore point out that I have not been remiss in giving attention to his contributions. I translated the articles he wrote in French and published them and all his other articles on Walras, with an extensive introduction, in a collected edition (Jaffé 1983). I wrote his obituary (Walker 1981a), an appreciation of his work (Walker 1981b), and an article on his career and beliefs (Walker 1983), and put together, edited, completed, in large part translated, and published his notes for the first chapter of a projected biography of Walras (Jaffé 1984). I now state again that the economics profession owes a great deal to Jaffé's lifelong study of the writings of Walras and, despite its defects, to his translation of Walras's major book. He brought Walras to the attention of English-speaking economists and explained much about his ideas for the first time in English. Moreover, Jaffé's edition of Walras's correspondence and related papers (Walras 1965) is a monumental contribution to Walrasian scholarship. It provides source materials for an understanding of the development of neoclassical economics, and has been of great value to me in writing this book.

In most respects I have had no reason to mention other students of Walras's writings. The chapters on his mature models are concerned with a phase of his work that has not even been identified by other modern writers, and my analysis and evaluation of his last phase of theoretical activity is also original. I see the book as a novel presentation of Walras's work, breaking new ground in the understanding of his writings and in the identification of his contributions, and the work of other interpreters has therefore not been relevant for my concerns. I could have drawn extensive contrasts between my views and the received interpretation of Walras's writings – for example, by pointing out in many detailed respects how other writers have misunderstood the last edition of the *Eléments d'économie politique pure* or by emphasizing that they have not even recognized many of the models and aspects of Walras's work that have interested me. That would not have been productive because I and the expositors of the traditional interpretations have perceived different subject matters.

I am grateful to Indiana University of Pennsylvania for Senate research grants that helped to support my efforts in writing the essays on which this book is based and in preparing the book itself, to Debbie Mahan and Mary-Anne Lupinetti for their secretarial efforts, and to Ronald Cohen for his editorial work on the book.

Acknowledgments

This book is based on nineteen of my essays on Léon Walras's work. The publisher and I wish to thank the publishers of the essays for permission to republish them with or without changes here.

"Léon Walras," *The New Palgrave: A Dictionary of Economic Theory and Doctrine,* edited by John Eatwell, Murray Milgate, and Peter Newman, Macmillan Press, London and Basingstoke; Stockton Press, New York; Maruzen Company, Tokyo, 1987. Permission given by Grove's Dictionaries Inc.

"A Primer on Walrasian Theories of Economic Behavior," *History of Economics Society Bulletin, 11,* Spring 1989, 1–23. Permission given by the History of Economic Society.

"Is Walras's Theory of General Equilibrium a Normative Scheme?" *History of Political Economy, 16,* no. 3, Fall 1984, 445–69. Permission given by Duke University Press.

"Walras's Models of the Barter of Stocks of Commodities," *European Economic Review, 37,* no. 4, 1993, 1425–46. Permission given by Elsevier Sciences Publishers B.V.

"Institutions and Participants in Walras's Theory of Oral Pledges Market," *Revue Economique, 41,* no. 4, July 1990, 651–68. Permission given by *Revue Economique.*

"Disequilibrium and Equilibrium in Walras's Theory of Oral Pledges Markets," *Revue Economique, 41,* no. 6, November 1990, 961–78. Permission given by *Revue Economique.*

"The Structure of Walras's Consumer Commodities Model in the Mature Phase of His Thought," *Revue Economique, 45,* no. 2, March 1994, 239–56. Permission given by *Revue Economique.*

"The Adjustment Process in Walras's Consumer Commodities Model in the Mature Phase of His Thought," *Revue Economique, 45,* no. 6, November 1994, 1357–76. Permission given by *Revue Economique.*

"The Structure of Walras's Mature Model of Markets for Capital Goods and Other Commodities," *European Journal of the History of Economic Thought, 3,* no. 2, Summer 1996. Permission given by Routledge Journals.

xv

"Walras's Theories of Tatonnement," *Journal of Political Economy, 95,* no. 4, August 1987, 758–74. Permission given by the University of Chicago Press. © 1987 by the University of Chicago. All rights reserved.

"Equilibrating Processes in Walras's Mature Comprehensive Model," *Revue d'Economie Politique, 100,* no. 6, November-December, 1990, 786–807. Permission granted by Editions Dalloz-Sirey.

"Walras and His Critics on the Maximum Utility of New Capital Goods," *History of Political Economy, 16,* no. 4, Winter 1984, 529–54. Permission given by Duke University Press.

"Le Modèle du Marché de la Monnaie de Walras Durant la Phase de Maturité de Sa Pensée Théorique," *Economies et Sociétés, Œconomia,* Histoire de la Pensée économique, P.E. no. 20–21, October-November 1994, 133–57. Permission given by the Institut de Sciences Mathématiques et Économiques Appliquées and Les Presses Universitaires de Grenoble.

"Iteration in Walras's Theory of Tatonnement," *De Economist, 136,* no. 3, 1988, 299–316. Permission given by *De Economist.*

"Walras's Theory of the Entrepreneur," *De Economist, 134,* no. 1, 1986, 1–24. Permission given by *De Economist.*

"Edgeworth versus Walras on the Theory of Tatonnement," *Eastern Economic Journal, 13,* no. 2, April-June, 1987, 155–56. Permission given by the Eastern Economic Association.

"The Structure of Walras's Barter Model of Written Pledges Markets," *Revue d'Economie Politique, 100,* no. 5, September-October, 1990, 618–41. Permission given by Editions Dalloz-Sirey.

"The Equilibrating Process in Walras's Barter Model of Written Pledges Markets," *Revue d'Economie Politique, 100,* no. 6, November-December, 1990, 786–807. Permission granted by Editions Dalloz-Sirey.

"The Written Pledges Markets in Walras's Last Monetary Model," *Economie Appliquée, 44,* no. 2, 1991, 87–107. Permission given by the Institut de Sciences Mathématiques et Économiques Appliquées and Les Presses Universitaires de Grenoble.

"The Markets for Circulating Capital and Money in Walras's Last Monetary Model," *Economie Appliquée, 44,* no. 3, 1991, 107–129. Permission given by the Institut de Sciences Mathématiques et Économiques Appliquées and Les Presses Universitaires de Grenoble.

Introduction

A biographical sketch

Walras's life in France

Léon Walras was the founder of the modern theory of general economic equilibrium.[1] He noted in his autobiography (1965, *1*, pp. 1–15),[2] from which most of the information in this sketch is drawn, that he was born on December 16, 1834, in Evreux in the Department of Eure in France, and christened Marie Esprit Léon. His father was Antoine Auguste Walras, a secondary school administrator and an amateur economist and literary critic; his mother was Louise Aline de Sainte Beuve, the daughter of an Evreux notary. After studying at the College of Caen from 1844 to 1850, he entered the *lycée* of Douai, where he received a *bachelier-ès-lettres* in 1851 and a *bachelier-ès-sciences* in 1853. He entered the School of Mines of Paris in 1854, but finding the course of preparation of an engineer not to his liking, he gradually abandoned his academic studies in order to cultivate literature, philosophy, and social science. Although those efforts resulted in a short story and a novel, *Francis Sauveur* (1858), it rapidly became apparent to him that social science was his true interest. Accordingly, in 1858 he agreed to his father's request that he give up literature and devote himself to economics, and promised to continue his father's investigations.[3]

During his youth in Paris, Walras became a journalist for *Journal des Economistes* and *La Presse* from 1859 to 1862, the author of a refutation (1860) on philosophical grounds of the normative economic doctrines of P.-J. Proudhon, an employee of the directors of the Northern Railway in 1862, and managing director of a cooperative association bank in 1865. He gave public lectures on cooperative associations in 1865, from 1866 to 1868 was co-

---

[1] For an account of the school of economic theory that he founded and references to the works of its members, see Walker 1996a.

[2] See the last section of this introduction for conventions on citations of Walras's writings.

[3] Auguste chose the opposite of the plan that he recommended to Léon. Auguste decided to give up economics and to concentrate on literature for much of his career, returning briefly to economics only at the end of the 1850s, without adding anything of significance to his earlier work (see the intellectual biography of Auguste by Pierre-Henri Goutte and Jean-Michel Servet in Auguste Walras 1990, CXXI–CLXXII).

1

editor and publisher with Léon Say of the journal *Le Travail,* a review devoted largely to the cooperative movement, and during those years gave public lectures on social topics (1868). After the failure of the association bank in 1868, he found employment with a private bank until 1870. During the 1860s he tried intermittently to obtain an academic appointment in France, but he lacked the necessary educational credentials, and the eleven economics positions in higher education in France were monopolized by orthodox economists who, he complained, passed their chairs on to their relatives. His fortunes ultimately changed as a result of his participation in 1860 in an international congress on taxation in Lausanne, for that brought him to the attention of Louis Ruchonnet, a Swiss politician who secured his appointment in 1870 to an untenured professorship of economics at the Academy (subsequently University) of Lausanne in Switzerland. He was made a tenured professor there in 1871, and held that position throughout his teaching career.

Walras's personal life was initially unconventional. He and Célestine Aline Ferbach (1834–79) formed a common law union in the late 1850s. She had a son, Georges, by a previous liaison, and she and Walras had twin daughters in 1863, one of whom died in infancy. In 1869 he married Célestine, thereby legitimizing their daughter, Marie Aline, and adopted Célestine's son. A long illness of Célestine's and the meagerness of Walras's salary made life very difficult for him for several years. His time and energy were sorely taxed not only by the need to care for his wife but by the need to supplement his salary by teaching extra classes, contributing to the *Gazette de Lausanne* and the *Bibliothèque Universelle,* and working as a consultant for La Suisse insurance company. Five years after Célestine's death in 1879, Walras married Léonide Désirée Mailly (1826–1900). The marriage was a happy one. Her annuity relieved his financial distress, and his situation was further improved in 1892 by an inheritance of 100,000 francs from his mother, which enabled him to pay debts incurred in publishing and disseminating his works and to buy an annuity of 800 francs.

Influences on his work. Walras's professional life was devoted to research and teaching. He frequently asserted that his research was a development of his father's, and that was true in some respects. It was under the influence of his father's classification of economic studies that Léon, as early as 1862, planned the division of his life's work into the study of pure theory, economic policies, and normative goals (Walras to Jules du Mesnil Marigny, December 23, 1862, in 1965, *1,* letter 81, pp. 117–24). He ultimately set forth those areas of study respectively in his book *Eléments d'économie politique pure*[4] and his two collections of essays, *Etudes d'économie social* (1896c) and

---

[4] The title of all editions of this work is shortened to *Eléments* throughout this book.

Etudes d'économie politique appliquée (1898b). Léon adopted his father's classification of the factors of production into the services of labor, land, and capital goods, regarding thc sourcc of cach service as a type of capital. He adopted his father's definition of capital as wealth that can be used more than once and of income as wealth that can be used only once, and revised his father's vague use of the term "extensive utility," using it to mean the quantity-axis intercept of a market demand curve. The topic of utility had been treated in French thought by writers such as the Abbe Fernandino Galiani (a Neapolitan diplomat at Versailles) and Etienne Bonnot de Condillac (a priest and philosopher), and it was given further development by Auguste and Léon Walras. Auguste used the word *numéraire* to mean an abstract unit of account, and Léon adapted the meaning of the word to his purposes. Auguste's philosophy of social justice and his belief in the desirability of nationalizing land were advocated by Léon throughout his adult life. Léon's major economic theories, however, were derived from his own original inspiration and from sources other than his father. Auguste's greatest contribution to Léon's development as an economist were to encourage him to study economics, to suggest that it should be a mathematical science (A.A. Walras 1831, ch. 18; Walras 1965, *1,* p. 493), and to give him access to a library of books on economics.

In that library was Antoine Augustin Cournot's *Recherches sur les principes mathématiques de la théorie des richesses* (1838), which Léon Walras credited with having demonstrated that economics could and should be expressed in mathematical form (Walras to A.A. Cournot, March 20, 1874, in 1965, *1,* letter 253, pp. 363–67; Walras to Henry L. Moore, January 2, 1906, in 1965, *3,* letter 1614, pp. 292–93; Walras 1905a). Cournot's work introduced Walras to the mathematical formulation of exchange between two locations, the theory of monopoly and the associated conditions for profit maximization, and the analysis of how prices are repeatedly changed in a search for equilibrium in a purely competitive market, all topics that Walras developed in his own work. The first demand curve that Walras beheld was Cournot's, and he found it immensely suggestive. He was critical of it, however, because he perceived that Cournot's postulate that the quantity demanded of a commodity is a function only of its own price is inaccurate if more than two commodities are exchanged, and that Cournot did not provide a theoretical rationale for the demand function. Those perceptions, Walras observed, were the starting point for his own inquiries (1965, *1,* p. 5; 1905a).

Other ingredients that went into the composition of Walras's theories were provided by Adam Smith, John Stuart Mill, François Quesnay, A.R.J. Turgot and Jean-Baptiste Say. Smith had revealed many of the consequences of unfettered competition and had formulated the concept of normal value. Mill had provided a supplement to and reinforcement of Cournot's and Smith's analyses of competitive pricing (Walras to Ladislaus von Bortkiewicz, February 27, 1891, in 1965, 2, letter 999, pp. 434–35), and also an extension and grand synthesis of classical doctrines that served Walras as a catalyst for critical studies. Quesnay, in his *Tableau économique,* had expressed the concept of a circular flow of income and the interdependence of the various parts of the economy. Turgot had clearly delineated the idea of the simultaneous and mutually determined general equilibrium of those parts. Say (1836) had suggested the distinction between the incomes of the factors of production and the demand for commodities. Walras sharpened those ideas and made them a fundamental part of his general-equilibrium models.

Achylle-Nicolas Isnard's *Traité des richesses* (1781), a book that Walras owned and that may have been in his father's library, was probably an important source of some of Walras's constructions (Jaffé 1969). Like Walras, Isnard was interested in determining equilibrium price ratios, set up a system of simultaneous equations of exchange showing the dependence of the value of each commodity on the values of the others, stressed the necessity of having as many independent equations as unknowns, and perceived that the use of a numeraire rendered his system determinate. Anticipating Walras's treatment of production, Isnard assumed given ratios of the inputs in a mathematical model and expressed the costs of production in equation form. Also like Walras, Isnard studied the allocation of capital among different uses, coming to the conclusion, as did Walras, that in equilibrium the net rate of income of different capital goods is the same.

Finally, Louis Poinsot's *Eléments de statique* (1803) exerted a powerful influence on Walras. He first read that book when he was nineteen, and kept it at his bedside for decades (Walras to Melle Dick May, May 23, 1901, in 1965, 3, letter 1483, pp. 148–49). Poinsot painted a picture of the mutual interdependence of a vast number of variables, of how the dynamic forces in physical systems eventuate in an equilibrium in which each object is sustained in its path and relative position. Inspired by the implications of Poinsot's work, Walras conceived a magnificent project. He would emulate Poinsot's vision and analysis in reference to the general equilibrium of the economic universe! That he tried to carry out the plan can be inferred from the striking similarity of the form of his work to Poinsot's, with its careful delineation of functional dependences and parameters, its sets of simultaneous equations, and its equilibrium conditions. Equipped, therefore, with ideas that he could take as building blocks and points of departure, with enough geometry and algebra to put together mathematical statements of economic relationships and conditions – his use of calculus in the *Eléments* came after the first edition – and with the explicit objective of developing a mathematical theory of general equilibrium, Walras began his scholarly activity in Lausanne in 1870.

Walras was an extremely conscientious teacher, but he was an uninspiring lecturer (Jaffé in 1965, *2*, p. 560), and the students at Lausanne were interested in careers in law, not in economics, so he failed to develop disciples among them. Moreover, he was with increasing frequency afflicted by bouts of mental exhaustion and irritability that made it difficult for him to lecture and to read and write. In 1892 he took a leave to regenerate his strength in order to be able to continue teaching, but soon realized he would find the strain of returning to his tasks insupportable and retired in that year, being at that time fifty-eight years old. In 1899 and 1900 he revised the *Eléments* once more. After 1900 he made no theoretical contributions but wrote some articles, and in late 1901 and 1902 made some inconsequential changes to the *Eléments* that were ultimately incorporated into the text of the fourth edition (1900) to produce the edition of 1926. He died on January 5, 1910, in Clarens, Switzerland, and was buried there.

Many models

Léon Walras's theoretical work is complex in several ways. Economists imagine that he presented a general economic model composed of submodels that are smoothly integrated into a seamless whole. This book will show that his work on markets is quite otherwise. He constructed many models of markets. They differ in a variety of respects in addition to dealing with different types of commodities. In some of the models, oral pledges are made; in some, written pledges are made; in others, pledges are not made. Some of the models deal with stocks, some with flows; some involve a numeraire, some do not; some are barter models, some are monetary; some are quite realistic, some are very unrealistic; some are complete, some are incomplete, and some are incompatible.

The models are united, however, by having a single fundamental concern – namely, the behavior of participants in markets. Walras grouped the models into categories that he called the theory of exchange, the theory of production, the theory of capital formation, and the theory of money, but those names do not bring out the fact that the models all deal with markets. What he called the theory of exchange comprises the models of market behavior that he constructed on the assumption that there are given total amounts of the commodities available to be traded. It is traditional to reserve the term "theory of exchange" for that situation, but that should not obscure the circumstance that the other models also deal with exchange, as is shown by the following considerations. First, Walras incorporated the monetary model of exchange of fixed available total stocks, epitomized by his model of the securities market, into his mature comprehensive model, which includes the production and sale of consumer commodities and capital goods. Second,

Walras indicated that all the models are concerned with pricing. He wrote that "by the *theory of exchange*" he had been able to achieve "the determination of the prices of consumer goods and consumable services" (1889, p. XIII). That was not a good description of his theory of exchange, inasmuch as it deals with situations in his models in which there are all types of commodities, including wholesale agricultural commodities and securities markets. Nevertheless, the statement makes clear that Walras regarded the determination of prices in a model of consumer commodities as an important part of the pricing process. "By the *theory of production*," he explained, he had been able to achieve "the determination of the prices of primary materials and productive services" (ibid.), so the theory of production is also concerned with price determination. The production to which Walras referred takes place in factories and workshops, but the determination of the prices and rates of production and use of services and consumer goods is effectuated by the participants in the markets of the model.

Thus, Walras's theory of production is largely a model of market behavior, not of activities in workshops. The name "the theory of production" is therefore not really descriptive of the model on which he bestowed it, and it is badly named for the additional reason that production also occurs in the model in which there is capital formation. "By the *theory of capital formation*" in particular, Walras explained, he had been able to achieve "the determination of the prices of capital goods" (ibid.). That occurs in a comprehensive model that is likewise principally concerned with markets – namely, those in which are determined the prices, rates of production and sale of services and of consumer goods as well as of new capital goods. Similarly, Walras's theory of money is concerned with models of markets – namely, markets for loans (ibid, p. XVI). Walras accordingly described his mature comprehensive model, which includes all commodities and money, as concerned with the behavior of "traders" – that is, with the behavior of participants in markets (1889, p. XVII; 1896b, p. XVI).

It has been written many times that Walras built a theoretical edifice architectonically by adding a model to a first model and another to the resulting model, and so on, until the grand edifice was finished. That is not true. The model of monetary exchange indicates how the pricing process is conducted on any market day in the market for any commodity, and that the pricing process takes place in every one of the models. The model of the production and sale of consumer commodities mentioned in the previous paragraph is one in which only nondurable commodities, including services, are produced, and there are no inventories. It cannot be said that Walras added capital goods markets to that model to produce the next stage of his construction because in every edition of the *Eléments* he discarded the nondurable consumer commodities model when he took up new capital goods. He replaced most of its leading features with a new set of assumptions about consumer behavior, about the kind of consumer commodities that are produced, and about inventories, and put that different assemblage of phenomena into a model with savings and capital goods markets. In his mature phase – at the same time as when he put consumer commodities and capital goods into a model – he also added the holding of money balances and a loan and money market. Similarly, it is recognized in this book that in the mature phase of his theoretical activity Walras did not develop a series of increasingly complex barter models and then add money in a final grand model. On the contrary, the mature models of nondurable consumer commodities, of new capital goods and all types of consumer commodities, and, of course, the model of the securities markets are all monetary. The book will show what transpired during the course of his efforts to revise his model in the fourth edition of the *Eléments*. Suffice it to say at this point that in that edition he did try to develop a barter model with consumer commodities and capital goods, and only subsequently tried to add money to it.

Phases of theoretical activity

The history of Walras's theoretical work is also complex because he went through four phases of theoretical activity, and changed most of his models to some degree and in some cases extensively during each phase. Accordingly, in order to identify the subject matter of Parts I and II of this book and to make clear their places in the scheme of his writings, some preliminary classifications and explanations must be provided. The phases merge into each other, so the dates given for their beginnings and endings are approximations except as noted later regarding the end of the fourth phase. The appropriateness of categorizing a particular publication of Walras's as being in a particular phase may therefore be debatable if the date of publication comes at or near the date given for the beginning or the end of a phase. Nevertheless, the phases are clearly there; indeed, most of Walras's writings are strongly marked by the characteristics of the phase in which they were written.

The experimental phase: First, Walras underwent an experimental phase, one of apprenticeship, mistakes, and exploration during the 1860s until 1872. In this period he made a number of attempts to model markets, but his efforts were confused and unproductive. He lacked the basic constructions that are necessary for that task. In particular, he did not have a theory of demand, and consequently lacked a theory of the determination of market prices.

The creative phase: Second, Walras experienced a creative phase, one of great originality and intense and substantial theorizing, which spanned the years 1872 through 1877. During that phase he wrote four brilliantly original memoirs (1877c) that he developed into the core of the reasoning and into much of the specific language of the first edition of the *Eléments* and completed that work. Walras insisted to his publisher that the first part appear in 1874, before the second part (1877b) was completed, because he learned in May of that year that William Stanley Jevons had published a mathematical theory of utility and exchange that was similar to his own (J. d'Aulnis de Bourouill to Walras, May 4, 1874, in 1965, *1*, letter 267, p. 388), and he was anxious to establish the independence of his discoveries and his priority in regard to most of them. For those same reasons he paid for the publication of his books, and sent copies of them and of his articles to his many correspondents. This book will not examine Walras's second phase in itself, but many of its constructions will be studied because he carried most of them, with modifications, forward into his next phase of work. The material in the first edition of the *Eléments* that is incorporated into the second edition is legitimately considered as contributing to the models that Walras presented in his mature phase.

Although the contents of the first edition suffer by comparison with the mature phase of Walras's work, it should be noted that the division, placement, and naming of sections in the first edition are clearer and better conceived than in any of the subsequent editions. In the first edition, Walras began by examining exchange with fixed stocks in barter models and in monetary models. Then he introduced a section on money to make clear that he was going to present monetary models in the remainder of the volume. Then he developed a monetary model of the production and sale of services and nondurable consumer goods. Finally, he presented a comprehensive monetary model of economic growth in which capital goods and durable and nondurable consumer commodities are produced and used and the national product grows. By titling that model "Conditions and consequences of economic progress" (1877b, p. 274), Walras indicated that it was a model of economic growth.

The mature phase: Third, Walras underwent a mature phase of theoretical activity during the years 1878 through the mid-1890s. He presented the theoretical aspects of his work during that phase in the second edition (1889) of the *Eléments* and in essays written during the first half of the 1890s. He asserted in the second edition that he had not changed the basic character of his models of market structures and behavior, noting that his theoretical system was "the same as [his] doctrine was fifteen years ago"[5] (1889, p. XII) and that was true in many fundamental respects. By the time he prepared the second edition, however, he had achieved a clearer view of certain aspects of the type of economy that he wanted to portray. Walras emphasized this in a

---

[5] He presented that statement again in the introduction to the fourth edition, but his insertion of the written pledges model into that edition rendered the statement invalid.

letter in which he described some of the major "modifications" he had introduced into that edition, including the models of tatonnement in the production of nondurables, the numeraire commodity, and new capital goods (see ch. 12), and additions or alterations to his work on exchange, the net income of capital and its rate of net income, the special equations of capital formation, and the theorem of the marginal utility of new capital goods (Walras to P.H. Wicksteed, April 9, 1889, in Walras 1965, *2,* letter 877, pp. 307–9). He also rewrote his model of the money market and behavior in regard to money. Accordingly, his mature phase was one of clarification and extension of important facets of his models. He refined many of their aspects, adding to the brilliant efforts of his second phase in the light of his increased experience and knowledge, and bringing his theoretical system to the best state it was to attain.

Of course, this does not mean that he brought it to perfection, because he did not complete all his conceptions or work out all their ramifications or reconcile all their differences or eliminates all their incompatible aspects. It is not to be expected that a pioneer would present a completely finished work. As Walras said, he had confined himself to solving the problem of general economic equilibrium in its broad outlines and left to those who came after him the tasks of correcting the details and filling in the gaps (Walras to Irving Fisher, July 28, 1892, in 1965, *2,* letter 1064, pp. 498–99). The examination of Walras's mature phase of theoretical work is interesting, however, because it reveals his contributions as they were before he contradicted and obscured them by forcing the written pledges model and other material of inferior quality into the fourth edition of the *Eléments.* The examination reveals a Walrasian system, unrecognized in this century and poorly understood in the last, which could have given rise to a stream of economic modeling that would have been a fruitful alternative to the one that actually transpired. By contrast with the reception given to the fourth phase of Walras's theorizing, his mature phase of modeling has been neglected since 1920 to such an extent that there does not exist, as far as I am aware, any modern exposition of it in the secondary literature,[6] a situation this book is intended to remedy. From it will emerge a fully documented picture of Walras's mature market models that differs from the received view based on his written pledges models. It is thought by some that his work was normative; it will be shown that his mature models were positive in intent. It is thought that he was concerned only with statics; it will be shown that the mature models are much concerned with dynamic processes and disequilibrium. It is thought that his work had no institutional content; it will be shown that he posited an institutional framework for the markets in his models. It is thought that his

---

[6] My essays on the subject are excluded from this remark.

work is purely abstract theory; it will be shown that his mature models are rich in detail drawn from real markets.

The question arises as to where the third edition of the *Eléments*, published in 1896, fits into the present classification of Walras's theoretical endeavors. His capacity for creative intellectual work had begun to diminish during the years that immediately preceded its publication, a situation he was well aware of. He wrote at the beginning of that edition that he feared he was no longer capable of finishing the plan of work that he had earlier projected, and represented his incapacity as the reason for not making any changes in the lessons that he carried over from the second to the third edition (1896b, p. V, n. 1).[7] Indeed, the only changes he made were some small alterations in the introduction and in the lessons, the elimination of four lessons on the applied theory of money, and the addition of three brief appendixes consisting of material that he had written during the period 1890 through 1895. The appendixes do not alter the character of the models of markets that Walras presented in the second edition, but they strengthen his mature theoretical system. The lessons in the third edition are therefore exactly the same as the corresponding lessons in the second edition, and the appendixes in the third edition are part of his mature work, so the edition is part of Walras's work during his mature phase of theoretical activity.

During that phase Walras presented the following models:

1. Barter models of the exchange of fixed total (market) stocks of commodities. These are all oral pledges models, as will be explained.
2. A monetary model of an organized purely competitive market with fixed total stocks of the assets. This is an oral pledges market.
3. A monetary model of the production and sale of productive services, primary materials, and nondurable consumer commodities, called "the nondurable consumer commodities model" in this book. It will be seen that its behavior is radically different from that of the written pledges model of nondurable consumer commodities that Walras introduced in the fourth edition of the *Eléments*.
4. A comprehensive monetary model of equilibration and equilibrium, called "the mature comprehensive model" in this book. This was Walras's crowning achievement.
   a. The model includes integrated submodels of the production and sale of productive services, primary materials, consumer

---

[7] At the beginning of his preface to the fourth edition and in a letter (Walras to Alfred Danbitch, January 22, 1900, in 1965, *3*, letter 1441, p. 106), Walras noted that it was "really the third" (1900, p. V) precisely because the body of what is called the third edition is, with a few exceptions, identical to that of the second.

commodities of all types, and capital goods, and of the rental of the latter. It contains a loan market, a stock market, and a bond market. The model is one in which all the types of economic behavior that Walras distinguished occur in disequilibrium as well as in equilibrium.

b. Walras provided a detailed version of the loan-market model that he had introduced in his initial discussion of his comprehensive model. The version adds some elements about the structure of the loan market and specifies an adjustment process concerning lending and borrowing and the holding of money balances.

In all those models, Walras incorporated his mature ideas about tatonnement[8] processes, and in the models involving production he introduced entrepreneurs who link markets for flows of inputs and outputs and undertake functions that lead the markets toward equilibrium.

The phase of decline

Fourth, Walras underwent a phase of decline in the quality of his theorizing. That phase began in the mid-1890s and lasted until he completed the fourth edition of the *Eléments*. The course of general-equilibrium theory after Walras was greatly influenced by the constructions of the fourth edition. The fact that he produced that edition and, for English-speaking economists, the fact that a very slightly amended version of it was translated by William Jaffé (Walras 1954), were taken by the economics profession as unquestioned indications that Walras had put his best ideas and definitive system of thought into it. Many economists will be reluctant to accept the judgment that that is not true. Having invested much time and effort in mathematical constructions that are founded on the supposition that the written pledges model is complete and sound, they will be loath to accept the notion that the source of their ideas is in serious disorder. That attitude was manifested by a referee of one of my most recent papers who offered two points of criticism. First, the referee wrote that I had simply asserted that Walras had a phase of decline without indicating the basis of my contention. The referee evidently had not read the articles, published long before the paper under review and now incorporated into this book (part II), in which I did so in detail. Second, the referee stated the related misapprehension that there is no reason to believe that Walras did not develop intellectually throughout his life. Why should it not be reasonable to believe, the referee wrote, that Walras continued to grow in perceptiveness and wisdom, and continued to improve his theoretical system until his death? Of course, the referee did not in any respect try to

---

[8] The anglicization of this word is explained on page 15.

substantiate that contention, and could not have done so; and, once again, the referee had not read the articles in which I demonstrated the deficiencies of the work of Walras's last phase and wrote about the debilitating impact of his health on his theoretical activity. I will show in detail in part II that although Walras introduced a few variations of exposition in the fourth edition, all the major theoretical changes he incorporated into it were fragmentary, and most of them were ill-conceived and poorly executed.

The decline of Walras's abilities is evidenced by his introduction of a written pledges model that is so incomplete and sketchy as to fail to be a functioning system; by its dealing with a hypothetical economy that is in many respects absurd; by many logical inconsistencies, inept definitions, nonsensical constructions, and obscure passages; by his abandonment of the dynamic analyses and period analysis that he had created during his mature phase; and by his abandonment of the goal of modeling real economic processes. The models of the phase of decline, through which he sought to convey the concept of an economy in which no sales, production, consumption, or saving take place except in equilibrium, give a distorted view of the nature of economic processes rather than clarifying them.

During his phase of decline, in the fourth edition of the *Eléments,* Walras presented the following submodels featuring written pledges and submodels in which they are not used:

1. Barter models of written pledges markets.
    a. A written pledges barter model intended to deal with of the production and sale of services and nondurable consumer goods. Walras wanted this to be a model with no disequilibrium production, and wanted exchange to occur only when the model is general equilibrium. The model is incomplete, and thus does not have either an adjustment phase or an equilibrium.
    b. A written pledges barter model intended to deal with markets for services, consumer commodities of all types, and capital goods. The model is incomplete, and does not have either an adjustment phase or an equilibrium. Walras did not construct written pledges markets of land, old capital goods, long-term loans, primary materials, or other circulating physical capital.
2. The last comprehensive model, which is monetary and contains these submodels:
    a. Written pledges monetary models. These are very sketchy and they are incomplete. For example, Walras's mention of the short-term market for loans consists of one sentence. Only by implication can it be considered as one in which written pledges are used.

b. A model of circulating physical capital. This is not a written pledges model.

c. A model of the market for money and loans. This is not a written pledges model.

The fourth edition also includes material that was presented in the second (and third) editions. Much of that material deals with the adjustment processes in markets and with convergence to equilibrium. It is not proper to regard that material as being joined to the passages that Walras wrote in his last phase of theoretical activity, and to regard the two sets of writings as constituting a single body of work, despite his intermingling of the two sets, because there are radical and incompatible differences between the models introduced in the fourth edition and his earlier work.

It cannot be said that Walras had a fifth phase of theoretical activity of any kind, whether of better or worse quality than his previous efforts, because after finishing the fourth edition he abruptly and completely gave up attempts at theoretical construction. Chapters 18 and 19 show that he stated that he was doing so and that he explained the reason for his behavior.

Citations and terminological conventions

To summarize about the dates of the editions of the *Eléments* that Walras prepared, the first edition was published in two parts, one in 1874 and one in 1877, the second edition was published in 1889, the third in 1896, the fourth in 1900, and the fifth, posthumously, in 1926. Walras called the 1900 edition the definitive edition (1900, p. V), but then the 1926 edition was labeled the definitive edition on its front cover and title page, so it is clearer to refer simply to the fourth and fifth editions or to use their dates of publication. A comparative edition, which contains the textual variations of all editions, was published in 1988. In the documentation in the present book, the edition of the *Eléments* in which Walras first introduced a passage is cited first. Except on occasion in this introduction, his name is omitted from citations of his publications; they are identified simply by their date of publication. Complete bibliographical information on each citation is given in the list of references at the end of the book, and the publication history of each reference is given in Walker 1987b.

There are really only three editions of the *Eléments* that have more than negligible differences in the body of the text: the first, the second, and the fourth. If relevant passages are the same in wording and pagination in the second and third editions, only the second will be cited. The differences in pagination will be indicated by citing both editions, and the appendixes in the third edition are cited when reference is made to them. The 1926 edition of the *Eléments* is identical to the 1900 edition in regard to the pagination, section numbers, and language of all passages to which reference is made in this book, and the two editions differ in only very minor respects. When the 1954 translation is cited it is because the focus of attention is on Jaffé's wording. The 1900 edition is cited in the chapters concerned with Walras's models of the barter of stocks of commodities (ch. 3) and the monetary oral pledges model (chs. 4 and 5) because those models were carried over from the second and third editions into that edition (and therefore into the 1926 edition) without the introduction of the device of written pledges, without any changes emanating from that device, and indeed without any changes of substance.

Some of the chapters of this book deal with the material that Walras introduced in the fourth edition. Following the policy mentioned in the previous paragraph, when that material is examined the fourth edition will be cited because doing so establishes the year in which the passages, which are in both the 1900 and 1926 editions, first appeared. The numbered subdivisions of the *Eléments* are called "sections" in this book because there is no other appropriate English word for them. To be consistent with that nomenclature, the divisions of the *Eléments* that Walras called "sections" are called "parts." The section (§) number in the fourth and therefore in the fifth edition is given in order that the passage can be found in Jaffé's translation (1954) of the latter and in the comparative edition, neither of which uses the original pagination. At the end of the book I have presented an adaptation of Jaffé's painstaking collation of the five editions of the *Eléments* so that any section in the 1900 edition that is cited can be located in the earlier editions in which the section or an earlier version of it appears. The superb comparative edition (1988; see Walker 1995) enables the reader to learn the editions in which any passage appeared. Even passages that Walras eliminated from an edition are reproduced in the comparative edition, and their original location is given. A reader of my essays commented, however, that he had difficulty locating passages from pre-1900 editions of the *Eléments* in the comparative edition. That circuitous procedure is not a good way to try to locate pre-1900 passages. The simple and straightforward way is to consult a copy of the edition that I cite. Thanks to the facsimile re-publication in 1988 of the first edition and the availability in libraries of the second or third edition, that poses no problem.

The correspondence cited in this book is published in Walras 1965, unless otherwise noted. The citations indicate the correspondents, the date of the letter, the volume in which the letter appears, the number of the letter, and the page or pages on which it appears. When materials other than correspondence that are published in Walras 1965 are cited, they are identified by the date, and are listed individually among the references to Walras's writings, together with their location in Walras 1965. Walras's letters and papers and those of Continental economists that are cited in this book are in French in Walras 1965; the letters written to him by English-speaking economists that are cited in this book are in English in that same source. All translations from the French of letters and of all other writings are mine, except a few of Jaffé's, which are analyzed and revised. It should be observed that my translations of passages in the *Eléments* differ from Jaffé's in detail and sometimes in respects of crucial importance.

When referring to the reader, to a consumer, to an entrepreneur, and so forth, I have used "he" and "him" – the standard male forms of the English language – for easy reading. I wanted to avoid giving the text a contrived appearance and to avoid distracting readers from its meaning by directing their attention to matters of language style. I have no intention of slighting anyone and apologize in advance if anyone takes offense at the convention I have followed.

Walras's terminology will be adopted, with the following exceptions. First, his use of the word "market" will not always be followed. He used it in the singular but actually had reference to groups of markets. For example, what he called for convenience "the market" for services actually consists of many markets in his model, one for each service. It will be convenient on some occasions to use Walras's terminology and on other occasions to refer to markets in the plural. As the context will indicate, the word "model" will sometimes be used to mean a submodel such as the one for a particular commodity, sometimes a submodel of a special group of markets, and sometimes a comprehensive model of the production and sale of all commodities.

In some recent publications in English, including mine, the word "tatonnement" has appeared without italics to avoid the distracting and unintentionally emphatic appearance of an italicized word repeated many times. That practice has been followed in this book, and in further recognition of the anglicization of the word, the circumflex over the "a" has been eliminated. Similarly, the French word *numéraire* is anglicized, being written without italics and without accent as "numeraire." In quotations of texts written in English, however, those terms appear in whatever form the authors used. The mathematical notation and font of the equations quoted in this book are Walras's. This includes such matters as putting some variables in parentheses, italicizing Greek and lower-case letters, not italicizing upper-case letters and subscripts, and so on. Words that are quoted that are in italics in the original source are italicized in this book without comment; if words in quotations are italicized by me, I indicate that the emphasis has been added. The citations of Jaffé's articles give both the original pagination and, in brackets, the pagination in the collected edition of them (Jaffé 1983). Finally, I have tried to minimize footnotes on the grounds that the book should contain only relevant and important material and that material of that type should, with certain exceptions, have an integral place in the text.

PART I

The models of the mature phase

Background and preliminaries

CHAPTER 1

Walras's conception of a competitive market economy

This chapter is concerned with Walras's conception of the major features of the behavior of a real market economy. He incorporated them into his mature market models and imprinted them on the character of neoclassical economic analysis.

I. Introduction

This chapter presents the general characteristics of economic behavior that Walras identified. His objective in the mature phase of his thought was to understand and model the behavior of a freely competitive capitalist market economy. He defined that as one in which there is private ownership of most economic resources and other commodities, and in which commodities of all types and money are exchanged in freely competitive markets. In his *Eléments* and other writings he elaborated on the properties of such an economy, setting forth his message about them in a number of propositions, models and analyses.

II. General features

Walras identified three important general features of a market economy. First, he conceived of a market economy as a system in which price competition is strong and widespread but not universal. He recognized that it is absent or very limited in some markets, and developed a theory of monopoly to take account of them. He believed, however, that "free competition is the principal mode of exchange in the real economy, practiced on all markets with more or less precision and therefore with less or more efficiency" (Walras to Ladislaus von Bortkiewicz, February 27, 1891, in 1965, 2, letter 999, pp. 434–35). Walras contended that it was therefore reasonable to make the assumption that all markets included within his model of an economy are freely competitive. "To be logical, it is necessary to proceed from the general case to the particular case, and not from the particular case to the general case, like a physicist who, in order to observe the sun, carefully chooses an overcast period instead of taking advantage of a cloudless sky" (1874a, p. 51; 1889,

p. 70).[1] By "freely competitive" in this passage, Walras meant not only a high degree of competition, as in organized markets such as the stock exchange and wholesale markets for agricultural commodities, but also a lesser degree of competition. He meant competition that is sufficient, together with market rules and institutions, to generate the operation of the laws of supply and demand (1874a, pp. 48–49; 1889, pp. 66–67; 1898b, pp. 197–98). They operate, he explained, through prices being changed by buyers and sellers in the same direction as the sign of the market excess demand, which will henceforth in this book be called Walrasian pricing. That, he argued, is the pricing adjustment mechanism of a competitive market (1874a, p. 50).

Nevertheless, in the models studied in this book, Walras assumed that the markets are not only freely competitive but organized, like the Bourse. He made that assumption not only because he thought it captured the essence of real competitive markets but also in order to simplify his field of study. If he had tried to deal in the same model with imperfectly competitive markets as well as with those that are highly competitive, he would have found it impossible to achieve the goal of constructing a comprehensive model of an entire economic system. The interactions of its elements, and in some cases their independence, would have been too complicated for him to incorporate into a model.

Second, Walras believed that in a freely competitive market economy all economic phenomena are interrelated. There are connections between the behavior of consumers, entrepreneurs, workers, capitalists, and landlords, and therefore there are connections between the prices and rates of output of different commodities. Walras's idea of the interrelatedness of all economic activities was expressed in his analysis of the dependence of excess demand functions on all prices and of the connections between input and output markets.

Third, Walras believed that in a market economy all economic agents strive to maximize their utility. He assumed that utility is cardinally measurable, and described the preferences of economic agents with total and marginal utility functions (1874a, pp. 79–81; 1889, pp. 98–99). About consumers, Walras argued that each individual's demand for a commodity is in principle a function of the prices of all commodities, and assumed that he regards utilities as independent. Walras explained,

Each individual consumer calculates the number of units of services or of products such as foods, clothing, furniture, etc., that he wishes to consume. He compares the intensity of their want satisfaction, not only of similar units of a given service or product, but of different units of diverse kinds of services or products. When a price is cried out or posted, he calculates how he ought to distribute his income among those diverse commodities in order to procure the greatest possible total utility. And,

---

[1] See, however, ch. 13, p. 366.

finally, he demands particular quantities of the various products and services (1898b, p. 197).

Professional traders and wholesale and retail merchants supply and demand commodities as functions of their preferences, their actual holdings of commodities, and all prices. They add to their holdings of each commodity, or sell out of their stocks of commodities, until they hold the batch of commodities that maximizes their utility. Similar considerations are true of the suppliers of economic resources. Workers try to maximize utility. Entrepreneurs and capitalists strive to maximize utility by maximizing their profit and interest incomes respectively. Thus, Walras believed that the driving force of all economic behavior is utility maximization, and he imprinted that view of the motivation of economic agents on Continental economics and modern general-equilibrium theory.

III. Special features

Walras fleshed out his concepts of the general features of a market economy with six special ideas about economic behavior. First, he explained that a fundamental aspect of his conception of capitalism is his theory of how entrepreneurs relate input and output markets. It is, he wrote, "the key to all economics" (Walras to Francis A. Walker, June 12, 1887, in 1965, 2, letter 800, p. 212).[2] The entrepreneur is the buyer of productive services and the seller of products (1877b, pp. 228, 233; 1889, pp. 211, 216). Functions he undertakes in other capacities – such as supervisory labor – are not entrepreneurial (Walras to Francis Amasa Walker, June 12, 1887, in 1965, letter 800, p. 212). In input markets, the entrepreneurs hire labor, land-services, and capital-goods services, and purchase raw and semifinished goods. In their capacity as managers of firms they supervise the use of the productive services to transform the raw materials and semifinished goods into products. The entrepreneurs then sell the products, which include consumer commodities and capital goods (1877b, pp. 228–29; 1889, pp. 210–11). Their earnings are profits, made by selling a commodity at a price that exceeds its average cost. They make a loss if average cost exceeds price (1877b, pp. 231–33; 1889, 213–15). Since costs are incurred by entrepreneurs in input markets, and since prices based in part on those costs are charged by them in output markets, their actions connect those two types of markets. Entrepreneurs also play a role in connecting input and output markets by paying incomes to the owners of economic resources, because those incomes are partially spent by their recipients on consumer commodities (1877b, pp. 228–29; 1889, pp. 210–11). As Francis Y. Edgeworth wrote in recognition of the importance of

---

[2] See p. 280, n. 2.

Walras's theory of the entrepreneur: "Professor Walras is one of the first to correctly conceive the entrepreneur as buying agencies of production ... and selling finished products in [different] markets, which thus become interdependent" (Edgeworth 1889, p. 435).

Second, Walras believed that the crucible of economic growth is the process of saving and investment, and he developed a comprehensive theory of that behavior, including the formulation of the first macroeconomic savings function (1877b, p. 284; 1889, p. 271). Capitalists – that is, economic agents who are savers – provide their money savings to entrepreneurs by making loans and purchasing stocks and bonds on the Bourse, an institution that is therefore fundamental to capitalism (1877b, p. 303; 1889, pp. 310–11). The entrepreneurs spend the funds to acquire materials and productive services and use them to make new capital goods. Walras explored these processes in a brilliantly original modeling of the capital market, of the determination of the rate of net income from the use of capital goods, and of market and equilibrium rates of interest (see chs. 9 and 10). His treatment reveals yet another way that entrepreneurs connect different economic sectors and markets. The incomes paid by entrepreneurs are partially saved by the recipients in their role as members of households, and the savings are used by entrepreneurs to produce new capital goods. These are bought by other entrepreneurs and used to make other capital goods and consumer commodities (1877b, pp. 294–95; 1889, pp. 287–88).

Third, Walras analyzed how the allocation of resources among different economic activities takes place in a capitalist economy. Once again, the entrepreneurs play a crucial role because their anticipation of obtaining profits and their desire to avoid losses motivate them to determine the allocation of resources by directing resources into and out of economic activities. Walras did not identify entrepreneurial activity in relation to the production of new commodities, although he considered the effects on prices of changes in the coefficients of production and of the introduction of new commodities. He regarded the assessment by entrepreneurs of the profit potential of an industry as being based mainly on its past history. "If, in certain firms, the price of the products that they sell is superior to their average costs, which constitutes a profit, entrepreneurs move into the industry or increase their production" (1877b, p. 231; 1889, p. 213). On the other hand, "if, in certain firms, the average cost is greater than the price, which constitutes a loss, entrepreneurs avoid the industry or restrict their production." The shifts of resources reduce the difference between price and average cost (ibid.), and would end if that difference were reduced to zero.

Fourth, Walras conceived of the economy as always undergoing processes of change, always in dynamic motion, always in disequilibrium. The incessant motion results from two circumstances. One is that parametric changes create states of disequilibrium. For example, preferences, the number of workers, and production functions change, altering supply and demand functions (1877b, p. 310; 1889, pp. 316–17). The other is that in the situation that succeeds any parametric change, the interrelationships between excess demand functions, the behavior of entrepreneurs, and the process of pricing cause the variables of the economy to undergo mutually interdependent adjustment processes. Prices are changed repeatedly, inducing changes in the amounts of commodities supplied and demanded at any given time. The disequilibrium adjustments, Walras maintained, continually move the economy toward a position of general equilibrium. He called the adjustments the process of tatonnement, which means "groping." He used that word to indicate that the participants in markets do not know the equilibrium magnitudes of prices and quantities of commodities produced and traded, but unwittingly grope their way toward equilibrium. They do so by quoting one set of prices after another and through reacting to them by producing and trading different amounts of the commodities.

Walras devoted many pages to discussions of this disequilibrium behavior, explaining the process of tatonnement with reference to organized exchanges, such as markets in which securities and wholesale agricultural commodities are traded; markets for productive services, such as labor and land services; retail markets for consumer goods; markets for capital goods and capital-good services; and markets for circulating capital and money. If the adjustment process were not disturbed by parametric changes, it would converge, Walras maintained, to a stable equilibrium of all economic agents. "That state of equilibrium . . . is the normal state in the sense that it is the one to which things tend automatically under a regime of free competition operating in production and in exchange" (1877b, p. 231; 1889, p. 213). Concerning the production of capital goods, for example, Walras explained that as prices are progressively adjusted in real markets, the quantities manufactured and their prices converge to equilibrium through processes of tatonnement (1889, p. 287). In equilibrium, the mutually determined set of prices and quantities of all commodities supplied and demanded would be such that all the plans of the participants in the economy would be reconciled with each other and fulfilled: "The equilibrium prices are those at which the quantities demanded and supplied of each service or product are equal, and for which, moreover, the price of each product is equal to its average cost of production" (1889, p. XV). Prices and rates of production and consumption would remain constant until some disturbing force upsets the equilibrium.

Equilibrium is never reached, however, because the parameters are just analytical parameters, not true constants in the real world or in Walras's account of it. The market, he concluded, is always "tending toward equilibrium without ever arriving there because it cannot move along a path toward it except by tatonnements, and before the tatonnements are finished they must begin again on the basis of new costs, all the parameters of the problem . . . having changed" (1877b, p. 310; 1889, pp. 316–17). Consequently, the "state of equilibrium of production is, like the state of equilibrium of exchange, an ideal state and not a real one. It never transpires that the price of products is absolutely equal to their average cost of production in productive services, nor does it ever happen that the quantities supplied and demanded of productive services or of products are absolutely equal" (1877b, p. 231; 1889, p. 213). No sooner is a set of equilibrium values determined, and no sooner does the economy start moving in the direction of that set of values, then the movement is disrupted by a change in a parametric condition. The market is "like a lake stirred by the wind, in which the water continually seeks its equilibrium without ever achieving it" (1877b, p. 310; 1889, pp. 316–17).

Realizing, therefore, that the economy is characterized by ceaseless change, Walras emphasized that the goal of economic science is to explain disequilibrium behavior. His efforts to provide such an explanation were offered in his theory that in disequilibrium, individuals strive in a variety of ways to maneuver themselves into a position of maximum utility; in his theory that the disequilibrium activities of pricing, exchange, and production are the mechanisms that drive the system; and in his theory that the tendency of the direction of change of variables in disequilibrium is toward a temporarily existing equilibrium but that the equilibrium constantly changes so the tendency is continually redirected. Walras argued passionately in favor of this view of a competitive market economy. He wanted

to demonstrate that the operations of the raising and lowering of prices, of the increases and decreases of the quantities of products produced, etc., on the markets are nothing other than the solution by tatonnement of the equations of exchange, of production, and of capital formation. . . . The object and goal of economic theory . . . consists above all and before all in the demonstration to which I am referring (Walras to Bortkiewicz, October 17, 1889, in 1965, 2, letter 927, pp. 363–64).

By "solution by tatonnement" he meant the dynamic processes of change in disequilibrium that cause the movements of the variable to tend to be in the direction of their equilibrium values.

Fifth, Walras identified consumer sovereignty as a fundamental characteristic of capitalism, contending that the pattern of production of consumer goods in a market economy reflects the pattern of demands of consumers. The entrepreneur, who "is only an intermediary between the worker and the consumer" (1871, p. 36), transmits the desires of consumers to the production side of the market. When consumers shift their demand in favor of a commodity, they bid up its price and make its production profitable, and that induces entrepreneurs to produce more of it. If consumers decided that they do not want to consume as much of a commodity as before, its price falls.

Entrepreneurs make losses in its production, so they produce less of it. The adjustments occur "as a result of the mechanism of the raising and lowering of prices on the market, combined with the fact of the turning away of entrepreneurs from enterprises in which losses are being made and their movement toward enterprises that are making profits" (1889, p. XVIII). Workers are hired to produce the commodities that consumers demand, and are laid off in industries in which consumer demand drops, so "the consumer is in the last analysis, the true demander of labor" (1871, p. 35). Changes of consumer demand are also transmitted to the capital goods industries that supply inputs to the consumer good industries. Consequently, the kinds and amounts of commodities that are produced reflect the demands of consumers, and the structure of economic activities responds to changes in consumer demand.

Sixth, a capitalistic competitive market economy, "contrary to the denials of the socialists" (1889, p. 305), tends to generate a maximum of well-being for its participants (1877b, p. 266; 1889, p. 251; 1900, § 221, p. 231; Walras 1877b, p. 305), a maximum that depends on their initial wealth and the dynamic characteristics of the market system that result in it moving toward a particular set of equilibrium values. In equilibrium the system would actually achieve that maximum. Walras emphasized that this is the outcome of the aspects of a competitive economy that he identified:

The development of economic theory in the mathematical form is an operation which ought essentially to consist in providing a system of equations based upon two conditions. One is the maximization of utility. The other is the equality of the quantities supplied and demanded of each service and of each product. The theory makes clear that the mechanism of free competition leads precisely to the solution by tatonnement of that system of equations. Accordingly, it follows that the market mechanism creates maximum satisfaction (Walras to Filippo Virgilii, October 17, 1889, in 1965, 2, letter 928, pp. 364–65).

The maximization of satisfaction tends to occur not only in markets for consumer commodities but in regard to saving and investment:

The mechanism of free competition is, under certain conditions and within certain limits, a self-driving mechanism and automatic regulator of the transformation of savings into capital goods as well as the transformation of services into products. And thus . . . free competition in regard to exchange and production procures the maximum utility of services and of products . . . , [and] free competition in regard to capital formation and credit procures the maximum utility of new capital goods (1889, p. 306).

Those general and specific aspects of Walras's work summarize his comprehensive and percipient conception of economic behavior in a freely competitive capitalistic economy, a conception conveyed in brilliant modelings and vivid characterizations of the essential elements of the changing mosaic of economic life. A competitive system of production and exchange is vast and complicated in its many details, but Walras divined its underlying order. He revealed that there is simplicity in the principle that directs it – namely, the consumers' desire to maximize utility; simplicity in the principle that makes the system responsive – namely, the entrepreneurs' desire to maximize profits and avoid losses; and simplicity in the uniformity of the mechanism whereby the system operates – namely, the Walrasian price and output changing processes. Walras's ideas on these matters have become standard parts of our conception of a system of freely competitive markets.

CHAPTER 2

The mature models: Not a normative scheme

I. Introduction

Jaffé's thesis

This chapter examines Walras's motives in constructing the models of his phase of maturity. It is a commonplace of writing on the history of economic thought that the work of one or another economist is alleged to have a normative bias in the sense that values and prejudices embedded in his ideational process and philosophical outlook have crept into his work without the writer being conscious of their influence. It is often maintained, for example, that value judgments operate in determining the selection of problems that a scientist finds interesting, or that a writer's treatment of his subject is affected by his being a member of a particular social class. The allegation made by William Jaffé about Walras's work was, however, of a different character, for he asserted that in developing the theory of general equilibrium in the *Eléments,* Walras consciously had the objective of constructing a normative system. Jaffé made that allegation about the constructions of Walras's creative phase and therefore about the models that Walras presented during his mature phase. Jaffé maintained that Walras's "latent purpose" was not "to describe or analyze the working of the economic system as it existed, nor primarily to portray the purely economic relations within a network of markets under the assumption of a theoretically perfect regime of free competition" (Jaffé 1977d, p. 386 [340]). Although Walras's theory superficially seems to be a treatment of the economics of pure competition, in actuality it "was deliberately designed as a normative model" (Jaffé 1974, p. 14) that "would satisfy the demands of social justice" (Jaffé 1977d, p. 386 [341]), and it is therefore "through and through informed and animated by Walras's moral convictions" (Jaffé 1977a, p. 31 [105]).[1] Walras's theory of general equilibrium, Jaffé emphasized, was constructed with "an ethico-normative purpose in mind and not, as is generally supposed, with a view to systematizing an all-encompassing theory of positive economics" (Jaffé 1974, p. 15).

[1] See also Jaffé 1977d, p. 371, and passim; 1980, pp. 530–32, 537, 538, 546; 1981, pp. 315, 334.

This thesis was expressed very forcefully by Jaffé in his penultimate article, in which he considered Michio Morishima's treatment of Walras's work: "In my estimation, Morishima got off on the wrong foot ... in supposing that 'the ultimate aim [of Walras's *Eléments*] was to construct a model, by the use of which we can examine how the capitalist system works.' That, I contend, was not the aim of the *Eléments*, either ultimate or immediate" (Jaffé 1980, p. 530 [345]). Instead, Walras's objective was "to portray how an imaginary system *might* work in conformity with principles of "justice" rooted in traditional natural law philosophy. ... The *Eléments* was intended to be and is, in all but the name, a realistic utopia" (ibid.). Walras condemned utopian schemes that totally disregard the realities of the world, but he nevertheless strove to achieve the implementation of his own ideal of social justice, one that was based on the concepts of commutative and distributive justice that are part of the humanistic tradition that stretches back to classical antiquity (Jaffé 1979, p. 15). Walras wanted a normative system, Jaffé maintained, for use as a guide to the formulation of policies that would change the structure of the economy. It would then conform to his ideal scheme and produce in reality the beneficial consequences that he deduced in his logical experiments (Jaffé 1978, p. 574).

Jaffé argued that his thesis aids in achieving a correct understanding of the meaning of Walras's theories and in evaluating them.[2] In particular, Jaffé contended, many criticisms of them are unjustifiable because Walras was concerned with a normative scheme and not with the problems in which his critics were interested (Jaffé 1977d, p. 386 [340]). "It is because our contemporary critics of Walras, our Patinkins, our Kuennes, our Garegnanis, our Morishimas, proceed blissfully unmindful of Walras's primary aim in creating his general equilibrium model that I suspect they misunderstand it and subject it to reformulations, emendations, and corrections that are beside the point" (Jaffé 1980, p. 547 [367]). "Ever since the 1920s these misdirected criticisms have given rise to a succession of corrections, emendations, modernizations, reconstructions, and outright rejections, each more ingenious than the last, but all ... mistaking the 'spirit' of the original" (Jaffé 1978, p. 575).

The implications of Jaffé's thesis are important issues for the history of economic thought. There is a major difference in character between the work of a scientist who strives as best as he can to discover what he believes is objective truth – an accurate description of facts or a theoretical explanation of them – and the work of someone who develops a system as a means of showing how his ideas about social justice can be distilled into rules of proper conduct, and as a way of demonstrating the desirable consequences

---

[2] See Walker 1981 and 1983 for accounts of Jaffé's outlook on the study of the history of scientific thought and on the nature of scientific knowledge, which helps to explain why he conceived his thesis regarding Walras's work.

those rules would have if they were adopted. In arguing that Walras's work was of the latter character, Jaffé made a very serious allegation about Walras as a scientist, about his models of general equilibrium, and about the relevance and value of criticisms and emendations of Walras's work. Furthermore, my discussions with many colleagues have made clear that they accept Jaffé's thesis because of his great authority and because of their predisposition, acquired during the course of studying philosophy, to believe that normative interests are important or even dominant in the development of any theory. Accordingly, the purpose of this chapter is to assess the validity of Jaffé's thesis, a task that entails the examination of some interesting unfamiliar parts of Walras's writings, and a reexamination of some of the familiar parts.[3]

Why, according to Jaffé, did Walras purposely conceal the normative nature of his general-equilibrium theory? The answer, Jaffé explained, is found in the circumstance that political economy was regarded with suspicion by the authorities in France in the nineteenth century. There was strict censorship during the Restoration and subsequently under Louis Philippe and Louis Napoleon, and economists had to be extremely circumspect. Consequently, when Walras decided to study economics to lay the foundation for the realization of his social ideal, he "was first obliged by the repressive regime of the Third French Empire to give his theory the appearance of a positive theory" (Jaffé 1974, p. 17). In substantiation of this position Jaffé cited letters in which Auguste Walras warned his son Léon of the need to be cautious in his treatment of sensitive social issues, and through which, according to Jaffé, he instilled in Léon a "sense of *petit-bourgeois* prudence" (Jaffé 1965, p. 231). An example of Auguste's admonitions was transmitted in a letter of 1859 prompted by Léon's authorship of a manuscript on the refutation of the economic doctrines of P.-J. Proudhon:

If you decide to publish your work, re-read it with care; don't allow anything to remain in it that would give even the slightest offense from a political point of view.

---

[3] Most of Morishima's reply (Morishima 1980, pp. 550–58) dealt with other issues, but he also responded briefly to Jaffé's thesis. He disagreed strongly with Jaffé, taking the position that Walras was concerned with obtaining "a first-approximation view of . . . reality," and describing his theory "as an abstract expression of the real world rather than a moral fiction" (ibid., p. 551, n. 2). "It is entirely clear," Morishima maintained, "that Walras's aim in the *Eléments* is to obtain a scientific description of the real world, which is the capitalist economy in his case" (ibid., p. 552). In fact, however, these were merely counter-assertions by Morishima. He did not examine or dispute the alleged evidence that Jaffé brought forward to support his thesis. Morishima's procedure instead was to present (ibid., p. 551) a few brief quotations from Walras, which Jaffé contended (Jaffé 1980, p. 530) could be done without resolving the issue in Morishima's favor. Jaffé's thesis, by contrast, was based on what he considered to be evidence, which he presented and analyzed in several articles. Jaffé's thesis was therefore evaluated for the first time in the article on which this chapter is based. I have seen no other evaluation of Jaffé's evidence since that article was written.

Place yourself and keep yourself always on scientific ground. Arrange matters, in a word, so that if by chance anyone decides to lodge charges against you, the Imperial Prosecutor would be obliged, in order to have you condemned, to maintain that the world does not turn, that the sun is no bigger than a pumpkin, that thunder is a bar of iron forged by the Cyclops and hurled by Jupiter (A. Walras to L. Walras, October 29, 1859, in A. Walras 1912, pp. 299–300).

Walras's normative ideas explicitly expressed: It is understandable that Auguste would have cautioned Léon about his book on Proudhon, because it was written in France in 1859 and was on "the social question," devoted to an examination of justice and property rights. In contrast, the character of the *Eléments,* written in Switzerland fourteen years later, is quite different, and Jaffé should not have alleged that the advice given by Auguste in 1859 led Léon to design it as a way of concealing a normative scheme.[4] Moreover, it should be noted that even in 1859 Auguste did not advise Léon to conceal normative doctrines with a positive façade, but to write a positive analysis, resting "always on scientific ground."

Intellectuals in France during the first three-quarters of the nineteenth century were fully aware of the dangers of offending the political authorities. When Walras recalled conditions in 1860, a year in which he delivered a paper on taxation in Lausanne, he observed that "in those days, one was hauled into the police court and put in prison for merely inquiring into the existing institution of property. That was precisely the fate of Vacherot. But my father had made me promise not to take this risk, though I for my part should have considered myself honored by it."[5] Nevertheless, when we examine the sort of inquiry that Walras believed that the government would suppress, we find that he was not referring to his theory of economic equilibrium, but to the politically sensitive issue of the ownership of land, for in his next sentence he went on to write: "This explains why I did no more than hint at the theory of the collective ownership of land, without enlarging upon it in my ... *Théorie critique de l'impôt.*"

The picture of Walras as a would-be reformer constrained to hide his politics by the repressive government of Napoleon III is inaccurate. In fact, Walras never at any time put aside a passionate and vocal interest in social

---

[4] Jaffé initially referred to Auguste Walras's letter as support for a contention quite different from the thesis evaluated in this chapter. Jaffé argued that Léon found pure theory more congenial than the anxiety-ridden occupation of a nineteenth-century reformer. "I would like," Jaffé wrote, "to draw your attention to a single incident at that time" – the letter from Auguste to Léon – "because I believe that we will find in it the psychological reason for his great attraction to pure economic theory, even though he was passionately interested in political and practical questions" (Jaffé 1956, p. 214 [125]). Similarly, in 1971 the inference that Jaffé drew from the circumstances of censorship and repression was that they led Walras to put aside his earlier enthusiasm for social reform and to take refuge in purely theoretical studies (Jaffé 1971, p. 93 [275]).

[5] This was Walras's statement in an unmailed letter to Charles Gide dated 1906, quoted in Jaffé 1975, p. 812 [38–39].

reform. Consider, for example, the preface to his novel *Francis Sauveur,* published in France in 1858, in which he expressed himself in the following unequivocal terms. "What is this society that we are supposed to serve?" he asked rhetorically,

And what revolting and iniquitous society is one divided into two classes of humanity: on the one side a mass of workers, despised proletarians, and on the other a group of idlers, fortunate owners of the earth on which we were born? And the leaders of this unruly society, who are they? They are these same idlers who are interested in maintaining a pact according to which they receive benefits without accepting burdens, imbecile legislators whose ineptitude is equalled only by their corruption and their venality! Serve this society! We would do that by betraying it and overthrowing it, if we knew what other to construct in its place (1858, pp. ix–x).

Similarly, Walras's concern with the censors did not prevent him from arguing in 1860 in favor of his brand of socialism (1860b, p. viii), and he spent much of his twenties involved with normative social issues, strongly influenced by the outburst of idealistic social and political schemes that followed the insurrections of 1848. All his adult life he advocated the nationalization of land; he wrote articles on "the social ideal" in the 1860s; he was active in the movement to establish workers' cooperatives; he published the aforementioned examination of Proudhon's ideas about property and justice; and in his *Recherche de l'idéal sociale,* delivered as public lectures in Paris in 1867 and 1868, he once again set forth his opinions about how society and the economy should be organized (1896c).

Moreover, there may have been repression in France, but Walras was not there when he wrote and published his *Eléments*; he was in free republican Switzerland. Far from discouraging policy proposals, the authorities who appointed Walras to his position at the Académie de Lausanne in 1871 had the objective of providing for the development of social studies that could be used to aid in framing solutions to social problems, rather than leaving the field to what they regarded as the destructive and nihilistic programs of the Internationale (1871, address by Louis Ruchonnet, pp. 8–9). The Swiss Councilor of State Louis Ruchonnet declared on the occasion of Walras's installation as professor of economics that the social question could be solved only with scientific thought: "It is necessary that science take up the problem of the future and that it speak with the complete freedom that is the privilege of science" (ibid., p. 8). To solve "social and economic questions," to find "fruitful solutions for the peace and happiness of humanity," it is necessary to begin "a serious study of the social sciences" (ibid.). Ruchonnet proudly introduced Walras, explaining that the author of the thoroughly normative *Recherche de l'idéal sociale* (1868) and the proponent of workers' cooperatives seemed to the authorities to be the best person to accomplish the purposes of the chair of economics they had just created (ibid.).

There was therefore no need for Walras to conceal an interest in social reform at the time that he wrote the *Eléments,* and he did not, revealing by the content of his speeches the improbability that he would have hidden his normative views behind the equations of an ostensibly pure theory. In his first address to a class at Lausanne, while still a visiting lecturer and therefore on probationary status, he declared his desire to inculcate in his students, with all the ardor of which he was capable, "the knowledge and love of the principles of economic science and social ethics which will definitively assure the growth of wealth and the triumph of justice" (transcript, December 16, 1870, in 1965, *1,* p. 251). It should be noted that even in that impassioned declaration, Walras distinguished positive and normative principles and re-sults. On the occasion of his installation as professor of economics at the Académie de Lausanne, he committed himself "to the careful cultivation of the notions of economic truth and social justice in order to give birth to them in the minds of my pupils" (1871, p. 42). He also wrote extensively on explicitly normative topics at the same time that he was conceiving and developing his economic theories,[6] and continually made a clear distinction between his normative and positive endeavors,[7] revealing in those additional respects the improbability of Jaffé's thesis.

There is one letter in which Walras gave a different account of the attitude of the Swiss authorities. He was asked by Charles Franklin Dunbar, the editor of *Quarterly Journal of Economics,* to write a paper on the effects of the law that established progressive taxation in the canton of Vaud. Walras answered that although he had benefited from the studies of the effects of economic policies that were made so readily during that epoch, he labored to try to establish economics on a scientific basis so that subsequent generations could proceed in a more rational fashion with their decision-making. He followed that course all the more closely at the time he was responding to Dunbar because, he wrote, "my greatly weakened health hardly leaves me the hope of finishing my work." Moreover, he continued, "I announced, when I came to this country twenty-one years ago, the intention of not taking part in economic discussions of a practical character, while claiming, on the other

---

[6] See, for example, Walras 1896c for normative essays written during the late 1860s and subsequently.

[7] Indeed, Jaffé was of the opinion in 1971 that Walras "confined his theoretical work to the rigorous plane of pure analysis. The very title of his major treatise, *Eléments d'économie politique pure,* announced unmistakably a study in the pure theory of economics, actually inspired by the pure theory of mechanics" (Jaffé 1971, p. 91 [273]). Jaffé went further to observe that Walras did not construct his pure theory for an audience that would include politicians or businessmen or humanistic scholars, but exclusively for professional economists who would be living a generation or two after his time, believing that his contemporaries could not appreciate his ideas (ibid.; see 1965, *1,* Walras's "Notice autobiographique," p. 12). It is unlikely that anyone with a message of social reform would aim it at such a select future audience.

hand, total liberty in my theoretical teachings. I have been well served by that arrangement; and, since it has been scrupulously observed by the governing officials, I am anxious to conform to it no less rigorously myself" (Walras to Charles Franklin Dunbar, February 10, 1892, in 1965, *1*, letter 1043, p. 479).

That was surely not an accurate characterization of the situation. It has just been seen that Walras was invited to Lausanne to contribute to the development of socially relevant analyses and that he had declared his interest in studying social ethics and social justice. It has also been seen that Walras in fact wrote many articles on applied economics during his tenure at the University of Lausanne. Perhaps his memory was betraying him, or perhaps he simply he wanted an excuse not to write the paper for Dunbar because he would find it too exhausting or not part of his immediate interests. In any event, it is certain that he did not just confine himself to the formulation of economic models and leave their applications and the analyses of the impact of government policy to others. Shortly after having written the letter to Dunbar, Walras plunged once more into precisely those types of policy discussions and analyses, writing on such topics as "Le Problème monétaire" (1894a), "La Monnaie de papier" (1894b), "Théorie de la propriété" (1896a), and even publishing in 1898 a manuscript full of policy prescriptions, "The State and the Railroads," which he had written in 1875 "at the request of two members of the Council of State of Vaud, at a time when the question of the purchase of the railroads [by the state], being considered again in Switzerland at the present time, had been raised in the canton of Vaud" (1898b, p. 193).

Equations to hide normative ideas: How did Jaffé support his contention that Walras adopted a theory of general equilibrium expressed in simultaneous equations as a means of concealing his normative scheme? According to Jaffé, Walras's private jottings and correspondence indicate that he came to realize from reading Achylle-Nicolas Isnard's *Traité des richesses* and Louis Poinsot's *Eléments de statique* that he could "give a neutral aspect to his model" by using a type of equation system similar to theirs (Jaffé 1974, p. 17). Jaffé did not present any evidence for that contention, and it is inconsistent with the evidence that is available on the matter, including Walras's private jottings and correspondence. Walras nowhere stated or implied that he learned from Isnard how he could hide his normative views. Walras never acknowledged receiving inspiration of any kind from Isnard's work, nor did he even mention it, except in bringing the title of his book to W.S. Jevons's attention in response to his request for titles of works on mathematical economics (Walras to William Stanley Jevons, July 13, 1878, in 1965, *1*, letter 410, pp. 570–72; and see Jaffé 1969, p. 25). Furthermore, although Jaffé's research (1969) on Isnard's work was directed at establishing that Walras drew upon it, the extent of Walras's indebtedness to Isnard is irrelevant for the present issue. The question is whether or not the reason that Walras used a system like Isnard's was that he found it a useful way of hiding the normative character of his message. When that issue is considered in the light of the direct and circumstantial evidence brought forward in this chapter, it seems reasonable to conclude that if Walras adopted Isnard's economic theories and method, he did so because he thought that they were scientifically valuable.

As for Poinsot's work, it undoubtedly stimulated and reinforced Walras's conviction that only by using mathematics and by emulating the methods of the natural sciences, and particularly the model of celestial mechanics, could economics become a true science (1860b, p. xiii; 1861, p. 93; Walras to Jules du Mesnil-Marigny, December 23, 1862, in 1965, *1*, letter 81, pp. 117–24). Indeed, Walras specifically indicated that his indebtedness to Poinsot was straightforwardly scientific. Walras reported, long after the event, that when he was nineteen years old, Poinsot's theory of equilibrium seemed to him so illuminating and comprehensive that he read the first half in one sitting and the second in another (Charles Gide to Walras, January 12, 1900, in 1965, *3*, letter 1438, p. 103), and he still owned and admired the book in 1901 (Walras to Henri Poincaré, September 26, 1901, in 1965, *3*, letter 1495, pp. 161–62). The reason that he found it so inspirational was that he wanted to express the interrelatedness of phenomena in his economic theory, and Poinsot showed how simultaneous equation systems can perform that function.

Walras's explanation of his motivation and procedure was explicit and credible. He did not write that a normative scheme was concealed under the garb of his formulas. He did not even indicate that equations were necessary in the exposition of his ideas. Far from using them to conceal a normative scheme, he asserted that he was describing his model in purely literary terms. He wrote that "there is, under the garb of my formulas, a complete system of economic theory, that is to say, a new and original conception of the mechanism of free competition in regard to exchange, production, and capital formation, which could not be demonstrated without mathematics, but which could be described very well outside of the mathematical form, and that I am concerning myself at this very moment to set forth in ordinary language" (Walras to Johan Baron d'Aulnis de Bourouill, September 10, 1878, in 1965, *1*, letter 416, pp. 579–80). Jaffé nowhere took account of those declarations, although he must have been familiar with them, as well as with comments like the following. "The use of the mathematical language and method," Walras explained, "enabled me not only to demonstrate the laws of the establishment of equilibrium prices, but also to demonstrate the laws of the variation of those prices, and to analyze the fact of free competition and in so doing to establish it as a principle .... Why not ... accept the description of the world of economic facts that conforms to the principle of free competition?" (1877b, pp. 365–66; 1889, p. 371). Thus Walras maintained that free competition was a fact and that his equations and economic reasoning expressed its workings. "I felt that I had to give both [mathematical and literary treatments]," he concluded, "in order to outline, as I wished to do, a truly scientific theory of social wealth" (ibid. p. 366; 1889, p. 372).

II. Examination of Jaffé's evidence

As far as I am aware, nowhere in Walras's writings does he state that his theory of general equilibrium has a normative purpose, and there are many places in which he states that it does not. Furthermore, an examination of the content of Walras's theory as set forth in the *Eléments* does not establish its normative nature, and there are extensive sections in that volume in which Walras argued against the introduction of normative elements into economic theory. It could therefore be argued that on balance the evidence obtained by an analysis of Walras's general-equilibrium theory is against Jaffé's thesis. Jaffé was unwilling to draw that conclusion, however. He took the position that the textual evidence in the *Eléments* is not sufficient to establish whether Walras constructed a normative scheme or had some other purpose in mind. "On this point the *Eléments* itself is not clear" (Jaffé 1980, p. 531 [347]). Unable to furnish direct evidence for his thesis in Walras's exposition of general equilibrium, Jaffé instead cited other writings in which Walras discussed ethics and economics, and used certain passages in the *Eléments* as a basis for speculations that went beyond their literal meaning. The nine considerations that Jaffé brought forward in support of his thesis will now be examined.

1. First, Jaffé placed his special interpretation on some sections of a paper that Walras submitted for a prize offered in 1860 by the Council of State of the Vaud canton in Switzerland. Referring to pure theoretical social science, Walras argued in his paper that the consequences of premises have an abstract and ideal character and should be criticized in the name of reason, truth, and absolute justice (see Jaffé 1975, p. 811, n. 10 [38 n. 10]). Jaffé also offered (1980, p. 530, n. 6 [345, n. 6]) as evidence Walras's statement that on the terrain of science we seek absolute concepts and rigorous perfection, and that "it is not sufficient to have half-utility or something close to justice, it is necessary to have complete utility, and full entire justice" (1896c, p. 188). Jaffé regarded these declarations as indicating that Walras thought that considerations of justice have a place in determining the content of pure theory. Walras did not, however, mean "ideal" in the sense of "good," but in the sense of a pure concept, like a perfect circle, which exists only as an idea and is never perfectly exemplified in fact. This he made evident in other writings, as will be seen, and by proceeding in his 1860 paper to explain that pure theory is on a different plane than policy, arguing that pure theory does not dictate the details of practical applications, since on the applied level compromises have to be made and the particular characteristics of individuals have to be taken into consideration.

Furthermore, Walras did not mean that economic science contains or is based on notions of what is just. His position on this issue and on the treatment of normative and positive economics can be made clear by presenting a representative sample of his writings. At the beginning of his career, Walras distinguished positive economics and considerations of justice, and this distinction runs consistently through his entire life's work. His opinion during the early 1860s was given in the *Théorie critique de l'impôt*, in which he wrote that economic policy is the result of the application of principles of justice to the laws of economics, and in which he made clear that his statement about "complete justice" refers to what he identified as the scientific study of justice. "Economics is an experimental science. It observes natural facts rigorously and determines their order and relationships. As for the principles of justice, they are the object of an *a priori* science; and reason, infallible reason, with the use of undebatable axioms suffices to establish ethical truths that are as incontestable as geometric theorems" (1861, p. 92). Once a set of norms is taken as given, Walras was arguing, the consequences of those norms in various derivative respects can be deduced. He declared that he needed a scientific theory of distribution, and socioeconomic laws as rational, as evident, as productive as the laws of astronomy. Such positive laws would form a secure foundation of pure scientific knowledge, and once in possession of them, he could turn to the investigation of the practical problem of taxation, which involves the normative question of justice (ibid., p. 93).

Six years later, in 1867 – just four years before beginning the development of his theory of general equilibrium – Walras expressed his outlook by dividing the study of economics into three parts (1868; 1896c, p. 31), a division which he also advocated in the *Eléments* (1874b, p. 22, lesson 5; 1889, p. 42 and lesson 3; 1900, § 20, p. 20) and in subsequent writings (see Walker 1995b). First, there is pure economic theory, which establishes *truth*, and which is the study of the natural laws of exchange, or the theory of social wealth. Second, there is applied economics, which deals with what is *useful*, and which is the study of the maximization of the production of wealth. This branch of economics is concerned with working out the consequences of given normative goals, as exemplified by the chapters that Walras was to collect in the *Etudes d'économie politique appliquée* (1898b). Third, there is social economics, which deals with what is *just*, and which is concerned with formulating goals and assessing their consequences in the areas of property and taxation. This is the normative theory of the distribution of wealth (1896c, p. 30), as exemplified by the chapters that he was to collect in the *Etudes d'économie sociale* (1896c).[8]

Then in 1874, in comments that introduced his theory of general equilibrium, Walras contended that practical expediency and material well-being on the one hand, and equity and justice on the other, are two different orders of consideration (1874b, p. 7; 1889, p. 28; 1900, § 5, p. 7).[9] Economics distinguishes, he explained, between *what is* and *what ought to be*. What ought to be, from the point of view of expediency and material well-being, is the object of applied science or art. What ought to be, from the viewpoint of equity and justice, is the object of moral science or ethics (1874b, pp.16–17; 1889, pp. 37–38). These distinctions are based on the difference between natural phenomena and phenomena that result from the exercise of human will. Two further matters are concerned with the consequences of human decisions. First, the theory of industrial activity has to do with the production of an abundance of wealth, considering the relations between people from the point of view of material well-being. Second, the theory of property is an ethical discipline that considers people in their capacity as moral beings. It has to do with the conditions of the equitable distribution of wealth, and therefore has justice as its guiding principle (1874b, pp. 38–44; 1889, pp. 57–62; and see also 1879b, pp. 15–17, 246).

Finally, from the large body of Walras's writing on the subject, all to the same effect, a sample written in the 1890s reveals him steadfastly identifying the branch of science that deals with material well-being and the branch that deals with justice (1898b, pp. 452–53). Economic laws and normative principles relate to different aspects of experience. Pure moral science is concerned with formulating the laws about facts that have their source in the exercise of human will. Pure natural science is concerned with formulating the laws about facts that have their origin in the play of the forces of nature (ibid., p.

---

[8] In a letter to Louis Ruchonnet, Walras repeated these ideas, enlarged on the content of the three divisions, and gave a remarkably prescient outline of the studies that he was to undertake over the course of the next thirty years (Walras to Louis Ruchonnet, September 6, 1870, in 1965, *1*, letter 148, pp. 204–12; see also Walras to Jules Ferry, March 11, 1878, in 1965, *1*, letter 403, pp. 561–62).

[9] In his theory of bank money, Walras analyzed (1880a) the consequences of an increase in the amount of liquid assets borrowed by entrepreneurs to finance the construction of new capital goods. He distinguished in this process between the consequences of investment financed by new savings, investment financed through bank notes, and investment financed by an increase in the quantity of money proceeding from new gold and silver discoveries. In all this reasoning, there are no normative assumptions or assertions, in contrast to those he explicitly made in his prolific writings on monetary policy (see 1898b, pp. 3–59, 150–59; 1965, *1*, letters 473, 483, 484, 513, 570; 1965, *2*, letters 618, 680, 683, 691, 731, 771, 780, 789, 1034, 1136, 1142, 1145, 1148).

452). Applied science, which is concerned with guiding the directions in which human will is exercised, is divided into applied ethics and applied natural science. Applied ethics deals with the principles of relationships between people, and is pursued from the point of view of justice. Applied natural science deals with the rules of relationships between persons or things, and is pursued from a viewpoint of what is useful. Applied economics, which enunciates the rules of what is useful, is an applied natural science that deals with the relationships between people, not as moral beings, but as workers undertaking tasks in accordance with their relationships with things. Thus the evidence all shows that Walras was very much aware of the distinction between normative and positive studies, and of the desirability of keeping them separate. It is also clear that he regarded economic theory as a positive study of economic behavior.

2. A second piece of evidence offered by Jaffé was Walras's 1868 statement that

in regard to science, we are on the terrain of ideas, of the ideal, of perfection. No one can prevent us from defining, that is to say, from abstracting from experience, such ideas as those of social wealth; of capital and revenues; of productive services and products; of landowners, workers, and capitalists; of entrepreneurs; of the market and prices; of man in society pursuing different occupations, reasonable and free (Walras 1896c, p. 187; cited in Jaffé 1980, p. 530, n. 6 [345, n. 6]).

Those observations in no way support Jaffé's thesis. Walras's statement asserts that science makes abstractions from reality and that it formulates concepts that are perfect and ideal in the sense that they are not influenced by extraneous complications and the idiosyncratic character of phenomena in the actual world. Once again, Walras was referring to the ideal and to perfection in the sense that characterizes the definitions of geometry or pure physics. He went on in the same passage to make a number of remarks that demonstrate not a fusion but a separation of positive and normative reasoning. On the foundation of the pure abstractions of economic science, he wrote, it is possible to establish the theory of production and distribution, a theory that demonstrates scientifically when private enterprise results in abundance and when it does not. It then becomes possible to formulate normative practical proposals as to when the state should intervene in the economy (1896c, p. 188).

3. Jaffé maintained on the basis of two considerations that Walras's theory of consumer demand embodies his normative views. One of Jaffé's contentions was that Walras's normative aim was manifested by his lack of interest in the characteristics of individual consumption, as contrasted with his concern for the relevance of the theory of demand to the conditions of market equilibrium (Jaffé 1974, p. 14). The absence of an area of study from a writer's work cannot be accepted as evidence of the manifestation of a normative intention in the areas that he does investigate. Jaffé's other assertion was that the purpose of Walras's theory of demand was to investigate the justice of the outcome of exchange in a competitive market (ibid., pp. 14–15). The history of the development of Walras's theory of demand disproves that contention.

Walras labored over the theory of demand for thirteen years. At first, in his own unaided efforts, he followed a futile maze of mathematical reasoning about scarcity, extensive utility, intensive utility, virtual utility, effective utility, ratios of supply and demand, and a number of other purely technical considerations – a maze that had nothing to do with social reform (1860a; 1860b, pp. xiv, xxxiv, xlviii, lix; Walras notes summarized in 1965, *1*, pp. 293–94; and see Jaffé 1972, pp. 392–97). Finally, in 1872 he asked a colleague at the Académie de Lausanne, Antoine Paul Piccard, for the answer to the problem of the derivation of the demand curve from the utility function. It is obvious from Piccard's response that Walras did not frame the problem in a normative manner, nor ask how a normative theory could be concealed within the theory of demand. Piccard provided him with a model of utility maximization and derived the demand function within it (undated transcript by Paul Piccard, in 1965, *1*, pp. 309–11). Walras took over that model in its entirety and utilized it in his economic analysis without adding normative elements to it. Subsequently, he modified his theory of demand in ways that were stimulated by scientific considerations brought to his attention by other writers. His adoption of nonlinear marginal-utility curves was almost certainly made in response to criticisms by Wilhelm Lexis. His discussion of the proportionality of marginal utilities under conditions of discontinuous marginal-utility curves was made in response to comments by Eugen von Böhm-Bawerk. His introduction of a second-order condition for a utility maximum was made in response to a suggestion by Ladislaus von Bortkiewicz (Bortkiewicz to Walras, April 27/May 9, 1888, in 1965, *2*, letter 831, p. 248; Jaffé 1977b, p. 302 [215]; Jaffé 1977c, pp. 210–12 [89–91]).

The Walrasian theory of demand as it ultimately emerged was therefore in large part composed of the ideas of scientists other than Walras. Jaffé himself in 1972 remarked on the circumstances of its origin in the following terms: "Does not," he asked, "the biographical narrative of Léon Walras's awesome voyage of discovery of marginal utility in terms of a differential coefficient reveal the voyage as an academic adventure, directed in large part by prevailing pedagogic winds?" (Jaffé 1972, p. 401 [307]). Since the same theory had been published by H.H. Gossen in Germany in 1854, and was independently discovered around 1870 by W.S. Jevons in England and Carl Menger in Austria, it was evidently the outcome of contemporary intellectual conditions, not the result of Walras's normative views.

Many other examples of Walras's work could be presented, such as his theories of interest, of bank money,[10] of production,[11] of capitalization; his treatment of business accounting and inventory; and his analysis of bimetallism and fiduciary money. An examination of them cannot fail to reveal their patently scientific and technical character. Like the theory of demand, some of them were to a considerable extent based on the ideas of other economists. It cannot accurately be maintained, therefore, that the parts of Walras's system were designed as embodiments of his normative views nor therefore that it is "through and through informed" by them.

4. The fourth piece of evidence that Jaffé brought forward (1980, pp. 530–31) is the change of the wording of a passage in which Walras described his theory of capital formation. In the second edition of the *Eléments* he stated that it is a faithful expression and exact explanation of real phenomena (1889, p. xxii). In the third and subsequent editions (1896b, p. XXII; 1889, p. 68; 1900, p. XVIII; 1954, p. 46), he described it as an abstract expression and rational explanation of real phenomena. The change to the latter wording is a manifestation of an effort to give a more careful exposition of the relationship of theory to reality, not evidence that his work is a moralizing fiction. This interpretation of the internal content of the passage is straightforward and it is also supported by the viewpoint established in the *Eléments* as a whole, and by its consistency with Walras's explicit methodological position. In the first and subsequent editions of the *Eléments,* he explained that

in applied geometry, for example, there are to be found only approximations of the pure ideal types defined in the science of geometry, but this does not prevent geometry from having many rich applications. Following this same method, pure economics ought to borrow from experience the concepts of exchange, of supply, of demand, of a market, of capital, of revenues, or productive services, of products. From these real phenomena, economics should abstract and define ideal types, and use them in its reasoning, not returning to reality to make its applications until the structure of the science is complete. We thus have, in an ideal market, ideal prices which have a rigorous relationship to ideal supply and demand (Walras 1874b, 32; 1889, pp. 51–52).

[10] The notion that inputs are used in productive processes is not normative, nor is the idea that they are combined in certain proportions. Was Walras's treatment of the way in which they are combined affected by his view of social justice? The answer must be that it was not. He initially assumed that their proportions were fixed, because he was unfamiliar with the mathematics that would have enabled him to assume that they are variable. When he made the latter assumption, it was because he finally achieved an understanding of the mathematics with which Enrico Barone presented it. In fact, the theory of marginal productivity that Walras embraced as part of his model of general equilibrium and presented in the *Eléments* was largely a creation of Barone's (Jaffé 1964). To sustain his thesis on this topic, Jaffé was by implication arguing the absurd notion that Barone developed the theory as a normative scheme and concealed that fact with mathematics, but that Walras perceived its normative nature, found it consistent with his own biases, and therefore adopted it.

[11] For the positive theorem of maximum satisfaction, Walras referred to the *Eléments*, lessons 20, 21, and 22 (1898b, p. 195, n.). For the normative conclusion, he referred (ibid., p. 197, n.) to his "Théorie de la propriété," which appears in his volume on social economics (1896c).

Walras believed it was necessary "to simplify as much as possible, to concentrate on the general case and to follow reality closely" (Walras to Charles Gide, April 11, 1891, in 1965, 2, letter 1000, pp. 435–36). Walras therefore intended his entire theory to be "an abstract expression and rational explanation of real phenomena" because he believed that was the true relation of his theory to reality, not because he wanted to construct a normative scheme.

5. To lend credibility to his thesis, Jaffé formulated characterizations of French traditions in philosophy and of the age in which Walras's work was conceived, noted Auguste and Léon Walras's objective of social reform, remarked on the characteristics of French rationalism, and concluded that the *Eléments* was designed in that tradition as "a theoretical representation of a just economy from the standpoint of 'commutative justice' " (Jaffé 1980, p. 532 [348]). Commutative justice refers to the ethical rightness of the results of exchanging commodities. Is it true that Walras wanted to develop a theory of exchange that embodied a scheme of social justice? Even in his earliest work he indicated that that is not appropriate. In *L'Economie politique et la justice,* written in 1860, he argued that it is possible to have a theory of value in exchange that is independent of considerations of justice (1860b, p. 11). The theory of value in exchange and the theory of property differ, he maintained, because of their different points of view. Value in exchange is a natural fact, because it has its origin in deterministic natural forces, resulting in part from the presence of humanity on earth and in part from the limitation in the quantity of useful things. It is as independent of free will as are the facts of mass, weight, and vegetation. Property, on the other hand, is an ethical phenomenon, because it has its origin in the free will of mankind. Mere appropriation arises because of scarcity, but property results from the ethical characteristics of ownership, which are features of the morality or immorality of the circumstances of the appropriation (ibid. p. 13). Thus there are two distinctly different theories dealing with different facts: the natural science of value in exchange, which is logically the first of the economic sciences, and the ethical science of property. "I would like to believe," Walras wrote,

that M. Proudhon never thought of being astonished that mathematicians or physicists are not preoccupied with the notion of justice. It is good to be upset about rights; it is not necessary to invoke them at all points. The binomial theorem of Newton is neither just nor unjust, and the hypothesis of two electricities is not constrained by the rules of morality. Nor is the theory of value in exchange, believe it well, Monsieur Proudhon. It is a natural science and independent of justice (ibid., pp. 18–19).

That Walras adhered to that idea throughout his career has been demonstrated in the exposition of his distinction between normative and positive economics and his related tripartite division of economic studies.

6. Jaffé argued that the normative convictions he believed underlie Walras's theory of equilibrium are revealed most clearly in his theorem of maximum social satisfaction (Jaffé 1977d, p. 371 [326]). Briefly, this is the theorem that traders can obtain the greatest possible satisfaction through trade at a single price in a purely competitive market (1874b, p. 99; 1877b, p. 67; 1889, pp. 251–52). In a Walrasian pledges market, trade on any particular day occurs only at the price that is the solution to the supply and demand functions that have the initial asset distribution as a parameter. Jaffé contended that Walras introduced the condition of a single price because he believed that any redistribution of aggregate asset values during the course of exchange would result in some traders benefiting at the expense of others, and he wanted to ensure that such an unjust process cannot occur. "Uniformity of competitively determined price represented for Walras not only an analytical ideal, but an ethical ideal as well, constituting an indispensable pillar of social justice" (Jaffé 1977d, p. 375 [330]). Jaffé concluded that "Walras's multi-equational system of general equilibrium thus appears profoundly moralistic" (ibid.).

There can be no doubt that Walras believed that a single trading price on a particular market day is desirable. He stated that thesis in his "Théorie de la propriété," which was avowedly devoted to normative economics. To be precise, he thought the condition of a single price is just, not because it eliminates changes in the value of a trader's assets, but because an inequitable situation would be created on a given market day if one buyer acquired a commodity for less than was paid by another, or if one seller received a higher price than another (1868; 1896c, p. 212). He also thought it would be unjust for changes in the value of money to occur, because otherwise, for example, a buyer might part with a smaller amount of real purchasing power than the seller subsequently finds that he has acquired. Finally, he also believed that it is just that commodities be produced and sold at as low a cost per unit as possible (ibid.). Jaffé contended that the last two arguments are in the *Eléments,* "though not in so many words" (Jaffé 1977d, p. 374 [329]).

What appears in the *Eléments,* however, is a theorem that in purely competitive equilibrium any commodity exchanges at a single price that equals its average cost of production, and that this produces a constrained maximum of satisfaction. Instead of mixing together science and his moral views, Walras first expressed that theorem, which he believed was an expression of a scientific truth, and then he made a normative judgment on it. This procedure is shown clearly in Walras's "L'Etat et les chemins de fer," written in 1875 (1875, in 1898b, pp. 193–236). He explained the difference between the theorem and his normative conclusion. He stated that economic theory teaches us that in pure competition the inputs in the productive process are combined in products of the kinds and in the quantities that give the greatest possible satisfaction of wants, subject to two conditions that result from competition. One is that there is a single price for each service, the price at which the supply and demand quantities are equal. The other is that the price of each output is equal to its average cost of production. These two conditions, he argued, can be reduced to the single condition that services are exchanged for each other in proportions that result from the preferences of their owners. Pure economic theory, he wrote, therefore deduces the principle that competition results in economic services being put to their most efficient use in producing want-satisfying commodities. Walras then introduced the normative judgment that this theoretical consequence of pure competition is socially desirable, so practical policies should be implemented to achieve it. It is "a condition of justice that social economics should establish," in the sense that policies should be devised to achieve it (ibid., pp. 196–97). Applied economics should discover the cases in which competition is not possible and devise for them some other means of accomplishing the condition of justice (ibid., p. 197).[12]

Jaffé believed that Walras, in his discussion of the theorem of maximum satisfaction in the *Eléments,* "momentarily dropped his pure theory mask" by developing an argument favoring pure competition based "on moral grounds rather than on grounds of economic efficiency" (Jaffé 1977d, p. 375 [330]). The implication that Walras framed his theorem as a means of expressing a concealed utopian scheme is an interpretation that cannot be sustained by the passage Jaffé refers to (1877, pp. 266–67; 1889, pp. 251–52). In that passage Walras followed the same procedure as in his "L'Etat et les chemins de fer." He was careful to state that in developing the pure science of economics he had assumed competition as a fact or even as a hypothesis. It is of little significance, Walras remarked, whether it is regarded as the former or the latter, because to achieve rigor it is sufficient that a conception of pure competition be formed. Simply because competition does not exist in all aspects of the economy does not mean it is not a useful or valid scientific assumption. In the first place, he observed, noncompetitive conditions may eventually be incorporated into the equations of the model. In the second place, he explained, he had studied the nature, causes, and consequences of pure competition, and among those consequences he had deduced the important result that, subject to certain limits, it results in a maximum of utility. About this theorem, Walras concluded with "a last observation of the greatest importance. Our demonstration of the characteristics of free competition deals with the question of material well-being, and takes no account of the

---

[12] Walras did not believe that the initial endowments – that is, the distribution of wealth and income existing at any particular time – are inherently just. That is why he developed the normative discipline of social economics, in which he proposed state intervention to change endowments by nationalizing land and to provide equality of opportunity so that wealth would be obtained as a result of merit.

question of justice." That normative question, he stated, is open for exploration. Only after an objective statement of the theorem did Walras introduce the explicit normative judgment that it is desirable to achieve maximum utility, and formulate the proposal that all obstacles to pure competition should therefore be eliminated (1877b, 268–69; 1889, pp. 251–254).

Could Walras have assumed that there are many prices in equilibrium in a purely competitive market if he had thought that this was a condition of social justice? The obvious answer is that he could not. Whether or not Walras approved of a single price, that market characteristic is not an axiom but a consequence of the basic institutional conditions and trading rules in a purely competitive pledges model, as he indicated on many occasions (1874a, p. 6; 1898b, pp. 197–98; see chs. 3, 4, 5). Having constructed the competitive pledges model and having deduced among its consequences the feature of a single trading price on a given day, Walras then considered whether or not it is good. "It remains only to be known," he wrote, "if the condition of a single price is a condition of justice. This is a question which is not within the province of pure economics, and one which I treat with the greatest care in the part of the science which is concerned with the distribution of wealth and in which the principles of social ethics intervene" (Walras to Carl Friedrich Wilhelm Launhardt, May 20, 1885, in 1965, 2, letter 652, pp. 49–50). Thus in his normative work, Walras investigated the welfare implications of a single price, and because of the rightness that he discovered in that condition, he advocated purely competitive markets or state intervention to achieve it.

Since a single price is a consequence of purely competitive exchange, in a pledges market, the question may be raised as to whether Walras assumed the basic postulates of pure competition as a way of introducing covert normative views. Far from substantiating Jaffé's thesis, the evidence shows that Walras had no such intention. Walras began his *Principe d'une théorie mathématique de l'échange* of 1873 – his first accomplishment in economic theory, and one that expressed his methodological point of view and scientific objectives at the time that he wrote the first edition of his *Eléments* – with a warning against the practice in French economics of mixing normative and positive economics together, and with a declaration that economics could be transformed into a proper science by use of the mathematical method (1874a, p. 5). Pure economics is the study of the necessary and natural effects of free competition on to production and exchange. On the other hand, applied economics is the demonstration of the conformity of these effects with the general material welfare, and consequently is the study of the application of the principle of free competition to agriculture, industry, commerce, and credit. Is it not necessary, he asked, to ascertain the results of *laisser-faire laisser-passer* in order to judge whether they are desirable? "Let us assume that there is pure competition, pure *laisser-faire laisser-passer*, making abstraction of any consideration of expediency or of justice. I do not to any degree assume free competition because it may be believed to be more useful or more equitable, but for the sole purpose of knowing its results" (ibid.). He did not assume free competition for a normative purpose.

From that assumption, Walras continued, necessarily proceed three derivative features: commodities are produced, commodities are exchanged at determinate prices, and productive services are exchanged at determinate prices. "These are the natural and necessary effects of free competition in regard to production and exchange. The study of these effects should be, in my opinion, pursued in a special manner, independently of any question and prior to any consequence that may result from their application" (ibid., p. 6). He did not study pure competition because of the normative qualities of its consequences.

That approach to his subject was expressed by Walras repeatedly throughout his career. In a letter written in 1877 to the philosopher Charles Bernard Renouvier, for example, Walras explained:

With respect to my pure economic theory, it studies purely and simply the facts of the determination of prices or proportions in exchange under a hypothetical regime of absolutely pure competition. It makes no conclusion either for or against that regime, and I believe that it is necessary to remove its study from the ethical point of view. You may be sure that when I introduce that point of view, it will find the field of inquiry free from any given preconception (Walras to Charles Bernard Renouvier, September 6, 1877, in 1965, *1*, letter 385, pp. 542–43).

Of course, Walras did introduce the normative point of view when he turned to the formulation of economic policies, like writers that preceded and followed him. Economists as diverse in their social philosophy as Joseph Schumpeter and Oskar Lange have subscribed to general-equilibrium theory, illustrating a relation that is often found between economic theories and value judgments. A particular structure of ideas is acceptable to people with different normative beliefs because of its scientific value and its intrinsic ethical neutrality, and is then used as a foundation or justification for moral judgments and economic policies that differ in accordance with the different normative convictions of their formulators.

7. Jaffé alleged that Walras introduced his equations of exchange (1874b, pp. 120–22, 142; 1889, pp. 143–45, 168), which are budget constraints, as part of the requirements for justice in exchange (Jaffé 1977d, pp. 373–74 [328–29]. An implication of the equations, as Jaffé pointed out, is that traders' asset values are unchanged by trade at the equilibrium price. Jaffé believed that Walras, aware of that circumstance, introduced the equations to prevent, in his models, the injustice of any trader's increasing his asset values, since on a given market day that could occur only at the expense of some other trader. That was a speculation on Jaffé's part, because Walras did not remark on any normative implications that his budget constraints might have, and an examination of them does not support Jaffé's thesis. Two considerations are relevant for judging Walras's procedure. First, by introducing the budget constraint of a trader, he was expressing a fact of economic life, not a normative condition. Second, the constancy of asset values that follows from exchange that occurs at a given price subject to a budget constraint is another fact of economic life. Walras could not have argued that the values are different after exchange if that had been the condition he preferred. Whether one likes it or not, it is simply a truism to say that a trader's money plus his stock of a commodity valued at a given price has the same total value before and after exchange at that price. Traders are able to change the value of their assets only by trading at a series of different prices, either on the same market day in a disequilibrium-transactions market, or from one day to another in a pledges market. It is therefore clear that Walras was describing an objective feature of the exchange process.

Furthermore, he had no adverse reaction to the circumstance that one day succeeds another in a pledges market, and that the values of the traders' assets consequently change. If Walras had wished to devise a market model in which no one changes the value of his assets, he would have had to ensure that equilibrium prices are always the same. That would have required him to introduce the absurd condition that market parameters never change, which of course he did not do. On the contrary, he specifically indicated that there is in actuality a continuous variation of the conditions that are parameters for a market day and that there is therefore a series of market days (1877b, pp. 310–11; 1889, pp. 316–17).

8. As part of his evidence, Jaffé argued that Walras displayed a normative bias by criticizing Gossen's theorem of maximum satisfaction on the ground that it implies that the initial endowments of the traders should be pooled and then divided up in such a way as to maximize joint utility (Jaffé 1977d, pp. 381–85 [335–340]). It is true that Gossen's scheme does not preserve the initial endowments, but Walras did not, contrary to Jaffé's interpretation, object to that implication of the theorem, but to two other aspects of it.[13]

First, he argued that it is scientifically faulty because it defines an absolute maximum rather than one that is constrained by the condition of a single price at which the supply and demand quantities are equal. Gossen's theorem is wrong, Walras stated, because it does not introduce relevant market conditions (1885, pp. 76, 78–79; 1889, pp. 188–89). In contrast, Walras explained, his own theorem of maximum utility takes cognizance of the fact that free competition results in a single price, and expresses the welfare implications of that condition, defining not an absolute maximum but a relative one.

---

[13] That statement was introduced in the second edition of the *Eléments* (1889, p. 287), except for the last four words.

Second, Walras also saw that Gossen's theorem is not a scientific description of the welfare consequences of an actual market process, but a policy proposal, and he argued that the normative position embodied in that policy is unjustifiable because it allows different people simultaneously to trade at different prices (1889, p. 189). It would, Walras observed, obviously be possible to generate levels of welfare that are higher than those that result from pure competition by using noncompetitive types of pricing systems, such as selling commodities at higher prices to the rich than to the poor; but what is the best system? (Walras to Carl Friedrich Wilhelm Launhardt, May 20, 1885, in 1965, 2, letter 652, pp. 49–50). Consideration of that question raises the normative issue of whether a single price, which would be provided by pure competition, is a necessary condition of justice. Walras argued that it is, and therefore that pure competition is the best plan. "The goal that should be pursued," he wrote, "is not maximum welfare, but a welfare maximum that is *compatible with justice*" (ibid.).

Walras's second criticism of Gossen's plan was therefore frankly normative, and as such it does not constitute evidence that Walras's theory of general equilibrium was a normative scheme. As has been observed, Walras was concerned with justice, like most economists. The conditions of justice were the reason for his development of a normative branch of economic analysis and argumentation, of which his second criticism of Gossen's theorem was a part. On the basis of that normative work, however, Jaffé made an erroneous inference. As in many of his other arguments in favor of his thesis, Jaffé's treatment of Walras on Gossen's theorem contains the confusion of supposing that Walras's expressions of concern with social justice are evidence that his economic theory is normative. It is not, however, legitimate to assert that because Walras explored and approved of the consequences of a single price he must have inserted that condition into his theory as a normative postulate. To observe that competitive markets produce a result that is compatible with a particular conception of justice is not evidence that the theory of those markets is itself a normative scheme.

9. Jaffé speculated that Walras's theory of tatonnement was not designed, as Jaffé had originally argued, to "lend an air of empirical relevance" to the theory of general equilibrium (Jaffé 1967, p. 2 [222]), but to portray a "feasible desideratum rather than an empirical fact" (Jaffé 1981, p. 315 [246]). The evidence does not support Jaffé's contention. There are two tatonnement processes in Walras's models. One is the changing of the price in any market in the same direction as the sign of the market excess demand quantity. The other is the adjustment of the rate of production of each commodity in the same direction as the sign of the price minus the average cost. Those cannot be regarded as normative propositions.

Walras did not assert that the tatonnement process was a policy proposal that he wanted to see implemented. On the contrary, he never deviated from the belief that real organized competitive markets actually employ Walrasian pricing and a pledges process, and he stated repeatedly that his model of market pricing is realistic (1898b, pp. 408–9, 432; Walras to Edouard Pfeiffer, April 2, 1874, in 1965, *1,* letter 256, pp. 370–74; Walras to Ladislaus von Bortkiewicz, October 17, 1889, in 1965, *2,* letter 927, pp. 363-64; Walras to Flippo Virgilii, October 17, 1889, in 1965, *2,* letter 928, pp. 364–65; Walras to Albert Aupetit, August 7, 1901, in 1965, *3,* letter 1491, pp. 155–56, n. 8). "We will now see," he asserted, "how the same problem of exchange of several commodities to which we have just found the scientific solution is also that which is solved empirically in real markets as a result of the mechanism of competition" (1874b, p. 126; 1889, p. 148; 1900, § 124, p. 129; and see 1889, p. 141). Repeatedly he wrote that actual markets generate trading prices that are the solutions to a system of Walrasian equations as a result of Walrasian pricing: "What is necessary," he asked, "to establish that the theoretical solution and the solution in the marketplace are identical? Simply that the raising and lowering of prices are a mode of solution by tatonnement of the system of equations of the equality of supply and demand" (1889, p. 149). Again, in his discussion of new capital goods, Walras set forth a Walrasian pricing model, and then observed that "the indicated tatonnement is exactly that which transpires in the market for new capital goods" (1889, p. 287).[14]

In the mature phase of his theoretical activity, Walras habitually thought of the tatonnement processes in his models as describing how real purely competitive markets come into a mutually determined equilibrium. "It remains only to demonstrate in regard to production as in regard to exchange, that the same problem to which we have given the theoretical solution is also that which is solved empirically in real markets by the mechanism of free competition" (1877b, p. 251; 1889, p. 234). Walrasian pricing and the adjustments of the rate of production that cause the difference between price and average cost to diminish are, he believed, a feature of the real market system:

The object and . . . goal of economic theory . . . consist above all and before all in the demonstration [that] the operations on the markets of raising and lowering prices, of increasing and decreasing the level of production of commodities, etc., are nothing other than the solution by tatonnement of the equations of exchange, production, and

---

[14] It is also true that in one place Walras formulated an iterative technique by which an economic theorist can solve the equations of equilibrium and thereby find the solutions that he believed are achieved simultaneously by real interrelated markets. He described both the iterative technique and real market behavior as tatonnement processes: "In considering that the tatonnements which I thus present successively by analytical necessity in fact operate *simultaneously* in real markets, do you not have exactly in its entirety the fact of the determination of the prices of several commodities under the regime of free competition?" (Walras to Maffeo Pantaleoni, September 2, 1889, in 1965, *2,* letter 913, pp. 343–47).

capital formation (Walras to Ladislaus von Borkiewicz, October 17, 1889, in 1965, *2*, letter 927, pp. 364–65; and see 1874b, p. 49; 1889, p. 67; 1900, § 41, p. 45).

Walras concluded with the assertion that he had formulated a system of equations that have a set of solutions, and that he had "demonstrated that the sequence of real phenomena generates in actuality the empirical solution of that system of equations. This I have done," he maintained, "successively for exchange, for production, and for capital formation" (1877b, p. 365; 1889, p. 370). Thus Walras did not design the tatonnement process in pricing or in production as a utopian scheme but, he thought, as a description of real adjustments. In no instance did he describe tatonnement processes as normative objectives, nor do they have any such role in his models.

III. Conclusion

The relatively permissive political climate prevailing in Switzerland at the time that Walras wrote his *Eléments* has been described. His methodological views and classification of scientific studies, which draw careful distinctions between normative and positive subject matters, have been examined. The fact that he did not hide his moral convictions and his cultivation of normative economics under that explicit title have been noted, as has his related lack of a motive to construct a covertly normative economic theory. His assertions that his theoretical works were positive and his condemnation of the intrusion of normative considerations into scientific investigation have been cited. The positive content and objectives of his comprehensive model of general equilibration and equilibrium as a whole and of a number of its components have been presented.

On the basis of the evidence it must be concluded that Walras's economic theory does not carry within it a particular conception of social justice, and that his objective during his mature phase was to analyze the workings of the economic system. The conclusion reached here is therefore the same as the one reached by William Jaffé in his studies during the forty-year period prior to 1974.[15] The basic idea expressed by Walras's general-equilibrium model is that markets are interrelated, which is not a normative concept. Walras's desire to analyze their interrelatedness was the reason for the character of his model of general equilibrium, not a desire to use simultaneous equations and the idea of interrelated markets as a vehicle and veil for his moral convictions.

Contrary to Jaffé's contention, Walras did not make the assumption of free competition in his models in order to construct a utopian scheme. He recognized the existence of deviations from freely competitive economic behavior

---

[15] See, for example, Jaffé 1935, pp. 192–94, 198–99; 1956, p. 215; 1969, p. 2; 1971, pp. 91–94, 98, 104; 1972, pp. 380–83, 401. See also notes 4 and 7.

and he believed that one day they would be given a place in a general-equilibrium model (1877b, p. 267; 1889, p. 252; 1900, § 222, p. 232), but that task was beyond him. Therefore, like dozens of theorists before and after him, in order to undertake the analysis of markets he assumed pure competition to simplify his subject matter, believing that it was a reasonable approximation to the real economy, that it was scientifically necessary because of the complexity and lack of generality of alternative assumptions, and that it resulted in a system that provided a guide to the understanding of reality.

Jaffé argued that Walras used mathematics to hide a normative scheme. Walras, however, made a different allegation: "My application of mathematics to economic theory has no objective other than the scientific determination of the relations among the variables: quantity, utility and marginal utility, demand, supply, the prices of commodities" (Walras to Charles Bernard Renouvier, September 25, 1874, in 1965, *1,* letter 303, p. 435). Jaffé believed that Walras purposely constructed his model as an "ideal fiction" (Jaffé 1980, p. 533 [349]). Walras, however, took a different view: "I continue to believe," he wrote, "that my conception of the equilibrium of production is not a *fiction* but an *abstraction* completely analogous to the conceptions of mechanics" (Walras to Johan Gustav Knut Wicksell, November 10, 1893, in 1965, *2,* letter 1170, p. 598). He stated that his intention was to construct an abstract account of reality, not a utopian dream, and he thought he had succeeded. His system, he wrote, is "très conforme à la réalité" (1879a, in 1965, *1,* letter 453, p. 628, n. 3). Whether or not he was unconsciously influenced by his normative views in developing some parts of his theoretical work, he did not intend it to be a normative scheme.

CHAPTER 3

The mature models of the barter of stocks of commodities

Walras's models of the barter of stocks of commodities are described with regard to those features that determine and express the pricing and exchange processes – namely, their physical characteristics, participants, institutions, procedures, rules, and behavioral patterns. It is shown that Walras's arbitrage model is defective and that Walrasian arbitrage is not an equilibrating mechanism in the other barter models. It is also shown that they are complete functioning systems, that the numeraire does not simplify pricing in the models, that the pricing process in the models does not involve a central or particular-market authority, and that the models do not use or logically depend on the assumption of large numbers of traders.

I. Introduction

This chapter has the general objective of describing and evaluating the processes of pricing and exchange in the models of the barter of fixed total stocks of commodities that Walras presented during the mature phase of his theorizing.[1] Walras placed these models at the beginning of the series of lessons on markets in the *Eléments*. The models were intended by him to display fundamental and elemental features of market behavior, as though they are logically antecedent to markets in which money is used. In fact, as will be seen, Walras took most of the characteristics of the barter markets from organized monetary markets, and his assumption of barter, as will also be seen, created situations that are not simpler but more complex than those found in monetary markets.

The chapter answers the following specific questions. First, what are the physical structures, market institutions, participants, procedures, rules, and behavioral patterns that determine and express the pricing and exchange

---

[1] Accordingly, Walras's models of the barter of stocks and commodities are examined as they appear in the second and third editions of the *Eléments*. As it happens, when Walras prepared the fourth and fifth editions, he made no changes in the models, although he added a few words, phrases, and very short explanatory sections to them (1900, § 82, pp. 83–84; § 122, pp. 127–28; § 151, p. 157). Thus, the work surveyed in this chapter is not only Walras's mature thought on the topic but also his final thought on it.

processes in those models?[2] Second, is arbitrage an equilibrating mechanism in them? Third, how does Walras's introduction of a numeraire affect their behavior? Fourth, did he construct a particular-market model of barter that is a complete system in the sense that it has structural and behavioral features that are sufficient to generate processes of pricing and trade in it and for the variables to converge to equilibrium? Fifth, did he construct a similarly complete model of a general-equilibrium system of barter markets? Sixth, did he assert that the behavior of the models depends on the participation of large numbers of traders in each market and does it in fact so depend? Seventh, does his assumption of barter provide illuminating insights into the characteristics of exchange in real markets?

It will be understood that except for the reference just made to Walras's barter flow markets, the term "barter model" and similar terms involving the word "barter" in this chapter refer to Walras's models of the type indicated by its title.[3] His simple barter models are considered because he assumed that most of their structural and behavioral features also characterize his general model of barter, without explicitly repeating mention of all of them in his discussion of the latter. Walras presented the models in logical order, beginning with the simplest case and proceeding to progressively more complex cases, and that is the order in which they are examined in this chapter.

II. The simple barter models

Two commodities

In Walras's first barter model, he assumed that two commodities are exchanged for each other. He assumed there is no money and no numeraire, so the model is not only one of barter but also one in which pricing is direct. That is to say, the price of each commodity is expressed in terms of the number of units of the other commodity that will be given in exchange for a unit of it, rather than the price of each being expressed in terms of a third item. Walras made a number of assumptions about the physical structure of the marketplace, the characteristics of the participants, and their trading procedures. It will be seen that he used a number of the features of his model of the structure and functioning of the Parisian stock and bond market (chs. 4, 5) in his models of the barter of fixed total stocks of commodities. The assumptions make it evident that he was thinking of a market process that

---

[2] Thus, this chapter is not concerned with such matters as Walras's treatment of preferences, how he derived the offer functions of the participants, the Pareto optimality of the equilibria, or the mathematics of the equations systems.

[3] It should be noted that Walras also constructed some models of barter that are quite distinct from those studied in this chapter – namely, models of the barter of rates of supply of services for rates of supply of consumer goods, and of the barter of rates of supply of services for rates of supply of new capital goods (see chs. 15 and 16).

takes place in an area sufficiently small and constructed in such a manner that all the traders can see and hear each other. Some people initially hold only commodity (A). They arrive "on one side" of the marketplace, and are prepared to give a part of their holdings in exchange for commodity (B). Some people initially hold only commodity (B). They arrive "on the other side" of the marketplace, and are prepared to give a part of their holdings in exchange for commodity (A) (1874a, p. 100; 1874b, p. 52; 1889, p. 70; 1900, § 44, p. 48).[4] Each trader has a supply or demand function. At any two reciprocal prices, p_a and p_b, the quantities supplied or demanded by each trader "would be determined without premeditated calculation, but nevertheless conforming to the condition of maximum satisfaction" (1874b, p. 98; 1889, p. 119; 1900, § 98, p. 98).

How prices are quoted

The manner in which Walras enabled the price to be quoted and changed in any particular barter market will now be examined. The received view has recently been expressed by W. Hildenbrand and A.P. Kirman, who are singled out for quotation here because they made their remarks in the last decade and made them specifically in reference to a barter model with fixed total stocks. They assert that Walras assumed that "individuals are *price-takers,* that is, they have no influence on prices and therefore take them as given" (Hildenbrand and Kirman 1988, p. 89; and see p. 7). As Kirman expressed matters, "if all the participants are price-takers by definition, then the actor who adjusts prices to eliminate excess demand is not specified" (Kirman 1992, p. 119, n. 1). Given that belief, the authors naturally have to find some mechanism other than the traders' behavior to bring about changes of prices in Walras's models. They find it, they allege, in "an ingenious idea of Walras, the so-called 'tâtonnement' process. Walras envisioned a situation in which a central auctioneer or 'crier' announces prices and then modifies them progressively until equilibrium is achieved" (Hildenbrand and Kirman 1988, pp. 102–3). Those authors could not furnish any evidence that Walras did so, for the reason that he did not state or imply that a central authority announces and changes prices, nor is there any logical necessity for such a personage in Walras's models. Nowhere in his five barter models is there any statement that could by any stretch of the imagination be construed as even hinting at such an authority, and in each of the many passages in which he discussed

---

[4] Walras expounded some ideas on barter in public lectures that he delivered in August 1873 and published in January 1874 (1874a), expressed in language that he modified only slightly when he introduced it into the first edition of the *Eléments*. He also presented some ideas on barter in public lectures in December 1875, published them in 1876, and incorporated them with changes into the second edition of the *Eléments*. For a listing and history of the lectures in 1873 and 1875, see Walker 1987b, entries 98 and 108.

the process of pricing he referred to a procedure totally different from the activity of a central authority.

The related question of whether Walras assumed that each market has its own authority who changes and quotes the price will now be examined. In this respect also, Walras's five barter models are the same. He began by assuming that all the people actually active on the trading floor are agents. By an agent he meant a professional trader who executes trades on behalf of a client on an organized market like the monetary oral pledges market he had presented in the *Eléments* (1874b, pp. 49–50; 1889, pp. 67–69; 1900, §§ 41–42, pp. 45–47), just two pages before he began his first barter model. Some of them are buyers on behalf of their clients and some are sellers on behalf of their clients. Walras assumed that the agents in his barter models quote prices by making oral pledges: "Since there must be an initial basis for the pricing process, we assume that an agent offers to give up n units of (B) for m units of (A), in accordance, for example, with the price on which the market closed on the previous day" (1874b, pp. 52–53; 1889, p. 70; 1900, § 44, p. 48). The offers to trade are proposals of prices. For example, if "an agent proposed to exchange 5 hectoliters of wheat for 10 hectoliters of oats, the price proposed for wheat in terms of oats would be 2, and that of oats in terms of wheat would be ½" (1874b, p. 53; 1889, p. 71). Thus prices are changed and quoted by the traders, not by a market or central authority. They deal directly with each other, each would-be buyer trying to reach an agreement with a would-be seller.

Walras then developed a variant of the model by assuming that the owner of a commodity goes in person to the marketplace and is a direct participant in the process of pricing and trying to reach agreements (1874b, p. 60; 1889, p. 78). Such a person, Walras assumed, does not think about buying or selling specific quantities until he knows what price is being quoted, whereupon he determines his desired trading quantity at that price. Nevertheless, the trader has desired demand or supply quantities at prices that have not been quoted (ibid.). On the other hand, Walras continued, the trader may be unable to go in person to the market, or may not wish to do so for any of a number of reasons. He will then "give his commission to a friend or his orders to an agent," to be executed. In that event he has to foresee the possible values of the price, determine explicitly his trading desires at alternative possible values, and inform his representative of them (1874a, p. 105; 1874b, p. 60; 1889, p. 78; 1900, § 50, p. 56). In other words, the owner of a commodity furnishes his demand or supply schedule to his agent.[5]

---

[5] In contrast, in the written pledges model, Walras assumed that the owner of a commodity provides his agent simply with a written pledge indicating a single supply quantity at the current price. After it has been determined that the price is a disequilibrium value, the agent therefore has to find out from the owner what new price should be quoted and what his supply

Up to a point, the traders in Walras's models take the quoted price as given and indicate their desired supply or demand quantities at that price. That does not mean they have "no influence on prices." On the contrary, Walras indicated that if would-be sellers discover that they are unable to elicit pledges by counterparts to buy from them all that they wish to sell at the ruling price, they no longer take it as given and proceed themselves to change it and to make new pledges at the new price; and if would-be buyers are unable to find counterparts who will or sell to them all they wish at the quoted price, they change the price (1874b, p. 69; 1889, p. 86; 1900, § 60, p. 64; ch. 5). The sellers and buyers do so, Walras asserted, in the manner known as Walrasian pricing. That is, the participants raise the price of the commodity for which their individual excess demand quantity is positive, and lower the price of the commodity for which their individual excess demand quantity is negative (ibid.). The magnitude of each change of price is a conventional fraction of a unit of the commodity.

Inasmuch as individual supplies and demands exist, aggregate quantities supplied and demanded of each commodity at the quoted price also exist (1874b, pp. 97–98; 1889, p. 119; 1900, § 97, p. 97). Walras did not, however, provide any mechanism for the latter magnitudes to be calculated in the market because he was aware they are not known in most real markets, and therefore reasoned there is no need for them to be known by the participants in his model. In this, as in every model that Walras constructed, they are known only by the theorist who is observing it. In his role as that theorist, Walras described the behavior of the participants by saying that they change the price in the same direction as the sign of the market excess demand, even though the participants know only the sign of their individual market-oriented excess demands (ch. 5).

The traders all recognize that they pledge to supply or purchase the quantities they specify only if the price is the equilibrium value. The assumption that disequilibrium transactions are not allowed is one that Walras adopted because that was true in the French stock market of his day (ch. 5). He originally employed that property in his design of the structure of his model of the securities market (1889, p. 68; 1900, § 42, p. 46) and carried it over into his models of barter. Eventually, in the market for any particular commodity the price is found at which "each buyer or seller finds exactly his counterpart in a seller or buyer" (1874b, p. 56; 1889, p. 74; 1900, § 46, p. 52). The traders look around and hear and see and infer from the absence of further cries of offers and the absence of further changes of the price that this is the case. Only then do they engage in trade, and they do so in the amounts

or demand quantity is at the new price. The owners of assets do this by writing out new pledges at each new price and transmitting them to their agents (1900, § 207, p. 215; § 251, p. 260; ch. 16).

that they have pledged. "The market is in equilibrium. At the equilibrium prices ... the quantity $D_a = O_a$ of (A) is exchanged against the quantity $O_b = D_b$ of (B), and, the market being concluded, the holders of the two commodities each go to their own side of the market" (ibid.). At no earlier point in his exploration of the properties of the model did Walras mention trade as occurring, and D_a and O_a are determined given the initial set of commodity holdings, so it is evident from his statement that no disequilibrium transactions take place in the model. The condition that each trader must find his counterpart before trade occurs – that the market supply and demand quantities must be equal – is the same in the barter and the monetary models of exchange of fixed stocks: "The law is that which we might have been tempted to formulate immediately after the study of the market on the Bourse; but a rigorous demonstration was necessary" (1874b, p. 69; 1889, p. 86; 1900, § 60, p. 64).

More than two commodities

In his second barter model, Walras assumed that there are three commodities and three groups of traders, each of whom initially holds only one of the commodities. That model has the same institutional, physical, procedural, and behavioral characteristics as the model with two commodities (1874b, pp. 106–8; 1889, p. 130–32; 1900, §§ 104–107, pp. 110–112). Walras introduced some new elements, in a third barter model. First, he assumed there are many commodities. Second, as before, each trader initially holds only one of them. Third, Walras carefully specified the physical and information-dissemination characteristics of the markets in the model. He specified that "the place which serves as a market for the exchange of all the commodities (A), (B), (C), (D) ... for each other has been divided into as many parts as there are trades between commodities taken two by two" (1889, p. 135; 1900, § 110, p. 115). Thus there are many "special markets." He specified that each market is "designated by signs." On each sign is "indicated the names of the commodities that are exchanged and the price at which they exchange determined mathematically by the foregoing system of equations. Thus: – 'Exchange of (A) against (B) and of (B) against (A) at the reciprocal prices $p_{a,b}$, $p_{b,a}$'; – 'Exchange of (A) against (C) and of (C) against (A) at the reciprocal prices $p_{a,c}$, $p_{c,a}$'" (ibid.). By $p_{a,c}$, for example, Walras meant the price of a unit of (A) stated in terms of the number of units of (C) that it is worth. Each market is therefore specialized for the trading of one commodity for one other and in each market the price of one of the commodities is calculated in terms of the second and posted, and the price of the second is calculated in terms of the first and posted.

Fourth, Walras assumed that trading is restricted to exchanges of commodities two by two. By "two by two" he meant, for example, that each holder of (A) who wishes to buy (B) and (C) exchanges (A) for (B) on the (A, B) market, and exchanges (A) for (C) on the (A, C) market, and similarly for other traders and combination of commodities (1889, p. 135). The demand for any commodity, say, (C), to be paid for with units of (B), equals the demand for (B) to be paid for with (C) times the price of (B) in terms of (C), and similarly for any two commodities. Walrasian pricing occurs in each market and as a result, Walras concluded, there would be "a certain equilibrium of the prices of the commodities taken two by two" in that way (1889, p. 135; 1900, §§ 110–11, pp. 115–16; and see 1876a, p. 376).

III. Walrasian arbitrage

The meaning of "Walrasian arbitrage"

Walras published the first version of what became his arbitrage model in 1874 (1874b, pp. 113–16), and a second version in 1876 in which he did not refer to arbitrage but to "complementary exchanges" (1876a, p. 379).[6] In 1889 he eliminated many of the passages in the latter model, combined some of them with terminology and ideas from his earliest exposition, and added new material, thereby constructing a definitive fourth model of the barter of given stocks of goods. It is characterized by a type of trading behavior that will be called Walrasian arbitrage. As far as I am aware, this model has not hitherto been interpreted correctly.

Walras assumed that each trader initially has only one commodity, that there is no numeraire (1889, p. 137; 1900 § 114, p. 118; and see 1874b, p. 115), and that traders are not restricted to the type of exchanges made in the third model. Relative to the resulting situation in the fourth model, the equilibrium of the third model then appears as "only an imperfect equilibrium" (1876a, p. 376; 1889, p. 135; 1900, § 110, p. 115). A better way to describe matters would be to say that there is an equilibrium in the third model, but that the nonoccurrence of Walrasian arbitrage in it is an arbitrary postulate – it is not a consequence of the properties of the model. Walras

---

[6] In this model, a trader sells, for example, (A) for (B) and (A) for (C), and he then exchanges some of the (C) that he has just acquired for more (B). "That operation disrupts the equilibrium of the (B, C) market by making the quantity of (C) supplied greater than the quantity demanded; and that equilibrium, thus disrupted, can reestablish itself only by a fall of $p_{c,b}$," (1876a, p. 378). Walras evidently interpreted the "complementary exchanges" as parametric changes initiating new market days, because he described the original prices as part of an equilibrium situation and the additional demand as leading to a new equilibrium. Other interpretations of the model are possible.

meant that when the postulate is removed, the result is Walrasian arbitrage. It remains to be seen whether that results in a different equilibrium or, indeed, whether equilibrium exists.

To understand the fourth model, it must be recognized that in its context Walras did not mean arbitrage in the ordinary sense of purchasing a commodity in one market and selling it in another market in which its price is higher, or even of buying or selling a commodity at different prices in one and the same market. Walrasian arbitrage is not a process of benefiting from price differentials of a given commodity, because there are none. In the fourth model, a given trader buys a particular type of commodity in only one market, and in every market trade occurs only at the equilibrium price on any given day; that is, there are no transactions at prices at which the market-day supply and demand quantities are unequal. By "arbitrage" Walras meant the process by which a trader who holds, for example, (A) and wants to acquire (B), first exchanges (A) for (C) and then (C) for (B), instead of exchanging (A) directly for (B). Walras accordingly repeated his assumptions that the traders each "hold only one commodity, and [that], in accordance with allowing arbitrage to occur, $m(m-1)$ prices of m commodities are cried two by two, not subjected to the condition of general equilibrium" (1889, p. 142; 1900, § 117, p. 122). That is the condition that "*the price of any two commodities in terms of each other is equal to the ratio of the prices of the two commodities in terms of any third*" (1889, p. 135; 1900, § 111, p. 115; and see 1874b, p. 116; 1889, p. 139). For example, the price of (C) in terms of (B) may be greater than the ratio of the price of (C) in terms of (A) to the price of (B) in terms of (A). If that is the case, the market equilibrium given by the third model "is not definitive or general, and . . . arbitrages will be made there, the result of which is a fall of $p_{c,b}$, a rise of $p_{c,a}$, and a fall of $p_{b,a}$. It is seen at the same time that, in the case in which $p_{c,b}$ would be $< p_{c,a}/p_{b,a}$, there would be, on the market, arbitrages which would have the result of a rise of $p_{c,b}$, a fall of $p_{c,a}$, and a rise of $p_{b,a}$" (1889, p. 138; 1900, § 115, pp. 118–19). The traders will engage in Walrasian arbitrage, because they can thereby increase their utility as compared with their utility in the model without arbitrage. "Maximum satisfaction will occur for each trader when the ratios of the marginal utilities of the commodities demanded to the marginal utility of the commodity held by the trader are equal, not to the prices that are cried, but to the true prices obtained by arbitrage" (ibid., p. 142; 1900, § 117, p. 122).

How the model works: Here is the explanation of the workings of Walras's model, using his figures. He assumed that some of the prices quoted in the markets in equilibrium are $p_{c,b} = 4$, $p_{c,a} = 6$, $p_{b,a} = 2$. The reciprocal values are prices such as $p_{a,b} = 0.5$. Assume now that some traders hold (B) and want (C). As compared with his complementary exchanges model, in the arbitrage model Walras changed the types of trades that are possible, not allowing a trader to buy, for example, (C), in both the (A, C) and (B, C) markets. Moreover, the traders do not want to buy any (C) in the (B, C) market. For half a unit of (B), a trader can get one (A), and for 6 (A)s a trader can get 1 (C). It follows that for 3 (B)s, a trader can get 6 (A)s and exchange them for 1 (C). What Walras unfortunately called the "true" price of (C) in terms of (B), but what will here be called the "indirect" price, is therefore 3 (B)s for one (C). That is the case, even though the price cried in the (B, C) market is 4 (B)s for 1 (C). Thus, the way that Walras wanted the model to work is that as a result of Walrasian pricing there are certain equilibrium quoted prices, and as a result of Walrasian arbitrage there are certain equilibrium indirect prices. Here are the values for three of the commodities:

	Quoted	Indirect		Quoted	Indirect
$P_{c,b}$	4	3	$P_{b,c}$	.25	.334
$P_{b,a}$	2	1.5	$P_{a,b}$	.5	.667
$P_{c,a}$	6	8	$P_{a,c}$	.167	.125

Problems with the model: In actuality, Walras's model cannot work as he wanted because it does not have the necessary structural characteristics. This becomes evident in considering his treatment of demand. He described the arbitragers' demand as a "supplementary" component that is in addition to the "principal demand" (ibid., p. 138; 1900, § 114, p. 118). The reader at first supposes that the latter is expressed in each market by some irrational or immobile traders who do not engage in Walrasian arbitrage, even though all traders must be aware of the advantage of doing so. If that were the case, then the markets would be complete in the respect that there would be some demanders and some suppliers in each market. Walras proceeded, however, to assume that all the traders act in the same way. The "supplementary demand will be made," he stated, "like the principal demand: by the holders of (A) in exchanging (A) against (C) and (C) against (B), but never (A) against (B); by the holders of (B), in exchanging (B) against (A) and (A) against (C), but never (B) against (C); by the holders of (C), in exchanging (C) against (B) and (B) against (A), but never (C) against (A)" (ibid.). The implication of this situation, according to Walras, is that

on the (A, B) market there will always be a demand for (A) and a supply of (B), but not a demand for (B) or a supply of (A); consequently $p_{b,a}$ falls. On the (A, C) market, there will always be a demand for (C) and a supply of (A), but not a demand for (A) or a supply of (C); consequently $p_{c,a}$ rises. On the (B, C) market, there will always be a demand for (B) and a supply of (C), but not a demand for (C) or a supply of (B); consequently $p_{c,b}$ falls (ibid.).

The first of the two passages just quoted is internally contradictory with respect to each commodity. For example, Walras stated that the holders of (A) buy (C) and sell it for (B), but he also stated that the holders of (B) never sell it for (C), so there cannot be a (B, C) market. He stated that the holders of (B) are willing to sell it only for (A), but that holders of (A) are not willing to exchange it for (B), so there cannot be an (A, B) market, and so forth. The second passage begins by focusing on that situation, and states again that one side of the market for each commodity is missing. On the (B, C) market, for example, whereas the traders who hold (C) want to trade it for (B), there is no one who offers (B) for sale to them. Thus in each market there is either no supply or no demand. Obviously there cannot be a pricing process in markets structured in that way and equilibrium prices cannot exist.

Although in those passages Walras introduced features that make pricing and trade impossible, he nevertheless also contradicted himself by tacitly assuming that supply and demand quantities exist in each market and that prices are called out and are changed until the supply and demand quantities are equal. In order to continue with an examination of his statements, the defective structural features of his model will be ignored, and his assertions that a pricing process occurs will temporarily be accepted and considered. When he stated that in one case $p_{c,b}$ and $p_{b,a}$ fall and that $p_{c,a}$ rises (ibid.), and when he described other price changes in other circumstances, he may have been thinking about Walrasian pricing that takes place before exchange occurs. That is what he should have been thinking about, and not about temporary equilibrium prices being replaced by final equilibrium values as a result of Walrasian arbitrage, because in his model the equilibrium quoted prices, once assumed to be found, do not change, and no transactions occur at any other prices. This is made clear by Walras's numerical example. In it he began by assuming that the equilibrium prices in the earlier table are quoted in the markets, then assumed that arbitrage occurs, then continued to use the same quoted prices as he worked out the indirect prices implied by purchases in different markets, and ended up with the set of indirect prices but also with those same quoted prices (1889, pp. 136–37; 1900, § 112, pp. 116–17). Similarly, Walras described what he called the situations before and after arbitrages – properly speaking, in a model without them and in a model with them – in a way that indicated that what is different is not the equilibrium prices but the arrangement of equilibrium prices in particular ratios and of the marginal utilities in particular ratios (1874b, pp. 117–18; 1889, pp. 154–55; 1900, § 132, pp. 135–36).

Thus in the exposition of the workings of his model, Walras assumed that $p_{c,b}$, $p_{b,a}$, and $p_{c,a}$ are unchanging equilibrium prices, existing and found in some inexplicable manner despite the absence of either suppliers or demanders. Accordingly, he indicated, as is shown by the table, not that the equilibrium price $p_{c,b}$ falls but that the indirect price of (C) in terms of (B) is lower than $p_{c,b}$, and similarly not that the equilibrium price falls but that the indirect price of (B) in terms of (A) is lower than $p_{b,a}$. Likewise, once the equilibrium price $p_{c,a}$ has been found, it does not rise, but the indirect price of (C) in terms of (A) is higher than $p_{c,a}$.[7]

In the course of the pricing process that Walras mistakenly asserted happens in his arbitrage model, there would be no possibility of the occurrence of disequilibrium transactions as defined with reference to a market day in a particular market. That is because the model is an oral pledges model, with all offers to buy or sell being contingent for their execution on the quoted price being the equilibrium price. Similarly, if the model were not defective and there actually were pricing and trading processes in a system of Walrasian arbitrage markets, there would be no possibility of disequilibrium exchanges occurring because trade cannot occur in any particular market until the entire set of markets has reached an equilibrium set of prices. Whether a commodity is bought by an ordinary trader or by an arbitrager making an intermediate purchase, trade in a Walrasian arbitrage model trade cannot occur at any price other than the one at which a commodity is sold – namely, the equilibrium price quoted in its market – not at what Walras called the "true" price. The latter is a calculated value, one that is calculated by comparing the equilibrium prices of different commodities. Doubtless in recognition of this, Walras did not carry over into his arbitrage model his statement, made in the complementary exchanges model, that indirect trading "disrupts the equilibrium" of the markets (1876a, p. 378).

Errors of interpretation: It has been seen that Jaffé misrepresented Walras's arbitrage model. Another writer makes a major part of his argument rest upon a misperception of the model. He states several times: "In the context of arbitrage, disequilibrium trading is carefully noted and discussed" by Walras (Kompas 1992, p. 2); "As mentioned above, Walras does allow for disequilibrium transactions (those associated with arbitrage) in the theory of exchange"

---

[7] When Walras wrote that in equilibrium the ratios of the marginal utilities are equal "not to the prices that are cried, but to the true prices obtained by arbitrages" (1889, p. 142; 1900, § 117, p. 122), he was making a distinction between equilibrium prices, which are cried, and the indirect ones, which are not cried. Jaffé made his own addition to the passage, however, representing Walras as having written "not to the prices *as they are first cried,* but to the true prices" (Jaffé in Walras 1954, p. 164; emphasis added). The words in italics are Jaffé's, not Walras's. Jaffé thus attributed his erroneous belief that there are changes in the equilibrium prices that are cried in the markets to Walras, whereas there are no such changes in his arbitrage model. Walras's careless phraseology in other passages explains why Jaffé adopted that belief, and Jaffé's desire to be helpful by explaining Walras's text was the reason for his procedure, but he should not have added words that Walras did not write.

(ibid., p. 3); "Walras discusses the effects of disequilibrium transactions associated with arbitrage" (ibid., p. 15 and again on p. 19). He then writes:

All of this is quite significant. The recognition of arbitrage in exchange *must* entail, as Walras rightly acknowledges, the presence of out-of-equilibrium trades until the $m(m - 1)$ prices in the pair-wise markets 'converge' to, what Walras (1954:119) calls, their 'true' equilibrium values, or the $m - 1$ prices consistent with a common *numéraire*. This clearly contradicts Walker (1972:347), who maintains that 'in the *Eléments* and elsewhere Walras simply asserted that disequilibrium transactions do not occur in exchange markets' (ibid., p. 23).

What that statement attributes to Walras unquestionably contradicts both Walras and me, because it is an erroneous attribution in every respect. First, Walras did not carefully note, allow, or discuss disequilibrium transactions in the arbitrage model – there are no such transactions in the model. Jaffé's translation and Walras's confusing manner of expressing his model are to be blamed for the error of supposing that there are; indeed, Jaffé's translation led me to make the same error in the past. Second, it is nonsense to speak of a numeraire in the model. Far from doing so, Walras explained that a numeraire eliminates the possibility of arbitrage, as is implicit in the foregoing account and documented in the following section. Misinterpreting him in that respect cannot be blamed on Jaffé or Walras. Finally, this book documents at great length that Walras assumed in all his models that all goods are sold only at prices at which the market-day supply and demand quantities in any particular market are equal.

IV. The general model

Barter plus a numeraire

Walras was not content to leave matters as they stood in his arbitrage model because it is characterized by unnecessarily restrictive assumptions. Returning to the mainstream of his development of a multimarket model, he took up the general case in his fifth barter model. He assumed that each trader holds several commodities, and "in order to prevent there being any place for arbitrage, $m - 1$ prices of $m - 1$ of the commodities are cried in the mth taken as the numeraire" (1889, pp. 142–43; 1900, § 117, p. 122). Thus Walras abandoned the topic of Walrasian arbitrage. Given the structure of the general model, traders who hold (B) and want some (C) will not seek to engage in trades such as (B) for (A) and (A) for (C) because there would be no advantage in doing so. Traders do not quote the prices of the commodities as rates of exchange between each pair of commodities in the model, but instead express the prices of all commodities in terms of the numeraire, so there cannot possibly be indirect prices that differ from the quoted prices. Walras described the situation as "the case of the substitution of a general market in place of special markets" (ibid., p. 139; 1900, § 116, p. 120).

It is useful to point out once more that by introducing a numeraire, Walras eliminated the possibility of arbitrage, as he stated in the above quotation, because various writers on the topic in addition to Kompas have simply failed to read his text on this matter. Arthur W. Marget, for example, wrote that "if, however, Walras had been asked, at this stage of his argument, whether he thought of this 'arbitrage' as taking place through an indirect exchange involving the commodity chosen as *numéraire,* I am sure he would have replied that it made no difference, so far as his argument had gone, whether one did or did not introduce the *numéraire* commodity as one of the links in the type of 'indirect exchange' which performs the 'arbitrage' function in his system" (Marget 1935, pp. 175–76). That is incorrect, as has been shown. It is certain that Walras would have replied that it is nonsense to speak of Walrasian arbitrage involving a numeraire.

When Walras assumed that the fifth barter model has a numeraire, he characterized it simply as "the commodity in which the prices of all the others are thus expressed" (ibid.). Later in his exposition, however, he referred to exchange as occurring "with intervention of the numeraire" (1874b, p. 136; 1889, p. 161; 1900, § 137, p. 142), and that may lead some readers to think that the numeraire is actually money. It is true that in his avowedly monetary models, by "the intervention of money" he meant that it intervenes in the process of exchange as a medium of exchange, but that is not the kind of intervention that he meant is made by the numeraire in the barter model. Walras explained at the beginning of his barter models that "the intervention of money in exchange is a particular phenomenon that will be studied later and should not be mixed in, as early as the beginning, with the study of the general phenomenon of value in exchange" (1874b, p. 52; 1889, p. 70; 1900, § 43, p. 48), by which he meant with the study of value in barter models. Furthermore, he terminated his treatment of the general barter model with the statement that by introducing a numeraire he was not thereby introducing money.[8] The true role of the numeraire, the kind of intervention made by it, he wrote, is to serve as a commodity in terms of which the prices of commodities are stated and in terms of which wealth can be measured, as distinct from the function of money, which is to be a medium of exchange (1874b, p. 149; 1889, p. 174; 1900, § 148, pp. 154–55). Signaling the fact that there are differences between his general barter model and a monetary

---

[8] In his exposition in the fourth edition of the *Eléments* of models of the exchange of rates of production for rates of supply of services in which there is a numeraire but no money, Walras emphasized that the exchange process is one of barter (ch. 15).

one, immediately after that statement he developed a completely distinct monetary model of exchange for the specific purpose of illustrating what happens when the numeraire is assumed also to be money (1874b, pp. 149–56; 1889, pp. 174–82; 1900, §§ 148–55, pp. 54–63).

Moreover, the structure and behavior of the fifth model makes it clear that each commodity is bartered for other commodities just as in the models without a numeraire. To reflect this property of the model, Walras first replaced the equations of exchange applicable to the third model – those that indicate the equality of supplies and demands for each separate pairing of commodities – with a single equation for each commodity that indicates that in equilibrium the total quantity demanded of it equals the sum of the amounts offered for it of all the other commodities multiplied by their respective prices in terms of it (1889, p. 140; 1900, § 116, p. 120). It is evident that those equations describe a barter situation because they indicate that the total supply of a commodity, such as (C), is made up of the amount of it that is offered for (A), plus the amount of it offered for (B), plus the amount of it offered for (D), etc., and because the total demand for (C) is the sum of the demands for it expressed by the offers for it of each other commodity (ibid.). Walras then changed the equation system to reflect the fact that the price of each commodity is quoted in terms of the numeraire (ibid.). Continuing to recognize that the markets are ones in which barter occurs, Walras indicated that the total quantity demanded of any given commodity is made up of the offers for it of each other commodity, and that the total quantity supplied is the amount of the given commodity offered for each other commodity multiplied by the ratio of the prices, stated in terms of the numeraire, of the two commodities that are traded in each separate market (ibid.). Walras thus combined the use of the numeraire with the barter nature of the process of exchange. In contrast, if there were money in the model, the aggregate supply of each commodity would be offered for money in its own market and the aggregate quantity of it demanded would be paid for with money. There would then be no occasion for introducing, in a statement of the equality of quantities supplied and demanded of a commodity, consideration of commodities other than the one in question and of money.

Walras also described trade in the fifth model as a barter process in a variety of other ways (1889, pp. 139–75; 1900, §§ 116–50, pp. 120–56). For example, he wrote repeatedly about the exchange of commodities for each other, explained that many holders of commodities who want to buy other commodities do not hold the numeraire commodity and therefore cannot use it to make purchases; they have to engage in barter to pay for the goods they buy. In a definitive statement he observed that the price of (B), for example, is quoted in terms of the numeraire (A), but that the traders nevertheless "offer (B) in demanding some (A), some (C), some (D)" (1889, p. 160; 1900, § 137, p. 141).

Equilibration and equilibrium

Walras's fifth model has an equilibrating process based on Walrasian pricing and on the structural features of the markets that make it possible. Those are the features described in the first three barter models, such as the well-defined physical properties of the markets, the participation of agents, the calling out of prices by the traders, and the making of oral pledges. Prices for the commodities are initially quoted at random, and each trader determines his demand or supply quantity of the different commodities. "That is done after reflection, without close calculations, but exactly as would be done by mathematical calculation with reference to the system of equations of the equivalence of quantities demanded and offered and of maximum satisfaction subject to the appropriate restrictions" (1889, p. 148; 1900, § 124, p. 129). Walras judged that, other things being constant, it is "probable" that Walrasian pricing would generate sets of prices that are progressively closer to the equilibrium set (ibid.).[9]

Walras then described the conditions that would prevail in the model in equilibrium. The equilibrium utility relations are "that maximum satisfaction will occur for each trader when the ratios of the marginal utilities of commodities other than the numeraire commodity to the marginal utility of the numeraire commodity will be equal to the prices that are cried" (1889, p. 143; 1900, § 117, p. 123). The equilibrium relationship of prices with respect to the numeraire is that the price of any two commodities stated one in terms of the other is equal to the ratio of their prices expressed in terms of the numeraire (ibid.), and since "the prices have been cried in numeraire, the equilibrium condition was fulfilled *ipso facto*. Otherwise, [that is, in the previous model] it was fulfilled by means of arbitrage" (1889, p. 154; 1900, § 131, p. 135). There is for each commodity a single equilibrium price in terms of the numeraire, that for which the total quantity demanded is equal to

[9] Walrasian scholars are well aware that Walras had originally written that it appears "certain" that convergence would occur (1874b, p. 131), but that he altered his opinion and his adjective evidently as a result of correspondence on the matter with Philip H. Wicksteed (Wicksteed to Walras, April 2, 1889, in 1965, 2, letter 875, p. 303; Walras to Wicksteed, April 9, 1889, in 1965, 2, letter 877, p. 307). J. M. Ostroy argued that in a multimarket barter system with sequential bilateral trading arrangements, if each trader knows the competitive equilibrium prices but not the excess demands of others, the competitive equilibrium would not be reached (Ostroy 1973). A barter model of sequential bilateral trading constructed by Ostroy and R. M. Starr, unlike the barter models contemplated by Walras, produces a general equilibrium only if the model has a centralized price-changing authority (Ostroy and Starr 1974).

the total quantity supplied. The equilibrium condition in the set of markets is that the excess demand for each commodity be simultaneously equal to zero for all commodities (1889, p. 152; 1900, § 129, p. 133).

V. Numbers of traders

Untenability of the received view

It is presumed in modern discussions of Walras's work that he assumed there are very many suppliers and demanders in each market. Hildenbrand and Kirman, for example, state that

> our first theme, due to Walras, is the decentralization by prices of the exchange problem. The idea, which will be familiar to the reader, is that the individuals in the economy takes prices as given. . . . We make the point at the outset that this price-taking behavior only makes sense when individuals view themselves as an insignificant part of a large market. Thus, our first theme is like Wagner – it can only be played with any success by large orchestras (Hildenbrand and Kirman 1988, p. 7).

The authors refer to "the fundamental importance of large numbers of agents in equilibrium analysis. . . . The competitive solution has as its basic behavioural justification the insignificance of the individual . . ." (ibid., p. 90). Once again they attribute those features of their analysis to Walras (ibid., p. 89).

The foregoing exposition of Walras's barter models can now be drawn on to evaluate the received view of his conception of the role of numbers of traders in freely competitive exchange. That view is evidently profoundly mistaken. First, the fundamental premise of the received interpretation is incorrect – namely, the supposition that Walras assumed that the traders are always price-takers. As has been indicated, stated many times – and assumed it is always true – that any individual trader can and does change the price, precisely as is in fact the case in most real organized freely competitive markets. Second, as in their discussion of Walras on price formation, Hildenbrand and Kirman – like all other commentators on the topic – are unable to cite any passages in which Walras made the assertion that large numbers of participants are significant for the pricing process or for the existence of competitive equilibrium in freely competitive markets because no such passages exist.

In Walras's models, the physical structure of each market and the activities of the traders in it make clear that he did not envision that there are very large numbers of direct participants in the trading process. Nor did he in any way state or imply that a direct participant may represent more than one owner, so he did not introduce large numbers of owners indirectly through assuming they are represented by a fairly small number of direct participants.

Instead, he always implied that on any given market day an agent represents only one client. In any event, the professional traders can act on behalf of only one client at any instant. Moreover, the pricing process and the existence and properties of equilibrium in his barter models are not in fact the outcome of large numbers of traders. In the models there could well be a sufficient number of traders in a particular market so that no one of them would cause the equilibrium price to be appreciably different by such variations as halving or doubling the amount of the commodity that he offers or demands at each alternative price. That situation would nevertheless not deprive any of the traders of the ability to change the price during the movement toward equilibrium in a particular market during a given day by calling out a new value. The pricing process and equilibrium in Walras's models are not affected by the number of traders except in the sense that will be indicated in the next paragraph. The way the price is changed is the result of the physical properties of the marketplace, the means of disseminating information, and the rules and procedures that impose certain forms of pricing, offering, and trading behavior on the traders. All traders must simultaneously hear the price that their fellow-traders propose, and all traders must be able more or less simultaneously to arrive at the understanding that new offers and changes of prices have ceased so that they know that the equilibrium price has been found.

Those conditions require that the trading area be relatively small and that there cannot be very many direct participants. If there were very many it would be impossible to impose the marketplace rules on them, such as the rules that trade cannot take place at disequilibrium prices and that all trade must take place at a single price on a given market day. It would also be impossible to secure the necessary direct personal contact and information dissemination among the traders that are features of Walras's models of freely competitive organized markets. The trading space would dissolve into a number of special markets with transactions occurring simultaneously at different prices, as happens, for example, in the real markets for municipal bonds, in which on a given business day different dealers simultaneously offer a range of different prices at which they will buy or sell a given bond, and as is exemplified by real local markets in the United States for wheat of a given grade, in which millers, food companies, and wholesalers buy the wheat on any given day at different prices in country markets all over the wheat-producing states. Accordingly, the traders in Walras's model act in a well-defined relatively small trading area like a pit on the Chicago Board of Trade or a station on the New York Stock Exchange, calling out proposals that are heard by their fellow-participants. What is important in Walras's model is that (1) the number of traders physically present in the marketplace is limited, and (2) the related condition that whether each trader represents many clients, only one, or himself, the prices he cries are simultaneously heard by all.

Walras's references to numbers of traders

Additional substantiation of the foregoing characterization of Walras's view will now be provided by considering his references to numbers of traders. In one place he assumed that the traders are "very numerous" (1874b, p. 142; 1889, p. 169; 1900, § 144, p. 149). His postulation of that condition did not have anything to do with the number of traders in a particular market or with the process of quoting or changing prices on a particular market. It was an assumption made about the aggregate number of traders in all markets in the economy, and has to do with the entire set of equilibrium prices in alternative situations. Walras was investigating the comparative-static impact of assumed variations in an individual's holdings of commodities subject to the constancy of the total value of the individual's holdings, an impact that he concluded would be negligible (ibid.). Obviously that is not an assertion that large numbers of traders in a particular market convert the traders into persons who do not change prices. Furthermore, Walras went on to state that he did not want to leave matters with the construction of a multimarket model that depends on the law of large numbers, because it produces only an approximate result. He wanted to be mathematically rigorous and "to be able to state that the prices are absolutely unchanged." For that to be true, he did not assume large numbers of traders in the economy and large amounts of commodities; instead, he stated, he had to assume only "the fulfillment of the two conditions of the equivalence of the [values of] quantities possessed and of the constancy of the total quantities" (ibid.).

There were only two instances in which Walras mentioned the number of traders in a particular market in the part of the *Eléments* in which he dealt with what he described as the theory of exchange. In neither case did he do so in order to construct a model in which traders do not change the price. In the first instance he was concerned, not with the definition of a freely competitive market or with the influence of the numbers of traders upon how prices are quoted and changed, but with the continuity of the market demand function. The individual demand curves may be discontinuous but the market demand curve can nevertheless be considered approximately continuous in virtue of the law of large numbers (1874b, pp. 61–62; 1889, pp. 79–80; 1900, § 52, p. 58). In Walras's example, when there is a small increase in the price of oats, "at least one of the traders, *out of the great number of them,* arriving at the limit that obliges him to do without [an extra] horse, will thereby cause a very small diminution in the total demand" for oats (1874b, p. 62; 1889, p. 80; 1900, § 52, p. 58). Walras's assumption in that case of a large number of traders in a given market was not made to study the question of price-taking behavior. He stated that the continuity or otherwise of the market demand curve was important to him because he wanted to establish the existence of precise solutions to his equations – that is, to establish the existence of equilibrium – or if the curve is discontinuous, determine the interval of values within which the equilibrium price falls (1874b, pp. 60–65; 1889, pp. 80–83; 1900, §§ 53–57, pp. 58–62). That is a separate matter from the market institutions and procedures by which prices are quoted and changed. The character of that process is not implied by the continuity or otherwise of excess demand curves nor does any particular set of pricing institutions and rules create their continuity or otherwise.

The second instance was, as far as I am aware, the only case in which Walras mentioned the number of traders in connection with a discussion of price formation in the *Eléments,* and in that instance he attached no importance to large numbers. W.S. Jevons's assumption of trading bodies, Walras asserted, led him to a formula for the equilibrium prices in a freely competitive market that is "valid for the restricted case in which only two individuals are present" (1889, p. 190; 1900, § 163, p. 171). Jevons had explained, as Walras was aware, that the individuals are subject to the institutions and rules of trading of an organized freely competitive market (Jevons 1957, pp. 88–100). Walras then considered numbers of traders in relation to the freely competitive markets represented by his models: "It remains thus to introduce the *general* case in which *any number* of individuals are present for the purpose of exchanging first two commodities for each other, and then any number of commodities for each other" (1889, p. 190; 1900, § 163, p. 171; emphasis added). Far from there being any hint in that analysis of a concern with large numbers of traders to establish the properties of a freely competitive market, Walras was arguing that the market will be freely competitive regardless of the number, provided that the rules are observed – there may be two traders or a few or many. Similarly, Walras never assumed there is an infinite number of traders, and he did not even mention the number of traders in his most definitive statement of the characteristics of a freely competitive market (1874b, pp. 48–52; 1889, pp. 66–70; 1900, §§ 41–43, pp. 44–48), nor indeed in any of his definitions of that type of market.

Walras did not address what happens if a trader has a supply or demand function that is so large relative to the market supply or demand that if he were to supply or demand a large different amount at each given price the equilibrium price would be different. There is a possible explanation for his neglect of the issue. He would have viewed it as a matter of comparative statics – that is, of a comparison of market days with different sets of individual supply and demand functions and hence of different market supply and demand functions. In the type of market model that Walras constructed, the amount of a commodity a trader demands or supplies relative to the market as a whole is not a matter that affects the characteristics of the pricing process within a given market day once the traders have settled on their supply and demand functions. Let it be assumed that on an initial market day there are a sufficient numbers of buyers and sellers so that if any one of them were not in the market, or if any one of them demands or supplies much more or less at each price, the equilibrium price would not be appreciably different. If, in successive alternate market days, there are progressively fewer buyers or sellers, the effect on the price of there being one trader less, or of a trader demanding or supplying widely different amounts on different days, would be progressively greater. The traders are constrained, however, to behave in the way mandated by the institutions and procedures of a Walrasian market. Consequently, within any market day, given the amounts that they decide to try to buy or sell at each alternative price, regardless of the size of those amounts relative to the market totals, the traders will indicate those quantities at each quoted price and will change the price in the way Walras described. The result will be that the freely competitive equilibrium price for a pledges market will be found. Walras realized – like Jevons (1957, pp. 88–100) and Francis Y. Edgeworth (1881, p. 39) in their treatments of two-person purely competitive exchange – that market models can be constructed in which the process of price formation results in the equilibrium price and quantity's being the solutions to the initial pair of market supply and demand functions even if any single trader's supply function is a significant part of the market supply function, and similarly regarding individual and market demand.

VI. Conclusion

Defective arbitrage model

Walras's arbitrage model is structurally and therefore functionally defective. That is not of any significance for his other models of barter markets, since they are structurally and behaviorally unlike the arbitrage model. His development of it was a detour because it deals with processes that cannot occur if there is a numeraire, and therefore cannot occur in Walras's general model of barter with fixed aggregate stocks, in his barter models that deal with services and the production and sale of consumer and capital goods, nor, of course, in any of his monetary models. Thus, Walrasian arbitrage is not a mechanism of intermarket adjustments of prices in those models. The following remarks refer to Walras's barter models other than the arbitrage model.

Cumbersomeness of assumption of barter: In his barter models, Walras did not describe satisfactorily the real process of pricing and trade in organized competitive markets, as evident from two considerations. First, no economic insights are gained by assuming that each commodity is bartered in hundreds of different markets, one for each other commodity that its possessors want to acquire. The postulation of that process obstructs an understanding of real exchange. The logistics of the process defy the imagination, and the transportation, storage, and transactions costs would be so enormous as to make many exchanges undesirable and to render a multimarket barter model unworkable. Second, although Walras's introduction of the numeraire brought his treatment of barter into closer agreement with real markets in that real prices are quoted in a numeraire, his retention of the assumption of barter after he had introduced a numeraire was a poor theoretical decision because the resulting trading process is absurdly cumbersome and obviously does not reflect or illuminate the characteristics of real markets. In his model, it is not enough for prices to be quoted in the numeraire. For the traders to know how much should be exchanged of two commodities, they must take the further step of calculating exchange ratios in accordance with the implications of the numeraire prices. For example, if $p_{b,a} = 2.65$ and $p_{c,a} = 3.15$, (A) being the numeraire commodity, then on the (B, C) market the traders have to work out the fact that one unit of (C), worth three and one-quarter (A)s, must be exchanged for approximately 1.189 units of (B), also worth a total of approximately three and one-quarter (A)s, and then work out the implications of that ratio for the total amounts they want to trade. That would be sufficiently burdensome that the traders would have a strong incentive to use the numeraire as money. Thus the conclusion drawn from an examination of Walras's barter models of the exchange of fixed total stocks is that the assumption of barter is not valuable for the understanding of real market behavior. Walras should have stayed with the monetary type of model with which he opened his analysis of markets in the *Eléments*.

Complete models of particular markets: As for their properties, Walras's barter models of particular markets, excluding the arbitrage model, are logically complete with respect to their operation in the sense that each market has the necessary physical structure, participants, institutions, and procedures so that prices are quoted and pledges to trade are made and the variables converge to a particular equilibrium. Each market has both supply and demand sides, means of expressing desired trades, market rules, a pricing procedure, and a trading space that enables all traders to know when the particular equilibrium price has been found. The traders themselves quote and change the price, and trade is allowed to take place only at the equilibrium price. Walras's statement of the equilibrium condition in any particular market as being the equality of the market supply and demand quantities is an accurate description of a property of his barter models – that equilibrium prices exist in them. Of course, to say that Walras's particular-market barter models are complete in the sense that they contain the features necessary for them to be functioning systems and to move them to particular equilibrium does not mean that they constitute a general theory. They do not describe other types of hypothetical or real markets; indeed, their structure and rules result in their being a very restricted type of hypothetical market.

Incomplete models of general equilibrium: With respect to intermarket general equilibrating adjustments, Walras's second and third models and his general model are not complete. This is true in two interrelated respects. First, for the models to work properly as multimarket systems, the traders in any one market would have to adjust their supply and demand quantities of their commodity, and hence their quotations of prices for it, in reaction to the prices of other commodities. That requires that the traders of one commodity be informed about current prices of other commodities, or have sufficient information about past prices in other markets to form a rational expectation of current equilibrium prices in those markets. It is possible that Walras believed that the traders' rational expectations of prices in markets other than their own would lead them to find the equilibrium set, but he did not provide information dissemination procedures that would enable the traders to have such information. Second, they would have to wait until a general equilibrium set of prices is reached before engaging in trade. That requires that there be a fully enforced rule that trade cannot occur until excess demand quantities in all markets are zero. That rule does not exist in Walras's models, and there is no institution that could promulgate or enforce it. Even if the rule existed, it would not be sufficient. There would also have to be a means of collecting and disseminating information so that all traders are informed when all excess demands are zero, features that also do not exist in his models. In short, the barter models lack the institutions, technology, rules, and procedures that would be necessary to generate the necessary characteristics of information, adjustment, and coordination.

Walras tacitly supposed that his general model has the features that would provide the traders in it with the same sort and degree of information processed by traders in real markets. He always wrote with the implicit presumption that the mechanisms for intermarket adjustment exist and operate efficiently in the real economy, making, in effect, an appeal to the reader to accept that they do so in the real economy and in some unexplained way in his models. "It remains only to show," he wrote, "and this is the essential point, that the same problem of exchange for which we have just furnished the theoretical solution is also that which is resolved practically on the market by the mechanism of free competition" (1889, p. 141, and see p. 148). How can that be shown? That is, "what is necessary to prove that the theoretical solution and the solution on the real market are identical? Simply that the raising and lowering of prices is a mode of resolution by tatonnement of the systems of equations of equality of supply and demand" (ibid., p. 149). Walras asserted that the prices that are the solutions to his system of equations "will always be, theoretically and practically, the equilibrium prices" (1874b, p. 139; 1889, p. 165), because "the mechanism of competition on the market is nothing other than the practical determination of the theoretically calculated prices" (1874b, p. 142; 1889, p. 168). Similarly, Walras assumed good intermarket information in his discussion of the impact on the set of equilibrium prices of changes in the holdings of one commodity and of the utility functions for it.[10] The difficulty with Walras's tacit assumptions is that there is in fact no mechanism in the real market system that produces the conditions needed by his model. Trade is not suspended in disequilibrium in all real markets until all excess demand quantities are zero, so his appeal to the features of the real economy is a fallacious way of contending that his models have the characteristics that he desired.

Accomplishments: Nevertheless, Walras accomplished a great deal in his barter models of particular markets, as is evident by comparing them with the relatively sketchy models constructed by his contemporaries. He provided his models with well-defined physical, institutional, and procedural features, many of which he drew from his observation of real markets. He assumed that agents make oral pledges to trade provided that the price is the equilibrium value. Prices are called out and changed by the participants in his barter models, and large numbers of traders are not necessary for their functioning, just as is true in organized exchanges. When Walras assumed there are large numbers of traders, it was for reasons other than to assert that any particular one of them is unable to influence the price, for that would have contradicted his repeated assertions that individual traders change prices. In summary, Walras's achievement in his barter model was to work out some of the foundations of the modeling of exchange in organized freely competitive markets.

---

[10] In this connection, Walras discussed the consequences for various variables of the existence of a large number of commodities – that is, of a large number of markets. That subject also has nothing to do with the processes of quoting and changing prices and of reaching an equilibrium price on a particular market within a given market day. In some of his discussions of large numbers of commodities, he was concerned with comparative statics, concluding that changes in the holdings of one commodity or the utility functions for it will change its price but will not appreciably change other prices (1874b, pp. 155–56, 168; 1889, pp. 160–61, 179, 181, 182). In his other discussions of large numbers of commodities he argued, first, that if the "commodities are great in number and in considerable quantities," the partial equilibrium market supply and demand curves relating to (B) would approximately indicate its price in general equilibrium (1874b, p. 154; 1889, pp. 179–180), and, second, that if the number of commodities is great, it is generally not possible for there to be multiple equilibria in exchange (1874b, p. 156; 1889, p. 182).

CHAPTER 4

Institutions and participants in the model of monetary oral pledges markets

For many years, the opinion has been expressed in the literature on Léon Walras's work that he did not pay attention to market institutions in his models of market behavior. It is shown that in fact he founded his model of a monetary oral pledges market on a detailed specification of the institutions and other structural features that condition the traders' behavior, including rules, conventions, kinds of firms represented, and kinds of commodities and trades. It is also shown that he explained how the phenomena and processes of organized markets arise from economic needs and are related to other economic processes. He drew on empirical information to construct his model, and illuminated that information with his theoretical perceptions.

I. Introduction

The current view

The current view of Walras's work is that he did not pay attention to market institutions – namely, to the complex of rules and procedures that regulate and influence the behavior of the participants. William Jaffé expressed that view by writing that "Léon Walras sought to systematize the economic forces that he regarded in *specie aeternitatis,* i.e. economic forces which he thought were independent of institutional constraints" (Jaffé 1971, p. 98 [279]). Jaffé agreed with Oskar Lange that "the general equilibrium model of the Lausanne type is devoid of any specification of the institutional framework, precisely because it consists in nothing more than a pure theory of exchange, production and capital formation, positing only a freely competitive market of the atomistic variety" (ibid., p. 100 [281]). It will be demonstrated in this chapter that the current view is erroneous. Jaffé did not quote any statement of Walras's to the effect that he believed he was systematizing economic forces that are independent of institutions. No such statements exist, as far as I am aware, and his work manifests the opposite objective. He dealt with several kinds of markets, and he expended much effort on specifying their institutional features and the institutionally shaped characteristics and behavioral patterns of the participants. His market models are rich in detail drawn from real markets and the real economy generally.

This chapter is concerned with Léon Walras's model of markets in which the participants make oral pledges to buy and sell commodities and in which money is used. In the real economy, these activities occur in several varieties of markets, so it will be understood that by an oral pledges market in this chapter is meant the freely competitive model of that type that Walras developed. The chapter examines the institutions, participants, kinds of commodities, and sorts of trades that are made in the model, reserving for the next chapter the examination of its equilibrating behavior and equilibrium conditions, and an evaluation of it. By the term "oral pledges model" in this chapter is meant the monetary version of that type of model, unless otherwise specified. Walras revised and refined the model extensively between 1877 and 1889 and thus produced a version that is part of his mature body of work. He did not alter the model after he published the second edition of the *Eléments* – that is, he did not modify it or introduce new material into it during his last phase of theoretical activity. He simply presented it again, with a few inconsequential changes, in the successive editions of the *Eléments* even though its structure and functioning contradict the written pledges model that he introduced in the fourth edition of the *Eléments*. The citations in this chapter and the next therefore also indicate where the model is to be found in the fourth (and fifth) editions.

The importance of Walras's model

There are three reasons for studying Walras's model of oral pledges markets. First, these markets are important in the modern economy, so it is interesting to learn what Walras contributed to their understanding. Second, the oral pledges model is an important part of his theoretical work. In that model, he constructed the type of trading situation that he assumed occurs in all his mature models. For example, the market days in his model of the sale of consumer goods are of the type examined in this and the next chapter. Third, the markets with which he dealt in his oral pledges model have been described as auctions, thereby greatly affecting perceptions of how organized competitive markets behave, and it is therefore interesting to determine whether the model is accurately described in that way. Despite those considerations, no interpretative study has been made of it, as far as I am aware, as distinct from brief comments on special aspects of the model. This neglect has probably occurred because Walras's work on oral pledges markets has unjustly been deemed less interesting and less important than his written pledges model of markets. Nevertheless, Walras became interested in oral pledges markets early in his career (1860c, 1867), retained his exposition of them in the successive editions of the *Eléments,* and retained an interest in oral pledges markets because they are a part of real economic life. He pointed out that at the time he was writing there was little understanding of organized securities and commodity exchanges, although there was a great deal of condemnation of the traders' activities. They are varied and complicated, he wrote, and are well-known only to business people who have no interest in divulging information about them. He therefore regarded his analysis of oral pledges markets as introducing the public to a significant subject (1880b, p. 453 [402]).

Sources for the model

In the *Eléments* (for example, Walras 1874b, pp. 49–51, 302–4; 1889, pp. 309–11; 1900, §§ 41–42, 45–47; 1900, §§ 269–70, pp. 292–94), in his article "La Bourse, la spéculation et l'agiotage" (1880b, 1880c) and in other writings, Walras drew on the features of the organized exchanges of his time for theoretical purposes. It would be wrong to suppose that "La Bourse . . .," for example, does not contain theoretical material or is irrelevant for this study simply because he republished it in a book with "applied economics" in the title (1898),[1] just as it would be wrong to deny the existence in the *Eléments* of empirical material on oral pledges markets, or to deny the relevance of that material for this chapter simply because the *Eléments* principally deals with theory. Consideration of writings of Walras's in addition to his *Eléments*, of "La Bourse. . ." in particular, enlarges our view of his theory of exchange. He used "La Bourse. . ." to express his theoretical vision by integrating statements of his model into each of the two parts in which the article was originally published (1880b, pp. 460–64 [408–11]; 1880c, p. 78 [432])[2]; by providing, in each part of the article, a theoretical treatment of the relation of the securities market to production, saving, and capital formation (1880b, pp. 456–59 [404–7]; 1880c, pp. 66–75 [422–29]); and by organizing and illuminating the empirical material with his theoretical perceptions. The empirical material in the *Eléments* and elsewhere is familiar to the readers of this study, except perhaps for some details of financial organization and practice peculiar to French organized markets in the nineteenth century. These facts are mentioned to show that Walras used empirical material, and to show how he organized it, used it for illustrative purposes, and drew conclusions from it.

Walras considered commodity bourses as well as securities exchanges in his oral pledges model. Indeed, he based his first exposition of a monetary

---

[1] The *Etudes d'économie appliquée* contains much theoretical material, including the "Theory of free exchange," the "Theory of credit," and, as Walras explained, the completion of the theory of money that he began in the *Eléments* (1898b, p. 286).

[2] If a reference is likely to be inaccessible to some readers, and it has been republished, the republication is also cited either in the text or in the list of references. The numbers in brackets are the pagination of Walras 1880b and 1880c in Walras 1898.

oral pledges market on a wheat bourse (1874a, pp. 102–3, and in 1877c, offprint pp. 10–11). In what follows, however, attention will for the most part be given to his treatment of the French securities market. This is done because he subsequently reworded his major statements of the oral pledges model to make them refer to a securities bourse, and because he devoted most of his attention to that type of market in considering empirical material about oral pledges markets. He did so for the reason that he regarded the securities bourse as "*le marché type,*" the standard form of a freely competitive market (1880b, p. 460 [408]; 1880c, p. 78 [432]).

In order to be structurally complete, a model of exchange must take account of the interrelated questions of the degree of competition, of who participates in the market, of the functions of the participants, of the assets they trade, and of the conventions regarding trading. It must also explain how the phenomena and processes of the market arise from economic needs and are related to other economic processes. These matters will now be considered with reference to Walras's monetary oral pledges model.

II. Market characteristics

Free competition

Walras stated that in his formal expositions of theoretical principles – that is, in all the models studied in this book – "we always assume a market perfectly organized under the regime of competition, just as in pure mechanics it is initially assumed that machines are frictionless" (1874b, p. 49; 1889, p. 67; 1900, § 41, p. 45). As will be shown in this chapter and the next, he did not adopt the assumption as an unexplained axiom; on the contrary, he specified with great care the institutions, physical features, and practices that result in that type of market. Many economists have supposed that Walras's market models are "perfectly" competitive. Joseph A. Schumpeter, for example, characterized Walras as dealing with "*perfect* equilibrium in *perfect* competition" (Schumpeter 1954, p. 1026, n. 72; see also ibid., p. 973).[3] In fact, Walras described the markets in his models as "freely" competitive, and stated they are perfectly *organized,* not that they are perfectly competitive in the sense of traders having perfect *knowledge.* That they are not perfectly competitive in that sense is evident from the workings of his oral pledges model, for such knowledge would mean that the traders or an omniscient price-setter know the market supply and demand functions and hence the solution price before trade occurs. That would eliminate the need for quoted prices, make pledges unnecessary, and render superfluous the rules and proce-

---

[3] An analysis that is relevant for evaluating Schumpeter's view of Walras's concept of freely competitive markets is given in chapter 5.

dures that Walras incorporated into his model. Nor are the markets perfectly competitive in the sense of there being infinitely many participants. On the contrary, the number of traders is limited for the same reasons as in his models of barter (ch. 3). Moreover, Walras stated that by describing the oral pledges model as "perfectly organized," he was indicating that he was making "abstraction from small perturbing circumstances" (1874a, p. 103, and in 1877c, offprint p. 11). He explained that he meant the model is free of the frictions that arise in markets that lack the rules and procedures of organized exchanges (1874b, pp. 49, 267; 1889, pp. 251–52; 1900, § 41, p. 45; 1900, § 222, p. 232).[4]

Walras emphasized that "in regard to exchange especially, he did not claim to have constructed the mathematical theory of all possible modes of trading. He had devoted himself solely to the mode that consists *of raising the price when the quantity demanded exceeds the quantity supplied and lowering the price when the quantity supplied exceeds the quantity demanded*" (1895, p. 630), the mode known as Walrasian pricing. He summarized the meaning of the term "free competition" in the following way:

In the question of tatonnement, for example, I take the almost universal regime of free competition in regard to exchange, that which was described by John Stuart Mill, and which consists in raising the price in the case of the quantity demanded exceeding the quantity supplied and lowering it in the case of the quantity supplied exceeding the quantity demanded, and I demonstrate that the process leads to equilibrium by establishing the equality of the quantities supplied and demanded (Walras to Bortkiewicz, February 27, 1891, in 1965, 2, letter 999, p. 434).

Thus, oral pledges markets are freely competitive in the sense that they behave in the way described by supply and demand functions and the associated action of market forces.

Walras also argued that the oral pledges model is applicable to markets with a spectrum of degrees of competition. Free competition "can be considered as the principal mode that is practiced on all markets with more or less rigor and accordingly with less or more friction" (ibid.; and see Walras 1874b, pp. 48–49; 1889, pp. 66–67; 1900, § 41, pp, 44–45). In addition to the organized exchanges, "there are others in which competition, although less well-regulated, functions in a sufficiently expedient and satisfactory manner: such are the markets for fruits and vegetables, for poultry." The streets of a town filled with retail stores "are markets organized a little more defectively in regard to competition, but where, however, it makes itself sufficiently felt" (1874b, pp. 48–49; 1889, pp. 66–67; 1900, § 41, pp. 44–45) – sufficiently, that is, for supply and demand analysis to be applicable to them. Walras proceeded to give other examples that depart progressively

---

[4] Walras recognized that in many markets there are perturbing circumstances but maintained that his model was nevertheless valuable (1874b, p. 267; 1889, p. 252; 1900, § 222, p. 232).

from the characteristics of *le marché type* but are nevertheless competitive to a degree (ibid.).

Walras regarded the oral pledges model as a realistic scientific account of markets. It describes the behavior of real "stock exchanges, organized commodity markets, the markets for grain, fish, etc." (1874b, p. 48; 1889, p. 66; 1900, § 41, p. 44). It incorporates the characteristics of the Paris securities exchange because that is where Walras found "the description of the mechanism of free competition in regard to exchange" (1877b, p. 303; 1889, pp. 310–11; 1900, § 270, pp. 293–94). Walras also drew the bases of his theory of exchange from the wheat market, a real oral pledges market: "Let us scrupulously take account of the operations that occur there. Perhaps the most delicate point in the physio-mathematical sciences is in this way to borrow from reality the experimental data upon which the intellect then establishes a series of logical deductions" (1874a, p. 102, and in 1877c, offprint p. 10).

The participants

Walras began his account of the structure of oral pledges markets by identifying the participants. In some such markets, he explained, the owners of assets act directly for themselves "without agents, or criers" (1974b, p. 69; 1889, p. 86; 1900, § 61, p. 65). Walras therefore sometimes assumed that "in our market, the sellers and the buyers," by whom he meant the owners of the assets, "are in the presence of each other" (1874a, p. 106, and in 1877c, offprint p. 14). For example, he explained in one formulation of a market in which rates of production and consumption are determined and in which prices are cried that "there is generally, for each service or product in the private sector, a crowd of consumer-demanders; and similarly, there is a crowd of producer-suppliers assured of selling to one person whatever they will be unable to sell to another" (1875/1897, and in 1898b, p. 197).[5] The owners of products that are traded on organized commodity markets include producers, wholesalers, and semi-wholesalers (1880b, pp. 469–71 [415–17]). The original owners of securities are the units of government and private corporations that issue them. The types of businesses that buy new and old securities and resell them include underwriters such as brokerage firms, investment banking houses, industrial credit companies, mortgage banks, and loan companies. Some bankers specialize in buying and selling securities and stand in the same relationship to investment houses as retail merchants do to wholesale merchants. Private individuals also buy and sell securities, although doing so is not their principal occupation (ibid., pp. 453, 469 [401, 415–16]).

---

[5] Walras subsequently assumed that in retail markets for consumer goods, the pledges are written, as is documented in chapter 16.

In some oral pledges markets – namely, organized exchanges – the traders are not the owners of the assets, the presence of whom "is not necessary: if they give their orders to agents, the market will be held among the latter" (1874a, p. 106; and in 1877c, offprint p. 14). "On the securities exchange," for example, "sales and purchases are made, not between sellers and buyers, but through the intermediation of agents" (1880b, p. 461 [408]). The agents who are active in commodities and securities exchanges and other organized markets include "*agents de change, courtiers de commerce, crieurs*" (1874b, p. 48; 1889 p. 66; 1900, § 41, pp. 44).[6] The question arises as to what sorts of participants Walras meant by those three terms. The first two clearly refer to trading agents. They are brokers who effect purchases and sales on behalf of owners of assets (1880b, pp. 460–61 [408]), and who arrange transactions. For example, capitalists who want to make short-term loans and speculators who want to buy securities but need purchasing power both "call upon the *agents de change,* who bring them together" (ibid., p. 466 [413]).

As for *crieur,* the word entered the French language in the twelfth century and meant a public town crier or bellman, a person who had the duty of announcing public proclamations in a loud voice. The word, with appropriate qualification, is now used for a newspaper seller, a street hawker, or more generally for a stationary or mobile vendor who cries out the name of the commodity he sells. It also means or has meant a crier, a bawler, a shouter, and a call-boy in a theater. *Un crieur* was sometimes used to refer to an auctioneer of the type that functioned in markets like Covent Garden, but never, so far as I am aware, to an auctioneer in an organized securities exchange. The French term for auctioneer is *commissaire-priseur.*

William Jaffé correctly translated *crieurs* as "criers" (Jaffé in Walras 1954, p. 84; Walras 1874b, p. 48; 1889, p. 66; 1900, § 41, p. 44) in his rendition of the passage quoted in the previous paragraph, but he then led his readers to believe that they are *auctioneers* by translating *crieurs* in that way in a subsequent passage (Jaffé in Walras 1954, p. 106; Walras 1874b, p. 69; 1889, p. 86; 1900, § 61, p. 65). Michio Morishima, for example, drawing his ideas about Walras's work from Jaffé's translation of the *Eléments,* believed that auctioneers are present in Walras's models of markets (Morishima 1977, p. 19).[7] In actuality, Walras did not think that a crier is an auctioneer, as will

---

[6] The brokers on *la coulisse,* the market for securities in France that operated outside of the Bourse (see Walras 1880b, p. 462 [409]), were called *courtiers.* Their positions were eliminated in 1961 when that market was eliminated. *Agents de change* were replaced by "sociétés de Bourse" on January 22, 1988.

[7] Jaffé criticized Morishima for having made the "gratuitous invention" of "the auctioneer," evidently meaning a single central entity that sets prices in every market (Jaffé 1980, p. 538, n. 27 [355, n. 27]; also see Jaffé 1978, p. 575). In actuality, Morishima made the different error of supposing that Walras assumed multiple auctioneers, one in each market. Morishima cited as his authority Jaffé's translation of the *Eléments.*

shortly be made clear by a discussion of the difference between an auction and the type of market that Walras modeled. He emphasized that all three types of agents are professional traders who are active in organized markets (1874b, p. 48; 1889, p. 66; 1900, § 41, p. 44). Their functions are not to auction off commodities or securities but to "centralize the offers in such a way that no exchange takes place without its conditions being announced and known" (ibid.). The meaning of that statement is that the agents, like those on the Chicago Board of Trade, the New York Stock Exchange, and the Paris Bourse, receive orders to buy and sell from many owners of assets, channel the orders into one locality for their execution, and shout out their price and quantity offers (see Walras 1880b, p. 461 [408]).[8]

Characteristics of assets and trades

There is much more to Walras's account of the commodities traded on oral pledges markets than his specification in his equation systems that commodities abstractly symbolized by (A), (B), and so on are arguments of the supply and demand functions. As has been seen, he mentioned a number of agricultural raw materials that are traded in oral pledges markets. He explained that a variety of different types of securities are sold on the Bourse – bonds issued by the central government and by communities, and stocks and bonds of banks, financial houses, and industrial enterprises (1880c, pp. 68–69 [424]). He identified some of the original issuers of stocks at the time he was writing as being primarily railroad companies, firms that construct canals, oceanic and canal shipping concerns, carriage and omnibus companies, mines, coking plants, factories for making gas, and iron foundries and forges (ibid., p. 454 [402–3]). In an effort to introduce even more empirical detail into his analysis of securities exchanges, he examined such matters as the par value of a security, its current price, the premium made by speculators who buy stocks at their issuance price and bonds at par and sell them at higher prices, the ownership of titles to capital goods, the ownership of evidences of debt, the types of incomes received by stock and bond holders, the details of the payment of interest and dividends, the sale of bonds with and without coupons, the difference between the official exchange and the market operated by brokers outside of the exchange, the timing of operations of different sorts, the structure of commissions, the distinction between settlements in cash and agreements to make future settlements, the differences between firm contracts and options, and the details of the delivery times of French govern-

---

[8] Since agents or owners or both function in one sort of Walrasian oral pledges market or another, for convenience of expression henceforward in this chapter the words "trader," "buyer," "demander," "seller," and "supplier" will be used in reference to either an agent or an owner, unless otherwise indicated.

ment bonds and of private securities (1867; 1874b, pp. 50–51; 1889, p. 95; 1900, § 42, p. 72; 1880b; 1880c).

Walras also classified the different types of operations in which buyers and sellers engage. The traders' activities vary according to whether they have sufficient funds for what they have pledged to buy, or possess the assets that they pledge to sell. Some take long positions, some sell short. Some of the activity on the floor of exchanges is pure gambling with no assets being actually traded, but that is not true of most of the activity. The trader who has pledged to supply securities ordinarily has to deliver them; the demander who has pledged to buy them has to pay for them; and in some cases the buyer can demand the securities before the due date for settlement (1880b, p. 464 [411]). In this connection, Walras described some sophisticated trading operations. For example, a trader who wants to sell securities in order to acquire money in the present and who also wants to own securities in the future needs to deal with a spot buyer and a future seller. On behalf of the trader, an agent searches for them, and finds them combined in a capitalist who is willing to buy the trader's securities during the current settlement and sell them back to him at the next settlement. A trader who wants to acquire securities but hold them only for a short time needs to find a spot seller and a future buyer. On behalf of the trader, an agent finds them combined in a holder of securities, who sells them to the trader securities during the current trading period and buys them back at the next settlement (ibid., pp. 465–66 [412–13]).

Oral pledges

The question then arises as to the character of the pledges that the traders make to each other. An oral pledge in Walras's model is a commitment to buy or sell all that is demanded or supplied at a proposed price if it is the price at which all individual excess demand quantities are zero on the particular market on a particular day, or, in another formulation, if all excess demand quantities are simultaneously zero in all markets. In all organized markets, conventions determine the way that price and quantity offers are made. In the oral pledges model, "sales and purchases," Walras wrote, "are made *à la criée*" (1874a, p. 106, and in 1877c, p. 14; 1874b, p. 48; 1889, p. 66; 1900, § 41, p. 44; and see Walras 1867, p. 1732, also in Walras 1987, p. 180). An understanding of his use of the term *à la criée* is crucial to achieving an understanding of the nature of his model of oral pledges markets. The term can be used with the meaning "by auction," which may lead both French-speaking and English-speaking economists to suppose it has that meaning in Walras's work. Indeed, Jaffé made a second important translation decision that influenced many English-speaking economists to perceive Walras's model as a theory of auction markets by rendering *à la criée* as "by auction" (Jaffé in Walras 1954, p. 84).[9] Nevertheless, when Walras used the term and wrote in other contexts that "prices are cried,"[10] he did not mean "by auction" or that prices are cried by an auctioneer. Nor did he state that securities are sold by the method – called *"la criée"* in France – of a market authority calling out the names of the securities that are listed, although such a system would not be inconsistent with his view of how prices and trades are determined. He implied that in a securities market the name of each listed security is called out in turn, but once a security has been called out in his model, its price is not then determined by auction. He used *à la criée* in its literal sense of meaning "by being cried out," and he was referring to the crying out of prices and the associated desired quantities.[11]

About the term *crié*, Jaffé asserted, long after preparing his translation, that "in the *Eléments* prices are said to be 'cried,' but Walras did not specify by whom they are 'cried.' It seems reasonable, therefore, to render Walras's '*crié*' by 'quoted' or 'called,' the quoting or calling being done by any-one," by the traders or an auctioneer (Jaffé 1980, p. 538, n. 27 [355, n. 27]). In fact, Walras specified precisely many times by whom prices are cried, and he made clear they could not possibly be cried by an auctioneer. He stated that suggested prices and the associated individual supply and demand quanti-ties are cried out by the buyers and sellers – the owners of the commodities and money – in some markets and by their agents in others. Walras indicated this in many passages, such as one he wrote when he first formulated the oral pledges model. "There are real markets," he noted, "on which the sales and purchases are made *à la criée* by the intermediation of agents such as trad-ing agents, brokers, and these markets are precisely the ones best organized under the regime of competition. Nothing prevents us from assuming that our market is organized in that manner." These agents, he continued, "un-dertake *la criée*" in order "to execute the orders written on their order books" (1874a, p. 106, and in 1877c, offprint p. 14). Thus, Walras stated that in the process of trading *à la criée* it is the traders who undertake *la*

---

[9] I was provided with an example of the influence of Jaffé's translation in that regard when I gave a paper on price iteration in Walras's theory of general equilibrium (ch. 12) at the Western Economic Association meeting in 1988. The discussant, Professor Mayo C. Toruño, criticized my paper on the ground that it did not reflect that Walras had dealt with what happens *in an auction*. Upon my questioning his interpretation, Professor Toruño provided me with documentation of its source. It was, he showed me, Jaffé's unqualified use of the word "auction" in his translation of the crucial passage in which Walras specified the type of markets he was going to consider.

[10] Walras used expressions like *on y crie des prix* (1874b, p. 127), or *un prix étant crie*, or *on crie un autre prix*, or *il faudra criér d'autres prix*. See, for example, 1886, pp. 26–27; 1898b, p. 86; 1889, p. 234; 1900, § 185, pp. 191–92; 1900, § 207, p. 214.

[11] As it happens, in the modern French Bourse all orders to buy or sell are supposed to be written, but, following custom, oral pledges are still accepted.

criée.[12] He stated directly that traders quote prices when he wrote about "sellers of commodities expressing their prices in gold" and "sellers of commodities expressing their prices in silver" (1874b, p. 191; 1889, pp. 439–40). He explained in the passage of the *Eléments* in which he used the term *à la criée* that an organized market functions with "the sellers being able to lower the price and the buyers to raise it" (1874b, p. 48; 1889, p. 66; 1900, § 41, p. 44).[13]

Walras specified that information is disseminated in oral pledges markets in three ways. First, the traders call out the terms of their offers so that their coparticipants in the trading area can hear them. Second, after the business day is over, prices are listed on in-house trade sheets, which are made available to the participants and the organizations for which they work: "It is necessary in a model market for there to be a market price list on which the current price is officially written; and the prices on the Bourse are many and complicated, since they include the spot cash prices, the firm share prices, the prices of options, the contango rates" (1880c, p. 78 [432]). Third, interested parties in the wider financial community are apprised of the prices at which trades have occurred "by the market price lists called *quotations* that all the newspapers reproduce" (1880b, p. 454 [402]).

III. Contrast with auctions

The process that takes place in Walras's monetary oral pledges market model is not an auction; indeed, none of his models deals with an auction. In an auction (see Cassady 1967; Smith 1987, *1*, pp. 138–41; Mester 1988), there is, of course, an auctioneer.[14] Using all his skill to try to get the highest price for the item, he is the agent of the seller, not a neutral party. The sellers do not compete against each other, do not interact in any way, do not act for themselves,[15] and do not hire floor traders to represent them. In contrast, Walras's oral pledges model has no auctioneer, the agents act on behalf of buyers as well as of sellers, and they trade directly with each other on behalf

---

[12] It can be inferred from Walras's descriptive passages that in some oral pledges markets, the traders not only call out their offers but also signal prices and quantities with stylized gestures. The latter procedure is equivalent to the crying out of offers. It could be included in the meaning of the term "oral pledges" if the question arose as to how such signaling fits into Walras's theory.

[13] For much additional evidence that the traders change the price in Walras's oral pledges model see ch. 11.

[14] Many special cases and variations of detail are not considered in this characterization of oral auction markets. Sealed-bid auctions are not mentioned in the body of this chapter because they are written pledges markets.

[15] A monopolistic seller acts for himself when he is the auctioneer, like the U.S. Treasury in its gold auctions during the 1970s or in its sales of securities, but those have been sealed-bid auctions.

of their clients. An auction market such as Sotheby's or Christie's or an estate auction or an auction market for cattle is not characterized by a crowd of buyers and sellers of a homogeneous commodity.[16] Instead, on each "day" a single item or a batch treated as a unit is put up for sale by a single seller. In contrast, in Walras's model of organized exchanges the commodity is homogeneous, and it often happens that selling agents offer to sell multiple units of it simultaneously. There are a number of selling agents, and they compete against each other, and there are a number of buying agents, who simultaneously offer to buy multiple units of the commodity (1874b, p. 50; 1889, p. 68; 1900, § 42, p. 46). The competitive behavior and multiplicity of units traded also characterize Walras's model of markets in which the traders are the owners of the purchasing power and the commodity. In some auctions, on rare occasions, the price may be quoted by demanders when they want to raise it by less than the standard increment called out by the auctioneer, and the quotation is then confirmed by the auctioneer. In most auction markets, however, prices are always changed and cried by the auctioneer.[17] In contrast, in Walras's oral pledges model it is always the traders who both quote and change the price.

In his passages dealing with the traders quoting prices, Walras used the terms *au rabais* and *à l'enchère* to describe their activities. Those terms can be used in reference to auction behavior, and thus constitute another reason why many economists, both French and otherwise, have been led to believe that Walras was discussing auctions. Nevertheless, the terms are not used in that way in contexts such as those in which they were employed by Walras. Jaffé correctly translated the terms in most of Walras's passages as respectively "lowering and raising the price" (Jaffé in Walras 1954, pp. 84–85).[18]

---

[16] In auctions of metals, for example, the units in the batches are homogeneous, but the markets are not conducted like an oral auction. The fixing of the price of gold in London, for example, is not determined in an auction market. A market authority cries the price but both buyers and sellers state desired quantities, which vary with the price.

[17] In an auction, by making a bid, a demander pledges to buy the item at the quoted price if the auctioneer awards the item to him, so an auction is a type of oral pledges market, but not the type with which Walras was concerned.

[18] In an entirely different context and in his last phase of theoretical work, Walras wrote that the auctions of many firms lead to competitive equilibrium, but that the same equilibrium would result if a single entrepreneur dealing in all products "demanderait les services à l'enchère et offrirait les produits au rabais" (1900, § 188, p. 194; emphasis added). In this case, however, Jaffé made another unfortunate translation decision by once again representing Walras as describing auction behavior, rendering the passage as: "if he bought his services and sold his products *by auction*" (Jaffé in Walras 1954, p. 225; emphasis added). This is not only an incorrect translation but also absurd, since there is only a single buyer, the monopsonistic entrepreneur, in services markets. There cannot be an auction if there is only one buyer. On reflection of the correct meaning of the French words in reference to Walras's work, and of his point about the monopolist acting like freely competitive firms, the correct translation of the passage is: "if he were to raise the prices he offers for services and were to lower the prices of the products" (1877b, p. 231; 1889, p. 213; 1900, § 188, p. 194).

That Walras was not referring to auctions in his oral pledges model is also made evident by his illustration of the pricing behavior of the traders in a bond market (1874b, pp. 49–50; 1889, pp. 67–69; 1900, § 42, pp. 45–47). If there is a positive market excess demand quantity, the demanders *vont à l'enchère,* that is, "*they raise the price.*" If there is a negative market excess demand quantity the sellers *vont au rabais,* that is, "*they lower the price*" (ibid.; emphasis added). In contrast, the price is not both raised and lowered in a given auction market. At an English auction, after the buyers become active, the price is always raised. At a Dutch auction, the price is always lowered. In Walras's oral pledges model, however, "as buyers, *the traders raise prices*; as sellers, *they lower prices,* and their competition thus leads to a certain value in exchange that is sometimes rising, sometimes falling, and sometimes stationary" (1874b, p. 48; 1889, p. 66; 1900, § 41, p. 44).

That type of pricing behavior, curiously enough, is called auction behavior in some modern models of exchange. For example, writers postulate a competitive market process in which "buyers and sellers are free to enter price quotes" (Smith and Williams 1981, pp. 1–2). The writers then describe that behavior as "double auction trading" (ibid.), although buyers characteristically do not make price quotes in an auction, and sellers never do in the sense meant in the models – that is, from the floor. Similarly, there are modern models in which buyers freely announce not only "bid prices" but also corresponding quantities, and accept offers, and in which sellers freely announce not only "offer prices" but also corresponding quantities that vary with the price, and accept bids. This behavior is then described as an "oral double auction" (Smith et al. 1982, pp. 58, 61), although it never happens in an auction market. A similar peculiar usage occurs when a central price-setter who never conducts an auction is called "the auctioneer" (Arrow and Hahn 1971, chapters 11, 12; Hahn 1987).

The introduction of genuine auctioneers into each market would result in a system that behaves very differently from the way Walras wanted his model to behave. An auction system would require that changes of prices in various markets lead the auctioneer in a particular market to halt the auction or to annul the winning bid and auction off the item again. Walras never mentioned anything remotely resembling those processes. He would have added to the logical problems of his model if he had done so, because if an auction were begun again, expectations would be changed as a result of what happened the previous time the item was being auctioned. Consequently, the equilibrium reached by a system of auction markets – if an equilibrium exists – would not be independent of the path to equilibrium and would therefore not be given by Walras's system of equations.

When Walras wanted to refer to an auction, he made clear that he was discussing a market that differed from his oral pledges model. He used terms that unequivocally have the meaning of an auction – *vente à l'encan* (1874b,

p. 155; 1889, p. 180; 1900, § 153, p. 161), *le système d'enchères anglais* and *le système d'enchères hollandais* (Walras to Ladislaus von Bortkiewicz, February 27, 1891, in 1965, 2, letter 999, pp. 434–35), and he alluded to "the particular form of bidding" that takes place in an auction (1874b, p. 155; 1889, p. 180; 1900, § 153, p. 161). If he had had auctions in mind when he discussed oral pledges markets, he could have used those terms in reference to them, or the term *audience des criées,* which means "auction market," but he did not. When he discussed oral pledges markets, if he had wanted to refer to an auctioneer who calls out prices and notes their acceptance by bidders, he could have used the term *commissaire-priseur,* but he did not. He did not want to encumber his theory with the behavior of auctions. He had, he asserted, developed a theory of the general case and relegated auctions to the category of special cases. He therefore complained about being told that he should have included them in his model, resenting having had "thrown at my head the market for English public debt, the system of English auctions, the system of Dutch auctions, etc." (Walras to Ladislaus von Bortkiewicz, February 27, 1891, in 1965, 2, letter 999, pp. 434–35). In summary, auctions are unlike the competitive markets Walras discussed throughout the *Eléments,* unlike the behavior that he proceeded to describe immediately after his remark about *à la criée,* and with the exception of a few fish markets, unlike any of the examples of markets that he mentioned.

IV. The economic functions of oral pledges markets

Walras's theory of exchange has always been represented in the interpretive literature as postulating that traders come to market with unexplained given endowments of money and an asset. In actuality, an important reason for Walras's interest in oral pledges markets was his concern with the underlying economic processes that are facilitated by the activities of the participants. That led him to develop, as a significant part of his model of oral pledges markets, an explanation of the complex activities by which the traders come to have command over purchasing power and by which the goods or securities they hold come into being. All those activities, Walras contended, except pure gambling, are economically useful (1880b, pp. 470 [416]). He identified three major economic functions of oral pledges markets. The first relates to both commodities and securities exchanges, and the other two relate to the latter.

Increasing efficiency

According to Walras, speculation in both commodity markets and securities exchanges leads to efficiency by linking parts of the economy. Commercial speculation operates on commodities, which disappear through consumption and reappear through production. The speculators in commodity markets are wholesalers who transmit products from manufacturers to retailers (ibid., pp. 469–70 [415–16]). The speculators in securities markets operate "on the securities that a continuous stream of investment puts at the disposition of a continuous stream of money savings" (ibid., p. 470 [416]). They are intermediaries in capital formation. They transmit the ownership of new capital goods from those who make them to those who have savings (1880c, p. 66 [422]).

A speculator is not a philanthropist and does not try to be a saint, Walras observed. His motive, like that of the other participants in oral pledges markets, is to make profits, and that results in economic efficiency:

It is his right, and one could say almost his duty, to aim solely at earning a lot of money. It is accepted as an axiom among competent people that the best farmer is the one who makes most profit. If it is true that the services and products that are most useful are those that people will pay the most for, why is it not true that the best industrialist, the best merchant, the best banker, the best speculator is the one who enriches himself the most, of course within the limits of honesty and fair dealing (ibid., pp. 91–92 [443])?

Speculation links the present with the future and, Walras contended, is necessary to the smooth functioning of a capitalist economy. Speculators make existing commodities available in the future by buying them from the producers, holding them in the hope that their prices will rise, and then selling them to retailers (1880b, p. 469 [415–16]). Speculators do the same with securities. The professional dealer may buy future commodities or securities at a price established now if he expects the future price to be higher, with the intention of reselling the assets in the future or he may agree to deliver future commodities or securities at a price established now if he expects to be able to buy them in the future at a lower price. A dealer in securities increases his inventory if capital formation and the attendant issuance of securities is increasing more rapidly than money savings, and decreases his inventory in the opposite event. In the former case, he helps to prevent a decrease in the price of securities; in the latter, he helps to prevent an increase in the price. By introducing the question of future needs, the speculator in securities, for example, diminishes the amplitude of changes in the stock of securities and also enables the stock to be as small as possible (ibid., p. 472 [418]). Thus, speculation in commodities and securities futures reduces the volatility of prices and the amplitude of their changes.

Transforming savings into capital goods

Walras asserted that the purchasing power in the securities market is generated by capitalists consuming less than their incomes and spending their savings there (ibid., pp. 456–57 [404–5]; 1880c, pp. 70–75 [425–29]). "In effect, in order to buy new securities there must be new money capital, that is to say, saving. By saving, we mean in a general sense the excess of production over the consumption of income" (1880b, p. 456 [404]). As Walras conceived of matters, savings are transformed into capital goods. That is made possible by the operations of the oral pledges securities market, operations that can be summarized as speculation and the extension of credit (1880c, p. 71 [426]).[19] "Thanks to credit and speculation, the totality of savings will be capitalized" (ibid.). "Capital formation is the goal, speculation is the means" (1880b, p. 456 [404]). Concerned to show how that happens, Walras explained that engineers and financiers make studies and calculations about the undertaking of a new venture. Businessmen then establish a company and are installed as managers and directors, and they issue stocks and bonds for the money capital they need. They produce securities just as industrialists produce manufactured goods. The newly issued securities thus represent capital goods that are planned or are in the process of being made (ibid., p. 459 [406–7]).

The securities, highly speculative at first, are bought by speculators, Walras's name for underwriters. They are merchants in securities at the wholesale and semi-wholesale levels. They intervene between the entrepreneurs and the securities retailers. After the capital goods are made, the profitability or otherwise of the firm that issues the new securities becomes apparent, in light of which their prices are established. The retailers of securities, who are counterparts of the retailers of goods, buy securities from the underwriters, inform the capitalists about their features, and sell them the securities (ibid., p. 469 [15–16]). Thus, by spending their savings on stocks and bonds, capitalists finance the creation of new capital. "The work of speculation is then finished; its profit or loss is realized. That shows how speculation is the intermediary between savings and new capital goods" (ibid., p. 459 [407]). The underwriters then use the funds to buy another batch of new securities (ibid., p. 458 [406]).

Allocating economic resources

Finally, Walras explained that the particular types of capital goods that are made "depend on the direction imprinted on savings by credit and speculation" (1880c, p. 71 [416]). The desire to maximize utility and competitive forces allocate the total annual amount of savings of the country so that some part of it goes to private demanders of capital and the rest to government entities (ibid., pp. 68–69 [424]). The use that private business makes of the

---

[19] Walras's models of loan and money markets lie outside of the scope of this chapter.

proceeds of the sale of its securities is also subject to market forces. These forces cause the aggregate amount of saving to be divided between the creation of fixed and circulating capital, and to be divided between agricultural and manufacturing activities (ibid., pp. 70–71 [425–26]). "Thus it is, thanks to the variety and flexibility of the combinations used on the Bourse, that the immense operation of the distribution of saving among the different uses of capital is effectuated without disorder or discontinuities other than those that result from exceptional circumstances" (1880b, p. 473 [419]).

V. Summary

The characteristics of Walras's model of oral pledges markets have been explained. It has been shown that he drew the structural properties of his model from economic reality, basing the model on the institutions of the organized markets of his day. By noting that the state undertakes "the organization of market operations on the Bourse" (1880c, p. 79 [433]), Walras emphasized his recognition that an oral pledges market is not a place where atomistic unregulated competitive forces act in the absence of institutional constraints. He also explored the significance of many conventions and rules that were adopted voluntarily by the traders. His conclusion about the securities exchange stresses the importance of its institutional structure and the characteristics of the participants: "If one examines without prejudice the organization of the Bourse of Paris and the functioning of the credit societies that operate there, one will be more and more convinced that it is an admirable mechanism for undertaking the work that it does" (ibid., p. 91 [443]).

It has also been shown that Walras provided many details about the structure of his oral pledges model. He specified the types of participants and their functions, the institutional provisions for changing and publicizing prices, the types of contracts, the settlement procedures, and the kinds of assets that are traded. He incorporated these facts of the marketplace into his model, organized them in accordance with the categories, relationships, and processes identified by it, and elucidated the significance of the facts in light of the theoretical considerations established in his model. He also showed the connections of organized commodity markets with production and retail sales, and the connection of securities markets with saving and investment. Thus, Walras's treatment of the structure of oral pledges markets is revealed to be remarkably complete and realistic. The next chapter will show how he explained the equilibrating process in the model and dealt with its equilibrium conditions.

CHAPTER 5

Disequilibrium and equilibrium in the model of monetary oral pledges markets

Oral pledges markets, such as securities exchanges, are an important part of the market system, and accordingly were assigned an important role in Walras's models of general equilibrium. His conception of their disequilibrium behavior was an essential part of his wider conception of the functioning of a freely competitive economy. The model of monetary oral pledges markets was fruitful in that major aspects of it were incorporated into the modern theory of competitive markets, but the model itself and the insights that can be derived from examining it have been neglected. Moreover, it has been incorrectly alleged that the features of auction markets can be substituted in place of the ones Walras assumed, without affecting the outcome. This chapter analyzes the functioning of the model, shows that its outcomes are different from auction markets, and identifies its merits and deficiencies.

I. Introduction

Expressing a view that has become general concerning Walras's model of exchange in oral pledges markets, William Jaffé maintained that Walras neglected their disequilibrium behavior (Jaffé 1981, pp. 327–28 [257–58], 322–23 [252–54], 330 [261]). According to Jaffé, Walras concentrated on equilibrium conditions, developed an analysis that was "consciously and deliberately confined within a strictly statical framework" (ibid., p. 327 [258]), and thus failed to "depict an actual process" of adjustments that traders make in markets (ibid., p. 327 [257–58]). Walras did not mean his treatment of price formation to be an account of "market events" (ibid., p. 327 [258]). Richard Goodwin similarly maintained that Walras did not deal with the events and processes that occur in disequilibrium in competitive markets (Goodwin 1950, p. 61). This chapter will demonstrate that that view is not accurate.

It has been shown in chapter 4 that in his model of a monetary oral pledges market, Walras identified the institutions, participants, and types of assets and trades; that he specified who quotes and changes the price; and that he incorporated many real trading practices into his model. The first purpose of this chapter is to show that Walras provided an extensive account of how those market features interact in disequilibrium to result in the determination of prices and quantities traded. It will be seen that he realized that to construct a complete model of exchange, he needed to specify whether or not disequilibrium transactions are allowed, the disequilibrium conditions in response to which the price is changed and that determine its direction of change, how prices change in accordance with the sign of the market excess demand quantity, and how it is signaled that trade is allowed to occur.

The second purpose of this chapter is to evaluate Walras's model of monetary oral pledges markets, as promised in the previous chapter. The evaluation will examine his account of the equilibrating process within a particular market and determine the degree to which Walras provided for the coordination of markets that is necessary for achieving multimarket equilibrium. The chapter will be restricted to an examination of those aspects of the equilibrium of exchange because Walras's mathematical treatment of the conditions that obtain in equilibrium has been thoroughly analyzed in the interpretive literature. The evaluation will be conducted in a way that is constructive and that recognizes the pointlessness of castigating a nineteenth-century economist for not having known all the things that were discovered by later economists.

II. Disequilibrium processes

Risk and uncertainty

In his analysis of oral pledges commodities and securities markets, Walras was not blind to the existence of the risk and uncertainty that are features of dynamic situations. He emphasized that risk and uncertainty are always present in real markets, and that different participants assess them differently. In organized securities markets, for example, savers are ordinarily risk-averters, conservative, and prudent. Many of them prefer to use their savings to buy old securities that yield a certain income rather than new ones with an uncertain yield (1877b, p. 302; 1889, p. 310; 1900, § 269, pp. 292–93; 1880b, p. 458 [406]). Professional speculators, in contrast, are willing to take substantial risks (ibid.). The traders' estimates of risk and their feelings about taking risks enter into determining the properties of their preference functions at the beginning of the trading day.

The degree of risk, Walras noted, differs for old and new securities. Old securities are well-known and have been evaluated, but they do not escape the hazards of uncertainty. The appearance of new securities creates some uncertainty about what will happen to the prices of old ones, and therefore causes some variations of their prices. In normal times, however, the variations are not extreme. The volatility of the prices of the bonds of the national government, for example, is limited because the size of the debt of the French government is known, as is the government's ability to service the debt.

Similarly, much information is available about the financial condition of big companies such as the railroads and the transatlantic steamer corporations, so ordinarily the securities of established firms are not highly speculative (1880b, p. 455 [403–4]).

New securities are issued to finance the production of assets that are planned or are being constructed. Neither the costs nor the revenue of new firms or projects can be predicted with great accuracy. For them, "the future is still uncertain," and strong elements of risk and uncertainty are associated with their securities (ibid., p. 455 [404]). Although success may seem probable, failure is also possible, and the difference between expected profits and the actual financial results can be very great (ibid., pp. 457–58 [405]). New securities are therefore the subjects of active speculation (ibid., pp. 455–56 [403–4]), and "the idea of speculation carries naturally and necessarily that of quite a high risk" (ibid., p. 458 [405]).

Walras then began his analysis of disequilibrium behavior in a particular oral pledges market by positing that at the beginning of a market "day" there is a particular group of buyers and sellers with given preferences that do not change during the day. In his oral pledges model, risk and uncertainty therefore influence the formation of the initial individual and market supply and demand functions and hence the outcome of the equilibrating process, but do not alter the functions once the process of groping for the equilibrium price has started. He also assumed that the traders have certain initial holdings of a commodity and of money. The question then arises as to what happens when the traders quote a series of prices in accordance with the Walrasian pricing procedure.

No disequilibrium transactions

Bertrand's argument: Joseph Bertrand believed that prior to 1883, Walras did not understand what happened when the traders quote prices. "It should be noted," Bertrand wrote,

that the curves that represent the orders of demanders at various prices must necessarily vary for each of them throughout the duration of the market, without their intentions changing as a result. The resulting curves, the intersection of which solves the problem, are incessantly modified in shape, and one can easily demonstrate the necessary variation of the abscissa of the point at which they intersect . . . For each price a similar problem arises, and the curve that represents the orders ought, after each transaction, to be calculated and remade (Bertrand 1883a, pp. 505–6).

Bertrand's argument implies that Walras did not realize that the traders' holdings of money and the commodity are parameters of the individual supply and demand functions and hence of the market supply and demand functions, that disequilibrium transactions occur, that the market functions change when trade occurs because the holdings change, and that the series of different market functions associated with each new distribution of the assets ordinarily have solutions that differ from the solutions to the initial pair of market functions. In that event, so also do the pair that obtain when the market reaches equilibrium, at least with respect to the solution quantity and ordinarily with respect to the solution price. That means that the equilibrium price would ordinarily differ from the initial solution price. In most cases, therefore, the equilibrium price could not be explained by Walras's analysis, for it is conducted with a knowledge of only the initial pair of market supply and demand functions.

Bertrand's opinion of Walras's grasp around 1883 of exchange phenomena has become generally accepted, and it is even believed by some economists that Walras learned about the impact of disequilibrium transactions from Bertrand. Jaffé, for example, contended that Bertrand's comments "were substantial criticisms that Walras, to the end of his working days, tried desperately to answer. On the subject of *tâtonnement,* he evaded the issue, to begin with by assuming in the theory of exchange that markets were institutionally so organized[1] as to preclude transactions at nonequilibrium prices," and later by introducing written pledges. "This," Jaffé commented, "was hardly a proper response to Bertrand's call for realism" (Jaffé 1977c, pp. 208–9 [87–88]).

Walras's comprehension of the situation: It will now be shown that Bertrand should not have alleged that Walras's theory as it stood in the early 1880s was indeterminate on the ground that he neglected to exclude disequilibrium transactions, and that Jaffé's characterization of the events in Walras's intellectual history relating to the oral pledges market is not accurate. Walras probably always believed that trading on any "day" in real oral pledges markets occurs only at the initial solution price. It is true that he did not mention that rule in his first descriptive accounts of oral pledges markets (1860c, 1867) nor in the first edition of the *Eléments* (see, for example, 1874b, p. 50; 1889, p. 68; 1900, § 42, p. 46). Nonetheless, he never stated or implied that trade occurs at disequilibrium prices in oral pledges markets in the sense of prices at which the market supply and demand quantities in a particular market are not equal on a given market day. Furthermore, at the time he was writing the first edition of the *Eléments* he made clear, contrary to Bertrand's supposition, that he realized that in order for the solutions of his equations to be the equilibrium values, not only the traders' preferences but also the asset holdings must be constant while the equilibrium price is found. Here is how he expressed the matter:

---

[1] That phrase constitutes a recognition by Jaffé, contrasting with his general opinion (see chapter 4), that Walras incorporated at least one institutional component into his oral pledges model.

It is the right of the theoretician to assume that the elements of [the formation of] prices are invariable during the time that he uses to formulate the law of the establishment of the equilibrium prices.. . . These elements are the utilities of the commodities and the quantities possessed of those commodities. They are therefore the causes and prime conditions of the variations of these prices[2] (1876, pp. 390–91; and in 1877c, offprint pp. 26–27; and with a minor addition in 1889, p. 125; 1900, § 101, p. 103; and see 1874b, pp. 102–4).

Walras knew that the aggregate quantities of the assets held during a market day must be constant because changes of them would imply changes in the set of individual holdings, which would cause changes in the individual excess demand functions. He stated that the equilibrium price will change if there is "a change in the quantity of [the] commodity possessed by one or several holders" (1874b, p. 102; 1889, p. 126; 1900, § 102, p. 104), and he dealt with the matter by specifying that the asset distribution is a parameter of a market day (1874b, pp. 59–62, 106–7; 1889, pp. 77–81, 130–32; 1900, § 50, pp. 55–58; §§ 105–6, pp. 110–12). Similarly, long before Bertrand's review, in discussing comparative statics Walras explained that it is necessary "to consider the changes in the absolute conditions of value," by which he meant the parameters. They are "the utility and the quantity of the commodities" – that is, the preference functions and the actual holdings of the assets. Demonstrating again that he understood the effects on equilibrium prices of changes in those parameters very early in his career, Walras observed that they cause the ratios of the marginal utilities to change, and that as a result the equilibrium prices change (Walras to A. A. Cournot, March 20, 1874, in 1965, *1,* letter 253, pp. 363–67; and see 1874b, p. 102; 1889, p. 126; 1900, § 102, p. 104; 1874b, pp. 103–4; 1889, pp. 126–27; 1900, § 103, pp. 105–6; 1874b, pp. 135–37; 1889, pp. 159–62; 1900, §§ 137–38, pp. 140–44). Thus, Walras indicated that there is in any market a different equilibrium price associated with each different disequilibrium distribution of the assets, and that he was aware that the different distributions can arise either as different initial conditions or as a result of disequilibrium transactions within a given market day.

Rule against disequilibrium transactions: Doubtless with those considerations in mind, Walras assumed the rule that trade can occur only at the equilibrium price in his first[3] analysis of oral pledges markets (1874a, pp. 106–7, and in 1877c, offprint pp. 14–15), written during the same period as the part of the first edition of the *Eléments* that deals with such markets. The assumption is evident from his argument that the equilibrium price that would be reached

---

[2] Walras repeated the sense of the last two sentences in almost the same words in the first edition of the *Eléments* (1874b, p. 135; 1900, § 137, p. 140).

[3] This excludes Walras's initial attempts (1860a, 1869–70) at the mathematical modeling of exchange because in them he was not concerned with the disequilibrium behavior of an oral pledges market but with equilibrium conditions.

by the oral pledges process is exactly the same as would be reached if the traders in a particular market, instead of dealing with each other, communicate their supply and demand functions to a calculator – a hypothetical authority in a particular market, Walras indicated, not a central supra-market institution. The price would be the same because if there is a calculator there are no disequilibrium transactions: "In place of crying out their bids, let them give their order-books to a calculator, and the calculator will determine the equilibrium price, certainly not as rapidly but assuredly more rigorously than can be done by the mechanism of raising and lowering the price" (ibid.).

John Maynard Keynes believed that the price is set by a calculator in Walras's oral pledges model. That, Keynes wrote,

is the actual method by which the opening price is fixed on the Paris Bourse even today. His [passage] suggests that he was aware that the Agents de Change used this method and he regarded that as the ideal system of exchange to which others were approximations. As a matter of fact, this is also the method by which opening prices are fixed on Wall Street. It is unfamiliar to us because the only London example which I can think of is the daily "fixing" of silver by the bullion brokers. In all these cases there is an application of Edgeworth's principle of recontract, all those present disclosing their dispositions to trade and the price which will equate offers and demands is arrived at by an independent person, known in New York as the specialist (Keynes to J. R. Hicks, December 9, 1934, in Hicks 1976, p. 151, n. 16).

Contrary to Keynes's belief, Walras did not postulate the presence of a calculator in his oral pledges model. He mentioned the calculator only as an expository device, comparing the way a hypothetical market with such a personage would work and the way that his model of a real market works. Moreover, Francis Y. Edgeworth and Walras contemplated situations in which the traders do *not* disclose their dispositions to trade, neither their preference functions nor their supply and demand functions. In Edgeworth's model, that is why the formation of new contracts is necessary day after day until equilibrium is found (Edgeworth 1904, pp. 193–94), and in Walras's oral pledges model is the reason for the quotation of a series of experimental prices. Such a sequence is of the essence of the tatonnement process that Walras elaborated at great length in his account of the disequilibrium behavior of oral pledges markets. In contrast, in disequilibrium in a market with a calculator there would be no experimental prices, no recontracting, no trading behavior of any kind prior to the discovery of the equilibrium price. As in the market for new U.S. Treasury bills, the traders would disclose their trading desires to the calculator. He would add up the individual supply and demand functions respectively, solve for the initial solution price, and set it as the trading price.

In 1880, Walras was explicit in setting forth the rule that trade is allowed only at the initial solution price. After an exhaustive study of the institutions and practices in oral pledges markets, Walras asserted that the rule was a feature of the securities exchange in Paris in the nineteenth century. He believed that it was important to draw attention to the presence of the rule in his model, as indicated by this assertion:

If the quantity demanded and the quantity supplied are equal, the price is an equilibrium one and exchange takes place at that price; the securities pass from the hands of the agents who are sellers to the hands of the agents who are buyers, or at all events the affair is finished, even if settlement has not yet been carried out. *Otherwise, exchange does not occur* (1880b, p. 461, and in 1898b, p. 408; emphasis added).

He enlarged on that statement, writing that

the market for securities ought to be the standard type of market, and the standard type of market, we have said, is one where the sales and purchases are made by the intermediation of agents who receive the orders of sellers and buyers and *who engage in trade only after having determined, as the trading price, the price at which the effective quantity supplied and the effective quantity demanded are equal* (1880c, p. 78; and in 1898b, p. 432; emphasis added).

As the quotations show, Walras stated that no trade is allowed during the process of quoting disequilibrium prices in an oral pledges market, and that trade occurs at the price at which equality exists between the market supply and demand quantities given by the initial market supply and demand functions. In that case, the initial solution price is the equilibrium price. Those empirically derived theoretical characterizations of market behavior are summarized in the single rule that trade occurs only at the initial solution price. Thus, Walras did not evade the issue of disequilibrium transactions in his theory of exchange in oral pledges markets. Striving for realism long before Bertrand's review, he assumed they do not occur because he believed that was a fact.

Walras's answer to Bertrand: Bertrand's assertions about Walras's oral pledges model were made in a review of writings on exchange by Walras in which the passage about a calculator occurs.[4] Walras could therefore have answered Bertrand's criticism very effectively by pointing out that disequilibrium transactions were excluded in the material that Bertrand reviewed. Walras could also have pointed out that he had indicated clearly his awareness that the distribution of assets is a parameter of his oral pledges model and that changes of the distribution would change the equilibrium price. Walras could have noted his explicit assertions, four years before Bertrand's review, that trade occurs only at the initial solution price. Walras could have argued that he believed he had given a realistic account of what happens on the kind

---

[4] Bertrand reviewed the book (1883a) in which Walras republished the mémoire (1874a) in which he discussed exchange with a calculator.

of organized market that he took as his subject. Instead, he answered Bertrand by stating that the rule is justified on theoretical grounds:

On the theoretical market, in the case of an excess of the quantity demanded over the quantity supplied or of the quantity supplied over the demand, no one is satisfied, and exchange remains suspended until the raising or the lowering of the price has led to the equality of the quantity supplied and the quantity demanded; after which everyone is satisfied. The theoretical equilibrium price is essentially a unique price that results, at a given moment, in a general exchange of the commodity (1885, p. 69, n. 1; and in 1896c, p. 352, n. 1).

Probably remembering that he had not made himself clear to Bertrand in the selection of writings Bertrand had read, Walras was careful to carry an explicit mention of the rule over from his 1880 model into his model of an oral pledges market in *Eléments* when he revised the book in 1889. As in the above quotation, he first formulated the rule in such a way that he can be interpreted as conceding that trade may occur at disequilibrium prices in real markets. If the price is a disequilibrium value, he wrote, "theoretically, trading should be suspended" (1889, p. 68; 1900, § 42, p. 46). In the next paragraph, however, as in other places in his work, he wrote simply that "trading is suspended" (1889, p. 68; 1900, § 42, p. 46). When he reviewed the controversy some years later, Walras cited Bertrand's comments and replied to them that he, Walras, had "rightly maintained" that his model of exchange is determinate because "exchange was suspended in the case of the inequality of the quantities supplied and demanded." At this point, however, Walras reverted to the type of formulation that appears in the quotation in the preceding paragraph, stating that the rule is a "hypothesis that no scientific spirit would hesitate to concede to the theoretician" (1895, in 1965, *2*, enclosure to letter 1200, p. 630; see also the enclosure to a letter from Walras to Charles Gide, October 23, 1909, in 1965, *3*, letter 1775, p. 437). Perhaps he had temporarily forgotten that he believed the rule really exists. Perhaps he meant that it is justifiable to adopt the rule as a theoretical assumption precisely because it is realistic. Perhaps he phrased his remark to indicate that although in reality the rule exists only in highly organized markets, he wanted to adopt it as a simplifying assumption regarding oral pledges markets in which some disequilibrium transactions occur, in order to extend his theory to them.

In any event, Walras indicated that the rule is incorporated into the pledges the traders make. They understand that their pledges are agreements that they will trade only if it becomes evident that the quoted price is one at which all traders would have their offers accepted. They pledge to buy or sell no less than the entire amount of their desired demand or supply quantity. Pledges therefore have two functions in Walras's oral pledges model. First, they are the means by which the traders communicate desired prices and the quantities they wish to trade. Second, they provide a way of communicating that information without the occurrence of trade being an integral part of the disclosures. No contracts have to be annulled, no money and goods have to be given back. To do so would be time-consuming and costly and would engender much bitterness, which is doubtless why no real markets permit recontracting during a market day or require the handing back of disequilibrium amounts of money and the commodity. The condition that no disequilibrium transactions occur in the oral pledges model can therefore be achieved with a minimum of difficulty to ease the process of finding the initial solution price.

Despite the clarity with which Walras expressed the rule, Sir John Hicks contended that "what, however, Walras does not make really clear is whether any exchanges do or do not actually take place at the prices originally proposed, when those prices are not equilibrium prices" (Hicks 1934, p. 342; and see Newman 1965, p. 102). As evidence of this, Hicks quoted Walras on the presence of professional traders in oral pledges markets and their making sales and purchases *à la criée* (1874b, p. 48; 1889, p. 66; 1900, § 41, p. 44; and see ch. 4). Hicks obviously had not noticed the sentences two pages later in which Walras explicitly enunciated the rule (1889, p. 68; 1900, § 42, p. 46). John Keynes was also unaware of those sentences, but the same passage that Hicks found ambiguous "convinces me," wrote the brilliantly intuitive Keynes, that Walras "assuredly supposed that [transactions] did not take place except at the equilibrium prices" (Keynes to Hicks, December 9, 1934, in Hicks 1976, p. 151, n. 16); and Keynes, of course, was right (see Hicks 1946, p. 128).[5]

Changing the price

Walras's traders not always price-takers: Joseph A. Schumpeter characterized Walras's view of pricing under free competition partially in the following terms: "The quantity produced by any one producer is too small to affect price perceptibly or," Schumpeter added, "to admit of price strategy" (Schumpeter 1954, p. 973). The first part of Schumpeter's statement is true. The second part, if intended as an assertion that traders in a Walrasian freely competitive market do not change the price, is incorrect. It would be contrary to reason and fact to suppose that a trader who is a price taker when that is possible will obdurately continue to be one when he learns that his assumption in wrong. In recognition of this, prices in Walras's oral pledges model are always quoted and changed by buyers or sellers or their agents (ch. 4).

---

[5] Evidently Keynes persuaded Hicks to change his mind, because he adopted the argument in Keynes's letter, including its erroneous attribution to Walras of a recontracting process but not the notion that the traders reveal their supply and demand functions (Hicks 1946, p. 128).

All traders initially take the quoted price as given and determine how much they would like to buy or sell at that price. Explaining what happens next, Walras first assumed that the price is one at which the market excess demand is positive. In that case, some or all demanders discover they have been wrong to suppose they would find sellers who would be willing to sell them all they wished at the quoted price. The response of the frustrated demanders, Walras explained, is to quote a higher price. It does not matter which demander speaks up first or if several speak in unison. The price on an organized exchange such as the Paris Bourse, Walras pointed out, is changed by a conventional fraction of a franc, so all those who want to change the price quote the same new price (1874b, p. 50; 1889, p. 68; 1900, § 42, p. 46). Taking the opposite case, Walras then assumed that the market excess demand quantity is negative. Suppliers find they have been wrong to assume that they could sell all they wish at the quoted price. The result is that one or more of them quote a price that is lower by the conventional minimum fraction (ibid.). This is the process called Walrasian pricing.

How traders know the price should be changed: The question then arises as to how information is generated to guide the traders in their pricing behavior. It has been seen that Walras stated that traders bid prices up or down according to the sign of the market excess demand, and that trade occurs when the ex ante market excess demand is zero, but how is the sign of the market excess demand quantity known? This question of economic coordination led Robert W. Clower and Axel Leijonhufvud to ask "how might we best proceed to modify standard theory so that it can be used to deal explicitly, at least in principle, with real disequilibrium?" Their answer:

On first thought, one's natural impulse is to eliminate the auctioneer and work instead with models in which individual economic agents engage in trade on a strictly "do it yourself" basis. No doubt that is the direction in which a definitive solution to the problem of economic coordination ultimately must be sought (Clower and Leijonhufvud 1975, p. 184).

As has been shown in chapters 3 and 4, that was Walras's natural impulse in his models one hundred years before Clower and Leijonhufvud made their suggestion, although, as will be seen at the end of this chapter, following that impulse did not lead him to a definitive solution of the problem of intermarket coordination. Walras did not postulate or describe or imply the functioning of institutions of any kind or any rules of behavior that provide for the calculation of the market excess demand quality. The reason is that he did not think it is calculated or needs to be calculated in real oral pledges markets.

It is true that Walras analyzed and explained the behavior of markets with the use of market supply and demand functions. Indeed, he pioneered their construction and use (see Van Daal and Walker 1990). Nevertheless, those functions, he believed, are exclusively devices used by the theoretician. The participants in his oral pledges model do not know the market supply and demand quantities. According to Walras, the traders are correctly guided by their individual situations to change the price in accordance with the sign of the market excess demand quantity even though they do not know that sign. That process works because the traders know the sign of their market-oriented individual excess demand quantities at the quoted price. The definitions of those quantities, which Walras incorporated in literary form into his discussions of freely competitive markets (for example, Walras, 1874b, pp. 49–50; 1900, § 42, pp. 45–47), will now be explained. To simplify matters, his procedure of dealing initially only with the price of the particular commodity in his discussion of pricing in any particular market will be followed, but it should be remembered that he also then went on to discuss the influence of other prices on the traders in the given market.

In Walras's monetary oral pledges model, both demanders and suppliers make pledges to buy and sell respectively, and instruct their agents as to the prices that should be quoted. Each demander's agent seeks one or more agents who will agree to sell the amount that the demander is offering to buy; each supplier's agent seeks one or more agents who will agree to buy the amount the supplier wants to sell. As Walras indicated, agents seek counterparts. In such a market, the concept of a vast anonymous pool of demands or supplies upon which an individual can draw as much as he wishes at each price is not appropriate. In Walras's models, as in real markets, buyers naturally have to make arrangements with particular sellers, and an individual's agent ordinarily acts simultaneously with other individuals. For example, in real organized securities markets, a seller of a stock is typically able to make an agreement at the current price with one or perhaps a few buyers. Other sellers are dealing with the other buyers, so they are not all available to any one buyer. If any purely competitive market is in disequilibrium, it is necessarily true that either demanders cannot buy as much of the service as they wish at the quoted price, or the suppliers cannot sell as much as they wish, even though the market is not thin. The demand for a seller's stock is therefore perfectly elastic only up to a relatively small quantity at a quoted disequilibrium price, and the elasticity is zero at that quantity. Similarly, the supply offered to a buyer is perfectly elastic only up to a relatively small quantity, and the elasticity is then zero. That is to say, at a disequilibrium price less than the equilibrium value, the quantity offered to some and perhaps every demander is less than they want. That situation is reflected, as a derivative matter, in there being a positive market excess demand quantity. Similarly, at a disequilibrium price greater than the equilibrium value, the quantity demanded from some and perhaps all suppliers is less than they want to sell. That is reflected, as a derivative matter, in a negative market excess demand quantity. Thus, at each disequilibrium price the market excess demand quantity is a reflection of the inability of every individual to buy or sell as much as he wishes.

Accordingly, in the oral pledges model, a demander's market-oriented individual excess demand function for a commodity is his demand quantity for it, transmitted to an agent, minus the quantity offered to his agent by one or more agents of suppliers of the commodity, at each price at which he would be offered less than or as much as he would want to buy. At other prices, suppliers may try to sell him more than he wishes, but his agent cannot thereby be led to disregard his instructions. His client's excess demand quantity is therefore zero at such prices. The sum of the demanders' individual excess demand quantities for a commodity at each relevant quoted price is the market excess demand function for that commodity over the range in which the function is positive.

A seller's market-oriented individual excess demand is the amount of his commodity demanded by one or more demanders, expressed by the demanders' agents, minus the amount of the commodity that the supplier pledges to supply, at each price at which he would want to supply more than or as much as is demanded from him. At other prices, his agent may learn that there is unsatisfied demand for more than he offers, but the agent would still want to sell only as much as he is instructed to sell and would disregard the requests for more. His client's excess demand quantity is therefore zero at such prices. The sum of the suppliers' individual excess demand quantities for the commodity they supply at each relevant quoted price is the market excess demand function for that commodity over the range in which the function is negative.

The pricing process: In Walras's model of a particular oral pledges market, the pricing process works in the following way. He explained how changing the price in the model is done with no more information than the traders' being aware of whether they can personally buy or sell all they wish, without knowledge of the market supply and demand quantities or direct knowledge of the sign of the market excess demand quantity, and without the intervention of a market authority. Let it be assumed that some of the agents who are demanders on behalf of their clients cannot find exact counterparts at the current quoted price. They inform their clients that their individual excess demand quantities are positive. At the same time, the agents for sellers are able to find exact counterparts, so they inform their clients that their individual excess demand quantities are zero. Demanders and suppliers change the price in the same direction as the sign of their individual excess demand quantity. The suppliers therefore have no desire to change the price. The demanders, on the other hand, raise the price by the amount that is conventional in the given market and reduce the quantity of the service they pledge to purchase per time period. The agents repeat the process of trying to find counterparts. If the price is one at which the agents of the suppliers find that their clients have negative individual excess demand quantities, they inform them of that fact. The suppliers then instruct their agents to lower the price and reduce the amounts they pledge to supply. The latter are informed that their individual excess demand quantities are zero, so they have no desire to change the price. Trade is allowed to occur, as Walras expressed matters, only when all agents have found their exact counterparts (Walras 1874b, p. 50; 1900, § 42, p. 46).

In his models of securities markets, which he presented as typical of oral pledges markets, Walras asserted that traders communicate their desired demand and supply quantities to each other in face-to-face encounters. Each trader "has to find a counterpart" – the person to whom he makes a pledge to trade (1880b, p. 467 [414]). At a low disequilibrium price, "agents for demanders no longer find their counterparts" – they do not find traders who will sell to them (1874b, p. 50; 1889, p. 68; 1900, § 42, p. 46). They know, therefore, that their own ex ante individual excess demand quantities are positive, and that is what leads them to raise the price. Walras illustrated his model with an example of the sale of a bond that yields three percent of its face value. The sign of the market excess demand quantity can be known by inference: the fact that the traders do not find their counterparts "proves that the market quantity demanded of the 3% bond at a price of 60 francs is superior to the market quantity supplied at the same price" (ibid.). At a high disequilibrium price, "agents for suppliers no longer find their counterparts" – they do not find traders who will buy from them (ibid.). They know, therefore, that their own ex ante individual excess demand quantities are negative, and that is what leads them to lower the price. The fact that the agents for sellers do not find counterparts is "what indicates that the market quantity supplied of the 3% bond at a price of 60 Francs is greater than the market quantity demanded at that price" (ibid.). Once more, incidentally, it is abundantly obvious from Walras's specifications of the behavior of the traders that his model has nothing in common with auction markets.

One price at any moment

Walras stated that there can be only one price in equilibrium in a freely competitive market (1874b, p. 99; 1889, p. 121; and 1900, § 99, p. 99; 1874b, p. 118; 1889, p. 155; 1900, § 132, p. 136; 1874b, p. 132; 1889, p. 153; 1900, § 131, p. 134) and apparently thought that there must also be a single price at any moment in disequilibrium also. According to Jaffé, Walras inserted this "law of indifference" into his model in an effort to construct an ideal type of model and a normative scheme, not in an attempt to give a realistic account of real markets. If there were only one price, then no seller would make more money per unit than another; no buyer would pay more per unit than another. "Uniformity of competitively determined price represented for Walras not only an analytical ideal, but an ethical ideal as well, constituting an indispensable pillar of social justice" (Jaffé 1977d, p. 375 [330]).

In actuality, Walras did not advocate the law as an analytical ideal if by that is meant something other than a description of reality. Nor did he introduce the law as a normative rule. In ordinary retail markets, he explained, there is often more than one price ruling at the same moment. Housekeepers buy groceries, for example, from retailers who have their shops or stalls at different locations, and any particular housekeeper, at the moment of making a purchase, is therefore not in touch with sellers and customers in other shops. Consequently, the commodity may be sold to different customers at different prices simultaneously, each price being quoted at a different location (1880b, p. 460 [408]). Walras noted that the spread between the prices cannot be great, and that it will tend to disappear because sellers will move where prices are higher and buyers will move where prices are lower. "On the bourse," however, Walras continued, "that difference is impossible; here is why" (ibid.). It is an oral pledges market, rigorously organized to be freely competitive. Therefore, "sales and purchases are made not between sellers and buyers, but through the intermediation of agents called *agents de change*" (ibid., pp. 460–61 [408]), who congregate in one location in a market with special conventions. One convention is that they call out their pledges, and since they are together, that results in the simultaneity of knowledge of price quotations for all of them. In disequilibrium, one or more of the traders call out one price and accompanying offers to buy or sell. Then one or more call out a single new price, which immediately displaces the previous one. As the traders quote the new price or hear it quoted, they respond to it. Different traders do not quote different new prices simultaneously when the price is changed, because, as has been indicated, the price is changed by a conventional fraction of a franc. Thus it cannot happen that the sign of the individual excess demand quantities is opposite for different demanders at the same time, or opposite for different suppliers, and consequently there cannot be multiple prices changed in different directions at the same time.

By a "uniform price" Walras also meant that trade cannot occur at more than one price simultaneously in a freely competitive oral pledges market. All the traders in such a market are together in one location, and inasmuch as no exchange takes place at any value other than the initial solution price, there obviously cannot be more than one price at which trade occurs at any given moment (1880b, pp. 460–61 [408]). Thus, although Walras approved of a single price, that was not why he identified the law. He did so, he stated, because it is a fact. He did not introduce it as a postulate into his model, but perceived that it was a derivative circumstance, generated as a consequence of the spatial characteristics, institutions, procedures, and type of participants in organized markets. Of course, he sometimes referred to it as a "condition" of a freely competitive market (1874b, p. 132; 1889, p. 153; 1900, § 131, p. 134), but that did not mean he regarded it as an axiom, but simply that it was a feature of that type of market. Once he had abstracted it from empirical behavior, he could describe it as a condition with the understanding that it implies the empirical behavior that gives rise to it.

The signal for trading

Walras's final task concerning market disequilibrium behavior was to indicate how it is determined that trade can occur. He did not believe or hypothesize or imply that a market authority signals that trade can or cannot occur. The picture Walras portrayed is that of a market in which the traders are milling around in a relatively small area and are calling out and gesticulating in efforts to elicit responses directly from each other. In this way he incorporated into his model precisely the situation that exists in organized commodities and securities exchanges. The exchanges that the traders propose are made publically, and so, according to Walras, they all learn whether or not their coparticipants have found counterparts. If some have not, none of the traders engage in trade, because they all know there is a rule against trading unless every trader has found his exact counterpart. The attempted matching of offers occurs at each price that the traders call out. Finally, when the initial solution price is quoted, each trader knows that he can buy or sell the amount that he wants at the quoted price, so none of them wants to change the price. "Each selling agent or buying agent finds exactly what is called his *counterpart* in another buying agent or selling agent" (1874b, p. 50; 1889, p. 68; 1900, § 42, p. 46). That is the signal, recognized by all the traders, that trade can take place in a particular oral pledges market.

III. Partial and general equilibrium

Walras stated in many places that in a particular oral pledges market the equilibrium amount of the commodity is then immediately exchanged for the equilibrium amount of money (1874b, p. 50; 1889, p. 68; 1900, § 42, p. 46; 1880c, p. 78; 1898b, p. 432; 1885, p. 69, n. 1; 1896c, p. 352, n. 1). The market supply and demand curves shift to the left to a position of nondivergency, indicating that equilibrium has been reached. Since each buyer and seller has traded all that he wished at the equilibrium price, the new market supply and demand quantities are zero at that price. The market remains in equilibrium, with the traders contentedly holding their stocks of the asset and money until a parametric change occurs. The market curves then shift to the right and the traders once more begin the process of trying to match pledges to buy and to sell.

In his theory of general equilibrium in a pledges system, however, Walras stressed that the equilibrium price must be found in every market before any trade is allowed. Particular equilibrium is "an imperfect equilibrium. The perfect or *general equilibrium* of the market [system] does not take place unless the price of any commodity in terms of a second one is equal to the ratio of the price of each of them in terms of any third commodity" (1876, p. 376; 1877b, p. 12; 1889, p. 135; 1900, § 111, p. 115). That does not happen until the market excess demand has become zero simultaneously in all markets. "We are thus led to formulate in the following manner the law of the establishment of equilibrium prices in the case of the exchange of several commodities for each other" – namely, "it is necessary and sufficient that at these prices, assumed to be a general equilibrium set, the quantity demanded of each commodity be equal to the quantity supplied" (1874b, p. 131; 1889, p. 152; 1900, § 130, p. 133 with some slight changes). If that condition does not obtain, there will be "a proportional rise in the prices of commodities of which the quantity demanded is greater than the quantity supplied" and the reverse (ibid).

Many markets appear temporarily to have reached equilibrium, but it is soon revealed that the interconnected system is still going through the adjustment process. These markets are repeatedly disarranged by changes in other prices, which are arguments of the market excess demand function in any given market. Each disarranged market then begins again with the process of Walrasian pricing, which, Walras asserted, leads the entire system of pledges markets to converge to general equilibrium (1876, pp. 381–82; 1889, p. 141; 1900, § 116, p. 121).

IV. Evaluation

Many markets not like Walras's model

It is true, just as Walras asserted, that there are markets in which the initial solution price is found before trade occurs, like the immediate-settlement market on the modern French securities exchange and markets on the New York Stock Exchange. There are also, just as Walras asserted, markets in which the initial solution price is not merely the opening trading price but is also the only price at which trade is allowed to take place during the business day, like the cash market on the Belgian securities exchange and the over-the-counter securities market on the Bourse in Paris (Spray 1964, pp. 76–80,

168). On the London gold market, for example, the price that is fixed at the beginning of a market day is the equilibrium value and the only price at which trade occurs on that particular day in that market.[6] That type of behavior, however, does not result from a rule against disequilibrium transactions and from the pricing interactions of the traders in the way Walras envisioned. It actually happens in a way he did not incorporate into his model – namely, through the traders' informing a specialist or a market authority of their orders. Furthermore, most real freely competitive organized oral pledges markets do not have a rule that trade can occur only at the initial solution price. One consequence is that even if there is a specialist, the opening price is frequently not an equilibrium value, but simply the price at which the market closed on the previous day. On the New York Stock Exchange, a specialist sets the initial solution price as the opening trading price only when he thinks that the flow of either buy or sell orders before the market opens has been relatively too great or too small. Another consequence is that even if the initial transactions have occurred at the initial solution price, during the rest of the business day disequilibrium prices are quoted and trade occurs at them. Thus, on the noncash markets on the Bourse and in markets on the New York Stock Exchange, an irregular stream of new orders comes to the traders for execution – some to buy, some to sell – at different prices, and the specialist does not periodically halt trade to ascertain if the market excess demand is zero.

It is true, just as Walras asserted, that the traders in many organized markets deal directly with each other without the intervention of a market authority. It is not true, however, that they look around to see if each of them has found a counterpart, and refuse to trade until that happens. A floor trader may call out an order to sell a certain number of shares of units of a commodity at a particular price, and a buyer may want more than that amount. The quoted price is therefore a disequilibrium one, but the buyer wants to acquire any part of his demand quantity and will therefore proceed to trade because it is to his advantage to do so. Obviously, the seller is also willing to trade even though his trading partner is not his exact counterpart in Walras's sense. The traders do not wait to trade until market equilibrium is reached.

In different types of real markets, the way that the available supply or demand quantity is divided varies. On the Paris Bourse, for example, if there is a positive market excess demand quantity and no likelihood of more sell orders forthcoming at the quoted price, the specialist divides the available supply proportionately among the demanders. On the New York Stock Ex-

---

[6] The price is fixed twice each business day, so there are two market days each business day. Of course, gold is traded in other markets during the course of the business day and frequently at different prices than the London equilibrium price.

change, if two traders simultaneously pledge to buy all that is offered by another trader, a coin is tossed to determine which buyer receives the shares. On that market, traders who speak up first are able to buy or sell some of the asset, although perhaps not all they want, whereas others who want to buy or sell at the price at which trade has just occurred are unable to do so. Their cries are swept aside in the noisy chaos of exchange behavior and they have to make trades later under other conditions. Thus, Walras's model is seen to be a special case. It is not applicable to the many real pledges markets in which disequilibrium pricing and trading behavior occur, and it cannot explain the volume of transactions or the equilibrium price in such markets.

Not a general equilibrium pledges model: As for the logical structure of Walras's work, his presumption that he had extended his model of monetary exchange in oral pledges markets to a general-equilibrium setting cannot be accepted because he did not provide a way of ensuring that trade does not take place until the excess demand quantities in all markets are simultaneously zero. To avert trading before that condition obtains, he should have devised a way for information about prices and market excess demands to be transmitted among all markets before the day is over in each particular market. In his model, the traders' knowledge of what is happening in their immediate vicinity cannot inform them about other markets or provide the signal for when trade can occur in all markets. Just as in the real economy, at the moment when the current initial solution price is found in Walras's model of a particular oral pledges market, the traders do not know or care whether general equilibrium has been reached. They conclude transactions, just as Walras described, even though the price is not a true equilibrium value from a general-equilibrium point of view (ch. 9). To reach the general equilibrium that would be determined by Walras's equations in a pledges system of markets, the traders in his model of each market would have to put aside their urge to trade at the price that currently equates the market supply and demand quantities. They would have to make that price known to traders in other markets. The initial solution price in any market would then change as traders take into account the prices that are emerging as tentative equilibrium values in other markets. The traders in the various markets would have to continue in this fashion, abstaining from trading until the general-equilibrium set of initial solution prices is found.

Walras mentioned the fact that price quotations are published in the newspapers, and that phenomenon can be accepted as being part of his model (ch. 4). The prices are, however, only highs, lows, and closing values, and they are not published before trade is allowed. Consequently, they cannot be used by traders to react to other markets during a given day or to determine, before trade occurs, whether the quoted prices are part of a general-equilibrium set of initial solution prices.[7] The published price information would help Walras's system of markets to move toward a general equilibrium, but it would not be the equilibrium given by his equations. It would be the equilibrium of a system in which transactions that are disequilibrium ones from a general-equilibrium point of view occur in each market during the series of market days that elapse before equilibrium is reached, even though the transactions occur at particular-equilibrium prices.

Walras's model a significant achievement: Nevertheless, Walras's monetary oral pledges model of a particular market provides the basis for a particular-equilibrium model of wider applicability. His model can be reformulated to take account of disequilibrium transactions within the given market. It can also be supplemented with the information that is commonly available to traders in the real economy regarding what transpires in related markets. Such a particular-equilibrium model of an organized commodity or security market would be of greater practical value than a logically complete model of general equilibrium in which no disequilibrium transactions occur, which would have little relation to the real economy.

Despite these observations on the respects in which Walras's model is of limited applicability or can be improved, it must be recognized that his model was a significant achievement. It was a brilliant expression of his recognition that traders' behavior is conditioned by and takes place within a framework of institutions and rules. Walras related his statements of theoretical principles to the functioning of real markets and in many respects provided a realistic theoretical treatment of the behavior of the traders in disequilibrium. At the time that he initially constructed the model, it was far more complete, rigorous, and advanced than the work that had been done by other economists on oral pledges markets. Moreover, its richness of structural and behavioral detail was a striking contrast to later work, such as Alfred Marshall's sketchy and elliptical treatment of a corn market (Marshall 1890, pp. 391–94) and the disembodied models of modern mathematical economics.

Walras not only identified but also used in a systematic analysis most of the components that are now recognized to be necessary parts of a particular-equilibrium model of purely competitive exchange: individual supply and demand functions, a means of making prices and offers known, the Walrasian pricing procedure, the identification of the consequences of changes in prefer-

---

[7] See also Walras 1877b, pp. 206–7; 1900, §§ 313–16, pp. 360–61. In his oral pledges model, Walras did not assume that a commodity has more than one organized market in which different prices could rule, so traders cannot profit by arbitrage. If they were able to do so, however, the effect would just be to equalize the net prices in the two markets. It would not provide for the adjustment of the price of a commodity in its own market in response to changes of prices of other commodities, which is the process of intermarket adjustment that would be required to achieve general equilibrium.

ences and asset holdings, a way that the traders learn that the market excess demand in their market is zero, and a statement of equilibrium conditions. With these components, and the rule that transactions can occur only at the initial solution price, Walras constructed a particular-equilibrium model of an oral pledges market that is logically complete and a seminal basis for later theoretical developments.

CHAPTER 6

The structure of the mature
nondurable consumer commodities model

This chapter explains and evaluates the structural aspects of the mature model of the production and sale of nondurable consumer commodities that Walras developed in the mature phase of his thought. It is shown that the structural characteristics of the model were carefully designed by Walras to throw light upon a hypothethical economy in which there are only services and nondurable goods.

I. Introduction

Walras developed a mature model of markets for consumer goods and services and of markets for the primary materials and productive services used to make those commodities. That description of the model and the introduction to this book explain why Walras will not be followed in calling the subject of this chapter "the theory of production." The model was poorly understood by Walras's contemporaries and has been unrecognized in the twentieth century. In this chapter and the next, this model is frequently called, for brevity, "the consumer commodities model," but it is not to be confused with the consumer commodities model discussed in section 2. It is also quite different from the consumer commodities model that he wanted to construct during the last phase of his thought and that has erroneously been considered as his best work on the subject. The objectives of the chapter are to identify the parameters of the model, to determine whether or not money is used in it, and to identify and explain those aspects of the structure of the model that are relevant for the determination of prices, rates of production, and sales of consumer commodities, and of the services and primary materials used to make them. The topic of the functioning of the model is reserved for chapter 7.

II. Parameters

The parameters of Walras's model will be explained in order to make clear the assumptions that determine important parts of the framework within which the action in the model takes place and its degree of abstractness. It is crucially important for the relationship between Walras's equation system and

113

his model that the phenomena he identified as parameters be truly unchanging. If they were to vary as a function of the endogenous processes of the model, then the equations, which incorporate those phenomena as constants, would not describe the model. Their solutions would not be the equilibrium values of the model, and a different set of equations would have to be constructed to describe the model properly.

Parameters affecting demand

Walras specified that one set of parameters is the consumers' utility functions for consumable services and products. A given set of the functions enters into the determination of a given set of consumers' demand functions. If the utility functions were to change, the demand functions would change, and that would change the equilibrium set of prices and quantities (1877b, pp. 269–70; 1889, p. 256). Walras assumed that the utility functions are not changed by the endogenous processes of the model, and that the exogenous factors that can change them are constant, except when he varied the utility functions in order to study the comparative statics of the system.

Parameters affecting supply

Walras classified economic resources as land, personal faculties, and capital goods proper, or, in modern terminology, natural resources, human capital, and capital goods. They respectively yield land services, personal services, and capital-good services. Walras specified that another set of parameters is the maximum aggregate amounts of those services that resource owners can provide (1889, p. 235). He assumed that there is a fixed maximum amount of services providable by a particular piece of land or worker or capital good. He therefore thought that in his model there would be only two reasons why the market supply function for a service would change. First, it would if the amount of the associated economic resource changes – namely, if there is a change in the natural resources of the nation or the size of the work force or the capital stock. Such changes would alter the sum of the maximum individual quantities that could potentially be offered. Changes in the number of workers would increase or decrease the number of individual supply functions for labor and therefore increase or decrease the market supply functions for labor of different types. If the aggregate holdings of land or capital goods increased or decreased, the market supply of the associated service would increase or decrease (1889, p. 257). Changes in the market supply function for any service would alter the equilibrium price of the service. Walras showed that the changes in the market supply functions of the services would also alter the equilibrium prices of the products that they are used to make (1877b, p. 270; 1889, p. 256).

Accordingly, Walras assumed that the amount of land (natural resources) is constant, and argued that that is very nearly true in reality (1877b, p. 219; 1889, p. 202). He assumed that the number of workers depends on conditions external to his model and is therefore a constant with respect to its endogenous processes, even though he realized that in reality there is some connection between economic conditions and changes in the size of the population (1877b, p. 224; 1889, p. 207). An implication of his assumption that the set of supply functions for each type of labor is constant is that workers do not change occupations. He then dealt with the characteristics of capital goods in the model. They are of two types: those that yield productive services, which are used to make other goods for sale, and those that yield consumable services, such as passenger trains, amusement parks, and all consumer goods that are used more than once, such as furniture, houses, jewelry, and clothing (1877b, pp. 217–20, 222–24; 1889, pp. 200–203, 205–7). Walras made three assumptions to ensure that the stock of capital goods in his model is constant (1877b, pp. 224–26; 1889, pp. 207–9). First, he assumed that there is no saving (1877b, p. 225; 1889, p. 208), so no new capital goods are produced. He remarked that if abstraction were made from saving, then abstraction could be made from money savings (ibid.). In other words, since he assumed there is no real saving, he could assume there is no money saving.[1] Second, he assumed that capital goods do not wear out. Third, he assumed that they are not accidentally destroyed. These assumptions are implied by his assertions that the capital stock in constant and that the only production in the model is that of primary materials and consumption commodities. There is therefore no replacement of capital goods (1877b, p. 224; 1889, p. 207) and no production of parts to repair them, but also no necessity for replacement or repair. Walras made the assumptions that render economic resources in his model constant in order that the maximum possible amounts of the productive and consumable services "remain, after all the simplifications that we have indicated, as the essential fixed conditions of the problem" (1877b, p. 245; 1889, p. 228).

The second possible reason for a change in the market supply functions for services is changes in the utility functions that enter into the determination of the individual net supply functions for services (1877b, p. 246; 1889, p. 229). Walras explained that changes of those utility functions in his model would

---

[1] In the introductions to the second and third editions of the *Eléments,* there are some slight differences in wording and differences in the numbering of the pages on which some passages cited in this chapter appear. The pagination in the introductions is in roman numerals. The differences in numbering will be noted.

result in a different set of equations of general equilibrium and hence in a different set of solutions (1877b, pp. 269–70; 1889, pp. 256–57). He assumed that the utility functions are not altered by the endogenous processes of the model.

The other parameters identified by Walras affect the entrepreneurs' supply functions for outputs. First, there are the entrepreneurs' preferences, which Walras summed up by stating that they want to make profits (1877b, p. 231; 1889, pp. XIV, 214). Second, there are the production functions of the firms, which embody the coefficients of production. These indicate the quantity of each input that is necessary for the production of a unit of a consumer good. They may be constant or there may be substitutability among the inputs, but in either case the production functions that Walras implicitly represented in his equations are parametric conditions (1877b, pp. 249–50, 312–14; 1889, pp. 232, 319–20). No introductions of new technology occur as a result of endogenous processes. Third, there is a given set of commodities, as Walras indicated each time that he specified the set of commodities in the model. The introduction of new products in his model stems exclusively from exogenous causes (1889, p. 258).

III. A monetary model

Statements that money is not used

Another question about the fundamental building blocks of the model is whether or not Walras assumed that money is used in it. In the second and third editions of the *Elements* this matter is somewhat obscured by Walras's having stated or implied in some passages that he was going to assume there is no money in the consumer commodities model. He asserted in one place that his model permits the determination of "the prices of all social wealth in numeraire, and it remains only to know, by the *theory of money,* what these prices become when the numeraire is at the same time money" (1889, p. XVI). That could be interpreted as indicating that he had in mind dealing with a barter system of markets until he introduced his theory of money. On the other hand, since he dealt with monetary exchange before the lesson entitled "Theory of Money," he may have just been stating that the theory gives an intellectual understanding of the way that money prices are determined and explains the details of their determination, without implying that money and money prices do not exist in the markets of the consumer commodities and capital goods models. That interpretation is strengthened by the difference between Walras's modeling of monetary exchange and his "theory of money." The former is a treatment of markets and the latter is the title he used for the subjects of the quantity theory and money balances.

Walras also stated, in a passage that will shortly be examined, that he was assuming in a special model that money is not used (1877b, p. 252; 1889, p. 237), and then in the next sentence wrote that "with the data and conditions that are ours here, we assume that capital goods properly speaking are rented out in kind. We have, however, explained that, in reality, the capital goods are rented out in money, for the reason that the capitalist forms his capital by saving [in money]. But it is only later that we will consider at the same time the creation of capital goods and their being rented out in the form of money" (1877b, p. 252; 1889, p. 237). Coming immediately after his assertion that no money is used, the phrase "the data and conditions that are ours here" and the rest of the passage appear to confirm that he was making that assumption in the consumer commodities model. Nevertheless, the connection between the statement that no money is used and the passage just quoted is tenuous, as will be made evident in an examination of the special model. Furthermore, Walras may have meant by the statements about capital only that there is no money savings, which unquestionably is a feature of the consumer commodities model. When he assumed that capital goods are rented out in kind, he did not mean to imply that money is not used in the model. Money is used to purchase services and goods and to pay the rental charges for capital goods.

In an introduction to the consumer commodities model, Walras stated that he would shortly demonstrate that it is easy to abstract from the use of money for transactions (1877b, p. 225; 1889, p. 208). Moreover, he concluded the remarks with which he introduced the equation systems of the consumer commodities model with the statement that he was going to assume that there is no circulating money held in balances by businesses, and that consumers have no circulating money or savings (1877b, p. 244; 1889, p. 227). Of course, there is a difference between asserting that money is not used in a model and constructing a model in which it is not used. The four passages mentioned here do only the former, so it is not possible to say that they establish the nature of Walras's model.

In another passage, Walras wrote that the assumption of the use of money is a theoretical complication, and "that is why we have abstracted from it in the scientific study of the phenomena of economic life" as though he were characterizing all his work in the *Eléments* up to that point. In the second edition of the *Eléments* (1889, p. 427), that statement appears after he had introduced money, after he had constructed his comprehensive monetary model, and after he had developed models of the money and loan market, and so on, so it is evidently out of place. In fact, he first introduced the statement in a lesson in the first edition that came just after the lessons on the barter of stocks of commodities (1874b, p. 175), which explains what would otherwise seem to be a totally erroneous statement and which is in actuality made erroneous by the place given to it by Walras in 1889. Walras eventually eliminated the statement and the lesson in which it appears from the *Eléments*.

A special barter model of consumption: Walras did in fact sketch a barter model of flows of consumer commodities, the special model in which the sentence mentioned earlier about the absence of money appeared. His paragraph on that model cannot be understood without tracing its history. In his original formulation of it (1876, p. 411; 1877b, p. 252), he initially assumed that the entrepreneurs borrow services from resource owners who are in a foreign country and subsequently repay them with amounts of the services that are not equal to amounts that were borrowed but are equal in value to the value of the services that were borrowed. Those transactions are highly peculiar. First, in any real economy, entrepreneurs do not borrow services; second, in exchange for their services, service suppliers want commodities other than the kinds of services they produce; and third, entrepreneurs do not possess services and therefore cannot use them in payment. In any event, in the special model, the transactions are done without money. Walras then altered the model by assuming instead that the entrepreneurs pay for the services with services that are not only equal in value but also equal in amounts. That being the case, he wrote, he could assume that the entrepreneurs buy services from resource owners in the domestic market, and he described the owners of the domestic resources as the landlords, workers, and capitalists to whom the entrepreneurs "*sell their products*" (ibid., emphasis added). The italicized words may indicate that he assumed that the entrepreneurs do not pay for the services with services, but with goods. Walras then wrote that "it is easily seen how this manner of proceeding makes abstraction, if not from the numeraire, at least from money" (ibid.). He meant that the numeraire fills its role of being a commodity in terms of which all prices are stated, but services are exchanged directly for products in barter markets.

In the second and third editions of the *Eléments* (1889, p. 236), Walras eliminated entirely the consideration of a foreign market in the special model and the reference to products being exchanged for services. Instead, on a first hypothesis he represented entrepreneurs as acquiring productive services and paying for them by later giving back to the original suppliers sufficient amounts of services so as to be, on an initial hypothesis, equivalent (equal in value). The services are paid back in different amounts and therefore at different prices than those which they had when they were borrowed. He then adopted the hypothesis that the services are paid back in the same amounts and at the same prices. Walras thus retained the procedure of paying for services directly with services, a construction that makes no sense in a model and sheds no light on the real economy. What is most relevant for this discussion, however, is that Walras was describing a barter process. He retained the sentence that declares that "it is easily seen how this manner of proceeding abstracts, if not from the numeraire, at least from money" (ibid., p. 236; and see Walras 1877b, pp. 231–32; 1889, p. 214), and that is true in the special model.

It has not previously been noticed in the secondary literature that Walras mentioned the special barter model of flows of consumer commodities in the second edition of the Eléments, for the reason that attention has been riveted on the fourth edition, in which the original character of the special model is obscured. It evidently has appeared to readers that the passage devoted to the model in the latter edition is perfectly unobjectionable and that it reveals Walras's best thought on the situation. It is interesting to see if that is true. In actuality, by the time that he prepared the fourth edition of the *Eléments,* Walras realized that something was wrong with the special model, and changed it radically. He first altered it so that "the entrepreneurs sell and that the consumers buy certain quantities of products," which was reasonable. That is, he eliminated the absurd payment for services with services and introduced instead the payment for services with goods. Unfortunately, his health by that time was so poor that he could not think clearly about the model and the rest of his amendments were inappropriate. He went on to write: "the one group buying and the other group selling quantities of productive services (T), (P), (K) . . . not equal but simply equivalent" (1900, § 208, p. 216), that is, not equal in amount but simply equal in value. Obviously that statement is nonsense, because purchases and sales of one and the same batch of services cannot be unequal in amount.[2] "We will next assume," he wrote, "that the entrepreneurs buy and the consumers sell quantities of productive services no longer only equivalent but also equal" (ibid.). With respect to their equality that was the obvious truism rather than an assumption. Walras then appended to the revised model the sentence that he had used before in reference to a different situation: "It is easily seen how this manner of

---

[2] William Jaffé added to confusion on this matter by making one of the changes that he thought were helpful in his translation of Walras's *Eléments.* Walras wrote: "In order to grasp better the operations that are going to follow, we will assume first that the entrepreneurs sell and the consumers buy certain quantities of products (A), (B), (C), (D) . . . *the one group buying and the other selling quantities of productive services* not equal [in amount] but simply equivalent [equal in value] . . ." (1926, § 208, p. 216; emphasis added). Jaffé did not want to translate that nonsense, so he offered the following in place of Walras's sentence: "To make the following operations easier to grasp, we shall assume, in the first place, that *entrepreneurs sell certain quantities of products (A), (B), (C), (D) . . . to consumers from whom, in turn, they purchase productive services (T), (P), (K) . . .* not in the same amounts but in amounts having the same value" (Jaffé in Walras 1954, p. 243; emphasis added). Jaffé's alteration of Walras's sentence was itself flawed inasmuch as his rendition involves a comparison of amounts of productive services and amounts of products, but they are incommensurable.

proceeding makes abstraction, if not from the numeraire, at least from money" (ibid.). In the fourth edition, that sentence makes no sense. Its appearance is inexplicable because after Walras had made the modifications to the preceding material, what he alleges to be the case cannot be seen at all. There is nothing in the revised special model that suggests that money is not used.[3]

Statements that money is used in the central model: It will now be established that Walras stated in many passages that he was assuming there is money in the central consumer commodities model he presented in the second and third editions of the *Eléments,* as distinct from the special model just discussed. He assumed without exception throughout his exposition of the central model that markets for services and for products are separate, stating that "as a consequence of this first conception of the role of the entrepreneur it is necessary that we conceive of two distinct markets" (1877b, p. 228; 1889, p. 211). "In place of a single market, two of them can be imagined" (1889, p. XV; 1896b, p. XIV). On one of the markets, services are sold. Here is how Walras described this market. "The landlords, workers, and capitalists as sellers meet the entrepreneurs as buyers of productive services" (1877b, p. 228; 1889, p. 211). There is "a market for services on which these services are offered exclusively by the landlords, workers and capitalists, and demanded in the following way: the consumable services by the same land-lords, workers and capitalists, and the productive services by the entrepre-neurs" (ibid.), and the payment for the services is made at the time that the price is determined and while it rules. In other words, in that market there are suppliers of services and demanders of them, dealing only in the services. Since only services are sold, they must be sold for money. Walras explained that the market for land services, for example, can be analyzed with a supply curve of those services and a demand curve for them, each as a function of the price of the service (p_t) with other prices held constant. Walras's diagram of this situation (1877b, plate III, fig. 12; 1889, plate IV, fig. 14) and his discussion of that diagram reveal that the land service is the only nonmone-tary commodity in its market, which implies that money must be used to purchase it. The demand is "a decreasing function of a single variable p_t, which can be represented geometrically by a demand curve T_dT_p and the second member is a function successively increasing and decreasing, from zero to zero, of the same variable p_t, which can be represented by a supply curve MN. The intersection of the two curves at T determines the price p_t" (1889, p. 258). It is evident that his diagram refers to a monetary market, as

---

[3] In the fourth edition of the *Eléments,* the passages are thrown out of context by Walras's insertion of the barter model of written pledges and are inconsistent with that model.

he also made clear with reference to a similar diagram with particular-market supply and demand curves in a model of exchange of fixed aggregate stocks of commodities. He stated with reference to that model and diagram that there is "a commodity" that is both "numeraire and money" (1874b, p. 151; 1889, p. 176). He believed that with "this hypothesis of the use of a numeraire and of money, we approach closer to the reality of things" (ibid.), and he explicitly stated that the supply curve is the supply "in exchange for numeraire" (1874b, p. 153; 1889, p. 178). That is, "if a holder supplies a quantity o_b of (B), he will obtain in exchange a quantity $d_a = o_b p_b$ of (A)," where (A) is money (1889, p. 177).

"The other market," Walras continued, "is the market for products" (1877b, p. 219; 1889, p. 212). Here is how Walras described it. "The entrepreneurs as sellers meet the landlords, workers, and capitalists as buyers of products" (1877b, p. 229; 1889, p. 212). There is "a market for products on which these products are offered exclusively by the entrepreneurs and demanded in the following way: the primary materials by the same entrepreneurs, and the consumption items by the landlords, workers and capitalists" (1889, p. XV; 1896b, pp. XIV–XV). The market for each product has its own locale and structure, so "we see how we have on the other hand a market, a supply and a demand and an equilibrium price for products" (1877b, p. 219; 1889, p. 212). In other words, in that market there are suppliers of the product and demanders of it, dealing only in the product, and with the products being purchased at the time the price is determined and while it rules. The demanders do not bring nonmonetary commodities to the market, so they must pay for the product with money. On each market day, a certain amount of the product is sold and is acquired on that day by the demanders. The reason for seemingly belaboring the obvious is because in the last phase of his theoretical activity, Walras tried to devise a barter model in which the price of each commodity would be determined in terms of the numeraire but the exchange of commodities would take place later, so that payment for any commodity would be made with another commodity (chs. 15, 16).

In each of the two types of markets, the commodities are sold "with intervention of a numeraire" (1877b, p. 229; 1889, pp. 211–12), which means that prices are quoted in terms of it. Walras reserved the word "money" for a medium of exchange. The numeraire is not, as such, a medium of exchange, although the numeraire may have that property added to it. He went on immediately to indicate that in the consumer commodity model, he was making that addition by stating that "these conceptions, it should be clearly noticed, are rigorously in conformity with the facts, with observation, with experience. In fact, and thanks to the use of money, the two markets are perfectly distinct in the reality of things just as they are in the regard of science" – that is, just as they are in the model (1877b, p. 230; 1889, p. 212;

emphasis added). By treating the markets for services and products as perfectly distinct, Walras was indicating that services are not bartered for products, because that would have to take place in one and the same market.

Emphasizing again that he was dealing with a monetary situation, Walras illustrated the verisimilitude of the model by describing a market for shoes in this way: "It is the entrepreneur who receives the productive service and who gives the money" to the worker (1877b, p. 230; 1889, p. 213). "It is with the money that they have received on the first [market] for their productive services that the landlords, workers and capitalists go as consumers to the second to buy products; and it is with the money that the entrepreneurs receive for their products on the second that they go to the first to buy productive services" (1877b, p. 230; 1889, p. 213). Walras also indicated (1877b, p. 229; 1889, pp. 211, 257) that the context of his discussion is the same as the context of his modeling of supply and demand in his monetary models of the redistribution of fixed aggregate stocks of commodities. In those models, he assumed that the numeraire commodity is "the numeraire and money" (1874b, p. 151; 1889, p. 176), explaining, as has been noted, that his assumption of the use of money makes his theory more realistic (1874b, pp. 49–51; 1889, pp. 67–69; 1874b, pp. 151–56; 1889, pp. 176–82).

Finally, it should be noted that Walras placed a discussion of the role of the entrepreneur in the model, and a realistic discussion of his flows of funds and his balance sheet (1877b, pp. 233–44; 1889, pp. 216–27) squarely in the middle of the lessons on the consumer commodities model. Walras conducted the entire description of the entrepreneur's operations in money terms, assuming that he borrows money, pays for inputs with money and sells goods for money, and repays loans with money. Walras commented that the discussion "proves that our theory of production is well founded on the nature of things" (1877b, p. 235; 1889, p. 218) and that accounting practice establishes the correctness of his theory of production (1877b, p. 238; 1889, p. 222). His "theory of production" is his consumer commodities model.

Evaluating seemingly conflicting statements: In evaluating the statements on barter and on monetary exchange concerning consumer commodities in the second and third editions of the *Eléments*, it is possible to argue that Walras did not have a clear idea of which assumption he wanted to pursue, or that he had in mind two different models. It could be argued that he should have realized that and drawn attention to it rather than indiscriminately mixing their descriptions together. Or it could be maintained simply that his work was contradictory. Those contentions do not, however, take account of some crucial facts about Walras's model. It will be recalled that Walras made the statement that he was going to assume no money is used in the model just before his presentations of equations. Here is the statement:

That shows how an entrepreneur can, in principle, by means of an accounting procedure, know at any moment that he is making a profit or a loss. At present, our definitions being established theoretically and on the basis of practice, we are going to suppose our entrepreneurs make neither profits nor losses; we are going, as we have said, to make abstraction from the working capital of the entrepreneurs in the form of primary materials, new capital goods, new income goods, circulating money in till as well as the working capital of consumers in the form of accumulations of income goods, circulating money and money savings; and we are going to show how the equilibrium prices of products and of services are mathematically determined in the state of equilibrium (1877b, p. 244; 1889, p. 227).

That is not the same as stating that he was going to assume those phenomena are absent during the equilibrating process. Walras did in fact assume consistently that the entrepreneurs "make profits or losses" during the equilibrating process in the consumer commodities model (for example, 1877b, p. 254; 1889, p. 238), and in the next chapter it will be seen that doubt is cast upon whether he always assumed that there is no accumulation of business inventories in the course of the equilibrating process. Similarly, in the foregoing statement he was probably indicating that he would assume no money is used just in his exposition of the mathematical relationships of the variables in equilibrium.

The foregoing thesis is strengthened by the consideration that Walras made a contrast between the consumer commodities model and a barter one by stating that only a limited aspect of the former – its equilibrium state – can be regarded as the equilibrium of a barter model: "Furthermore, we may remark that, *with respect to the state of equilibrium* of exchange and production, it is possible, as we have said, to make abstraction, if not from the numeraire, at least from money" and see that resource owners provide services to entrepreneurs in return for products (1877b, pp. 231–32; 1889, p. 214; emphasis added). That can be seen by throwing the veil of money off the state of equilibrium. Thus, Walras commented upon the possibility of constructing a barter model in such a way as to suggest that he had been assuming in his foregoing exposition that money is used, and that he was going to assume that it is used in his following exposition of the model's equilibrating process. When he stated in the second and third editions of the *Eléments* that products are exchanged for services in his model, he meant that its outcome in real terms is that entrepreneurs receive services and consumers receive products, and thus that services and products can be considered theoretically as being exchanged for each other in the state of equilibrium, even though in actuality in the model they are each bought with money, just as he described in his discussion of the shoe market. If he believed that money could actually be eliminated from his model in equilibrium as distinct from disregarding its presence, he was incorrect because each commodity is the only one nonmonetary one in its market and exchange takes place in the marketplace at the time the price is determined, and the commodity therefore must be sold for money.

The plan that Walras followed was to discuss the separate markets for goods and for services in which monetary exchange occurs, then the monetary activities and accounting practices of the entrepreneur, then to give an exposition of the mathematical relationships of the variables in an equilibrium in which he abstracted from the use of money, and finally to take up the equilibrating process on the assumption that money is used and to try to show that his model is stable. In that latter effort, he assumed the occurrence of all the disequilibrium phenomena that he had naturally eliminated from his discussion of equilibrium – namely, disequilibrium production, disequilibrium consumption, actual money profits and money losses. He also assumed the occurrence of the exchange activities in separate markets that necessarily require the use of money. He never stated that he was going to assume in all circumstances that there is no money in the model, and, whether or not that was at one time his intention, certainly he did not adhere to that plan. It is true that he mentioned a barter flow model in the second edition, but that special model is sketchy, incomplete, and illogical, and after writing the single paragraph devoted to it, Walras abandoned consideration of it.[4] It has been described here as constituting a special model, unreconciled with his central model, precisely because Walras did not employ its peculiar conditions in his subsequent constructions in the second edition.

Moreover, Walras's statements in the second and third editions about monetary exchange, instead of being merely assertions about the central consumer commodities model, constitute fundamental parts of its structure and specifications of its manner of functioning in disequilibrium and in equilibrium. Even if he had not made many references to money in the lessons on the central consumer commodities model, the conclusion would still have to be reached that money is used in its markets, because money is an essential part of the processes that Walras described as occurring in them.

IV. Services

Productive services

In his mature monetary consumer commodities model, Walras specified that some of the services provided by economic resources do not yield utility directly but are instead used to make commodities. He called them productive services. He observed that the question of the production of consumer goods

---

[4] He introduced a written pledges version of it as his central consumer commodities model in the last phase of his theoretical activity (see chs. 15 and 16).

becomes injected into the analysis of their exchange when it is recognized that they are the result of the use of productive services either combined exclusively with each other or with primary materials (1889, p. XIV). He therefore developed a model of the determination of the prices and rates of sale of services that are used to make consumer goods or are consumed directly.

Productive services and consumer commodities in Walras's model "are sold according to the mechanism of free competition" (1889, p. 211; and see 1877b, pp. 228–29). Walras therefore conceived of buyers and sellers in any particular market as being in direct contact with each other in a place sufficiently small that they can all simultaneously hear the prices that are quoted (1877b, p. 48; 1889, p. 66). One commodity is sold in each market and its price is quoted in terms of the numeraire. Since the participants in a given market are all in the same physical area and hear all offers and the associated price, there can be only one price at any moment.

Walras specified that the suppliers of productive services are their owners – namely, landlords, workers, and capitalists. They hire out their economic resources in the markets that Walras postulated exist for their sale (1889, pp. XIII–XIV), and the resources render the services as flows over time (1877b, p. 245; 1889, p. 228). The owners of the economic resources are capable of providing certain maximum amounts of the services but they do not necessarily offer those amounts for sale. Many or all of the owners vary the amount of each service they offer for sale as the price of the service varies (1889, p. 235; 1889, p. 245; 1877b, plate III, fig. 12; 1889, plate IV, fig. 14). Walras specified that the demanders of productive services are entrepreneurs. They use the services to make commodities for sale. The entrepreneurs' demands for services are functions of their prices, of the amounts of commodities that the entrepreneurs want to produce, and of the coefficients of production (1877b, p. 249; 1889, p. 232).

The different types of land produce different types of productive land services (1877b, p. 245; 1889, p. 228). Examples are land supporting factories, workshops, and stores (1877b, p. 223; 1889, p. 206). There is a marketplace for each such type, and they each have their own price (1889, p. 430). Different workers provide different types of productive personal services. Examples are salaried workers, lawyers, and doctors (ibid.). There is a marketplace for each such type, and they each have their own wage rate (1889, p. 430). There are different types of capital goods, each producing a different type of productive service. Examples are factories, workshops, trees that yield commercial fruits, work animals, machines, and tools (ibid.). There is a marketplace for each type of productive capital-good service in which a price is determined for each type (ibid.; 1877b, p. 229; 1889, p. 211).

Consumable services

Some of the services yielded by the three types of economic resources are consumable. Landlords, workers, and capitalists are the owners of the economic resources that yield such services (1877b, p. 234; 1889, p. 217). Those economic resources include roads, land such as parks, and land supporting homes and public buildings; the human capital that is used to provide such consumable services as those of servants and government employees; durable consumer goods such as houses, furniture, clothing, and jewelry (1877b, pp. 217–18, 222–26; 1889, pp. 200–201, 205–9); and public buildings (1877b, p. 223; 1889, p. 206).

Walras considered the supply of consumable services. The owners of economic resources may offer positive amounts of those services for sale. At any price, the excess of the sum of the positive individual quantities supplied of any particular consumable service over the sum of the negative individual quantities supplied is the total quantity supplied on the market (1877b, p. 246; 1889, p. 229).

Walras considered the demand for consumable services. The owners of economic resources may wish to consume some of the services provided by their own land, human capital, and capital goods (1877b, p. 228; 1889, pp. XIV, 211). If so, the amounts they want to consume are negative offers of supply and are therefore quantities demanded. Owners of resources may wish to consume services produced by other such owners. Those demands are registered on the market. The amounts of consumable services demanded by the owners of resources, whether produced by their own resources or by the resources of others, vary as functions of the prices of the services (1877b, p. 259; 1889, p. 244).

Market supplies and demands

Walras aggregated the individual net supplies of each service to obtain the market supply function (1877b, p. 248; 1889, p. 231). He aggregated the individual demands for each service (1877b, p. 224; 1889, p. 244) by adding the demands by all consumers for a service, such as the demand for a type of land service, to the demands by all entrepreneurs for that service for productive uses (1877b, p. 259; 1889, p. 244) in order to obtain the total demand for it.

In summary, Walras constructed a market for each service so that it has buyers of it dealing with sellers of it, instead of barter occurring between sellers of the service and sellers of a product. The service is the only nonmonetary commodity in the market, so it must be sold for money. In the model, the services are sold "following the mechanism of free competition with intervention of numeraire" (1877b, p. 229; 1889, p. 211). That means that they are sold in purely competitive organized markets, as Walras indicated by referring the reader to the passages (1877b, pp. 49–51; 1889, pp. 67–69) in which he modeled such a market in which the numeraire is also money.

V. Goods

It is not generally recognized that Walras restricted the production and sale of goods in the consumer commodities model to nondurables (1877b, pp. 225–26; 1889, pp. 208–9). There are no markets for durable goods of any kind in the model. The goods that are produced in the model are primary materials and nondurable consumer goods. Since services are used only once, all commodities in the model are nondurable. As Walras put it: "We can restrict ourselves for the present to . . . the production of new income commodities: things that are consumed and primary materials" (1877, p. 226; 1889, p. 209) – income commodities being nondurables. Primary materials are those commodities that are used to make other commodities and that can be used only once. They result from the use of productive services with each other, or with each other and with raw materials (1877b, p. 250; 1889, p. 233). Walras assigned the role of organizing the process of production to the entrepreneurs, which they undertake in order to make a profit. Accordingly, entrepreneurs are the demanders of the primary materials in the marketplaces and some entrepreneurs are also the suppliers of them (1889, p. XIV). Walras assumed that primary materials are sold as soon as they are produced and used as soon as they are bought (1877b, pp. 225, 244; 1889, pp. 208–27).

The nondurable consumer goods result from the combination of productive services with primary materials or with each other. The combination is organized by entrepreneurs. They are the suppliers of the consumer goods on the marketplaces (1877b, p. 245; 1889, p. 228). The demanders of the consumer goods are the landlords, workers, and capitalists (1889, p. XV). Walras assumed that the consumer goods are sold as soon as they are produced and consumed as soon as they are bought (1877b, pp. 225, 244; 1889, pp. 208–27), and there are therefore no household or business inventories; but it remains to be seen whether he adhered consistently to that assumption. Walras summed up the quantities demanded of each consumer good at each price by each individual to obtain the aggregate demand function for it (1877b, pp. 246–48; 1889, pp. 229–31).

Walras specified the characteristics of the marketplaces in which the suppliers and demanders of products meet. "The entrepreneurs as sellers meet the landlords, workers and capitalists as buyers of products," and the products are sold, like services, "according to the mechanism of free competition"

(1877b, p. 229; 1889, p. 212), by which Walras meant that they are sold in purely competitive markets that are organized (1877b, p. 49; 1889, p. 67). Paralleling his treatment of services, Walras specified that the goods are sold "with intervention of a numeraire" (1877b, p. 229; 1889, p. 212), which means that the price of each good is quoted in terms of a numeraire. Walras treated the numeraire in goods markets as also being money, because he assumed that the good in any market is not bartered for services or for another good. It is the only nonmonetary commodity in the market, so it must be sold for money.

VI. Conclusion

It has been shown that in the mature phase of his thought, Walras carefully specified the structure of a consumer commodities model. The only commodities produced are services and nondurables. He assumed that there are many types of land, many types of labor, and many types of capital goods, each with its associated service. He specified that the parameters of the model are the maximum potential supplies of services, the production functions, and the utility functions for services and goods. The model contains the following structural properties that are necessary to enable it to be capable of functioning: There is a separate market for each type of service and for each type of primary material and consumer good. Each market has a physical locale. Suppliers of productive and consumable services – landlords, workers, and capitalists – have supply functions for those services and demand functions for consumer commodities, and the entrepreneurs supply consumer goods. Both demanders and suppliers are present in the marketplaces, and there is a procedure by which they are enabled to express their offers. There is a numeraire and it is money. Each market is organized and is freely competitive, which implies the rules and procedures of such types of marketplaces. The functioning of the model will be examined in the next chapter.

CHAPTER 7

The equilibrating processes in the mature nondurable consumer commodities model

This chapter shows how Walras's mature nondurable consumer commodities model functions in regard to pricing, exchange, production, and consumption. It is shown, for the first time, how Walras explored the interesting field of possible alternative paths of disequilibrium production and sales of consumer commodities and services. After the discussion of the endogenous processes of the model, the conditions that he specified as parameters and that were discussed in chapter 6 are reexamined to see if they are in fact unchanged by those processes.

I. Introduction

The chapter describes the process of equilibration in Walras's mature nondurable consumer commodities model. It is shown how the model moves toward equilibrium by means of a pricing process in which disequilibrium transactions, disequilibrium production, and disequilibrium consumption occur. It is also shown that Walras explored an adjustment mechanism with prices as independent variables and another with both prices and quantities as independent variables. It is determined whether or not the conditions he considered to be parameters of his model are in fact independent of the equilibrating process, and thus it is determined whether or not his system of equations truly describes the model.

II. Services

Who changes the price?

The first aspect of the functioning of the mature model of the production and sale of nondurable consumer commodities to be considered is by whom the price of a commodity is changed. In this model, as in all of Walras's models, regardless of the phase in which he constructed them and regardless of their subject, there are no particular-market or central authorities that change and quote prices. With respect to services, for example, Walras assumed on the contrary that the price of each service is quoted in its market by the buyers or the sellers: "For each of [the services], a price is cried in numeraire; if, at the price cried in that way, the quantity demanded is greater than the quantity supplied, the entrepreneurs raise the price; if the quantity supplied is greater than the quantity demanded, the landowners, workers, and capitalists lower the price" (1877b, p. 229; 1889, pp. 211–12). At any quoted price, each supplier of a service offers a certain rate of supply of it to the potential buyers with whom he is in contact, and demanders offer to buy a certain rate of it.[1]

About each service market, Walras assumed that price is the independent variable and that a series of prices is cried in disequilibrium in the market. He wrote that if the price of the service of land, for example, is one at which the market demand quantity exceeds the market supply quantity, "a certain number of entrepreneurs would not be able to buy land services; alternatively all the entrepreneurs would not be able to buy as much as they would wish" (1877b, p. 373; 1889, p. 431). If the price exceeds the equilibrium value, "a certain number of landlords would not be able to sell, or alternatively all the landlords would not be able to sell as much as they would wish" (ibid.). Walras went on to describe the same types of disequilibrium situations in markets for capital-goods services and for labor (1877b, pp. 373–74; 1889, pp. 431–32).

Irrevocable disequilibrium sales of services: The question is whether irrevocable sales of productive services actually take place at the disequilibrium prices. In several places in the second edition of the *Eléments,* Walras may have implied that productive services are sold only at prices at which the supply and demand quantities are equal in each particular market. For example, he stated that "productive services are exchanged following the mechanism of free competition with intervention of the numeraire. For each of them a price in numeraire is cried; if, at this price thus cried, the quantity demanded is greater than the quantity supplied, the entrepreneurs raise the price; if the quantity supplied is greater than the quantity demanded, the landlords, workers and capitalists lower the price. The equilibrium price is the one for which the quantity supplied and the quantity demanded are equal" (1877b, p. 229; 1889, pp. 211–12). That, and other similar passages, do not state that disequilibrium transactions occur or are prohibited, but it is probable that Walras meant that they do not occur.

Nevertheless, there is unequivocally a different answer to the question posed at the beginning of this paragraph about the mature model of consumer

---

[1] Walras described one of his models of a particular market, in which there is in fact no calculator, as resulting in the same price *as if* individual supply and demand functions were submitted to an authority in the market who calculates and quotes the equilibrium price (1874a, pp. 106–7). Walras's models do not have a calculator, however, and during the equilibrating process do not behave in the same way as if there were a calculator. See p. 98.

commodities. Hiring and use of productive services occur at disequilibrium prices. As Walras described the situation: "Certain prices of services being cried, and certain quantities of products being produced, if these prices and these quantities are not equilibrium prices and quantities, it is necessary not only to cry other prices," and hence to produce different quantities of services, but also "to produce other quantities of products" (1889, p. 235). Walras specified that disequilibrium amounts of services are actually purchased and used: "A reprise of the tatonnement" in the model, he wrote, "consists in this: at the prices of services cried first at random, and subsequently raised or lowered according to the circumstances, the entrepreneurs will borrow from the landlords, workers and capitalists the quantities of these services that are necessary to produce certain quantities of products determined initially at random and subsequently increased or decreased according to the circumstances" (ibid.). Walras's use of the word "borrow" in that sentence is another instance of his use of the peculiar notion that payment would be made for the services by rendering the same amounts of services back to their original providers (ch. 6). Nevertheless, in effect the word "borrow" really means "purchase," inasmuch as the entrepreneurs acquire the services and pay for them.

Continuing with his discussion, Walras stated that he accepted those disequilibrium phenomena as a feature of his model (ibid.), thus indicating that he wanted to construct a model in which the adjustment processes in each market are variations of disequilibrium prices, disequilibrium rates of supply of services, and disequilibrium production and sales.

Not all-or-none offers: The next aspect of the model to be considered is the conditions of the offers made by the buyers and sellers of services. These conditions are made evident by the way that Walras conceived of the equilibrating process. His assertion that disequilibrium amounts of services are actually purchased makes clear that the offer of an entrepreneur to buy a certain amount of a service is understood by the other participants to mean that he wants to buy the amount he specifies but that he will buy any lesser amount at the quoted price. The offer of a seller of the service is understood to mean he wants to sell the amount he specifies but that he will sell any lesser amount at the quoted price. If the quantity demanded is less than the quantity supplied, all demanders are satisfied. If the reverse, then all suppliers are satisfied. After all possible sales of services have been made at a disequilibrium price that is lower than the equilibrium price, the demanders who have positive individual excess demand quantities quote a higher price. After all possible sales have been made at a higher price, the suppliers who have negative individual excess demand quantities quote a lower price. The offers to buy or sell a service that are accepted take effect immediately at the quoted price even if it is not one at which all excess demand quantities in the multimarket model are zero.

Depending on whether the price at which transactions have occurred is lower or higher than the equilibrium value, either demanders or suppliers of services find they still have unsatisfied individual excess demand quantities. That produces a situation that the theorist who is examining the model sees is reflected in the inequality of the sum of the demands for the productive and consumable uses of the service on the one hand and the sum of the supplies of it on the other (1877b, pp. 258–61; 1889, pp. 244–46). The participants do not know those sums, but they know the signs of their individual excess demand quantities, and those signs lead them to change the price in the market for each particular service.

III. Goods

Justification of the use of particular equilibrium functions

Before beginning the analysis of Walras's adjustment processes in the markets for goods, three interrelated issues must be examined. First, purely for the sake of simplicity and to allow a graphical treatment, supply and demand curves will be used – that is, particular-equilibrium curves. There is ample justification in Walras's work for the use of such curves. He explained that the solution shown by Rudolph Auspitz's and Richard Lieben's partial-equilibrium supply and demand curves could not be the one that would rule in general equilibrium, because in the course of moving to equilibrium the prices of other products and services would change, shifting the supply and demand curves for the particular product (1896b, pp. 482–84). Having criticized those author's construction as being contradictory, however, Walras modified his position by stating that although the "two curves would not be able to serve as a point of departure for a complete and rigorous theory of determination of prices" (ibid., p. 484), there is a place in economic analysis for them if they are properly defined. He reproduced Auspitz's and Lieben's supply and demand curves, with output on the base axis and price on the vertical axis, displaying a negatively inclined demand curve and a supply curve that is monotonically increasing (ibid., Appendices, figure 9), and used the curves to show that at quantities less than the equilibrium amount, producers would make profits, and that at quantities greater than the equilibrium amount, they would make losses and production would be restrained (ibid., p. 484). Moreover, he wrote that "thus envisaged," by which he meant properly understood and used, the particular-equilibrium demand curve "served me to construct the pure and applied theory of money" (ibid.,

p. 484), and he declared that he "would not want to maintain, with reference to one or another different question, that it would not be advantageous to use the supply curve also" (ibid.). In other words, he sanctioned the use of particular-equilibrium supply and demand curves. He used them on several occasions (1877b, pp. 370–72; 1889, pp. 257–58, 476, 478–79, 481; 1877b, plates II, III; 1889, plate IV) and used literary particular-equilibrium analysis of demand and supply in isolated markets on many occasions.

Walras described in detail the way to construct industry particular-equilibrium curves of the type that this chapter and chapter 13 use to convey the essential nature of the relationship of market-day and long-run equilibrium goods markets in his model. He provided an unequivocal example of the use of particular-equilibrium industry supply and demand curves in his discussion of the production of a capital good (1896b, p. 479). He assumed with reference to them that the prices of other commodities are constant, except for the prices of the productive services used in the industry. There and in passages such as the one just discussed, he indicated that the industry demand curve is negatively inclined. As for the shape of the industry supply curve, he indicated repeatedly that the relation of average cost and output is governed by these considerations: "The average cost of a product is a function of the prices of the productive services which enter into the confection of the product; and it is because the prices of the productive services increase or decrease that the average cost itself increases or decreases with the quantity produced" (ibid., p. 482). The market supply curve is therefore an increasing curve that shows the average cost of the product at each industry rate of output.[2]

Second, there is no evidence in Walras's writings before 1896 nor in the consumer commodities model in the third edition of the *Eléments* that he was aware that his assumption of constant coefficients of production implies that production functions are homogeneous of the first degree. Indeed, it appears that he rejected the assumption of production functions of that type when they came to his attention (Jaffé 1964, p. 97 [207]). Even if the production functions in his model had that property, however, they would not conflict with the ascending industry supply curves that he described and graphed and that are used in this chapter, because in his models the prices of the inputs vary as a function of the industry output, not as a function of the output of a firm. His industry supply functions manifest the effects of the firms' being subject to net external pecuniary diseconomies of scale, which Walras described in his discussion of the effects of increases of input prices. It should also be observed that the two-part process described later with reference to

---

[2] The diagram that Walras drew and his explanation of the shape of the supply curve are more fully explained in chapter 13.

Figures 7.2a and 7.2b would occur in essentially the same way if the supply curve were horizontal. That would, however, entail the assumption that input prices are constant, which is contrary to the assumption that Walras made.

Third, it will subsequently be emphasized that the process is more complicated than is shown by the diagrams, because the curves shift. They are used simply to illustrate the relation of the market day to the long run during a given period of time in Walras's analyses. The shifts of the curves are omitted because of the complexity that would otherwise be introduced without any corresponding gain in clarity of explication of the relationships that are of interest in this chapter.

Price as the independent variable

Walras specified many times in the second edition of the *Eléments* that disequilibrium sales of consumer goods occur in the markets of his model. An example of his conception of the situation was given in the quotations presented that refer to the necessity of producing different quantities of products if disequilibrium quantities are being produced (1889, p. 235). He also explained in different incompatible ways the process of adjustment that ensues. In one of his articles, he treated price as the independent variable and the rate of production as a dependent variable. It will be noted that in the following quotation in which he adopted that procedure, he was not referring to sales out of a given stock of previously produced commodities. He was describing a situation in which production and sales occur in disequilibrium amounts, whereas in a fixed-stock situation there is no production, and in his models of those situations sales occur only at the equilibrium price on the given market day. He was describing a situation of desired and actual flows of production and sales, because he was dealing with production and its average cost, and with consumers and producers, not with persons who are simply professional traders. The dependent variables in the model discussed later are the desired rates of production and purchases.

Behavior of the model: As in all of Walras's models, the participants meet directly and quote and change the price:

Thus there is generally, for each service or product in the private sector, a crowd of consumer-demanders; and similarly, there is a crowd of producer-suppliers assured of selling to one person what they will not sell to another. Therefore, competition can function. The quantity demanded of certain products being found to be greater than the quantity supplied, the consumers will want to bid the price up and will raise it; the price will rise above the average cost, and output will increase. The quantity supplied of certain products being found to be, on the contrary, greater than the quantity demanded, the producers will want to cut the price and will lower it; the price will fall below the average cost and production will diminish. Order and proportion will

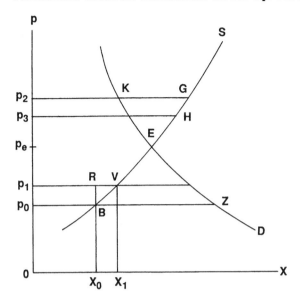

Figure 7.1 Price tatonnement: consumer goods industry

establish themselves of their own accord with the attainment of equilibrium (Walras 1875, pp. 197–98).

At some prices, some demanders may not be able to buy any of the good and others may be able to buy only some of the quantity they would prefer. At other prices, some suppliers may not be able to sell any of the good and others may be able to sell only some of the quantity they would prefer.

This process will be explained by reference to particular equilibrium market supply and demand functions. This is done because Walras was contemplating a particular-equilibrium situation in the passage quoted. He generally regarded markets in that way when he discussed the direct impact of a change in the price of a good on the sales of that good. The functions are defined, of course, on the assumption that all other prices that affect supply and demand in the particular market are constant, except the prices of the inputs used in the production of the commodity. In actuality, in the wider setting of Walras's consumer commodities model, the supply and demand curves shift as other prices change, but with respect to each new set the process that occurs is illustrated in Figure 7.1.

The output is shown on the base axis simply to be consistent with Figures 7.2a and 7.2b. At the price p_0, the quantity demanded, p_0Z, exceeds the quantity supplied, p_0B, so there is a positive excess demand, BZ. The amount actually sold is the quantity produced and supplied, X_0. The ordinate of any point on the S curve shows the average cost in each firm when the industry total rate of production is the one shown by the abscissa of the point. Thus the average cost of X_0 is X_0B. The demanders bid the price up to p_1, and the excess of that price over the average cost is RB. That means that the firms in the industry are making profits, so output expands to X_1, the average cost of which, X_1V, is equal to p_1. There is still an excess demand, so demanders bid the price up again, and the process continues until the equilibrium price is reached. If the price is p_2, the quantity supplied exceeds the quantity demanded, but only the quantity demanded is purchased. What then is the meaning of KG? If the suppliers have actually produced p_2G units of output, then KG would go into inventories. The producers would cut the price to p_3, which is $p_2 - p_3$ less than the average cost ($= 0p_2$) of p_2G units of output. Thus, following Walras's account, the producers would diminish their rate of production, moving down the supply curve from G to H, where the average cost of p_3H units of output is equal to p_3. The price would then be lowered again and the process of adjustment would be repeated until E is reached.

The problem with the process is that Walras may have assumed that there are no business inventories under any conditions in his model (see ch. 6). If there is no inventory accumulation, then p_2G cannot be produced when the price is p_2; if p_2G is produced, there must be unintended inventory accumulation. It cannot be supposed that the producers offer to produce p_2G at p_2 but actually produce only the amount that demanders will buy – namely, p_2K (which, to simplify the lettering and number of lines on the figure, has been made equal to $0X_1$) – because the average cost of that amount is only X_1V. The producers would then be making a profit of KV dollars per unit of output and expand output, whereas the process Walras was describing in the foregoing quotation is one in which at prices higher than p_e the average cost exceeds the price, so entrepreneurs are making losses and output falls toward the equilibrium value. It may be therefore that Walras made the assumption of no inventories only in reference to the equilibrium state in the belief that there would then be no need for them, but assumed that inventories exist and are varied in disequilibrium. Otherwise, the adjustment process illustrated by Figure 7.1 does not make sense. If Walras dropped the assumption of no business inventories in disequilibrium, however, then his equations no longer describe the model, as will be explained in a subsequent section.

It should be noted that it is not possible to interpret the quotation Figure 7.1 refers to as describing a series of market-day equilibria, with all transactions occurring at market-day prices that equate supply and demand quantities. The reader who tries to make such an interpretation will find himself describing a cobweb process that may or may not be stable and would have the price alternating between being greater than average cost and less than average cost. That process would contradict the general features and the details of the situation that Walras described.

Price and output as independent variables

Walras conceived of another process of adjustment of output markets in the consumer commodities model. He described it as "the demanders bidding prices up in the event of an excess of the quantity demanded over the quantity supplied, and the suppliers lowering prices in the event of an excess of the quantity supplied over the quantity demanded; the entrepreneurs who make products increasing their production in the case of the excess of the price over the average cost, and, on the contrary, decreasing it in the case of the excess of the average cost over the price" (Walras 1892a; and in 1896b, p. 476). This is a two-part process.

Price tatonnement: In the first part, the price in each market is the independent variable and the dependent variables are the desired supply and demand quantities of the good. Walras thought of the amount of any good is brought to market on a given day as selling only at the market-day particular-equilibrium price. In his model of the barter of fixed total stocks of commodities (ch. 3) and in his treatment of organized securities and commodities exchanges (ch. 5), he explicitly assumed that transactions occur only at market-day equilibrium prices. Furthermore, in the sale of consumer goods and consumable services, "prices are raised or lowered until the quantity demanded and the quantity supplied of each object or service are equal. At that moment, the prices are current equilibrium prices, and exchange takes place" (1889, p. XIV). It is evident that Walras meant that exchange does not take place at other prices. In other passages in which he described Walrasian pricing in a given product market in his model of consumer commodities, Walras did not state that trade occurs only at equilibrium prices, but on the other hand he did not state that disequilibrium transactions occur. For example, he wrote that "products are exchanged . . . according to the mechanism of free competition," so that "for each [product] a price is cried in numeraire; if, at the price thus cried, the quantity demanded is greater than the quantity supplied, the landlords, workers and capitalists raise the price; if the quantity supplied is greater than the quantity demanded, the entrepreneurs lower the price. The equilibrium price is the one for which the quantity supplied and the quantity demanded are equal" (1877b, p. 229; 1889, p. 212).

Production tatonnement: The second part of the process involves the circumstance that during the disequilibrium phase of the model the price and the average cost are unequal: "The prices (of products) ordinarily being different from the average costs of production . . ., the entrepreneurs who produce (B), (C), (D) . . . will make profits or losses" (1877b, p. 254; 1889, p. 238).

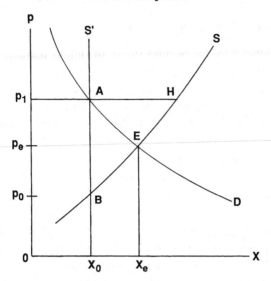

Figure 7.2a Price and production tatonnements: profitable consumer-goods industry

Entrepreneurs will then want to change their rates of production. Walras assumed that output cannot be changed immediately to the rate that entrepreneurs would like to produce at the current price; instead, increases or decreases of the rate of production occur in relatively small amounts from day to day until general equilibrium is reached. The "quantities of products are determined initially at random, and subsequently are increased or diminished according to the circumstances" (1889, p. 235). The entrepreneurs sell the varying disequilibrium amounts of consumer goods at varying prices: "Then they will come to sell these products on the market for products, following the mechanism of free competition, to these landlords, workers and capitalists" (ibid.). Walras referred frequently to the mechanism of free competition as one in which trade occurs only at a price that clears the market. It is very likely, therefore, that he was thinking in that passage of amounts that are disequilibrium ones in relation to long-run equilibrium in the industries but that are sold, once they are taken to market, at market-day particular-equilibrium prices. This is a different process from the one shown in Figure 7.1 in which the price is rising when there are profits.

Behavior of the model: Walras began by assuming that the entrepreneurs in an industry are making a profit. Under the regime of free competition, "if, in certain firms, the price of products is superior to their average cost of production in terms of productive services, which constitutes a profit," the result is that "entrepreneurs will move into the industry or increase their production, which will increase the quantity of products on the market, resulting in a lowering of the price and a reduction of the difference" (1877b, p. 231; 1889, p. 214). Those considerations are taken into account in Figure 7.2a. The rate of production and sales per day are shown on the base axis. The current market-day supply is shown by S', a line parallel to the price axis at the current amount of production per day, X_0. That can be presumed to have been the long-run equilibrium output when the demand curve passed through B. The demand then shifted to the position shown. The average cost of X_0 is X_0B. The initial price may be p_0, in accordance with Walras's suggestion that the price opens at the value at which it closed on the previous day (Walras 1874b, pp. 52–53; 1889, p. 70). At p_0, the quantity brought onto the market is less than the quantity demanded. Since the market is freely competitive and organized, if Walras were consistent with his earlier accounts of such markets, then there would be no disequilibrium sales on the given day. The price would be raised to p_1, whereupon p_1A ($= 0X_0$) would be sold at the market-day equilibrium price p_1. Alternatively, if the initial price is cried at random, in accordance with Walras's occasional assumption of that in the *Eléments* (for example, 1877b, pp. 252–53; 1889, pp. 236–37), and if the initial price is greater than p_1, there would be an excess supply quantity, as shown by the relation of S' to D, and the price would be lowered to p_1. Whatever the initial price, the participants would change the price until p_1 is found, whereupon exchange takes place. The market would then be in temporary equilibrium at A.

The next part of the process involves the adjustment of the rate of production. At p_1, the excess of the price over the average cost of X_0 is AB. The firms are making profits in the industry, and, precisely following Walras's account, that would lead to an increase in production by the firms already in the industry and to an increase in the number of firms in the industry. At the price p_1, the producers would want to produce in the aggregate p_1H immediately, but Walras assumed that they would be unable to expand output sufficiently rapidly to do so. On the next day, more firms would enter the industry and existing firms would be able to hire more labor, purchase more raw materials, and expand the plant and equipment that they hire. Output could therefore be increased to some quantity larger than X_0 but less than p_1H and less than X_e. As output expands, the S' line would shift to the right. Thus, on each day before equilibrium is reached, as the price falls from p_1 toward p_e, the entrepreneurs would want to produce in the aggregate an amount that is more than X_e but that progressively diminishes. That is, the desired rate of output falls from p_1H down the supply curve to p_eE as the actual rate of output rises from X_0 to X_e. By demanding and purchasing more services, the entrepreneurs "make the price of services rise" (1877b, p. 264; 1889, p. 250). The average cost of output therefore rises, as reflected by the ascending path

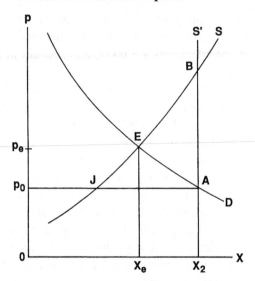

Figure 7.2b Price and production tatonnements: unprofitable consumer-goods industry

of S. On each subsequent day, trade would take place only at the equilibrium price for that particular day as given by the intersection of the shifting S' line and the D curve, following the downward course of the demand curve from A to E. The average cost rises along the supply curve from B to E. The excess of the market-day equilibrium price over the supply price of the product therefore diminishes. At E, the current rate of production would be X_e, at which the market supply and demand quantities would be equal and the market-day and long-run equilibrium price p_e would be equal to the average cost X_eE.

Walras then considered the case in which the initial output exceeds the long-run equilibrium quantity and the firms are making losses. The current market-day equilibrium price would be less than average cost and the entrepreneurs would diminish production: "If in certain firms, the average cost of production in terms of productive services is superior to the price, which constitutes a loss, the entrepreneurs will turn away from the industry or diminish their production, which diminishes the quantity of products in the market, resulting in a rise of the price and similarly reducing the difference" (1877b, p. 231; 1889, p. 214). As the entrepreneurs reduce production, they purchase smaller quantities of services and thereby "they make their prices fall" (1877b, p. 264; 1889, p. 250), and that lowers the average cost.

The case of losses is shown in Figure 7.2b. If the initial output is OX_2, the market-day supply curve is S' and the average cost is X_2B. The market-day equilibrium price at which all the output is sold is p_0 ($= X_2A$). The loss per unit of production in each firm is AB. The suppliers would want to produce p_0J at p_0, but they can reduce output only gradually, so the rate of output would fall from X_2 toward X_e. The market-day supply curve S' would shift to the left, intersecting the D curve progressively closer to E on the path from A to E. As that happened, the market-day equilibrium price would rise from p_0 to p_e, which is also the long-run equilibrium price, and the amounts that the producers would want in the aggregate to produce but would be unable to produce would rise along the supply curve from J to E. The average cost would fall along the path BE from X_2B to X_eE, and the long-run equilibrium rate of production per day would become X_e. The two-part process just described, for both of profits and losses, is precisely what Walras described when he wrote that disequilibrium quantities are "then transported to the market" and are sold there "according to the mechanism of free competition" at prices that are closer to being equal to the costs of production than were the previous set of prices (1889, p. 239).

Walras wrote on more than one occasion that when there are losses, it is to be expected that the entrepreneurs "would completely cease production" to avoid the losses (1877b, p. 374; 1889, p. 493; 1896b, p. 433). In that case, instead of diminishing gradually, output would immediately change from an initial disequilibrium quantity that exceeds X_e to one at which there is no loss and which must therefore be equal to or less than the long-run equilibrium amount. In fact, Walras did not explain what the initial new output would be nor how it would be determined. Evidently it would be only by accident that the new output would be the long-run equilibrium one. If the new output is less than X_e, such as p_0J, profits would become positive and output would expand following the procedure discussed in relation to Figure 7.2a. The submodel is asymmetrical in the sense that except for the initial situation and the initial fall in output, profits are always positive in disequilibrium, and changes of output are always increases. Walras assumed, however, in most of his passages on production that the rate of production would fall gradually toward the equilibrium amount.

Adjustments in the price and production of the numeraire: The same type of adjustment process illustrated in Figures 7.2a and 7.2b also occurs in the case of the numeraire commodity, (A). The price of the numeraire, p_a, is, of course, unity in terms of itself, but stated in terms of some other commodity, as in the discussion in Walras's model under consideration, it may "by chance" equal 1, "but generally we will have ... $p_a'' \gtrless 1$" (1877b, p. 262; 1889, p. 248). If so, entrepreneurs produce disequilibrium rates of it and sell them at prices that differ from their average costs, and hence make profits or losses in disequilibrium. The variables converge to equilibrium because the entrepreneurs who produce (A), "like those of (B), (C), (D) ... have only to increase their production in the case of the excess of the price over the average cost, as in fact they do, and to reduce it in the case of the excess of the average cost over the price" (1877b, p. 264; 1889, pp. 249–50).

In the former case, the producers of (A) are making profits. Their increased production leads to increases in the prices of inputs, which cause the average cost of (A) to rise, and leads the price of the numeraire commodity and its average cost to approach each other. In the latter case, the producers of (A) are making losses, so they diminish their production. If the reduction of output is gradual, Walras observed, the diminution of the production of (A) causes the prices of inputs into the industry to fall gradually, and that causes the average cost of (A) to fall gradually. The reduction of the quantity supplied causes the price of (A) to rise. Thus the average cost and the price of the numeraire commodity approach each other (ibid.). In fact, Walras observed, the entrepreneurs are free to avoid losses by not producing any output when the average cost of production of the numeraire commodity is greater than its price (1877b, p. 264; 1889, p. 249). As in the case of other commodities, Walras did not explain how the adjustment process would work in the latter case. It would be asymmetrical in the sense that the only gradual adjustments of output would be increases.

The processes discussed with reference to Figures 7.2a and 7.2b and the numeraire commodity combine Walras's implication in his consumer commodities model that transactions of goods occur only at a price at which the supply actually available on a market on a given day and the quantity demanded are equated, and his assertion that there is disequilibrium, resulting in changes of the rate of output when average cost does not equal the current price. Even though a service or product is sold at a price at which there is temporary equilibrium in the particular market, and even though the market demand is always satisfied, if there are profits or losses the transactions and the price are disequilibrium magnitudes in two interrelated respects. First, the desired long-run desired market supply quantity at the market-day equilibrium price is not produced and sold. Second, the market-day equilibrium price is a disequilibrium one in relation to the one that will eventually be established as the equilibrium price in the market and in relation to the set of prices that will eventually be reached in all the markets in general equilibrium.

Contrast of services and goods markets: It can be seen from the foregoing discussion that the adjustment process that Walras specified as occurring in productive service markets in the mature consumer commodity model is not the same as in goods markets. In a market for a good in that model, and indeed in all Walras's models, on a given market day trade occurs only at the price at which the market-day supply and demand quantities are equal. In a market for a productive service, however, the participants do not pledge to buy and sell only at a market-day equilibrium price. Walras indicated that in his model, disequilibrium sales of productive services actually occur on any given market day – that is, sales that are disequilibrium ones with reference to the market-day supply and demand functions. It appears impossible to interpret Walras as having assumed, in the particular passages that were quoted, that a productive service is sold only at market-day equilibrium prices that are, during the adjustment phase, disequilibrium prices with respect to a long-run situation and to the general-equilibrium set of all prices. Throughout Walras's model of consumer commodities, he assumed there is a given number of workers with given preferences. The quantity supplied of a service cannot be accumulated and hence is not a produced stock, and the quantity supplied varies with the price of the service and with other variables. Consequently, Walras's work done on those assumptions presents no possibility of defining a market-day supply function for a service that differs from a longer-run supply function, and the type of process illustrated for goods in Figures 7.2a and 7.2b is not true for productive services in Walras's model. The lack of refinement of Walras's thought on these matters is indicated by the fact that in contrast, in one model he described the market for consumable services as one in which exchange occurs on any market day only at the initial solution price (1889, p. XIV), as was noted earlier.

Other alternatives

Walras also referred to a model in which the average cost of some consumer commodities falls when their output increases, thus implying, in particular-equilibrium terminology, a forward-falling long-run supply curve. The entrepreneurs quote progressively lower disequilibrium prices for goods, and trade occurs at them. In Walras's words, as output increases, "the average cost is lowered and the price of products follows it" and "thanks to that lowering they [the owners of services] receive more products while giving up less services" (Walras to Vilfredo Pareto, July 19, 1894, in 1965, 2, letter 1181, p. 607). Eventually, equilibrium is reached in product and services markets (ibid.). Walras did not elaborate on this model or explore the consequences of external economies of scale.

Walras also wrote a number of ambiguous passages on the topic of adjustment processes in the consumer commodities model. For example, a page and a half after the passage in which he assumed that given batches of consumer goods are sold only at market-day equilibrium prices (1889, p. XIV), he stated that when production is considered in relation to consumer goods, primary materials, consumable services, and productive services, "on each market, the prices are raised in the case of an excess of the quantity demanded over the quantity supplied and lowered in the case of an excess of the quantity supplied over the quantity demanded. And the current equilibrium prices are those for which the quantity demanded and the quantity supplied of each service or product are equal and for which, moreover, the *price* of each product is equal to its average cost in terms of productive services" (1889, p. XV). That may have simply been a statement of the double condition of long-run equilibrium. On the other hand, Walras may conceivably have had in mind a process in which there are disequilibrium transactions on market days, or one in which transactions occur only at market-day equilibrium prices, or alternatively, one in which transactions occur only at the prices that rule in general equilibrium – that is, in long-run equilibrium. If he meant the latter, he was either thinking briefly of a totally different model from the one discussed in relation to Figures 7.2a and 7.2b, or he was momentarily confused when he wrote the sentence. The sentence is incompatible with the fact that in his mature consumer commodities model, it is impossible for trade to be suspended until firms have changed their size, until firms have moved in and out of industries, and until production rates have been adjusted so that average cost equals price. The significance of the production of a series of different rates of output during the adjustment process in Walras's model is that different amounts of the product, with different average costs, are brought onto the market and sold on successive market days until the two equilibrium conditions obtain. In his mature model, disequilibrium production necessarily occurs before general-equilibrium values of the input and output prices are reached, and therefore during the adjustment process sales of services and goods necessarily occur at prices that are disequilibrium ones in relation to the eventual general equilibrium.

IV. Convergence and equilibrium

Stability of the model

Walras's discussion of mathematical iteration concerning the prices and rates of supply of services reflects his belief that those variables converge to equilibrium in his model. The theorist solves the equations of the model by mathematical iteration. Contemplating an equation that sets the market supply of a service equal to the market demand for it, Walras observed that a set of values of the arguments of the equation can be found that is closer to making the two sides equal than did the previous set. The change in the price of, say, a type of land service has a direct effect, and it is wholly in the direction of leading to an equalization of the two sides, whereas the changes in the prices of other services, which may have the opposite effect, have effects that are indirect and to a degree cancel each other out. "The system of new prices p''_t,

$p''_p, p''_k \ldots$ is thus closer to equilibrium than the system of previous prices $p'_t, p'_p, p'_k \ldots$ and it is necessary only to continue following the same method in order to approach it more and more" (1877b, p. 261; 1889, p. 246).

Walras's discussion of mathematical iteration concerning product prices also reflects his conception of his model as being a system in which disequilibrium transactions and disequilibrium production follow equilibrating paths. He observed that variations in prices and average costs of production result from variations of the quantities produced of consumer goods, "these [disequilibrium] quantities being substituted for [the equilibrium quantities] in the tatonnement" (1889, p. 239).

He then mixed descriptions of the behavior of the model in with mathematical iteration, writing that disequilibrium amounts of output are taken to the market and sold (ibid.). It is certain (ibid., p. 240), he stated, that the change in the quantity produced of each good in disequilibrium has a direct effect on its price. The changes in the disequilibrium quantities produced of other products have only indirect effects on the price of a given good, and those changes influence it in opposite ways and therefore cancel each other out to a certain degree. "The system of new quantities produced and of new prices is thus nearer to equilibrium than the former set, and it is necessary only to continue the tatonnement in order to approach equilibrium more and more closely" (ibid., p. 241). "Free competition in regard to exchange," however, "that is to say the liberty given to landlords, workers and capitalists and to the entrepreneurs to sell and buy services and products by raising and lowering the prices, is the practical means of solving the equations" (1877b, p. 266; 1889, p. 251), and is the way the processes of convergence work in the unconstrained model.

This process occurs not only in the model (1877b, p. 255; 1889, p. 241) but in reality: "Now this tatonnement occurs naturally, on the market for services, under the regime of free competition, since, under that regime, the price of services is raised when the quantity demanded is greater than the quantity supplied, and is lowered when the quantity supplied is greater than the quantity demanded" (ibid.). By raising or lowering the prices of the services "on the market for those services," just as the theorist does in his iteration process, the entrepreneurs "tend to produce equilibrium" (1877b, p. 264; 1889, p. 250). Equilibrium, Walras asserted, exists in his model – "l'équilibre existera" (1877b, p. 257; 1889, p. 243). The equilibrium values, he asserted, are given by the solution to his equation system, in which market supplies and market demands are prominent.

Equations and the model. Walras's general equilibrium system of equations ostensibly related to his consumer commodities model is not, however, the same thing as that model. It should always be asked whether the equations a theorist writes down are descriptive of the behavior that transpires in his model. That the equations and the model are different things can be illustrated in regard to Walras's writings by two examples. First, it should be observed that nowhere in the foregoing expositions was it asserted that knowledge of the market supply and demand functions is necessary for the process of equilibration of either goods or services in Walras's model. Of course, he wrote that if the market supply and demand quantities for any good or service are not equal, the price is changed, but the participants in the model do not know the market quantities. The market functions are known only to the omniscient theoretician, who calculates them to obtain an index of the conditions in the model, whereas the knowledge that produces change in the model and drives its markets toward equilibrium is the knowledge by participants of their individual situations – that is, of the signs of their individual market-oriented excess demand quantities. Those signs lead individuals to quote higher or lower prices, quite without knowledge about or concern for the market as a whole, and certainly without concern for general equilibrium.

Second, the difference mentioned is illustrated by the following example. Walras specified the budget equation for a consumer (1877b, p. 248; 1889, p. 230) and then summed the budget equations for all consumers (1877b, p. 248; 1889, p. 231). He thus arrived at the statement that the sum of the values of all the commodities purchased by consumers must equal the sum of the incomes they earn from the different productive services they sell (1877b, p. 251, 1889, p. 234). In the passage that follows, unlike the confusing procedure that he adopted elsewhere in the *Eléments,* he did not use the demand notation to indicate the entrepreneurs' equilibrium supplies of goods, but straightforwardly to indicate the market demands of consumers:

To the quantities effectively demanded D'_b, D'_c, D'_d ... of [the consumer commodities] (B), (C), (D) ... at prices that are equal to the average costs p'_b, p'_c, p'_d ..., there correspond the quantities O'_t, O'_p, O'_k ... effectively supplied of [the productive services] (T), (P), (K) ... conforming to the equations of the aggregate supplies of services ... which form, with the equations of the aggregate demands for products, a system of equations of exchange answering to the three conditions of maximum satisfaction, a single price in any market, and general equilibrium (1877b, p. 255; 1889, pp. 241–42).

By postulating that the price of each commodity equals its average cost, Walras introduced by assumption the equilibrium condition for production and implied that the quantities of services offered are valued at their equilibrium prices. He had to assume those conditions arbitrarily, because the equilibrium values of the variables are not determinable with the equations he mentioned. That reflects the circumstance that contrary to his assertion, the equations he mentioned – of the supplies of inputs and the demands for outputs – do not form a model of exchange. If those equations actually described the model, the service suppliers would be the only ones represented in the market, for they are the ones who offer services for sale and they are also the would-be demanders of goods. Since the service suppliers do not make or possess goods, they cannot trade them with each other. Consequently, no trade could occur except insofar as they sell consumable services to each other. Thus, Walras should have stated that the equations are simply aggregates of the budget constraint for each consumer in an assumed equilibrium.

Equilibrium conditions: Walras explained the equilibrium conditions for the disequilibrium transactions and production model. There is a state of equilibrium of exchange, one "first, in which the quantity supplied and the quantity demanded of the productive services are equal, and in which there is a stationary equilibrium price on the market for the services" (1877b, p. 230; 1889, p. 213; and see 1877b, pp. 258–61; 1889, pp. 244–49). "It is one, next, in which the quantity supplied and the quantity demanded of products are equal, and in which there is a stationary equilibrium price on the market for products" (1877b, p. 230; 1889, p. 213; and see 1877b, p. 264; 1889, p. 250). It will be noted that Walras therefore stated that it will not only be true in general equilibrium that there are market-day equilibrium prices, but that those market-day prices have ceased changing; the market-day equilibrium price has reached the long-run equilibrium value. In Walras's model, the equalities obtain simultaneously for all commodities, a situation that, together with some other features, is now called a "Walrasian equilibrium." Finally, the equilibrium of production is ensured by the condition that "the price of the products is equal to their average cost of production" (1877b, p. 231; 1889, p. 213), simultaneously for all products (1889, p. XV).

If the circular flow is considered in real terms, it can be seen that in equilibrium the consumer goods made by entrepreneurs are acquired by the providers of productive services, and the quantities of those commodities are precisely enough to remunerate the latter for those services, while the entrepreneurs receive exactly the quantities of services needed to produce the commodities. The quantity demanded times the price of each good summed over all goods is equal to the quantity purchased times the price of each service summed over all services. The expenditures of consumers on commodities are therefore equal to the payments to the consumers for services: "The tatonnement will be finished when, in exchange for the products that they will have fabricated, the entrepreneurs will obtain from the landlords, workers and capitalists precisely the quantities of land services, labor and capital good services for which they [the entrepreneurs] will be indebted to them, and which they [the entrepreneurs] will employ in the confection of products" (1889, p. 235). The entrepreneurs have undertaken either to produce a fixed batch of commodities or to produce a rate of output and are therefore able "either to pay off their debts and stop at that point, or more likely, to continue indefinitely the production with which the functioning of the system will be regularized from that time forward" (ibid.). For the sake of clarity, it is worth mentioning once more that Walras's use of the terminology of borrowing and repaying debts harkened back to his concept in the first edition of entrepreneurs borrowing services and paying back services, but in the passage just quoted, which was introduced in the second edition, that terminology nevertheless simply means that the entrepreneurs pay for the services provided by the resource owners.

V. Parameters and endogenous processes

Are the supposed parameters truly constant?

Walras explained that in his model, the solutions to the general-equilibrium system of equations are found on the assumption that the parameters of the model are constant, and that the equilibrium continues until a parametric change alters the market supply or demand function for a service or product (ibid., p. 234). The question to be examined now is whether Walras was right in supposing that the endogenous processes in his model – the adjustment processes just discussed – do not change any of the conditions that he believed are parametric constants in his equations. If the supposed constants are really variables, the equilibrium conditions that have just been stated would not be affected, but the equations would be invalidated because they would not be descriptive of the model. They would not identify some magnitudes as being variables, and their solutions would not be the true equilibrium magnitudes of any of the variables.

There are no endogenous processes in the model that necessarily alter the utility functions of consumers for consumable services and consumer goods, the utility functions of resource suppliers that enter into the determination of their offers of productive services, the aggregate amounts of land or labor, the entrepreneurs' desire to maximize profits, the production functions that old or new firms have, or the set of commodities. In other words, Walras's assumptions that those elements of the model are unchanging are not contradicted by its workings.

A variety of situations would cause the equilibrium values in most consumer commodities models to differ from the solutions to Walras's equations, but most of those situations do not arise in his model. First, the hiring of services at disequilibrium rates and the consequent flow of disequilibrium payments of income has the effect of providing individuals with the wherewithal to save in disequilibrium. That would lead to positive savings at varying rates in disequilibrium and change the capital stock. Walras eliminated this problem in his consumer commodities model by assuming that all income is consumed. That was a purely arbitrary assumption; that is, it created a condition that does not follow reasonably from the characteristics of the economic agents in Walras's model.

Second, the earning of disequilibrium incomes from the sale of services does not affect the consumers' demand functions for commodities. This is evident from the fact that Walras specified that a consumer's demand for a commodity is a function of the prices of all commodities and of income (ibid., p. 239), where the latter is determined by the prices of the services sold by the consumer times the amounts sold. The quantity demanded of any commodity by the consumer is determined simultaneously along with the prices of all commodities and the consumer's corresponding income. The individual and therefore the market demand function for a consumer good therefore do not change with disequilibrium incomes; income is simply one of the arguments of those functions. They would be affected by changes of income only if those changes led to changes in wealth, which could occur through savings or inventory accumulation or changes of the values of inventories or other assets. Walras avoided those possibilities, however, by eliminating changes in wealth through his supposition that all income is immediately consumed (1877b, p. 225; 1889, p. 208) and that there are no markets for consumer durables and therefore no prices for them. The consumer goods produced in the model can be used only once, and consumers do not hold inventories (ibid.; 1877b, p. 244; 1889, p. 227).

Third, disequilibrium incomes do not alter the supply functions for services. For personal services, for example, at any wage rate the preferences of the worker lead to a certain amount of work and a certain daily income from the sale of that work. Those two variables are determined together. A change in the income earned by the worker does not even shift the supply *curve* of labor as a function of the wage rate; that curve is derived from a stable offer curve, which, in modern terms, has income and hours of work as the coordinates of the points of tangency of the opportunity line and the work-income indifference curves. If a worker sells less labor than he wishes or as much as he wishes at a disequilibrium wage rate, his supply quantities at different subsequent wage rates are therefore unchanged. In the real economy, changes of inventory of product held by its suppliers will affect their supply of it, but in regard to services, the circumstance that less of a type of service may be purchased than is offered at a particular price cannot lead to accumulation of inventory of the service by the sellers, nor can a positive market excess demand lead to sales out of inventory, because amounts of a service cannot be accumulated.

The supply functions for services would be affected by changes of income only if they led to changes in wealth. It is probable that changes in wealth would affect the service suppliers' subsequent offers of services at each of their possible prices. In the real economy, if a service supplier's holdings of commodities or other wealth – for example, his consumer nondurables, durables, money savings, or ownership of stocks or bonds or other financial assets – is affected by the level of his income, then his supply function for the service will change after he sells a disequilibrium amount of it. Those changes are, however, eliminated by Walras's assumptions. First, the sellers of services do not accumulate or reduce inventories of nondurable consumer goods, because there are no such inventories in Walras's model. Second, there is no savings and no wealth in the model in any functional sense. There may be such items as houses, furniture, and jewelry, but there are no markets for them and therefore no prices for them. There are no stocks or bonds or other financial assets. The service supplier simply starts each new working day with zero holdings of marketable wealth. Consequently, the individual and market supplies of services functions do not change as a result of disequilibrium sales of services.

As for the demand for a service, the quantity demanded by the entrepreneurs is the profit-maximizing amount, which depends on the price of the service, the production functions, the price of output, and other prices. The production functions are unchanging in the model. The price of output varies during the equilibrating process, but it is simply a variable in the individual and market demand functions for the service. The entrepreneurs who demand a service can have no stocks of it on which to draw if there is a positive excess market demand. They start hiring at each new price of the service with no reserves of it and zero stocks of other commodities except land and capital goods. Consequently, the entrepreneurs' demand functions for the service do not change as a result of disequilibrium purchases of it. Thus, neither the market supply nor the market demand functions for services changes as a result of disequilibrium sales of them.

Fourth, variations of entrepreneurs' inventories of primary materials would change their supply functions for products. This problem was eliminated by Walras's assumption that they have no inventories; they use primary materials immediately upon their purchase (1877b, pp. 225, 244; 1889, pp. 208, 227).

Fifth, in constructing his equations, Walras assumed that there is no production of new capital goods and that capital goods are indestructible and imperishable. Thus, not only the total stock of capital goods but also the particular batch of goods in existence is constant. The model therefore does not cause the capital stock to change as a result of endogenous processes, nor therefore the supply functions for capital-good services insofar as they depend on the stock of capital goods. Consequently, Walras's equations are not invalidated by such changes. Walras achieved this, however, only at the cost of a loss of realism, as will now be explained. He constructed the supply function for any primary material or consumer commodity on the assumption that the amount of capital goods in the industry varies with each industry rate of output, for the reason that during the equilibrating process the number of firms in an industry changes and the size of the firms in the industry changes. Given his assumptions about the batch of capital goods, those changes force some peculiar conditions on his model. In each industry in which output increases, new firms are created and old ones expanded without the production of new buildings, machinery, or tools. The capital goods must come from firms that are abandoned or diminished in size. The capital goods in the model must therefore be nonspecific, that is, usable in any industry and perfectly mobile. If the wine industry is expanding and the fishing industry is contracting, the wharfs and boats and nets used in the latter must be perfectly usable on the hills and in the aging cellars of the vintners. Inasmuch as Walras identified different types of capital goods, each producing its own particular service and each of which has its own price, it is evident that the idea of a homogeneous capital-substance never occurred to him and that his consumer commodities model is essentially contradictory in regard to the kinds of capital goods that are actually in it and the kind that is required by its adjustment processes.

Sixth, disequilibrium sales of land and of capital goods would result in the acquisition of those resources during the equilibrating process by persons with preferences that differ from those of their original owners. That would change the set of supply functions for the services of the resources, and that would change the equilibrium prices of the services. Walras eliminated such sales, and thus their invalidation of his equations, by his assumption that there are no markets for land or capital goods. Walras assumed that each resource supplier controls, throughout the equilibrating process, constant maximum possible amounts of services (1889, p. 235). The cost in terms of loss of verisimilitude of that assumption, however, is severe. First, firms change size and are created and disappear without any changes in the amount of capital goods owned by any capitalist, which cannot be considered as a reasonable state of affairs. Second, there would either have to be institutions and other structural features that would prevent participants from being able to sell land or old capital goods, or participants would have to have preferences not to sell land or old capital goods, regardless of what happens to their prices and hence to their rates of return, each of which suppositions would be highly unrealistic. Walras did not introduce structural features that would eliminate the sales as a result of the model's character and workings, and he did not offer any rationale for why anyone in his model would have such preferences. Instead, he eliminated the sales by arbitrarily assuming they do not occur, an assumption that contradicts his general assumption of freedom to trade. The assumption that land and capital goods are not sold is therefore not defensible. From a purely logical point of view, however, it avoids the invalidation of Walras's equations.

The role of profits: Another disequilibrium phenomenon in the model is the payment of profits. There are no changes in the quantity of durable capital, so entrepreneurs do not reinvest the profits. The profits are revenue in excess of the amounts that are spent on inputs, and are therefore a true surplus. Walras indicated that the profits are taken by the entrepreneur (Walras 1877b, pp. 232–35; 1889, pp. 215–18), but regardless of whom their ultimate recipients are, the profits are used by them in their role as consumers, and since there is no saving, the profits are not saved. When Walras specified that income is one of the variables on which an individual's demand for a commodity depends, he defined it as the sum of the products of the amounts of services of land, labor, and capital goods sold by the consumer and their respective prices. The profits change the recipients' demand functions for consumer goods, introducing new variables into it, because the profits are varying augmentations of income that are a function of the price of the product sold by the entrepreneur minus its average cost. The result is that the demand equations set forth by Walras in relation to the model do not reflect the changes of demand that occur during the equilibrating process, and the equations of supply do not reflect the resulting changes of the pattern of production. Nevertheless, the payment of profits is not a source of a path-dependency of the model. As equilibrium is approached, profits approach zero, and when they are eliminated the patterns of demand and supply become those that are the outcome of the preferences of consumers and service suppliers, the maximum available amounts of services, the prices of goods and services, and the production functions. Those conditions are then free of the influence of the augmentations of income resulting from the transitory profits.

Path dependency in one model but not the other: The model shown in Figure 7.1 displays path-dependency. The supply curve for the product shows the actual amount that would be produced at each price that rules, not just the ex ante desired amount, and Walras assumed that supply functions are defined with no inventories. At prices higher than p_e, however, it is impossible for firms to sell all that they produce as soon as they produce it because the market quantity demanded is less than the quantity supplied. At those prices, there must be inventory accumulation. When that happens at one price, the quantities supplied in the industry at other prices would not be as large as before. In other words, the supply function in each industry changes during the equilibrating process. The result is that the price at which the final supply function and the demand function are equated is affected by the series of previous actual prices.

It is not an answer to this problem to say that Walras's supply functions represent the rates of supply at each price after all such adjustments have been worked out. The supply functions do not have that meaning in the model shown in Figure 7.1. They are supposed to describe the behavior of the producers during the adjustment process – that is, the rates of supply at alternative prices that may succeed each other fairly rapidly. Of course, those particular equilibrium curves shift as a consequence of changes of the prices of other commodities, but Walras's discussion of the market incorporates the assumption that the curves do not shift as a consequence of changes of the price and rate of sales of the industry's own output, an assumption contradicted by the behavior of the market to which the figure refers. When Walras's model employs the process shown in Figure 7.1, therefore, the equilibrium values are path-dependent and his equation system does not describe the model or give its equilibrium values.

Those problems do not arise for the model illustrated by Figures 7.2a and 7.2b. The equilibrating process illustrated for a particular market in those figures ensures that all output is sent to the market and is all purchased without delay. Consequently, there is no inventory accumulation by the producers to give rise to path dependency. Moreover, the model is free of path-dependency because there is no marketable economic wealth in it; it is purely a model of flows of input, output, income, and consumption. If preferences, resources, and technology are constant, as is true in Walras's model, path-dependency would be created by changes in the amounts of savings that people have, or of the amounts or the prices of their assets, but in the model there are no savings and no holdings of assets, except durable capital and consumer goods and land, which have no markets and therefore no prices. Walras never mentioned that feature of the model. Indeed, the evidence indicates that he thought that the model is path-dependent (see chs. 15 and 16).

VI. Conclusion

This chapter is a voyage of discovery into the model of consumer commodities in its various forms that Walras presented in the mature phase of his thought. The model is exceedingly simple and highly abstract. The available amounts of all economic resources are constant. The only commodities produced are services, primary materials, and consumer nondurable goods, or, in short, services and nondurable goods. The markets, including those for consumer commodities sold at retail, are organized and freely competitive. There is no saving. There is no using up of the capital goods that are employed in production, no accidents, and no obsolescence. The same is true of consumer durables. Any particular capital good can be moved and used in any production process. There are no sales of capital goods even though there are changes of their location, of the firms in which they are used, and of the uses to which they are put. Similarly, there are no markets for land or consumer durables. In the model discussed in relation to Figures 7.2a and 7.2b there are no business inventories of any kind, and no consumer inventories of nondurables.

Some of the assumptions Walras made to simplify the mature consumer commodities model detract seriously from its verisimilitude, and it is obviously not a model that can be used to explain or predict the behavior of the real economy. It is not, for example, a virtue of the model that it avoids the path-dependency that characterizes the real economy. Nevertheless, the mature consumer commodities model has laudable characteristics. The markets in the model are complete. For each good and service there is a physical locale in which the participants meet. Money is used in the markets. Both demanders and suppliers are able to make offers in the markets and are the persons that quote and change prices. The procedure they follow in changing prices – namely, Walrasian pricing – is specified. Moreover, the model is a remarkable pioneering construction because it deals with an interconnected system of markets that moves toward equilibrium by means of a process of disequilibrium hiring, disequilibrium production, and disequilibrium sales. Walras thus anticipated by many decades modern efforts to develop general-equilibrium models in which transactions and production occur in disequilibrium. His accounts of the adjustment processes are full of suggestive ideas and creative theorizing.

The mature consumer commodities model was a preliminary exercise. In subsequent chapters it will be seen that Walras replaced it with a comprehensive model in which he made very different assumptions about consumer commodities and consumer behavior.

The mature comprehensive model

CHAPTER 8

The structure of the mature comprehensive model

This chapter begins the examination of the comprehensive model that Léon Walras constructed during the mature period of his theoretical work. This model constitutes the culmination of his work on capital and on what he regarded as the essentials of general economic equilibration and equilibrium. The chapter answers fundamental questions about Walras's definitions, his assumptions about the nature of capital goods in the model, and his treatment of productive services, consumer commodities, participants, market institutions, money, and the types of economic activities with which the markets in the model are concerned.

I. Introduction

This chapter continues the study of the mature phase of Walras's theoretical work, which spanned the years 1878 to the mid-1890s. Chapters 6 and 7 dealt with his mature model of the production and sale of productive services, primary materials, nondurable consumption goods, and consumable services in an economy in which there is no saving and in which capital goods are not subject to wear and tear or accidents. Walras did not use that model in his mature comprehensive model, but he employed some of its features in developing the latter. By the "mature comprehensive model" is meant his all-inclusive mature model of general equilibration and equilibrium, which he introduced and largely completed in the lessons in the *Eléments* he titled "Theory of Capital Formation and of Credit." The model includes all the basic components of his theoretical system. Following the presentation of the principal features of the model in this chapter and in chapter 9, the details of its characteristics are explored in the subsequent five chapters.

In the mature comprehensive model, Walras assumed the production and sale of productive and consumable services and nondurable and durable consumer goods, introduced a submodel of markets for the pricing of old capital goods and other resources, and introduced submodels – henceforth often simply called models – of savings and of a number of aspects of the financing, production, sale, and rental of new capital goods and of other economic activities. By "durable goods" is meant goods that are used more than once. He developed the comprehensive model in three stages. In the

157

first, which is the subject of this chapter, he assumed that there are no inventories (1877b, p. 306; 1889, p. 312). In the second, he introduced inventories and explicitly considered money balances (ch. 9). In the third, he provided the details of the functioning of the money and loan market in the model (ch. 11). As contrasted with Walras's models of exchange with fixed aggregate stocks (ch. 3) and of the production and sale of nondurable consumer commodities, the major novel feature of the comprehensive model is the production and sale of new capital goods. Consequently, much of this chapter and of chapter 9 is concerned with the market activities associated with them, and chapter 10 is entirely devoted to them.

The mature comprehensive model, presented in the second and third editions of the *Eléments,* is a significant improvement over the version Walras published in the first edition. He not only refined and clarified the latter version but also changed its substance in some respects, added important new structural and behavioral elements, broadened the scope of his treatment, and increased the detail of the modeling. He drew on realistic elements concerning the structure and dynamic behavior of markets and used them in a scientific formulation. Nevertheless, the model was poorly understood by its readers during the nineteenth century, and indeed was not given much attention and was not discussed from the points of view taken in this book. The mature model is also vastly superior to the models that Walras presented in the last phase of his theoretical activity. Those models have been the exclusive source of modern ideas about his treatment of inventories, consumer durables, capital formation, and general equilibrium, so instead of deriving inspiration from the mature phase of his work, economists have drawn on the notions he conceived during the period of his intellectual decline. Thus the mature comprehensive model is a novel subject for the modern reader.

Several of the mature submodels dealing with capital goods have not previously been analyzed or even identified, and they are in great need of an explanatory treatment because they were not clearly presented by Walras and were not mature in the sense of being finished.[1] They do not have the elegant logical qualities of modern theory and, as mentioned in the introduction to this book and as will now be shown in detail, are far from constituting a seamless whole. They were an early attempt at theoretical construction in a complex field, characterized by speculations, brilliant insights, solid constructions, experiments, and mistakes. In short, Walras's mature work on capital, like many other pioneering and seminal works in economics, is brimming with suggestive ideas, not all of which are complete. For all these reasons,

---

[1] Walras first published models dealing with capital goods in 1876. He incorporated much of that work into the first edition of the *Eléments*. All the models of markets for capital goods that he developed in the mature phase of his theoretical studies were published in the second and third editions of the *Eléments*.

the model of markets relating to inventories and durable goods and the mature comprehensive model that includes it merit investigation.

In order to bring out clearly the characteristics of the structure of Walras's mature comprehensive model, the chapter will pose and answer the following fundamental questions. What are the characteristics of the marketplaces in the model? Is it a barter or a monetary model? What are the characteristics of used capital goods in the model? Where is the rate of net income determined? What is Walras's treatment of savings? Are there stocks and bonds in the model? Did Walras construct a genuine model of capital formation? Who supplies and demands capital goods that have been produced? Is the key to Walras's model of capital formation found, as he maintained, in the rental market for capital goods?

II. General characteristics of the markets

What are the characteristics of the marketplaces in the model?

Walras was careful to define his subject matter and to specify the structure and institutional characteristics of his mature comprehensive model. With one exception, the parameters he specified for it are exactly the same as the parameters of his model of nondurable consumer commodities. The exception is that in the latter, the batch of capital goods is a parameter, whereas in the mature comprehensive model there is net saving and investment. Briefly, the other parameters are the technology embodied in the production functions, the set of kinds of commodities, the preferences of the participants, the aggregate amounts of land and personal faculties, the maximum amounts of services providable from land and personal faculties, and the quantity of money.

Walras endowed the markets in his mature comprehensive model with features that make them functioning systems. He provided them with individuals who supply services and savings and who demand consumer goods and capital goods, with entrepreneurs who demand services and supply consumer nondurable and durable commodities and primary materials (1877b, p. 288; 1889, p. 277), and with "entrepreneurs who, instead of making primary materials or consumer goods, make new capital goods" (1889, p. XVI; 1896b, p. XV). He provided the participants in the model with marketplaces in which to trade. He had specified many of the structural features of marketplaces for primary materials, nondurable consumer goods, and consumable services in lessons in the *Eléments* prior to the ones on the comprehensive model, and made the marketplaces operating systems by furnishing them with institutions, physical structures, rules, and practices that enable the participants to quote prices and express their supplies and demands. Those markets are part of the comprehensive model in which he also included capital goods and other economic resources, and therefore they function in that model with the structure and behavioral characteristics he assumed in lessons that precede the ones on economic resources.

Noting that it is not possible to have a price except as a result of market activity, Walras began the task of constructing a model of "a market that we will call the market for capital goods on which these capital goods will be sold and purchased" (1877b, p. 273; 1889, p. 262). That sentence contains examples of two of Walras's terminological usages. First, he used the term "capital goods" to refer to land, personal faculties, and capital goods properly speaking because they are used more than once. By "capital goods properly speaking," Walras meant all inanimate produced goods that are used more than once, not just capital goods that are used to make other goods for sale. In this chapter, however, except when Walras is quoted, the term "capital goods" means only inanimate produced goods that are used more than once to produce goods for sale.[2] Thus, Walras included durable consumer goods, such as furniture, houses, jewelry, and clothing (1877b, pp. 222–23, 226; 1889, pp. 205–6, 209) in the category of capital goods, as he made clear when he wrote that "capital goods properly speaking . . . are consumed gradually. Houses and buildings deteriorate; furniture, clothing, objects d'art and luxury goods are used up. The same is true of buildings used by businesses, machines, instruments and tools" (1877, p. 226; 1889, p. 209). Walras noted that in the first stage of his comprehensive model he was principally concerned with capital goods properly speaking that are used to make other goods for sale (1877, p. 274; 1889, p. 262), and consequently those goods are also the principal concern of this chapter. Second, Walras often used the word "market" in the singular to refer to a group of markets. For example, with respect to the services of the three types of capital, he wrote that "it is appropriate to distinguish the market for the renting of capital goods proper from the market for the hiring out of land and of personal faculties" (1877b, p. 303; 1889, p. 311). Similarly, he wrote with respect to the sale of capital that "it is appropriate to distinguish the market for capital goods properly speaking from the market for land and personal capital" (ibid.). Nevertheless, within each general category that he called "a market," Walras indicated that there is a supply and a demand and a price for each particular kind of commodity, and thus assumed that each commodity grouped in the category is sold in its own market. Concerning capital goods represented by shares, for example, Walras assumed that they are all sold on one general market, the Bourse, and that there are many markets within the Bourse, one for each listed security. Accordingly, reference will sometimes

---

[2] Walras's terminology will be followed in other respects.

be made to "the market" for capital-good services or to "the capital goods market" or to "the market" for commodities of one type or another, but sometimes it will be indicated explicitly that Walras was dealing with a system of many markets, one for each kind of commodity.

When Walras wrote about markets for capital goods properly speaking he frequently meant markets in which goods that are used more than once to make other goods for sale are represented by stock certificates. He made it perfectly clear when that was his subject matter, as when he wrote that "it is necessary to distinguish the market for capital goods [properly speaking] from the market for land and for human capital. This market for capital goods is the *Bourse*" (1877, p. 304; 1889, p. 311). Unless otherwise noted, Walras's model of that market for capital goods is the one discussed in this chapter. It should also be noted that the model will sometimes be described as dealing with economic resources, by which is meant land, workers, and capital goods, as distinct from the services they provide.

Walras expected the reader to realize that the general characteristics of the markets for services and consumer commodities are also characteristics of the markets for capital goods and to understand that it was not necessary to repeat in detail the features of free competition. This is evident because he explicitly assumed that the capital-goods markets in his model are organized and have the other properties that make them freely competitive. He indicated this when he wrote regarding the securities market in the comprehensive model that

all attentive readers will recognize here what happens on the market of the Bourse when new capital goods, represented by their certificates, are exchanged there against savings in proportion to their incomes, in accordance with the mechanism of the raising and the lowering of prices, and will agree that my theory of capital formation, which rests entirely, I repeat, on the preceding theories of exchange and of production, is really what a theory of that nature ought to be: the faithful expression and exact explanation of the phenomena of reality (1889, p. XXII).[3]

Walras also indicated his assumption about the structure of the market for capital goods when he specified (1877b, p. 303; 1889, p. 311) that they are sold according to the organized and freely competitive mechanism that he assumed to be operative in his model of the Bourse (1874b, pp. 49–50; 1889, pp. 67–69).

A barter or a monetary model?

Jaffé contended that "the whole development up to and including [the theory of capital formation] presupposes a barter or moneyless economy, for Walras'

---

[3] It was noted in chapter 2 that in 1896, Walras changed this to read "the abstract expression and rational explanation of the phenomena of reality" (1896b, pp. XXI-XXII).

standard commodity (*numéraire*) is on a par with all other commodities or products, except that its value is taken as a standard of measurement of values" (Jaffé 1942, p. 37 [139–40]). If Jaffé was referring to the written pledges models that Walras presented in the fourth edition of the *Eléments* in lessons earlier than the ones on money, then he was correct. That is not, however, how Walras conceived of the model of the markets for capital goods that he presented in the mature phase of his thought, as is evident from a passage in which he concluded that in order for savings to be amassed and lent in his model, "numeraire capital" is necessary (1877, pp. 276–77; 1889, pp. 264–65). On that isolated occasion, however, he went on to make the curious implication that numeraire capital differs from money: "Let us also remark that, since we are abstracting from money, we must speak hencefor-ward not of *money* capital, but of *numeraire* capital" (1877, p. 277; 1889, p. 265). Walras thus asserted, first, that there is a numeraire; second, that there is no money; and, third, that there is a kind of capital funds in the model. The second assertion is incompatible with the third and with the monetary nature of Walras's model of capital. If numeraire capital does in fact differ from money, introducing it would have resulted in another model, but, as it turned out, Walras did not accurately describe his model in the foregoing quotation. Despite the passages quoted here and similar ones in the lessons on capital in the *Eléments,* he did not construct a barter model of capital in the mature phase of his work. If those passages are assertions that the model is one of barter, then they contradict the character of the model that he actually devel-oped. There is much evidence to that effect, as will now be shown.

Of decisive significance is that Walras not only stated that his models of capital are monetary but made the use of money an integral part of their structure and behavior. It is indubitable that the markets for services, primary materials, and consumer commodities that Walras included in the mature comprehensive model are monetary markets, as has been fully documented elsewhere (Walker 1994a). It would be absurd to suppose that he assumed that money is used in the consumer commodities markets in the comprehen-sive model but not in the capital-goods markets in that same model, or to suppose that payment is made for productive services with money but that the income recipients do not save in money. Near the conclusion of his lessons on capital, he wrote that it would be recalled that in discussing "the elements of production" he had made abstraction from circulating money and money savings (1877, p. 306; 1889, p. 312). It is true he did so in that discussion (1877, pp. 223–25; 1889, pp. 207–8), but he did not do so in his mature model of the production and sale of nondurable consumer commodi-ties, nor in his mature capital-goods model. He obviously did not mean he made that abstraction in the latter, because he immediately proceeded to state straightforwardly that there are "circulating money and money savings" in it

(1877, p. 306; 1889, pp. 312–13). Similarly, Walras made explicit the monetary nature of the capital-goods markets by stating in the first edition of the *Eléments* that he would deal with the "lending of savings *in money,* or *credit,* and the demand for productive new capital goods by the entrepreneurs" (1877, p. 273; emphasis added to "in money"). In the second edition, he again presented the statement about the "lending of savings in money" (1889, p. 261) and emphasized his intention by adopting the title "Theory of Capital Formation *and of Credit*" for the section on capital (1889, p. 259; emphasis added). In both editions, he dealt with "the equations of capital formation and of credit" (1877, pp. 291, 299; 1889, pp. 274, 281). In Walras's models, credit means the lending of *money:* "The capitalist forms his capital by successive savings and he lends the *money* to the entrepreneurs for a certain time; the entrepreneur converts this *money* into capital goods properly speaking and, at the maturation of the loan, pays back the *money* to the capitalist. That operation constitutes *credit*" (1877, p. 234; 1889, p. 217; emphasis added to "money").

Walras made many other unambiguous statements that the markets in the capital-goods model are monetary. In a lesson on the finances of the entrepreneur in which Walras considered "fixed capital" and "capital goods properly speaking," he naturally described the entrepreneur's balance sheet, including the aspects relating to capital goods and their profitability, in money terms (1877, p. 237; 1889, p. 220). Similarly, he specified that the demand for new capital goods is measured and expressed "in numeraire, whether by the savers themselves or by the entrepreneurs who have borrowed the savings in the form of *money* capital" (1889, p. XXII; 1896, p. XXI; emphasis added to "money"). Obviously, in that passage Walras stated that money is used and that it is the numeraire. "Numeraire capital" is not a real capital good like a machine or a tool; numeraire capital, Walras explained, must be distinguished from "capital *in kind*" (1889, p. 289). The former is, in fact, a medium of exchange, as Walras implied. In his model, the rate of interest "is manifested on the market for numeraire capital, which is to say, in the banking system" (ibid., pp. 288–89). He thereby indicated that he was using the term "numeraire capital" to refer to something that is not merely like money but is in fact identical to the money used by banks in the real economy. Thus "numeraire capital" is just a redundant term meaning "money."

It is abundantly evident from the monetary phenomena that Walras embedded in the construction of the models described here and in the following pages, and from the monetary terminology he used and is quoted as documentation, that they are monetary models in all respects, and notably in relation to the payment of incomes, saving, lending, rentals, repayments of loans, and purchases of capital goods and all other commodities. Walras's procedure reflects the fact that there is no way other than by money savings that savers could amass and then transfer purchasing power to the entrepreneurs, and, given the conditions of the model, no way other than by the use of money that payment could be made for capital goods in their markets. The savings of the capitalists are distributed by them among the producers of different capital goods through the monetary mechanisms described later, and therefore must be made in money. The numeraire capital borrowed by the entrepreneurs is spent by them in different services markets and in various markets for primary materials, using the numeraire as a medium of exchange. Moreover, all the markets for services and consumer goods, which are also a part of the comprehensive model in which there are new capital goods, are monetary markets. Thus the only way of reconciling his statement about "abstracting from money" with what he actually did is to suppose that he meant that he was not going to consider it explicitly in some respects in some of the passages in the lessons on capital formation, but intended to incorporate it into others. It would otherwise have to be concluded that he made contradictory statements about his model.

III. Markets for used resources

Land and personal faculties

One component of Walras's comprehensive model is his treatment of the market for land, and another is his treatment of the market for personal faculties. He specified that the quantities of those two types of resources are parameters for his model, on the grounds that they are not produced by the economic system (1877b, pp. 224, 276; 1889, pp. 207, 264). Land and personal capital are necessarily hired out in kind (1877b, pp. 234, 277; 1889, pp. 217, 265). In Walras's terminology, the landlords lend their land to the entrepreneurs and the workers lend their personal faculties to the entrepreneurs, and the entrepreneurs use the services of those resources. The fees for the services are paid by the entrepreneurs in money. The landlords and workers resume control of their land and personal faculties respectively when the contracts they have made expire.

The reason that the entrepreneurs demand those economic resources, Walras indicated, is that they yield valuable services, so the prices of land and personal faculties depend on the prices of those services (1877b, p. 274; 1889, p. 262). The latter prices are determined by supply and demand in the way indicated in the model devoted to the production and sale of consumer nondurable commodities. The price of land itself is equal to the gross price of its service divided by the rate of net income (1877b, pp. 224, 301; 1889, pp. 207, 308), the determination of which is discussed later. There is no subtraction from the gross price of land to arrive at a net price because there is no amortization or insurance of land (1877b, p. 278; 1889, p. 266). Personal faculties – human capital – are valued by calculating the net price of their service, which is the gross price minus charges for replacement and insurance, and by dividing the resulting net income by the rate of net income (ibid.). Of course, since there is no slavery, human capital is not bought and sold and its price is a virtual one (1877b, p. 303; 1889, p. 311).

What are the characteristics of used capital goods?

The other economic resource that is given in amount is the particular batch of capital goods properly speaking (1877b, p. 276; 1889, p. 264) in use at the beginning of the disequilibrium phase of the model. Walras began his analysis of markets for used capital goods by recognizing that in the real economy, the yields of different assets are not the same (1877b, pp. 302–3; 1889, p. 310). He wanted it to be true in his model, however, that old capital goods are maintained in the same state as new capital goods of the same type, so that he could focus on net saving and the growth of the capital stock and avoid the complications that would arise from differences in the rate of net income earned by different capital goods. He therefore made his model differ from reality in this connection in three respects. First, in the real economy, differences in risk and uncertainty cause differences in the valuations, amortization rates, and insurance premiums of capital goods. In his model, in contrast, Walras assumed that all conditions giving rise to such differences are absent (ibid.). Second, in the real economy, capital goods are not fully maintained, and may eventually be used up. In his model, in contrast, Walras assumed they are all fully maintained by the expenditure on them of amortization funds set aside from the income produced by the sale of the services of the good, at whatever rate is necessary to maintain the particular type of capital good. Third, in the real economy, capital goods are destroyed by accident and are often not fully insured and hence are not all replaced by the proceeds of insurance claims. In his model, in contrast, Walras assumed that insurance premiums are set aside from the income generated by a capital good at whatever rate is necessary for that particular type of good to be fully insured against its accidental destruction or damage, so they are fully replaced or repaired (1877b, pp. 274–75; 1889, p. 263).

The gross income generated by an old capital good is the price of the service it renders. The net income is the gross income minus the amortization of the capital good and the cost of insuring it (1877b, p. 279; 1889, p. 267). The net income divided by the price of the capital good is its rate of net income. Obviously the price of each old capital good is equal to its net income divided by the rate of net income.[4] Inasmuch as old capital goods are just like new capital goods in the highly special conditions of Walras's model, the net income of an old capital good and of a new capital good of a given type are the same, and the rate of net income that the former earns and that the latter will earn are the same. Therefore the prices of old capital goods are the same as the prices of new ones of the same type (1877b, p. 301; 1889, p. 308).

Since each type of capital good provides the same rate of return in Walras's model, there would appear to be no reason to sell one capital good in order to purchase another that would simply yield the same amount of money (1877b, p. 302; 1889, p. 309). Walras explained that there are, however, reasons to buy and sell capital goods in the model. He ensured this by introducing assumptions he described as being drawn from reality – namely, that there are on the one hand, people who save and therefore want to buy capital goods, and on the other hand, people who *want to dissave* and therefore want to sell capital goods (ibid.). In the passage in which he discussed this matter, Walras was evidently thinking about old capital goods, because he gave as an example a rental dwelling that is yielding a return (ibid.), and he may also have been thinking about old capital goods represented by stock certificates. He must have been thinking about old capital goods, because in his model there is a source of capital goods other than dissavers, which he would otherwise have had to recognize and thus alter his statements, namely, entrepreneurs who want to produce and sell new capital goods in order to make money, not to dissave.

Where is the rate of net income determined?

Walras's treatment of where the rate of net income is determined is one of the ways he changed the structure of his model after 1877. In that year, he wrote that the "principal result" of his study of the capital market was "the determination of the rate of net income on the market for numeraire capital – that is to say, on the market for productive services, in conformity with the law of supply and demand" (1877b, p. 300). The market for numeraire capital is the market for loans (which is not, despite Walras's statement, the market for productive services in his model). Thus he thought the rate of net income is determined on the market for loans. In 1889, however, he viewed "the price of lending numeraire capital" as the rate of interest (1889, p. 295), so it, and not the rate of net income, is manifested on the market for loans. He

---

[4] The terms in the equations that Walras used to show the relationship of the price of a capital good to the price of its service are arranged differently in the first and second editions of the *Eléments* (1877b, p. 280; 1889, p. 267).

asserted, in contrast to his 1877 treatment, that the rate of net income is determined, not on the market for numeraire capital nor on the services market in which capital goods are rented, but "on the market for capital goods, in conformity with the law of supply and demand" (ibid.).

In fact, Walras's definition of the rate of net income indicates that it cannot be determined in that market alone. The rate is the ratio of the net price of the service rendered by a capital good, which is determined in the rental market for the capital good, and the price of the good itself, which is determined in the market in which that type of good is sold. Walras should therefore have noted that in his model, the rate of net income is determined by what transpires in both the rental market for capital goods and the capital-goods market, which reflect what happens in other markets also. In his model, the price of the service of a capital good, the price of the good, the rates of interest and net income, and all other prices are mutually interdependent.

Walras also asserted that the rate of interest is not different "in any respect" from the rate of net income (1889, p. 288). He blurred their differences even more by stating that the former is manifested in the banking system but "in reality is determined on the market for capital goods properly speaking, that is to say, on the Bourse, as the rate of net income, which is the common ratio of the price of the net service to the price of landed capital, personal faculties, or capital goods" properly speaking (ibid., p. 289). In any event, more clearly put, Walras was expressing the idea that the activities that determine the rate of net income are the valuations of services and the economic resources that yield them and that the market for loans to finance the production of capital goods and circulating capital reflects those valuations. He also indicated, however, that the two rates are not the same phenomenon in his model. The rate of interest is the rate paid to borrow money; the rate of net income is the rate of return generated by the use and valuation of capital goods. As he expressed matters, the "two rates tend to equality" (ibid., p. 381). Accordingly, when he wrote as though the behavior of the participants would prevent the rate of interest from differing from the rate of net income (ibid., p. 288), he meant that they cannot be different in equilibrium.

IV. New capital goods

Walras had four interrelated objectives in his theorizing about new capital goods. First, he wanted to explain how their production is made possible; that is, to develop a model of saving and investment. Second, he wanted to model the institutional arrangements by which new capital goods are bought and used. Third, he wanted to develop a model of the disequilibrium behavior of a competitive economy in regard to the prices and rates of production of new capital goods. Fourth, he wanted to establish the equilibrium conditions in the markets in the model, including the equilibrium welfare conditions. To explore these subjects, he constructed or sketched several submodels.

What is Walras's treatment of saving?

To construct a model in which the stock of capital goods can be replenished and increased, Walras had to begin by dropping the assumption, made in his consumer commodities model, that income recipients consume all their income. In Walras's comprehensive model, an individual's income is derived from his sales of services. His supplies of services are functions of their prices, the prices of other commodities, given the amounts of economic resources that he owns and his preferences. His demands for consumer goods and services are determined by their prices, his preferences, and his income. The excess of an individual's income over his consumption therefore depends on his preferences and on the prices of the services of his land, human capital, and capital goods. More briefly, Walras wrote, apart from the conditions that he considered to be parameters, the excess depends on the rate of net income and on the prices of consumer goods and services (1877b, pp. 283–84; 1889, pp. 270–71). The excess is equal to the individual's income minus the value of the services that he consumes of his own and of other persons' land, personal faculties, and capital goods, and minus his expenditures on consumer services and nondurable goods (1877b, p. 281; 1889, p. 269).

Walras then examined the question of what the individual does with that excess. Writing as though a private person amortizes and insures his capital assets, as is true of a proprietor or a partner in a firm, Walras asserted that the individual can follow any of three alternatives. He may generate an excess that is just sufficient to maintain and insure his capital goods and is used for those purposes, and thus may neither add to nor decrease his stock of them. He may generate an excess that is insufficient fully to maintain and insure his capital goods, in which case his stock of them will diminish. He may have some part of the excess left over after fully maintaining and insuring his capital goods. That part is his saving (1877b, pp. 281–83; 1889, pp. 269–70). To construct a model in which the capital stock grows, the third alternative must be assumed to be followed. "It is necessary," Walras explained, "to assume [the existence of] landlords, workers, and capitalists who *save*, that is to say who, instead of demanding consumable services and consumer goods for the total value of the services they offer, demand new capital goods for a part of that value" (1889, p. XVI; 1896b, p. XV). Elsewhere he made clear that he defined "saving" as net saving after payments for amortization and insurance premiums. "It will be understood," he emphasized, "that it [the excess of income over consumption] is truly saving only if it is not only positive but also greater than the total of amortization and insurance of existing capital goods properly speaking" (1877b, p. 282, 1889, p. 270).

Walras therefore posited that an individual's savings is a function of the prices of all commodities, including the prices of services, of consumer goods, and the rate of net income (1877b, p. 283; 1889, p. 271). He described the savings function as empirically based, by which he meant that he specified the variables on which an individual's saving depends but did not derive the function from an underlying structure of preferences. He noted that the function could be given a theoretical foundation by considering the difference between present and future utility, but he chose not to do that, justly remarking that his equation system was not damaged thereby (1877b, pp. 283–84; 1889, p. 271).

Are stocks and bonds in the model?

Jaffé argued that Walras's theory of capital formation "was designed entirely in real terms" that precluded a place for securities (Jaffé 1980, p. 541 [359]). Jaffé alleged, uncertainly and obscurely, that "in Walras's static model, from which all transfer payments are excluded, securities, if they have any place at all, cannot be viewed as anything but a veil" (ibid., p. 542 [361]). It has already been shown that Walras's mature model was couched in monetary terms. Moreover, if Jaffé meant transfer payments in the usual sense of that term – such as pensions or welfare payments – his remark makes no sense; and if he meant that Walras excluded the transfer of money from one economic agent to another that occurs when a stock or a bond is sold, he was mistaken. That has already been made clear by the foregoing discussion, and now it will be shown that Jaffé's allegation that there are no securities in Walras's model is incorrect if that allegation is interpreted as an account of his mature model.

In regard to that model, it would be absurd to say that securities have no place, inasmuch as Walras stated, as has been shown, that the market for capital goods with which he was concerned "*is* the Bourse" (1877, p. 303; 1889, p. 311; emphasis added), an institution created for the purpose of buying and selling securities. It will now be shown that Walras not only made such statements but also incorporated the market for stocks and bonds directly and formally into his mature comprehensive model. Walras did not present his *detailed* model of the securities market in the lessons on capital goods but in the section of the *Eléments* devoted to the theory of exchange with fixed total amounts of the assets (1874, pp. 49–51; 1889, pp. 67–69) and in the article on the Bourse (1880b, 1880c) to which reference has already been made. The model in the first part of the *Eléments* deals with the mechanics of the process of buying and selling them on the Bourse. Jaffé tried to dispose of it by contending that it is a "quasi-anecdotal narrative," not part of Walras's theoretical work (Jaffé 1967, p. 4 [225]). Jaffé misinterpreted Walras's work in that regard. Walras's treatment of the securities market in the first part of the *Eléments* is a full-fledged model with a theoretical nature that is evident from his use in it of the concepts of supply and demand functions, of equilibrium, and of the convergence to equilibrium of the price and the desired market demand and supply quantities (1877b, pp. 49–51; 1889, pp. 67–69; ch. 4). His extension of the model in his article deals with the sources and uses of savings as well as with the mechanics of exchange of securities. Walras adopted the properties of his model of the securities market – the "*marché type*" – in all the markets for different commodities in the comprehensive model and incorporated it directly into the mature comprehensive model as his model of the Bourse. He stated, as has been noted, that "all attentive readers will recognize" in the submodel of capital goods "what happens on the Bourse when the new capital goods, represented by their certificates, are brought there to be exchanged against savings" (1889, p. XXII); and squarely in the middle of his exposition of capital formation he introduced the determination of the rate of net income as a phenomenon that occurs on the Bourse (ibid., p. 289).

Totally decisive on this matter is that in the last part of his lessons on capital goods, Walras specified that the securities market is part of his comprehensive model. He explained that he had taken up the securities market in the early part of the *Eléments* to give a preliminary idea of exchange, but that he also wanted to develop a model of barter of consumer commodities, so he had to put the monetary model of the Bourse aside temporarily (1874b, p. 52; 1889, p. 70). In a lesson on capital and the comprehensive model, he wrote that he was fulfilling his promise to return to the study of the securities market, which he had examined to discover the characteristics of a freely competitive organized market and which he had "put aside in order not to return to it until the present, after having successively taken account of all the complications of exchange, of production, of capital formation, and of credit" (1877b, pp. 303–4; 1889, p. 311). That does not mean that securities are absent from Walras's initial exposition of capital formation but simply that he had wanted to defer a detailed discussion of the securities market. When he made the comment just quoted, he had not finished his discussion of his model of capital formation, and so he immediately proceeded to emphasize that the system of eight sets of equations (1877b, p. 289; 1889, p. 278) – which he had developed earlier in the lessons on capital formation in relation to his mature comprehensive model – refers to the securities market as well as to other markets. He asserted that the equations take account of "all the variations of prices that occur there" – namely, on the Bourse (1877b, p. 304; 1889, p. 311). He then gave two examples of the types of securities transactions that are included in the capital-goods model and therefore in the comprehensive model of which it is a part. The first deals with shares and the second with bonds:

We have, *in the system [8] of equations,* the means of discussing all the variations of prices that occur. If the capital (K) is a railroad, and p_k is an annual sum received as a dividend, the price P_k in numeraire of the shares of the railroad will vary because of past or expected variations in the dividend. If the capital (K′) is a capital sum lent to a factory or to a State, and if $u_{k'}$ is a rate corresponding to the risks of bankruptcy of the factory or of the State, the price $P_{k'}$ of the bonds of the factory or of the State will vary because of the past or expected variations of those risks (1877b, pp. 303–4; 1889, p. 311; emphasis added).

Walras continued in that vein, discussing the forms of the demand and supply functions for the assets, and concluded that it thus becomes comprehensible how "on the market of the Bourse, the raising or lowering of the price" of securities affects the supply and demand quantities of them (1877b, p. 304; 1889, p. 312).

Did Walras construct a genuine model of capital formation?

To answer that question, it is necessary to examine the salient features of Walras's use of the terms "new capital goods" and "existing capital goods" in the submodels. It is important to know whether or not he meant that new capital goods are planned. There are passages in the *Eléments* that, if they were the only ones Walras had written on the subject of savings and real capital, would lead to the conclusion that he did not have a model of capital formation. In those passages, real saving and investment have already occurred before the goods become the subject of action by the participants in the model. He treated the quantity of real saving and investment as a postulate, and dealt only with the question of the pricing of a given stock of newly produced capital goods. Ordinarily in the *Eléments* he used the term "new capital goods" to mean capital goods that have been constructed, and hence are "existing" just like used ones, but are new in the sense that they have not been sold or used. In passage after passage, he referred to new capital goods being constructed and then subsequently being brought to market. For example, he stated that entrepreneurs "will fabricate certain quantities of new capital goods. Then they will come to sell these new capital goods on the capital goods market" (1889, p. 280). Unequivocally in those sentences, Walras stated that new capital goods have been produced and are then brought to market. Moreover, he gave a formal definition of "new capital goods" as goods that are "momentarily unproductive of income, on sale by their producers as products: newly constructed houses and buildings on sale; plants, animals, furniture, clothing, objects d'art, luxury goods, machines, instruments and tools, in inventories of shops or on display for sale" (1877, p. 223; 1889, p. 206). The quotation indicates that new capital goods are held in inventories and on display for sale; they are not merely planned but existing. In those passages, therefore, Walras regarded new capital goods as being already produced and differing from existing capital goods only by being unsold and unused, and he was therefore not dealing with a genuine model of investment and capital accumulation.

It is a weakness of Walras's exposition of his model of capital accumulation in the *Eléments* that he did not explicitly state that securities are offered on the Bourse to finance planned investment. Nevertheless, there are a few passages in the *Eléments* in which Walras unambiguously used the term "new capital goods" to mean capital goods that are planned and hence are yet to be produced. In one such passage, he referred to "capital goods properly speaking, existing *or to be produced*" (1877, p. 279; 1889, p. 267; emphasis added). Even so, that passage related to the production functions and not to the processes of saving, planning investment, and the pricing and sale of new capital goods.

Similarly, Walras's discussion in the *Eléments* of the difference in the attitude of savers toward "new" and "existing" capital goods (1877, pp. 302–3; 1889, p. 310) has to be interpreted with care. His remarks in that regard refer to the real economy, in which there are different degrees of uncertainty about costs and the income that will be derived from different capital goods. Nevertheless, his usage of terms in his discussion of the real economy throws light on the meanings he attached to those same terms in the construction of his model of capital formation, because he stated that in order to provide a reason for individuals to buy and sell capital goods "it is necessary to borrow some decisive circumstances from reality and from experience" (1877, p. 302; 1889, p. 310). He did not state that new capital goods are planned rather than simply unsold and unused prior to the sale of the associated securities (1877, pp. 302–3; 1889, p. 310). He explained, however, that savers are afraid to buy new capital goods because of their uncertain incomes. They prefer to buy existing capital goods, by which he meant old stock certificates, because the incomes they yield are more certain. In contrast, speculators subscribe to new capital goods (1877, pp. 302–3; 1889, p. 310). Thus he used the verb "to subscribe" in reference to the placement of funds, with the likely implication that speculators finance planned investments. Even there, however, he referred to the amount of income from new capital goods being not as well-known as that of existing capital goods, as though the new capital goods have just been put in service. Of course, he could have meant that the income of the new capital goods is uncertain because it is just a prediction, the goods not having yet been sold and put into service, or conceivably having not yet been produced, but he did not state those things directly in the *Eléments*.

In fact, however, Walras elaborated on that discussion, which he had first published in the *Eléments* in 1877, in a theoretically informed and molded treatment of the real Bourse that he presented in the article mentioned earlier. Walras wrote in that article that he was dealing with "that branch of credit which treats the transformation of savings into new capital goods, otherwise called capital formation" (1880a, p. 456 [404]).[5] He used the term "new capital goods" to mean planned investment or investments that have not been completed and therefore have need of additional financing, distinguishing "old securities that are yielding an established return, in consequence known and evaluated, and new securities *in the course of being created,* and for which, in consequence, the future is still uncertain" (1880a, p. 455 [403]; emphasis added). Walras gave as an example the planning of the formation of a new railroad. Engineers project the costs of production and financial experts project the revenues from the sale of the product. "It is necessary to portray the engineers and the financiers making the studies and the calculations relative to such and such new business, then the men who, after these studies and these calculations, form a society or a company of which they are the administrators and directors, and issue stocks and bonds for the amount of social capital of which they have need. They produce securities just as industrialists produce manufactured objects" (ibid., p. 459 [406]). If it is not evident that the enterprise will be profitable, capital funds will not be made available in response to the appeal to sell the shares in the enterprise. Walras thus made it clear that the new securities are sold to finance planned investment; the funds obtained from their sale are "consecrated to the creation of new capital goods" (ibid., p. 456 [404]).

Here is how the process works. It has been noted that Walras stated that many savers prefer to purchase old securities because the income from them is more certain than from new ones. He then explained that "among all the securities sold on the Bourse, it is above all these new securities that are the subject of speculation. In effect, in order to buy the new securities it is necessary to have new capital, that is to say savings" (ibid., pp. 455–56). To cause the new savings "to be exchanged for the titles of ownership of these new capital goods, that is what speculation proposes to do" (ibid.). The new securities representing capital goods that are not started or not completed are purchased by speculators such as credit institutions and bankers. The money provided by the speculators is used to construct new capital goods. They subsequently sell the securities, after the capital goods have been produced and are in operation, to savers. "The speculators always have in their possession a certain number of securities that they sell to capitalists.. . . And as soon as they have thus sold the capital goods that have been formed, they buy others that are *in the course of being formed*" (ibid., p. 458 [406]; emphasis added).

[5] The numbers in brackets give the pagination of the article in 1898b.

In summary, "the stocks and bonds thus issued ... pass through two distinct phases. They are first purchased by the institutions that provide credit for capital goods, by bankers and by speculators, who keep them or resell them to each other during the entire period of construction. It is then that these securities are speculative securities, the price of which is determined in the Bourse" (ibid., p. 459 [407]). Then "the period of construction is finished, the value of the business is known. The securities then become investment grade securities, the price of which is established according to the income [they yield] and they are purchased by the capitalists. The securities are *graded*. The work of speculation is then finished; its profit or loss is determined. That is how speculation is the intermediary between saving and new capital goods" (ibid.).

In light of that discussion, it seems likely Walras believed his account in the *Eléments* made it clear that he was referring to the purchase of securities by speculators to finance planned investment and to the subsequent purchase of those securities by savers. Nevertheless, Walras did not incorporate the material on uncertainty and speculation in that account into the comprehensive model presented in the *Eléments*, because such matters were, he explained, properly a part of applied economics. He would, he wrote (1877, p. 302; 1889, p. 310), put them into his course devoted to that type of study, and he subsequently did so by reprinting his article on the Bourse that elaborated on those matters in his volume of applied economic studies (1898b, pp. 401–45).

There can be no doubt that other parts of the *Eléments* are also concerned with the construction of a genuine model of capital formation – namely, those which present a model of the market for loans. In that submodel, Walras specified that money is saved and lent to finance planned investment. "The capitalist forms his capital by saving in money" (1877, p. 277; 1889, p. 265) and he uses those funds to finance real capital formation. "He lends this money to the entrepreneur" (ibid.). Capital goods, with the exception of buildings and, on occasion, furniture and instruments, are "hired out" – that is, lent – not in kind but "in money" (1877, pp. 234, 277; 1889, pp. 217, 265). The money savings are used by the entrepreneurs to buy inputs that they transform into capital goods (ibid.). At the expiration of the period of the loans, they pay back the money to the capitalists (1877, p. 234; 1889, p. 217). Furthermore, it has been shown that Walras formally incorporated his model of the Bourse into his mature comprehensive model. It can be accepted that he intended his remarks in the *Eléments* about speculation on the Bourse to be an *application* of his model to a situation in which there are different degrees of uncertainty regarding different planned investments, inasmuch as his remarks appear to refer to the processes he described in his article on the Bourse.

It can therefore be concluded that Walras alluded in the *Eléments* to the sale of stock certificates and bonds to finance the construction of capital goods that are still in the planning stage or are partially finished at the time the securities are sold. The financial processes on the loan market and the Bourse in Walras's model genuinely lead to capital formation because they show how people's decisions to save permit resources to be used in the production of capital goods instead of consumer goods. The processes channel purchasing power into the hands of the entrepreneurs so they can purchase and hire the services and resources necessary to produce new capital goods. Thus, Walras was able to make the "assumption of the production and of the supply of productive new capital goods" (1877, p. 273; 1889, p. 261), and was able to show how those processes occur as a function of the workings of his model. Real saving and investment occur in his model when the capital goods are constructed.

V. The sale and rental of capital goods

Who supplies and demands capital goods that have been produced?

It has been shown that Walras considered not only planned investment but also what happens to new capital goods after they have been produced. His work on the latter matter will now be examined. To provide his comprehensive model with a market in which their sales could take place, he sketched the structural features of two submodels. In one, he observed regarding the supply side that "it is necessary to assume that the entrepreneurs, instead of producing [non-durable] consumer goods, have produced new capital goods" (1877, p. 276; 1889, p. 264; in 1877 this reads "have produced new capital goods in order to sell them"). He emphasized that the capital goods are first produced and then brought to the market: entrepreneurs "will fabricate certain quantities of new capital goods. Then they will come to sell these new capital goods on the capital goods market" (1889, p. 280), by which in this context he meant the Bourse. He meant that producers in the model figuratively bring produced capital goods to the Bourse and literally sell them by means of selling new securities that represent the goods. About the demand side, he assumed that the demanders of those goods are savers. "It is necessary to assume that there are landlords, workers, and capitalists who, having bought consumer goods and services for a sum less than the total of their incomes, have the means of buying these new capital goods with the difference" (1877, p. 276; 1889, pp. 264–65). They use their money savings to buy shares and thus to buy capital goods from the entrepreneurs that have produced them.

The securities issued by any given firm are offered and demanded and are

priced by the Walrasian process. Walras explained the price of the newly
constructed capital goods as being the outcome of traders' behavior in relation
to the amount of money saving on the one hand and the amount of produced
new capital goods on the other: "A certain sum of savings, on the one hand,
and certain quantities produced of new capital goods, on the other hand,
being given, these savings and these new capital goods are exchanged for
each other on a *market of new capital goods* according to the mechanism of
the raising and lowering of prices" (1889, p. XVI; 1896, p. XV; and see, for
example, 1877, pp. 276–77; 1889, pp. 264–65). This is "what happens on the
market of the Bourse when new capital goods, represented by their certificates, are exchanged there in proportion to their incomes, in accordance with
the mechanism of the raising and lowering of prices" (1889, p. XXII). That
is not a model of capital formation because the capital goods have already
been financed and produced. Nevertheless, in the real economy, firms sometimes use the proceeds from new securities sales to retire debt, and that must
be what happens in Walras's submodel. Thus it explains how the production
of new capital goods that is financed by loans is subsequently "justified," in
J.A. Schumpeter's sense of the word, by the acquisition of the assets by
savers through purchases of shares and the repayment of the loans by the
debtors.

In the other submodel, Walras specified that savers "in part" save in
numeraire and lend the money to producers to enable them to acquire capital
goods for use in their businesses. As he expressed matters, the savers "hire
out" – lend – the value of "new capital goods evaluated in numeraire to those
entrepreneurs who produce products" (1889, p. 288). Therefore the savers do
not themselves buy new capital goods; instead, "it follows that it is the
entrepreneurs that produce products, who demand the new capital goods on
the market" and not the capitalists, the creators of the savings (1877, p. 277;
1889, p. 265). The entrepreneurs "will present themselves, in place of the
savers, as buyers of the new capital goods on the market for those capital
goods" (1889, p. 288). The suppliers of the capital goods are the entrepreneurs who have produced them. After the entrepreneurs who buy the capital
goods have generated revenue with their use, they pay the savers back their
money (1877, p. 277; 1889, p. 265). It appears that the capital goods have
already been produced before the activity described in the model takes place,
and if so, that submodel is also not one of capital formation.

Is the key to the model of capital found in the rental market for capital goods?

Walras stated that the creators of savings "in part" rent out capital goods "in
kind on the market for [capital good] services to the entrepreneurs who

produce products" (1889, p. 288). After writing that the rate of net income is determined "on the market for capital goods, that is to say on the Bourse," Walras asserted that "it is seen here clearly that the key to the entire theory of capital is found in this elimination of the lending of capital *in numeraire* and in the exclusive consideration of the lending of capital *in kind*" (1889, p. 289),[6] the latter activity being the renting out of capital goods. Presumably he meant that his subject matter is both the acquisition by savers of capital goods on the Bourse and their renting of the goods to entrepreneurs. In any case, he erred in stating that the key to the whole of the broad subject of the theory of capital, including the theory of saving and investment, is found by consideration of the renting out of capital goods. Capital goods rented out have already been produced, so although the structure of their rental market and their rental prices are relevant for a model of saving and investment, their market is a different aspect of economic behavior. If Walras had in fact concentrated on the lending of capital in kind he would have confined his model to a secondary feature of the economics of capital goods. Certainly he could not have found the key to the theory of capital in the rental market. In his model, the prices of capital goods are only partially the outcome of what happens in that market. Furthermore, in the real economy, most of the capitalists who acquire stocks on the Bourse do not rent out the capital goods that they thereby come to own. They hire entrepreneurs to operate the capital goods. The exceptions are firms that are formed and capitalized for the purpose of buying capital goods and renting them out, but even so, the acquisition of the shares of those firms and the functions that are subsequently exercised by the owners because of owning the shares are not ones of renting out capital goods, and the capital goods bought by such firms are rented by them on a market totally different from the Bourse.

Walras's exposition of the rental market for capital goods is confusing because he neglected to mention the sequence of economic behavior that links the Bourse and the rental market for capital goods. After stating that "the key to the entire theory of capital is found in this elimination of the lending of capital *in numeraire* and in the exclusive consideration of the lending of capital *in kind*," he immediately went on to write that "the market for numeraire capital thus having nothing other than a practical and not a theoretical interest, we will leave it aside to return to the market for capital goods and search there for the equilibrium price of new capital goods" (1889,

---

[6] Contrary to Jaffé's interpretation of that passage (Jaffé 1980, p. 541 [359]), Walras did not mean that he was going to develop a barter theory of capital formation. By "the lending of capital *in kind*" he meant instead that he wanted his model of that particular type of economic activity to be one in which savers buy capital goods and then rent them out, instead of making loans. Renting out capital goods is the act of lending in kind, but the savers save in money and buy the capital goods with money, and the rental fees are paid in money.

p. 289). In the first of those sentences, he referred to the necessity of studying the rental market for capital goods – the market for the services of capital goods in which capital is lent (rented) in kind. In the second, however, without noticing the change in his subject matter and as though he were developing the logical consequences of the first sentence, he stated that in order to find the prices of capital goods it is necessary to study their market, the Bourse. That is not the market on which capital is lent in kind; it is the market on which shares of enterprises and their bonds are sold for money.

Fortunately, Walras did not carry out his plan to "leave aside" the market for numeraire capital and give "exclusive consideration" to the rental market for capital goods. Instead, he retained the market for capital funds on which the lending of numeraire capital occurs – namely, the loan market, and he retained what he called the market for capital goods – namely, the securities market, as the central parts of his model of saving and investment. He argued that the market for capital funds reflects the fundamental forces manifested in the market for capital goods, and he did in fact "return to the market for capital goods" to "search there for the equilibrium price of new capital goods" (1889, p. 289).

The major deficiency of Walras's exposition is the confusion he engendered throughout the *Eléments* between the prices of capital goods and the prices of shares of corporations. In the examples he gave, he even appeared to define the capital good as the entire enterprise, so it appears as though the price of that capital good and the total value of the shares of the corporation are the same thing (1877, p. 303; 1889, p. 311). Thus, in the passage reproduced earlier, he wrote initially as though the price P_k of a railroad (K) and the price of the railroad corporation are the same, and similarly as though the price of a company that constructs and operates a canal is the price of that canal and the associated physical and administrative installations. Nevertheless, by "the prices of capital goods" that are determined on the Bourse he meant the prices of shares, as he indicated by proceeding to state that P_k is not the price of the company but the price of one of its shares (ibid.). In general, the value of a share is obviously not the same as the price of any specific capital good. For example, let it be assumed that a firm produces tractors and combines, which it sells at different prices, and that the firm has sold shares that are currently valued at $79.00 each and at $100 million in the aggregate. It is sufficient to observe that the firm sells the products at different prices to make clear that the price of its shares cannot be the same as the prices of the capital goods it produces. Moreover, the different capital goods that constitute the physical assets of the firm – for example, its factory building, its assembly line equipment, its trucks – would sell for a variety of different prices if sold individually. Obviously, those prices are also different from the price of one of its shares. Walras's model of sales of securities on the Bourse does not indicate what the prices of either the products or the individual assets are; they cannot be deduced from the value of the shares sold on the Bourse. To find, for example, the price of a tractor in a model it is necessary to go to the market for tractors, to examine the supply produced by the firm and other firms, and to identify the demand – quite different from the demand for the shares of the firm – for tractors, and find the price established by the workings of the multimarket system. There is of course a relation between the prices of a firm's products and the value of the firm, but Walras's model of capital formation does not identify it. A second deficiency of his model is that it does not contain a process of the financing and valuation of unincorporated enterprises.

It is gratifying to know that Walras did develop a model of the determination of the prices of specific capital goods. The process in the model is one of capital formation but does not focus on the channeling of money savings into investment. There are many instances in which Walras wrote about capital goods such as tractors and combines and the determination of their prices in their own markets rather than the value of the shares of corporations. He did that on the many occasions when he specified that the sum of the amounts spent on the inputs used to make a unit of a capital good equals the price of the good – not, of course, the price of a share. He did that when he described how the prices of capital goods are raised or lowered until they are equal to their average cost of production. That is quite different from the pricing of the shares of the corporation, regarding which, it would, of course, be absurd to say that they are produced until their average cost equals the share price. Evidently Walras was dealing with the pricing of new capital goods – physical instruments of production such as tractors and combines. In examining his true model of the pricing of specific capital goods, which is considered in the next chapter, his occasional unfortunate interjection of the statement that new capital goods are priced on the Bourse will be disregarded. His discussion of the Bourse has been and will continue to be relegated to its correct place as an account of how corporations are valued in the model and of how the rates of return on bonds and shares are determined.

VI. Conclusion

This chapter has answered the fundamental questions it posed about the structure of the comprehensive model that Walras developed in the mature phase of his thought. First, it has explained the characteristics of the markets in the model, showing that he laid out the components of an impressively comprehensive multicommodity, multimarket model. He assumed that all markets are freely competitive and organized. He outlined the basic structure of the markets for productive services, consumer commodities, land, personal

faculties, used capital goods, loans, stocks, bonds, planned and newly produced capital goods, and of markets in which the rental of capital goods
occurs. Second, the chapter has shown that the model is monetary. Third, it
has explained the characteristics of old capital goods in the model. Fourth, it
has established that the rate of net income is determined in both the rental
market for capital goods and in the stock market. Fifth, it has explained
Walras's submodel of individual saving behavior. Sixth, it has demonstrated
that there is a securities market in the model. Seventh, it has shown that
the comprehensive model contains the fundamental elements of a genuine
submodel of capital formation: money savings, planned investment, means of
channeling the savings to entrepreneurs, and their use of the funds to construct new capital goods. Eighth, it has explained who supplies and demands
capital goods that have been produced. Ninth, it has shown that some of the
keys to Walras's model of capital formation are found in his submodels of
the market for loans and of the financing of corporations on the Bourse. The
other keys are found in his model of the production and pricing of specific
capital goods, to which we now turn.

CHAPTER 9

The equilibrating processes in the mature comprehensive model

This chapter is concerned with aspects of the second stage of Walras's mature comprehensive model. He developed the second stage by assuming the existence of inventories and by explicitly considering money balances. The chapter investigates the equilibrating processes in the markets, showing that the model is characterized by disequilibrium production and sales of all types of commodities. It examines the conditions of the variables in general equilibrium. Finally, it assesses the capacity of Walras's equation system to identify the equilibrium values of the variables in his model.

I. Introduction

This chapter continues the examination of the mature comprehensive model. The first concern is to identify the structural properties of the second stage of the model, which Walras presented, like the first, in the lessons of the *Eléments* that also deal with new capital goods. It is shown how Walras began by identifying the components of national wealth, and then introduced business and consumer inventories and made explicit some features of the holding of money balances. The chapter goes on to examine the actions of the participants in the markets and the dynamic behavior of the variables, with particular attention to the market for new capital goods. In dealing with the behavior of the model in disequilibrium, it shows the reconciliation of two seemingly contradictory phenomena: the occurrence of trade only at equilibrium prices during the adjustment process, and the fact that the model is not in equilibrium at those prices. It also examines the equilibrium conditions of the model, and investigates whether the equations that Walras presented in connection with it are descriptive of its general equilibrium and whether their solutions are its equilibrium values.

II. The structure of the second stage

The components of the capital stock

Walras's first objective in the elaboration of the second stage of his model was to identify and classify the constituents of the capital stock in it and to devise a method of measuring and summing them. When Walras had used the unqualified term "capital" in earlier lessons, he meant land, human capital, and capital goods. When he wrote about capital in his classification of the wealth in the second stage of his model, however, he did not include natural resources and human faculties because he meant the total wealth produced by the economic system. Furthermore, he explained that he was not interested in analyzing how much there is of each type of component of produced total wealth. In a given economic state, he assumed, the amounts result "from the nature of things"; that is, from the conditions of production and consumption (1877b, p. 306; 1889, p. 312). He remarked that in examining wealth he assumed, as always, that markets exist and that there are economic processes through which productive services are transformed into products, fixed capital, and circulating capital (ibid.).

The first component of the total capital stock in Walras's model is the circulating capital held by consumers in their personal inventories. Walras specified that this capital has three components: the consumer goods in the possession of consumers that can be used only once and are then replaced, the numeraire held as a commodity, and the numeraire held as money (ibid.). The latter is divided into two parts. A certain amount of the numeraire is held as money in transactions balances and a certain amount as money in savings balances (ibid.). Thus, Walras defined wealth as including not only physical capital but also money, which is reasonable in a model with a commodity money. He then obtained a single number to measure the consumers' aggregate circulating capital by multiplying the quantity of each consumer nondurable good held in personal inventories by the price of the good and summing the results to obtain the total money value of such inventories. To that total he added the total amount of the numeraire held as a commodity times its price of unity, and the totals of all consumers' transactions and savings balances (ibid.).

When Walras considered the nature of a numeraire commodity used as money, he often indicated that he was thinking of it as being silver or gold (see, for example, 1877b, pp. 183–91; 1889, pp. 433–40). If so, the numeraire held as a commodity by consumers is such objects as gold bracelets and rings, silver ornaments and silverware – namely, durable goods that are used many times, yielding a stream of consumable services. In that event, Walras's inclusion of the amount of the numeraire held as a commodity as a part of consumers' circulating capital is an error. He should have classified gold and silver commodities with consumers' durable capital goods because they do not circulate – that is, they are not used only once and then replaced. Walras also indicated, however, that in principle, money could be a nondurable consumer commodity such as wine or cigars (Walras 1877b, pp. 174, 178; 1889, p. 376). If that were the case in his model, his classification scheme would be consistent, although it would involve an assumption that is not true regarding money in any modern economy.

The second component of the total capital stock in the model is the fund of circulating capital held by entrepreneurs. Walras began his discussion of it as part of an analysis of the rate of interest (1889, p. 295). By circulating capital in that context he meant goods that are produced and sold and are replaced, as distinct from the broader definition shortly to be examined. He indicated that since a market exists in his model for the lending of money, it can be lent for more than one purpose. Since money is lent to finance the production of fixed capital in his model, he stated that he could and would assume that money is also lent to finance the production of circulating capital (ibid.). About circulating capital, the entrepreneurs borrow money to finance the purchase of primary materials which they put into inventory to replace those that they have used, and they borrow money to buy other inputs which they use with the primary materials to replace the consumer goods that they have sold out of their inventories (ibid.). Apart from the effects of certain frictions, the money lent to finance circulating capital is lent at the same rate of interest as the money lent to finance fixed capital. This follows from the fact "that it is completely indifferent to the capitalist who lends numeraire whether the entrepreneur who borrows it transforms the numeraire into machines, instruments, tools, or into primary materials held in his inventory and products on display that are for sale" (ibid.).

In his broader definition of business circulating capital, introduced in his discussion of the measurement of wealth, Walras identified five components: the amount of the numeraire commodity that businesses hold in inventory for use in the production of other commodities or to be worked up into a saleable product; the amount of the numeraire commodity held as money in business transactions balances; the money value of the new capital goods that firms have produced and are holding for sale, obtained by multiplying the amount of each good by its price and adding the results together for all such capital goods; the money value of the primary materials held by firms in inventories; and the money value of the consumer goods held by enterprises in inventories (1877b, p. 306; 1889, p. 313). The sum of the consumer and business circulating capital is the total amount of circulating capital in the model.

The third component of the total capital stock in the model is fixed capital that has been purchased and is in use. In this paragraph, for simplicity of expression, "capital" means durable goods whether they are used to make goods for sale or not. Of course, fixed capital is not a new component of Walras's modeling inasmuch as he had introduced it at the beginning of his construction of his mature model of the production and sale of nondurable consumer commodities. The capital goods are fixed in the sense that they are used more than once and thus render a stream of services. Some of the capital goods are held by consumers. Those include objects such as furniture, houses, and jewelry. Some are used in firms. Those include buildings, machines, and tools. Walras multiplied each used durable capital good by its price in order to be able to sum the amounts.

Through the procedures indicated in the two previous paragraphs, Walras obtained a measure of the total capital in the model (1877b, pp. 306–7; 1889, p. 313) – namely, the sum of the consumers' and producers' circulating capital and fixed capital (1877b, p. 307; 1889, p. 313).

Inventories, money, and the equation system

In the comprehensive model that appears in the second and third editions of the *Eléments,* presented prior to the lesson (33) on the details of the loan and money market, there are money, transaction balances, savings balances, loan and securities markets, and business and personal inventories. All the components of the structure of Walras's mature comprehensive model were in place, and he proceeded to analyze its functioning with "all the accessory phenomena of which we had made abstraction being reinserted" (1877b, p. 307; 1889, p. 314). He noted (1877b, p. 306; 1889, p. 312), however, that he was reserving the detailed discussion of money for a subsequent section of the *Eléments* (ch.11).

Walras believed that inventories and money balances have no effect on the system of eight sets of equations that he had developed in reference to the first stage of the model (1877b, p. 307; 1889, p. 313). Therefore, he explained, he was not introducing those phenomena as separate variables in the equations alongside the quantities of commodities already specified and "to which they are added, inasmuch as there is nothing simpler and easier to do than to assume them to be included there now" (ibid.). Consumer and business inventories, consumer and business circulating balances of money, and consumers' balances of money savings, he claimed, can be considered as being included in the magnitudes symbolized in the system of equations (ibid.). The eight sets of equations (1877b, pp. 285–90; 1889, pp. 274–79), according to Walras, are consequently also descriptive of equilibrium in the second stage of the model.

Whether or not Walras's contentions about the effects of the inclusion of inventories and cash balances in his equations are warranted, a matter that will be considered later, his model is fundamental and the equations are not. The model, like the real economy, is not an equation system but a system of institutions, physical structures, physical items, procedures, technology, participants and behaviors, some aspects and consequences of which any particular set of equations may or may not accurately describe. The behavior that transpires within the homes, workplaces, markets, and other parts of the economy simulated in the model forms an interrelated functioning system. The participants include landlords, workers, and capitalists. They provide the services of their resources, and thereby earn incomes. There is a set of markets in which those services are sold, and in those and in the other markets there are certain institutions, rules, and procedures followed by the buyers and sellers. The service suppliers save part of those incomes in their role as capitalists, and they spend part in the set of markets that Walras provided for nondurable consumer goods and consumable services. The participants also include entrepreneurs. They purchase the productive services and primary materials. There is a set of markets for the latter. The entrepreneurs produce nondurable consumer goods and services, primary materials, and capital goods. They accumulate money for the purchase of inputs. Savers accumulate money balances and finance the production of primary materials and consumer goods by lending money, and they finance the production of capital goods by lending money, purchasing new shares, and buying bonds. Walras provided a loan market and a bourse for those activities. Capital goods incorporated into the productive processes in firms are sold on the Bourse through the sale of the shares of the firms. Capital goods are also sold on their own particular markets without any change in the ownership of shares occurring.

Entrepreneurs in the model draw on their stocks of primary materials and roughly simultaneously replace them; they produce consumer and capital goods and put them into inventories and on display, and sell them out of those sources and replace them; and they use the stocks of fixed capital goods in their businesses and maintain and fully insure them. Consumers accumulate balances of money to buy consumer goods and services. They hold stocks of nondurable goods, draw down those stocks, and roughly simultaneously replace them. They use their stocks of consumer durables and maintain them and fully insure them.

III. Equilibrating processes in capital goods markets

Adjustments between loan and rental markets

Walras explained the adjustment processes various parts of the model undergo when it is in disequilibrium. One part of its dynamics that he needed to consider is the adjustments between the market in which money is lent and the market in which capital goods are rented. He began his modeling of this matter by discussing the rate of interest and the rate of net income. The rate of interest is paid to lenders by entrepreneurs who borrow money to buy capital goods or to construct them. It is the rate of return on the capital goods used by the entrepreneurs – that is, "the ratio of net profit to the price of capital goods, which manifests itself on the market for numeraire capital, which is to say, in the banking system" (1889, pp. 288–89). The rate of net income, in contrast, is the "ratio of the net price of the service" of any type of capital good "to the price of the capital" good (ibid., p. 289). It is paid to the owners of capital goods by the entrepreneurs who use them. In modern terminology, Walras was distinguishing the rate of interest on loans to finance new capital goods and the rate of dividends on capital goods, both of which derive from the net productivity of capital goods, but which can temporarily be different. If the rate of interest were higher than the rate of net income, savers would find it advantageous "to lend their capital in the form of numeraire on the market for numeraire capital, rather than to lend it in kind on the market for services." In other words, they would lend their money savings, rather than using them to buy capital goods that they would then rent to entrepreneurs. Entrepreneurs, however, would find it advantageous "to rent capital goods in kind on the market for services" – and thus to pay the rate of net income – "rather than to borrow it in the form of numeraire on the market for numeraire capital" and pay the rate of interest (ibid., p. 288). Accordingly, the quantity of numeraire capital supplied would increase and the quantity of it demanded would diminish. The rate of interest would fall until it came into equality with the rate of net income. The reverse would happen in the opposite case (ibid.).

Adjustments in the market for shares

Generations of writers have repeated Walras's statements that the prices of new capital goods are determined on the Bourse. In fact, in his model the prices that are determined on the Bourse are the prices of the shares of enterprises and the prices of their bonds, not the prices of new capital goods. Much of Walras's mature modeling of capital in the *Eléments* and elsewhere is concerned with the pricing of shares. Unfortunately, he described the process in an indirect and inaccurate way.

In one type of exposition he specified that the quantities of capital goods supplied and demanded are "led to equality by means of the raising or the lowering of the prices of the new capital goods accomplished by the lowering or the raising of i according to whether the quantity demanded is superior to the quantity supplied or the quantity supplied superior to the quantity demanded" (ibid., p. XXII). By the symbol i in that particular exposition, Walras stated, he meant the annual rate of interest (ibid). That was not a clear description of the behavior of the model. In the first place, the prices of shares are changed directly. In the second place, the rate that is partially determined in the market for new capital goods in the sense of the Bourse is the rate of net income, not the rate of interest (ibid., pp. 280, 289), although

Walras's terminology would be pardonable in reference to equilibrium, inasmuch as in that case, i takes the value of the rate of net income. Moreover, despite Walras's statements to the contrary, the rate of net income is only partially determined in the Bourse because it is the ratio of the price of the services of capital goods to the price of those goods, and hence is partially determined in the market for those services.

In a second type of exposition, Walras wrote about "a certain rate of net income . . . being cried" (ibid., p. 280) in the capital-goods market in the sense of the Bourse. "A rate of net income [is] cried first at random, and then revised or lowered according to circumstances" (ibid.). He thereby once again introduced a fictional process into his model. In the real economy, neither the rate of net income nor the rate of interest is quoted and changed in the capital goods market in the sense of the Bourse. Walras elsewhere recognized this by stating that the prices of capital goods, by which, in this context, he meant the values of shares, are raised and lowered on the Bourse directly through the changes in the prices of shares (for example, ibid., pp. 311–12).

Adjustments in the market for newly produced capital goods

Walras also specified, as indicated in the previous chapter, the structural features of a submodel of the pricing of particular new capital goods and of the determination of their rates of production – in the example given in the preceding chapter, a submodel of the price of tractors as distinct from the price of the shares of the tractor-producing corporation. In this chapter, it is shown how he treated the dynamics of the determination of the prices and rates of production of specific new capital goods. By considering those matters he was able to present a general treatment that included all new and old capital goods, whether produced by incorporated or unincorporated enterprises. It is clear that Walras considered specific new capital goods because he devised an adjusted process in which the rate of production of each capital good is varied until its average cost equals its price. As pointed out in the previous chapter, it would be absurd to say that the average cost is equated to the price of a share of the enterprise, and Walras did not make any such statement. Any comments he may have made asserting that the capital goods are priced on the Bourse must therefore be disregarded in this connection and relegated to their proper place, which is to a discussion of the evaluation of enterprises.

Changes of prices: One of Walras's tasks was to design the equilibrating process regarding new capital goods in the mature comprehensive model. He did that by positing two equilibrating mechanisms. The first is changes in prices. That process works in the following way. On the one hand, Walras specified, there is a demand for capital goods that proceeds from the volume of money savings (ibid., p. XVI). This is "the demand for new capital goods in numeraire, either by the creators of savings themselves or by the entrepreneurs who have borrowed these savings in the form of money capital" (1889, p. XXII; 1896b, p. XXI; "in numeraire" added in 1896b). On the other hand, there is the quantity of capital goods of a given type that have been produced and are offered for sale (1889, p. XVI; 1896b, p. XV). Walras assumed there is some initial disequilibrium state of the market in which there is a set of prices at which the quantities supplied and demanded of capital goods are not equal. During the equilibrating process, he specified, the service suppliers "possess the same [maximum] quantities of services" – that is, have unchanged quantities of resources (1877b, pp. 224, 246, 276, 280,; 1889, pp. 207, 229, 264, 268) and "the same needs for consumer services and products and the same preferences for saving" (1889, p. 280). He assumed that Walrasian pricing occurs on the market for new capital goods – the price is changed in the same direction as the sign of the market excess demand for the capital goods. This does not take place because anyone knows the market excess demand quantity but as a result of the participants' reactions to their individual excess demand quantities. As in all Walras's market models, the prices are quoted by the buyers and sellers. They meet face-to-face and deal directly with each other. Capital goods and money are exchanged: "A certain sum of savings, on the one hand, and certain quantities produced of new capital goods, on the other hand, being given, these savings and these new capital goods are exchanged for each other on a *market for new capital goods* according to the mechanism of the raising and lowering of prices" (1889, p. XVI; 1896b, p. XV).

Walras implied that the sale of capital goods occurs only at prices at which the market supply and demand are equal, as when he wrote that "the sales of new or existing capital goods, once decided on, are made following the mechanism of free competition and the law of supply and demand" (1877b, p. 303; 1889, p. 310). Similarly, he wrote that when the entrepreneurs have produced new capital goods, and thus necessarily after shares have been priced and sold to finance their construction, "then they will come to sell these new capital goods on the capital goods market following the mechanism of free competition, that is to say, at a price equal to their net income divided by the rate of net income" (1889, p. 280). For Walras, the capital goods markets are, like all markets for goods in his model, organized and freely competitive, which to him meant that trade occurs only when the market excess demand is zero. He always stated or implied that sales of goods occur at prices at which the market supply and demand quantities are equal.

The ratio of exchange between savings and a type of capital good, Walras explained, depends on the prices of the consumable or productive service that it yields, but he marred his work on this topic by engaging in circular reasoning. The pricing of the service, he wrote, results in a certain rate of net income for that type of capital good, and the price of the capital good is equal to the ratio of the price of its service to that rate of net income (1889, p. XVI). That is true in his model in equilibrium for a share, in which case the rate of net income is the dividend divided by the price of the share, and it is true for a capital good as just described. The problem in Walras's exposition is that he represented the pricing of the service as determining the rate of income, and the price of the service and the rate of income as determining the price of the capital good. The price of the service, according to Walras, therefore determines all the parts of the equation, whereas in fact the price of the capital good must be determined independently of the rate of income in order to establish the latter. The price of the service is the income generated by a capital good, and that income must be compared with the price of the capital good to discover the rate. Walras should also have remarked that the price of a service of a capital good that is new and has therefore never been used depends on the price of the service of old capital goods of that type. There is, however, no problem posed for his model in this regard by differences in the productivity of old and new capital goods of a given type because old capital goods are just like new ones, so there are no such differences.

Changes of disequilibrium rates of production: The second equilibrating mechanism in the markets for new capital goods in the model is changes in their disequilibrium rates of production. Walras specified this equilibrating mechanism with much greater clarity and detail in the second edition of the *Eléments* than in the first. Focusing on the market in which capital goods that have been produced are sold, he wrote that during the equilibrating process the capital goods are produced and are "brought onto the capital goods market" and are sold "at prices that differ from the average costs" of the capital goods (ibid., p. 292). Sales of them therefore occur at prices that "are not equilibrium values" (ibid., p. 280). New capital goods are products whose prices are subject to the law of the cost of production (1877b, pp. 278–79; 1889, p. 266).[1] When their prices and average costs are unequal, which Walras asserted is ordinarily the case in his model, "the entrepreneurs that produce new capital goods will make profits or losses" (1877b, p. 295; 1889, p. 289), just as is true of the producers of consumer commodities when their prices and average costs diverge. If the average cost of a type of new capital good is less than its price, profits are made, and its production will be

---

[1] He emphasized the parallel between the equilibrating processes for capital goods and consumer goods by using the word "products," which he ordinarily reserved for the latter.

increased by the entrepreneurs. If the reverse is true, there are losses, and its production will be decreased (1877b, p. 276; 1889, pp. XVI, 265). Thus, resources are directed into or out of capital-goods industries by entrepreneurs.

Simultaneity of the two equilibrating mechanisms

Walras referred to the two adjustment processes many times. Here is a typical statement, already partially quoted here, in which the production of capital goods in disequilibrium is specified in the first part of the passage, and the sale of capital goods only at equilibrium prices is implied in the second part of the quotation by the statement that the goods are sold under the conditions and procedures of freely competitive markets:

A reprise of tatonnement will consist in this, in regard to the formation of capital goods viewed in isolation. At a rate of net income cried first at random, and then raised or lowered according to the circumstances, the entrepreneurs that produce new capital goods will fabricate certain quantities of new capital goods determined first at random and then increased or diminished quantities according to the circumstances. Then they will come to sell these new capital goods on the capital goods market following the mechanism of free competition, that is to say, at a price equal to their net income divided by the rate of net income (1889, p. 280).

Thus, production and sales occur at disequilibrium prices, but it is also the case that sales occur only at equilibrium prices. In order to understand the adjustment processes, it is necessary to understand how Walras reconciled those ostensibly contradictory assertions.

Particular-equilibrium supply and demand functions: The manner in which he did so is shown in Figures 9.1 and 9.2, in which particular-equilibrium supply and demand curves are used. It has been demonstrated in detail in chapter 7 that there is complete justification for the use of such curves in the *Eléments* and that Walras's assumption of constant coefficients of production is in no way incompatible with the shape of the industry supply curve shown in Figure 9.1. Here the specific justification for the use of particular equilibrium curves in connection with capital-goods industries will be presented.

The long-run supply curve and the demand curve in the figures are not my constructions. They are precisely the curves that Walras drew and used. He assumed that the prices of all commodities are constant except those of the capital good under consideration and of the services used to make it. He asserted that the market demand curve is negatively inclined. The shape of the industry long-run supply curve is influenced by the changes in the prices of the services as the industry expands or contracts: if the quantity produced of a capital good "is increased or decreased, the prices of all the services that enter into the confection of the capital good (K) are increased or decreased; that is to say, the average cost of that capital good is appreciably increased or decreased" (1877b, p. 297; 1889, p. 291). In other words, there are net external pecuniary diseconomies of scale. Walras applied those considerations to the construction of an example of supply and demand curves in a capital-good industry (1896b, p. 479). Referring to a figure that he drew with money per unit of the capital good on the base axis and the quantity of the capital good on the vertical axis (1896b, Appendices, fig. 7), he asserted that "we are equally entitled to enunciate that, in increasing or diminishing the quantity of the same capital good (K), the marginal utility and the prices of the productive services which enter into the confection of that capital good are increased or decreased and, as a consequence, its average cost of production; that is to say, *the curve of the quantity as a function of the average cost is an increasing curve XY*" (1896b, p. 479; emphasis added). That diagram is precisely the one that is used as a model for the demand curve and the long-run supply curve in a capital-goods industry (Figures 9.1 and 9.2).

These figures are a temporary expository device. After using them to make clear the relationship of marketdays to the long run over a given period of time in Walras's analyses, they will be replaced by a general description of the adjustment processes. It will be emphasized that the processes are more complicated than is shown by the figures, because the curves shift. The shifts of the curves are omitted in the figures simply because of the complexity that would otherwise be introduced without any corresponding gain in clarity of explication of the relationships of interest in this chapter.

Interaction of price and rate of production adjustments when price exceeds average cost: The essence of the double process of adjustment was expressed by Walras in this manner: "If the price is superior to the average cost, the quantity produced will increase and the price will fall; if the price is lower than the average cost, the quantity produced will diminish and the price will rise" (1877b, p. 279; 1889, p. 266). The equilibrating process in production and the equilibrating process in pricing occur simultaneously in the model because the changes in the rate of production of the capital goods have an impact on their prices, and the prices that are paid have an impact on the rate of production. Walras explained that as long as the quantities of new capital goods supplied and demanded are unequal, Walrasian pricing will occur, and that as long as the price of each type of new capital good is not equal to its average cost, there will be "an increase in the quantity of the new capital goods for which the price exceeds the average cost, and a decrease in the

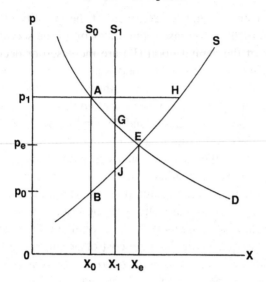

Figure 9.1 Price and production tatonnements: profitable capital-goods industry

quantity of those for which the average cost exceeds the price" (1889, p. 294; 1877b, p. 300, with slight differences).

This is explained by Figure 9.1, in which it is assumed that the market is initially in long-run equilibrium at B and that the market demand curve then becomes the one labeled D. The amount brought onto the market on the day of the shift of demand is the old equilibrium quantity X_0, so the market-day supply curve is X_0S_0, which intersects the market demand curve at A. In accordance with Walras's first assertion about pricing, trade occurs only at the price at which the quantities of the capital good supplied and demanded are equal on any given market day, so all sales on the first day after the shift of demand occur at p_1. By his first assertion, Walras therefore had reference to a price at which the market-day excess demand quantity is zero. In accordance with Walras's second assertion, however, that price is not an equilibrium price with reference to the long-run supply, which has the average cost as its ordinates. The price is greater than the average cost X_0B of the good; the profit per unit of output is AB. The producers in the long run would want to produce and sell a larger batch of it – namely, p_1H units, which is AH more than demanders want to buy. There is a long-run negative market excess demand. Thus, the market is in market-day equilibrium but not in long-run equilibrium.

In Walras's model, the producers can increase output only by degrees because it takes time for firms to expand and for new firms to enter the industry. Consequently, they are able initially to increase output per day only to X_1 units. The vertical market-day supply curve shifts right to that new quantity, intersecting the demand curve at G. The price on the second day is $X_1 G$. Of course, the increase of output might occur by small increases each "day," in which case the market-day supply line would shift almost continuously to the right and the price would fall almost continuously.

The price $X_1 G$ is still greater than average cost, but the difference GJ between price and average cost is smaller than before. This is true because the increased quantity supplied causes the market-day equilibrium price to be lower, and because the effort of increasing the size of the batch of capital goods causes the prices of the inputs used in making them to be bid up, thus increasing the average cost. As long as the difference is positive, however, the dual process continues, converging to the point E. Thus the series of market-day equilibrium prices falls down the ordinates of D from A toward E, the production per day that would be desired in the long run falls down the abscissae of S from H toward E, the actual output rises from X_0 toward X_e, and the actual average cost rises along the ordinates of S from B to E.

In actuality, in Walras's model the adjustments take place in a general-equilibrium setting. The prices of other commodities change from day to day during the adjustment process, leading to shifts in the demand and long-run supply curve for X. Nevertheless, the character of the dynamic process in the given market is the one just described. The curves should be thought of as having a given locus on one market day, with the market adjustment occurring and the rate of production undergoing one day's adjustment. Then the demand curve and the long-run supply curve shift up or down to another pair of loci, and there is again another market day and rate-of-production adjustment. The process of shifting and adjustment is then repeated.

Adjustments when price is less than average cost: Walras probably gave two accounts of what happens if the price is less than the average cost. When he wrote that producers "restrain" or "diminish" their production (1889, pp. XVI, 266, 280), he probably implied that gradual diminutions would occur in that case. Let it be assumed that the market demand curve in Figure 9.2 initially runs through B and that it shifts left to the position shown by D. On the first day, the output is X_2, the average cost is $X_2 B$, the market-day equilibrium price is $p_0 = X_2 A$, and the loss per unit of output is AB. At the current price the actual and potential suppliers would prefer to produce amounts that add up to $p_0 Z$ units per day, but it takes time for firms to go out of business and for reductions of output to occur, so the quantity supplied falls initially only to X_3 and losses per unit of output become GJ. The process continues, and the series of market prices rises along the ordinate of D from A to E; the desired production per day rises along the abscissae of S from Z toward F, the actual output falls from X_2 toward X_e, and the actual average

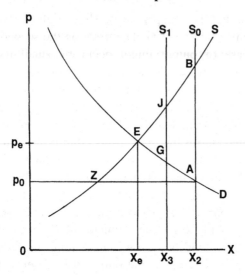

Figure 9.2 Price and production tatonnements: unprofitable capital-goods industry

cost falls along the ordinates of *S* from *B* toward *E*. It may be, however, that when Walras wrote that production "diminishes" he meant the process about to be described.

In what may be a second account, Walras asserted that when the *D* curve shifts left, production is temporarily entirely suspended. He observed that in his model, the entrepreneurs that produce new capital goods know the prices of services and know the rate of net income before they select a particular rate of production. They also know the average cost and the prices of the capital goods they produce. They are therefore theoretically "free to produce only in the case in which they will make profits and not to do so in the case of losses" (1889, p. 295). Since they know in advance when the average cost exceeds the price, they do not produce capital goods on the sale of which they would incur losses. They suspend production until enough firms leave the industry so that the new industry output is sufficiently small for profits to be positive or zero – that is, for the price to be greater than average cost or to be equal to it. Obviously there are some aspects of this process that Walras did not work out. Notably, he did not explain how the price is determined when no goods are being offered for sale, why all the firms do not go bankrupt, which ones survive, how the survivors know when the industry output would be low enough for profits to become nonnegative, despite the fact that no offers to sell are made in the adjustment situation, and, when production is resumed, whether it is equal to or less than the equilibrium amount and how that matter is resolved.

Walras then connected his capital-goods model to the real economy by stating that the real capital-goods market goes through a tatonnement like the one in the model: "Now, the indicated tatonnement [in the model] is exactly that which occurs on the [real] capital goods market when the new capital goods are sold there following the mechanism of bidding up and lowering prices, proportionately to their net incomes" (ibid., p. 287). "Now, this tatonnement" – the one in the model – "is precisely that which generates itself on the [real] market for products, under the regime of free competition, when the entrepreneurs that produce new capital goods, just like those that produce consumer goods, move toward firms or turn away from them according to whether profits or losses are made in them" (ibid., p. 294).

IV. Equilibrating processes in all markets

It must be remembered that the capital-goods model is embedded within and is an integral part of Walras's comprehensive model that includes all other types of commodities. He repeatedly drew attention to this circumstance in the lessons that he devoted primarily to the capital-goods model, as will now be shown. First, it will be noticed that in the foregoing and in the following quotation, he made reference to the functioning of consumer commodities markets alongside the capital-goods markets. Second, he emphasized the functioning of markets for services as an integral part of the system of markets treated in those lessons when he wrote that "a certain rate of net income and certain prices of services being cried, and certain quantities of consumer goods and of new capital goods being produced, if this rate, these prices and these quantities are not equilibrium values of the rate, prices and quantities, it is necessary not only to cry another rate and other prices, but also to produce other quantities of products and of new capital goods" (ibid., p. 280). Third, he indicated that the functioning of the market for the numeraire commodity is part of the comprehensive model treated in those lessons. The adjustment processes undergone in relation to that commodity are like those of the other commodities (ibid., p. 294). Its quantity, average cost, and the amounts of other commodities that are exchanged for a unit of it vary during the equilibrating process. It is produced during disequilibrium, so the stocks of it held as money and as a commodity change in disequilibrium. Other prices can be quoted in terms of it because it is the unit of account, but its use as a medium of exchange in the model entails variations of the price level, resulting from changes in the amount of it that is available. Fourth, he asserted that his system of eight sets of equations includes all commodities and money balances, as has been seen. Walras wrote that he accepted the occurrence of the interrelated complex of disequilibrium activity involving all markets, consumers, entrepreneurs, savers, and service suppliers, and asserted that he would endow his model with properties that would, he thought, result in its convergence to equilibrium (ibid., p. 280).

The equilibrating process in each market has the same general characteristics as those discussed in reference to the market for a type of capital good. It has been shown in chapter 7 that Walras devised a pricing process in the market for each consumer commodity whereby sales of it occur only at the market-day equilibrium price. He stated the same thing in a discussion of the comprehensive model: "On the market for products, the equilibrium prices being determined, the exchange of these products is done immediately" (1877b, p. 302; 1889, p. 309).[2] That implies that in the comprehensive model Walras continued to assume regarding consumer goods that transactions occur only at equilibrium prices, subject to the special interpretation of the term "equilibrium price." As in the submodel of capital-goods markets, it is defined in reference to a market day as the price that equalizes the consumer-good market supply and demand quantities on that day. As in the submodel of capital-goods markets, this process is part of a larger adjustment mechanism in which, during the adjustment phase, the market-day equilibrium prices of consumer commodities are disequilibrium values with respect to the given market as long as average cost and the price are not equal and are disequilibrium values with respect to the ultimate general-equilibrium set of prices.

The market-day equilibrium prices of each consumer good change not only as production changes, but also in reaction to the changes of prices in other markets. The point of intersection of the market demand curve and the long-run supply curve changes because those curves shift, the quantity demanded and the desired rate of production being functions, in principle, of the prices of all commodities. The adjustment of market-day prices and average costs of consumer commodities and capital goods is accompanied by the adjustment of the prices of services and primary materials, and of the rates of interest and net income. These changes occur in a dynamic model in which, according to Walras, all markets move in an interrelated fashion toward equilibrium.

V. Equilibrium

Capital-goods markets

Walras asserted that there are two conditions which, taken together, are necessary and sufficient for equilibrium in the capital-goods market to obtain

---

[2] By the word "products" in that sentence he was referring to consumer goods, unlike the usage described in note 1. That is evident because the rest of the sentence reads in part as follows: "on the market for capital goods, on the contrary, exchange does not necessarily take place" (1877b, p. 302; 1889, p. 309).

in his model. He identified the first equilibrium condition in the following way: "In order that there may be equilibrium in the capital goods market, or a stationary price in numeraire of all the new capital goods, it is necessary and sufficient: 1^0 that at the prices determined by the ratio of the net incomes to the common rate of net income the quantity demanded of these new capital goods be equal to the quantity supplied" (1889, p. 294; 1877b, p. 300, without reference to the ratio; and see 1877b, pp. 276, 279; 1889, pp. 265, 266). When the model is in equilibrium, the connection between the financing of the process of constructing new capital goods and the sale of newly produced capital goods is clearly seen. Part of the financing of production is by loans made from savings. These are repaid with funds obtained by the sale of the capital goods to businesses. Part of the financing is by the sale of new stocks and bonds by the capital-goods producing firms initially primarily to speculators. They subsequently sell them to savers, so the funds raised in those ways are also new savings provided by capitalists (chs. 12 and 15) Drawing attention to these characteristics of his model, Walras constructed a macroeconomic equation describing the fact that in equilibrium the total amount of new saving is equal to the aggregate value of the new capital goods (1877b, p. 284; 1889, p. 271).

Walras then identified the second condition. It is "2^0 that the price of these new capital goods be equal to their average cost" (1889, p. 294). The equilibrium average cost of a type of new capital good and its long-run equilibrium price are determined together. The latter is the one that is part of the set of general-equilibrium prices, and hence is both the long-run equilibrium, price at which the number and size of the firms in the industry are in equilibrium and a market-day equilibrium price. Since the price of old and new capital goods of any given type must be equal, the price of old ones is also determined. The rate of net income is the outcome of the determination of the prices of capital goods and of the prices of their services (1877b, p. 276; 1889, p. 265). In equilibrium, that rate is the same for all old capital goods and for land and personal faculties also (1877b, p. 275; 1889, pp. 263–64). At the time that its equilibrium value materializes, the equilibrium rate of interest also materializes, and has the same value (1889, p. 295).

Walras also dealt with the consequences for utility of the equilibrium in the market for new capital goods in his theorem on the maximum utility of new capital goods (ch. 10). In disequilibrium, the holders of capital goods adjust the quantities they demand of them to try to maximize utility (ibid., p. 273). The equalization of the ratios of net incomes to the prices of the new capital goods is, except for certain qualifications, the condition that secures maximum utility for all relevant participants. "Capital formation on a market ruled by free competition is an operation by which the excess of income over consumption can be transformed into new capital goods of the kind and the quantity proper for giving the greatest possible satisfaction of wants within the limits of the condition that there is a single rate of net income for all the capital goods on the market" (ibid., p. 305).

Equilibrium conditions in all markets

The eight sets of equations that Walras used to try to describe some of the characteristics of the equilibrium state of the model are as follows: First, the aggregate excess of income over consumption, and for each individual, the equation of the equality of the value of services offered to the value of commodities demanded and the equations of maximization of utility, from which are derived the individual's offers of each service and demand for each commodity, including the individual's demand for the numeraire; second, the aggregate offers of each type of productive and consumable service; third, the aggregate demand for each product by consumers, including the aggregate demand for the numeraire commodity; fourth, the equality of the demand of each productive service to the offer of it; fifth, the equality of the sum of the values of each input used to make a unit of output to the price of that output – that is, the equality of price to average cost for each consumer good; sixth, the equality of price to average cost for each type of new capital good; seventh, the equality of the value of all new capital goods to the aggregate excess of income over consumption, always considered to be positive; and, eighth, the equality of the price of each capital good to the price of its service divided by the rate of net revenue plus the rates of amortization and insurance premiums (1877b, pp. 285–289; 1889, pp. 274–78). Expressed as has just been done, in a literary way and without mention of the parameters that Walras specified for the equations, those conditions accurately describe some of the features of the model in equilibrium.

Contrary to Walras's belief (1877b, p. 307; 1889, p. 313), that equation system is incomplete. It fails to include the outcomes of certain processes that are in the model and that affect all the outcomes that the equations are supposed to describe. He should have added an equation that describes the equality of the quantities of money supplied and demanded in equilibrium, inasmuch as the first and second stages of his comprehensive model include the use of money, a loan market, and the holding of money balances. Similarly, the influence of inventories is not revealed by his equation system. In the first place, he did not provide the model with a process of adjustment of the size of business inventories and consumer inventories to the desired level, although they are both functions of variables that change as the model moves toward equilibrium. In the second place, his equations are confined to describing relations between flow variables in equilibrium, but to indicate the levels of inventories in equilibrium they would have to indicate equilibrium conditions in the holding of stocks of commodities.

Walras then turned to a description of equilibrium in terms of the welfare of the participants. According to him, the purely competitive economy he modeled achieves in equilibrium "a maximum of effective utility, on the one hand; a single price, on the other hand, whether it be for consumer goods on the market for consumer goods, or for services on the market for services, or for net income on the market for capital goods: that is therefore the double condition in accordance with which the world of economic interests tends to regulate itself" (1877b, p. 305; 1889, p. 306).

Economic growth

The foregoing equilibrium conditions must be interpreted as either a description of equilibrium at a point in time or, with appropriate modification of some of the phrasing, as conditions that prevail in a moving equilibrium. This is because Walras's comprehensive model is one in which there is economic growth. He stated that he had developed a model of economic growth by assuming that new capital goods are produced:

And, in that respect, one of the characteristics of the economic progress can be pointed out. Let us assume, in effect, that at the end of a certain time we stopped the functioning of the economic production process, again for an instant, as we have already done, and that we found a larger quantity of capital goods: that would be the sign of a progressive state. Thus, one of the characteristics of economic progress consists in the increase in the quantity of capital goods. Since our following section will be specially devoted to the study of the conditions and consequences of economic progress, we can reserve the question of the production of new capital goods for later (1877, p. 226; 1889, p. 209).

He explained that after the tatonnement is finished – after general equilibrium is reached – saving and investment will be equal, and "production and capital formation can then continue" (1889, p. 280). He explicitly asserted that the rate of net saving (and therefore net investment) is positive in all states of the model: "The sum of individual net savings [is] henceforward always assumed to be positive" (1877b, p. 284; 1889, p. 271).

Walras also made clear and emphasized the continuous occurrence of net new savings and investment with a numerical illustration of the working of his comprehensive model (1877b, pp. 308, 310; 1889, pp. 314, 316). In the moving equilibrium during a particular year, "out of 10 billion of annual aggregate income, 8 billion are consumed, and 2 billion are capitalized, of which 1,500 million are used for amortization and insurance of existing capital goods properly speaking, *and 500 million for the creation of new capital goods properly speaking"* (1877b, pp. 309–10; 1889, p. 316; emphasis added). "The tatonnement will be finished" regarding capital formation when saving equals investment and the average costs of new capital goods equal their prices. "Production and capital formation can then continue, but, it is understood," the model undergoes "the changes that proceed from the existence of new capital goods" (1889, p. 280). The subsequent output of the economy grows: "In order to have a supply and a demand and prices of capital goods it is necessary to substitute in place of the conception of a stationary economic state that of a progressive economic state" (1877b, p. 276; 1889, pp. 264–65). In short, a flow of new capital goods is produced in Walras's mature comprehensive model; consequently he conceived of it as a model of economic growth, even though he did not examine the moving equilibrium that actually resulted from his assumptions.

VI. The model vs. the equations

Capital goods a supposed parameter

Walras constructed his model on the assumption that the stock of capital goods is constant during the adjustment process – that is, while the system moves from disequilibrium to the equilibrium path. The set of equations he wrote out to indicate the amounts of capital-good services and other services employed in the production of a unit of each type of capital good referred to the situation that would exist in equilibrium (1877b, p. 279; 1889, p. 267). In those equations, Walras introduced the services of "capital goods properly speaking, existing *or to be produced*" (ibid.; emphasis added). Thus, the new capital goods in those equations do not exist during the equilibrating process. Similarly, in his discussion of an individual's saving equation, Walras assumed the individual holds given amounts of resources: "Assuming there is, at present, an individual who owns q_t of (T) ... q_p of (P) ... q_k of (K), $q_{k'}$ of (K'), $q_{k''}$ of (K'')" etc. (1877b, p. 280; 1889, p. 268), where (T) is land, (P) is personal faculties, and the (Ks) are different capital goods. Walras went on to specify how the individual offers the services of his resources and demands consumer commodities and to identify the excess of the value of what the individual offers over what he demands. The individual evidently cannot own nor therefore offer the services of capital goods that are not in existence, so the equations for saving assume that the existing capital goods are those that exist at the beginning of the equilibrating process. They are intended to describe the offers of services in general equilibrium, when the amount of new savings and therefore of planned capital goods has been determined, as though no capital goods had been planned and actually constructed during the equilibrating process. Thus, Walras tried to determine the equilibrium amount of new capital goods to be produced and the corresponding net saving and therefore the equilibrium amount of the capital stock on the basis of the assumption that the amount of capital goods is a constant during the equilibrating process.

Durable goods not constant

In his model, however, consumers are paid incomes in disequilibrium; they save some part of those incomes and their net savings are used to increase the capital stock during the equilibrating process.[3] New capital goods and new durable consumer goods are therefore acquired by consumers during that process. This has the following consequences. The amount offered for sale of any particular capital-good service in Walras's model is a function not only of the prices of all commodities but also the maximum available supply of the service, which depends on the amount of the capital good. Since the amounts of the capital goods increase during the disequilibrium phase, Walras's assumption in his equations that the maximum available supplies of productive and consumable services of capital goods are constant is invalidated. Inasmuch as the maximum available supplies keep changing during the equilibrating process, changes keep occurring in the amounts of capital-good services that would be offered to entrepreneurs at each possible price for the production of both capital goods and consumer goods. The equilibrium prices and outputs of the services and goods they produce therefore differ from the solutions to Walras's equations. They do not describe the equilibrium of the model.

Other consequences are entailed by the process of net saving and investment. Demand functions in the model undergo changes. Businesses in the model purchase capital goods with borrowed money at the disequilibrium prices that rule in any given stage of the adjustment process. Consequently, the businesses demand lesser amounts of those goods at each subsequent possible price. The changes of the businesses' demand functions for new capital goods keep occurring through the entire equilibrating process. Similarly, as a result of their purchases of new capital goods in disequilibrium, the demand functions of businesses for other inputs and their supply functions for output undergo changes. Moreover, after individuals acquire new capital

---

[3] The changes of income that result from increased productivity of the economy through the use of an augmented supply of capital goods do not in themselves invalidate Walras's equations of the demand for consumer goods and services, because a consumer's income is simply one of the variables in his demand functions for those commodities. Changes of it therefore do not change those functions. The changes of income do, however, change the rate of saving.

goods that yield productive services through the purchase of shares at disequilibrium prices, the subsequent quantities they demand of capital goods are different at each possible rate of net income. Likewise, after they purchase bonds or make loans at one stage of the adjustment process, the subsequent quantities they demand of bonds or promissory notes respectively are different at each possible rate of interest. In other words, the amount of saving and investing that actually occurs at one disequilibrium rate of net income and of interest changes the amounts that consumers want to save subsequently as a function of subsequent possible rates of net income and interest, and therefore changes the amount they actually save at the next rate that materializes.

Since capital goods that yield consumable services are also acquired at any given set of disequilibrium prices by consumers, the demand functions for such goods at subsequent possible prices are altered. Furthermore, consumers buy nondurables at disequilibrium prices and put them into inventories. Some of them are used almost immediately, but others are used only after various lapses of time, and acquisition of them at one set of disequilibrium prices changes the subsequent demand functions for them. Each of the foregoing changes invalidates Walras's equation system.

Changes in individuals' holdings of nominal and real cash balances also occur during the course of the equilibrating process, and those changes alter the demand and supply functions for commodities.[4] Disequilibrium prices change the wealth of the participants in the model, leading to various kinds of wealth effects. For example, changes of the values of the inputs and outputs held in business inventories occur during the equilibrating process when their prices change. Changes of the prices of new capital goods occur in the course of the equilibrating process, which change the value of old capital goods because they are exactly like new ones of the same type. Changes in the disequilibrium prices of consumer durables and nondurables alter the value of the holdings of those durables by consumers. Nevertheless, whether or not or how such changes alter supply and demand functions for net additional amounts or replacements of inventories in Walras's model cannot be determined because it is not specified in sufficient detail to determine the degree to which wealth effects are offset by cost effects. For example, higher prices of new commodities increase the value of inventories, but that effect tends to be offset because the higher prices also increase the cost of their replacement and of their insurance. Decreases in their prices cause offsetting influences in the opposite sense. Nor did Walras explore the consequences in other respects of the introduction of inventories into the model. The supply of output functions is not changed by unintended inven-

---

[4] An analysis of cash balances and of the role of money in the model generally is reserved for the study in chapter 11 of Walras's detailed account of those matters.

tory changes. There are no such changes because all output that is brought to market is sold the same day. Nevertheless, Walras's specification that businesses keep amounts of inventory of inputs and outputs in some relation to the level of sales (1877b, p. 306; 1889, p. 313) implies that they purchase more inputs than they use and produce more output than they sell at some prices during the equilibrating process, or the reverse, in order to augment or deplete inventories. The model is incomplete, however, in these matters and their consequences for the equilibrating process and equilibrium, inasmuch as it makes no mention of them.

The equations not descriptive of the model

The fact that Walras's equations do not relate to his model is their weakness and not its deficiency. Even if they gave the true equilibrium values of the variables, they would be far from being the essence of the model. First, they are static equilibrium equations and therefore indicate nothing about its dynamics. Second, even if they were correct, the aggregate equations would not be part of the workings of the markets. The behavior of the participants concerning pricing and all other activities is conducted in ignorance of the supply and demand quantities in the particular market for any commodity and naturally in ignorance of its macroeconomic supply and demand quantities. If the model converges to equilibrium, it does so without market and macroeconomic functions playing any role in that process. Third, even if Walras's system of static equations were altered and supplemented by additional static equations in an effort to take account of the variables he thought were parameters, the equation system would fail to indicate the equilibrium values of the variables because the model is path-dependent. By path dependency is meant that the equilibrium values of the variables are affected by the behavior that occurs at the particular series of sets of disequilibrium prices that are quoted in the markets during the equilibrating process. If the series were different, the equilibrium values would be different. The model is path-dependent because the amounts of saving would be different at different series of interest rates and incomes, and the production and acquisitions of durable and nondurable goods would be different at different series of disequilibrium prices. Walras's equations do not indicate the particular series of prices that is quoted. Consequently, the equilibrium values cannot be deduced from the equations. To discover the equilibrium values of the variables in the model, the initial conditions would have to be specified and a system of dynamic equations would have to be found that identifies the particular series of prices that is quoted and that has the equilibrium values of the variables as its solutions.

VII. Conclusion

Major characteristics of the model

This chapter has demonstrated four major matters regarding Walras's mature comprehensive model. First, it has shown that in his mature phase of theoretical work, Walras developed a comprehensive model in the lessons that appear in the *Eléments* before his detailed lessons on money. Second, it has explained the essence of the equilibrating process in each market, showing how he devised an interrelated market-day and rate-of-production adjustment process. The occurrence of exchange only at prices at which supply and demand quantities are equal works together with a process in which those exchanges are seen to be occurring in disequilibrium. Third, it has been shown that some of the conditions that Walras treated as parameters in his equations are actually endogenous variables in his model, with the result that its equilibrium is not described by his system of equations. Fourth, it has been shown that Walras's mature model is a remarkable achievement for several reasons. It is very comprehensive, containing markets for all nonfinancial commodities, consumption, savings, a loan market, a securities market, inventories, and cash balances. New capital goods are produced in it, so that unlike in his consumer commodities model, the firms can expand and new ones can be created without it having to be assumed that capital goods are nonspecific. All economic activities occur in its disequilibrium phase, including saving, capital formation, production of primary materials and consumer commodities, and sales of commodities of all types, just as is true of the real economy. Disequilibrium production serves as part of the equilibrating mechanism that generates the dynamic path by which the model moves toward equilibrium. Yet another strength of the model is that its equilibrium is a moving equilibrium because there is a continuing flow of saving and net new investment, just as there is in the real economy. Finally, the fact that the model is path-dependent is another of its strengths, because outcomes in the real economy depend on the particular paths that are taken by economic variables.

Contrast with the written pledges model

It should be recognized that the mature comprehensive model is very different from the written pledges model.

First, the mature model is logically and substantively independent of the latter, having been constructed for a different purpose – namely, to model real competitive economic processes.

Second, disequilibrium production and sales, which Walras made a central feature of his mature comprehensive model, were a basic part of his conception of general equilibration for almost his entire career, whereas the written pledges model was an attempt to eliminate them. He developed the mature model in the early 1870s and drew on it throughout the first edition of the *Eléments*; he elaborated greatly on the economic processes that involve disequilibrium production in the second edition of the *Eléments* and presented them again in the third edition; and he wrote about it repeatedly in his correspondence during more than twenty-five years. In contrast, he introduced the written pledges model in the last months of his years of theorizing, and by its characteristics revealed the weakening of his creative powers. It was extremely unrealistic; it was an incomplete afterthought; his presentation of it was sketchy; and he forced it into the structure of the *Eléments* without eliminating or revising the older theorizing that contradicted it.

Third, Walras's mature comprehensive model was the one that was familiar to nineteenth-century economists and was discussed and criticized by them. It was carried forward in the stream of economic theory in the nineteenth and early twentieth centuries by the work of Pareto (1896/1897, pp. 45–47, 86–90; 1909, pp. 181, 213, 606–7, 632–33, 635), until it was overwhelmed by the attention given to the written pledges model.

Fourth, Walras constructed theoretical formulations of a number of real and important dynamic aspects of economic behavior that depend crucially on the occurrence of disequilibrium production and sales. Those formulations are essential parts of the processes presented in all editions of the *Eléments*. Consequently, despite his declared desire to adopt the written pledges model in the fourth and definitive editions of the *Eléments,* he was compelled to retain in those editions the language he had adopted in reference to the mature model. His book would otherwise have been shortened to a few pages. That explains why scholars could read about the written pledges model in those editions and conclude from the passages that surround it and are interspersed between its expositions that Walras had tried to present a realistic account of economic dynamics in it.

The character of Walras's last two phases of theoretical activity obscured by conflations

Two examples will be given of Walras's formulations of phenomena that depend on disequilibrium production and sales that were introduced in the first edition of the *Eléments* and that Walras failed to eliminate from the fourth edition, and one of a construction of that type that was introduced in the third edition and that was similarly retained in the fourth edition.

1. Walrasian profits per unit of output are the actual (ex post) difference between price and average cost and are therefore a disequilibrium-production and sales phenomenon (1877b, pp. 231, 254; 1889, pp. 214, 238; 1900, §§ 188, 210, pp. 194–95, 218). They are the remuneration to the entrepreneur

for buying and selling in disequilibrium, not surpluses or quasi-rents, and can accordingly materialize, as Jaffé observed, "only in the course of the emergence (établissement) of equilibrium via a tâtonnement process" (Jaffé 1980, p. 536 [353]; see also ch. 13). They exist through time in Walras's theory of general equilibrium, and are eliminated as time passes. In the written pledges model, in contrast, if it were a functioning system, actual profits would never be anything but zero, for in disequilibrium they would be only hypothetical and unrealizable, and in equilibrium they would be zero.

2. A major part of Walras's work on tatonnement processes in the mature comprehensive model deals with the allocation of resources among different economic activities. He repeatedly described how "this tatonnement is precisely that which occurs automatically on the market for products, under the regime of free competition, when entrepreneurs move toward or turn away from firms according whether profits or losses are made in them" (1877b, p. 255; 1889, p. 241; 1900, § 212, p. 221; see also Walras 1889, p. XVIII; ch. 13). In Walras's mature models, this process is not and cannot be a rehearsal without any real economic action because the entrepreneurs must actually move from one industry to another, abandoning and establishing firms, and expanding and contracting the size of existing firms. To do so, they must actually change the allocation of resources during the course of the equilibrating process, and that means they must hire and produce at disequilibrium prices.

3. The theory of marginal productivity that Walras presented in the third edition of the *Eléments* (1896b, Appendix III, pp. 485–92) – that is to say, during his mature phase of theorizing – deals with economic behavior in a setting of disequilibrium production and sales and was intended to be realistic. Walras explained that entrepreneurs, through a process of time-consuming experimentation, discover and adopt the optimum amounts of the inputs used in making a unit of output. "The entrepreneur, by a process of tatonnement, increases or reduces each productive service" until profit is maximized. In this way free competition leads to the minimum cost of production (ibid., pp. 490–91). Walras indicated that this dynamic process of experimentation in production should be considered as part of his general-equilibrium model although he had not incorporated it into his exposition of the model because he feared to do so would make it so complicated as to become hard to grasp in its totality (1900, § 326, p. 376). Nevertheless, he moved the theory of marginal productivity from an appendix into the main body of the Eléments at the same time as he introduced the written pledges model, but in his account of the former there is not a word about pledges. Indeed, since Walras assumed that the entrepreneurs do not know the production functions in the manner of an omniscient engineer, there is no way that they could experiment with written pledges to find the optimum proportions of the inputs. That can

only be done by actually hiring and using disequilibrium amounts of the inputs. This was indicated with great clarity by Walras when he wrote:

The "minimum average cost of production" [is] obtained through tatonnement by the entrepreneur who does not know the function ø [the production function] or Θ [the function specifying and relating the optimum coefficients of production], nor amuse himself by differentiating them, but who increases the quantity of service A as long as [the value of the marginal product of A exceeds the marginal factor cost] and who decreases it as long as [the reverse is true] (Walras to Enrico Barone, October 30, 1895, in 1965, 2, letter 1217, pp. 650–51).[5]

Walras's account of how the best combination of inputs is found is therefore part of his mature comprehensive model and is incompatible with the tatonnement process he wanted his written pledges model to have.

Walras's best work

Finally, incorporating as it does important aspects of the behavior of real markets, the mature comprehensive model, including Walras's detailed mature treatment of money (ch. 11), was his best work on the subject of general equilibrating processes and general equilibrium. The mature model is an almost complete system, and it is suggestive about the aspects that are missing from it. It is a brilliantly conceived forerunner of modern dynamic models that feature disequilibrium production, consumption, and savings, and the fact that it deals with the determination of a long-run flow of net savings and investment makes it a major neoclassical contribution to the literature on economic growth. The fruitful direction for future general equilibrium modelling lies in the development of that model through such means as the assimilation into it of imperfectly competitive market structures, and the exploration of its behavior during business fluctuations and in regard to the trend path of economic growth.

---

[5] In the last two sets of brackets are statements of conditions that Walras expressed in equations.

CHAPTER 10

Walras and his critics on the maximum utility of new capital goods

A part of the history of economic thought that has not previously been examined is the reception and resulting modification of Walras's theorem on the maximum utility of new capital goods. The reactions of his contemporaries and his responses to them, hidden for decades in his correspondence, reveal why and how he modified his theorem. His efforts to explain it to his correspondents and to persuade them of its correctness are invaluable as aids to understanding it because the presentation of the theorem in the *Eléments* is in some places difficult to follow and in some places incomprehensible. In this chapter, the criticisms of the theorem and Walras's responses are examined and evaluated, and a reformulation of the theorem is given.

I. Introduction

This chapter examines the details of Walras's modeling during his mature phase of theoretical activity of the behavior of savers, the determination of the batch of capital goods that savings are used to construct, the way that capital goods are treated with respect to depreciation and insurance, and the relation between the amount of capital and the services that it renders. The chapter thus continues the study of Walras's mature model of the capital-goods market as distinct from his model of the pricing of shares and bonds on the Bourse.

Walras presented a model of saving behavior in the first edition of the *Eléments*. In that model, a saver is influenced by a variety of variables as summarized by the individual gross saving relation:

$$e = f_e(p_t \ldots p_p \ldots p_k, p_{k'}, p_{k''} \ldots p_b, p_c, p_d \ldots i)$$

(1877b, p. 283) where e is the excess of income over consumption, p_t is the price of the productive services of land, p_p is the price of the services of personal capital, p_k etc. are the prices of the services of different capital goods, p_b etc. are the prices of different consumption goods, and i, in the notation Walras adopted in that particular exposition, is the rate of net income common to all capital goods. The function identifies gross rather than net savings because e includes income that is used to insure capital goods and

208

income that is set aside for their replacement. Walras summed the individual gross savings functions to obtain an aggregate gross saving function $E = F_e(...)$. He then specified D_k, $D_{k'}$, $D_{k''}$ ... as the quantities of new capital goods, and P_k etc. as their prices, with the price of each capital good equal in equilibrium to its cost of production as well as to the present value of the net income that the capital good will produce. In equilibrium the aggregate demand for new capital goods equals the aggregate supply of saving. Walras was therefore able to write the equation (ibid., p. 284):

$$D_k P_k + D_{k'} P_{k'} + D_{k''} P_{k''} + ... = E$$

Walras also provided eight sets of equations of general equilibrium (ibid., pp. 285–89), but in part they describe again the relations just discussed, and in part they deal with general equilibrium in the markets for productive services, products, and new capital goods rather than with the issues introduced by his theorem on the maximum utility of new capital goods. Although Walras based the aggregate savings function on individual savings functions, the latter were, as he observed (ibid., pp. 283–84), simply postulated on the basis of empirical considerations, not derived from an underlying theory of preferences and economic conditions.[1]

It can be seen that Walras's original model of saving was incomplete. It did not explain the motives for saving and investment, how the utility from saving is maximized, nor how the savings are directed toward the production of particular sorts of capital goods.

II. The initial statement of the theorem

About a decade after the publication of the foregoing analysis – in the mature period of his theoretical work – Walras began to think about extending his system to include consideration of those issues, and early in 1889 he produced a first version of a theorem he regarded as having the utmost importance, a theorem, he wrote, that not only crowned but confirmed his entire system of economic theory.[2] He called it the theorem on the maximum utility of new capital goods.

---

[1] In the second edition of the *Eléments* (1889, p. 271), Walras repeated his remarks on the empirical basis of the savings function as it was presented in lesson 23. In that same edition, he provided its theoretical basis in lesson 26, which is devoted to the theorem on the maximum utility of new capital goods.

[2] Walras to Foxwell, December 16, 1888, in 1965, *2,* letter 859, p. 279; Walras to Foxwell, March 13, 1889, in 1965, *2,* letter 869, p. 294. For evidence about some of Walras's earliest work on the subject, see his correspondence with the mathematician Hermann Amstein and Jaffé's notes to those letters (Walras to Amstein, October 2, 1888, in 1965, *2,* letter 850, pp. 268–69; October 3, 1888, in 1965, *2,* letter 851, pp. 269–70).

To judge by the correspondence on the matter, the theorem as it appeared on the galley proofs that Walras sent to a few economists must have been similar to what eventually appeared in the second edition of the *Eléments,* but with some different notation and lacking some explanations and important qualifications. After an introductory exposition of utility maximization with respect to all types of commodities, Walras began by observing that a trader's utility from new capital goods can be expressed as a function of either the consumption of the services yielded by the goods, or as a function of the goods themselves. Maximum total utility is achieved when the differential increments of the utility derived from each capital good are equal:

$$\Phi'_k(\delta_k)d\delta_k = \Phi'_{k'}(\delta_{k'})d\delta_{k''} = \Phi'_{k''}(\delta_{k''})d\delta_{k''} = \ldots \tag{1}$$

where δ_k etc., are the services of the capital goods (K), (K'), (K'') ..., and $\Phi'_k(\delta_{k''})$ etc. are their marginal utilities. Otherwise it would be advantageous to produce less of a good with a relatively small marginal utility and more of a good with a relatively large marginal utility (1889, pp. 298–99). It follows from general considerations of utility maximization that the marginal utilities must be directly proportional to the prices p_k etc. that are the measures in numeraire of the gross incomes produced by capital goods, or, more simply, that are the gross incomes from the goods or the prices of their services per time period. Using r rather than Φ', Walras stated (ibid., p. 299) the condition

$$\frac{r_k}{p_k} = \frac{r_{k'}}{p_{k'}} = \frac{r_{k''}}{p_{k''}} = \ldots \tag{2}$$

He then considered the problem of how society distributes its gross savings among the construction of various kinds of capital goods. To do that in such a way as to maximize utility, the differentials of the quantities produced of various capital goods must be inversely proportional to their prices P_k etc. in accordance with the equations

$$P_k d\delta_k = P_{k'} d\delta_{k'} = P_{k''} d\delta_{k''} = \ldots \tag{3}$$

With no further explanation, he concluded this section of the theorem by observing that the foregoing equations can be replaced by

$$\frac{p_k}{P_k} = \frac{p_{k'}}{P_{k'}} = \frac{p_{k''}}{P_{k''}} \tag{4}$$

These equations express the condition of maximum total utility from new capital goods for each saver (ibid.).[3]

In the second part of the theorem, Walras assumed that the new capital goods yield "productive income" – income that is not consumable directly, but is used in the production of other commodities (ibid., pp. 300–5). By an unintelligible process of reasoning, he arrived at two conclusions.[4] First, he stated that the equilibrium condition for capital goods that yield productive income is the same as condition (4). Second, he asserted that the price (π) of the services of a capital good net of the sums that must be set aside to provide for amortization and insurance must bear the same ratio to the price of the capital good for all capital goods for each trader:

$$\frac{\pi_k}{P_k} = \frac{\pi_{k'}}{P_{k'}} = \frac{\pi_{k''}}{P_{k''}} = \dots \tag{5}$$

III. Bortkiewicz's criticisms

Walras asked Ladislaus von Bortkiewicz, the brilliant young Polish Russian who was subsequently to become an eminent statistician, for his opinion on the preliminary version of the theorem.[5] Bortkiewicz immediately replied with an extensive criticism of it (Bortkiewicz to Walras, February 5, 1889, in 1965, 2, letter 865, pp. 282–86).[6]

---

[3] The rest of the text of the *Eléments* (§ 258) dealing with this topic was written after Bortkiewicz's criticism of the proofs.

[4] Jaffé's judgment was that Walras's mathematical exposition in the second part of his theorem is "obscure to the point of almost complete incomprehensibility," and that his method of analysis is "undecipherable" (Jaffé in Walras 1954, translator's notes, p. 539).

[5] The draft that Walras sent to Bortkiewicz, and subsequently to Edgeworth, was the galley proof of the theorem prepared for the second edition of the *Eléments* (Walras to Bortkiewicz, January 9, 1889, in 1965, 2, letter 863, pp. 281–82). Walras had sent Herbert Somerton Foxwell a copy of the theorem a day earlier (Walras to Foxwell, January 8, 1889, in 1965, 2, letter 862, pp. 280–81), but Foxwell did not comment on it.

[6] The fact that the theorem had its critics was briefly mentioned by David Collard (1973, p. 466), but he was interested in matters other than an explanation of it and its modification as a result of their comments. Jaffé was primarily concerned with the more general issue of Walras's model of capital formation. When Jaffé considered the theorem he did so, as will be seen, in order to try to correct what he believed were its notational deficiencies, not to review Walras's correspondence about it (see Jaffé 1953, pp. 311–13 [170–72]. See the translator's notes to Lesson 27 in Walras 1954, pp. 536–41, which are a summary of Jaffé 1953). Jaffé also wrote (Jaffé in Walras 1954, translator's notes, p. 536) that he had given an account of Francis Edgeworth's criticisms of the theorem, but none appears in the place to which he directed the reader (ibid., pp. 596–97), nor is there such an account elsewhere in Jaffé's writings, as far as I am aware, apart from one sentence (Jaffé 1935, p. 203 [31–32]) in which he mentioned Edgeworth's objection to Walras's treatment of the services and quantities of capital goods, and a footnote in which he reproduced Edgeworth's letter on the topic (ibid. [32]).

1. His first objection was that Walras had neglected to consider the amortization and insurance of capital goods that produce only consumable services (Bortkiewicz to Walras, February 5, 1889, in 1965, 2, letter 865, 283). The fact that a capital good produces income necessarily implies a period of time during which the income is gathered, or, as Walras had expressed it, a period during which capital goods gave birth to income (1889, p. 198).[7] Since they exist through time, they deteriorate. Having assumed in the first part of the theorem that all the proceeds from the use of capital goods are in the form of consumable services, rather than that they yield services that produce commodities, Walras should have taken account of the fact that those proceeds cannot provide for the amortization and insurance of the capital goods. If they are not repaired or replaced, as they deteriorate they yield less income. Eventually they are either used up or cease to function because of damage incurred in accidents. Arguing that these considerations necessitate a reformulation of the theorem, Bortkiewicz produced a revised set of equations.

2. Bortkiewicz's second objection related to another implication of the necessity of accounting for depreciation and insurance in Walras's theorem. To determine the conditions of the maximization of the utility of new capital goods, Bortkiewicz maintained, it is not appropriate to consider the utilities of the gross incomes generated by the capital goods. Bortkiewicz believed that by identifying the utility of new capital goods with the utility of the gross income that they produce, or rather, by measuring the former utility with the latter, Walras had committed a mistake. That mistake had led him to the system of equations

$$ p_k d\mathrm{D}_k = p_{k'} d\mathrm{D}_{k'} = p_{k''} d\mathrm{D}_{k''} = \dots $$

where Dd_k etc. are the differential increments of the aggregate quantities demanded of the capital goods.[8] Bortkiewicz argued in contrast that the utility of a new capital good is a function of its *net* income, because if it is maintained in good condition, then part of the gross income is absorbed by amortization and depreciation and only the net income is available to the owner. He therefore suggested replacing Walras's system by

---

[7] Walras had treated these considerations in connection with some aspects of his model of capital formation (1877b, pp. 279–82, 293–98; 1889, pp. 263–72).

[8] The transcript of Bortkiewicz's letter to Walras (Bortkiewicz to Walras, February 5, 1889, in 1965, 2, letter 865, pp. 282–86) records Bortkiewicz as writing "les quantités D_k, $D_{k'}$, $D_{k''}$ ... seraient donc les quantités de profit (K), (K'), (K'') ... consommées par N échangeurs." This is confusing unless it is remembered that the word "profit" in Walras's system means "capital services in kind," not the difference between revenue and cost. For the latter concept, Walras used the word "bénéfice." It must also be remembered that Walras often used the symbols (K), (K'), (K'') ... to indicate both different kinds of capital goods and the services yielded by different capital goods.

$$\pi_k d D_k = \pi_{k'} d D_{k'} = \pi_{k''} d D_{k''} = \ldots \tag{6}$$

where the π_k etc. are the incomes of the capital goods minus depreciation and insurance. This system can be combined with the equations

$$P_k d D_k = P_{k'} d D_{k'} = P_{k''} d D_{k''} = \ldots \tag{7}$$

where the P_k etc. are the prices of the capital goods, as distinct from the values p_k etc. of their services. The result of dividing (6) by (7), according to Bortkiewicz, is the correct way of deriving Walras's utility-maximizing condition (5).

Walras did not agree with this manner of derivation of the utility maximizing condition, even though he granted that Bortkiewicz's aggregative equations summarized the essence of the theorem (Walras to Bortkiewicz, February 20, 1889, in 1965, 2, letter 868, pp. 288–92). Walras pointed out that his equations differ from Bortkiewicz's by the substitution of the differentials of the quantities of capital goods (K), (K'), (K") ... produced for trader 1, namely the differentials $\partial_{k,1}, \partial_{k',1}, \partial_{k'',1} = \ldots$ in place of the differentials of the quantities $D_k, D_{k'}, D_{k''} \ldots$, which are quantities of capital goods produced for all traders. It seemed to Walras (ibid., p. 290) that this change in his exposition made it easier to demonstrate that the system

$$p_k d\delta_{k,1} = p_{k'} d\delta_{k'',1} = p_{k''} d\delta_{k'',1} = \ldots \tag{8}$$

expresses correctly the maximum satisfaction of trader 1. When all traders attain the condition of maximum satisfaction, the savings of society are distributed in a particular way among the various new capital goods that are to be produced. Walras made the galley-proof corrections that were necessary to clarify his meaning (ibid., p. 289), thus incorporating them into the *Eléments* (1889, pp. 289–304).

Nevertheless, Bortkiewicz was right in the main points made by his first and second criticisms. There is a question as to how capital goods are maintained if they produce only consumable services, and there is a question as to whether gross or net values of capital services should enter into the equilibrium conditions. Walras was therefore obliged to take account of amortization and insurance. In a letter to Bortkiewicz (Walras to Bortkiewicz, February 20, 1889, in 1965, 2, letter 868, pp. 288–92), he first assumed that amortization and insurance are paid "bénévolement" by the owners of capital – namely, at their own expense – rather than being added into the prices of the services. That is not a realistic assumption, and Walras did not elaborate on it, but turned instead to the assumption that amortization and insurance are paid by the consumers of the services (ibid.). Admitting to Bortkiewicz that his criticism made necessary a justification of the latter assumption, Walras proceeded to explain (ibid., pp. 290–91) that if consumers pay for amortization and insurance, the prices p_k etc. of the capital services are composed of two parts. For the capital good (K), for example, the part $(\mu_k + v_k)P_k$, is the sum that pays for amortization and insurance of the capital good, where μ is the proportion of the price of the capital good set aside for amortization, and v is the proportion set aside for insurance. The other component, $\pi_k = p_k - (\mu_k + v_k)P_k$, is the part that pays for the service itself. Under these conditions, the differentials of the quantities of services consumed, instead of being inversely proportional to the gross prices p_k, $p_{k'}$, $p_{k''}$ ... in accordance with equations (8), are inversely proportional to the net prices π_k, $\pi_{k'}$, $\pi_{k''}$ ... in accordance with the equations

$$\pi_k d\delta_k = \pi_{k'} d\delta_{k'} = \pi_{k''} d\delta_{k''} = ... \tag{9}$$

Dividing (9) by (3) results in

$$\frac{\pi_k}{P_k} = \frac{\pi_{k'}}{P_{k'}} = \frac{\pi_{k''}}{P_{k''}} = ... \tag{10}$$

The value of the ratio of π to P is the net rate of return on capital, or for each (K) for each trader, $\pi/P = i$ (1889, pp. 267, 305). System (10), identical in form to (5) but not restricted to capital goods that yield only productive services, assures the maximum utility of new capital goods, subject to the condition that amortization and insurance are paid by the consumers of the income from capital goods (Walras to Bortkiewicz, February 20, 1889, in 1965, 2, letter 868, pp. 288–92). Walras explained to Bortkiewicz that once the provision for amortization and insurance of capital goods has been made by setting aside part of the price of their services, there nothing else need be done to provide for their continuance (ibid.), and within the framework of his static analysis, Walras was correct in this respect. He therefore took account of Bortkiewicz's first two objections.

It is evident, nevertheless, that Bortkiewicz's criticism led to a modification of the *Eléments*, because the wording on the topic of amortization and insurance in Walras's letter is almost the same as in the passage on that topic that he added to the *Eléments*. Furthermore, in a letter to Herbert S. Foxwell (Walras to Foxwell, March 13, 1889, in 1965, 2, letter 869, pp. 292–94), Walras wrote that he was adding a section to his text to demonstrate that the equality of the rate of net income from capital goods, instead of the equality of the rate of gross income, requires that amortization and insurance be charged to the consumers of the services of the capital good.

3. Bortkiewicz, in his third objection, observed (Bortkiewicz to Walras,

February 5, 1889, in 1965, *2*, letter 865, pp. 282–86) that his suggestion that Walras use the ratio of π to P does not fully solve the problem of the conditions that ensure the maximum utility of new capital goods. The equations involving π are based on the supposition that a certain part of the gross income from a capital good is annually withheld for its upkeep, and that only the remainder is used for consumable services. Withholding funds for depreciation because of usage and accidents, however, constitutes in itself a particular use of income. The funds are used for the maintenance of the capital that produces them and for the production of new capital goods in replacement of those that are accidentally destroyed. Are these uses compatible with the maximum utility of new capital goods? The question, Bortkiewicz wrote, cannot be answered a priori. Although he did not elaborate on this matter, he appears to have been arguing that there has to be an optimum disposition of sinking funds and insurance premiums. Walras never responded to this minor but formally correct criticism, and his failure to do so allowed his statement of the conditions for maximization of utility to remain incomplete.

4. In his fourth objection, Bortkiewicz argued (ibid., p. 285) that Walras should have taken account of the time of receipt of the utility obtained from consuming the services of a capital good. The total utility of a given quantity of income differs depending on whether the moment when it can be consumed is more or less close to the moment at which the consumer makes a judgment about the utility of the product. Let it be assumed that a quantity q of income payable one year hence is believed by the consumer to have the same utility as a quantity $\epsilon_k q$ of income payable now, and a quantity payable two years hence to have the same utility as a quantity $\epsilon^2_k q$ payable now, and so on. According to Bortkiewicz, the distinction thus recognized between present and future utility necessitates a modification of Walras's formulas. The system of equations corresponding to a maximum utility of new capital goods in the case in which their incomes are all utilized as consumable services has to be written:

$$\frac{p_k}{P_k(1 - \epsilon_k + \rho_k \epsilon_k)} = \frac{p_{k'}}{P_{k'}(1 - \epsilon_{k'} + \rho_{k'} \epsilon_{k'})} = \ldots$$

Where $\rho_k, \rho_{k'} \ldots$ are coefficients of depreciation of capital through use and through use and accident.

Walras correctly rejected this criticism. He pointed out to Bortkiewicz (Walras to Bortkiewicz, February 20, 1889, in 1965, *2*, letter 868, pp. 288–92) that the theorem does not specify the length of time of the production or enjoyment of the services of a capital good, and has no need to do so, and he added the same observation to the proofs of the *Eléments* (1889, pp. 299–

300). The ratio p/P in the theorem is therefore simply the rate of gross income produced by a capital good, whether considered per year, per month, or per day. In Walras's particular formulation, it was assumed to be the annual rate of gross income. Similarly, he did not see (Walras to Bortkiewicz, February 20, 1889, in 1965, 2, letter 868, pp. 288–92) any relevance to Bortkiewicz's comments about the time that utilities become available. Since Walras considered interest as the price of the services of a capital good, or as the price of obtaining the income it produces, he had no need to explain the existence of interest by reference to the difference between present and future values in the manner of William Stanley Jevons and Eugen von Böhm-Bawerk. Walras recognized that their theories and his own are entirely different in that respect (ibid.).

5. One last matter troubled Bortkiewicz. On the galley proof, Walras described the theorem of the maximum utility of new capital goods as the point of departure for normative economics, which he called "social economics." He then used the theorem in defense of "free competition" (1889, pp. 306–7). In contrast, Bortkiewicz believed that it is erroneous to interpret the theorem as an argument either for or against the regime of free competition. Whereas normative economics properly considers alternative possible distributions of income and evaluates their justice, the theorem is part of positive economics, and positive economic theory in general and the demonstration of the theorem in particular therefore assume the distribution of income as a given datum (Bortkiewicz to Walras, February 5, 1889, in 1965, 2, letter 865, pp. 282–86). Bortkiewicz quoted Walras in support of his argument: "Our demonstration of free competition, while bringing forward the question of utility, leaves entirely aside the question of justice, because it limits itself to observing the distribution of output that follows from a particular distribution of productive services, and the question of justice still remains" (1889, p. 254).

Concerning the normative implications of the theorem, Walras refused to retract his opinions (Walras to Bortkiewicz, February 20, 1889, in 1965, 2, letter 868, pp. 288–92). In addition, he argued in favor of the necessity for a normative proof of the right of the capitalist to own his capital, and maintained that normative economics should also prove the right of the capitalist to make the consumer of the income from capital goods pay for the amortization and insurance of capital goods. Only after that two-fold proof has been developed, he contended, can applied economics transform the conclusion of economic theory on the maximum utility of new capital goods into the rule of conduct that there should be laissez-faire with respect to speculation and credit. Walras believed that there is nothing in those views that goes beyond premises that can be taken for granted (ibid.).

In this argument, both Bortkiewicz and Walras were correct, which is possible because they addressed different issues. Bortkiewicz was right to state that the theorem is not in itself a justification for the market system. It describes the process of individual choices concerning the demand for new capital goods and the reconciliation of those choices within the limits imposed by technology and the aggregate supply of savings. Walras agreed with this position, and indeed emphasized that the theorem does not establish the justice of that process. On the other hand, Walras was free, if he chose, to make an argument that he recognized as being dependent on assumptions and reasoning employed in the sphere of normative economics – free to go beyond positive economics to make the normative judgment that the process is good. He did so explicitly, approving of the maximization of utility that is facilitated by the system of competitive markets concerning to the construction of new capital goods, and hence approving of that system.

IV. Edgeworth's criticisms

A first model; Walras and Edgeworth interpreted by Jaffé

The other critic of Walras's theorem during the time it was in galley-proof stage was Francis Y. Edgeworth. Edgeworth's first criticism was that it was unclear why Walras used both equations (4) and (10) (Edgeworth to Walras, March 19, 1889, in 1965, 2, pp. 295–96). Jaffé believed (Jaffé 1953, p. 312 [170–71]) that Edgeworth was puzzled because he thought the two sets of equations were incompatible. Superficially, that appears to be the case, Jaffé argued, because they seem to have the same P. Believing that the two sets coexist in a given model, he contended that if P were defined in the same way in each system, the relationships described by the equations could be true only if $p = \pi$ for all capital goods, or if amortization and insurance are the same proportion of P for all capital goods (ibid., p. 312 [171]). Since those assumptions are unreasonable, Jaffé developed an explanation of how the equations should be interpreted in order to reveal their true compatibility.

Actually, Jaffé maintained, they refer to the behavior of different types of individuals, and P is defined differently in the two situations. System (4), according to Jaffé, is the calculation made by the consumer of capital-good services (ibid., p. 313 [172]). The value of p includes charges for amortization and insurance, and P, when used by Walras in (4), includes the price of the capital good "*plus* the provision of supplementary capital that consumers must make for each unit of each new capital good in order to ensure a regular flow of income to cover the depreciation and insurance charges of that capital good" (ibid.). Jaffé identified the price of the capital good plus the supplementary capital by the special symbol P*, called it "the cost of the capital good to the consumer," and rewrote (4) by using it in place of P.

Jaffé argued that "in a stationary state the cost to the consumer of a new capital good that ultimately wears out is not equal to the market price received by the producer of such a good" (ibid.), and that the true cost is P^*. That view cannot be accepted. In actuality, the capital good that the consumer buys is one with a certain length of life – one that is capable of yielding a certain amount of services. The cost to the consumer for that good is P, the market price received by its producer – not P^*. The consumer may, however, elect continually to repair a good so as to maintain it in a state like a new capital good, or may elect to replace the capital good and its successors when they wear out. In that case, over time he obtains and pays for more than the services that are locked up in the original capital good. He actually buys more than the original amount of the good, in reflection of which the addition of the present value of amortization to the price of the good results in counting the cost of the good more than once.

Jaffé continued by stating that "it is the P^*_k values and not the P_k that appear in the calculation made by the consumer to achieve a maximum of his effective utility" (ibid.). Jaffé therefore defined a fund $(P^* - P)$ that is actually established by the consumer at the time the capital good is bought. If Jaffé believed that a fund is actually established, then it must be observed that his belief is not realistic. Two paragraphs after his statement, however, he appears to have described a different procedure. Consumers must "provide an annual amount of saving in each future year sufficient to replace that unit when it is used up or destroyed. That annual provision, which must be made for all future time if the stationary state is to be preserved, is equivalent to the permanent investment of a sufficient amount of capital to produce that annual provision each year" (ibid., p. 315 [173]). In this ambiguous statement Jaffé may have implied that a fund is not actually established, but is a present value calculated for accounting purposes. Whatever he may have intended, the two procedures are not equivalent in their actual consequences. Establishing a fund now, on the one hand, and paying amortization and insurance charges as they arise periodically, on the other, are fundamentally different activities that have different effects on the owner's net worth. In the one case, he saves the amount of the fund, thus adding to his net worth; in the other, maintains his present consumption; and there are other obvious differences also.

Thus Jaffé argued that system (4) refers to the calculation made by the consumer of capital-good services. System (10), according to Jaffé, is the calculation made by the producer of a capital good. "What is of concern to the producer of a new capital good in his search for maximum profits are the P_k. It is therefore the P_k values, and not the P^*_k, which ought to appear" in equation (10) (ibid., p. 313 [173]). Objections to Walras's equations would not have arisen, Jaffé concluded, if Walras had used appropriate notation to distinguish P^* and P.

The correct interpretation

In actuality, Walras's letter to Bortkiewicz and the *Eléments* indicate that the two sets of equations are the result of different assumptions. They do not refer to a single model, but are descriptions of different models, and therefore should not and cannot be reconciled. Amortization and insurance are features of set (10), but they do not exist in set (4) or have no function that affects that set and Jaffé should not have introduced them into it. This is not an interpretation of Walras's work but a description of it, as is abundantly clear from his repeated assertions. For example, he wrote regarding set (4): "Nor does this take account of amortization and insurance of capital goods; alternatively said, it supposes that amortization and insurance are made gratuitously by the owners of capital goods at their own expense, and that the prices p_k, $p_{k'}$, $p_{k''}$. . . pay only for the services" (Walras to Bortkiewicz, February 20, 1889, in 1965, 2, letter 868, pp. 288–92). Again, Edgeworth indicated that Walras made clear in one set of proofs that set (4) "exists only provisionally, abstraction being made of 'amortissement' and insurances" (Edgeworth to Walras, March 19, 1871, in 1965, 2, letter 871, pp. 295–96). Subsequently, Walras wrote that "free competition leads to a rate of net income corresponding to or equal to the ratio of the net prices of the services of capital goods to the prices of the capital goods (*I here abstract from amortization and insurance*) following the equalities p_k/P_k etc. expressed by set (4) (Walras to Edgeworth, April 4, 1889, in 1965, 2, letter 876, pp. 305–06; emphasis added). With the italicized clause Walras was obviously identifying the assumption that results in the circumstance that the p_k etc. are the net prices as well as the gross prices in his first model. Similarly, in the second edition of the *Eléments*, Walras wrote down set (4), and then said of it: "Nor does this take account of amortization and insurance of capital goods; otherwise stated, it assumes either that the capital goods are indestructible or imperishable, or that their amortization and insurance are made gratuitously by the owners at their own expense" (1889, p. 300).

A second model

Walras used the model described in part by set (4) only as a first approximation – as a simple way of demonstrating the necessity for equality of the rate of return on different capital goods. He recognized that its assumptions are not satisfactory because they are purely formal in nature, rather than reflecting economic realities. Taking heed therefore of Bortkiewicz's criticisms, he turned to the construction of a second model, in which he assumed that capital goods wear out and that they are subject to accidents, and that amortization and insurance are not borne by the owners. After the second edition of the *Eléments* had been published, Bortkiewicz wrote to Walras that whether amortization and insurance are paid by the owners or the consumers, more savings will be channeled into capital goods that are indestructible than into those that are subject to wear and tear or accidental destruction (Bortkiewicz to Walras, September 12, 1889, in 1965, 2, letter 918, pp. 350–51). Furthermore, Bortkiewicz pointed out, to suppose that the owners gratuitously pay for the expense of amortization and insurance is contrary to the basic postulate that individuals try to maximize their own utility. That Walras agreed with this view was indicated by his saying so explicitly, by his assertion of the unrealism of set (4), and by his replacement of it by set (10) (Walras to Bortkiewicz, September 14, 1889, in 1965, 2, letter 919, p. 353). "I do not," he responded to Bortkiewicz, "attach any economic value to the maximum expressed by the system $p_k/P_k = p_{k'}/P_{k'} = ...$" (ibid.).

Bortkiewicz also argued that whether the expense of amortization and insurance is made by the owners or the consumers, the correct equilibrium condition is the proportionality of the net prices of capital services to the prices of the capital goods (Bortkiewicz to Walras, September 12, 1889, in 1965, 2, letter 918, pp. 350–51). Walras quite properly did not interpret Bortkiewicz's remarks as criticisms, since, as Walras observed, they were in full agreement with his own treatment of the issues (Walras to Bortkiewicz, September 14, 1889, in 1965, 2, letter 919, p. 353).

Here is the second model that Walras constructed: "If we *now* assume," he wrote, "that amortization and insurance are paid by the consumers of the services, the prices p_k, $p_{k'}$, $p_{k''}$ ... become constituted of two parts" (Walras to Bortkiewicz, February 20, 1889, in 1965, 2, letter 868, pp. 290–92; emphasis added), the part that pays for the service and the part that pays for amortization and insurance, as explained in the discussion of Bortkiewicz's criticisms. The services are priced so that they generate a flow of income that is adequate to replace the good when it is worn out and to insure it (ibid., p. 291). Taking cognizance of the fact that this model differs from set (4) posed no difficulty for Bortkiewicz, as was evident, for example, when he wrote to Walras about "the case in which the capital goods are no longer assumed to be indestructible and imperishable." Bortkiewicz argued "that once that assumption is relaxed, it is necessary to substitute the magnitudes π_k, $\pi_{k'}$ ... in place of the magnitudes p_k, $p_{k'}$ ...." (Bortkiewicz to Walras, September 12, 1889, in 1965, 2, letter 918, pp. 350–51), a comment with which Walras agreed in his reply (Walras to Bortkiewicz, September 14, 1889, in 1965, 2, letter 919, pp. 353–54) to Bortkiewicz's letter. Walras showed once more that the relaxation of the assumption leads to the second model and thus to set (10), in which the π magnitudes must be used because amortization and insurance are deducted from the gross income generated by the capital goods (Walras to Bortkiewicz, September 14, 1889, in 1965, 2, letter 919, pp. 353–54; and see Walras to Bortkiewicz, February 20, 1889, in 1965, 2, letter 868, pp. 288–92). In his second model, as formulated for Bortkiewicz, Walras therefore treated the costs of amortization and insurance as a component of p, but not as an addition to the denominator of (10). Thus he did not define P differently in systems (4) and (10). In both systems, the denominator is the price at which the capital good is purchased on the market.

In his treatment of the matter in the *Eléments* (1889, p. 300), Walras set forth a variation of (10):

> If one now wished to introduce the condition that amortization and insurance are made at the expense of the consumers of the services, it would be necessary, while leaving the maximum satisfaction of wants to be established by the proportionality of the *raretés* of incomes to their prices, to add *to the cost of production* of each unit of capital the sum necessary to provide, at the rate of net income of that capital, both amortization and insurance (1889, p. 300).

Jaffé interpreted that variation as an abandonment of the initial assumptions behind set (4), leading to an amendment of (4) (Jaffé 1953, pp. 314–15 [172–73]), but in fact it has nothing to do with that set. Walras had put (4) to one side and was analyzing a model in which amortization and insurance are relevant. His concern in the quoted passage and subsequent mathematical analysis was to identify an alternative description of the consequences of the model that results in (10). This he did by adding the annual amortization and insurance charges into the numerator so as to make it equal to p, and by adding the present value of those charges into the denominator, using i, the net rate of return to the capital good and the equilibrium rate of interest, as the rate of discount. Thus,

$$\frac{\pi + a + y}{P + \dfrac{a + y}{i}} = i \tag{10'}$$

where a is the annual amortization charge and y is the annual insurance premium. It can be seen by simple algebraic manipulation, however, that (10') reduces to $\pi/P = i$, which is a simple way of stating (10). Systems (10) and (10') therefore state precisely the same rate of return; they are descriptions of the same model.

Economic agent to whom the theorem refers

Walras's account of the economic behavior related to (10′) leaves much to be desired, however. It is evident that he was referring in the quoted passage to calculations made by the owner of a capital good, because in the sentence that preceded it he noted that he was dealing with "les propriétaires." The details of the procedure he described therefore make no sense, because a person who buys a capital good and sells its services – a "pure owner" – does not calculate the cost of production of the good. He is concerned only with the price he pays for it, and with the price, including the expenses of amortization and insurance, he charges for its services. The latter price depends on the cost of producing the capital-good services, which ordinarily will have no relation to the cost of producing the capital good, except for the amortization and insurance components. Alternatively, despite the sentence that precedes it, the assumption could be made that Walras's reference to additions to the cost of production of the capital good describes the behavior of a manufacturer who sells the capital goods he constructs – a "pure producer." That would not make sense either, because a pure producer of a capital good has nothing to do with providing for its amortization and insurance. He receives no money for these purposes, inasmuch as he does not possess the capital good after he has sold it, and has no interest in whether or not it is subsequently amortized and insured. Moreover, Walras could not have been stating that a consumer who buys capital-good services and does not own the capital that yields them – a "pure consumer" – calculates the rate of return, because such a person has nothing to do with calculating the cost of production of the capital good.

The question therefore arises: To what type of economic actor does Walras's theorem refer? The answer given by Jaffé resulted from his belief that (4) and (10) refer to the same model. That belief required him not only to define the cost of capital goods differently in the two sets, but also to represent the calculations as being made by two different types of economic actors. This led him to postulate economic processes that are inconsistent with Walras's models and with economic behavior, as will now be shown. Contrary to Jaffé's view, system (4) does not refer to a person in his capacity as a consumer of capital-good services. It is not appropriate to suppose that a pure consumer adds the present value of amortization and insurance onto P to calculate Jaffé's P*, for the reason that the consumer does not buy the capital good and therefore does not pay its price or provide for its replacement. Furthermore, a pure consumer has no interest in calculating the rate of return on a capital good, because the rate of return accrues not to him but to the owner of the capital good. In contrast, a consumer who owns the capital good that yields the services he consumes is in a different situation. This is the only instance in which system (4) would be calculated by a consumer, and he would do so in his capacity as an owner. Jaffé's interpretation of that system therefore requires the supposition that the consumer buys all the capital goods that yield the services he consumes, whereas in reality he frequently purchases the services of capital goods that he does not own.

Reference of the theorem to an owner

In fact, the answer to the question posed above is that Walras expressly and repeatedly indicated that system (4) refers to the same type of person, the owner of capital goods (1889, pp. 299–300, 305; Walras to Bortkiewicz, February 20, 1889, in 1965, 2, letter 868, pp. 288–92; Walras to Foxwell, March 13, 1889, in 1965, 2, letter 869, pp. 292–94; Walras to Edgeworth, March 22, 1889, in 1965, 2, letter 872, pp. 297–98; Walras to Edgeworth, April 4, 1889, in 1965, 2, letter 876, pp. 305–06; Walras to Wicksteed, April 9, 1889, in 1965, 2, letter 877, pp. 307–9). Even in the absence of Walras's explanations, it would be evident from the definition of the terms and from the nature of the equations as measuring the rate of return on a capital good that set (4) is a calculation made by the owner of a capital good. Since there are no amortization or insurance charges in the model described by (4), p is both the gross and the net income received by the owner through the sale of the services of the good, and P (the price that he pays for the good) does not include amortization and insurance. Clearly, the owner calculates the ratio of p to P in order to determine his rate of return.

Similarly, contrary to Jaffé's view, system (10) does not refer to a producer of capital goods but to an owner of them, as Walras repeatedly stated (ibid.). The type of economic actor of whom Jaffé was writing, the pure producer, would be happy to manufacture a capital good even if its purchaser obtained no return at all from it, and even if its amortization and insurance absorbed its entire revenue. The numerator of (10), which is the flow of net income from the sale of the services of the good, cannot refer to the income of a pure producer, because he does not own the good. In fact, even without Walras's explanations, it is evident that in system (10) the numerator is the net income received by the owner of a capital good. The only circumstance in which the calculation indicated by (10) is made by a producer of a capital good is when he retains it and uses its services himself, and he makes the calculation as an owner to determine whether the good is worth replacing or augmenting. The producer who retains a capital good and uses or sells its services is in exactly the same position as a consumer who buys a capital good and uses its services himself, or as a buyer of a capital good who sells its services to others. They are all owners of capital goods who pay P for their capital good, or incur P as its cost of production; they make provision for amortization and insurance charges and therefore add them into the calculation of p, but subtract them from p to determine π; and they calculate π/P, because that is their rate of return.

Edgeworth's perplexity

There is no need to speculate about why Edgeworth was puzzled by (4) and (10), because he explained the reason. "I find . . . a difficulty," he wrote to Walras,

in the establishment of *both* the systems of equations. . . . In your last proof you have inserted some additional matters, importing as I understand that the system (1) exists only provisionally, abstraction being made of "amortissement" and insurances. *But at p. 305 (January proof) I do not find any such explanation.* Perhaps there has been some *lapsus calami* (Edgeworth to Walras, March 19, 1889, in 1965, 2, letter 871, pp. 295–96; emphasis added to the sentence).

Edgeworth did not understand the reason for stating both (4) and (10) because on the particular page that Edgeworth had under review, Walras had not made clear that he was making alternative assumptions whereby in (4) there are no amortization or insurance charges, and in (10) there are. Evidently, Walras's amplifications in his letter of April 4, 1889, quoted earlier, conveyed his meaning, for Edgeworth subsequently wrote (Edgeworth to Walras, April 12, 1889, in 1965, 2, letter 878, p. 310) that the reason for using both sets of equations had become evident to him. Utilizing the market for geese as a synecdoche, Edgeworth expressed his understanding that when using π, Walras made allowance for the goose's food and for the risk of its' flying away – for amortization and insurance – and when using p in his first model he assumed that no provision need be made for those matters. Walras and Edgeworth therefore had a meeting of the minds on the interpretation of systems (4) and (10), although Edgeworth rightly continued to believe (ibid.) that Walras's exposition of the sets of equations at the end of the theorem in the *Eléments* (1889, p. 305) is unclear.

Edgeworth's second criticism was directed at an aspect of the theorem that Walras confessed was "knotty" in letters to Foxwell and Bortkiewicz – namely, Walras's contention that "the quantities of capital goods produced are also the quantities consumed of services," and that a given utility function therefore has two different sets of differentials – those of the services and those of the goods (Walras to Foxwell, February 13, 1889, in 1965, 2, letter 867, pp. 287–88; Walras to Foxwell, March 13, 1889, in 1965, 2, letter 869, pp. 292–94). Edgeworth remarked, after reading the proofs of the theorem and the letter to Foxwell, that "the knot is to me a Gordian one" (Edgeworth to Walras, March 19, 1889, in 1965, 2, letter 871, pp. 295–96) for the reason that the amounts of services and of capital goods are not the same nor equal in magnitude. There is, he maintained, no necessary equality between such things as, for example, the price paid to rent a bottle and the price of a bottle, or between the wear and tear of old bottles and the production of new bottles (Edgeworth to Walras, March 29, 1889, in 1965, 2, letter 874, pp. 299–300). In the case of an indestructible capital good such as silver plate, it can be clearly seen that the amount of services of the plate demanded by a person and the amount of plate that the person wants as a possession are not the same thing. For a person to use a certain amount of the annual services of a capital good, Edgeworth argued, it is not necessary for a capitalist to produce capital goods equal in number to the services consumed of those capital goods (Edgeworth to Walras, undated postmarked May 7, 1889, in 1965, 2, letter 886, pp. 317–18). For the consumption of additional services of a capital good to occur it is not necessary that a capitalist produce a new capital good. Walras's view was therefore unacceptable, Edgeworth wrote to him: "The implied correspondence between the capital used . . . and the capital newly made is still to me unintelligible" (ibid.). The quantity of silver plate, for example, may be constant, and it would nevertheless be true that the amount of services yielded by the plate may vary from time to time. Accordingly, Walras's use of two different sets of differentials was incomprehensible (Edgeworth to Walras, March 29, 1889, in 1965, 2, letter 874, pp. 299–300). Referring once more to his synecdoche, Edgeworth argued that there is no relationship between the egg market and the goose market like the one implied by those differentials (Edgeworth to Walras, April 12, 1889, in 1965, 2, letter 878, p. 310). They cannot be both of the nature of services and of the nature of capital goods (Edgeworth to Walras, March 29, 1889, in 1965, 2, letter 874, pp. 299–300; Edgeworth to Walras, April 12, 1889, in 1965, 2, letter 878, p. 310).

Walras admitted (Walras to Edgeworth, March 22, 1889, in 1965, 2, letter 872, pp. 297–98) that he also had been troubled by the difficulties that Edgeworth found in the theorem on new capital goods, but Walras felt that he had resolved them. The utilities to a trader of the goods (K), (K'), (K'') . . ., Walras insisted, may be expressed as functions either of the quantities consumed of the capital services or of the quantities of capital produced, since the same number indicates those two different kinds of quantities (Walras to Edgeworth, March 25, 1889, in 1965, 2, letter 873, pp. 298–99). A person who owns 10 silver plates worth 100 francs each is a capitalist who possesses a capital good worth 1,000 francs that he rents to himself, for 40 francs if the annual rate is 4 percent. He is also a consumer who annually uses 40 francs' worth of services of silver plate. The quantity of services of silver plate he consumes is 10, and that is also the quantity of silver plate he owns (Walras to Edgeworth, April 4, 1889, in 1965, 2, letter 876, pp. 305–6). In the general case, Walras argued, the quantity δ can therefore be introduced into the individual's utility function either as a quantity of capital services consumed, or as a quantity of new capital goods produced, even though utility is derived from the services of capital, not from the capital itself (Walras to Edgeworth, May 3, 1889, in 1965, 2, letter 881, pp. 314–15).

It follows, Walras reasoned, that the differentials ($\partial \delta$) of the quantities of services consumed and the differentials ($d\delta$) of the quantities of new capital goods are not the same. Walras had earlier expressed this same view to Bortkiewicz (Walras to Bortkiewicz, February 20, 1889, in 1965, 2, letter 868, pp. 288–92) and Foxwell (Walras to Foxwell, March 13, 1889, in 1965, 2, letter 869, pp. 292–94). The partial differentiation can first be done with respect to the quantities of services consumed, which results in the system of equations

$$r_k \partial \delta_k = r_{k'} \partial \delta_{k'} = r_{k''} \partial \delta_{k''} = \ldots$$

where, as before, r is the derivative $\Phi'(\delta)$ of the utility function (Walras to Edgeworth, March 25, 1889, in 1965, 2, letter 873, pp. 298–99). These equations express the maximum satisfaction of wants. The differentiation can then be done with respect to the quantities of new capital goods produced, which results in the system of equations

$$r_k d \delta_k = r_{k'} d \delta_{k'} = r_{k''} d \delta_{k''} = \ldots$$

These equations express the maximum utility of new capital goods (ibid.). Walras wondered whether the same type of circumstance arose in any other branch of applied mathematics – the singular circumstance of functions in which the variables can at the same time express two different sorts of quantities that are necessarily equal but that have different differentials. The more he thought about the problem, the more he was convinced that the equations furnish the key to the theorem of the maximum utility of new capital goods (ibid., p. 299). Edgeworth was provided by Walras with a numerical example designed to reinforce his position (Walras to Edgeworth, March 22, 1889, in 1965, 2, letter 872, pp. 297–98), and with a copy of a diagrammatic explanation he originally constructed for Foxwell (Walras to Foxwell, March 13, 1889, in 1965, 2, letter 869, pp. 292–94). These materials do not clarify Walras's argument in any respect, however, because the assumptions that Edgeworth questioned are presented in both the example and the diagram as unexplained axioms. To improve the clarity of the exposition in the *Eléments*, Walras informed Foxwell, he was introducing different symbols for the two differential increments (Walras to Foxwell, March 13, 1889, in 1965, 2, letter 869, pp. 292–94). In short, Walras did not accept Edgeworth's argument, but an examination of his rebuttal reveals that all he did was to restate his position without providing a rationale for it.

Who was right? Walras's assumption of a fixed proportional relationship between capital goods and their services has some merit, because it is true with reference to working capital such as coal, and because it may sometimes be a useful simplification with regard to durable capital. The difficulty with Walras's procedure is that he did not regard himself as making a simplifying assumption, useful in some contexts, but as describing a literal and general truth, and Edgeworth was right to reject that view. Walras's assumption is often contrary to the facts of the relation between services or output and the capital good used in the process of producing them, and is often an assumption that distorts rather than clarifies. In many cases, the services or output and the capital good will not be equal in number, and in many cases a capital good can be used to produce varying amounts of services or output per year. Furthermore, it is ordinarily not possible to determine precisely how much of a capital good is used up as it yields its services, a circumstance that is reflected in the arbitrary nature of depreciation allowances.[9]

The charge of redundancy

Edgeworth's third criticism made use of the fact that Walras had demonstrated in the first edition of the *Eléments* that maximization of utility is a general outcome of competitive markets. The sale of capital goods occurs in markets, Edgeworth observed, so the maximization of utility that Walras had shown to occur in any market necessarily also occurs in the markets for capital goods (Edgeworth to Walras, March 29, 1889, in 1965, 2, letter 874, pp. 299–300). Edgeworth felt that there is therefore no need to demonstrate maximization for the special case of the markets for capital goods, and thus no need for Walras's theorem on the maximum utility of new capital goods (ibid.). This observation led Walras to comment to Wicksteed (Walras to Wicksteed, April 9, 1889, in 1965, 2, letter 877, pp. 307–9) that at the time of writing the first edition of the *Eléments* he had thought his general theorem of maximization of utility applied directly to the marginal utility of new capital goods also, but he subsequently saw that a special analysis was necessary for their case because of the difference between income and capital.

Enlarging on this thesis, Walras wrote to Edgeworth that a fundamental aspect of economics (Walras to Edgeworth, April 4, 1889, in 1965, 2, letter 876, pp. 305–6) is the distinction between income – things that are used only once – and capital – things that are used more than once (1877b, p. 213;

---

[9] I am indebted to Vernon Smith, Robert Clower, and David Collard for comments on this issue. Smith's point of view is that the concept of capital-good services is not illuminating. He argues that the essential property of capital is its presence as a physical entity when current flow inputs are transformed into current output. Capital, in his view, does not provide something productive distinct from its presence as a nonconsumed input in the productive process (Smith 1964, pp. 131–32).

1889, p. 197). The theories of exchange and of production, Walras continued (Walras to Edgeworth, April 4, 1889, in 1965, 2, letter 876, pp. 305–6), both deal with the allocation of income by individuals to satisfy their various wants on the assumption that the aggregate quantities of capital goods are given. Each theory consists of two distinct parts. In one part, it is established for each type of income or service that free competition leads to the price at which supply and demand are equated. In the other part, it is established that there is a maximum satisfaction of wants because marginal utilities are made proportional to prices. In contrast, the object of the theory of capital formation is to solve the problem of how a society distributes its total annual savings among the creation of different kinds of new capital goods, and they are therefore unknowns that have to be determined. In accordance with the distinctions that have just been made, the theory of their determination is composed of two parts. One part establishes that free competition leads to a rate of net income that is uniform for all capital goods. The other part establishes that, as a result of the foregoing process, there is a maximum utility of the aggregate quantities D_k, $D_{k'}$, $D_{k''}$ ... of new capital goods produced. On introducing the quantities of capital goods produced for each trader as variables in the utility function, instead of the quantities of services consumed, it can be demonstrated (ibid., p. 306; and see Walras to Wicksteed, April 9, 1889, in 1965, 2 letter 877, pp. 307–9) that the condition of maximum utility in the production of new capital goods for each trader is

$$\frac{r_k}{P_k} = \frac{r_{k'}}{P_{k'}} = \frac{r_{k''}}{P_{k''}}$$

On reviewing Walras's arguments, Edgeworth made an effort to be diplomatic by describing himself (Edgeworth to Walras, April 12, 1889a, in 1965, 2, letter 878, p. 310) to Walras as being "in complete agreement with the views which you have so kindly restated in your last." He understood Walras to be saying precisely what he, Edgeworth, had suspected – namely, that the utility maximization that had been proved for the markets for services and products is also true for the markets for capital goods. Walras had proved that the price of goose eggs is determined by maximizing utility, and Edgeworth agreed that Walras had then proved that the same is true for the price of geese. The latter proof was of course precisely what Edgeworth felt was unnecessary, as he proceeded to indicate once more in his review (Edgeworth 1889a, p. 435) of the second edition of the *Eléments*.

Commenting on the issue to Bortkiewicz after reading the review, Walras gave a particularly clear statement of his position. "As I expected," he lamented,

Edgeworth continues to fail to understand that the theory of capital formation raises two problems of maximum effective utility. One is the question of knowing which capital goods ought to be constructed, and the other, the question of knowing how the services of those new capital goods ought to be distributed (always, it is understood, taking account of the conditions of a uniform rate of net income for the capitalists and a uniform price of the capital-good services for the consumers). He maintains that everything has been said when the second problem is solved, and he honestly believes that I am amusing myself by inventing the first for the pleasure of complicating matters. In thinking of all the trouble that the theorem of the maximum utility of new capital goods has given me, I found that idea most diverting (Walras to Bortkiewicz, October, 17, 1889, in 1965, *2*, letter 927, pp. 363–64).

Edgeworth was surely wrong in his judgment. The markets for capital goods have characteristics that distinguish them from markets for directly consumable goods, and that, given the logic of the Walrasian system, make necessary a separate theorem regarding the equilibrium of their markets for the reasons that Walras indicated. Furthermore, it is interesting to establish the conditions of equilibrium of capital-goods markets, as Walras, in his fashion, did in this theorem.

No meeting of minds about the charge of redundancy

As their correspondence dragged on, Walras began to lose patience with Edgeworth, despite his protestation to the contrary, and he delivered what could not have failed to be an irritating lecture. He explained to Edgeworth that it was not until after writing the first edition of the book – that is, until his mature phase of theorizing – that he had seen the necessity of the theorem. He had become convinced that Edgeworth would also see its necessity and appreciate its value if he would carefully reread the entire theory of production and capital-formation in the *Eléments:*

Recall that almost always at the introduction of important mathematical theories it is difficult to grasp the principle involved. This difficulty is surmounted when one has the conviction that it is necessary to surmount it and the resolution to do so. You stand at the threshold of the theory of capital. I will wait patiently, in the expectation that you will cross it (Walras to Edgeworth, April 4, 1889, in 1965, *2*, letter 876, pp. 305–6).

Walras maintained that he had taken account of the aspects of the theorem that puzzled Edgeworth, and had corrected the second edition of the *Eléments* in order to make his thought clearer. He would, he wrote, be overjoyed to learn that Edgeworth completely accepted the proof of the theorem and agreed that it confirmed the theory of capital (Walras to Edgeworth, May 3, 1889, in 1965, *2*, letter 881, pp. 314–15). On that note, the debate between Edgeworth and Walras on the theorem ended. When Walras mentioned the theorem in his subsequent letters to Edgeworth, he did not try to argue in favor of his views. It was without comment that he sent Edgeworth a copy of a correction to the preface of the second edition of the *Eléments* (Walras to Edgeworth, July 17, 1889, in 1965, *2*, letter 892, pp. 320–21), modifying the equation relating the demand for the services of new capital goods and the quantities of capital goods produced (Walras 1896b, XXI–XXII). Walras once more expressed his desire that the theorem be accepted by Edgeworth, but regretfully remarked that "since that is impossible, I renounce the effort to persuade you" (Walras to Edgeworth, March 8, 1890, in 1965, 2, letter 964, pp. 399–400). Edgeworth refused to cross the threshold to the theoretical edifice that Walras had constructed, and Walras refused to demolish it in accordance with Edgeworth's analysis.

V. The mature theorem

It is now possible, using the *Eléments* and the clarifications furnished by Walras's correspondence, to provide a reasonably clear and concise statement of the theorem as it was presented by Walras in the mature phase of his theoretical activity.[10] The theorem which, as is now apparent, is actually an exposition of considerable length, was divided by Walras into two parts. In the first part, he assumed that all the income from new capital goods is in the form of consumable services. He then analyzed two problems. One (1889, pp. 296–98) was the question of how a consumer distributes his income among the diverse services of different capital goods to maximize his satisfaction, on the assumption, not stated explicitly in the *Eléments* but explained in Walras's correspondence (Walras to Edgeworth, April 4, 1889, in 1965, 2, letter 876, pp. 305–6; Walras to Wicksteed, April 9, 1889, in 1965, 2, letter 877, pp. 307–9), that the aggregate amount and composition of the capital stock is already determined. Throughout the theorem it is assumed that the prices of capital services and goods are determined as part of the general

---

[10] Walras's statement of the theorem in his article "Théorème d'utilité maxima des capitaux neufs" (1889) was republished as §§ 257 and 258 of the second edition of the *Eléments*. The theorem was presented again without change in the third edition of the *Eléments* (1896b, pp. 296–307). In the fourth edition, the two parts of the theorem were put into separate chapters (1900, lesson 26, pp. 275–80, and lesson 27, pp. 281–87), but all the conclusions were the same as in previous editions, and all the analysis, except that in one respect Walras changed the exposition of how the conclusions are reached. Providing another instance of the deterioration of the quality of his analyses after the mature period of his work, instead of using system (3), he adopted, for each trader, an incredibly cumbersome procedure. He paired every capital good with (K), the first capital good, and set the sum of the values of the differential increments of each pair equal to zero (ibid., pp. 276–77, 279, 285). For trader 1, the equations are

$$P_k d\delta_{k,1} + P_k d\delta_{k',1} = 0$$
$$P_k d\delta_{k,1} + P_{k''} d\delta_{k'',1} = 0$$
$$\cdots\cdots\cdots\cdots\cdots\cdots$$
$$P_k d\delta_{k,1} + P_{k^n} d\delta_{k^n,1} = 0$$

Walras's exposition in the second edition is clearly superior.

equilibrium of the entire economy. When a trader's utility is maximized, he consumes amounts of the services of capital goods so as to achieve the equalities

$$r_k d\delta_k = r_{k'} d\delta_{k'} = r_{k''} d\delta_{k''} = \dots \tag{1}$$

where $d\delta$ is the differential increment of the services. It is also true in equilibrium that the value of the marginal quantity of services consumed of each capital good is the same:

$$p_k d\delta_k = p_{k'} d\delta_{k'} = p_{k''} d\delta_{k''} = \dots \tag{8}$$

Dividing (1) by (8) the condition of maximum satisfaction of wants is obtained:

$$\frac{r_k}{P_k} = \frac{r_{k'}}{P_{k'}} = \frac{r_{k''}}{P_{k''}} = \dots \tag{2}$$

Today we would say that this common ratio attained in equilibrium by a trader is equal to the marginal utility of income. In his analysis of this problem, Walras explained the reason for the existence of a market for the services yielded by capital goods. The services are bought because of their utility, and the amount and kinds of services bought by any trader are those that maximize his utility.

The second problem is the question of how a society distributes its savings to obtain the production of particular amounts of the various kinds of new capital goods. In this analysis, the quantities of new capital goods are unknowns that are to be determined (1889, p. 299). To examine the problem, Walras chose to regard utility as a function of δ interpreted as the quantity of a capital good, but in this reformulation, utility will be regarded as a function of the services that are themselves a function f of the quantity (x) of a capital good, or $u_k = \Phi_k(f_k(x_k))$, and similarly for the other capital goods. The rest of Walras's theorem then follows without the difficulty caused by assuming that the quantity of capital is the same as the quantity of services. When a trader's utility is maximized, he buys amounts of capital goods such that

$$r_k dx_k = r_{k'} dx_{k'} = r_{k''} dx_{k''} = \dots \tag{11}$$

where dx is the differential increment of the amount acquired of a capital good. It is also true in equilibrium that the value of the marginal quantity of each kind of capital good acquired is the same:

$$P_k dx_k = P_{k'} dx_{k'} = P_{k''} dx_{k''} = \ldots \tag{12}$$

Dividing (11) by (12), the condition obtained is

$$\frac{r_k}{P_k} = \frac{r_{k'}}{P_{k'}} = \frac{r_{k''}}{P_{k''}} = \ldots \tag{13}$$

Equations (13) state that to maximize utility, each owner of capital goods makes the ratio of the marginal utility of the services to the price of the good equal for all goods. This condition, which is central to a statement of Walras's theorem, is not mentioned in the statement of the theorem in the *Eléments,* but is given in his correspondence (Walras to Edgeworth, April 4, 1889, in 1965, 2, letter 876, pp. 305–6; Walras to Wicksteed, April 9, 1889, in 1965, 2, letter 877, pp. 307–9) and in an article entitled "Geometrical Theory of the Determination of Prices" (1892a) that he added as an appendix to the third edition of the *Eléments* (1896b, pp. 463–80).

Walras initially assumed that either capital goods do not require amortization or insurance, or if such charges are made, they are not paid out of the gross incomes the capital goods produce. Each owner calculates the rate of return obtained by dividing the price of the services yielded by a capital good by the cost of the good. As long as one capital good yields a higher rate of return than another, more of it will be demanded and less of those that yield a lower return. This will lead to an adjustment of yields and of capital-good prices until, for each owner of capital goods, the following condition (1889, p. 299) is fulfilled:

$$\frac{P_k}{P_k} = \frac{P_{k'}}{P_{k'}} = \frac{P_{k''}}{P_{k''}} = \ldots \tag{4}$$

In the second part of his theorem, Walras assumed (1889, pp. 300–05) that new capital goods do not produce consumable capital services directly, but instead produce services that are used in the production of commodities. He continued to assume that no amortization or insurance charges are made against capital-good incomes. Putting aside his obscure mathematics,[11] the model leads, by the same reasoning as in the preceding case, to the conclusion that the maximum total utility of the income from capital to each owner occurs when, for each capital good, the ratio of the income to the price of the good is the same for all capital goods. This is the same condition as (4), except that it refers to goods that produce productive services.

Walras then assumed that capital goods that yield consumable or produc-

---

[11] See note 4 and Jaffé in Walras 1954, translator's notes, 534–41; and Jaffé 1953 [151–75].

tive services wear out and are subject to accidents, and that provision for amortization and insurance is made out of the sums that are paid for their services or, he implicitly assumed, is charged to the imputed value of their services. The purchasers of consumable services are pure consumers or consumer-owners; the purchasers of productive services are producers who rent the capital goods or are owners of the goods who use them in their own businesses and who make an imputed charge for the services. In accordance with the analysis that Walras developed in his correspondence, the owners of the capital goods calculate a net rate of return, what Walras called the net rate of income, by dividing π by P. In an effort to maximize his total return, each owner acquires more of capital goods with higher yields and less of those with lower yields until, for each owner, the following condition obtains:

$$\frac{\pi_k}{P_k} = \frac{\pi_{k'}}{P_{k'}} = \frac{\pi_{k''}}{P_{k''}} = \dots \tag{10}$$

This net rate of return, which in equilibrium is the same for capital goods of all types, is the condition for the maximization of the utility of new capital goods, and is the essence of Walras's theorem on the subject. Buyers of capital goods indicate to the producers of the goods what kinds are desired. When supply and demand are equal in the market for each newly produced type of capital good, each purchaser acquires the particular kinds and amounts of the capital goods that maximize his utility. Those amounts, when added for all traders, are the aggregate quantities of new capital goods produced.

In his analysis of the problem of how the kinds and amounts of new capital goods are determined, Walras explained the reason for the existence of a market for capital goods, as distinct from a market for capital services. Some traders want to acquire capital goods, rather than simply to hire their services; and some traders find it convenient – as with household goods – to own the capital goods that yield the services they use. The traders acquire the batch of new capital goods that maximize utility, and thus the savings of society are transformed into new capital goods which yield consumable and productive services. Walras therefore provided a basis in individual motivation for his model of the formation of new capital goods.

VI. Conclusion

Walras realized, he wrote, that it was not a great discovery to have recognized that there is an increase in utility to society if capital is taken out of employments where it yields relatively low returns and transferred to employments where it yields greater returns (Walras to Edgeworth, May 3, 1889, in

1965, 2, letter 881, pp. 314–15). He believed, however, that it was a considerable achievement to have furnished a mathematical demonstration of so
plausible a fact, and that the agreement with experience of the outcomes of
his model proves that it uses realistic definitions and analytical techniques.
Walras maintained that the truth of his theoretical system in general and of
his theory of capital in particular is confirmed by the theorem (ibid., pp. 314–
15; and see Walras to Foxwell, March 13, 1889, in 1965, 2, letter 869, pp.
292–94; 1889, xxiii), because it reveals the operation in the capital-good
markets of the same principles that operate in all other markets: the principles
of maximum total utility for each trader and of a single price for any given
commodity. "A formula of two lines therefore expresses the double condition
by which the world of economic interests regulates itself. The formula
comprehends the entire science and furnishes the explanation for an innumer-
able multitude of particular facts" (1889, p. 306).

Walras was right to believe that his theorem, despite its defects and the
defects of his exposition of it, was a contribution to early general-equilibrium
analysis. The theorem was necessary to complete his analysis of markets by
furnishing a rationale for the conduct of savers and investors and by completing his description of the conditions of equilibrium in the markets for capital
goods and capital services in his mature comprehensive model. The theorem
should also be viewed as an early contribution to welfare economics – a
statement of what in later versions would become known as the marginal
conditions for a Pareto optimum in markets for capital goods and capital
services. Walras showed that capital formation in a purely competitive model
is a process by which the excess of income over consumption is transformed
into new capital goods of a kind and quantity that under certain conditions
and within certain limits, maximizes utility for each trader. Are those conditions just? That, Walras rightly concluded, is for normative economics to
decide (ibid.).

CHAPTER 11

The mature models of the money market

The purpose of this chapter is to explain Walras's mature models of the money market. It is shown how he first constructed a model with a fiat money. He specified the structure and behavior of the market for money, the institutions of the market, and the procedures related to the borrowing and lending of money. To analyze these matters he utilized a dynamic period analysis and assumed that in disequilibrium there is exchange, production, consumption, and saving. Walras then assumed that there is a commodity money and that certain payments are made with fiduciary money. His innovations in the third stage of the comprehensive model were significant theoretical advances which anticipated some of the analyses made during the nineteen-twenties and 'thirties by J.M. Keynes, D.H. Robertson, and J.R. Hicks.

I. Introduction

This chapter explains the structure and functioning of the market for money in Walras's mature comprehensive model. The market for money is the same thing as the market for loans of money capital in his model, as will be seen, and his discussion of it also includes his treatment of circulating capital. He added the detailed modeling of these matters to his mature comprehensive model, thus constructing the third and last stage of its development. It has been shown in earlier chapters that Walras's mature comprehensive model is the basic model that he presented in the second and third editions of the *Eléments* in the lessons titled "Theory of Capital Formation and Credit." In the subsequent lessons on money where he filled in the details of the place of money in the model, he did not change its fundamental structural and behavioral features, such as the organized and competitive character of the markets, the use of money, the available commodities, the participants in markets, and the pricing processes. Moreover, he had already introduced many of the features of the money market in lessons that precede the ones devoted especially to money. He made a series of special assumptions in the latter, however, varying one or another of the characteristics of the model and thus constructing a variety of special models.

The justification for the chapter is three-fold. First, there has been no study in the secondary literature of the market institutions and procedures relating to money in Walras's mature model, as distinct from an examination of his cash balances equations (see Marget 1931). The exclusive source of modern ideas about his monetary model (see, for example, Kuenne 1954, 1961) has been the notions that he sketched in the fourth edition of the *Eléments,* which differ considerably from his mature work on money. Indeed, he eliminated from the fourth and fifth editions of the *Eléments* almost all of the passages with which this chapter is concerned. Second, Walras's exposition of the model is difficult to follow and is in great need of a clear explanation. Third, the mature model is worth studying because it is superior to his monetary constructions in the final phase of his theoretical activity (see ch. 18). In fact, by turning away from his mature model in the last period of his theoretical activity, Walras lost the opportunity to encourage his followers to elaborate on the theoretical approaches and analytical techniques that he introduced in that model and which were instead developed much later by Keynes, Robertson, and Hicks.

Walras incorporated parts of the first edition of the *Eléments* into the *Théorie de la monnaie* (1886), but added much new material. He then incorporated much of the *Théorie* into the second and third editions of the *Eléments.* Arthur W. Marget judged that the *Théorie* was an advance in Walras's monetary thinking, as shown by the quotation in the next paragraph. Marget therefore approved of the changes that Walras made in preparing the second edition of the *Eléments* insofar as they were incorporations of parts of the *Théorie,* and therefore agreed with the view taken in this chapter that during his mature phase of theoretical activity, Walras improved on the treatment of money he had made in the first edition of the *Eléments.*

Marget differed, however, in his judgment on other changes in the monetary modeling that Walras presented in the second and third editions of the *Eléments.* Although Marget stated his position diplomatically, he made it clear that he thought that Walras did his best monetary thinking prior to the second edition of the *Eléments:*

Aspects of Walras's later treatment might justify the assertion that the net effect of most of Walras' elaboration after the first edition of the *Théorie* is to confuse the clear line of his general argument without a corresponding definitive gain in analytical content. The same thing might be said of the other new features introduced into the second edition of the *Eléments* – such as, for example, the attempt to introduce into the general analysis the effect of the rate of interest, as well as the beginnings of an attempt, which reached its most elaborate development in the fourth (1900) edition of the *Eléments,* to incorporate the equations representing the demand for money into his more general system of equations, particularly those dealing with "circulating capital" (ibid.).

Marget's opinion of the monetary model in the second and third editions is surely mistaken, as this chapter will show. Although it cannot be denied that

Walras did not achieve perfection in his attempt in the second edition of the *Eléments* to introduce the effect of the rate of interest and the demand for money into his model, it is not accurate to maintain that his attempt to do so merely confused an argument that was better expressed without them. They are fundamental aspects of behavior related to money, of the essence of a monetary economy, essential components of a monetary model of general equilibration and general equilibrium. No monetary model that fails to give them a place can be regarded as anything other than primitive, and Walras's introduction of them into his mature model is a notable reason for its superiority over his previous work.

II. The content of the "Theory of Money"

It is important to classify and explain the content of Walras's lessons in the part of the *Eléments* titled the "Theory of Money" because much of it is not part of his monetary model, and because it is sometimes difficult to detect when he was constructing and analyzing a model, when he was applying a model to empirical questions, and when he was describing the real economy. He presented four groups of subjects.

First, he dealt with general aspects of the valuation of money, postulating them in and deducing them from equations that are largely definitional. In examining them he was concerned with the valuation of a fiat money and of a commodity money, with the valuation of the commodities that people intend to buy in terms of any arbitrarily selected commodity, with converting the equation that expresses those valuations to one in which the commodities are valued in money prices, and with manipulations of equations related to his definition of cash-balances.

This chapter does not directly consider such matters, which fall under the rubric of what has been called Walras's "theory of money" but that in fact deal with the mathematical epiphenomena of that theory.[1] The problem of how to convert prices expressed in one numeraire to prices expressed in another, for example, is not relevant for this chapter, however interesting it may be for other studies. It is a statistician's or a national income accountant's problem, one that he hopes to resolve by manipulating the equations that are related to a model. The participants in the model, however, have no knowledge of the equations or of the abstract questions posed by the accountant, and the behavior of the model is not affected by them. The cash balances equations, for example, have a mechanical quality that results from Walras's having constructed them to deal with relationships that follow as a matter of course from definitions that he made, rather than being descriptions of the

---

[1] Much of that material has been exhaustively and admirably studied by Marget (1931, 1935).

behavior of the participants in the households, businesses, and markets of the model. The equations cannot specify market institutions or technology; and they are static, so they cannot describe the dynamic adjustments that are of interest in this chapter. What Keynes wrote about the equations of the quantity theory of money is true of Walras's equations, which are an expression of that theory: "They are particular examples of the numerous identities which can be formulated connecting different monetary factors. But they do not, any of them, have the advantage of separating out those factors through which, in a modern economic system, the causal process actually operates during a period of change" (Keynes 1930, p. 133). Walras addressed the latter question in his literary discussion of the functioning of the markets in his model. Accordingly, the chapter is concerned with his equations only indirectly and insofar as his literary discussions of them indicate additional elements of the structure of the markets for commodities and money in the model.

Second, Walras dealt with aspects of the ways in which monetary obligations are settled in international trade in the real economy, and in particular with the uses in international trade of letters of credit (1874b, pp. 202–5; 1889, pp. 418–21). His discussions of these matters are largely straightforward accounts of international settlement practices rather than discussions of a model, and insofar as that is the case they are not directly relevant for this chapter. He did not present a model of international adjustments of imports and exports and international general equilibrium in the second and subsequent editions of the *Eléments*. Nevertheless, he did devote a few pages to the analysis of currency arbitrage and the general equilibrium of exchange rates, and that material can be considered as adding to his model (1874b, pp. 205–8; 1889, pp. 421–24).

Third, in the section titled "Theory of Money" in the second edition of the *Eléments,* Walras included (1889, pp. 425–85) four lessons on money that he described as "applied theory" as distinct from "pure theory" (ibid., p. IX). He felt that those lessons, "truly speaking, ought to be transferred to the *Eléments d'économie politique appliquée*" (1889, p. X).[2] They are devoted to practical questions of measurement, to actual monetary conditions, and to the characteristics of gold and silver. He finally acted on his judgment of the character of that material and excluded it all from the third edition of the *Eléments*, transferring it, with changes, to his collection of writings on applied econom-

---

[2] In those lessons, he discussed the definition of the numeraire, the desirability that the thing selected as a commodity money be portable, malleable, and so on; the physical characteristics of gold and silver; ways of regulating the price level; European monetary history; the doctrines of A.A. Cournot and W.S. Jevons on a measure of variations in the value of money; the determination of the price of social wealth and money; and policies for stabilizing the value of money.

ics (1898b, pp. 93 ff.). The material does not add to or explain the properties of the markets in his model or the behavior of its participants, so it is not considered here.

Fourth, Walras discussed how money is used by the participants in the markets in his model (1889, pp. 375–424). This is the material of direct interest for this chapter. In many passages it is obvious he was writing about his model as distinct from describing the real economy. That is the case when he stated he was doing so or when he was explicit in making assumptions to create a hypothetical special situation, as when he wrote that "I have simplified, as I ought to have done, as much as possible" (1886, p. 382), in order to reduce the mechanism of monetary circulation "to its essential elements" (1889, p. 379). In this connection, he frequently repeated aspects of the use of money that he had already presented, often in greater detail, in earlier lessons on the comprehensive model, presumably in order to collect his remarks on money in one place. He also added details about the behavior of the participants in his model of the money market, without which it would have been incomplete. Those aspects became an integral part of the operation of the comprehensive model he had introduced in earlier lessons. In reference to other passages, analysis of his procedure and their contents reveals their underlying analytically structured character. In still other passages, he filled in details of his model or presented variants of it in the course of dealing with issues of monetary policy. He did that when he used his model to examine a policy that was not a feature of the real economy, as distinct from discussing actual conditions. As has been emphasized, it is not always easy to distinguish modeling, applications, and description in the lessons on money in the *Eléments*. The lines between them are particularly blurred in passages in which Walras was trying simultaneously to establish some of the principles by which a policy issue that arose during his career could be analyzed and to apply the principles.

III. The fiat money model

Fiat money balances

In the first special model that Walras developed in the section entitled the "Theory of Money," he assumed that a single sort of thing is chosen by fiat to be money and that it is also the numeraire in terms of which prices are cried (1886, pp. 38–39; 1889, p. 377). Examples of such a sort of thing are horse chestnuts, pebbles, shells, and pieces of paper bearing an engraved image (1889, p. 377). There are no other means of payment in the model – no checks, no offsetting of mutual debts, no notes issued by banks, no circulating promissory notes. He assumed that the medium of exchange has no utility of its own and therefore has no exchange value on its own account. Consequently, a consumer or an entrepreneur in the model does not want to hold fiat money for its own sake. It is not the money in itself that interests him, but the utility of the commodities that he can obtain in exchange for it (ibid., p. 378). In order to purchase them, "the landlords, workers and capitalists and the entrepreneurs" therefore hold a certain amount of money (ibid., p. 377). Throughout much of his ensuing discussion, Walras grouped the first three of those types of participants together and called them consumers and referred to the entrepreneurs as producers. The balances held by consumers to purchase consumer commodities and the balances held by producers are "circulating money" (1877b, p. 306; 1889, pp. 312, 375). Consumers also hold balances as a way of accumulating savings (1889, pp. 312, 376). Consumers and producers aim at establishing balances of a particular size, which Walras called their desired cash balances (ibid., p. 379).[3]

The size of a consumer's desired cash balance depends on the value of the consumer commodities he intends to acquire and the magnitude of his desired savings (1886, pp. 40–41; 1889, p. 377). His intentions to consume and to deploy savings depend, among other things, on his character and habits (1886, p. 40; 1889, p. 377), on his income (1877b, pp. 280–84; 1889, pp. 268–71), and on the rate of interest. The size of an entrepreneur's desired balance also depends on his situation, character, and habits (1889, p. 377), and on the rate of interest. Consumers' and entrepreneurs' desired cash balances, and hence the aggregate desired cash balance, vary inversely with the rate of interest (ibid., p. 381). The greater the saving, the smaller the part of the desired cash balance held to purchase consumer commodities, the greater the part of the cash balance held to finance production, and the lower the rate of interest; and the reverse (ibid., pp. 381–82).

The desired balances are those that will enable the purchase of a specific amount of goods and services, so they are desired real balances. The aggregate desired real cash balance is the nominal aggregate value of all commodities that consumers and producers want to buy divided by the price level (ibid., pp. 378–79). In Walras's formulation, the price level is the inverse of the price of money calculated in terms of any arbitrarily selected commodity. The aggregate desired real cash balance held at one time represents the aggregate demand for consumer commodities and capital goods to be purchased at a future time.

In two respects, Walras adopted procedures in his model of the loan market that are confusing to the reader because Walras did not draw attention to them. First, in contrast to his previous assertions that savings are used to

---

[3] Walras also specified in the section titled the "Theory of Capital Formation and Credit" that they do so (1877b, p. 306; 1889, p. 313).

finance durable capital goods – that is, capital goods properly speaking (1877b, pp. 277, 282; 1889, pp. 265, 270) – he assumed in his model of the loan market that some part of savings balances is used to finance the production or acquisition of nondurable capital. He introduced his statement on this matter just before assuming that he was dealing with fiat money, but in the fiat-money model he assumed that savings are used in the ways described in the following quotation, so by the word "commodity" in it he obviously did not mean to restrict what he was saying to the case of a commodity money: "There is a commodity," he wrote, "in which the excess of income over consumption is formed and in which fixed *and circulating* capital is lent on the market for money capital, and which serves as money savings" (1889, p. 376; emphasis added). Savings are used to finance the production and purchase of "machines, instruments, tools, *primary materials,* fabricated things that are displayed for sale" (ibid.; emphasis added). Circulating capital does not outlast its first use; it consists of nondurables. It is held by consumers in the form of stocks of consumer goods and money savings (1877b, p. 308; 1889, p. 315) and by entrepreneurs in the form of stocks of primary materials, consumer goods ready for sale, and circulating money balances (ibid.). Walras therefore broadened his usage of the words "capital" and "savings" when he dealt with circulating capital (see 1877b, p. 213; 1889, p. 197). Savings balances in his models of the loan market are used to finance the production of both durable and nondurable goods used to produce other goods or services for sale, or to finance the purchase of goods for resale.

Second, Walras mentioned different exclusive uses of savings, and hence in effect referred to different special models without remarking on his changes of definitions, and he sometimes interjected the uses into contexts in which they did not fit. Thus, in one place he assumed that money savings are used by capitalists exclusively to buy durable capital goods. Funds are accumulated, he specified, by "the creators of savings in order to purchase new capital goods with the intention of lending them in kind" (1889, p. 381); in other words, to purchase durable capital goods which they rent to entrepreneurs. In other passages, some of them on the same page on which he presented a contrary assumption, he assumed that the capitalists use their savings balances exclusively to make loans. They lend to entrepreneurs to enable them to finance the production or purchase of durable capital goods and primary materials, and the production of finished goods (ibid., pp. 313, 376, 380–81). In yet another place he chose to make his model like reality, he wrote, by assuming that "fixed capital is hired out in part in money and that circulating capital is all hired out in money" (ibid., p. 379; and see p. 295). By the words "in part in money" he meant that capitalists use their savings partially to make loans and partially to buy fixed capital goods and rent them out. That was the assumption he had made in his discussions of savings and investment in the section titled "Theory of Capital Formation and Credit" (see ch. 8). In that case, it is the entrepreneurs who purchase not only the circulating but also the fixed capital goods. It will be necessary to sort out the special models implied by each of Walras's different assumptions about the uses of savings.

The structure of the money market

Walras had assumed the existence of a loan market and that loans are made in money in his initial exposition of his comprehensive model (ibid., p. 295), and he repeated and elaborated on elements of the structure and functioning of the market in part V of the *Eléments*. In the real economy, he contended, each type of physical capital generates income that pays the interest on the loans of the money used to finance it (ibid., pp. 295, 380). Fixed and circulating capital each have their own rate of interest and are lent in different markets, although the markets are related, so the rates are interdependent (ibid., pp. 295, 379–80). Walras chose to make his first special model differ from reality, however, by adopting four major simplifying assumptions in addition to the assumption of fiat money.

First, he assumed there is no difference between fixed and circulating real capital (ibid., p. 379), although in fact he continued to refer to them. He meant that there is no difference between them that affects the loans made to finance them (ibid., pp. 379–80).[4] The loans are all made in a single market that he called the market for money capital (1889, p. 380), at the same rate of interest and for the same duration. Moreover, since producers and consumers borrow money in the market not only to finance the purchase of durable goods but also the purchase of nondurable goods and to replenish their cash balances, it "is both the market for money capital and the market for money" (ibid., p. 381). Second, Walras made the simplifying assumption that in regard to the renting of fixed and circulating capital, there are no differences between the landlords, workers, and capitalists in their role as consumers and the entrepreneurs in their role as producers. Durable and nondurable consumption goods yield to the consumers the same services as machines, instruments, tools, primary materials, and fabricated products yield to the producers. The services, Walras assumed, have the same prices and pay for themselves, whether yielded to consumers or producers (ibid., p. 380). Third, Walras assumed that all savings are used to make loans (ibid., p. 382). Fourth, he assumed "that all of the existing quantity of money was brought every day

---

[4] Walras remarked that he would reintroduce those distinctions when he took up the applied theory of credit (1889, p. 380).

to the loan market" and thus assumed that there is no reservation demand for money (ibid.).[5]

In the model, there are three components of the aggregate daily demand for money that is exercised on the loan market. First, Walras posited that consumers come to the loan market every day and borrow the money they need in order to construct, complete, and maintain their fixed and circulating capital. With the money, they buy furniture, clothing, objets d'art, luxury goods, and other consumption goods (ibid., p. 380) during the day. Second, the entrepreneurs come to the loan market every day to borrow money for two general purposes: to construct, complete, and maintain their fixed capital goods, which consist of machines, instruments, and tools, and to replenish their physical circulating capital, which consists of primary materials and products they have made (ibid., p. 380; and see p. 295). Third, savers come to the loan market every day to borrow money (ibid., p. 381). By taking the first two demands for money and adding to them the demand for money "which will be made by the creators of savings with the objective of buying new capital goods in order to lend them in kind, we have the daily demand for money which is exercised on the market for money capital" (ibid., p. 381). In that passage, Walras created the curious situation that savers are borrowers, whereas elsewhere, as will shortly be seen, he represented them as saving out of income. It should also be noted that in the passage just quoted, he specified that savers save exclusively in order to buy new capital goods they rent out in kind, thus deviating temporarily from his supposition that they use savings exclusively to make loans.

The daily demand for money exercised in the market is nothing other, Walras asserted, than the demand for that fraction of the fixed and circulating capital of society that is renewed every day – "as we explained (271)[6] in speaking of the continuous market" (ibid., p. 381). What is happening behind the veil of money therefore is that the borrowers of it are really thereby borrowing the fixed and circulating capital on which they spend it (ibid.). The interest they pay on the borrowed money is actually the interest generated by the fixed and circulating capital that the borrowed money finances and therefore represents. That explains, Walras wrote, why the rate of interest cried on the market is the rate on money capital (ibid.).

The supply of money also consists of three parts. It is brought each day to

---

[5] See also 1889, pp. 379 and 381, where Walras repeated that the daily offer of money is equal to the total quantity, and that all of it is lent.

[6] Here, Walras noted the number of the relevant section in lesson 27 in the section titled "Theory of Capital Formation and Credit." Lesson 27 is titled "Laws of the Establishment and of the Variation of the Prices of Capital Goods. The Continuous Market" (1889, p. 308; and see 1877b, p. 305, where that material has the title "Of the Continuous Market").

the loan market, first, by entrepreneurs who have received money on the previous day from consumers in exchange for durable and nondurable consumption goods (ibid., pp. 380–81); second, by entrepreneurs who have received money on the previous day from other entrepreneurs in exchange for new fixed and circulating capital goods (ibid.); third, by the landlords, workers, and capitalists who have received money on the previous day in exchange for services (ibid., p. 381).

Adjustment processes

Walras then explained how the model adjusts when it is in disequilibrium, specifying, as he put it, the characteristics of the mechanism of free competition in regard to monetary circulation (ibid., p. 379). Mainly explicitly, but partially implicitly, he sketched the dynamic adjustments that were presented later by the Cambridge cash balances theorists. Walras's account of this matter is, however, exceedingly difficult to follow, and it is impossible to make sense of what he wrote unless distinctions are made between nominal and real cash balances and between changes in quantities desired and changes in the entire demand-for-cash balances function, distinctions that evidently he made but did not label as such in the passages in question.

Period analysis: Walras began his consideration of the timing of the operation of markets by passing "from the hypothesis of a market which is held once and for all to that of a market which would be held periodically, we could say once a day, we will say rather once per year in order to take better account of the change of seasons" (1877b, p. 307; 1889, p. 314). He then created the definitive framework for the period analysis used in his model of the money market by assuming two conditions. First, he assumed that production and consumption "extend over all the moments of the entire year" (1877b, p. 310; 1889, p. 316). Commodities of all types then "are like stems which, cut continuously at one of their ends, continuously grow at the other end" (1877b, p. 310; 1889, p. 316). They disappear as they are used and reappear at the same time through production of them. Workers, capital goods, and money are also used up and reproduced (ibid.). Second, he assumed that markets function every day and that different types of related behavior occur sequentially on different days (1889, pp. 381–83). Thus, he developed a continuous-production and periodic-market version of his model, its most highly developed form with respect to the treatment of time.

Here is the flow of activity in Walras's first special model. Money is held overnight by those who have received it on one day, lent by them in the morning, and spent in the afternoon by those who borrow it: "All the money is savings in the morning when it is brought to the market and all of it is circulating money in the evening when it is exchanged for fixed and circulating capital goods" (ibid., p. 382). Walras appears to have meant not that money is held in circulating balances in the evening, but the truism that it circulates when it is spent; and he clearly indicated that circulating and savings balances are not both present in the morning. In those circumstances, the transformation of money savings into circulating money and the transformation of circulating money into savings is as rapid as possible (ibid.). The holding of money overnight determines how long on the average a dollar is held before it is spent, which is the velocity of circulation of money, although Walras did not use that term. It is therefore wrong to suppose, as did Marget (1931, pp. 576, 590), that in the second edition of the *Eléments* Walras rejected the velocity approach to the analysis of monetary behavior he had used in the first edition; rather he blended it with a cash balances approach, as evidenced by his literary construction. Marget should have detected this because he asserted with reference to J.M. Keynes's work that "the problems for which the 'cash balance approach' is helpful – is, indeed, indispensable," are those "associated particularly with what is commonly referred to as the velocity of circulation of money" (Marget 1931, p. 595, n. 60). Marget was deceived by the circumstance that Walras did not express the velocity of money in the equations he used in the second edition and subsequently.

Effects of changes in the quantity of money: To initiate a disequilibrium state, Walras assumed that the quantity of money decreases (1889, p. 383). Here he employed what is today called a type of Hicksian or Robertsonian period analysis (albeit without the notation of lagged variables) but that more justly should be known as a Walrasian period analysis. The entire process of equilibration takes three days. Immediately after the decrease, at the old equilibrium rate of interest that is still being cried in the market, the quantity of money demanded to be held is greater than the quantity supplied, with the following consequence. "If, at the rate of interest that is cried, the quantity demanded is greater than the quantity supplied, the rate is raised and the producers and consumers will reduce their desired cash balance" (ibid., p. 381). On the second day a temporary equilibrium is attained: "The equilibrium would not establish itself the next day on the market, except at a new higher rate of interest at which the desired cash balance would be reduced" (ibid., p. 383). Walras's subsequent analysis indicates that the equilibrium to which he referred is temporary, and that in those sentences he must have been referring to the nominal desired cash balance.

The higher rate of interest does not induce a greater quantity of money. None of the fiat money is held as a commodity because it has no direct utility of its own, so no reserves of it are available to be monetized. During the course of the second day, the prices of all consumer goods, capital goods, land, services, and primary materials fall proportionately to the decrease in the quantity of money, and the aggregate nominal desired cash balance remains permanently lower. Walras explained, however, that as for the aggregate desired real cash balance, "as a result of that fall" of prices it will be "able to become again what it was before" (ibid.). Then "on the day after that" – the third day – "equilibrium would be able to reestablish itself at a rate of interest equal to the rate of net income" (ibid.). Since the prices of the services of capital goods and the prices of capital goods all fall proportionately, the latter rate is unchanged, so Walras meant that the rate of interest falls back to its old level. He asserted that the same sequence of events will happen if there is an increase in the aggregate desired real cash balance, by which he must have meant an increase in the desired cash balance function.

Production, hiring, the payment of incomes, consumption, and savings occur continuously during the three days of adjustment, and producers and consumers therefore acquire and use goods and services on each day while the economy is in disequilibrium. On the day that the quantity of money decreases, for example, the purchases of all commodities are made at the old set of prices, which have become disequilibrium prices. Purchases continue to be made while prices are falling on the second day. The model consequently is characterized by real and irrevocable disequilibrium behavior in regard to transactions, savings, production, and all other economic variables, and moves toward equilibrium along paths traced out by those real disequilibrium variables.

If there is an increase in the quantity of money, the opposite adjustments occur. The quantity of money supplied is initially greater than the quantity demanded. Those who find themselves holding an increased amount of money spend it off in an effort to reduce the size of their nominal balances in order to achieve the same real balances as before. That causes prices to rise, which induces participants to increase the size of their nominal cash balances (ibid., p. 381), thus leading to an increase in the quantity of money demanded that eventually equals the increase in the quantity available. The aggregate desired real cash balance becomes what it was originally because, at the higher price level, the larger nominal balance has its old real value.

Effects of changes of desired balances: If some participants in the model want to decrease their real balances and therefore to decrease their nominal balances at the existing price level, they increase their demand for goods and services. That is, they spend off some of their cash. That causes prices to rise, which ultimately leads to nominal balances returning to their previous levels but decreases the real balances that people are holding. The opposite sequence occurs if people decide to increase their real balances. It was not until forty years later that J. M. Keynes developed a very similar model (Keynes 1930, pp. 225–28).

If the real cash balance increases, that the utility of money is greater, and the reverse (1889, p. 383). If the quantity of money increases, its marginal utility falls, and the reverse. "The regime of free competition" in the markets in the model then comes into play. It generates "the self-maintaining tendency" to establish a direct proportionality of prices to the quantity of money and an inverse proportionality of prices to the size of the aggregate desired real cash balance (ibid., p. 379). As Walras summarized: "If, everything else remaining constant, the existing quantity of money increases or the desired cash balance diminishes, prices will rise proportionally. If the existing quantity of money diminishes, or the desired [real] cash balance increases, prices fall proportionally" (ibid., p. 383). "This law extends to money the principle by virtue of which value increases with utility and decreases with the quantity" (ibid.). Walras claimed with justice that his analysis thereby incorporates the determination of the value of money into his general theory of value (ibid.).

IV. Other special models

Walras constructed a second model, more general than the first, by assuming that there is a rental market for capital goods. This implies that the money brought to the market is partially spent by consumers on capital goods and is partially lent by them (ibid., p. 381). In this model, in addition to the processes described in relation to the first model, there is activity in disequilibrium concerning shifting between the markets in which capital goods are rented and the market in which money is lent. In the rental markets for such goods, the entrepreneurs must pay the prices of the capital-good services. The ratio of the prices of the services of capital goods to the prices of the capital goods themselves is the rate of net income. In the loan market, the entrepreneurs must pay interest to borrow money. That gives savers three choices. They can buy capital goods, rent them, and earn the rate of net income, or can lend their funds and earn the rate of interest, or do both. The rate of interest and the rate of net income are therefore compared by both entrepreneurs and lenders. The two rates tend to equality, because if one were higher than the other borrowers and lenders would move from one market to the other (ibid.).[7] For example, if the rate of net income exceeds the rate of interest, savers would prefer to buy capital goods and rent them, thus reduc-

---

[7] Walras explained this matter in detail in the "Theory of Capital Formation and Credit" (1889, pp. 288–89, 295; see chs. 9, 10).

ing the supply of funds in the loan market. Entrepreneurs, on the other hand, would prefer to borrow funds and buy capital goods with them rather than to rent capital goods, thus increasing the demand for loans. The rate of interest would therefore rise and the rate of net income would fall (ibid.).

Walras then introduced banks, creating a third special model (ibid., p. 382). It differs from the others only in regard to the size of cash balances and the velocity of money, because the banks have no function other than that of being passive depositories of money. Consumers and entrepreneurs deposit the revenue from sales into the banks, and subsequently withdraw all the cash they are going to spend on goods and services, or use to make loans. In that ideal situation, the quantity of money held in cash registers, wallets, and moneyboxes would be greatly reduced (ibid.). In fact, Walras could have noted, money would be held in cashboxes by merchants only fleetingly overnight or during the time elapsing between their receipt of it and their depositing it in banks later in the day, and only fleetingly by consumers after receiving it in payment for services and depositing it in their bank accounts.

Walras sketched a fourth model of the loan market by assuming that there is a reservation demand for money on the part of some participants.[8] "During the day," he wrote, "the entrepreneurs will buy the fixed and circulating capital with their money; and the next day the sellers will bring to the money market the money that they have received, *except for the sums they need that they will keep for themselves*" (ibid., p. 380; emphasis added). Some of the recipients of money on one day – the sellers of fixed and circulating capital – thus lend only the part they do not need to those who have to wait an interval of time between when they need to spend money and when they will earn some and therefore do not have sufficient ready money. Including in the gross supply of money the money that entrepreneurs hold for their own use and therefore supply to themselves, the aggregate daily quantity of money supplied is equal to the existing quantity of money (ibid., p. 381).

Walras created a fifth model by introducing yet another assumption about the velocity of money – namely, that all money is kept in containers such as cashboxes and other receptacles or billfolds from the moment it is received until the time when it is given in payment or lent. The idle money renders very few services, and those that hold it, whether producers or consumers, uselessly lose the interest on the capital that it represents (ibid., p. 382). Many businesses and consumers do not lend at all, and others lend only a part of their receipts. The daily net supply of money is diminished by the amount of the existing quantity that is held in reserve in cash containers, and the net demand is diminished by the corresponding fraction of the aggregate

---

[8] Walras mixed this model in with his discussion of the components of the demand for money in his first model.

desired cash balance (ibid.). Nevertheless, the current rate of interest is determined by the mechanism of Walrasian pricing – changing prices and the rate of interest in the same direction as the sign of excess demand quantities (ibid.).

The conditions of equilibrium are the same for all five special models. In equilibrium, the aggregate desired real cash balance is equal to the quantity of money times the price of money in terms of any arbitrarily selected commodity. "The equilibrium rate of interest will be the one at which the quantities of money capital that are supplied and demanded are equal" (ibid., p. 381), and it is equal to the equilibrium rate of net income. When there is monetary equilibrium, the entire comprehensive model is in equilibrium in all respects. There is "the equilibrium of exchange, in view of the fact that, the prices being always proportional to the marginal utilities, the consumers would always have the maximum satisfaction of their wants" (ibid., p. 379). There is the "the equilibrium of production, in view of the fact that, prices being always equal to their average costs, entrepreneurs would always make neither profits nor losses." There is "the equilibrium of capital formation, in view of the fact that, the rate of net income not having varied, the prices of capital goods [land, human faculties, and capital goods proper] would always be proportional to the prices of their services." Finally, there is "the equilibrium of circulation, in view of the fact that the exchangers would have the cash balances that they desire at the announced rate of interest" (ibid.).

V. Non–fiat money models

One commodity money

Walras then took up the case of a thing chosen to be money that has utility as a commodity. The exposition of this aspect of his monetary thought will not be lengthy because as far as all developed and developing nations are concerned, commodity moneys have not been used as everyday circulating mediums of exchange for many years, and unless some great upheaval causes a reversion to bygone ways of conducting affairs, will never be used in that way again. The metallic moneys in circulating use today are not commodity moneys because they do not have the value of their constituent metals, and are not minted or melted for industrial or commercial uses in accordance with changes of relative prices, thus eliminating the situations and adjustments that Walras created and explored in his model. Marget's criticism that the picture in the *Théorie* of the adjustment of the *encaisse désirée* (1886, pp. 41 ff.) in the commodity money model "principally by means of an interflow between the arts and the money-use, left much to be desired from the standpoint of realistic description" (Marget 1931, p. 581, n. 29) has therefore been deprived of significance. His criticism was in any event questionable as a judgment on Walras's perception of past economic processes.[9]

In Walras's single commodity money model, a part of the special commodity (A) is held in consumers' and entrepreneurs' inventories as a commodity, and has a price as such (1889, p. 383). A part is held in consumers' and entrepreneurs' balances as money, and has a price as such (ibid.). The equation that expresses the relation of the quantity of (A) used as money (Q''_a), the price (P_a) of (A) in terms of (B), and the aggregate desired real balance (H) is $Q''_a P_a = H$.[10] Obviously, the price of (A) in terms of (B) equals the aggregate desired real cash balance divided by the quantity of the commodity that is used as money (ibid., p. 384).

Walras established rigorously the intuitively obvious condition that if there is a single thing used as money, the price of the part of it used as a commodity and the price of the part of it used as money are the same in equilibrium. In disequilibrium, however, the price of money may be greater or less than the price of (A) held as a commodity (ibid., p. 386). If the price of money exceeded the price of (A) as a commodity, monetization of some of (A) would occur. The price of (A) used as money varies inversely with the quantity of (A) used as money, so an increased supply of money would lead to a lowering of its price, and the reduction of the supply of (A) available as a commodity would raise its price in that use (ibid.) The opposite processes and results would take place if the price of (A) used as a commodity exceeded the price of money. The outcome in each case would be that the prices would be brought to equality. The same processes would occur if the rate of interest rises because more money would be minted and circulated and as a result the rate of interest would fall back to the old level, equal to the rate of net income.

The price of (A), Walras also showed, increases or decreases with the increase or decrease of the magnitude of the desired aggregate cash balance and the utility of the part of (A) that is used as a commodity (ibid., p. 386). It follows from the basic relations $Q''_a P_a = H$ and $P_a = 1/p$, where p is the price level (1889, p. 384), that changes in the quantity of money result in proportional changes in the money prices of commodities (ibid.), just as Walras had established for the case of a fiat money (ibid., p. 379).

Walras explained further the characteristics of the model when it is in equilibrium, formulating his questions and the answers in a determinedly mathematical way, writing about unknowns and the equations necessary to solve for them, whereas he would have approached the matter on a more fundamental level if he had discussed the market behavior of the participants.

---

[9] As far as I am aware, the realism or otherwise of Walras's model of that adjustment has not been assessed by an economic historian.

[10] This neglects a small term, as Walras explained (1889, p. 384).

He posed the question of how the equilibrium values of the following three variables are determined: the price of (A) held as a commodity and used as money, the quantity of (A) used as a commodity, and the quantity of (A) used as money (ibid., p. 387). His answer was that there are three equations with which the unknowns are found, by which he meant the equilibrium values. First, the sum of the amounts of (A) held as a commodity by the participants plus the sum of the amounts of (A) held as money are equal to the total quantity of (A). Second, the price of (A) used as a commodity results from the quantity of (A) used as a commodity, by which he presumably meant in behavioral terms that the equilibrium quantity and the price result from the supply and demand for (A) used as a commodity. Third, the price of (A) used as money results from the quantity of it used as money (ibid.), by which he presumably meant in behavioral terms that the price and equilibrium quantity result from the supply and demand for (A) in that use.

Money substitutes

Walras then constructed a model in which there is a single commodity money and some payments are made without the use of metallic money. Some of his discussion of metallic money substitutes is a straightforward description of characteristics of the real economy. Nevertheless, he formally put some of those features into his model, and he began his discussion of the phenomena with the statement that the theory of money considers how the use of metallic money can be avoided (ibid., p. 412).[11] Walras's accounts of transactions being effectuated without cash exchanging hands should therefore be regarded as assumptions and analyses made as part of a model.

Walras assumed that there are four means of making payments without metallic money. The first two, bills of exchange and bank notes, comprise fiduciary money, which Walras also called paper money (1886, p. 44; 1889, p. 416). Bills of exchange are made by businesses by writing an acknowledgment of a debt and indicating the date on which the debt will become due. The bills can be used as payments many times, in each instance being signed over to another business, with only the last recipient actually presenting the letter to the originally indebted party for payment in money on the date that payment was promised (1874b, pp. 198–99; 1889, p. 414). Such bills have an important place in both domestic and international trade. Merchants in one country sell to merchants in another and vice versa, and the creditors obtain bills of exchange whereby their debtors agree to settle their debt at a future date. From the relationship of the magnitude of aggregate indebtedness of

---

[11] Walras incorporated the discussion of those topics in the *Théorie* into the second edition of the *Eléments* and retained the lesson on them in the third edition, thus indicating that those topics are part of his pure theory of money.

one country to another and the gold content of the unit of currency arises the exchange rate between the two currencies. Walras explained how bills of exchange are made, bought, and presented to the original maker to settle international debts without the use of metallic currency (1874b, p. 203; 1889, p. 419). Clearing house operations with bills of exchange permit payments for a vast amount of trade to be made without the use of metallic currency (1874b, p. 208; 1889, pp. 423–24). Walras presented the formulas developed by A.A. Cournot that show equilibrium conditions among international exchange rates, and explained how that equilibrium is reached by a species of arbitrage by dealers in bills of exchange (1874b, p. 206–7; 1889, pp. 422–23).

Bank notes are paper money issued by a bank with entrepreneurs' promises to repay their bank loans as collateral. The promises to repay take the form of bills of exchange and promissory notes. Once issued, a bank note does not have to be endorsed by each recipient and is payable in metallic money to the bearer on demand (1874b, pp. 198–99; 1889, p. 414). Consequently, bank notes circulate much more readily than bills of exchange. The total amount of bank notes issued by a bank can equal the value of its cash, bills of exchange, and promissory notes, and can therefore have a much larger value than the amount of cash held by the bank (1874b, p. 199; 1889, p. 415).

The third means of making payments without metallic money is "book credit," the process of canceling debts of equal magnitude by merchants who incur them to each other. Walras sometimes referred to book credits as "compensations" in order to stress their use in the offsetting of claims. Metallic currency is used to pay each merchant the excess of what he is owed over what he owes to others (1874b, pp. 196–97; 1889, pp. 412–13). The fourth means is checks drawn on banks (1874b, pp. 199–200; 1889, p. 416). Clearing houses enable banks to offset the value of checks drawn on them with the value of checks that they hold that are drawn on other banks and to pay only the excess of their debts in metallic money. Banks in the model under discussion are therefore not merely passive depositaries. They issue bank notes and thereby "put capital into circulation" (1889, p. 417), and checks are drawn on them to pay for a volume of transactions that has a much greater value than the amount of cash that has been deposited in the banks (1874b, pp. 199–200; 1889, pp. 415–16).

Walras reasoned that the size of the aggregate desired cash balance depends on the settlements that have to be made with cash (1886, p. 45; 1889, p. 416). Consequently, the existence of book credits and checks diminishes the amount of metallic money needed to effectuate a certain amount of transactions. The size of the aggregate desired cash balance therefore varies inversely with the level of usage of book credits and checks. Walras assumed that level of usage is fixed. He then reformulated his statement of the relation of money, its price, and the aggregate desired cash balance to take account of fiduciary money (1889, p. 416). He assumed that it is part of the money supply and satisfies the need to hold money just as metallic money does. He therefore put fiduciary money on the supply side of the equation, not modifying the demand side, which is the aggregate desired cash balance. He argued that his equation shows that if the quantity of the special commodity used as money increases or decreases, prices would still increase or decrease proportionally. The aggregate value of fiduciary money would also increase or decrease proportionally, and the aggregate desired real cash balance would remain constant (1886, pp. 44–45; 1889, pp. 416–17). "Indeed," Walras observed,

all the essential conditions of the four equilibria of exchange, production, capital formation and circulation continue unchanged, as we have seen. With the increase or decrease of prices occurring proportionately to the increase or to the decrease of the quantity of money, there would not be any reason why the entrepreneurs and the banks would not put into circulation the same quantity of capital for a proportionally greater or smaller nominal[12] total of bills of exchange and bank notes, or why the same quantities of commodities would not be sold and purchased through offsetting of claims for a proportionately greater or smaller nominal amount. Thus the two facts of the circulation of paper money and of the offsetting of claims do not imply any invalidation of the theorem of the proportionality of prices to the quantity of money (1889, p. 417).

Walras then assumed that fiduciary money supplants metallic money to a greater degree. In that event, he concluded, a new fixed proportionality between metallic money and prices would be established (1886, p. 46; 1889, p. 417).

The assertion that an increase in the quantity of metallic money leads to a proportional change in prices implies certain personal and market behavior on the part of the participants in the comprehensive model. The implications are familiar features of the model. First, the mechanisms of adjustments of ratios of marginal utilities and of the flexibility of prices operate freely. Second, people's habits concerning their intended consumption and savings and hence the size of the real balances they want to hold for those purposes are unchanged. Third, the features of the payment system – such as the income period; the degree of use of checks, bills of exchange, and bank notes; and the degree of offsetting of claims – do not permanently change when the quantity of money changes, even if there are short-term changes of those variables.

---

[12] This is the exact word that Walras used, manifesting his differentiation of nominal and real monetary magnitudes.

Two commodity moneys

Walras explained that if there are two commodities that are used as money, as would be the case with bimetallism,[13] it is impossible simply to inject the second commodity money into the framework of the single commodity money model. Its structure becomes incomplete, so it cannot function. To take account of this problem, Walras introduced a new participant, the state, and thus constructed yet another variation of his comprehensive model. In the new model, he assumed that politicians make a decision about some aspect of the problem, such as fixing arbitrarily the quantity of one of the types of money (1889, pp. 388–89) or adopting some constant of proportionality between the value of the two commodity moneys (ibid., p. 392). Then the market system in the model would determine the other prices and quantities, so that each of the following six variables would be determined: the price of each money, the quantity of each commodity used as money, and the quantity of each special commodity used as a commodity (ibid., pp. 391–95). If there were more than two commodity moneys, more political decisions, – that is, arbitrary assumptions regarding the structure of the model – would have to be made (ibid., p. 388).

Walras went on to explore the properties of his bimetallism model, assuming the freedom of participants or of the state to monetize or demonetize the special commodities, which he began calling gold and silver (ibid., pp. 390–91, 397–99, 401–11); but, as mentioned, that exploration is not of interest.

VI. Conclusion

It can be seen that the models of the money market that Walras set forth in the second and third editions of the *Eléments* become progressively richer in detail and more realistic. In the first model, all lenders are also borrowers. A worker, for example, does not retain some of his wages to purchase consumption commodities; he saves all the income he earned the day before and lends it. He therefore must borrow from other savers in order to finance his purchases of services and of fixed and circulating capital goods. Sellers receive money from the sale of finished goods at the end of one day and are suppliers of money on the morning of the next day. They are also demanders of money if they buy fixed or circulating capital goods. In the second model, however, recipients of money retain the amounts they need to finance their own expenditures. In subsequent models, Walras introduced banks, metallic

---

[13] Walras's discussion of bimetallism was viewed by him as a constituent of his theory of money. He placed it in the part with that title in the second and third editions of the *Eléments*, as he did also his discussion of the value of the bimetallic standard.

money, substitutes for metallic money, and finally two metallic moneys, as was characteristic of the economy of his day.

Walras's other accomplishments in his mature model were to develop a fiat-money model; to introduce the rate of interest and integrate it into the dynamics of his model; to make the demand for cash balances a function of it; to introduce the concept of desired real and nominal cash balances; to distinguish between circulating and savings balances; to analyze conditions that result in different velocities of money; to create a dynamic period analysis and use it in application to a model of the money market; and to develop a model that has real disequilibrium paths of transactions, production, consumption, and savings. Except for the concept of cash balances, Walras did not introduce those elements in his work prior to the second edition of the *Eléments*, which clearly reveals its superiority over his earlier work. For example, in the first edition of the *Eléments* and in the *Théorie*, Walras did not even mention fiat money, nor did he differentiate between circulating and savings balances.

Walras's innovations were very substantial advances in modeling, which, taken together, resulted in the most sophisticated and realistic monetary model that any economist developed by 1889. It is greatly to be regretted that in the fourth edition of the *Eléments* he replaced the dynamic sequence-analysis and irrevocable disequilibrium transactions and production model with the written pledges model in which he wanted no trade, production, or consumption to occur out of equilibrium.

CHAPTER 12

Iteration in the mature model
of tatonnement

Some writers have contended that Walras did not have a theory of economic tatonnement but was instead exclusively concerned with a technique of mathematical iteration for the purpose of finding the solutions to the equations of his model of general equilibrium, that his models lack an account of a means whereby prices are changed, and that he was uninterested in real economic adjustment processes. These allegations are examined, and it is concluded they are incorrect. It is shown that Walras wanted to develop a realistic model of time-consuming economic adjustment processes in a freely competitive economy, and that he incorporated into it the processes of iterative pricing, of iterative entrepreneurial behavior, and of a presumed convergence of the variables to equilibrium.

I. Introduction

This and the following two chapters fill in the details of Walras's conception of the dynamics of a freely competitive market model. Walras gave many accounts of markets undergoing repeated price adjustments that bring them progressively closer to equilibrium. It has been asserted by some writers that in all these accounts he was not really discussing the behavior of markets at all but was instead trying to design a mathematical technique of iteration to find the solutions to his equations of general equilibrium. For example, after quoting a passage in which Walras wrote that the market moves toward equilibrium through the raising and lowering of prices, Richard M. Goodwin asserted that Walras stated that "the use of this kind of market adjustment . . . is only a mathematical method of solution and not the practical one exemplified in the behavior of real markets" (Goodwin 1951, p. 5).[1] Kenneth J. Arrow and Frank H. Hahn wrote that:

There is yet another procedure we might take the auctioneer as following, a procedure that also fails to mimic the market, but deserves attention if for no other reason than that Walras found it worthy of attention. As a matter of fact, it is useful to consider it also as an example of a process taking place in discrete rather than continuous time.

We now take the auctioneer as concentrating on one market at a time. By this we

---

[1] Goodwin also stated that "at other points, however, he seems to assert the contrary" (Goodwin 1951, p. 5).

mean, in the first place, that if the system is not in equilibrium at t, then in the time interval, $(t, t+1)$, only one price is changed. Secondly, if it is the ith price that is changed, then the auctioneer changes it to the value that, given all the other prices, will ensure that the ith market is in equilibrium. . . . Indeed, this successive tâtonnement procedure has rather little to recommend it. Not only does it not imitate the market, but it is doubtful whether it imitates an efficient computational program for finding an equilibrium. It is in fact, what is known as a Gauss-Seidel method of solving a set of simultaneous equations, a method that is not particularly attractive as a computational means (Arrow and Hahn 1971, pp. 305, 306). . . . Walras [1874b, 1877b] first formulated the idea of a tâtonnement although in his more formal account of it he seemed to conceive of it as the Gauss-Seidel process discussed [above] (ibid., p. 322).

William Jaffé agreed that Walras's work on tatonnement that deals with changes of prices is not an economic theory but an exposition of a mathematical technique that should be "perceived as a translation into market language of the Gauss-Seidel algorithm for the solution of simultaneous equations by iteration" (Jaffé 1981, p. 330 [261]).

Jaffé also argued that in contrast to Walras's *mathematical* tatonnement, he had a theory of *economic* tatonnement that does not involve a sequence of adjustments of any kind. Walras's work on economic tatonnement, Jaffé argued during the final years of his career in two well-known and widely accepted chapters (Jaffé 1980, 1981), did not deal with the dynamic path by which markets move toward equilibrium, is purely static, and is not an attempt to understand the behavior of real markets. Walras's model of tatonnement, Jaffé contended, was not intended to be realistic in regard to either exchange or production (Jaffé 1981, p. 324 [255]). It was "consciously and deliberately confined within a strictly statical framework" (ibid., p. 327 [258]). Walras's tatonnements were not meant "to be market events in a dynamic sequence" (ibid.). "No idea of temporal sequence was implied in L.W.'s *tâtonnements*" (ibid., p. 327 [258]). They were intended as "metaphorically representing elements of a quasi-instantaneous operation" (ibid., p. 327 [257]). The economic tatonnements in his model were not "meant to depict an actual process that would require time to work itself out" (ibid., p. 327 [257–58]). They were instead "simultaneous aspects of a single, complex, virtually timeless event" (ibid., p. 330 [261]) that takes some amount of clock time but that "can still be regarded as theoretically instantaneous" (ibid., p. 322–23 [253]). Jaffé maintained that the idea that Walras's model of tatonnement was intended to deal with the dynamic path of real markets is a "myth," originated by Edgeworth (Jaffé 1981, pp. 326, 328 [257, 259]) and perpetuated by Pareto (ibid., p. 328 [259]). Admittedly, according to Jaffé, Edgeworth had only the first (1874, 1877b) and second (1889) editions of the *Eléments* as a basis for his opinion when he formed it in 1889, but his view of them was a "misapprehension." He was "misled" by Walras's presentation in those editions (Jaffé 1981, pp. 327 [257]). Edgeworth should have detected that even in them, Walras's tatonnement was "metaphorically representing elements of a quasi-instantaneous operation," not "an actual process that would require time to work itself out" (ibid., p. 327 [257–58]). Goodwin took an even more extreme view – namely, that Walras did not have a theory of economic tatonnement at all, no theory about "the motion by which an actual economy reaches equilibrium" (Goodwin 1950, p. 61). "I find support for this," Goodwin wrote, "in Joseph A. Schumpeter's statement that 'I remember a conversation with Walras in which I tried, but completely failed to elicit the slightest symptom of interest both in dynamical approaches and in a theory of economic evolution' " (ibid.).

This chapter evaluates the foregoing views. They will be examined in relation to the model of economic tatonnement that Walras incorporated into his mature comprehensive model. Whether or not there is valid support for them can be established only by reference to Walras's writings, not to statements such as Schumpeter's. The task requires an examination of Walras's investigations of mathematical iteration, his concern with the behavior of real markets, and the properties of his mature comprehensive economic model concerning iterative pricing and iterative adjustments of rates of production, including the means by which prices and production rates are changed and the rapidity of their adjustment. This chapter will examine those matters as they appear in a model in which there are disequilibrium rates of production, sales and use of consumer commodities and capital goods, and in which the related sales of productive services and goods occur at prices that are disequilibrium ones in relation to long-run supply functions and the eventual set of prices in general equilibrium.

There are three reasons for dealing with Walras's work on iterative processes in that context. First, the mature comprehensive model has a dominant place in Walras's writings, and was espoused by him during most of his entire career – that is, from about 1877 to 1899. Pointing out some of the major respects in which his mature model of tatonnement was an improvement over his previous work, Walras wrote to P.H. Wicksteed:

I will indicate to you here, as I did concerning the *theory of exchange,* the modifications made to the 1st Edition.

§ 203. I defined the tatonnement in production.

§ 204–216. I rectified on several points the demonstration of the law of the establishment of the prices of products and services, and especially I justified the tatonnement in consideration of the equality of the price of the average cost of production of products. . . .

§ 247. I defined the tatonnement in capital formation.

§ 248–256. I rectified on several points the demonstration of the law of the establishment of the rate of net income and especially I justified the tatonnement in consideration of the equilibrium of the supply and the demand of new capital goods;

(§51) distinguished the market for numeraire capital and for new capital goods and related them to each other; and justified (§ 254) the tatonnement in consideration of the equilbirium of the price and the average cost of new capital goods (Walras to P.H. Wicksteed, April 9, 1889, in 1965, 2 letter 877, pp. 307–9).

Second, when he applied mathematical iteration to the equations in the *Eléments,* he did so in all cases in reference to a model with disequilibrium production and sales – that is, with the idea that he was finding the general equilibrium values of that type of model. Indeed, he undertook all his explorations of mathematical iteration during the period in which he developed and adhered to the mature comprehensive model. Third, the economic tatonnement model that Walras incorporated into the mature comprehensive model was the only one that he developed (chs. 17, 18), inasmuch as his attempt to construct a different one in his last phase of theoretical activity was no more than an incomplete and illogical sketch.

II. Mathematical iteration

The first objective of this chapter is to establish the general character of the mathematical iterative technique by which Walras believed that a theorist can solve a set of simultaneous equations, and thereby to lay the foundation for distinguishing his model of economic tatonnement from that technique. Although Goodwin believed that Walras was not "altogether clear as to whether he was talking about an iterative solution or about an actual temporal process" (Goodwin 1951, p. 4), it will be shown that which of the two subjects he was discussing can be detected in any of his particular treatments of price changes.

In his investigations of mathematical iteration, Walras described how the theorist, who is sitting in this study pondering a model, must hold some prices constant by assumption and increase or decrease other prices in order to find the solutions of its system of equations of general equilibrium. Walras initiated those investigations at the time he began to work out his theory of general equilibrium. The theorist, he explained, must transform the equations relating economic variables repeatedly to diminish the difference between the demand and supply quantities of each commodity. It is evident from his statement that Walras was referring to the manipulation of equations by a theorist:

Now, that will be recognized as definitely occurring if it is realized that the multiplication of all the prices $p_{a,b}$, $p_{a,c}$, $p_{a,d}$ ... by the factor α, which has made the first function equal to zero, has had effects all in the same sense, while the division of each of these prices by the factors β, γ, δ ... some greater and some smaller than 1, a division which has moved the second function away from the zero, has had effects in the contrary sense and up to a certain point compensates some changes with other changes. The system of new prices is therefore closer to equilibrium than the preceding system, and it is necessary only to continue following the same method in order to approach it more and more closely (1874b, p. 131; 1889, p. 152, with changes).

In 1877, Walras extended his ideas about a mathematical technique for finding the solutions, showing how the theorist can vary output in his model to cause the average cost to be closer to the value of the price: "One would thus arrive at the determination by tatonnement" – by which Walras meant mathematical iteration – of the equilibrium outputs (1877b, p. 254; 1889, pp. 221; 238, 241). Concerning productive services, Walras also devised a mathematical procedure of progressively adjusting the values of the variables (1877b, p. 261; 1889, p. 246), and he used that method to try to find the solution values of the outputs and prices of new capital goods (1877b, pp. 297–98; 1889, pp. 291–92).

Walras formulated his most fully developed statements of mathematical iteration during the period 1891 to 1892. His language makes clear that he was referring to a mathematical activity. With respect to finding the prices of commodities when their stocks are fixed, he wrote:

For the moment let us *make abstraction from p_c, p_d...* . and seek initially to determine p_b *provisionally*. And to do so, we ask how, p_c, p_d... . *being supposed constant,* the variations of p_b influence the quantities demanded and supplied of (B) (1891a, in 1896b, p. 467; 1900, Appendix 1, § 3, p. 469). . . . Passing then to the determination of the current price of (C), then of the current price of (D)... . one obtains them by the same means. . . . [O]ne will always be closer to equilibrium at the second reprise of tatonnement than at the first (ibid., in 1896b, p. 469; emphasis added).

Concerning finding the equilibrium prices of commodities when disequilibrium production occurs, Walras explained that

we are going to assume that the quantities . . . are produced at random and *leaving p_t,* p_p, p_k . . . *as they are,* we are going to determine the prices of (B), (C), (D)... . [I]f, initially *making abstraction from the prices* of (C), (D)... . we seek to determine *provisionally* the price of (B), we can vary its price from zero to infinity . . . (1892a in 1896b, pp. 472–73; emphasis added).

Walras indicated that "after this first tatonnement, we would proceed to a second, to a third reprise . . . and so forth until we had obtained a series of prices" at which all excess demand quantities are zero (ibid., p. 473).

Similarly, regarding consumer goods, when it is assumed that all prices other than the price of (B) are "*determined and constant,* and we make the price of (B) change from zero to infinity . . . we find a quantity of (B) at which the price and average cost are equal" (ibid., p. 474; emphasis added). Repeating the procedure for each commodity, "we obtain new prices which will again be a little bit different from the previous set, and we continue in that fashion" (ibid.). Mathematical iteration can then be applied to finding the equilibrium prices of productive services, "and consequently, *one arrives at the equilibrium of the market for services* like that of products . . ." (ibid., p. 476; emphasis in the original). The same procedure of "successive reprises of tatonnement" (ibid., p. 479) can be used to find the equilibrium prices and outputs of capital goods, initially assuming the prices of their productive services are "determined and constant" (ibid., p. 478).

The foregoing quotations express the equation-solving technique that Walras applied *"successively* for the needs of analysis" (Walras to Maffeo Pantaleoni, September 2, 1889, in 1965, *2,* letter 913, p. 345). By "successively" he was referring to two aspects of mathematical iteration – the theorist's successive consideration of temporarily isolated markets, first repeatedly adjusting the price in one market, then in a second market and so on, and the theorist's successive treatment of types of commodities, dealing first with the prices and outputs of products, then with the prices and outputs of productive services. In Walras's discussions of those matters, he made clear he was dealing with mathematical iteration by indicating that he was performing those operations on a model, and by stating that he was "determining the prices mathematically" (1874b, p. 126; 1889, p. 148), or was considering the "logical," "scientific," or "theoretical" solution of the equations, determining one price "provisionally" by adjusting its value while "making abstraction from other prices" or "holding them constant." As will be seen in subsequent quotations, by the word "solution" in this context and in his references to economic tatonnement, Walras generally meant "the process of finding the equilibrium values," although in some passages he used the word to mean "the set of solutions to the equations."

III. Reality and Walras's objective

Concern with real markets

The next objective of this chapter is to show that Walras was concerned with real markets in his mature comprehensive model in general and in his model of economic tatonnement in particular. The writers who believe that his work on iterative processes is exclusively an attempt to find a way a theorist can solve equations, or is purposely concerned with an unrealistic hypothetical model, have neglected a large body of evidence. In this section, which deals not with his technique of mathematical iteration but with his mature model of economic tatonnement, it will be shown that, rightly or wrongly, he thought the latter was an abstract account of real economic behavior. The demonstration of Walras's concern, consisting in large part of straightforward quotations of statements in which he expressed an interest in real tatonnement processes, does not constitute a judgment that his model was in fact realistic in some narrow literal sense. His model of tatonnement obviously refers to the behavior of an artificial construction – namely, a freely competitive model with many simplifying assumptions. This is one reason why this book refers to his models rather than to his theories.

Walras stressed that he was dealing with abstractions when he contended that he had identified the absolutely essential elements of economic behavior. They are, he stated, few in number and are "sufficiently in conformity with reality" that it is possible to add to them secondary materials that enable the study of economic question in mathematical form to be pushed as far as is wished (1895, p. 639). Writing in the third person, Walras declared that Vilfredo Pareto, better than anyone else, has

assimilated the system of economic theory of M. Walras that consists of expounding from a purely objective point of view the mechanism of free competition in regard to exchange and production, and instead of reproaching the author for having, as a first step, reduced that mechanism to its essential elements, has understood that it is appropriate to introduce into his model one by one all the complications that reality presents (1894c, p. 624).

By making successive approximations, economists can "approach more and more closely to the reality of things" (1877b, p. 310; 1889, p. 316).

Walras stressed that he was interested in reality when he observed that his conceptions of a market, the tatonnement process of raising and lowering of prices, supply and demand, and an equilibrium price "are rigorously in conformity with fact, with observation, with experience" (1877b, p. 230; 1889, p. 212). He maintained that the mechanism of "free competition" – by which he meant a high degree of competition – that he incorporated into his model of tatonnement really exists: "In the question of tatonnement, for example, I take the almost universal mode of free competition in regard to exchange" (Walras to Ladislaus von Bortkiewicz, February 27, 1891, in 1965, 2, letter 999, p. 434). "Why not accept . . . the description of the world of economic facts that conforms to the principle of free competition?" (1877a, p. 564; 1877b, p. 366; 1889, pp. 371–72). He contended that his "theory of production is well-founded on the nature of things" (1877b, p. 235; 1889, p. 218), that his analysis of the market for new capital goods made a "relatively simple statement of the most complicated economic phenomena and a relatively facile statement of the most important economic truths" (Walras to Herbet S. Foxwell, December 16, 1888, in 1965, 2, letter 859, p. 277), and, as indicated at the end of chapter 1, that his model of the economy in general "is very much in conformity with reality" (1879a, in 1965, 1, p. 628). Similarly, Walras was concerned to make clear that the location of the action of changing prices that he wanted to model is the marketplace. His model, he wrote, answers the question of "What happens *on the market?*" (1876a, p. 384; 1889, p. 149; emphasis added). The adjustment of prices and the tendency to equilibrium that it produces are real: equilibrium "is the normal state in the sense that it is the one toward which *things tend of themselves* under the regime of free competition applied to production as to exchange" (1877b, p. 231; 1889, p. 214; emphasis added). The economy "always tends toward equilibrium" and "can lead there only by tatonnements" (1877b, p. 310; 1889, p. 316). That is the reality that Walras perceived.

Walras believed that his model of economic tatonnement mirrored that reality. He had been able "not only to demonstrate the laws of the establishment of a given set of equilibrium prices, but also to demonstrate the laws of the variation of those prices, and to analyze the fact of free competition and in so doing to establish it as a principle" (1877a, pp. 563–64; 1877b, pp. 365–66; 1889, p. 371). He showed "that the mechanism of free competition leads precisely to the solution by tatonnement of [the] system of equations" (Walras to Filippo Virgilii, October 17, 1889, in 1965, *2,* letter 928, p. 365). His model of economic tatonnement noted "all the phases of the economic phenomenon": the crying of prices, the offers of buyers and sellers, and the progressive diminution of excess demand quantities (Walras to Charles E. Wickersheimer, February 11, 1897, in 1965, *2,* letter 1297, pp. 727–28). He wanted, he declared, to put "economic reality into the equations" (ibid., p. 728). By considering the real iterative pricing process that transpires in markets "we enter into the theory of tatonnement that I have set forth in my work," and

thanks to the concurrent use of the analytical formulation and of the geometric representation, we obtain not only the idea but the image of the phenomenon of the determination of prices on the market in the case of the exchange of several commodities for each other; and, in achieving that, in my view, we at last possess the theory (1891a, p. 8; 1896b, pp. 469–70).

Through analytical reasoning, Walras attained his idea of how the market works and was consequently able to develop his model of economic tatonnement. It was, he believed, the *image* of the equilibrating process in real markets.

The behavioral basis of Walras's model of iterative pricing

The final objectives of this chapter are to enlarge on the explanation given earlier in this book of the character of Walras's model of how freely competitive markets move toward equilibrium and to controvert some additional erroneous interpretations of his work. The model consists of several overlapping components. The first is a conception of how prices are changed. The received view is that he lacked such a conception. Goodwin, for example, remarked of Walras's model of competitive pricing that "unfortunately for the theory no one raises or lowers any price under perfect competition" (Goodwin 1951, p. 5). Repeating that statement several years later, Arrow maintained that the theory of pure competition as formulated by writers such as Walras has a fatal flaw because all traders in competitive markets are price takers and there is therefore "no one left over whose job it is to make a decision on price" when there is disequilibrium (Arrow 1959, p. 43). Michio Morishima had a different view of Walras's construction. Morishima also contended that Walras assumed that buyers and sellers do not change prices, but Morishima believed that Walras's theory was not flawed as a result, for the reason that Walras assumed that prices "are proposed and adjusted by auctioneers" – that is, by an auctioneer in each market in his model (Morishima 1977, p. 19).

Goodwin's criticism and Morishima's interpretation of Walras's model of economic tatonnement are not accurate. Walras was not intellectually paralyzed by the supposition that traders are always price takers and that therefore no trader changes the price. Although I have never argued that he made that supposition, I lent support to the view that he did by asserting that he failed to indicate who changes the price in his model. As evidence I pointed to the instances in which he wrote only that prices are raised or lowered, without stating who does the raising or lowering (Walker 1972, p. 347). I was mistaken. Morishima was even further from the truth. He was unable to offer any evidence that Walras made either of the assumptions that Morishima attributed to him, for the reason that there is none. It is now obvious to me, and should always have been, that Walras thought he could without confusion occasionally adopt an abbreviated description of economic tatonnement in which he stated simply that prices are raised and lowered, for the reason that he had written so many times that prices are changed by buyers and sellers. That behavior is a major part of the realistic foundation of his mature model of the economic iterative pricing process.

Walras described buyers and sellers in freely competitive markets as being price takers at the current price only until that becomes impossible. If the price is a disequilibrium one, some of those on the short side of the market inevitably discover that they cannot buy or sell all they wish. Walras's assertion about what they do next has a simple and obvious basis. An individual buyer or seller cannot alter the price by variation of the amount he wishes to buy or sell at that price, but that does not mean he cannot or does not change the price by quoting a different value. What does any buyer or seller do in a purely competitive market, such as the market for a widely held stock on the New York Stock Exchange, when told by his broker that his trade cannot be executed at the current price for lack of supply or demand? He instructs the broker to have the floor trader offer a different price, or to buy or sell "at the market," meaning to change the price he quotes until the desired supply or demand quantity is forthcoming. This is the behavior

Walras believed occurred in reality and incorporated into his model of economic tatonnement.

Here are some of his expressions of that behavior and of his explicit and repeated identification of the economic agents that change prices – floor traders, specialists, landlords, workers, capitalists, and entrepreneurs, in their capacities as intermediaries, employers, suppliers of services, suppliers of products and consumers:

> The markets that are best organized under the regime of competition are those in which sales and purchases are made by being cried out *by the intermediation of agents* who execute trades, commercial brokers, criers, who centralize them in such a manner that no exchange takes place without the conditions being announced and known and without *the sellers being able to lower prices and buyers to raise them* (1874b, p. 48; 1889, p. 66; emphasis added; see also chs. 4, 5).

Walras was convinced that freely competitive markets in which buyers and sellers change the price were the "almost universal mode" of exchange (Walras to Bortkiewicz, February 27, 1891, in 1965, 2, letter 999, p. 434). He knew there was no auctioneer in such markets, and he resented that on his having delineated the general case without such a figure, Francis Edgeworth had dredged up special cases in which there is (ibid., pp. 434–35; ch. 4). Moreover, Walras did not think that trading agents or criers are necessary features of freely competitive markets; "One can see, on large markets functioning even without trading agents or criers" – that is, on markets in which the direct participants are the owners of the commodities and money, "the current equilibrium price being determined in a few minutes and considerable quantities of merchandise being exchanged at this price in two or three quarters of an hour" (1874b, p. 69; 1889, pp. 86–87).

In many markets, prices are changed in the same way as on the stock market, so Walras "started by examining the *Bourse* when we began this course in economic theory, in order to seek there the description of the mechanism of free competition in regard to exchange" (1877b, p. 303; Walras 1889, p. 311), and as he indicated in that sentence, he adopted the characteristics of his model of the Bourse for all the markets in his freely competitive models. Here is the description he found and expressed in an illustration of the operation of competitive pricing with reference to different situations that arise in an organized securities market. When a new price, say 60 francs, is quoted for a bond by an agent for a buyer or a seller, all traders initially take it as given. If some demanders do not find their counterparts at 60 francs, however, those "who have orders to buy at 60 francs 05 centimes *or more* ask for the bond at that price. *They raise the price*" (1874, p. 50; 1889, p. 68; emphasis added to the last sentence). If some suppliers do not find their counterparts at 60 francs, those "who have orders to sell at 59 francs 95 *or less* make offers at that price. *They lower the price*" (ibid.; emphasis added to the last sentence; see also 1874a, in 1883, p. 16; and see 1880b, 1880c).

Not just agents on securities exchanges but traders of all kinds change prices when they learn they can no longer be price takers: "If the effective quantity demanded is greater than the effective quantity supplied, the land-lords, workers and capitalists raise their bids and the price rises; if the effective quantity supplied is greater than the effective quantity demanded, the entrepreneurs undercut the price and it falls" (1877b, p. 229; 1889, p. 212). Walras's straightforward statement that the price is changed by those parties is repeated in the next section in the *Eléments,* in which an example of shoe production is presented that illustrates the mechanism again with unmistakable clarity:

You enter a shoemaker's place in order to buy shoes; it is the entrepreneur who gives the product and who receives the money: the operation is done on the market for products. If the quantity of output demanded exceeds the quantity supplied, another consumer will bid the price up above your offer; if the quantity supplied exceeds the quantity demanded, another producer will offer a lower price than the shoemaker. At your side, a worker states the price he needs for making a pair of shoes; it is the entrepreneur who receives the productive service and who gives the money: the operation is done on the market for productive services. If a greater quantity of work is demanded than is offered, another entrepreneur will raise the price above the one offered by the shoemaker; if a great quantity is offered than is demanded, another worker will undercut the worker's price (1877b, p. 230; 1889, p. 213; 1900, § 187, p. 193).

Following his descriptions of freely competitive markets, Walras expressed their properties in his formal model of pricing behavior (1874b, pp. 68–69; 1889, p. 86), explaining that the model "is that which we might have been tempted to formulate immediately after the study of the market on the Bourse; but a rigorous demonstration was necessary" (1874, p. 69; 1889, p. 86). The resulting model of Walrasian pricing describes "the demanders bidding prices up in the event of an excess of the quantity demanded over the quantity supplied, and the suppliers lowering prices in the event of an excess of the quantity supplied over the quantity demanded" (1892a in Walras 1896b, p. 476). The model therefore establishes how "value in exchange left to it-self generates itself naturally on the market under the sway of competition. As buyers, *the traders raise prices;* as sellers, *they lower prices,* and their competition thus leads to a certain value in exchange of commodities that is sometimes rising, sometimes falling, and sometimes stationary" (1874b, p. 48; 1889, p. 66; emphasis in the original). In competitive markets there are "demanders bidding prices up" and "suppliers lowering prices" (1892a, in 1896b, p. 476). Thus prices are changed by buyers and sellers or by their agents in Walras's mature model of economic tatonnement. It does not have and does not need a central auctioneer or an auctioneer in each market to change prices.[2]

IV. Economic tatonnement in the mature models

Intent to develop a realistic model

Many distinguished scholars have contended that Walras tried to develop a theory of the equilibrating behavior of real competitive markets.[3] Adherents of that view include Francis Y. Edgeworth (1889, p. 435), Vilfredo Pareto (1896/1897, *1*, pp. 24–25), Oskar Lange (1944, pp. 94–97), Don Patinkin (1956, pp. 377–85; 1965, pp. 531–540), Michio Morishima (1977, pp. 27–45), and, for the first forty-three years of his career, William Jaffé. Jaffé interpreted all editions of Walras's *Eléments* in that way (Jaffé 1967, pp. 2, 8 [222, 229]), revealing the strength of his conviction by asserting that "we may be certain" that Walras's aim (ibid., p. 8 [229]) was to show that the mathematical problem of equilibrium in exchange and production "is the self-same problem which is solved in practice in the market by the mechanism of free competition" (1954, p. 242; quoted in Jaffé 1967, p. 8 [229]). Walras's theory of tatonnement "is a theory of the process by which the . . . market does this" (Jaffé in Walras 1954, p. 520, n. 12). It was in order "to link his model to the real world" that Walras developed a "quasi-dynamic theory of the emergence (or *establishment*) of equilibrium via the operation of the competitive market mechanism. He called the process of automatic adjustments of the network of real markets to equilibrium one of *tâtonnement*" (Jaffé 1968, p. 449 [131]).

Those views are unquestionably correct. Edgeworth's view was not a myth. He expressed his opinion in a review (Edgeworth 1889) of the second edition of the *Eléments* and gave a correct representation of the contents of that edition. In it, Walras unequivocally presented a dynamic process of equilibration in the models of exchange when there are fixed total stocks and in the models in which production occurs. He intended the models to be abstract and general but realistic accounts of the way in which competitive markets actually move toward equilibrium. The fixed stocks models and the production models will be considered in turn.

---

[2] It has been demonstrated rigorously that an exchange economy without auctioneers in which prices are changed by firms can converge to equilibrium (Fisher 1972). Moreover, a disequilibrium production and sales model does not need a central auctioneer to declare that an equilibrium set of prices has been found, and the enormity of the informational requirements of such an institution (Saari 1985), not to mention the price dissemination requirements, would make it a great hindrance to efficient adjustment.

[3] Since this chapter is concerned only with Walras's view of real economic adjustments, mathematical iteration, and modeling of market adjustments, no exposition is given of his work on the existence of equilibrium and its properties.

First, in all editions of the *Eléments,* Walras based his account of tatonnement in markets with fixed total stocks on the behavior of real organized competitive markets in which the traders in each market are in the same physical area and are therefore in direct communication to be able simultaneously to learn each other's offers (1874b, pp. 48–50, 126; 1889, pp. 66–69, 148; 1900, §§ 41–42, pp. 44–47; § 125, p. 129), as shown by the quotation given earlier in this chapter (1874b, p. 48; 1889, p. 66). Walras adopted those conditions in his model. Moreover, observing that market-day disequilibrium transactions were not allowed in the nineteenth-century Bourse, he incorporated that rule into his model (1880b, p. 461; 1880c, p. 78; 1889, p. 68).[4] Thus, he believed that it described a realistic adjustment process. He also believed that it was representative, explaining that "in the question of tatonnement," he assumed "the almost universal regime of free competition in regard to exchange" (Walras to Ladislaus von Bortkiewicz, February 27, 1891, in 1965, 2, letter 999, p. 434–35). It was therefore, he explained, from the behavior of the majority of real markets that he drew the Walrasian rule of purely competitive pricing, "which consists of raising the price when the quantity demanded exceeds the quantity supplied, and lowering the price when the quantity supplied exceeds the quantity demanded. This can be considered the principal mode that is practiced on all markets with more or less rigor, and consequently with less or more frictions" (1895, in 1965, 2, p. 630).

Second, all the discussion of tatonnement in the production and sale of consumer commodities and capital goods in the first edition of the *Eleménts* is based on and conveys the assumption that production and sales occur in disequilibrium. In the second edition, Walras introduced detailed and clear statements that the process is one of real irrevocable disequilibrium production, and irrevocable disequilibrium sales in the sense of sales that occur at prices that are not part of a general equilibrium set. In the mature models with production, two variables undergo tatonnement – namely, the price and the average cost of production. Walras's account of Walrasian pricing in service and product markets has been presented in chapter 9. The price in each market is changed by the participants in the same direction as the sign of their individual market-oriented excess demand quantities and therefore in the same direction as the unknown market excess demand quantity, as explained in chapter 5. The second aspect of the adjustment process, also presented in chapter 9, is that at each new set of disequilibrium prices a new set of disequilibrium quantities of commodities is produced, which changes the average cost of production. As long as the average cost does not equal the

---

[4] This does not mean that Walras copied exactly in his models all aspects of the functioning of the nineteenth-century Bourse. He utilized only those elements that he thought were representative of all organized competitive markets.

price, the rate of production is changed again, a process that occurs through entrepreneurs' changing the rate of production in existing firms and creating new firms or abandoning old ones. "The system of new quantities produced and new prices is thus closer to equilibrium than the former one, and it is only necessary to continue the tatonnement in order to approach it closer and closer" (1889, p. 241; 1900, § 212, p. 221; see also 1877b, p. 261). Finally, if no disturbing influences intrude on the system, the equilibrium set of prices and quantities is found: "Production is undertaken according to the mechanism of free competition, that is to say, if the average cost of production exceeds the price, output increases; if the average cost of production is equal to the price, equilibrium is established" (1879a, in 1965, *1*, p. 628; see also Walras 1877b, pp. 231, 264, 266, 294–95; 1889, pp. 234–35). Thus, Walras's account in the first three editions of the *Eléments* of the equilibrating process in situations with production depends on the pricing and use of disequilibrium quantities of labor and land and on the pricing, production, and use of disequilibrium quantities of capital goods and consumer goods and services. It is an attempt to model real dynamic phenomena.

Inaccurate and accurate interpretations of Bortkiewicz on Walras

Nevertheless, William Jaffé, in the interpretation he adopted at the end of his career – as was indicated at the beginning of this chapter – denied that Walras tried to develop a dynamic model, and claimed the support of Ladislaus von Bortkiewicz on that matter. According to Jaffé, Bortkiewicz regarded Walras's "*tâtonnement* as an essentially static (and therefore timeless) adjustment process" and therefore wanted "to nip in the bud any attribution of a dynamic character to L. W.'s *tâtonnements*" (Jaffé 1981, p. 328 [259]; see also Walras 1965, *2*, p. 378). Bortkiewicz, Jaffé argued, consequently shared the view that Edgeworth was mistaken in thinking that Walras had tried to describe the way in which the economic system adjusts from a disequilibrium to an equilibrium position (Jaffé 1981, pp. 327–28 [258]). Jaffé believed that this interpretation of Bortkiewicz's opinions was approved by Walras (ibid., p. 328 [258–59]).

Jaffé did not interpret accurately the position taken by Bortkiewicz and Walras. They were writing in 1889 about Walras's theories as they stood in that year, whereas Jaffé represented Bortkiewicz as supporting an interpretation of ideas that Walras did not have until ten years after Bortkiewicz's remarks were made. It is true that Bortkiewicz, and sometimes Walras, used the word "static" to describe an exchange model in which preferences are assumed to be parameters and asset holdings are assumed to be constant prior to trade at the equilibrium price. Jaffé followed the same terminology, but whereas he used it in the additional and illegitimate sense that Walras's model does not contain a dynamic process, Bortkiewicz did not. Bortkiewicz began by granting that Walras did not take up "dynamics" *if* that word is used, as Jevons used it, to mean the analysis of a system undergoing changes in asset holdings and preferences (Bortkiewicz 1890, p. 86). Walras's equations of equilibrium are confined to static analysis *"in the sense* that he assumes the quantities of products possessed as being constant quantities, and the utility functions as invariant" (ibid.; emphasis added). Bortkiewicz was referring to markets in which the total stocks of the assets are constant. He rightly stated that Walras assumed that there are no variations in the parameters of the static equations of supply and demand when they are examined to determine the existence of equilibrium.

Drawing on the first and second editions of the *Eléments,* Bortkiewicz then went on to distinguish between that aspect of Walras's theory and the aspect that deals with the process by which the market moves toward equilibrium. Arguing that Walras's model was not purely static, not a mathematical device, not hypothetical, and not quasi-instantaneously equilibrating, Bortkiewicz expressed in three statements the opposite of the view that Jaffé attributed to him. First, Bortkiewicz noted that Walras analyzed the dynamic "question of the solution of the equations of exchange by the raising and lowering of the price" (ibid.). Second, he defended Walras's attempt to describe the general characteristics of the dynamic path of the economy: "Mr. Edgeworth honestly believes that it is quite simply useless to try to demonstrate the path by which the economic system is led to equilibrium, and he finds a confirmation of that view in the opinion given by Jevons that the problems relative to economic equilibrium ought to be treated from the static point of view and not the dynamic one" (ibid., p. 85). Edgeworth's rejection of Walras's objective, Bortkiewicz argued, was a mistake. Third, Bortkiewicz observed that there could be more than one method for solving a system of equations, but what was under consideration was not "a problem of algebra" but "a question of showing what is the real procedure, actually used in the market, that constitutes the manner of solution of the given equations" (ibid.). To explicate this matter, referring to tatonnement in pricing and the expansion and contraction of the size of industries that change output and average costs, Bortkiewicz quoted Walras's statement that "the mechanism of raising and lowering of prices in the market, combined with the fact of the shifting of entrepreneurs from enterprises that are making losses to those that are making profits, is nothing other than a mode of solving by tatonnement the equations of those problems" (1889, p. xviii; quoted in Bortkiewicz 1890, p. 85; see also Walras 1877b, p. 266). Bortkiewicz's conclusion was that the model of tatonnement is a dynamic theory of the behavior of real markets. That is the interpretation of tatonnement of which Walras approved in 1889, not Jaffé's rendition of

Bortkiewicz's opinions. That conclusion is also supported by a mass of additional evidence dating from before, during, and after the time when Bortkiewicz's article was written.

Additional evidence of Walras's concern with dynamics

First, there are Walras's expositions of the nature of static and dynamic analysis. For example, he explained their difference clearly with reference to markets. The "static theory of exchange," he wrote, may be defined as "the exposition of the equilibrium formula." The "dynamic theory," in contrast, is the theory of tatonnement, which demonstrates "the attainment of that equilibrium through the play of the raising and lowering of prices until the supply and demand quantities are made equal" (1895, in 1965, 2, p. 630). By those statements, Walras indicated that he did not regard his model of exchange as being rendered static by his assumption that preferences and the distribution of assets are constant during the process of finding equilibrium prices. To emphasize this point, he continued by observing that whereas Jevons had not adequately treated the static problem to which his work was confined – that is, the exposition of the equations of equilibrium – he, Walras, had not only given it a full development but had also been the first economist to examine and formulate the dynamics of competitive market behavior (ibid.). Similarly, concerning his theory of production, he pointed out that the static part of his analysis was his exposition of the conditions of equilibrium and that when considering the process of adjustment in disequilibrium, he introduced disequilibrium phenomena and gave a dynamic treatment of economic behavior (1889, pp. XVII–XVIII; 1896b, p. XVII).

Second, there are Walras's repeated assertions that his model of tatonnement as it stood during both the creative and the mature phases of his theoretical work describes how real markets follow a dynamic path until they reach the equilibrium values. The prices are "determined empirically on the market, by the mechanism of free competition," he wrote, "exactly as they are determined mathematically" in accordance with the economic conditions of his model: maximizing utility, equality of supply and demand quantities, and general equilibrium (1876a, p. 389). The "same problem of the exchange of several commodities for each other, for which we have just found the scientific solution, is also that which is solved empirically on the market by the mechanism of competition" (1877b, p. 126; 1889, p. 148). "The mechanism of free competition produces by tatonnement precisely the solution of that system of equations" (Walras to Filippo Virgilii, October 17, 1889, in 1965, 2, letter 928, pp. 364–65). Real market processes also provide the practical solution of the equations of the general equilibrium of production

(1877b, p. 266; 1879a, p. 628; 1889, p. 251). Similarly, Walras maintained, his description of tatonnement was "justified" by the attainment of the equality of price and the average cost of production of new capital goods (Walras to Philip H. Wicksteed, April 9, 1889, in 1965, 2, letter 877, pp. 307–9). By "justified" he meant that the materialization of the equilibrium values of the variables in the formation of capital shows that the tatonnement process has been at work.

Third, there are Walras's communications to Bortkiewicz. Even before Bortkiewicz defended the model of tatonnement, Walras had written to him about the materialization of the equality of price and average cost of production as evidence that tatonnement occurs (Walras to Bortkiewicz, January 9, 1889, in 1965, 2, letter 863 pp. 281–82; Walras to Bortkiewicz, January 9, 1891, in 1965, 2 letter 996, pp. 428–29), by which statement he was indicating that the adjustment process ensures the stability of equilibrium. Again expressing to Bortkiewicz the opposite of what Jaffé alleged to be the content of his letters, Walras insisted on the importance of his model of tatonnement and explained that Edgeworth was right to interpret it as both dynamic and intended to be realistic but was wrong to criticize it for being an attempt to deal with those matters: "Edgeworth believes . . . that I am making absolutely useless efforts to demonstrate that the operations of raising and lowering prices, of the increase and decrease of the quantities of products manufactured, etc. on the markets are nothing other than the solution by tatonnement of the equations of exchange, of production, and of capital formation" (Walras to Bortkiewicz, October 17, 1889, in 1965, 2, letter 927, pp. 363–64). Later, Walras praised Bortkiewicz for agreeing with him on that matter and for his accurate interpretation of the *Eléments* (Walras to Bortkiewicz, January 18, 1890, in 1965, 2, letter 954, pp. 387–88; Walras to Bortkiewicz, February 6, 1890, in 1965, 2, letter 957, pp. 389–90).

The entrepreneur

Another component of Walras's model of economic tatonnement is the role of the entrepreneur in it. This is examined in detail elsewhere (ch. 13), and it is necessary here only to emphasize the four iterative aspects of entrepreneurial behavior that Walras identified.

First, Walras wrote, entrepreneurs are very important in the process by which excess demand quantities are diminished because they constitute an entire side of the market in factor and product markets and follow the iterative Walrasian pricing rule. They are the demanders in markets for productive services, bidding prices up repeatedly as long as they are unable to purchase all they want, whereas the suppliers lower prices if they cannot sell all they want (1877b, pp. 228–29, 364; 1898b, pp. 211–12). Entrepreneurs are the suppliers in markets for products, lowering prices repeatedly as long as they cannot sell all they want, whereas demanders of all types raise prices if they cannot buy all they want (ibid., pp. 229–30, 364).

Second, since entrepreneurs are the buyers of inputs and the sellers of outputs, they relate the prices of the latter to their expenditures on the former. Entrepreneurs therefore provide the connections between input and output markets that disseminate the impact of repeated price changes throughout the economic system, thus enabling its equilibrating activity to occur.

Third, in their efforts to maximize their incomes, entrepreneurs diminish excess demand prices iteratively by producing a series of disequilibrium rates of output:

If, in certain enterprises, the prices of products are greater than their average cost in productive services, which constitutes a *profit,* the entrepreneurs enlarge their productive activities, which increases the quantity of products, and results in lowering the price and reducing the difference; and if, in certain enterprises, the average cost of products in productive services is greater than their price, which constitutes a *loss,* the entrepreneurs turn away from the industry or restrict their productive activities, which reduces the quantity of products, thus resulting in raising the price and again in reducing the discrepancy (1877b, p. 231; 1889, p. 214).

Fourth, the iterative activity of entrepreneurs in disequilibrium includes their repeated experiments with finding the best combination of inputs during the course of the equilibrating process (Walras to Enrico Barone, October 30, 1895, in 1965, 2, letter 1217; 1896b, p. 489).

Walras therefore emphasized that his model of economic tatonnement deals not only with changes of prices and quantities traded but also with repeated reallocations of economic resources. He summarized those two aspects of iterative adjustment behavior in this way:

Free competition in regard to production, that is to say the freedom of entrepreneurs to increase their production in the case in which they are making a profit and to restrict it in the case of a loss, joined to free competition in regard to exchange, that is to say the liberty allowed to landowners workers, and capitalists on the one hand, and to entrepreneurs on the other, to buy and sell productive services and products by bidding prices up or down, is the practical method of solution of the equations of [general equilibrium] (1877b, p. 266; 1889, p. 251).

It is evident that Walras's theoretical accounts of the iterative processes of entrepreneurs moving into and out of industries, of their experiments with the amounts of inputs, and of buying and selling by service suppliers and entrepreneurs are attempts to model real time-consuming processes and are not part of a mathematical solution technique.

Convergent pricing

The final component of Walras's work on tatonnement is his assertion that the set of general equilibrium values found by mathematical iteration is found by the real economy because the iterative pricing process generates values that converge to the equilibrium set. He was incorrect in that belief insofar as it expresses the notion that his static equations give the equilibrium values of a model in which disequilibrium production and sales occur, but that problem is not the focus of the present discussion. The point to be made here is that Walras insisted that the real economy is convergent and claimed that circumstance is what makes his mathematical iteration worthwhile. In this respect he went far beyond a modeling of immediately perceivable behavior, making two theoretical statements. One is that markets in the real economy are interrelated because the excess demand quantity for any commodity is a function of all prices. The other is that the forms and interrelations of supply and demand functions in the real economy imply that iterative competitive pricing leads to a progressive diminution of excess demand quantities.

Despite his claim to have given a rigorous proof of the stability of equilibrium, Walras did not do so in fact, as many writers have observed. Nevertheless, he explicitly made the claim that the real economy is stable after each of his discussions of mathematical iteration in the lessons in the *Eléments*. Regarding the exchange of given stocks of commodities, Walras described the theoreticians's method of solving equations by iteration, and in the next sentence observed: "It remains only to show, and this is the essential point, that the same problem of exchange for which we have just furnished the theoretical solution" – found by the mathematical iterative technique – "is also that which is solved in a practical way on the market by the mechanism of free competition" – and described in the model of economic tatonnement (1876, pp. 381–82; 1889, p. 141). "The scientific solution" is found "empirically on the market by the mechanism of competition" (1877b, p. 126; 1889, p. 148). Just as mathematical iteration converges to equilibrium, so does economic tatonnement: "What must be proved in order to establish that the theoretical solution and the solution by the market are identical? Quite simply that the raising and lowering of prices are a mode of solution by tatonnement of the system of equations of equality of the quantities supplied and demanded" (1889, p. 149).

Regarding the production of consumer commodities, Walras set forth his method of mathematical iteration, and in the next sentence wrote: "It remains only to demonstrate, in regard to the equilibrium of production as in regard to that of exchange, that the same problem for which we have given the theoretical solution is also that which is solved practically on the market by the mechanism of free competition" (1877b, p. 251; 1889, p. 234). The convergent economic tatonnement "occurs of itself on the market for products" (1877b, p. 255; 1889, p. 241). Immediately after discussing mathematical iteration with reference to the market for services, Walras stated: "Now, this tatonnement occurs naturally and of itself on the market for services,"[5] through the raising and lowering of prices in accordance with the signs of excess demand quantities (1877b, p. 261; 1889, p. 246). Immediately after discussing mathematical iteration with reference to the capital market, Walras stated: "Now, the indicated tatonnement is exactly that which transpires on the market for capital goods" (1889, p. 287).

On one occasion, Walras reversed the procedures, discussing the real economic tatonnement first, "Let us go to the market," he wrote, where prices are cried. "At these prices, cried in this way, each trader determines his demand or supply of (A), (B), (C), (D) . . . That is done without reflection, without calculation, but exactly in the way it would be done by calculation in virtue of the system of equations of equivalency of quantities demanded and supplied and of maximum satisfaction" (1874, p. 127; 1889, p. 148). Walras believed he had found a mathematical technique of tatonnement that did for his equation system what the real market system does for economic variables: "It is a question of basing on the fact of that uncalculated determination a method of solution by tatonnement of the equations of the equality of the total demand and supply quantities. Here is how this can be done" (ibid.). Walras then proceeded to discuss mathematical iteration.

Returning to the subject of economic tatonnement, Walras concluded that "the mechanism of raising and lowering of prices in the market, combined with the fact of the shifting of entrepreneurs from enterprises that are making losses to those that are making profit, is nothing other than a mode of solving by tatonnement the equations of these problems" (1889, p. XVIII). His assertion that the market solves the equations is the assertion that the set of prices converges to equilibrium. As late as 1901, he was still repeating that message: "The increase and decrease of prices," he wrote, is "are a procedure of solving the equations by tatonnement, which identifies the solution by the market with the mathematical solution" (1901, in 1965, *3*, p. 158). Thus a mass of evidence makes it impossible to accept the view that he did not have an idea of real economic tatonnement or was uninterested in the dynamic behavior of the real economy.

V. How mathematical and economic iterative pricing differ

First, they differ in kind. One is a mathematical technique, the other is an attempt to model economic reality. Walras's view of the ontological status of

---

[5] In the 1889 edition of the *Eléments,* Walras deleted the words "and of itself."

his model of economic tatonnement was made evident when he stated repeatedly that on the one hand there is his model and its equations and on the other hand there is the tatonnement of the real economy, as has just been documented. He represented his model as reflecting the essential elements of real competitive pricing and adjustment of rates of production. When he did so, he was obviously referring to his modeling of the behavior of real competitive markets, not to the attempts of a theoretician to solve a set of equations.

Second, Walras's notions of mathematical and economic tatonnement differ in form. In his technique of mathematical iteration, he held some prices constant while one is changed, whereas in his model of economic iterative pricing, all prices change together. He emphasized the latter – in an age before computers – by writing that when one recalls that the tatonnement process occurs *"simultaneously* on the market," does one not see "exactly in its totality the fact of the determination of the prices of several commodities under the regime of free competition?" (Walras to Maffeo Pantaleoni, September 2, 1889, in 1965, *2,* letter 913, p. 345). Jaffé interpreted "simultaneously," to mean "theoretically instantaneously" and the passage to indicate that Walras's model of economic tatonnement did not describe sequential pricing (Jaffé 1981, pp. 222–23 [253]). In fact, when Walras used the word "simultaneously," he did not mean that the adjustments occur *instantaneously* either in reality or in his model. He indicated the opposite frequently and consistently, as when he wrote that the economy never actually reaches equilibrium because sufficient time elapses for parametric changes to occur before equilibrium is reached (1877b, pp. 231, 310–11). By *"simultaneously* on the market" as a whole he meant that different particular markets undergo a series of price changes during the same protracted period of time.

This is evident in all Walras's discussions of economic tatonnement, but he also expressed it explicitly in a passage that he published several times. In that passage, which he placed in the *Eléments* immediately following the republication of the explorations of mathematical iteration he had undertaken during the years 1891 and 1892, he emphasized that:

We must picture to ourselves as taking place simultaneously all the operations that, for the needs of the demonstration, we have had to assume taking place successively, that is to say, on the market for products and on the market for services, the demanders bidding prices up in the event of an excess of the quantity demanded over the quantity supplied, and the suppliers lowering prices in the event of an excess of the quantity supplied over the quantity demanded; the entrepreneurs in product markets increasing output in the case of an excess of the price over the average cost, and, on the contrary, decreasing it in the case of an excess of the average cost over price; and here again, we will have, thanks to the geometric representation, an exact and complete image of the general phenomenon of the establishment of economic equilibrium under a regime of free competition (1892a, in 1896b, p. 476; and see 1892b, p. 60).

Walras was explaining that it was for the need to work out mathematical iteration that he had assumed successive changes of prices in the sense that first one price is changed while others are held constant, then another is changed, and so on. He was striving to make clear that in contrast, his model of economic tatonnement reflected reality by treating the adjustments of different markets as taking place simultaneously in the sense that while the price is changing in one market, prices in other markets are also changing at the same time. For example, he was explaining, prices in the markets for products and the markets for services change at the same time, not successively as he made them do in his mathematical iteration procedure.

Third, economic tatonnement and mathematical iteration differ in that the former is efficient whereas the latter – in an age before computers – takes so long that it is not: "The practical solution is of a rapidity and a surety that leaves nothing to be desired. One can see, on large markets functioning even without agents or criers, the current equilibrium price being determined in a few minutes. . . . In contrast, the theoretical solution would be, in almost all cases, absolutely impracticable" (1874b, p. 69; 1889, pp. 86–87).

VI. Conclusion

Walras tried to develop a technique of mathematical iteration to solve the equations of a general equilibrium model. There was no confusion in Walras's mind about the difference between the methods of solution – the processes of moving toward the solution set of values – that mathematical and economic tatonnement constitute:

One sees clearly now what the mechanism of competition on the market is; it is the practical solution, by the raising and lowering of prices, of the problem of exchange for which we have furnished the theoretical and mathematical solution. One should understand moreover that it is not our intention in any respect to substitute one solution for the other (1874b, p. 69; 1889, pp. 86–87).

Walras also constructed a model of what he conceived to be the real process of economic tatonnement. He believed that his model mirrors the iterative pricing and related adjustment processes of real markets and explains how they converge to equilibrium. After constructing his system of simultaneous equations of equilibrium, he wrote that "it is necessary to establish that the result of the flow of the interrelated phenomena of reality is truly the empirical solution of that system of equations. That is what I have done successively in regard to exchange, production, and capital formation" (1877b, p. 365; 1889, p. 371; 1900, § 370, p. 427).

In fact, Walras's mature model of economic tatonnement is not a complete dynamic system because it does not trace the paths that the economic variables follow, nor prove that the variables in a model of interrelated purely competitive markets would converge to equilibrium. Nevertheless, his model describes the character and outcome of a process of economic tatonnement in general terms. He constructed it by identifying the economic agents that change prices, by summarizing their iterative economic behavior in the model of Walrasian pricing and of adjustments of rates of production and of average costs, by identifying the role of the entrepreneur in the tatonnement process, and by asserting that the markets of his model converge to equilibrium through iterative economic processes.

CHAPTER 13

The mature model of the behavior
of the entrepreneur

This chapter eliminates the obscurity into which Walras's mature model of the activities of the entrepreneur has fallen. An exposition of the three parts of the model is given: Walras's definition of the entrepreneur, an account of the entrepreneur's role in effectuating dynamic market adjustments, and a description of his situation in an equilibrium state of the market. Criticisms of the model are presented and evaluated, its contributions are identified, and its impact on the work of Vilfredo Pareto, Enrico Barone, and Joseph Schumpeter is described. It is concluded that the model was a significant addition to economic analysis, providing the foundation and inspiration for some important aspects of the modern theory of the entrepreneur and of profits.

I. Introduction

This chapter continues the examination of the adjustment processes in Walras's models. Its subject is the role of the entrepreneur in those processes. The fact that Walras's mature model of the behavior of the entrepreneur provided a significant part of the foundations of the modern theories of the entrepreneur and of profits has been obscured by misunderstandings[1] and decades of neglect. The major reasons for those conditions are that he did not provide a complete and clear statement of the model in one place, and that there has not been, as far as I am aware, any such statement in the interpretative literature on his work. The character of Walras's exposition resulted from the circumstance that his ideas on the nature and significance of the functions of the entrepreneur evolved gradually during the period 1874 to the late 1880s as an integral part of his maturing conception of the interrelationships in his comprehensive economic model and of its functioning. During his creative phase, Walras conceived some of the ideas that he incorporated into his mature model of the entrepreneur. He added significantly to his conception of the entrepreneur in the second edition of the *Eléments*. There he achieved a clear conception of his economic model as one in which production occurs

---

[1] Some pre-Walras literature on the entrepreneur is relevant for the formation of Walras's model and is reviewed in this chapter. For a modern brief controversy about his model, see Jaffé 1980 and Morishima 1980.

in disequilibrium, with profound consequences for the functioning of the entrepreneur. The entrepreneur in the mature model is active in disequilibrium situations that involve actual hiring, production, and sales. In the models of Walras's phase of decline, by contrast, that behavioral content is eliminated and the entrepreneur is stripped of his functions.

Walras presented some of his mature ideas on the entrepreneur in his correspondence and related papers. He provided some of them in his responses to his critics, and his supporters explained others by their responses to his critics. The second edition and those materials will be used to formulate a complete and clear statement of Walras's mature model of the entrepreneur, to interpret it, and to evaluate it. The model can be divided into three parts: a definition of the entrepreneur, an account of his role in effectuating dynamic market adjustments, and a description of his situation in an equilibrium state of the market. These parts will be considered in turn.

II. Definition of the entrepreneur

Defects of previous conceptions

Walras stated that "the definition of the entrepreneur is, in my opinion, the key to all economics."[2] He cleared the ground for his definition by characterizing and criticizing the doctrines of previous writers. The English classical economists, he argued, did not distinguish between the entrepreneur and the capitalist, so they used the word "profit" to include both the interest on capital and the profit of the entrepreneur (1877b, p. 359; 1889, pp. 364–65). Capitalists own capital; entrepreneurs perform a different function. It is true, Walras granted, that many capitalists are entrepreneurs, but many are not. As evidence he referred to individuals who are capitalists by virtue of owning bonds or commercial paper or because they are silent partners, but who take no part in the operation of businesses. Similarly, some entrepreneurs are not capitalists. Even if the two roles were more intermingled than is the case, they should be separated for theoretical purposes (1877b, pp. 359–60; 1889, p. 365). The failure to do so, in Walras's opinion, was typified by the work of William Stanley Jevons. His *Primer of Political Economy* (Jevons 1878) was

---

[2] Walras originally wrote "the key" but then replaced "key" by "noeud" (Walras to Francis Walker, June 12, 1887, in 1965, 2, letter 800, p. 212). The latter word, which translates literally as "knot," has the meaning in this context of "that which ties the loose ends together." Since that meaning is not well-conveyed by the word "knot" in the translation of Walras's dictum, his original word has been retained. Walras evidently felt that the door to economic knowledge could be unlocked with more than one key. He wrote that the distinction between capital goods and their services is "the key to all economic theory" (1889, p. XIII), and he also asserted that the substitution of marginal utilities in place of values in his equations "is the key to all the problems of economics" (1886, p. 36).

incomplete because of the absence of a definition of the entrepreneur. Lacking a recognition of his intervention in the market, Jevons was unable to construct determinate theories of rent, wages, and interest (Walras to W. S. Jevons, July 13, 1878, in 1965, *2,* letter 410, p. 470), and could not understand how those factor prices are determined (Walras to Johan Baron d'Aulnis de Bourouill, September 10, 1878, in 1965, *2,* letter 416, pp. 579–80).[3] Walras continued by asserting that once it is recognized that the roles of the entrepreneur and the capitalist are distinct, it becomes clear that the conditions that determine their incomes are different. The entrepreneur earns profit; the capitalist earns interest. The part of net income that constitutes the profit of enterprise is not like interest. The English school should learn that profit "is correlative to a possible loss, that it is uncertain, that it depends upon circumstances that are exceptional and not normal, and that theoretically, abstraction ought to be made from it" (1877b, p. 360; 1889, p. 365).[4] By the last seven words, he presumably meant that profit does not exist in equilibrium. Unlike interest, in other words, profit exists only when there is uncertainty, in disequilibrium states of the market in which there is also a chance of incurring a loss.

The French school, Walras contended, was also defective in its treatment of the entrepreneur. For fifty years prior to the mid-1870s, it had not taken a single step in the direction of constructing a satisfactory theory of the economy (1877b, p. 363; 1889, p. 369). Jean-Bapiste Say, in particular, was like Jevons in lacking a definition of the entrepreneur. He had no conception of the differences between the markets for products and for productive services, and therefore, like Jevons, could not adequately explain the services of which wages, rent, and interest are the prices (ibid.). It is necessary to avoid the error of "a certain number of French economists who make the entrepreneur a worker by considering him as being specially charged with the work of directing the firm" (1877b, p. 228; 1889, p. 211). By those comments, Walras did not do justice to French economists. As Francis A. Walker noted, "the French writers have always recognized profits and interest as separate shares in distribution. J.B. Say treated Adam Smith's neglect of the entrepreneur as creating a serious hiatus.[5] All of Say's successors down to Courcelle-Seneuil have dwelt strongly on the importance of that industrial function" (F.A. Walker 1887, p. 269, n.). Indeed, Say constructed a well-developed definition of the entrepreneur, distinguishing him from a pure capitalist as well as from

---

[3] Jevons replied that he agreed about the entrepreneur, "but must remedy the omission in some future work" (Jevons to Walras, July 16, 1878, in 1965, *1,* letter 411, pp. 572–73).

[4] On a secondary aspect of Walras's critique (1877b, p. 357), Francis Edgeworth granted that English economists had made an error by supposing that the entrepreneur controls a fund of which he predestines certain parts to be spent on particular types of factors of production. Working capital cannot by divided into one part intended specifically for wages, one for rent, and another for capital costs (Edgeworth 1889a, p. 435; Edgeworth 1891, p. 20).

[5] See Say 1836, p. 346.

an ordinary worker. Nevertheless, it is true that Say regarded the entrepreneur as one who directs the operations of the firm (Say 1836, pp. 144–45, 331–46), which Walras considered to be managerial labor, not entrepreneurship. Say also frequently fused the ownership of capital with other attributes of the entrepreneur (ibid., pp. 331–46). Walras was therefore more accurate when he argued not that the French school had no conception of the entrepreneur, but that their conception differed from his and failed to identify what he regarded as important entrepreneurial activities. Say and Walras both recognized that there is an intimate connection between entrepreneurship and the ownership of a firm, but Say emphasized the frequent identity of those roles, whereas Walras saw that they are fundamentally different.

Walras's definition

Walras began with that consideration when he turned to the construction of his own definition of the entrepreneur. The entrepreneur, Walras maintained, may own and provide the services of one or more of the other factors of production, but his function is nevertheless distinct from theirs (1877b, p. 228; 1889, p. 211). He is the person that purchases raw materials from other entrepreneurs and the services of the factors of production from workers, landowners, and capitalists, and that sells output (1877b, pp. 228, 233; 1889, pp. 211, 216; Walras to Johan Baron d'Aulnis de Bourouill, September 10, 1878, in 1965, 2, letter 416, pp. 579–80). Walras explained with great clarity that

I consider [the entrepreneur] exclusively as the person who buys productive services on the market for services and sells products on the market for products, thus obtaining either a profit or loss. If he owns some of the land or the capital goods that are used in his firm or if he [directs or supervises][6] takes part in the capacity of a director or otherwise in the operation of the transformation of services into products, he is then by virtue of that activity in actuality a landowner, capitalist, or worker, and combines their distinct functions with his own. As a matter of actual practice, for the entrepreneur to combine them is frequent and perhaps even generally necessary; but his doing so ought, I believe, to be put to one side for the purposes of theoretical investigation (Walras to Francis Amasa Walker, June 12, 1887, in 1965, 2, letter 800, p. 212).

Combining the factors of production in the firm or supervising their application to raw materials are therefore activities undertaken by the entrepreneur not as an entrepreneur but as a managerial worker.

Walras's statements are so explicit and assertively formulated on that precise point that there can be no question of the function of the entrepreneurs in his models. Moreover, that his statement remained his mature position on

---

[6] The words in brackets were written by Walras but then crossed out.

the matter was indicated by his repetition of his adherence to it in 1895. Maintaining that Alfred Marshall assumed in most of his theorizing that the owner of productive services is a worker who produces output and sells it, Walras explained that in his own model he proceeded differently. He envisioned the supply of productive services and the demand for products as being determined by the maximization of utility or net advantages by the owners of the factors of production. Then, he wrote, he introduced the intervention of the entrepreneur, "a distinct person whose role is essentially that of demanding services and selling products" (1895, p. 629). Thus, Walras made his model of the entrepreneur's behavior consistent with his analysis of the factors of production and their remuneration by eliminating the activities of coordination and supervision from the entrepreneur's functions. Those activities, he asserted, are part of routine management and are remunerated by the payment of the wages of management (1877b, p. 232; 1889, pp. 214–15; Walras to Francis Amasa Walker, June 12, 1887, in 1965, 2, letter 800, p. 212).

III. Dynamics

Walras then described the role taken by the entrepreneur in the dynamic adjustments by which the markets in the mature comprehensive model tend to equilibrium. The entrepreneur, he explained, is an essential part of the dynamics of the market system. He is not merely active in disequilibrium states of the model but exerts the principal equilibrating force in the market system by propelling the mechanism of free competition. This operates in three types of markets, to the identification of which Walras was led, he stated, by his idea of the entrepreneur as an intermediary who buys and sells (1877b, p. 228; 1889, p. 211). Walras's models of the markets, he believed and wanted to emphasize, "are rigorously in conformity with facts, with observation and experience" (1877b, p. 230; 1889, p. 212; and see Walras 1879a, p. 628).[7]

Entrepreneurs' roles in different markets

First, Walras referred to a model of markets on which the productive services of persons, land, and capital goods proper are supplied by workers, landowners, and capitalists respectively, and are demanded by entrepreneurs (1877b, pp. 228–29, 364–65; 1889, pp. 211, 370). On any such market, if the quantity demanded exceeds the quantity supplied, the entrepreneurs bid the price up.

---

[7] See chapter 2 for the evidence that Walras believed that his theory was a positive abstract account of the main features of economic reality and not a normative scheme.

If the quantity supplied exceeds the quantity demanded, the suppliers of the services lower the price. In examining the shoe trade, for example, one might observe a worker setting a price for making a pair of shoes. He quotes that price to the entrepreneur, who receives the productive service from the worker and pays him money in return. If the quantity demanded of a shoe-worker's labor exceeds the quantity supplied, some entrepreneur will offer a higher price than the first one did; if the quantity supplied exceeds the quantity demanded, some worker will offer his labor at a lower rate than the first one did (1877b, p. 230; 1889, p. 213).

Second, Walras referred to a model of markets for products. On the various markets within that general category, consumer goods and services and new capital goods are supplied by entrepreneurs and demanded by workers, land-owners, and capitalists (1877b, pp. 229, 364; 1889, p. 212; Walras 1879a, p. 628). For each commodity, a price is cried. If the quantity demanded exceeds the quantity supplied, then workers, landowners, and capitalists bid the price up. If the quantity supplied exceeds the quantity demanded, entrepreneurs lower the price (1877b, p. 230; 1889, p. 213). For example, a buyer might enter a cobbler's shop to buy some shoes. It is the entrepreneur who hands over the product and who receives the money. If the quantity demanded of the product exceeds the quantity supplied, some consumer will make a better offer than the first one did; if the quantity supplied of the products exceeds the quantity demanded, some entrepreneurs will ask a lower price than the first one did (ibid.).

Third, Walras referred to a model of a market on which money capital is supplied in the form of loans by capitalists and demanded by entrepreneurs (1877a, p. 562; Walras 1883, p. 113). The entrepreneurs purchase capital goods, make money from their use, and repay the loan to the capitalists. It is therefore not the capitalists but the entrepreneurs who are the demanders of new capital goods (1877b, pp. 234, 277; 1889, pp. 217, 265). It is through the latter's acquiring and using more of the capital goods that yield the greatest return that the net rate of return on all capital goods is made equal and becomes equal to the equilibrium rate of interest.[8] Since the entrepreneurs on the capital market and on the other markets buy from suppliers of services and sell to them, the entrepreneurs are not the only part of the adjustment mechanism within each market, but they are an essential part of it.

Connecting input and output markets

Walras also considered the role of entrepreneurs in relating input and output markets. His models of markets for services and for products are connected

[8] This aspect of Walras's theory of the entrepreneur is discussed in detail in chapter 14.

by payments that are made in accordance with the forces of supply and demand and therefore in large measure in accordance with the actions of entrepreneurs. The demand for productive services, the demand for money capital, and the supply of products are determined by entrepreneurs, motivated by the desire to maximize profits and avoid losses. The supply of productive services, the supply of money capital, and the demand for products are determined by workers, landowners, and capitalists, motivated by the desire to achieve the greatest possible satisfaction of wants. Consequently, what the entrepreneurs pay in money to the owners of factors of production for their services is spent by the latter as consumers in the product market, and what the entrepreneurs receive in money for their products they spend in the market for productive services (1877b, p. 230; Walras 1879a, p. 628; 1889, p. 213). By their activity in the market for services they contribute to the determination of the rates of remuneration of the inputs. By their activity in the market for commodities they contribute to the determination of the prices of products, the rate of net income, and the prices of personal capital,[9] land, and capital goods proper (1877a, pp. 113–14; Walras 1877b, pp. 277, 364–65; 1889, pp. 265, 370). Their activities therefore connect the input and output markets. Entrepreneurs are not the only participants in the processes whereby price adjustments between markets are made, but they are an essential part of them.

Allocating resources

As a central feature of the dynamic behavior of his model, Walras developed an account of how entrepreneurs allocate resources between and within purely competitive markets, and of how in so doing their behavior automatically gives rise to the tatonnement process in the markets for services and products (1877b, p. 255; 1889, p. 241; Walras 1879a, p. 628). Walras first considered the motives and remuneration of the entrepreneur. He is the recipient of profits and the bearer of losses, and he therefore seeks to make profits and avoid losses. Walras defined profits as the excess of the price over the average cost of production, multiplied by the number of units of output, and defined a loss as the reverse.[10] The entrepreneur draws his profits from the general revenues of the firm, after all costs, including his own salary as a manager, have been paid (1877b, pp. 231–32; 1889, pp. 214–15). Walras's statement that the entrepreneur bears losses reveals that in his theory – as in

---

[9] Walras must have meant the virtual price of personal capital. See Jaffé 1983, p. 153.

[10] In one place, Walras stated that a profit or a loss is the difference between what the entrepreneur obtains for his own services rendered for his firm and what he would be able to earn elsewhere (1877b, p. 232; 1889, p. 215). That opportunity cost or comparative earnings definition is incompatible with the definition that Walras used everywhere else in his work.

any theory that identifies entrepreneurial losses – the entrepreneur should be
an owner of the firm. An employee such as an entrepreneur can obtain cash
bonuses that are paid out of profits but how can he sustain a loss? His
managerial salary may be reduced, which sometimes happens when losses
are incurred, but that is a reduction of a cost, not a loss by the individual of
part or all of a previously possessed fund or asset. Losses are borne in the
form of a reduction of the worth of the firm, and are reflected in changes
such as a diminution of cash reserves and other liquid assets, sales of assets
and use of the proceeds to pay the costs of the business, and elimination of
dividends or payment of reduced dividends out of cash reserves. For these
changes to come partially or wholly at the entrepreneur's expense, he must
have an ownership interest in the firm,[11] a circumstance that does not imply
that the function of the entrepreneur is the same as an owner's because, as
Walras pointed out, the latter is frequently not an entrepreneur (1877b, p.
359; 1889, p. 365). In Walras's model, an owner is not necessarily an
entrepreneur but an entrepreneur must be an owner. Walras recognized that
the entrepreneur is ordinarily an owner of the firm but he did not regard
ownership as an essential characteristic of entrepreneurship (1877b, p. 228;
1889, p. 211; Walras to Francis Amasa Walker, June 12, 1887, in 1965, 2,
letter 800, p. 212). He should, however, have either made ownership a
necessary aspect of entrepreneurship in his model or he should have arranged
matters so that losses are borne by someone other than the entrepreneur.

Adjusting rates of production

Walras then considered the way that the adjustment process operates in
production. In his model, there are no impediments to the mobility of the
factors of production, including the entrepreneurs, and there is good knowledge of the profitability of industries. The adjustment process is initiated by
the response of entrepreneurs to the emergence of a profit or a loss – that is,
by a state of disequilibrium. They increase or diminish the quantities they
demand of services and the quantities they supply of products according to
whether the prices of the products are higher or lower than their average cost
(1895, p. 629). Attracted by profits, entrepreneurs enter an industry, and those
already in it increase the output of their firms. The increased supply leads to
a fall in the price and the increased demand for inputs leads to an increase in
their prices, thus diminishing the difference between the price and average
cost. If the cost of production is higher than the price of the product, losses
are made. Some entrepreneurs then leave the industry, and others restrict their

---

[11] See Knight (1921, pp. 299–310) for a discussion of the relation of ownership to the receipt of
profits. For a contrasting view, see the work of Schumpeter (1911/1926), whose entrepreneur
does not earn profits for bearing risk.

output. The decreased supply leads to a rise in the price of the product and the decreased demand for inputs leads to a decrease in their prices, thus diminishing the difference between price and cost (1877b, p. 231; 1889, p. 214). Walrasian pricing in the markets for services and products, and the processes through which inputs and output are varied and the difference between price and average cost is diminished, occur largely because of the actions of entrepreneurs. In Walras's system, therefore, the entrepreneurs provide the practical means by which the equations of the general equilibrium of production are solved (1877b, p. 266; 1889, p. 251). They are essential for the adjustment of the rates of production and the diminution of the difference between price and average cost to occur, and are consequently essential for part of the mechanism that leads the model to converge to equilibrium.

IV. Equilibrium

In the final part of his model, Walras identified the situation of the entrepreneur when the economy is in static equilibrium. When there is equality of the quantities supplied and demanded and equality of price and average cost, a state of equilibrium of production prevails (1877b, p. 230; 1889, p. 213). It follows that since total profit is the difference between price and average cost, multiplied by the number of units of output sold, in equilibrium the entrepreneur makes neither a profit nor a loss (1877b, p. 232; 1889, p. 215). That is Walras's notion of the zero-profit entrepreneur.

Even though the entrepreneurs in Walras's model are indispensable for creating the tendency for prices and quantities to move toward equilibrium, it cannot be the case that the entrepreneurs cause them to be a particular set of magnitudes. Walras's position on this matter was presaged by his first remarks on the entrepreneur, when he argued that notwithstanding John Stuart Mill's thesis, the consumer is in the last analysis the true demander of labor (1871, p. 35) – a proposition that had already been enunciated by J.B. Say (1836, p. 336). Walras made its implications explicit by asserting that "the entrepreneur is only an intermediary between the worker and the consumer." This comment, made in 1871, indicates that Walras had not by that time developed a view of the entrepreneur as the equilibrating force in the market system. He did not mention that function, and he appears to have depreciated the entrepreneur's role by describing him as "only" an intermediary and by remarking that he can be neglected after that role has been made clear (1871, p. 36). Walras subsequently wrote that workers, landlords, and capitalists receive income from the entrepreneur in exchange for productive services. In contemplating these exchanges in a state of equilibrium, it becomes clear that it is possible to abstract from the intermediation of the entrepreneur and regard the services and products, or even services alone, as if they exchanged directly for each other (1877b, pp. 231–32; 1889, p. 214). Thus, consumers are truly sovereign in Walras's system. Given the technological possibilities and their incomes, they determine the pattern of consumer commodities produced, and they determine the volume of savings. Entrepreneurs cannot do more than give effect to the decisions of consumers.

V. Criticisms

Walras's model of the entrepreneur was assailed by several eminent economists. Their criticisms will be evaluated in order to clarify its meaning.

1. Rudolph Auspitz and Richard Lieben argued that Walras's idea of a zero-profit entrepreneur is wrong because the entrepreneur does earn profits in equilibrium (Auspitz and Lieben 1890, p. 603). The reason for Walras's error, they contended, was his supposition that average cost is constant and the same for all producers in equilibrium. In fact, marginal cost is an increasing function of output, price is equated to marginal cost, and entrepreneurial profit is therefore earned in equilibrium on intramarginal units of output. Moreover, although price is sometimes made equal to average cost in equilibrium in an industry, that is true only for the marginal firm. The price is the same for all firms in the industry, but the average cost of production is not, so a profit is made in equilibrium by the entrepreneurs in more favorable circumstances than the marginal firm (ibid.). Anthony Beaujon criticized Walras's theory on much the same grounds. Supply is governed by the cost of production (Beaujon 1890, p. 6), which varies from firm to firm because they have different rates of output and because their efficiency differs in accordance with the ability of their entrepreneurs. Inframarginal entrepreneurs obtain producers' surpluses, and because these differ from firm to firm, entrepreneurs do not obtain a common rate of return on their capital in equilibrium (ibid., pp. 7–13). Irving Fisher similarly observed that marginal cost could be the same for producers of greatly different size, although the fixed and variable costs could be very different, and that Walras consequently did not need to assume that sellers produce equal quantities in order to have "a common cost price equal to the selling price" (Fisher 1892, p. 46). Fisher also contended that it is misleading to say that "the equality of [marginal][12] cost and selling price implies neither gain nor loss," because there exists a normal gain or producer's rent which is distinct from and independent of any speculative gains or losses (ibid., pp. 46–47). In a similar effort to give a new theoretical underpinning to Walras's account of entrepreneurial profits, Enrico Barone argued that they exist in disequilibrium because the entrepreneur remunerates services according to the value of his marginal products, whereas

---

[12] The brackets and the word "marginal" are Fisher's.

the intramarginal units of the services produce larger amounts of value. Thus the entrepreneur maximizes his own net revenue in equilibrium when the price of each factor is equal to the value of its marginal product (Enrico Barone to Walras, September 20, 1894, in 1965, 2, letter 1191, pp. 619–21). Barone thought mistakenly that this analysis was fully consistent with Walras's work, putting it into a new light and showing its seminal qualities (Enrico Barone to Walras, September 20, 1894, in 1965, 2, letter 1191, pp. 619–21). Nevertheless, most of Barone's other writings on profit and the entrepreneur were genuine extensions of Walras's theory (see Barone 1896).

Those objections and observations were not valid because they were based on a situation that differed from Walras's model in two interrelated respects. First, Auspitz and Lieben and Beaujon misinterpreted the nature of short-run surpluses by alleging that they are entrepreneurial rewards. The gains to which those critics referred are quasi-rents or rents, surpluses that are obtained by capitalists and possibly by workers and the owners of land, and that are not determined by the same principles as determine the profits of Walras's entrepreneur. The surpluses exist in equilibrium and are not earned by the entrepreneur for performing an entrepreneurial function. Walras was perfectly aware of these surpluses or "permanent profits," as he called them, and indicated that they should be added into the cost of production, but that he had not pursued the matter of how to deal with them (Walras to Irving Fisher, July 28, 1892, in 1965, 2, letter 1064, pp. 498–99). That he did not do so, however, cannot be considered a defect in his analysis of the transitory profits and losses of the entrepreneur in his model.

Second, Walras's critics were castigating him on the basis of considerations that are true only of the short run, whereas his analysis dealt with the long run. Walras did not, in the formal structure of his mature model, concern himself with the conditions of short-run equilibrium in production, did not use the term "marginal cost" nor the concept of marginal as distinct from average cost, and did not deny that entrepreneurs earn normal profits in equilibrium, if by that term is meant managerial earnings and a necessary minimum return on the capital they have invested in the firm. Fisher's statement that it is misleading to say that the equality of marginal cost to price implies zero profits was inappropriate. Walras wrote that it is the equality of average cost and price that implies zero profits, which is true. Walras's critics neglected his implicit assumption that short-run surpluses are capitalized so as to increase the value and hence the cost of the assets of the firm and thereby to make long-run average cost equal to price. These critics therefore disregarded his conclusion that in the long-run equilibrium of production, the price is equal to the long-run average cost of every firm, whereas to justify their strictures they would have had to show that his conclusion was mistaken.

2. Auspitz and Lieben charged that Walras's notion of the zero-profit entrepreneur is wrong because it depends on the erroneous assumption that all costs are variable. They quoted his statement that "since we suppose that the entrepreneurs make neither profit nor loss, we can also suppose them to be making equal quantities of products, in which case all the expenses of all kinds can be considered as proportional" (1877b, p. 250; 1889, p. 233), by which he meant "variable." In actuality, they maintained, the quantity of each productive service is not proportional to the quantity of output, notably because there are fixed factors, the existence of which was neglected by Walras (Auspitz and Lieben 1890, pp. 604–5). Apparently, their point was that the presence of factors that are fixed in amount implies that average costs cannot be constant.

Auspitz and Lieben's argument was incomplete and did not support their contention that marginal costs increase, and was ill-considered because Walras's theory dealt with the long run, in which there are no fixed factors. Their remarks nevertheless led him, in some *obiter dicta*, to consider the situation of firms in the short run, although he would not concede that his model needed correction (Walras to Ladislaus von Bortkiewicz, September 18, 1891, in 1965, 2, letter 1027, pp. 466–67). "It is certain," he maintained, that the assumption that the entrepreneurs produce equal amounts of output "is necessary in order that they make neither profits nor losses, and in consequence is necessary for equilibrium" (1895, p. 631).[13] If some firms produce less output than the average amount for a firm, they incur losses and go bankrupt. If some produce more output, they make profits, and would then increase output still more, driving out other firms. One firm would eventually become a monopoly (1891b, p. 467; 1896b, pp. 473–74, n. 1). Fixed expenses consequently have an enormous importance, Walras concluded (1895, pp. 631–32).[14]

In this analysis, Walras appears to have assumed that firms have the same total fixed cost, so that if they produce the same output they have the same average fixed cost. He also appears to have assumed that the average variable cost functions are the same for all firms. It follows that at the common rate of output all firms have the same average cost, which he assumed is equal to the price.[15] Walras then reasoned that if a firm reduces output below the one

---

[13] Thus, in this instance, Walras put the argument in the opposite order from the way it appears in the *Eléments*.

[14] Pareto commented that he did not understand why Walras conceded to Auspitz and Lieben that his formulas implied that fixed expenses ought to be assimilated to the variable expenses of production. Pareto believed that Walras's formulas took account of fixed costs (Vilfredo Pareto to Walras, February 19, 1892, in 1965, 2, letter 1048, pp. 482–83).

[15] Jaffé maintained in this context that fixed coefficients of production imply identical production functions in the industry, which he believed is a sufficient condition for equal rates of output (Jaffé in Walras 1954, p. 528). Putting aside the consideration that different firms

he identified as the common equilibrium amount, the average fixed cost rises, thereby raising average cost above the price; and that if a firm increases output, the average fixed cost falls, thereby lowering average cost below the price. That argument makes no sense, for it implies that average cost is falling in the neighborhood of the equilibrium output of a firm whereas, as is well-known, that condition is incompatible with purely competitive equilibrium and contradicts the assumption Walras ordinarily made in other contexts that the prices of services rise as output is increased and that the average cost therefore rises with output (chs. 7, 9). It is true he made that assumption in reference to the long run, but he would have argued that it is doubly true in the short run because of the presence of fixed factors. Moreover, there is no necessity for firms in a purely competitive industry to produce equal amounts of output in order for there to be equilibrium. Walras's response to Auspitz and Lieben on the issue of fixed costs therefore involved some inconsistencies and some confusion of thought, although those defects did not invalidate his model of the functioning of the entrepreneur.

3. Auspitz and Lieben also maintained on empirical grounds that Walras was wrong to suppose that entrepreneurs do not make profits. According to those critics, he believed that the equality of average cost and price occurs as expeditiously as does the equality between supply and demand. In actuality, they maintained, although the latter is established every day, that discrepancies between price and average cost persist for years for many firms. Consequently, profits are earned for long periods of time, and only when a renewed surge of competition occurs are they rendered equal (Auspitz and Lieben 1890, p. 603).

Walras's answer to this objection was provided in his original exposition. He argued that equilibrium is the normal state of the market not because it is attained but because it is the one to which the variables tend automatically in a regime of free competition, as a result of Walrasian pricing and of entrepreneurs expanding or reducing the size of firms and changing the number of firms in industries depending on whether profits or losses are made in them (1877b, p. 254; 1889, pp. 240–41). Like the equilibrium of exchange, he stated, the equilibrium of production is a theoretical concept that is never achieved in reality. The supply and the demand in real markets for productive services or for products are never exactly equal, and "it can happen and in actuality frequently does, that the price is persistently above the average cost,

could have different fixed coefficients and hence different production functions and costs, there is no reason why firms with identical long-run constant average cost curves could not produce different amounts of output. Furthermore, the assumption of fixed coefficients is not germane to Walras's problem of fixed and variable costs. That assumption eliminates the possibility of changing the proportions of the inputs by using more or less of a factor with a fixed amount of another, and thus eliminates the distinction between fixed and variable costs.

without the increase of output correcting the situation" (1877b, pp. 310–11; 1889, p. 317; and see Walras 1877b, p. 231; 1889, p. 214).[16] Walras's argument was that as a result, entrepreneurs are frequently able to make profits for extended periods of time. He therefore made precisely the point that Auspitz and Lieben alleged he neglected, long before they studied the issue. Unlike them, however, he did not regard it as evidence of a flaw in his model but as a description of frictions in the real economy. His view of the matter was correct, whereas Auspitz and Lieben were wrong to criticize his characterization of equilibrium on the grounds that disequilibrium is not like equilibrium and that disequilibrium exists in fact.

4. Auspitz and Lieben (1890, p. 603) charged that Walras's model is not robust because his entrepreneur would have no motive to act if the economy were in equilibrium and would perish from lack of income. Walras's answer was that although the entrepreneur would not receive profits in equilibrium he would not perish because he would not be destitute. This can be seen, Walras indicated, by applying rational accounting procedures to the firm. If the entrepreneur owns the land he farms or occupies, he should credit himself with wages; if he has capital funds invested in the firm, he should credit himself with an interest income. Each of those incomes should be calculated at the market rate for the associated productive service, and they should each be considered as part of the general expenses of the firm. It is on them that the entrepreneur subsists, in his own firm or in a firm owned by others, when he is making neither a profit nor a loss as an entrepreneur (1877b, p. 232; 1889, p. 215). Thus the individual who performs entrepreneurial functions and earns the rewards they may bring in disequilibrium sustains himself by other income when he suffers losses or when equilibrium occurs. Despite this answer, it must be recognized that Auspitz and Lieben's criticism had a certain amount of validity. Walras's theory was defective in failing to indicate the terms of the entrepreneur's remuneration with sufficient clarity, as will be seen in assessing Francis Edgeworth's view of the matter (see 7 following).

5. Auspitz and Lieben contended that by assuming the entrepreneur makes neither profit nor loss in equilibrium, and regarding services as exchanging directly for each other in that state, Walras was led to construct a set of equations (1877b, p. 248; 1889, p. 231) in which the offer of services by entrepreneurs is neglected (Auspitz and Lieben 1890, p. 604). In fact, their

---

[16] An interesting extension of this aspect of Walras's theory was given by Pareto, who explained that in a given industry in equilibrium, some of the entrepreneurs will be making profits and others will be making losses. "It is thus understood that when reference is made to a state in which the entrepreneurs make neither gains nor losses, it is an average state that is being considered, precisely as one speaks of the level of the waters of the ocean" (Pareto 1896/1897, 2, p. 87). Pareto therefore endorsed the conception of a statistical equilibrium – a notion associated with the work of Alfred Marshall – in which profits for some entrepreneurs would be positive even if equilibrium were actually attained, although the algebraic sum of profits and losses for all entrepreneurs would be zero.

argument was based on a misinterpretation of his reasoning. They erroneously implied that he assumed the entrepreneur does not exist in equilibrium and that Walras developed an account of equilibrium involving that assumption, which was not the case. In equilibrium, Walras's entrepreneur performs the role of an intermediary, buying inputs and selling output, as well as the role of a supplier of nonentrepreneurial services. Walras's remark about the exchange of services (1877b, p. 232; 1889, p. 214) was therefore not an assertion that the entrepreneur does not exist in equilibrium but a commentary on its properties, analogous to saying that one can measure and describe the level of a stable lake without giving an account of the flows of water into and out of it. Since the entrepreneur does not induce any change after equilibrium has been reached, Walras made the methodological observation that its conditions can be expressed in statements that make no mention of him.

Walras was right, because if the supply and demand quantities are equal for each product and for each productive service, including the services for which entrepreneurs, as managerial workers, are paid a regular salary, the model is complete. Separate expression in mathematical terms of the mediation of the entrepreneurs would result in a redundant equation. As Barone observed, the situation of Walras's entrepreneur, who makes neither profit nor loss after having paid for all services, corresponds exactly to the concept represented symbolically by the equation that sets the total revenue equal to the sum of the expenditures on the factors of production (Barone 1895, p. 186).

6. Francis Edgeworth also believed, for his own reasons, that Walras was in error in arguing that the entrepreneur makes neither profit nor loss in equilibrium (Edgeworth 1889a, p. 435). Edgeworth interpreted Walras's doctrine as having three implications, and evaluated them. First, it implies that "the maximum of income the entrepreneur aims at realizing is zero" (Edgeworth 1904, *1*, p. 26).[17] In this belief Edgeworth was of course wholly mistaken. Walras's entrepreneur aims at making as large a profit as possible; it is unwelcome competitive forces that reduce his gain to zero. Second, the doctrine implies that the addition to the entrepreneur's income due to the last increment hired of any factor is zero. In that belief, Edgeworth was entirely accurate, because the marginal condition is a necessary consequence of achieving maximum profits. Third, the doctrine implies that the total income to the entrepreneur, in his capacity as such, is zero in equilibrium (ibid.). This is of course a valid interpretation of Walras's doctrine by Edgeworth, and it is the proposition that Edgeworth denied.

On two occasions, Edgeworth wrote as though he had come into agreement

---

[17] When reference is made to an article of Edgeworth's that is republished in his *Collected Papers,* the volume and pagination given in the citation is that of the *Collected Papers,* but the article is given the date when it was first published. This establishes the chronology and enables the article to be found in the references.

with Walras on this matter. The theory of the zero-profit entrepreneur, he remarked ambiguously, was held by "grave doctors on the European Continent" (Edgeworth 1900, *3*, p. 101), and may accordingly be adopted, "notwithstanding the misgivings of common sense" (ibid., p. 100). Then Edgeworth made the disarming comment that "it is always pleasant to believe that one's differences with high authorities are only verbal. This satisfaction may now be enjoyed with respect to M. Walras's doctrine that the entrepreneur makes neither gain nor loss," because Vilfredo Pareto had made clear the compatibility of Walras's doctrine with modern theory (Edgeworth 1904, *1*, p. 25). Nevertheless, Edgeworth repudiated those statements and remained throughout his life in opposition to Walras's theory. The phrase "neither gain nor loss," Edgeworth contended, is misleading and "violently contrary to usage; it lends itself to a dangerous equivoque; and it has led distinguished economists to paradoxical conclusions." The entrepreneur makes a large income, and strives to make it larger, so why describe him as making neither a gain nor a loss? (ibid., p. 25). Since distribution is an aspect of exchange, "it seems undesirable to employ a phrase so foreign to the general theory of exchange as the dictum that one of the parties to an exchange normally gains nothing" (ibid., p. 31). Edgeworth was unable to agree with the literal interpretation that the Lausanne school gave to Walras's "peculiar proposition" (Edgeworth 1910, *2*, p. 378). It is a simplification that might be permitted to a pathbreaker, but one that deserves "pardon rather than praise" (Edgeworth 1925, *2*, p. 311). Edgeworth had the same reservations about John Bates Clark's theory of the entrepreneur, which follows Walras's in asserting that price equals cost in the static equilibrium of a purely competitive economy and that there is therefore "no net surplus to the *entrepreneur*, as such" (Clark 1899, pp. 78–79, quoted in Edgeworth 1900, *3*, p. 101; and see Clark 1889, pp. 290–91, 410–11).

Elaboration of criticism

Edgeworth began the development of his criticism of the doctrine – a criticism that is involved and difficult to follow – by suggesting that Walras's view of the remuneration of the entrepreneur would have been different if he had considered the disutility of labor in relation to economic equilibrium, rather than confining his attention to marginal utility (Edgeworth 1889a, p. 435).[18] Walras appeared "to have altogether made abstraction of the cost of production considered as importing sacrifice and effort" (Edgeworth 1889b, *2*, p. 281) and to have stated only the marginal conditions of commercial

---

[18] After noting this comment, Ladislaus von Bortkiewicz, who undertook to reply to Edgeworth at Walras's urging (Walras to Ladislaus von Bortkiewicz, October 17, 1889, in 1965, *2*, letter 927, pp. 363–64), could not help observing: "And that is all. It must be admitted that it is not much" (Bortkiewicz 1890, p. 81).

competition – the competition that occurs in output markets. In the *Eléments*, the services of workers are regarded as not costing them any effort, so they experience pleasure from their rewards but no pain from their labor (Edgeworth 1891, p. 21). This is illogical, Edgeworth contended, because in Walras's model there is industrial competition – the competition between occupations made possible by the mobility of labor. Marshall had analyzed the consequences of that mobility in his doctrine of the equalization of net advantages, and had shown that it leads to equilibrium in input markets (Edgeworth 1891, pp. 21, 28; Marshall 1890, pp. 279, 584–86; Marshall 1920, pp. 73, 557–58). The conditions of that equilibrium refer to total net utility, not to marginal conditions, and they contradict the idea of a zero-profit entrepreneur (Edgeworth 1925, 2, p. 311). Specifically, the doctrine of net advantages requires an explicit account of the disutility of labor (Edgeworth 1891, p. 22), and demonstrates that the entrepreneur earns his income by effort. He makes nothing from monopoly, or his conjuncture, or rent-of-ability; his income "is totally unmixed with rent" (Edgeworth 1915, 2, p. 470).[19] Consequently, just as wages are the supply price of a worker's effort, so also is there a supply price for entrepreneurial services, a necessary compensation in equilibrium as well as disequilibrium for the real costs of entrepreneurship. That compensation is profit (ibid., pp. 470–71). Edgeworth also stated, however, that the entrepreneur "is paid out of a surplus," whereas a worker's wage is a marginal outlay (Edgeworth 1915, 2, p. 471). It is puzzling that Edgeworth simultaneously maintained that the remuneration of the entrepreneur is not a rent and that it is paid out of a surplus. Perhaps he meant that although it is paid out of a rent, it is paid for a economic function that is performed. This does not solve the problems posed by Edgeworth's statements, however, because he believed that the entrepreneur, through the performance of his functions, generates the income that is paid for them, which means that he is not paid out of a surplus.

If Walras were correct, Edgeworth continued, then by analogy the consumer would have no utility as a result of competition, but, as Auspitz and Lieben also observed (1890, p. 603), in fact he obtains a surplus in equilibrium. Laymen "may be helped by [that] analogy to understand the nature of entrepreneur's profits. They may be encouraged to question the paradox propounded by the school of Lausanne" that the entrepreneur makes neither profit nor loss. His profit is reduced by competition (Edgeworth 1915, 2, pp. 469, 471), and "the remuneration of the average occupied person, measured in the pleasure that money can command, may in fact be small. But that it is normally *zero* neither common sense nor economic theory compels us to believe" (ibid., p. 469). On the contrary, in equilibrium the entrepreneur earns

---

[19] Edgeworth cited this analysis as originally appearing on page 570 of his entry entitled "Probability" in the eleventh edition of the *Encyclopedia Britannica* (1911), but that entry is on pages 376 to 403, and I have been unable to find any mention of entrepreneurs in it.

a steady flow of profits. In equilibrium, different levels of positive profits prevail in different occupations and equalize their attractiveness, for otherwise entrepreneurs would keep moving to industries with greater net advantages (Edgeworth 1925, 2, p. 311). Finally, the entrepreneur's profits should be included in the "general expenses" of a business, as appears to have been done by the more moderate adherents of the school of Lausanne. Walras failed to recognize those expenses, and therefore cut himself off from an understanding of the nature of entrepreneurial profits and the process of industrial competition (Edgeworth 1915, 2, pp. 469–70; 470, n. 1). Edgeworth concluded that the publication of the doctrine of net advantages in Marshall's *Principles* had rendered uninteresting any further discussion of Walras's entrepreneur. He is henceforward, Edgeworth declared in a sweeping condemnation, an irrelevant person (Edgeworth 1891, p. 28).

Walras's rebuttal

Walras's model was not so easily dismissed, however. In reaction to Edgeworth's criticisms, Walras explained that he had not assumed that labor entails no disutility. He alleged that on the contrary the term *personal services* he used in his model is an "exact synonym for the *disutility of labor*" (Walras to Ladislaus von Bortkiewicz, February 27, 1891, in 1965, 2, letter 999, pp. 434–35; and see Bortkiewicz 1890, p. 84); and he contended that he had adopted or developed the doctrine of net advantages. To him, those phenomena did not imply positive profits in equilibrium for entrepreneurs, and he rightly believed that he did not need to reconstruct his model of the activity of the entrepreneur to bring it into accordance with Marshall's theory of net advantages (1895, p. 629). Those constructions are compatible, as is shown by two considerations. First, the relevant monetary and nonmonetary considerations in the selection of occupations are reflected in the set of equilibrium factor prices and quantities of productive services, and the nonmonetary considerations do not give rise to an additional set of variables. Workers may find that the physical conditions of a job are pleasant and thus may have a lower supply price for their efforts in it than in an unpleasant one, but that does not invalidate the proposition that in equilibrium the supply price of their labor is equated to its demand price. Second, Walras's model is like Marshall's in recognizing that there is an equalizing structure of managerial earnings.

Differences of definitions of profits

The difference between the two models becomes apparent by considering Marshall's use of the word "profits." To him, "profits" include interest, and in his view "what remains of [a businessman's] profits after deducting interest on his capital at the current rate may be called his EARNINGS OF UNDER-TAKING or MANAGEMENT" (Marshall 1890, p. 142; and see Marshall 1920, p. 74). Whether or not a component of those earnings in disequilibrium may be Walrasian profits, it is evident that Marshall was asserting that profit is equal to the businessman's interest plus his managerial earnings, which are not entrepreneurial earnings in Walras's sense of the term. Other passages in the *Principles of Economics* make clear that when Marshall referred to profits, he had in mind normal interest plus the normal earnings of management that are payments for the conduct of the ordinary business of the firm and that are positive in equilibrium:

That share of the expenses of production of any commodity which is commonly classed as profits, is so rigorously controlled on every side by the action of the Law of Substitution, that it cannot long diverge from the normal supply price of the capital needed, added to the normal supply price of the ability and energy required for managing the business, and lastly the normal supply price of that organization by which the appropriate business ability and the requisite capital are brought together.

We have called the price of the first of these three elements "Net Interest"; we may call the price of the second taken by itself "NET Earnings of Management," and that of the second and third taken together "GROSS Earnings of Management" (Marshall 1890, p. 642, and see pp. 629–62; and see Marshall 1920, pp. 313, 596–605).

Marshall's use of the word "profits" is therefore not the same as Walras's.

Since Edgeworth followed Marshall's usage, it was inappropriate for him to insist that he was refuting Walras's model by arguing that managerial earnings are positive in equilibrium and that they are "profits." Edgeworth erroneously imagined that competition in Walras's model eliminates managerial earnings, producer's surpluses, and a necessary return on capital, whereas all it eliminates is the temporary difference between price and average cost that exists in disequilibrium in a freely competitive system, the difference that may be called "true Walrasian profits." Like Marshall, Edgeworth was referring to an equalizing equilibrium structure of Marshallian normal profits, whereas Walras was referring to disequilibrium gains and losses that necessarily become zero in equilibrium. Far from denying that Marshallian profits exist in equilibrium, Walras emphasized that in that situation, as in disequilibrium, capitalists receive interest and entrepreneurs receive an income as managers of their firms. To Walras, the interest that Marshall called a part of profit and that is earned by the businessman who invests in his own business is earned by that person in his role as a capitalist, not as an entrepreneur. Walras granted that there may be producer's surpluses, and that these may be paid to entrepreneurs in equilibrium. He also realized that from a long-run point of view those are necessary payments to induce the retention of capital and managerial ability. Furthermore, he explicitly recognized general expenses, and counted managerial income as part of the cost of production:

Thus, in the state of equilibrium of production, the entrepreneurs make neither profit nor loss. They subsist then not as entrepreneurs, but as landlords, workers or capitalists in their own firms or in others. It is clear that, in order to have a rational accounting, an entrepreneur who owns the land that he uses or that he occupies, who participates in the direction of his firm, who has funds invested in his business, ought to charge his general expenses and to credit himself with a land-rent, a wage and an interest amount, calculated at the rates on the market for productive services, and by means of which he subsists, without making, as an entrepreneur, either profit or loss (1877b, p. 232; 1889, p. 215).

Walras therefore correctly concluded that in equilibrium all of what Marshall called "profit" is part of the cost of production (ibid.; and see Pareto 1896/1897, *1,* pp. 39, 57) and that the firm's revenue minus all costs is equal to zero.

7. The element of truth in Edgeworth's criticisms – and it is a substantial one – is that Walras did not adequately deal with the issue of the real costs of operating a firm. This general observation can be refined into a precise criticism that identifies the major defect of Walras's exposition. The defect can be seen by evaluating William Jaffé's contention that "only when deviations from equilibrium are signalled by differences between selling price and cost of production does Walras's entrepreneur spring into action" (Jaffé 1980, p. 534 [351]). That cannot be true. The obvious character of economic processes and the content of Walras's model indicate that the firm continues to transform inputs into output in equilibrium just as in disequilibrium, and therefore the person who buys inputs and sells outputs does so continuously, not just when price differs from average cost. As Walras emphasized, the entrepreneur constitutes an essential link between the markets for productive services and products in all states of the market. He discharges the functions of buying and selling and incurs the real cost of doing so, and is therefore remunerated for those functions, in equilibrium as well as in disequilibrium. Walras also stated, however, that the entrepreneur does not earn any income for entrepreneurial functions in equilibrium. Those propositions are ostensibly contradictory, so Walras should have reconciled them. His assertion that equilibrium never actually prevails (1877b, p. 231; 1889, p. 214) so that the entrepreneur in fact always makes profits or losses does not solve the question of what would happen if it did prevail, and would have to be considered an evasion of the question if it were not for the circumstance that Walras was oblivious to the problem created by his constructions.

The statements are reconcilable, however, by recognizing that the buying of inputs and the selling of output involve two types of activities. The first consists of the routine aspects of buying and selling, aspects that transpire in both equilibrium and disequilibrium. Contracts for services have to be renewed, the delivery of services and raw materials has to be monitored, payments have to be made periodically for the inputs, agreements to supply output have to be renewed, and the output has to be delivered and its purchase price obtained. These routine processes are compensated by managerial wages. Thus the contractual salary that the entrepreneur earns in his capacity as a manager for undertaking supervisory and coordinating functions is paid to him in part as compensation for the real cost of his routine activity of buying and selling, and is paid day after day without regard to whether equilibrium or disequilibrium prevails. The second type of activity consists of the novel aspects of buying and selling in disequilibrium. These entail difficulty and risk, because the prices of inputs and outputs are changing and have to be learned, average cost is not equal to the price, and calculations and unprecedented decisions have to be made. As a result of undertaking the second type of activity, the entrepreneur makes a profit or a loss, which is added algebraically to his other income. In equilibrium, buying and selling involves the first type only, so the entrepreneur's profits or losses disappear. That is the complete answer to Auspitz and Lieben's allegation that Walras's entrepreneur would perish from lack of income in equilibrium.

VI. Conclusion

Walras made a number of contributions in his theory of the entrepreneur. First, by identifying profits as the difference between price and average cost, he originated the view that true profits emerge only in phases of economic transition. Second, he developed a dynamic model of the process whereby true profits and losses are reduced by the competitive forces brought into play by entrepreneurs, including the theory of the instrumentality of entrepreneurs in the allocation of resources. He integrated that process into his model of the general equilibrium of interrelated markets, and drew the conclusion that true profits and losses become zero in competitive equilibrium, a conclusion that is now a fundamental tenet of the model of pure competition in the long run. Third, he mentioned the uncertainty of receiving profits and the risk of incurring losses, although he did not develop that line of thought. Those three contributions are indicative of the fact that despite the detailed analysis of the conditions of static equilibrium in Walras's work that has led to the erroneous opinion that it is solely devoted to statics, his theory of the entrepreneur, though not involving dated variables, was largely concerned with dynamics in the sense of the processes of adjustment in disequilibrium. Fourth, Walras emphasized the difference between routine managerial functions and entrepreneurial activity, and the difference in the associated remuneration. Fifth, he sharpened the definition of the entrepreneur by making a clear distinction between his profit-seeking market activity and the role of the provider of capital-good services. Sixth, Walras provided a basis for a theory of monopoly profit. As was realized by him (1891b, p. 467; 1896b, pp. 473–74, n. 1) and elaborated on by Pareto, since the difference between price and average cost is eliminated by competitive forces, it follows that when they are absent the entrepreneur has a monopoly and can make a surplus in equilibrium (Pareto 1896/1897, *1*, pp. 68–69; pp. 78–81; Pareto 1909, p. 321; and see Schumpeter 1911/1926).

As a result of the foregoing contributions, Walras's theory of the entrepreneur became a part of the foundations of Continental entrepreneurial theory. There can be no question of the seminal quality of his theory, because Pareto, Barone, and Joseph Schumpeter acknowledged its importance and its influence on their own work. Pareto and Barone both defended Walras against Edgeworth's criticisms, Barone maintaining that the English economists did not understand Walras's theory of the entrepreneur (Enrico Barone to Walras, October 26, 1895, in 1965, *2*, letter 1216, pp. 648–49), and Pareto believing that they had systematically closed their eyes to it (Pareto 1896/1897, *2*, p. 78, n. 1). Even Edgeworth credited Walras with priority in defining the entrepreneur as the agent that links the input and output markets, and regarded Walras's definition as his second most important contribution to economic theory, preceded only by his marginal utility theory of demand (Edgeworth 1889a, p. 435; Edgeworth 1891, p. 20; Edgeworth 1909, *2*, p. 378).[20] Edgeworth's debt to Walras was manifested by his introduction of a Walrasian entrepreneur into his own work, without of course adopting Walras's theory of the entrepreneur's income (Edgeworth 1889b, *2*, pp. 297–98). Pareto repeatedly drew on Walras's theory of the entrepreneur, restating it, refining it, and using Walras's definitions of the entrepreneur and of profits, his zero-profit equilibrium condition, and his analysis of the dynamic role of the entrepreneur as the foundation for his own contributions to entrepreneurial theory (Pareto 1896/1897, *1*, pp. 46–47, 57, 59–61, 68–69, *passim; 2*, pp. 78–80, 181, 183, 206–7, *passim;* Pareto 1909, *passim*). Walras's exposition of entrepreneurial dynamics, Pareto observed, supplied a crucial element in economic theory: "Mr. Walras has shown that the competition of entrepreneurs and traders is a means of solving the equations of the equilibrium of production through successive attempts. This idea, in general, seems very fruitful for economic science" (Pareto 1896/1897, *1*, pp. 45–46). Barone based all his work on the entrepreneur on Walras's theory, which he described as "profound and correct" (Barone 1896, p. 145, and see pp. 132, 145–46; Enrico Barone to Walras, September 20, 1894, in 1965, *2*, letter 1191, pp.

---

[20] It is worth noting that Edgeworth singled out Walras's definition of the entrepreneur for praise and emulation, considering that the general-equilibrium theorists who wrote after the 1920s virtually neglected the entrepreneur's existence (Kirzner 1979, p. 53). Of course, Edgeworth took both possible extreme positions: that Walras's conception of the entrepreneur is a great contribution and that it is irrelevant. The general-equilibrium theorists apparently believed the latter.

619–21). That anyone could be critical of Walras's theory of the zero-profit entrepreneur he considered simply incomprehensible (Barone 1896, p. 145).

Schumpeter, at the time he was working out his own theory, identified Walras's rigorous analysis of the role of the entrepreneur in the market system as one of his contributions (Schumpeter 1910, p. 78), adopted Walras's view that routine coordination and supervision are not entrepreneurial functions, and commended his analysis of the zero-profit entrepreneur (Schumpeter 1911). Subsequently, Schumpeter emphasized again the importance of Walras's theory of the entrepreneur, praising his notions that profits arise only in dynamic situations and that they are zero in equilibrium – "the proposition from which starts all clear thinking on profits" (Schumpeter 1954, p. 893).[21] After the Schumpeterian innovating entrepreneur has established a new product, he becomes a Walrasian entrepreneur. To the framework provided by Walras, Schumpeter added a special type of entrepreneur who initiates disequilibrium by the activity of innovating – an idea that never occurred to Walras – and conceived of that activity as constituting another explanation of the source of true profits (Schumpeter 1911/1926). In Schumpeter's resulting theoretical amalgam, the type of entrepreneurs identified by Walras constitute a "secondary wave" of business persons. The profitable lines of production initiated by the Schumpeterian innovating entrepreneurs are entered by Walrasian entrepreneurs until the zero-profit condition is reached, and entrepreneurs are therefore seen as both disequilibrating and equilibrating forces in the economic system.

Thus, Walras's definition of the entrepreneur, his account of the entrepreneur's role in the dynamics of disequilibrium, and his identification of the situation of the entrepreneur in equilibrium provided the foundation and inspiration for some important aspects of the modern theory of the entrepreneur and of profits. It must be concluded, and it should be recognized, that his model of the entrepreneur's activity was a significant contribution to economic analysis.

---

[21] For some inexplicable reason, however, Schumpeter (1954, p. 893) also described Walras's contribution as "negative" (ibid.).

CHAPTER 14

Walras versus Edgeworth
on tatonnement processes

This chapter evaluates Francis Y. Edgeworth's criticisms of Walras's mature work on tatonnement as expressed in his mature model of nondurable consumer commodities and his mature comprehensive model. The reason for undertaking the evaluation is that Edgeworth's criticisms deal with basic issues in the interpretation of Walras's ideas about adjustment processes, their importance within his general-equilibrium model and to the economic theory of his time, their methodological soundness, and the breadth of their applicability. An examination of Edgeworth's criticisms therefore contributes to an understanding of the characteristics, function, and value of the mature comprehensive model.

I. Introduction

Walras had developed the major outlines and the details of his mature conception of the adjustment process of a competitive market system by 1889, when he published the second edition of the *Eléments*. Edgeworth's criticisms were first presented in his review (1889a) of that edition. He had warned that Walras might not like the review (Edgeworth to Walras, August 20, 1889, in 1965, 2, letter 910, pp. 338–39), but Walras feigned unconcern about the matter, commenting that because he expected some more or less lively criticisms, he had been careful not to go to the library in Lausanne to read them (Walras to Charles Gide, September 20, 1889, in 1965, 2, letter 923, 2, p. 357; and see Walras to Luigi Perozzo, October 13, 1889, in 1965, 2, letter 925, p. 359). Of course, he soon succumbed to temptation, and became involved in a vigorous and sometimes acrimonious controversy with Edgeworth. Very early in the debate, Walras's feeling for Edgeworth became close to dislike. Walras had hoped, he confided to Charles Gide, that the mathematical method in economics would eliminate the posturing and charlatanism Edgeworth displayed (Walras to Gide, November 3, 1889, in 1965, 2, letter 933, p. 370). Walras thought him a humbug and a puffist who was quite capable of discrediting the new method offered by mathematical economics (Walras to Gide, April 11, 1891, in 1965, 2, letter 1000, pp. 435–36), "a man who seems competent enough as a mathematician, but who is mediocre as an economist, and who in addition has a superficial and inconsistent intellect"

(Walras to Maffeo Pantaleoni, January 5, 1890, in 1965, *2*, letter 953, pp. 384–86).

Ladislaus von Bortkiewicz joined the debate in response to Walras's request that he answer Edgeworth, in order, as Walras put it, to try to prevent mathematical economics from straying into sterile fantasies (Walras to Bortkiewicz, October 17, 1889, in 1965, *2*, letter 927, pp. 363–64; see also Walras to Bortkiewicz, November 3, 1889, in 1965, *2*, letter 932, pp. 369–70); and, as will be seen, Vilfredo Pareto delivered his judgment on an aspect of the controversy. Bortkiewicz felt, like Walras, that Edgeworth was "extremely superficial as an author and a critic" (Bortkiewicz to Walras, December 29, 1889, in 1965, *2*, letter 952, pp. 383–84), a sentiment that was reciprocated by Edgeworth. In the hope, Edgeworth wrote, of providing "a sufficient defence against the accusation of having unjustly attacked one of those whom I consider to be a master," he recalled that in his review he had described Walras as one of the small number of persons who had made an original contribution to economics (Edgeworth 1891, p. 11), although not by his theory of tatonnement.[1] Any commentary that tries to be impartial without being insipid, Edgeworth continued, is liable to the sort of criticisms that Bortkiewicz had made (ibid., pp. 11–12, n. 1). Edgeworth was incensed that the critique of his work by Bortkiewicz was presented "in a tone of continuous denigration," and maintained that his own remarks were not. Nevertheless, they were in fact interspersed with barbed comments calculated with unerring precision to irritate their target. Edgeworth charged, for example, that Bortkiewicz did not bring to the subject the degree of attentiveness that is indispensable in mathematical studies (ibid., p. 18, n. 1). He was a true believer who, having become attached to a particular literal interpretation of Walras's work, became confused on discovering contradictory passages in his holy books (ibid., p. 17, n. 1). In the course of the debate, Edgeworth elaborated on and added to his criticisms, and during the rest of his life he intermittently reiterated them. Walras also commented on the issues for many years in his correspondence, which, with the exception of two or three relatively unimportant letters, has not been used before in the examination of his model of tatonnement. We shall now see what inspired such strong and enduring passions in such eminent scholars.

II. Edgeworth's criticisms

Edgeworth freely acknowledged Walras's contribution to the formulation of the conditions of static equilibrium in exchange, referring to Walras as "the

---

[1] Edgeworth identified the discovery of marginal utility as Walras's major contribution (Edgeworth 1889a, p. 435; Edgeworth 1891, p. 11).

economist who first stated the theory of exchange in all its generality" and to the justice of claiming priority for him with respect to it (ibid., p. 13; and see Edgeworth 1889b, 2, pp. 281, 296–97; Edgeworth 1915, 2, pp. 452, 453).[2] Edgeworth distinguished Walras's statements of static equilibrium, however, from his model of tatonnement, correctly interpreting the latter as an attempt to describe how the market system works its way to equilibrium (Edgeworth 1891, p. 13). That model, Edgeworth thought, was "not a very good idea" (Edgeworth 1889a, p. 435), for several related reasons.

1. The content of the model, Edgeworth maintained, is so limited that it can be stated briefly, so Walras should not have devoted so much of the *Eléments* to it (ibid). His "prolonged and reiterated" analysis of the dynamic problem (Edgeworth 1891, p. 20) was "out of proportion to the importance of its results" (Edgeworth 1889a, p. 435) and risked appearing purely speculative to the economist and insignificant to the mathematician (Edgeworth 1891, p. 20).

Walras regarded that criticism as mistaken (Walras to Bortkiewicz, October 17, 1889, in 1965, 2, letter 927, pp. 363–64; Walras to Edgeworth, March 8, 1890, in 1965, 2, letter 964, p. 399). "Some critics," he wrote, "are ... amused at the number of pages that I take to demonstrate that the equilibrium price must be reached by raising the price in the case of the quantity demanded exceeding the quantity supplied and lowering the price in the case of the quantity supplied exceeding the quantity demanded" (1896b, p. 470). Walras reported that when he had asked one of his critics how he would demonstrate the stability of equilibrium, the critic had replied in surprise that he thought it self-evident. Walras had replied: "There is nothing self-evident but axioms, and this is not one of them" (ibid.). In fact, Walras's model of tatonnement does not deal at excessive length with a minor or purely speculative matter. It is an attempt to accomplish the important task of identifying the occurrence and characteristics of equilibrating processes in a competitive multimarket system. Walras realized that the solutions to his equations have no significance unless there is a dynamic process in the model that causes its variables to tend to move toward those solutions. That question is of such complexity that it involved Walras in a lengthy consideration of market iterative processes, of the effects of changes in any particular price on other prices, and of the behavior of average costs. His investigation of those issues was a significant part of the beginnings of modern general equilibrium analysis, and their resolution, far from being a simple matter that can be briefly stated, has

[2] Articles of Edgeworth's that are reprinted in his *Papers Relating to Political Economy* (1925) are cited by first giving the date of original publication. This identifies the chronology, and enables the article to be found in the list of references. Then the volume of the *Papers* in which the article was republished is given, and the pages in that volume on which the material appears.

still not been achieved. Moreover, Edgeworth was in error in believing that the model of tatonnement involves nothing more than the raising and lowering of prices. Although that process and its impact on excess demand quantities are essential parts of the equilibrating process, a number of other important related disequilibrium economic phenomena, such as the behavior of average costs and emergence of economic profits and losses and their role in guiding the reallocation of resources, form the substance of Walras's analysis of tatonnement (chs. 9, 12, 13). He studied such matters not only in connection with stability analysis but in order to understand the dynamic behavior of the economy for its own sake.

2. Edgeworth took the position that all purely competitive markets behave in the same general way, so there was no need for Walras to give a separate exposition of tatonnement in the markets for different types of commodities. There was, for example, no need for Walras to have discussed the equilibrating process in the capital-goods market because the forces of supply and demand operate in that market in just the same way as in other markets (Edgeworth to Walras, March 1889, in 1965, 2, letter 874, pp. 299–300; Edgeworth 1889a, p. 435).

Edgeworth was mistaken in that criticism, for the reason, made clear by Walras, that the tatonnement process has different characteristics in the four differing situations of exchange when there are fixed aggregate stocks of commodities, of production and sale of consumer commodities, of production and sale of capital goods, and of the money and loan markets (1889, pp. xiv–xviii).

Walras's models of the exchange of fixed stocks deal with the general features of the dynamic path of prices in organized purely competitive markets on a number of assumptions that impart special characteristics to the tatonnement process (chs. 3, 4, 5). First, the amounts of the commodities available for exchange and the preferences of the traders are given (1877b, pp. 126–31), the latter being a condition that is also assumed in the tatonnements in Walras's other models. No production or consumption occurs during the tatonnement in the fixed-stock markets. Second, transactions in any market are allowed only at the equilibrium price. Third, prices are cried by traders in each market until the equilibrium price is found, following the procedure of changing the price in the same direction as the sign of their individual market-oriented excess demand quantities and therefore in the same direction as the sign of the market excess demand (1880b, p. 461; 1880c, p. 78; 1889, pp. 68–69). The result of those conditions is that the set of equilibrium prices and the quantities of each commodity traded are those that are the solutions to the set of equations of general equilibrium in which the initial asset distribution is a parametric condition.

In contrast, for an economy in which the production of consumer commodities occurs, Walras considered tatonnement processes in relation to the determination of the prices of productive services and rates of production of commodities. His treatment of those was incorporated in the mature comprehensive model, which was the model with which Edgeworth was familiar when he wrote his review and which he referred to in his subsequent criticisms of Walras's ideas about tatonnement in production. It describes the efforts of entrepreneurs to make adjustments of rates of production of commodities when markets are in disequilibrium, efforts that are very different from the bidding activities of traders in the model of tatonnement in a pure exchange economy. In the process of production, driven by the desire to make profits, entrepreneurs grope their way toward equilibrium by shifting resources among industries in two ways. They establish new firms in profitable industries and expand the output in existing firms in such industries. As the output expands in any industry, the price of the commodity falls in its market. Simultaneously, the prices of productive services are bid up, thus raising the average cost of production. Eventually, the output price and the average cost of each commodity become equal, and at the same time the supply and demand quantities become equal in all markets. The level of economic profit is then zero, the adjustments of production and the adjustments of prices cease, and the influxes of resources end. Driven by the desire to avoid losses, entrepreneurs reduce output and abandon firms in unprofitable industries. As the output in any industry decreases, the opposite of the changes just mentioned concerning prices and average costs take place until equilibrium is found. The level of economic profit is then zero, the production and price tatonnements cease, and the exits of resources end (1877b, pp. 231–32, 258–65; 1896b, p. 477; ch. 14).

The adjustment process in markets for capital goods has some additional characteristics. Nevertheless, Walras complained, Edgeworth "honestly believes that I am amusing myself by inventing" the problem of determining which capital goods ought to be constructed, "for the pleasure of complicating matters" (Walras to Ladislaus von Bortkiewicz, October 17, 1889, in 1965, 2, letter 927, p. 363). In reality, Walras contended, the capital-goods market requires special attention, which he gave it under the title of the theorem of the maximum utility of new capital goods (Walras to Francis Y. Edgeworth, April 4, 1889, in 1965, 2, letter 876, p. 305; Walras to Philip Henry Wicksteed, April 9, 1889, in 1965, 2, letter 877, p. 307; ch. 10). As in his treatment of consumer commodities, in his mature comprehensive model Walras presented a disequilibrium-production model of tatonnement in the capital-goods market, and that was the one scrutinized by Edgeworth. Walras's contention regarding it was justified, because the capital-goods tatonnement is conditioned by the institutions, rules, and equilibrating processes in the markets for savings and credit, and by the circumstances of the production, purchase, and use of commodities that yield a flow of revenue. The resulting tatonnement is one of entrepreneurs interacting with capitalists, workers, landlords, and sellers of raw materials in an effort to select the particular kinds of new capital goods that should be produced and to adjust the output of them to maximize profits (1877b, pp. 297–98; 1889, pp. 279–80). It eventuates in the equilibrium conditions that the ratio of the net price obtained from the sale of the services of a capital good to its price is equal for all such goods, that saving and investment are equal, and that the prices of new capital goods are equal to their costs of production (1877b, pp. 289, 300–301; Walras to Johan Gustav Knut Wicksell, November 10, 1893, in 1965, *2,* letter 1170, p. 598). The process determines the desired additions to the durable capital stock and the equilibrium net rate of return on capital goods, which is the pure rate of interest (ch. 10). Thus, the tatonnement in capital formation involves a variety of phenomena not present in exchange with fixed total stocks or in the production and sale of consumer commodities.

In his mature model of tatonnement in the money market, finally, Walras had to deal with the special phenomena involved in the circumstance that transactions in the mature comprehensive model are made with money. Cash balances are needed, he argued, because ordinarily income is not forthcoming in the necessary amounts when planned purchases must be made. The balances were regarded by Walras as yielding a service of availability – a convenience of possession – just like physical circulating capital; they are valuable because they ensure that goods and services can be acquired when they are needed. Capitalists have excess cash balances and supply money. It is demanded by consumers to make purchases of productive services, raw materials, and semi-finished goods. The tatonnement concerning money, Walras explained, is one of groping for optimum cash balances and for an equilibrium rate of interest (1889, pp. 375–81). If the net quantity of cash balances demanded exceeds the net quantity supplied at the quoted rate of interest, the rate is raised, and entrepreneurs and consumers reduce the net quantity demanded and capitalists increase the net quantity supplied. In the opposite case, the rate is lowered, and the quantity demanded decreases and the quantity supplied increases. The tatonnement continues until the equilibrium rate of interest on money capital is determined – namely, the rate that equates the quantities of cash demanded and supplied (ibid., p. 381). These matters were then related by Walras to the determination of the money prices of commodities and the price level (1889, pp. 383–86).

Thus, exchange, production of consumer commodities, production of capital goods, and a monetary economy each have special structural and behavioral features. In attempting to deal with them in his various discussions of tatonnement, Walras was not repeating himself or manufacturing complexities where none existed.

3. Edgeworth argued that Walras's model of tatonnement confuses the meaning of the static equations of exchange with the process of dynamic adjustment toward equilibrium. Walras tried, Edgeworth contended, to base his dynamic theory on the static equations and to derive its properties from their characteristics, but "as Jevons points out, the equations of exchange are of a statical, not a dynamical, character. They define a position of equilibrium, but they afford no information as to the path by which that point is reached" (Edgeworth 1889a, p. 435). Walras should have realized that they do not deal with "the play of supply and demand by which that position is attained" (Edgeworth 1891, pp. 12, 14).[3]

That was not a legitimate criticism of Walras's work. As Bortkiewicz rightly observed, Walras did not mix up statics and dynamics. His procedure conforms perfectly to the idea that Jevons expressed of the nature of the static equations – namely, that they are accurate representations of equilibrium conditions provided that certain conditions are constant during the equilibrating process (Bortkiewicz 1890, p. 85). Walras confined himself to the static point of view, "in the sense that he assumes the quantities of products possessed as being constant, and the utility functions as invariant." He maintained those assumptions without deviation when he dealt with the dynamic question of "the solution of the equations of exchange by the raising and lowering of the price" (ibid., p. 86). Bortkiewicz manifested by those remarks his realization that contrary to Edgeworth's opinion, Walras had a sound conception of the difference between statics and dynamics. Walras made this evident by the careful and correct distinction he preserved between statics and dynamics in his theorizing and by his analysis of the difference between them. The "static theory of exchange," he explained, "may be defined as the exposition of the equilibrium formula of the maximum satisfaction that obtains when there is proportionality of the value of each commodity to the intensity of the last want it satisfies." The static aspect of the theory is the statement of equilibrium conditions and the study of the existence of equilibrium. The "dynamic theory," he continued, is a different matter. It may be defined as "the demonstration of the attainment of that equilibrium through the play of the raising and the lowering of prices until the equality of the supply and demand quantities is established" (1895, p. 630). Thus, dynamics is the study of the stability of equilibrium. He went on to refer again to statics

---

[3] Edgeworth mistakenly referred (1891, p. 14, n. 1) to the seventh instead of the fifth appendix to his *Mathematical Psychics* as the place where his interpretation of Jevon's theory of exchange appears.

and dynamics as two different problems, and claimed priority in examining the latter (ibid.).

Furthermore, Walras did not confuse *comparative* statics with dynamics. His view of the character of the former, formulated as early as 1875 and repeated many times subsequently, was a model of clarity, revealing the soundness of his grasp of the methodological characteristics of static analysis. It is the right of the theoretician, he explained, to assume that utility functions and endowments are constant when he formulates the law of the establishment of equilibrium prices. It is his duty, however, once that operation is finished, to remember that in real markets those parameters are subject to change, and accordingly to examine the results of their variations in a model and to formulate the laws of the variation of equilibrium prices (1875, pp. 390–91; 1877b, pp. 135–37; 1889, p. 125), that is, to study comparative statics.

Finally, Walras did not try on any occasion to derive dynamic market processes from the conditions of static equilibrium. He repeatedly indicated the impossibility of such a derivation and the consequent necessity for a dynamic theory based on considerations logically antecedent to the statement of the conditions of static equilibrium. He rightly emphasized that Edgeworth, in one of his treatments of equilibrium, had neglected part of the problem. As a result of examining only the static equations and of indicating nothing about the mode of their solution by tatonnement in the marketplace, Edgeworth's treatment of the general equilibrium of exchange (Edgeworth 1889b, 2, pp. 296–97) was incomplete. It is not enough, Walras argued, to consider only the mathematical solution of the equilibrium equations. It is also necessary to explain how the real market system works dynamically and eventuates in their empirical solution (Walras to Maffeo Pantaleoni, January 5, 1890, in 1965, 2, letter 953, pp. 384–85; Walras to Luigi Perozzo, March 18, 1890, in 1965, 2, letter 969, pp. 403–404). That essential process was the subject of his model of tatonnement.

4. Edgeworth maintained that Walras's model of tatonnement could not accomplish its purpose because, Edgeworth thought in 1889, the problem of modeling the dynamic behavior of markets is very difficult. Even in regard to exchange in a competitive market for a single commodity, he contended, the dynamic problem is so difficult that although we know that such a market tends to reach equilibrium, economic theory has not been able to describe how that happens. The "economic problem of several trading bodies distributing and exchanging *inter se* under the influence of self-interest, and in a regime of competition, is much more hopelessly difficult than the as yet imperfectly solved dynamical problem of several material bodies acting on each other *in vacuo*" (Edgeworth 1889b, 2, p. 280). Furthermore, if there is

mobility between different occupations, it is virtually impossible not only to formulate a model of the dynamic path of the system but even to find its equilibrium:

When we advance from the simplest type of market to the complexities introduced by division of labour, it is seen to be no longer a straightforward problem in algebra or geometry, given the natures of all the parties, to find the terms to which they will come. Here, even if we imagine ourselves in possession of numerical data for the motives acting on each individual, we could hardly conceive it possible to deduce *a priori* the position of equilibrium towards which a system so complicated tends (ibid., p. 281).

By 1891, Edgeworth had come to believe that a knowledge of dynamics is impossible in principle. According to him, the unsatisfactory character of Walras's model of how prices are adjusted in such a way as to lead markets to equilibrium may be shown by drawing an analogy between market behavior and the flow of a liquid down the sides of a valley. Walras sometimes arbitrarily represented the liquid as flowing in a specific and determinate course, whereas the only thing that can be stated is that somehow it arrives at equilibrium (Edgeworth 1891, p. 19). The same is true about the progress of the economy from disequilibrium to equilibrium, so "the better position is that *only* the position of equilibrium is *knowable,* not the path by which equilibrium is reached" (Edgeworth 1904, *1,* p. 39; emphasis added). Although economic theory has succeeded in achieving a description of the conditions that prevail in static equilibrium, "we have no general *dynamical* theory determining the path of the economic system from any point assigned at random to a position of equilibrium. We know only the statical properties of the position" (Edgeworth 1925, *2,* p. 311). Edgeworth took the extreme position that "the give and take of bargaining by which the price is determined, the direction that the system follows to arrive at the equilibrium position, *is not part of the domain of the science*" (Edgeworth 1891, p. 12, emphasis added; see also Edgeworth 1904, *1,* p. 39). Consequently, he concluded, the dynamic behavior of markets can be discussed only in an abstract manner (ibid.), evidently regarding the theory of recontracting as an account on that level (Edgeworth 1881).

Walras did not, incidentally, owe an awareness of the invalidation of his static equations by disequilibrium transactions or production to a study of Edgeworth's theory of recontracting. He had read Edgeworth's *Mathematical Psychics* as early as 1886, but his only comments on it, as far as I am aware, relate to Edgeworth's use of the theory of marginal utility as a basis for the theory of value and exchange (Walras to Alfred Marshall, November 25, 1886, in 1965, *2,* letter 749, p. 159; Walras 1886, p. viii; see also Edgeworth to Walras, November 8, 1888, in 1965, *2,* letter 856, pp. 274–75), and he made those comments years before he abandoned the mature comprehensive model (see 1965, letters 744, 903, 912, and 960). Walras did not draw on Edgeworth for inspiration on dynamic processes because Walras did not detect any treatment of dynamics in Edgeworth's work. Walras repeatedly stated that Edgeworth did not deal with the problem of market dynamics, which Walras found "not at all astonishing, since he considers it to be insoluble" (1895, p. 630). Edgeworth had treated the equilibrium conditions, Walras remarked, but his model was incomplete because he did not show that the market converges to them (ibid.).

Walras rejected Edgeworth's imposition of a ban upon the investigation of dynamic paths, disagreeing with his opinion that

I am engaged in absolutely useless exercises in my efforts to demonstrate that the operations of the raising and lowering of prices, of the increases and decreases of the quantities of products produced, etc. on the markets are nothing other than the solution by tatonnement of the equations of exchange, of production, and of capital formation (Walras to Ladislaus von Bortkiewicz, October 17, 1889, in 1965, 2, letter 927, pp. 363–364).

Walras considered Edgeworth's argument that it is useless to try to demonstrate the way the economic system moves to equilibrium as a council of despair and as the product of a fundamentally erroneous conception of economic studies. His opinion, according to Walras, "shows that he has no idea of the object and proper goal of pure economics, which consists above all and before all in the demonstration to which I refer" (ibid.). Walras pointed out again that dynamic theorizing is not only a legitimate but also a necessary part of economic science. He was aware that a detailed dynamic model is difficult to construct, but he also believed that his objective of establishing the general character of adjustment processes could be attained without such a model. For his purposes, he observed, the precise path of the price in each market need not be known. Edgeworth should have seen, Walras continued, that a discussion on the level of abstraction of the theory of tatonnement is sufficient to establish the general features of the dynamics of competitive markets and, in particular, to establish their stability. He had not, he explained, tried to give a complete description of reality, but only to sketch its outlines, and he left the task of finishing the picture to others (Walras to Irving Fisher, July 28, 1892, in 1965, 2, letter 1064, pp. 498–499; 1895, pp. 629–30).

5. Edgeworth argued that the tatonnement process is not the only way that markets reach equilibrium. "Prof. Walras's laboured lessons indicate *a* way, not *the* way of descent to equilibrium" (Edgeworth 1889a, p. 435; and see Edgeworth 1891, p. 20). The idea of tatonnement, Edgeworth contended, is not an appropriate conception of its object because, unlike the idea of equilibrium, it does not typify reality (Edgeworth 1891, p. 20). In fact, Edgeworth claimed, he had provided a better description, not precisely of the dynamic

path, but of the economic behavior underlying it: "Walras's laboured description of prices set up or 'cried' in the market is calculated to divert attention from a sort of higgling which may be regarded as more fundamental than his conception, the process of *recontract*" (Edgeworth 1925, 2, p. 311). No real market behaves in the way described in the theory of purely competitive exchange (Edgeworth 1891, p. 12).

To show that there are other types of markets that could equally well be taken as having some generality, Edgeworth constructed a number of examples in which the different structural features of the markets give rise to different dynamic processes and equilibrium outcomes (ibid., pp. 15–17). He also pointed out the unique characteristics of a number of real markets. In the market for government securities in England, for example, there are two prices, one for the seller and one for the buyer. In the English labor market, there are coalitions that can exercise a great influence over the price (ibid., p. 12). In some markets, different prices are cried simultaneously. In some markets, there are quantity reactions, in others price reactions. In some markets, there are few traders, in others many. Some markets use the English auction system; some use the Dutch auction system (ibid., pp. 13, 16; p. 17 n. 1). Edgeworth consequently refused to admit that there is any single method of empirical solution of the equilibrium equations. The determination of prices cannot be brought under one rule (ibid., p. 20, n. 1). Thus, the question raised by Edgeworth, and answered in the negative, was whether it is useful to construct a model of the economy on the assumption that it is purely competitive.

Walras's position on that issue was explained in part by Bortkiewicz, who argued that Edgeworth was wrong to say that it was not a good idea for Walras to have supposed that the competitive mechanism of raising and lowering prices is the way that the equations of equilibrium are solved. Is there, Bortkiewicz asked, another process that actually occurs on the market and that can be regarded as a way of solution of the equilibrium equations? No, he declared (Bortkiewicz 1890, p. 85). It is obvious that the market system adjusts by changes of prices (ibid., p. 86). The tatonnement process is not *a* way, but *the* way that real markets do in fact move toward equilibrium (ibid., p. 85). Pareto agreed: "*M^r* Walras has shown that the bargaining established with free competition is the means of solving the equations of exchange by successive attempts. *M^r* Edgeworth has objected that the tatonnement process is only *one* way. He is right; but the way indicated by *M^r* Walras is truly that which describes most cases" (Pareto 1896/1897, *1*, pp. 24–25). Pareto therefore disagreed with Edgeworth's view that Walras's account of tatonnement in the mature comprehensive model was unrealistic and lacked sufficient generality.

Repeating and enlarging on Bortkiewicz's argument, Walras indicated his disagreement with Edgeworth's assertion that the tatonnement theory does not deal with a representative equilibrating process. Pure analytical economics, Walras maintained, is essentially the theory of "how prices are determined in a hypothetical regime of absolutely free competition" (1877b, p. 267; 1889, p. 252; and see 1900, p. XI). He rejected Edgeworth's view that such a theory is rendered useless by the variety of actual pricing processes. Walras recognized the existence of noncompetitive markets, and had a vivid appreciation of their complexity. He even developed a theory of monopoly pricing and production (1877b, pp. 376–88; 1889, pp. 493–505), but he had to leave it outside of his general-equilibrium model. The state of the discipline, he explained, did not permit the incorporation into a general-equilibrium model of market structures in which there are impediments to competition, although he hoped that would eventually be possible. In his theory of general-equilibrium, he wrote, he accordingly did not have the objective of constructing a mathematical theory of all the possible ways of conducting trade but of developing a model of those markets that follow the Walrasian pricing process (1877b, p. 267; 1889, p. 252; and see ch. 2). It was, he believed, perfectly legitimate to leave the noncompetitive market structures aside in developing that general model, for the reason that pure competition is the principal mode of exchange in the real world, practiced on all markets with more or less precision and accordingly with less or more frictions (Walras 1895, p. 630). He assumed it, therefore, as a reasonable simplification, believing that "the secret of science is to give primary importance to the general case and to relegate particular cases and exceptions to a secondary level of importance." That was, he declared, the basis of his quarrel with Edgeworth. A passage quoted earlier in this book must be quoted again here, for it relates directly to that quarrel. "In the question of tatonnement, for example," Walras elaborated,

I take the almost universal regime of free competition in regard to exchange, that which was described by John Stuart Mill, and which consists in raising the price in the case of the quantity demanded exceeding the quantity supplied and lowering it in the case of the quantity supplied exceeding the quantity demanded, and I demonstrate that the process leads to equilibrium by establishing the equality of the quantities supplied and demanded. Whereupon there is thrown at my head the market for English public debt, the system of English auctions, the system of Dutch auctions, etc., etc. (Walras to Ladislaus von Bortkiewicz, February 27, 1891, in 1965, 2, letter 999, pp. 434–35).

The point of contention was whether economics should be broken up into the study of particular market structures or be concerned with a freely competitive general-equilibrium model. Walras's assumption of free competition throughout the nonmonopolized parts of the economy and the treatment of them as a single system had great merit. It recognized and generalized the fact that price competition was extensive in the economy of his time. It enabled him to construct a model that could provide a very substantial beginning for general-equilibrium analysis, one that could serve as a stepping stone to a more general model which will eventually deal satisfactorily with disequilibrium exchange, disequilibrium production, imperfectly competitive behavior, and a variety of other phenomena that characterize the real economy (see Walker 1991, p. 565). His model is also the origin of general-equilibrium models which can be adapted for statistical implementation in the manner of Wassily Leontief's input-output system and in other ways also (Piggott and Whalley 1985). The clearly defined properties of a purely competitive model approximate those of reasonably competitive sectors of our economy, and furnish conditions and standards in the light of which we can conceive of imperfectly competitive models and evaluate the conditions they generate. The conclusion that the assumption of pure competition is useful for these and other well-known reasons (Walker 1970, p. 690) was reached by many of Walras's great contemporaries, including Alfred Marshall, Vilfredo Pareto, and Knut Wicksell, and by many subsequent economists, including J.M. Keynes and J.R. Hicks.

Edgeworth was unable to incorporate the different pricing processes he identified into a single manageable model, nor did he wish to do so. His rejection of Walras's freely competitive tatonnement model, coupled with his refusal to entertain the possibility of dynamic theorizing, led him to reject the goal of achieving a general theory of the economy of his day. Nevertheless, the alternative approach he recommended has great merit. His point that there are a variety of pricing processes is valid, and it is important because it leads to the analysis of different market structures in a partial equilibrium setting.

It would be inappropriate to pronounce Walras's analysis as right and Edgeworth's as wrong, or the reverse. To reject one approach or the other, as did the original protagonists, would lead to an impoverishment of economics. There are many questions aimed at discovering the impact of changes on the various parts of the economy that can be answered only with a general microeconomic model. There are many questions of limited scope best treated by the examination of a particular market structure. The conclusions of this section are therefore that both Walras and Edgeworth were right, inasmuch as they both identified important fields of economic analysis and approaches to the study of economic behavior, and that they were both wrong in condemning each other's field of inquiry.

III. Conclusion

Edgeworth alleged that Walras's model of tatonnement was unimportant, had very little content, was methodologically unsound because it tried to derive dynamics from statics, was a failure because the dynamics of the market place are not amenable to scientific formulation, and was useless because it was concerned with the equilibrating process of an unrepresentative model. Walras brought forward arguments against all those propositions, summarizing his response by charging that Edgeworth had not taken the trouble to read the *Eléments* with care. He answers me, Walras complained, without supporting evidence on one of the points "on which I am most confident: the theory of tatonnements, which is the essence of the theory of the determination of prices" (Walras to Charles Gide, November 3, 1889, in 1965, *2,* letter 933, p. 370). Walras nurtured the hope that the model would not be unfavorably judged by the public, because all the points of Edgeworth's critique appeared to him to be extremely weak (Walras to Francis Y. Edgeworth, March 8, 1890, in 1965, *2,* letter 964, p. 399).

Without deprecating Edgeworth's many and important contributions to an understanding of market behavior, and without forgetting that there were deficiencies in Walras's treatment of tatonnement in the mature comprehensive model (ch. 9) that are not considered here because Edgeworth did not mention them, the conclusion reached in this chapter is that Walras was right in the position he took in opposition to Edgeworth on the first four points of contention. The conclusion is also reached that both Walras and Edgeworth were advocating worthwhile analytical approaches in their discussions of the fifth point.

This concludes the examination of Walras's mature comprehensive model. He had completed it in almost all important respects by 1892 and in all major and minor respects by 1895, and then entered quite rapidly into his last phase of theoretical activity, to the study of which we now turn.

The models of the phase of decline

The written pledges models

CHAPTER 15

The structure of the
barter model of written pledges markets

Walras's barter model of written pledges markets is his solution to the problems created for his theorizing by endogenously induced economic changes. This chapter examines the structural aspects of the model that influence its equilibrating process. It presents and interprets his treatment of the parameters of the model, of written pledges, of the numeraire, and of the participants and trading conventions in the markets for consumer commodities, capital goods, and productive services.

I. Introduction

Decline of intellectual powers

It was stated in the introduction to this book, and it will be shown in the remaining chapters, that there was a marked decline in the quality of Walras's work during his final phase of theoretical activity. During that phase he tried to revise the *Eléments* into a written pledges system of markets. The reader should have some understanding of the reasons for the poor performance that is going to be described in the following pages. Why did it happen? A large part of the answer to that question is surely to be found in the state of his health. For all of his adult life, Walras was inconvenienced by headaches, "cerebral congestions," pain in the neck and spine, and an "affliction of the nerves" (Walras to William Stanley Jevons, February 26–27, 1877, in 1965, *1*, letter 376, p. 532). In 1887, he wrote about "suffering as usual from nervous fatigue and cerebral excitation" (Walras to Rawson William Rawson, April 10, 1887, in 1965, *2*, letter 796, p. 207), and explained that "all my nights are passed in crises of obsessiveness and neuralgia" (Walras to Luigi Bodio, April 19, 1887, in 1965, *2*, letter 796, p. 207). By 1890, teaching had become so difficult for him that he asked for a leave of absence from the University of Lausanne (Walras to Louis Jaquemot, November 24, 1890, in 1965, *2*, letter 988, pp. 419–20). "Each lesson," he wrote in 1892, "caused me a cerebral congestion for as much as two or three hours, sometimes for five or six, sometimes all day long, with difficulties of my circulation." Stating he had reached the extreme limit of his forces, he requested and subsequently took retirement (Walras to Eugène Ruffy, July 2, 1892, in 1965, *2*, letter 1060, pp. 495–96).

More ominously, Walras found that writing also became increasingly onerous. In 1892, he remarked that his health was so weakened that he scarcely
had a hope of finishing his work (Walras to Charles Franklin Dunbar, February 10, 1892, in 1965, 2, letter 1043, p. 479). To his mother he wrote: "My
back and my head are not very solid; but provided that I strictly limit my
writing, my lectures, and my conversation, and lie down for a half an hour
before dinner . . ., I succeed in finishing my day" (Walras to his mother,
March 7, 1892, in 1965, 2, letter 1050, p. 484). Walks were no longer
therapeutic; instead, they fatigued him. He installed himself in his country
cottage, put in his workroom a couch on which he would rest from time to
time, and interspersed his studies with manual work to prevent himself from
pursuing extended and fatiguing chains of thought (Walras to his mother,
August 1, 1892, in 1965, 2, letter 1065, pp. 499–500). Those measures could
not, however, prevent his deteriorating condition from being reflected in the
quantity and quality of his research.

In 1894, Walras gave a clear indication of the condition of his brain, and
once more recognized the deterioration of his powers of concentration and
the diminution of his intellectual energy:

My brain is still in quite a piteous state; and it is not probable that I will be able to
undertake new work. I have had to renounce writing completely my *Eléments d'économie politique appliquée* and my *Eléments d'économie sociale*. I will substitute in
place of them two volumes of *Etudes,* comprising the fragments I have already
published, if possible linked by an Exposition of Doctrine which will make the whole
collection comprehensible. But, it is not really certain that I will be able to write that
Exposition: I wanted [to put myself to work on it] and that caused me painful cerebral
troubles (Walras to Maffeo Pantaleoni, May 27, 1894, in 1965, 2, letter 1175, pp.
603–4).

Walras contemplated revising the *Eléments* in 1896, but made only a few
changes, explaining his incapacity to undertake a more ambitious project
(1896b, p. V). By that year he was publishing very little theoretical work,
and occupied himself, on a greatly diminished scale, primarily with applied
topics and with his old papers. Reflecting on his situation, he wrote that "I
am no longer involved with economic theory and normative economics. I am
tranquilly going to take two years to have the volume of Applied Economics
printed and my work will be finished." During the boring days of winter, he
explained, "my head can no longer work and even distractions exhaust me"
(Walras to Gustav Maugin, November 11, 1896, in 1965, 2, letter 1268, p.
702). This is not to suggest that Walras was then or ever became senile. His
problems were that in the ordinary course of everyday life he found it onerous
to conduct conversations, to take walks, and to read; and in regard to
scientific activity, by 1899 theoretical construction had become very difficult

for him, and undertaking long chains of reasoning and carrying out extensive tasks of revision were beyond his capabilities.

It will be shown in this chapter and in the rest of the book that the weakening of his intellectual powers manifested itself in many ways in the revision of the *Eléments* he undertook in 1899 and early 1900. One can imagine the struggles of the exhausted savant as he tried to work out his last comprehensive model, feeling all the weight of his sixty-six years, grimacing and blinking at the paper in front of him, trying to clear his mind and order his thoughts, lying down to rest, taking up his notes only to put them aside to rest again. One can imagine his trying desperately to concentrate, struggling with a tangle of variables and equations that became increasingly unmanageable and progressively less supported by a structural and behavioral foundation as he worked his way painfully forward through the pages of the *Eléments*. As the fourth edition cruelly reveals, his illness had become virtually incapacitating concerning creative work during his unhappy final phase of theoretical activity.

Two types of models

Walras outlined two types of models during that phase, presenting them in the fourth edition of the *Eléments* and without significant changes in the fifth edition. The first type was written pledges models.[1] Although he wrote in the introduction to the fourth edition about its revision that he had introduced the written pledges device in his model of the production and sale of consumer commodities and had "maintained that assumption in the subsequent analysis" (1900, p. VIII),[2] in fact he was unable to accomplish the exhausting task of carrying it forward into all subsequent models nor even to apply it to all the markets that should logically have been included in the written pledges models. His references to written pledges became less and less frequent and his models incorporating them more and more sketchy. Finally, he ceased to make the assumption, and outlined a number of models in which they are not used, thus presenting a second type of model in his last phase of theoretical activity, as will be seen in section 2 of this part of the book.

---

[1] Walras first introduced written pledges in 1899 in a brief note appended to his article "Equations de la Circulation" (1899, p. 103). He republished much of that note, with changes and a few additions, in two places in the 1900 edition of his *Eléments* (1900, §207, p. 215; §274, p. 302).

[2] It is perhaps useful to repeat here – at the beginning of the part of this book for which the 1900 and 1926 editions of the *Eléments* are the principal primary sources – some of the remarks made in the introduction to this book. The two editions are the same in wording, section number, and pagination of the passages cited in this part. Therefore, only one of those editions need be cited, and the 1900 edition is chosen for citation because the material appeared in it first.

This chapter introduces the barter model of written pledges that Walras developed concerning all consumer commodities and new capital goods, often referred to more briefly in this chapter and the next as the written pledges model or the barter model (not to be confused with the barter model of fixed total stocks of commodities examined in chapter 3). The study of the model is important to those who wish to understand Walras's work because it is his solution to the problems that are created for his equation system in relation to his mature comprehensive model by the occurrence of disequilibrium production and sales (ch. 9). The model is also of interest because the same type of solution is used in modern theory and the model was Walras's attempt to develop a general-equilibrium model on the assumption of barter.

Walras's presentation of the barter model of written pledges markets is extremely hard to understand and evaluate. This results in part from the incompleteness of his work on it, the defects in his constructions, and the difficulties inherent in the model. The many references to it in the secondary literature are sketchy and have been made without the benefit of an adequate understanding of its characteristics. Many of its features have never been discussed by its commentators. Moreover, Walras created severe problems for those who wish to understand his work by mixing together his accounts of the mature flow models dating from the second and third editions of the *Eléments* and passages on the written pledges model introduced in the fourth edition. Of course, Walras was entitled to use some of the material developed for the mature models as part of the new model. He could without contradiction use, for example, his definitions of capital and revenue, his identification of landlords, workers, and capitalists, and his definition of the numeraire. Accordingly, the documentation of the source of some aspect of the written pledges model will often be a citation of the first or second edition of the *Eléments,* written long before Walras conceived of that model. There are, however, structural and behavioral aspects of the mature models that are incompatible with the written pledges model, but naturally Walras did not point out that he had retained such elements. For example, those aspects of the mature models that result in irrevocable disequilibrium transactions and production are incompatible with the purpose of written pledges. For all the foregoing reasons there is a need for a clear exposition, interpretation, and evaluation of the written pledges barter model, and the purpose of this chapter and chapter 16 is to provide them.

This chapter examines the structural aspects of the model that Walras introduced for the purpose of determining the way that prices are quoted and exchanges are made in the markets for consumer commodities and capital goods. It is therefore concerned with the characteristics of written pledges and with related features such as the market institutions, participants, procedures, and trading conventions. It is not concerned with such matters as the form of the utility functions, the form of the production functions, the treatment of insurance premiums, the equations for saving, the perpetual net income commodity, and so on. The chapter will give special attention to aspects of the model that have been misunderstood in the secondary literature or that have not been recognized as constituting problematic features of the model. These include the questions of what its parameters are, whether the markets for services and products are separate, whether it is a barter model, the function of the numeraire in the model, why written pledges are made, their content, by whom they are made, and by whom they are used in the marketplace. Exposition and evaluation of the dynamic behavior of the model will be undertaken in chapter 16. The structure of the model will also be evaluated there, because its influence, effectiveness, and deficiencies are manifested in the features of what is supposed to be the equilibrating behavior of the model.

Terminology

For convenience of reference, some principal terminological conventions will be repeated here. The unqualified word "commodities" is used to mean productive services, consumer goods and services, and capital goods. Reflecting Walras's usage and his scheme of classification of commodities (1877b, lessons 36 and 37; 1900, lessons 17–18), the word "products" is used to mean consumer goods or capital goods or both, depending on the context. Products, often called goods, are made and sold by producers, who, following Walras's procedure, will sometimes be called entrepreneurs. Consumer commodities include goods and services. Also following Walras's usage, the owners of resources will sometimes be called consumers because they want to sell some or all of the productive and consumable services of the resources in order to acquire consumer commodities. In the interests of clarity, consumers will also sometimes be called "service suppliers." Consumers want to sell productive services to producers and want to sell consumable services to other consumers in exchange for services (1877b, p. 276; 1900, § 234, p. 244; 1877b, p. 285; 1900, § 244, p. 254). Henceforward, for the sake of brevity, the word "services" used alone will be used to mean productive services. Consumable services are always identified as a separate group.

It will be understood that unqualified references to "changes that occur during the equilibrating process" and similar phrases are references to changes that Walras wanted to occur in his barter model of written pledge markets without its' being implied that the model does in fact have those processes. Moreover, the changes are those he wanted to occur at disequilibrium prices, as distinct from the equilibrating changes he wanted to occur at equilibrium prices. The reason for introducing the phrase "wanted to occur" and similar ones is that the model is incomplete and is not a functioning system with various processes. With some exceptions, however, henceforward the tiresome repetition of phrases such as "wanted to occur" will be avoided. It will be understood that Walras wanted his model to function in certain ways and believed that it does, but that he was mistaken, as will be shown in chapter 16.

The commodities that Walras indicated are bartered on written pledges markets are labor, land-services, capital-services, retail nondurable consumer goods, new durable consumer goods, and new durable capital goods. His treatment of consumable services and primary materials will be dealt with in chapter 16. He first constructed a written pledges barter model that deals with services and nondurable consumer goods, and then replaced it with new assumptions. That is, he replaced it with a broader model in which he assumed that both nondurable and durable consumer commodities are produced and that consumers not only consume but also save, and in which he assumed that durable capital goods arc produced. Thus, there are two barter models of written pledges markets. This chapter and the next one are concerned with the features of all the barter markets in which Walras assumed that written pledges are used and hence are concerned with the broader model. Nevertheless, the chapters will frequently refer to and draw on the parts of the *Eléments* in which Walras presented the written pledges model of the barter of nondurable consumer goods because he incorporated aspects of it into the broader model.

II. Parameters

Walras believed for most of his career that the equilibrium prices and quantities reached in the mature comprehensive model (chs. 8–14) are the solutions to his system of equations of general equilibrium in production. That is not true because those equations are constructed on the assumption that, among other things, the amounts of consumer goods held by consumers, the stock of capital goods, and the maximum available amount of capital-good services are constant, whereas the disequilibrium production of consumer and capital goods causes those conditions to vary during the tatonnement process and thus results in the failure of his static equations to give the true equilibrium values of that system. The reason Walras decided to reject the disequilibrium production model and adopted the written pledges model was that he became aware of that problem.

Walras noted that two types of situations could be considered in relation to the constant conditions that he incorporated into his system of equations of equilibrium. First, he stated that it has to be true, with respect to both consumer goods markets and new capital goods markets, "that the given conditions of the problem are whatever they may be, but that they are invariable during a certain time" (1900, § 207, p. 214; § 251, p. 259).[3] In that statement, Walras was evidently indicating that he was going to determine the equilibrium values of the model for a given set of parametric conditions. That meant he had to ensure that the conditions he wanted to be parameters in his equations were invariable with respect to its endogenous process. Otherwise, he would have been dealing with a model in which endogenous processes cause those supposed parameters to change and hence cause the equilibrium values to differ from those given by his equations. Turning to another matter, Walras realized it should not be presumed that exogenous changes that affect the model never occur. Therefore he explained that it would "next be possible to assume that those constants are variables in order to study the effects of their variations" (ibid.). By that he almost certainly meant that the comparative-static effects of variations in the parameters could also be studied inasmuch as he did in fact undertake such studies or, less likely, he may have meant that the phenomena vary continuously. The comparative statics of his model or a model in which they vary continuously are not, however, the concern of this chapter except insofar as his treatment of them revealed his awareness of the parameters that his model must have.

Walras made it clear that in every instance, his reason for specifying a parameter or establishing some other structural feature of his model was in order to prevent changes in the individual supply functions of entrepreneurs and service suppliers that would otherwise result from economic activity at disequilibrium prices.[4] In order to ensure that his model had the necessary constant conditions, he adopted two procedures. First, he established by assumption that some conditions are parameters. Second, he adopted structural features of the model he believed result in its working in such a way that certain conditions turn out to be constants. In order to deal with some phenomena that would have invalidated his equations, he introduced structural features of the model that eliminate the phenomena.

Realistic parameters

The conditions that Walras thought he could reasonably hold constant by assumption in his model were those he believed were not affected by equilibrating processes in the real economy. He specified those conditions, long before thinking of the written pledges model, in a model that he used in some respects as a basis for it. One of them is technology, that is, the production functions (1877b, p. 310; 1900, § 322, p. 370), for if they change, the

---

[3] Walras wrote the same words about the markets for both types of commodities.

[4] The relevance of Walras's treatment of demand functions for this and other matters will be considered in the next chapter, for reasons that will be made evident.

entrepreneurs' individual supply functions for consumer goods and capital goods change. Another is the preferences of the participants in economic processes (1874b, p. 132; 1900, § 131, p. 134; 1877b, p. 246; 1900, § 201, p. 302), for if they change, the entrepreneurs' individual supply functions for commodities and the resource owners' supply functions for services change. It will be remembered in all that follows, but generally not repeated, that technology and preferences are among the conditions that must be constant to ensure the constancy of the individual supply functions for which they are relevant.

The other conditions that Walras held constant by assumption are the aggregate stock of land and the stock of personal faculties (1877b, p. 224; 1900, § 179, p. 187; 1877b, p. 276; 1900, § 234, p. 244). He was concerned with changes in the aggregate stocks of resources insofar as they reflect changes in individual holdings of resources, and he was concerned with the individual holdings of resources because, as he specified in many places in the *Eléments,* they are parameters of individual supply functions for services (1877b, pp. 246–68; 1900, § 201, pp. 209–10; 1877b, p. 270; 1900, § 227, p. 236; 1877b, p. 280; 1900, § 239, p. 248). About the stock of land, Walras observed that it could reasonably be assumed constant in his model because there are in reality, with insignificant exceptions, no changes in individual holdings of land that arise from the acquisition of new land (1877b, p. 219; 1900, § 174, p. 182; 1900, § 236, p. 246). There are consequently no changes in individual supply functions for land services that arise from that source. Similarly, Walras asserted that he could reasonably assume that the aggregate stock of personal faculties is constant with respect to the endogenous processes in his model, on the ground that the stock depends in reality on "variations of the population, not upon variations of agricultural, industrial, and commercial production," although the size of the population is not totally unrelated to production (1877b, p. 224; 1900, § 179, p. 187; see also 1877b, p. 278; 1900, § 237, p. 246). Furthermore, since workers are not bought and sold (1877b, p. 219; 1900, § 175, p. 183), there is no occasion for considering changes in the distribution of the ownership of personal faculties. Thus, by assuming that the stock of personal faculties and the preferences of the workers are constant in his model, Walras eliminated two sources of changes in the set of individual supply functions for labor.

Potentially endogenously variable phenomena

Walras was concerned with three groups of phenomena that vary as part of endogenous dynamic processes in the real economy. He realized that his equilibrium equations would be invalidated by the phenomena if they varied as part of the process of equilibrating adjustments in his model, and that he had to devise ways to deal with the phenomena.

1. The first group includes the disequilibrium hiring of services, the related disequilibrium production and, he implied, the occurrence of the economic processes that they entail, such as the payment of incomes: "Certain prices of services being cried, and certain quantities of (consumer) products being made, if those prices and those quantities are not equilibrium prices and quantities, it will be necessary not only to cry other prices, but also to produce other quantities of products" (1898b, p. 235; 1900, § 207, p. 215). Disequilibrium hiring and production would have an impact in three ways on the elements that Walras admitted into his model, and each way would invalidate his equilibrium equations by converting their parameters into endogenous variables.

First, consumption and saving depend on income in Walras's model (1877b, pp. 239, 281; 1900, § 212, 240, pp. 219, 248–49), so the payment of disequilibrium incomes would generate actual disequilibrium saving in his model. That would affect the size of the capital stock in disequilibrium. Second, even if new capital goods were to be produced and sold in disequilibrium only to replace goods that wear out, as the prices of the services used to make the goods change, incomes would be paid at different disequilibrium rates to the providers of the services. That would affect their supply functions for savings. Third, the disequilibrium phenomena make possible the accumulation of inventories. About producers, if the price of a commodity is one at which the quantity supplied exceeds the quantity demanded, actual production in excess of the latter will lead to the unintended accumulation of inventories of finished goods. If producers do not produce as much as they had planned, they will have unintended accumulations of inventories of raw materials and semifinished goods. In the real economy, the values of producers' inventories, which depend on their physical amounts and their prices, are parameters of the supplies-of-commodities functions. Changes of the values during the equilibrating process therefore alter producers' individual supplies-of-commodities functions during that process. About consumers, if the services they provide as resource owners are bought at disequilibrium rates of remuneration, they will be paid incomes during the equilibrating process. They will then accumulate inventories as consumers for the sake of convenience. In the real economy, the values of consumers' inventories are parameters of the supply functions for productive services and of the supply functions for saving. Changes of the amounts of the inventories and of their prices in disequilibrium therefore alter the values of the inventories, thus affecting the functions just mentioned.

Walras realized, as shown by his statement about production at disequilibrium prices, that the first group of phenomena occur in disequilibrium in the real economy. Consequently, he could not argue that their elimination in his model would be justified on the basis of realism. On the other hand, he did not want simply to postulate that they do not occur. Instead, he wanted to devise structural properties for his model that would result in an equilibrating process in which those phenomena do not materialize. He indicated this by stating his desire to establish "the equilibrium of production [of consumer commodities] in the same way that we established the equilibrium of exchange" (1900, § 207, p. 214), and by stating that he wanted "to achieve a rigorous tatonnement in regard to production [of consumer commodities] as in regard to exchange" (ibid., p. 215). By "in regard to exchange" he meant "in the barter and monetary models of exchange of fixed aggregate stocks of commodities" in which trade occurs only at general-equilibrium prices. His statements and others like them (1900, p. VIII) are confusing because the reader is led to believe that in his written pledges model, Walras was dealing with production as opposed to exchange, whereas in fact he was very much concerned with exchange in it.

By his statements, Walras meant that he wanted to devise institutions, rules, and procedures for the markets of the written pledges model that would generate an adjustment process that is rigorous in the sense that no production or sales occur until all excess demand quantities in all markets are simultaneously equal to zero – that is, until all the equilibrium prices are found (see chs. 3 and 5). That process would be very different from the dynamics of the mature comprehensive model. Walras indicated that he was introducing the written pledges model because "it is a question of establishing *ab ovo* the equilibrium of production in the same way that we have established the equilibrium of exchange, that is to say, by supposing that the given conditions of the problem are whatever they may be, but that they are invariable during a certain time . . ." (1900, § 207, p. 214). In the model of exchange of fixed total stocks, the parameters are invariable because if a disequilibrium price is quoted "another price is cried to which there corresponds another quantity demanded and another quantity supplied" (ibid., pp. 215–16), and the implicit rule against transactions except at a general equilibrium set of prices prevents any change in asset holdings until the equilibrium prices are found (1874b, p. 139; 1889, p. 165; 1876, p. 376; 1877b, p. 12; 1889, p. 135; 1900, § 111, p. 115). In a model in which production occurs, however, "the tatonnement of production presents a complication which does not exist in the tatonnement of exchange" (1900, § 207, p. 214) because "transformation of productive services into products takes place. Certain prices of services being cried, and certain quantities being produced, if these prices and these quantities are not equilibrium prices and quantities, it is necessary not only to cry new prices, but to produce other quantities of products" (ibid., p. 215).

Walras was indicating that disequilibrium production would change "the given conditions," a statement that he repeated when he introduced capital formation (ibid., § 251, pp. 259–60). Accordingly, he eliminated from the 1900 edition of the *Eléments* one of the principal passages in which he had described the tatonnement with disequilibrium production and sales (1889, p. 235) and replaced it with his new account (1900, § 207, pp. 214–15; and see § 251, pp. 259–60). How is it possible, he asked, for the type of tatonnement process he wanted to occur in the fixed total stocks model to occur in the markets for productive services and consumer commodities? As will be seen, he also wanted the pledges made by the sellers to have a role in the model after prices have been determined in the markets. Actuated by the same concerns, he asked how it is possible for the suppliers of services to the producers of capital goods to offer the services without becoming parties to binding contracts at disequilibrium rates of remuneration, and hence without actually supplying such services and being paid disequilibrium incomes (1900, § 251, pp. 259–60)? Again, he wanted the pledges to have a role after the pricing process has terminated, so the pledges cannot be oral, unlike the situation in his model of the exchange of fixed total stocks (chs. 3, 4, 5).

Introduction of written pledges: Walras's answer was to introduce written pledges and a market setting in which they are supposed to be used. He began by considering the behavior of the producers of consumer goods. He concluded that "it is necessary only to assume the entrepreneurs representing the successive quantities of *products* with *written pledges*" (ibid., § 207, p. 215), by which he meant that they pledge themselves to sell specific amounts of consumer goods if the price turns out to be a general-equilibrium price instead of producing and selling them at disequilibrium prices (1900, §§ 207, 214, 251, 273, 274, pp. 215, 224, 260, 298, 302). Thus "with respect to production . . . the preliminary tatonnements for the establishment of equilibrium are no longer made in actuality but *with written pledges*" (1900, p. VIII). The word *bons* in Walras's exposition is translated here as "written pledges"[5] because in his usage they are written out on pieces of paper and are markers in the sense of pledges, like bonds, that the issuers are *good* for the commitments they make. In contrast, Jaffé translated *bons* as "tickets," and in the absence of any other suggestion, that word has been used by English-speaking writers. If Walras had wanted to refer to tickets, however, he would have used the French words *tickets* or *billets,* words that unequivocally have precisely that meaning, but *bons* – with its emphasis on a commitment and on the idea that on presentation of the pledge to its maker the latter

---

[5] In some essays (for example, Walker 1987a), I translated this simply as "pledges," which does not bring out Walras's idea that in the model under discussion, the pledges are written.

would provide the promised amount of the commodity because the slip of paper is *good* for that amount – was better for his purposes. The pledges are written, and hence have a physical embodiment so that they can be handed back and forth. That makes it possible for them to play a role in the model after the pricing process is finished.

Walras then considered the behavior of landlords, workers, and capitalists who supply services to the producers of consumer goods. He concluded that it is necessary only to assume them "in the same way representing successive quantities of *services* with *written pledges*" and offering the services for sale (ibid.), by which he meant that they do so instead of actually hiring themselves out and earning incomes at disequilibrium rates of compensation. Walras then considered the behavior of the workers, landlords, and capitalists who supply services to the producers of capital goods. He concluded that it is necessary only to assume them in the same way as "representing the successive quantities of *services* with *written pledges*" at the successive quoted prices (ibid., § 251, p. 260), by which he meant there is no discquilibrium hiring of the services. Thus, in the written pledges barter model of consumer commodities, the suppliers in each service market make written pledges to sell all they have offered at the quoted price if it turns out to be the general-equilibrium price and none if it does not.

No inventories: Walras also dealt specifically with business and consumer inventories. He was thought by Jaffé to have arranged matters so that their values are constant (Jaffé 1967, pp. 17 18 [240–41]). In fact, in Walras's model the assets in question – unused items such as goods held by businesses in storage and for display, and such as those held by consumers in cupboards and closets – do not exist. There are two reasons for that situation. The first is Walras's introduction of the written pledges process. That eliminates the production of the items during the equilibrating process and therefore eliminates the possibility of accumulation of inventories of outputs because of an ex post excess quantity supplied and eliminates the possibility of unintended accumulation of inventories of inputs. The second is Walras's assumption that those items are used up "as soon as they are produced, without being stocked in advance" (1877b, p. 225; 1900 § 179, p. 188; 1877b, pp. 224–25; 1900, § 179, pp. 187–88; 1877b, p. 244; 1900, § 199, p. 277). That ensures that items produced in past equilibria are not held during the process of moving to a new equilibrium. Changes in the experimental prices of prospective items of the kind that are held in inventories in the real world therefore do not affect the wealth of firms and consumers in Walras's model and hence do not affect their desires to supply products and services respectively.

2. The second group of phenomena that vary in disequilibrium in the real economy is the holdings of capital goods. Walras wanted those holdings to be constant during the equilibrating process in his model, as he indicated by

assuming that an individual's holdings of capital goods is a parameter for his supply function for capital-good services (1877b, p. 280; 1900, § 239, p. 248; 1877b, pp. 285–86; 1900, § 244, pp. 254–55). If the holdings were to change during the course of finding equilibrium, the individual supply functions would change during that process. That would change the aggregate supply functions for those services during that process and that would invalidate Walras's equilibrium equations.

Alterations in the individual holdings would occur if positive or negative aggregate net investment occurs. Walras recognized that in reality, new capital goods are produced and sold during the process of disequilibrium adjustments, just as is true of consumer goods:

A certain rate of net income and certain prices of services being cried, and certain quantities of [consumer] products and of new capital goods being manufactured, if that rate is not an equilibrium rate, and those prices and quantities are not equilibrium prices and quantities, it is necessary not only to cry another rate and other prices, but to manufacture other quantities of products and of new capital goods (1889, p. 280; 1900, § 251, pp. 259–60).

Thus, Walras realized he could not reasonably argue that the individual holdings of capital goods are unaffected by equilibrating processes. Accordingly, he could not simply make the capital stock a parameter in his model by assumption as he did with the stocks of land and personal faculties. How is it possible, he asked, to devise a model in which economic processes result in equilibrium rates of production of new capital goods without their being produced at disequilibrium prices (1900, § 251, p. 259)? How could he arrive at "the equilibrium of capital formation in the same way that we have arrived at the equilibrium of exchange and the equilibrium of production" (ibid.)? His answer was to assume in his model that the producers of new capital goods "represent certain successive quantities of those *products* with *written pledges*" (ibid., p. 260). Capital goods are therefore not produced during the process of finding the equilibrium set of prices, so the individual holdings of capital goods are not changed by such production. Consequently, Walras reasoned, the individual and market supply functions for the services of capital goods do not change during the equilibrating process. New capital goods would be produced in the written pledges model only if an equilibrium set of prices exists and is found, and they would not pass into use until the following time period (ibid.). Walras believed that his procedure disposed of the problem of the impact of net investment, but that was not the case. In fact, if capital goods were to be produced, the individual holdings of capital goods would change, the individual supply functions for capital-good services would change, and it would be revealed that the system could not have reached static equilibrium (Walker 1987c, pp. 860–61; ch. 9). This matter is discussed further in chapter 17.

Alterations in the individual holdings of capital goods also occur in disequilibrium if old capital goods are sold in disequilibrium. Walras neglected to mention this problem. It is an example of the incompleteness of his construction of the written pledges model that he did not state that written pledges are used in the markets for old capital goods nor introduce markets of any kind for them into his model. Such sales are an important component of an economic system, and Walras should have dealt with them, but he did not take account of them in relation to the written pledges barter model.

3. The third group of phenomena that vary in disequilibrium in the real economy is the holdings of land. Disequilibrium sales of land change the disequilibrium holdings of land and hence change the individual and market supply functions that obtain in disequilibrium for the services of land. Consequently, if disequilibrium sales of land occurred in Walras's model, they would invalidate his equilibrium equations. Walras could not reasonably convert the holdings of land into a parameter in his model by simply postulating that they are constant on the ground that they do not occur in reality. He had specified that individual holdings of land are parameters of the individual supply functions for land-services in his mature model (1877b, p. 280; 1900, § 239, p. 248; 1877b, pp. 285–86), and since he presented the same passage in the fourth edition of the *Eléments* (1900, § 244, pp. 254–55), it can be presumed he continued to make that assumption. It was, however, an assumption and not the result of the structure of the model, because, as in the case of old capital goods, he neglected to assume that written pledges are used in the market for land or even to mention that important type of commodity in connection with the written pledges model. His neglect of the markets for old capital goods and land means either that his model is incomplete or that their markets function in the way described in his mature model. In the latter case, transactions that are not at general-equilibrium prices take place in their markets, which contradicts the properties he wanted his written pledges model to have. Thus, in either case, the model is defective.

In summary, Walras wanted it to be true in his model that "there are given quantities of land, personal faculties and capital goods" (1877b, p. 276; 1900, § 234, p. 244; and see 1900, § 273, p. 301). He introduced written pledges so that there could be no new commodities produced or sold in disequilibrium. He evidently wanted there to be no redistributions of existing productive resources, but failed to make that true with respect to old capital goods and land.

Other opinions

Don Patinkin argued that the parameters that the written pledges model needs but that Walras did not mention are the supplies of services: "Walras seems to forget that the given data of a production economy are not the quantities of commodities, but the quantities of productive services" (Patinkin 1956, p. 380; Patinkin 1965, p. 534). In fact, Walras's model does not require constancy of the quantities of productive services offered for sale.[6] In his model, those quantities are functions of quoted prices and thus are variables during the equilibrating process (1877b, pp. 286–87; 1900, §§ 244–45, pp. 255–56).

William Jaffé, strangely enough, did not believe that Patinkin held the opinion that he expressed in the foregoing quotation. Patinkin left Jaffé "with the impression that what is needed is constancy in the physical components of the individual endowment collections" (Jaffé 1967, p. 17 [240]). Jaffé argued, paraphrasing his translation (1954, p. 185) of a passage of Walras's (1874b, p. 142; 1900, § 143, p. 149), that it is wrong to assume that the physical asset-holdings must be constant. "In fact what is required for a unique equilibrium is constancy in the *values* of these separate endowments plus constancy in the sum total over all individuals of the physical quantities of the several commodities or services making up their initial endowments" (Jaffé 1967, p. 17 [240–41]; emphasis added). The values are the physical amounts times their prices. It does not matter if the individual holdings of physical stocks of assets are altered, Jaffé alleged, because

only if the redistribution of individual endowments of which Patinkin speaks affects their values will a change in the set of equilibrium prices ensue. Otherwise the equilibrium set is invariant with respect to redistributions of the physical items making up to separate endowments, provided always that the total quantity of each commodity remains constant over the entire "array of endowments." This, as has been seen, follows from Walras' "theorem of equivalent redistributions" (Jaffé 1967, p. 17 [240]).

Jaffé's view is inaccurate in three respects. First, contrary to Jaffé's supposition, a change in the physical amount of an economic resource held by a person changes his supply function for the service produced by the resource, as indicated here and as is well known. Changes in those supply functions would change the equilibrium set of prices. Walras's model therefore requires that supply functions for services be unchanged, and accordingly he ensured there is constancy of the individual holdings of the physical stocks of economic resources in it, as documented here and as is shown by his statement

---

[6] Walras asserted that it is necessary to assume the supplies of services are constant in reference to the mature consumer commodities model and the mature comprehensive model (1889, pp. 235, 280). Actually he meant constancy of the stocks of the resources from which the services are provided, but not the supplies, as is evident from his treating the stocks as parameters and the supplies of services offered for sale as variables that are functions of prices. Moreover, in 1900 he abandoned the passages cited in this note and replaced them with his assumptions about written pledges. He also assumed that the maximum possible amount of capital-goods services is proportional to the amount of capital, and indeed that the constant of proportionality is unity (ch. 10).

that in the model of written pledges markets, Walras wrote, it is necessary to have "a selected period of time during which there will be no changes in the given conditions of the problem." That is also why he gave the landlords, workers and capitalists "given quantities of fixed capitals: landed, personal and capital goods proper" (1900, § 273, p. 301).

Second, Jaffé's appeal to Walras's theorem of equivalent redistributions (1874b, p. 142; 1900, § 143, p. 149) has no merit, because the theorem is not relevant for the issue of the effects of changes in asset holdings when prices change. It states that the equilibrium prices will not change if the assets are redistributed, provided that the "sum of the quantities possessed by each of the traders remained always equivalent" (1874b, p. 142; 1889, p. 168; 1900, § 143, p. 149). The only way different assets such as land, human capital, and capital goods can be summed is in value terms, so obviously Walras meant that equilibrium prices will not change if the value of the sum of the traders' assets remains constant; and, in fact, by "equivalent" in different propositions he always meant "constant in value" or "the same in terms of value." Walras stated that the theorem follows from the fact that the equilibrium prices are unchanged by trading at those prices, so it is evident that he had in mind exchange at a fixed set of prices. The theorem is therefore little more than a truism, for if the physical quantities of the assets and their prices are constant, the sum of prices times quantities for each trader cannot be other than the same before and after trade, and consequently the aggregate value of each asset must also be unchanged. The matter under consideration is this chapter, however, is quite different. We are concerned with the conditions that must be constant in order for Walras's equilibrium equations to be valid when there are *changes in disequilibrium prices*. Such changes would alter the values of the amounts of economic resources during the course of disequilibrium adjustments. Far from asserting or implying that there is any need to prevent changes in those values during those adjustments, Walras wanted, in every one of his models, including the written pledges model, to devise an equilibrating process that would necessarily cause such changes. If he had constructed the written pledges barter model correctly, these changes would result from the quotation of a series of different disequilibrium prices of the services, a series that is an essential part of the tatonnement process.

Third, Jaffé was incorrect in supposing that changes of the values of the stocks of resources would invalidate Walras's equation system. Jaffé's reasoning was that such changes at disequilibrium prices would alter the supply functions for the services yielded by the resources. Of course, the value of the stock of a resource depends on the price of the service it provides, a matter that Walras explored in detail (1877b, pp. 273–80; 1900, §§ 231–38, pp. 345–55). In the case of a worker, for example, a change in the quoted wage rate not only generates the offer of a new quantity of labor by him, it also changes the value of the worker's faculties. Contrary to Jaffe's supposition, however, the change in the value of the human capital does not change the individual supply function for labor. A valuation of the worker's personal faculties and the supply quantity of his labor are determined simultaneously when a wage rate is quoted. Similarly, the valuations of land and old capital goods are determined together with the supply quantities of their services at their quoted prices. Moreover, since Walras specified that the individual supply quantity of any service is a function of all prices (1877b, p. 286; 1900, § 244, p. 255), changes in the price of one type of service in his model do not change the supply function of another type of service. The price of each service is simply one of the variables on which the quantity offered of any given service depends, and the variations of that price do not result in new equilibrium equations for the written pledges model. Jaffé was therefore mistaken in his notions of the parameters and variables that are relevant to the supply of services, and mistaken in his belief that changes in the values of resource endowments would invalidate Walras's equations.

III. The institutional setting of written pledges

Issuers of pledges and agents

A fundamental structural aspect of Walras's written pledges model is that its markets are organized. He indicated at the beginning of the *Eléments* that he was going to assume throughout his theoretical work on general equilibrium that markets are "perfectly organized" and freely competitive, and he explained that the standard type of such a market is an organized exchange (1874b, p. 49; 1900, § 41, p. 45; 1880b, p. 460, and in 1898b, p. 408; 1880c, p. 78, and in 1898b, p. 432). That the written pledges markets are of that type is indicated by the circumstance that suppliers in Walras's organized markets express their trading desires by transmitting their pledges to individuals that Walras called *"market agents"* (1874b, pp. 48–50; 1900 §§ 41–43, pp. 44–46; Walras 1880b, pp. 460–61, 466, and in Walras 1898b, pp. 408, 413; 1880c, p. 78, and in 1898b, p. 432), and Walras stated that the persons who are directly active in the markets of the written pledges model are agents (1900, § 214, p. 224).

In some passages in the first three editions of the *Eléments*, Walras employed the terminology that "prices are cried" in connection with markets for services and products (for example, Walras 1889, § 203, p. 234–35). He subsequently incorporated some of those passages into his account of the written pledges model. In that model, the agents are the representatives of the suppliers of products and services, there is no auctioneer or other market authority, and the agents are the only persons who are physically present in the markets. Consequently, when Walras wrote that "the price is cried" in the written pledges model (1900, § 207, p. 215; § 251, p. 260), he evidently meant that the crying is done by the agents of suppliers just as is done by agents in the oral pledges model and in many real organized exchanges. In the written pledges markets, if the price of any commodity is somehow discovered to be a disequilibrium value, the agents return the pledges to their makers, who dispose of them (ibid., § 257, p. 272). The makers of pledges then instruct their agents as to what the new price should be, and the agents call it out in the marketplace. The agents do not know their clients' entire supply functions; that is why Walras stated that new pledges to sell are written out at each new price by the entrepreneurs and the suppliers of services (ibid., § 207, p. 215; § 251, p. 260).

Organized markets: Walras's comments about the pricing process also make it evident that the markets in the written pledges model are organized. Just as in organized oral pledges markets (see chs. 4 and 5), the agents of the sellers in each written pledges market are physically present in the same location. This can be deduced from the consideration that Walras would not have asserted that the price is cried out (ibid.) without assuming that the cries are heard by the agents. Walras stated that as the price changes during the adjustment process, the pledges are issued repeatedly by sellers until the market supply and demand quantities are equal (1900, § 207, p. 215; § 251, p. 260) – a type of trading behavior that could be enforced only in an organized market. That he was thinking of organized markets can also be deduced from the fact that he intended that there be only one price at any moment in disequilibrium and in equilibrium in a written pledges market. Walras had described the property of a single price at any moment in the mature consumer commodities model, and it is evident that he reviewed and approved of that feature at the time he inserted the written pledges model because he added some language to the passage, as the following italicized words indicate: "On a market ruled by free competition" there is maximum satisfaction "within the limits of that *double* condition that each service like each product has only a single price on the market, *that at which the quantity supplied and the quantity demanded are equal, and that the price of the products be equal to their average cost in services*" (1877b, p. 266; 1889, p. 251; italicized words added in 1900, § 221, p. 231; emphasis added). In an oral pledges market, he had explained, a single price at any moment results from the circumstance that professional traders are assembled together and thus have simultaneous knowledge of the price that is quoted (1880b, p. 460, and in 1898b, p. 408; ch. 5). For there to be only one price at any moment in a written pledges market the same circumstance is necessary.

Why the pledges must be written: The role the pledges are supposed to have that necessitates their being written is now clear. Walras could not assume that the pledges in the markets discussed in this chapter are oral. The pledges must be written on pieces of paper because they not only, first, have to be given by the sellers to their agents, but second, be given by the agents to consumers and producers, and third, presented by them to their makers for fulfillment (ch. 16). Walras therefore used the word *"bons"* in the written pledges model to indicate not only commitments to sell but also their physical evidence. Written pledges are markers, like IOUs, made out for the amounts the traders pledge themselves to sell at the quoted price. Pledges are made in a variety of real markets, in all of which they are commitments in a general sense, but their specific terms in any particular market determine the precise role they play. It could be the case, for example, that a trader's pledge is to sell a maximum amount at the quoted price but also to sell less if less is demanded at that price, which is actually the case in many real organized exchanges. As has been noted, however, the pledges in Walras's written pledges model reflect a market rule that transactions are allowed only at general-equilibrium prices. That is, the sellers commit themselves to selling no more and no less than their individual supply quantities at the quoted price and to doing so only if it is the price at which the desired excess demand quantities of traders in all markets are zero. In this way, the written pledges enable offers to be made without entailing the occurrence of trade. Consequently, producers need not have already produced the amounts of consumer goods and capital goods they pledge themselves to sell, nor do they need to be in the course of producing them, and service suppliers do not have to provide services at disequilibrium rates.

IV. A barter model

Marget's misinterpretation

To explain further the structure of the written pledges model, it is necessary to examine Arthur W. Marget's claim to have demonstrated "once and for all, that the Walrasian system of general economic equilibrium is *not* constructed upon barter assumptions" (Marget 1935, p. 169). Of course it is not. As shown in previous chapters, the mature nondurable consumer commodities model and the mature comprehensive model are monetary. The model that Walras tried to construct in his lessons on money in the fourth and fifth editions of the *Eléments* is also monetary. He intended that it include all commodities, money, and inventories; in other words, that it be comprehensive. Marget was absolutely general in his assertion, however; he argued that in all lessons after the early ones on barter, Walras's model was monetary in all editions of the *Eléments*. Therefore, he was denying that exchange is a barter process in the written pledges model discussed in this chapter, and in that respect he misunderstood Walras.

The basic reason for Marget's misinterpretation was the confusing mixture of different models that Walras presented in the fourth edition of the *Eléments*. It has been shown in chapter 6 that Walras made statements in the first and second editions that are related to or describe barter flow markets (as distinct from the barter models of the exchange of stocks of commodities). He wrote about abstracting from money, about entrepreneurs and service suppliers meeting "face to face" in markets to exchange their commodities (1889, p. XV; 1900, p. XII), about there being no transactions or savings balances of money, etc. He stated in one place that there is a single market for consumer goods and services in a barter flow model (1898b, p. XV; 1900, p. XII) in order to indicate that no good or service is sold for money in that model. It has also been shown, however, that Walras developed monetary models of the production and sale of nondurable consumer commodities and a monetary comprehensive model in the first, second, and third editions of the *Eléments*. Walras's references to barter flow processes in the first three editions must therefore be considered as a contradiction of those models or as referring to another model that he did not actually construct during that phase.[7]

It has been noted several times in this book that, unfortunately for the comprehensibility of the 1900 edition of the *Eléments*, Walras failed to eliminate many of the discussions that related strictly to the mature model when he introduced the written pledges model. The 1900 edition is also confusing because it contains inconsistent passages on the matter of whether or not services and commodities are sold in separate markets. It is confusing because if there are separate markets in each of which there are buyers and sellers of a given commodity who conclude purchases and make settlements in the marketplace, as in consumer goods markets, then money must be used, and if there is barter, it would seem that the separate markets to which he referred cannot exist. Moreover, Walras did not clarify the way to think about markets by describing the identification of separate markets and of a single market as being merely the result of differing points of view, implying that the decision on which view to adopt depends on the aspects of economic behavior that happen to be of interest at a particular moment (1889, p. XV; 1900, p. XII). His wording also misleads the reader because by "two separate markets" (ibid.; 1877b, pp. 228–29; 1900, 185, 186, pp. 191–92) he really

---

[7] Those statements are not related to the "special" consumer commodity barter flow model that Walras sketched briefly and then abandoned in the second edition of the *Eléments* (ch. 6).

meant two complexes of individual markets. He grouped together the various markets for services and referred to them as one market, and similarly for goods. Finally, the written pledges model is confusing because Walras did not describe it consistently and because it is flawed in a number of crucial respects.

The 1900 edition therefore presents a mixture of passages dating from 1877b that refer an unrealized barter flow model, passages referring to the mature monetary models, confusing comments about markets, and a defective written pledges barter model. As will be shown, it is also the case that a barter model of general equilibrium is an absurdity. It is no wonder that Marget focused on the mature parts of the monetary models that Walras retained in the fourth and fifth editions of the *Eléments* and formed the opinion that there is no barter flow model in it.

Another reason for Marget's confusion was his failure to analyze the written pledges models. Nowhere in his treatment of whether or not Walras constructed this theory of general equilibrium on the assumption of barter did Marget even mention the radical changes that Walras made in the fourth edition of the *Eléments* – namely, the introduction of written pledges and of the market models that he introduced in the part on money. The facts of the matter are these. If one considers the material relating to the written pledges models that Walras introduced into the fourth edition of the *Eléments,* it becomes clear that he wanted them to be considered as a barter model. He began with the construction of a written pledges barter model of the production and sale of nondurable consumer commodities, and then went on to outline a written pledges barter model that included all consumer commodities and capital goods. Concerning those models, it was only subsequently, in the lessons on money, that he introduced money and inventories and thus tried to construct a comprehensive model. He made this clear in several passages. He wrote in the fourth edition that "we will make *circulating capital* and *money* intervene" in economic processes in part VI (1900, § 207, p. 215). Part VI comes after the barter models of written pledges markets. Walras opened the lessons in that part by indicating that he had previously been assuming there is barter. He drew attention to "circulating money held by consumers, circulating money held by producers, money that is saved," and in the next sentence stated that "the moment has come to introduce these elements into the general and complete problem of economic equilibrium" (1900, § 272, p. 297). Then he contrasted the monetary model with the barter model of written pledges markets by noting twice that he was going to consider various economic quantities *"no longer in kind,* but in *money"* (1900, § 273, p. 299; emphasis added to "no longer"). Thus, Marget's opinion is not sustainable.

Meaning of intervention of the numeraire and of money

Marget nevertheless raised an interesting issue by basing his opinion on an interpretation of the meaning of Walras's phrase "intervention of the numeraire." Walras referred several times to exchange as occurring "with intervention of the numeraire" in passages (1877b, p. 229; 1900, §§ 185–86, pp. 191–92; 1877b, p. 264; 1900, § 220, p. 230; 1877b, p. 300; 1900, § 260, p. 274) that he placed in the *Eléments* before his lessons devoted to the details of the models of the money and loan market.[8] Marget assumed that phrase meant the numeraire is used as a medium of exchange and believed that in all of Walras's flow models – as distinct from the barter models of exchange of stocks of commodities – the numeraire is "a money-commodity serving as the intermediate link" in indirect exchange (Marget 1935, p. 177).

It is true that Walras assumed the numeraire is used as a medium of exchange in the mature model of production and sale of nondurable consumer commodities and in the mature comprehensive model and, of course, in his mature models of the money market, but never in the written pledges models discussed in this chapter. Walras distinguished between "the intervention of money and the intervention of the numeraire" (1874b, p. 150; 1900, § 150, p. 156). When he assumed that the commodity or thing that is the numeraire is also money, by "intervention of the numeraire" he may perhaps have sometimes meant simply that money is used. In the written pledges models, however, there is no money, as has been seen. Consequently, by "intervention of the numeraire" in reference to those models he could not have meant its use as money. In general, by "intervention of the numeraire" he meant its use as "a commodity in terms of which the prices of other commodities are cried or to the value of which the values of other commodities are related, whether on the market for services or the market for products. That commodity then serves as the *numeraire*" (1886, p. 38; 1889, p. 375). Thus, by its intervention he meant its use not as money but as the "instrument of measuring value and wealth," which he called its "true role" (1889, p. 174; 1900, § 148, pp. 154–44; and see 1874b, pp. 148–50; 1900 §§ 147–50, pp. 154–56). It differs, he explained, from "a commodity for which services are sold on the market for services, and with which products are bought on the market for products, and which serves as *circulating money*" (1889, p. 375; and see 1886, pp. 38–39).

For some inexplicable reason, Marget asserted that Walras distinguished between the intervention of the numeraire and the intervention of money in order to indicate that there is no distinction between the two (Marget 1935, pp. 177–78). Marget offered as evidence that Walras wrote that there is "a

---

[8] That topic appears in various places with various titles in different editions of the *Eléments* (1877b, part III; 1889, part V; 1900, part VI). It will be remembered that the word "part" replaces Walras's "section."

perfect analogy between the intervention of money and the intervention of the numeraire" (1874b, p. 150; 1900, § 150, p. 156). To support his interpretation, Marget quoted a passage in which Walras explained that the analogy lies in the fact that "just as one can turn, when one wishes, from indirect prices to direct prices by abstracting from the numeraire, so can one turn also, when one wishes, from indirect exchange to direct exchange by abstracting from money" (1874b, p. 150: 1889, p. 175; 1900, § 150, p. 156). In fact, the passage indicates the opposite of Marget's thesis. Indirect exchange occurs when a (nonmonetary) commodity is sold for money and then the money is used to buy another commodity; direct exchange occurs when a commodity is exchanged for another. Indirect pricing is valuing a commodity in terms of a medium of exchange; direct pricing is valuing a commodity in terms of another commodity. Thus, contrary to Marget, Walras's statement does not mean that money and the numeraire qua numeraire are analogous in both being used as a medium of exchange. Walras was stating that the presence or absence of the numeraire affects the manner of pricing but not the manner of exchange. The presence or absence of a numeraire does not determine whether exchange is indirect or direct. That is determined by the presence or absence of money. Walras was indicating that if there is money, there is indirect exchange and indirect pricing; if there is no money, then there is direct exchange – namely barter; if there is a numeraire when barter is conducted, prices are calculated indirectly; and if there is no money and no numeraire, barter occurs with direct prices. "On the assumption of direct exchange," Walras asserted, commodities exchange for commodities. "But, on the assumption of the intervention of money," commodities exchange for money (1874b, p. 149; 1900, §§ 148–49, p. 155). Thus, Walras assigned the role of medium of exchange to money and not to the numeraire.

As if the foregoing were not sufficiently clear, Walras spelled out the difference between the intervention of the numeraire and the intervention of money. "There is," he wrote, "a certain quantity of exchanges that will be effectuated without the intervention of metallic money; but, nevertheless, the operation implies the invention of and the existence of the numeraire and of money; and the precious metals, if they are absent in fact, are always present in principle. It is thanks to the existence of the numeraire that it has been possible to maintain accounts of debits and credits" – that is the intervention of the numeraire – but "it is thanks to the existence of money that it has been possible to consider each transaction between [business persons] X and Y as an operation of complete and definitive exchange, needing only to be settled by the payment of money" (1874b, pp. 196–97; 1889, pp. 412–13) – that is the intervention of money. Knowing exactly how much money X owes to Y or the reverse and having an exact account of that at the time of settlement "would have been impossible without the intervention, not actual, but virtual, of the numeraire and of money" (1874b, p. 197; 1889, p. 413) – of the numeraire to keep the accounts, and of money to settle up the net debt. Walras then gave another example of the intervention of the numeraire – namely, to express the value of a piece of commercial paper used several times to settle debts, with the final settlement being made by the payment of money to either the final recipient or the original issuer: "Here again the existence of the numeraire and of money is necessary and their intervention is virtual if not real" (1874b, p. 198; 1889, p. 414) – the intervention of the numeraire to denominate the amount of the debt and the intervention of money to settle the debt. As he expressed matters concerning evaluation and payment in a monetary model, "the payment for these services, evaluated in numeraire, will be made in money at fixed dates. . . . The payment for these products, evaluated in numeraire, will also be made in money" (1900, § 273, pp. 298–99). The mode of intervention of the numeraire – evaluation versus that of money payment – is clear.

If it had been true, as Marget contended, that Walras introduced the numeraire in order that it serve as a medium of exchange, he would have eliminated the difference between the numeraire and money and would have had no reason to distinguish them. He asserted, however, that the numeraire differs from money precisely in the respect that money is the instrument of indirect exchange; he would not have made that statement if they were not different. Walras noted that in real economies "generally the same commodity that serves as numeraire serves also as *money* and plays the role of medium of exchange. The numeraire standard then becomes the monetary standard. Those are," he nevertheless went on to emphasize, "two functions which, even when added to each other, are distinct" (1874b, p. 149; 1900, § 148, pp. 154–55; see also 1900, p. XIV).

Non-monetary nature of the numeraire: Walras did not add the property of a medium of exchange to the numeraire in the written pledges model discussed in this chapter. There is no ambiguity about this aspect of the written pledges barter model of nondurable consumer commodities and the written pledges barter model including all consumer commodities and new capital goods that Walras presented in the fourth edition of the *Eléments*. He not only inserted statements that they are barter models into that edition, as has been seen, but, even more significantly, he structured the markets in it with the intention that goods would be exchanged directly for services in them. If he had wanted the numeraire to be money, he would have had to provide features of the model that would make that possible. Walras did not do so. On the contrary, in contrast to the mature comprehensive model, in the written pledges barter model the consumers do not hold balances of money or stocks of any commodity except consumer durables, and the producers do not hold inventories, fiat money, or stocks of commodity-money. In the passages devoted to the written pledges barter model, Walras eliminated the discussion of inventories and cash balances that had appeared in the second and third editions in the part just mentioned (1877b, pp. 306–7; 1889, pp. 312–13), delayed the introduction of inventories and money until the part on circulating capital and money (1900, § 273, pp. 298–301), and moved the mature discussion of inventories and cash balances and his treatment of the continuous market[8] to an even later place in the *Eléments* (1900, § 317, pp. 365–66). That does not mean, of course, that he removed all sources of confusion on this matter. In fact, since he retained discussions of the mature comprehensive model in the 1900 edition in the same lessons that he introduced the barter model of written pledges markets, he also retained contradictorily in those places accounts of the use of money and therefore implicitly of the holding of cash balances.

Contradictory market structures

Walras's treatment of the structure of barter markets in the written pledges model provides yet another example of the weakening of his analytical powers in the last phase of his theoretical activity. He posited two different market structures on which the same commodities are exchanged and that are therefore contradictory. To understand the situation, it is necessary to recognize that a fundamental property of the written pledges models is that producers of consumer commodities and capital goods make pledges to sell products but do not make pledges to buy services, and that consumers – landlords, workers, and capitalists – make pledges to supply services, but do not make pledges to buy products. No participants in the model express demands. This point is emphasized because the feature in question has been either misunderstood to its implications, or unrecognized or incorrectly described in the secondary literature. Its implications will be discussed here and in chapter 16. An example of incorrect description will be given immediately. Walras wrote, in one account of the use of written pledges, about the actions of service suppliers. William Jaffé inserted into his translation of that passage a phrase and a meaning that was purely of his own invention. He represented Walras as having written that the suppliers of productive services "use *tickets* [written pledges] to represent the successive quantities of *services* which are offered *and demanded* at prices" (Jaffé in Walras 1954, p. 282; emphasis added to "and demanded"). In fact, Walras wrote only that *suppliers* of productive services represent "with *written pledges* successive quantities of *services* at prices" (1900, § 251, p. 260). He nowhere mentioned pledges to represent quantities that are *demanded*. The words "and demanded" were added by Jaffé. Furthermore, Jaffé's translation wrongly conveys the nonsensical idea that Walras stated that the suppliers of productive services are also the demanders of them. The consequences of Jaffé's translation will be made clear in chapters 16 and 17.

The first type of market structure found in Walras's presentation of the written pledges models is that of a market for each product in which entrepreneurs make written pledges to sell, and change the quantities they offer as the price of the product changes, the price being expressed in terms of the numeraire. Here is Walras's statement of that process: "It is necessary only to suppose the entrepreneurs representing with *written pledges* successive quantities of *products* determined first at random and then increased or decreased according to whether there is an excess of the price over the average cost or reciprocally until equality of these two variables" (1900, § 207, p. 215). There can be no question but that the price in question is the price of the product, with the quantity supplied varying with the price. The price is not expressed as a rate of exchange between the product and a service, because the market is a separate one – that is, for each commodity only that commodity is sold in its market. Walras then continued that sentence by taking up the activity of the service suppliers. He did not put them into the same market as the entrepreneurs. That is evident, because the service suppliers act with respect to the prices of services, in separate markets. Here is his statement: ". . . and the landlords, workers and capitalists representing similarly with *written pledges* successive quantities of *services* [supplied] at prices cried first at random and then raised or lowered according to whether there is an excess of the quantity demanded over the quantity supplied or reciprocally, until the equality of the two" (ibid.). Similarly, Walras stated regarding the producers of any type of capital good that they represent their supply quantities with written pledges at the various prices of that type of good that are quoted in the market for it (1900, § 251, p. 260).

A single commodity in each market

It is obvious that those strange types of barter markets, if indeed that is what they ought to be called, are not ones in which the prices of products and services are expressed as ratios of exchange of products for services. Each commodity has its separate price, expressed in terms of the numeraire (ibid., § 273, p. 298). The entrepreneurs do not meet the service suppliers face-to-face in markets. There are many organized markets, one for each commodity, like stations on the New York Stock Exchange. In each organized assemblage of agents, the price of one service or of one product is quoted, and written pledges of suppliers of the particular commodity that is being priced are submitted at each such price, with no money being involved. In the written pledges model, Walras intended that consumers pay for consumer goods, not with a commodity-money such as gold and silver nor with fiat money – but directly with labor, land-services, and capital-good services; that is, with many different commodities, and that entrepreneurs pay for services directly with many different goods, but the payment of goods for services and reciprocally is supposed to take place after the market pricing process has occurred. Walras intended that after the prices are determined, the pledges are distributed and fulfilled by the direct exchange of services for products between the participants. They are supposed to meet face-to-face in the workplaces – that is, in locations that differ from the organized exchanges in which the prices of the commodities are determined. Concerning capital goods production, for example, the goods are supposed to be priced in their markets and labor is priced in its market. Then workers who save hire out their labor part-time in capital-goods industries and part-time in consumer goods industries. Similarly, landlords rent out their land to the entrepreneurs who make the products that the landlords desire, and capitalists deliver the services of their capital goods in exchange for commodities.

A complication in Walras's exposition of these matters in regard to the market for new capital goods is that he made the mistake of stating that the suppliers of services to the producers of new capital goods change the prices of services, not in accordance with the supply and demand quantities for services, but as a function of the supply and demand quantities of the amount of new capital goods (ibid., § 251, p. 260). This matter is discussed in chapter 16. Another confusing aspect of Walras's exposition of the written pledges markets is that he referred to both supply and demand in the quotation given in the preceding paragraph, but there are no demanders in the markets to which his discussion refers. This matter is also discussed in chapter 16.

Suppliers of goods meet suppliers of services

The second picture that Walras presented of the structure of the written pledges markets is one in which producers of goods and sellers of services meet face-to-face in markets and trade the commodities directly with each other. This is the idea conveyed by passages on the market for consumer goods and services such as the following:

... the producers selling by written pledges $D'_a + D'_b p'_b + D'_c p'_c + D'_d p'_d$... of products in order to purchase $D'_t p'_t + D'_p p'_p + D'_k p'_k + ...$ of services, and the consumers selling by written pledges $O'_t p'_t + O'_p p'_p + O'_k p'_k + ...$ of services in order to purchase $D'_a + D'_b p'_b + D'_c p'_c + D'_d p'_d + ...$ of products (ibid., § 213, p. 223).[9]

---

[9] Walras's use of "D" in this passage is a notation he adopted long before thinking of the written pledges model. It can be seen that he used "D" to indicate the offers of products as well as the consumers' demands for products. Thus his notation was ill-chosen, for it appears to specify that in disequilibrium as well as equilibrium at each possible price, the producers automatically offer the same physical amounts of each commodity as are demanded by the consumers. In fact, he meant to indicate an equilibrium condition, not a description of the state of affairs during the tatonnement.

Once again it is seen that one of the striking features of the market is that producers make pledges to sell products, but do not make pledges to buy services and that consumers make pledges to supply services, but do not make pledges to buy products.

If Walras had made the statement that services are exchanged products in the context of a monetary model, it would mean only that the outcome in real terms of a process of monetary exchange is that in effect the entrepreneurs produce various types of commodities and the service suppliers produce other types, and that they end up selling them to each other via the intermediation of money. About the written pledges model under discussion, however, as has been seen, Walras stated that he was treating the exchange of commodities "in kind." The ill-considered nature of the second type of written pledges model then becomes clear. Prices are not formed for the commodities in a manner consistent with face-to-face barter. They are not formed through two-by-two pairing of commodities with the price of each stated in terms of the quantity to be exchanged for the other, in the manner of barter without a numeraire. Walras assumed there is a numeraire in all the written pledges models and that commodities are priced in terms of it, as is evident from the price notation in the quotation in the previous paragraph, and from statements such as: "Equilibrium took place when the total of services and the total of products in numeraire were equal" (1900, § 273, p. 298). The commodities therefore all have their own markets. Thus, Walras's description of the second species of written pledges model is internally contradictory, and there is really only one type of written pledges market – namely, markets in each of which the participants are concerned with only one commodity and in which its price is expressed in terms of the numeraire.

V. Summary

The structure of Walras's written pledges model has been surveyed, establishing the institutions and participants in the markets for services, consumer goods, and new capital goods. The written pledges markets are purely competitive organized exchanges. The structure of the model is designed to ensure that the supply functions for newly produced goods and services cannot change in disequilibrium. Walras intended the use of pledges to have the effect of eliminating the endogenous processes in disequilibrium that would invalidate his equations of general equilibrium – namely, disequilibrium production and sales and all the processes in disequilibrium that they make possible, such as hiring, the payment of incomes, consumption, and savings. It has been shown that Walras did not assume the use of written pledges in markets for old capital goods and land, that written pledges are made only by suppliers, that they transmit all-or-none written pledges to agents, that the agents are the direct participants in the markets, that producers and service suppliers are supposed to exchange goods and services but do not meet face-to-face during a process of price formation, and that trade in the model is supposed to be a barter process. Walras's objectives for the written pledges model have been illuminated and it has been shown how he tried to provide it with properties that would enable him to achieve his objectives. It remains to be seen how or if the model functions in disequilibrium and to evaluate it.

CHAPTER 16

Disequilibrium features of the barter model of written pledges markets

This chapter focuses on the behavior of the market participants in relation to the use of written pledges in Walras's barter model of written pledges markets, analyzing and evaluating the structure and functioning of the model. The structural features of the model are shown to make it impossible for it to have equilibrating processes. The model is incomplete because the participants do not express their demands for consumer commodities, capital goods, or productive services. Even if the model is arbitrarily assumed to reach a set of equilibrium prices, there would be further insurmountable equilibrating problems because of the difficulties of distributing the pledges to consumers and producers and of arranging fulfillment of the pledges.

I. Introduction

This chapter concludes the explanation and evaluation of Walras's barter model of written pledges markets. Many matters that have not been discussed elsewhere in the interpretive literature are analyzed, and it is shown that the model has a number of logical deficiencies that have not previously been recognized, as far as I am aware. The behavior of the market participants in relation to the use of written pledges is explained, showing how Walras wanted the exchanges of products and services to be effectuated. Then the consequences of his assumptions are examined in regard to the equilibrating behavior of the model after an equilibrium set of prices is assumed to be found. It is shown how structural features of the model and the market procedures assumed by Walras are insufficient to result in the occurrence of equilibrating processes in the model. In order to generate a pricing process, assumptions have to be supplied by the reader. Moreover, other equilibrating processes would be necessary in order that exchange, production, and consumption take place in the model, but it is shown that there are no reasonable assumptions that can generate them. The chapter concludes with an evaluation of the structure and functioning of the model and it is shown that a multimarket written pledges barter system is unworkable.

II. Changing prices

Services

Individual excess demands for services: Walras stated that in his barter model of written pledges markets, the price of each service is changed in accordance with the sign of its market excess demand quantity (1900, § 207, p. 215). That requires that someone have knowledge of the direction in which the price should be changed. As indicated in chapter 5, one of the ways in which that knowledge can be obtained is by the traders' knowing the sign of their individual market-oriented excess demand quantities at the quoted price. It has been shown that Walras explained how changing the price in the organized markets of his oral pledges model of particular equilibrium is done with no more information than that. That model is properly constructed and complete inasmuch as there are suppliers and demanders in the market for each commodity, that they are able to express their trading desires, that they consequently have individual excess demand functions, and that they respond to their individual situations by changing the price. Individual market-oriented excess demand quantities exist because both sellers and buyers make oral pledges and their agents deal directly with each other. Each agent obviously knows whether or not he has reached an agreement with a counterpart, and informs his client as to the situation. If any agents do not reach an agreement, their clients instruct them to change the price.

In contrast, Walras wrote very little about those matters concerning the written pledges markets. He stated that the markets are freely competitive, that the participants are represented in markets by agents (ibid., § 214, p. 224), that the price is cried (ibid., § 207, p. 215; § 251, p. 260), and that new pledges to sell are written if the price is a disequilibrium value (ibid.). He did not mention how or whether sellers learn individual market-oriented excess demand quantities. Nevertheless, since the markets are organized in the same way as the oral pledges markets, except in the respect about to be discussed, Walras doubtless reasoned that as in the oral pledges model, traders would be guided by their individual circumstances to cause the price to move in the same direction as the sign of the unknown market excess demand quantity.

A major problem in the written pledges model, however, is that entrepreneurs and service suppliers cannot learn of individual excess demand quantities for services used to produce consumer goods. That is because entrepreneurs do not make pledges to buy services, nor do they express individual demand quantities for services in any other way (ch. 15). The demand side of the market pricing mechanism for services is missing. Walras did not realize that this lack of pledges to buy services renders his model unworkable, and indeed, he thought his procedure was sound. "The quantities demanded of productive services," he stated, are "a function of the quantities of products that are produced" (1889, p. 342; 1900, § 213, p. 222). He appears to have omitted pledges-to-buy not by carelessness or inadvertence, but because he believed that there is no need for explicitly expressed individual or market demands of services in the written pledges model. He apparently held that opinion on the ground that in a barter system there is a single exchange involved in the trading of any pair of commodities. It is only in reference to a monetary market, he believed, that there is a need to identify buying or selling as separate activities: "The intervention of money breaks down the single exchange of commodity for commodity into two exchanges, one of which is the exchange of commodity for money and which is called *selling*, and the other of which is the exchange of money for commodity and which is called *buying*" (1874b, p. 175; 1889, p.428). Walras's opinion was that entrepreneurs express their demands for services in his barter model of the written pledges market by their offers of consumer goods to the suppliers of those services.

No demand functions for services in the model: Walras's opinion was not correct. His design of the written pledges model is faulty, revealing the deterioration of his analytical abilities in the last phase of his theoretical activity. First, the producers do not meet the service suppliers face-to-face in barter markets. Each commodity is supposed to be priced in its own market with participants that are concerned only with that commodity (ch. 16). Each commodity is supposed to be priced in terms of the numeraire. Consequently, demands for services are not expressed in markets for products. Second, although it is of course true that in the real economy the quantities of services demanded vary with output, any product is made using a variety of services, as Walras emphasized (1877b, p. 227; 1900, § 182, p. 190). The amount demanded of each component service, however, is not deducible from a knowledge of the amount of the output offered for sale by the producers. The specific amounts demanded of each of the inputs result from the intermediation of the production functions, a circumstance of which Walras showed himself to be fully aware in many contexts (1877b, pp. 248–49; 1900, § 203, pp. 211–12; 1877, p. 254; 1900, § 212, p. 221; 1898b, pp. 486–92; 1900, §§ 324–26, pp. 372–76) other than that of the written pledges model. An employer's need for labor, for example, is implicit in his offer of a product, but the amount he needs cannot be deduced from the offer. In the organized markets of the written pledges model, in order for a worker to be able to learn the quantity demanded of his service, and hence to experience an individual excess demand quantity, the agent who receives his pledge to sell labor and represents him in the marketplace would have to communicate with an employer's agent who tells him how much of the worker's labor is wanted at the quoted wage rate. Then the worker's agent would be able to calculate his client's individual excess demand quantity. Employers in the written pledges model do not, however, write pledges to buy services, and have no agents in the marketplace representing their demands for services. There is no arrangement of any kind in the model whereby employers who make consumer goods can express how much of each service they want to hire. Therefore, inasmuch as a service supplier's excess demand for labor or land-services or capital-good services would be the quantity demanded minus the quantity supplied, and inasmuch as the first term of that equation is missing, there is no way that suppliers of services can have individual excess demands for them. As a result, there is no mechanism that can provide a signal to suppliers of services as to when they should lower the prices of services. Similarly, since entrepreneurs do not express demand quantities for services, there is no way that they can have individual excess demand quantities for them. As a result, there is no mechanism that can provide a signal to them as to when they should raise the prices of services.

Regarding the written pledges market for services used to make new capital goods, Walras also thought that the producers' offers of the goods indicate the demand for each of the services used in their confection (1900, § 251, p. 260). Obviously, that is not true. First, producers do not meet suppliers of services in markets. Second, if an entrepreneur offers to provide five cranes per month, that does not indicate the quantity of labor he needs to make the cranes; it does not indicate the quantity of land services he needs, and so on. The production of a capital good influences the demand for each input used to make it only via the intermediation of the production function, as Walras indicated in contexts (1877b, p. 288; 1900, § 246, pp. 256–57) other than his specification of the structure of the written pledges markets. In Walras's model, the entrepreneurs who make capital goods do not make pledges to buy services and have no alternative way of expressing demands for them (ch. 15). As a result, service suppliers do not have individual excess demand quantities for services used to make capital goods, and entrepreneurs do not have individual excess demand quantities for the services. Neither suppliers of services nor entrepreneurs know in what direction the price should be changed or if it should be changed at all.

Market excess demands for services: The second type of knowledge on which changes of the price of a service can be based is knowledge of the market excess demand quantity for it. That would require the model to contain economic behavior that generates market supply and demand quantities for each service. Markets would have to have a procedure by which individual demands and supplies are respectively added to obtain market demand and supply quantities, and by which these are used to calculate the market excess demand quantity.

There are no individual demands and there is no such procedure in Walras's market models. It is interesting, nevertheless, to analyze his treatment of market supply and demand in the written pledges model. About the market for services used to produce consumer goods, Walras provided economic behavior that gives rise to a market supply function for each service – namely, the making of pledges to sell services by their suppliers (ch. 15). As for market demand functions for those services, the *Eléments* gives the impression that such functions exist in the written pledges model. That is because Walras intermingled passages that describe the mature models with passages devoted to the written pledges models. In many passages and with equations that he wrote long before he thought of the written pledges model, he postulated that the demand for each service is a function of its price and other prices, that the price is adjusted to diminish the market excess quantity of the service, and that the condition of the equality of the market quantities supplied and demanded of services must obtain in equilibrium (1877b, pp. 252, 255, 258, 260–61, 264; 1900, § 208, p. 216; 1900, §§ 212–14, pp. 221–24; 1900, § 217, p. 226; 1900, § 220, p. 230). Walras also stated in specific reference to his written pledges model that disequilibrium adjustments in the market for services used to produce consumer goods occur through the prices of the services being "raised or lowered according to whether there is an excess of the quantity demanded over the quantity supplied or reciprocally, until equality of the two is achieved" (1900, § 207, p. 215; see also 1900, § 251, p. 260). If the market excess demand quantities for the services are not zero, he explained, "it becomes a question of initiating the tatonnement again on the basis of rational changes in the prices of services" (ibid., § 214, p. 224). It would seem, therefore, that a market excess demand function for each service used to produce consumer goods plays a role in the equilibrating process in his model. This matter will be examined shortly.

About services that are used to produce new capital goods, Walras established the conditions that generate a market supply of each of them in his model by assuming that their suppliers express their individual supply quantities in the marketplace by making written pledges (ch. 15). Furthermore, he gave the impression that there are market demands for services used to produce capital goods in his model, and referred to a market mechanism whereby their prices are changed (1900, § 251, p. 260). Manifesting in yet another respect the deterioration of the quality of his reasoning in his last phase of theoretical work, however, he did not state that the prices of services are changed in accordance with their market excess demands, but "according to whether there is an excess of the quantity demanded over the quantity supplied of the total of new capital goods in numeraire, or reciprocally, until the equality of the one and the other" (ibid.). That statement cannot be justified on either of the following possible interpretations of it. First, Walras was probably thinking in macroeconomic terms of the supply and demand for each service-in-general, suggesting that there is a mechanism whereby the aggregate supply and demand quantities of each service-in-general are adjusted to each other by the impact on its average price of the excess demand quantity for all capital goods in the aggregate. Second, Walras may have been thinking in less aggregative terms, referring to the "total of new capital goods" of each particular kind.

Regardless of which interpretation is accurate as an account of Walras's thoughts, contrary to Walras's statement, the market excess demand for capital goods does not influence the price of a service directly. It does so indirectly by affecting the market demand for the service, which in turn affects the market excess demand for it. It is the latter that affects the price of the service directly. The market excess demand for a service is also, however, a function of the market supply of the service, but that is neither a direct nor an indirect function of the market excess demand for capital goods. The supply of labor, for example, in reality and in Walras's model, is affected by the workers' preferences for work and income, and those preferences respond to influences that have nothing to do with the excess demand for capital goods. Accordingly, a parametric change that alters the supply of a service used in making a capital good will throw the market for the service into disequilibrium independently of what is happening to the market excess demand quantity for the good, even if that quantity is zero. The price of the service will then be adjusted in response to the change. Walras's statement of why the prices of services change therefore cannot be accepted in reference to the real economy or his model.

The role of market demand in the markets of Walras's written pledges models will now be examined. Inasmuch as Walras mentioned market excess demand functions in connection with services used to produce consumer goods and services used to produce capital goods, it is natural for the reader to think that the functions must exist in Walras's barter model of written pledges markets and play a role in its equilibrating process. On that supposition, the reader further presumes that someone in the model must have knowledge of them and acts upon that knowledge. All commentary on the model in the interpretive literature (excluding the present author's work), from Walras's time to the present, explicitly or tacitly assumes that the latter happens. In actuality, however, Walras did not state that it does. As was indicated in chapter 5, he did not believe that knowledge of those functions by the participants is necessary for Walrasian pricing to occur. He thought that market demand, market supply, and market excess demand functions for any type of commodity are known exclusively by the theoretician who contemplates the written pledges model.

In fact, those functions cannot be known even by that theoretician. Walras's many statements about market demands for services and formulations of equations involving them, made largely, as has been explained and documented, in reference to the mature models, give a false impression of the functioning of the written pledges model. Those statements do not imply or describe the behavior on which they should rest in the latter model; they do not establish the behavior to which they should refer; the written pledges markets do not have the structural features that would be necessary to generate individual demand functions for services used to produce either consumer goods or capital goods; and the statements would require behavior by the participants that would conflict with the behavior that Walras specified as occurring in those markets. He specified that only suppliers of services make written pledges, which are used to express their supply quantities in the markets of the model. Demanders have no means of expressing their demands. His statements involving demands for services therefore cannot be descriptive of the behavior of the participants in the written pledges model. Confounding the reader's suppositions and Walras's statements, there are no individual demands for services nor therefore market demands for services nor therefore market excess demands for them in his written pledges model.

Products

Consumer goods: Walras mentioned the quotation of prices by demanders of consumer goods (for example, 1877b, pp. 229–230; 1889, p. 212; 1900, § 187, p. 193; 1889, pp. 241–42; and see ch. 7), market demands for consumer goods, and market excess demands for them (1877b, pp. 255–56; 1900, § 213, pp. 221–22) in his descriptions of market adjustments dating from before the time that he developed the written pledges model, and carried those descriptions over into the fourth and fifth editions of the *Eléments*. He asserted there must be equality in equilibrium of the amounts supplied and demanded of each consumer good (1877b, pp. 264–65; 1889, p. 250; 1900, § 220, p. 230). Those statements make it appear that market excess demands for consumer goods are expressed in the written pledges model.

No demand functions for consumer goods in the model: In the written pledges market for consumer goods, there are pledges to sell them, so the model generates individual supply functions for them and therefore also market supply functions. There are, however, no pledges to buy consumer goods, and no other expressions of demand for them, and the consumers have no agents in consumer goods markets (ch. 15). Consequently, no information is generated about individual excess demand quantities for consumer goods, so such quantities cannot be identified by either would-be demanders or suppliers of them. As a result, the participants have no information on which to base a decision as to whether prices of consumer goods should be raised or lowered or left unchanged, and there is no one to bid prices up. The written pledges model does not have the structural features that would be necessary to generate or permit that behavior. Walras's descriptions of consumers' raising prices, and his references to market demand functions and market excess demand functions for consumer goods, are therefore not part of the written pledges model. They describe either behavior in the mature models or in real markets or part of the otherwise unrevealed structure of some unidentified model.

William Jaffé argued the contrary, contending that

a close examination of Walras' *tâtonnement* model in production reveals that he actually did make provision, albeit indirectly, for consumers to make use of tickets in bidding for products. In terms of Walras' model of *tâtonnement* in production, there is no trading of products among consumers, so that the only way consumers can obtain products is to purchase them from entrepreneurs in exchange for productive services. Since consumers are none other than Walras' "landowners, workers and capitalists," the tickets they use to represent their offer of services in exchange for products implicitly represent their demand for consumable products. It would, therefore, have been redundant "for consumers [qua consumers] also to make use of tickets" [Jaffé quoting Don Patinkin] in the case of production (Jaffé 1967, p. 18 [241]).

Examination of Jaffé's contention reveals not only its inaccuracy but also the absurdity of a general-equilibrium model based on barter and with a numeraire.

Walras thought of each supplier of a service in his model as offering all that he wants to supply on a single pledge at the rate of remuneration that is currently quoted in the market for that service. The service supplier does not offer the service for a variety of consumer goods at different rates of exchange quoted for each pair of commodities two by two, as would be the case if there were no numeraire. Each service is valued in numeraire. For example, let it be assumed that a consumer has no land or capital goods and therefore supplies only labor. The labor is priced in the labor market. The worker's weekly income may be a wage rate of ten numeraire units per hour times forty hours, or 400 numeraire units. That is his demand for numeraire income to spend on consumption. Obviously, contrary to Jaffé, the worker's demand for any particular consumer good cannot be detected from that homogeneous magnitude. Furthermore, if Walras's model were a functioning system, it would be the service supplier's misfortune that although his income is stated in numeraire, he would be paid only in the goods produced by the few employers who use the services he offers, not in all the different kinds of commodities he wants as a consumer. Obviously the service supplier's demand for the hundreds of consumer goods that he wants cannot be detected from the few commodities in which he would be paid. Thus, Walras and Jaffé erred in supposing that the quantities of services offered can indicate the amounts of each consumer commodity that are demanded.

Moreover, although Walras's ostensible variant model of markets in which producers and service suppliers supposedly meet face-to-face would seem to require that the service suppliers and the producers determine the prices of commodities in direct dealing with each other, this is precluded by the separate organized markets of that submodel and by the use of a numeraire in these markets. If producers and service suppliers meet face-to-face in the model during an assumed pricing process, that circumstance is irrelevant; it cannot in any way condition their market behavior. That is to say, the confusion of Walras's modeling in the 1900 edition of the *Eléments* is starkly revealed by the contradictions in the features that he attributed to the face-to-face model. Inasmuch as there is a numeraire in both variants of the written pledges of barter markets (ch. 15), in neither of them do service suppliers come into contact with the producers of consumer goods during the pricing process. In the market for a service, *its* price is cried, not the prices of goods. The amount of labor offered for sale, for example, is offered at a wage rate quoted in numeraire, taking all other numeraire prices into account (1877b, pp. 246–47; 1900, § 201, pp. 209–10). The workers do not transmit pledges of labor to agents who are crying the price of bananas or hairpins; they transmit their pledges to agents in the labor market. Similarly, in the market for a consumer good, *its* price is cried, not the prices of services, and the supply of the good is offered at its price quoted in numeraire, taking all other numeraire prices into account. In the markets of the written pledges model, the offers of services and of products therefore respond to different variables quoted in different places by different agents, although both types of offers are affected by all prices. Thus, even if a worker, having in mind a particular commodity and its cost, were to write out a pledge to supply ten minutes of labor at the quoted wage, he cannot thereby give a signal that he wants that particular commodity because labor is not offered in that commodity's market. There is therefore in fact just one type of market in the barter model of written pledges; in each market, there is only one commodity, and it is supposed to be priced in terms of the numeraire.

To summarize, in reality and in Walras's model, the offers of productive services do not tell the producers in any consumer-good industry whether there is a positive or negative excess demand for their commodity in disequilibrium, how much they should make of each particular consumer good in equilibrium, or whether any particular commodity should be produced at all. Walras recognized those matters when he wrote that "in effect, we sell our services to entrepreneurs who do not make the products which we need, and we buy products from entrepreneurs who do not employ our services. From this arises the necessity of a medium of exchange or money" (1886, pp. 38–

39; 1889, p. 376). Unfortunately, he was not guided by those considerations in his construction of the written pledges model. He should have designed it to reflect the fact that for entrepreneurs to learn how much of each of their products is demanded, the consumers' demand quantities for each of them must be registered in the marketplace. He should have assumed that service suppliers make pledges to buy consumer goods.

New capital goods: In the market for new capital goods, entrepreneurs write out pledges to supply them, so the model generates individual supply functions for the goods and therefore generates market supply functions for them (ch. 15). Walras also asserted that the difference between the market demand and supply quantities of new capital goods diminishes as the rate of net income is changed, and that those quantities must be equal in equilibrium (1877b, p. 300; 1900, § 260, p. 274). He therefore implied that individual and therefore market demand quantities and market excess demand quantities for new capital goods exist in his model. This is not the case.

No demand functions for new capital goods in the model: Walras did not think through the implications of his design of the written pledges model. In it, the would-be demanders of capital goods do not make pledges to buy any of the thousands of different capital goods, nor do they have any alternative means of expressing demands for them. The producers of capital goods cannot deduce the demand for them from any of the phenomena in the model. In it, savings are supposed to occur by individuals providing services to capital-goods producers (ch. 15), but the specific new capital goods or fractional parts of them that a supplier of services may want to acquire are not indicated by such offers. This is because the organized markets of the written pledges model do not permit would-be savers to offer their services to each producer of a capital good that they want to own. Walras thought of the supplier of a service who is planning on saving as offering some or all of the service on a single pledge intended for an employer in a capital-good industry. Whether the service is offered in a market in which service suppliers and producers of capital goods meet face-to-face with or without a numeraire or in a market in which the service is offered at its own price in numeraire, the action of offering a quantity of the service cannot indicate the supplier's demands for different capital goods. In Walras's model, therefore, the value of the amount pledged indicates the service supplier's demand for income to be used for saving-in-general measured in numeraire, but not his demand for any specific capital good.

Furthermore, in Walras's model – if it were a functioning system – the service supplier would have the misfortune to be paid only in the capital goods of the employers who hire the services that he offers. He may wish to own several or many different capital goods. A worker, however, can work in only one or two industries; and in reality, of course, workers in capital-goods industries work there in order to acquire income primarily for consumption, not to acquire the capital goods produced by their employer. The services of a particular piece of land can be sold only to capital-goods producers who like its characteristics and location. The services of a particular capital good are specific to one or a few capital-goods industries. Thus, the capital goods the service supplier receives in payment for his services are not likely to be those that he wants as a saver.

Since individuals do not express demands for capital goods in the written pledges model, individual excess demand functions for capital goods do not exist for either entrepreneurs in capital-goods industries or suppliers of services to them. Consequently, there are no market demand functions for capital goods in the model. The market demand for new capital goods and therefore the market excess demand for capital goods to which Walras referred cannot be part of the written pledges model, and in fact, those market functions and the system of equations in which they are incorporated were part of a quite different model, the mature comprehensive model of the second edition of the *Eléments*. Walras's equations involving demands do not themselves establish the behavior in the written pledges model that would be necessary for demands to be expressed; the behavior in the model is incompatible with those equations and it lacks the structural characteristics and behavioral processes necessary to generate those market equations.

III. Changing pledges to supply commodities

Walras was so deliberate in his decision to assume that no written pledges to buy are made – spurning that assumption in every one of the passages he wrote about the written pledges model (ch. 15) – that it would be a direct violation of his design if they were introduced into his model. Their introduction would create a radically different model. Instead, at this juncture, in order to facilitate constructive discussion of the remaining aspects of the model that he mentioned, his wish that prices be adjusted in his model will be recognized by making the assumption that there is an unexplained pricing mechanism in it.

Walras described adjustments of rates of output in the written pledges model in terms of what has been called the Marshallian stability process, which he identified independently and published (1876b, pp. 403–4, 424; 1877b, pp. 231, 264–65) before Alfred Marshall did (Marshall 1879). Walras expressed the process by writing that the rates of output of consumer goods and capital goods pledged by producers are "increased or decreased according to whether there is an excess of price over the average cost of production or the reverse, until equality of those two values is achieved" (1900, § 207, p. 215; § 251, p. 260). That adjustment process implies that at the quoted price of a product, the producers already in the industry predict the expected average costs of alternative possible rates of output and find the profit-maximizing rate. Entrepreneurs in reality estimate the prices and average costs of output they have not actually produced, but they make errors, whereas the entrepreneurs in Walras's model make accurate predictions. Entrepreneurs who produce capital goods and the numeraire commodity, for example, "know . . . their average costs . . . and their prices . . . and know in advance if they will make a profit or a loss" (ibid., § 257, p. 272).[1] Entrepreneurs who are not currently in the industry also take part in the written pledges process, according to Walras's account of entrepreneurial activity, set forth long before he developed the written pledges model and in fact impossible within that model but tacitly presented by Walras as part of it (1877b, p. 231; 1889, pp. XVIII, 214; 1900, § 188, p. 194). His assertion that entrepreneurs "move toward" industries that are profitable (ibid.) will be accepted temporarily as part of the written pledges model in order to allow the discussion to proceed with an examination of what he explicitly claimed as transpiring in that model. Would-be entrepreneurs in that model, it will be assumed, estimate what the average cost will be in firms they have not yet established.

If entrepreneurs who are already in an industry calculate that they would make profits at the quoted price, they issue written pledges to supply the profit-maximizing quantities of output (1900, § 207, p. 215; § 251, p. 260). Potential entrants also issue pledges to supply quantities, thereby committing themselves to entering the industry. The entrepreneurs' estimates of average cost and pledges to supply output change with each alteration of the quoted prices of services and of the product. Walras should have assumed that the entrepreneurs concomitantly pledge themselves to acquire different amounts of productive services and primary materials. Instead, he stated only that there is a rational adjustment of the prices of services used to produce consumer goods (ibid, § 214, p. 224). Given the lack of pledges to buy services, he was unable to explain how that occurs in his model. Assuming, nevertheless, that increases in the prices of services occur, the expected average cost calculated by the entrepreneurs increases and the expected profit decreases.

The entrepreneurs in capital-goods industries may calculate that average

---

[1] Walras alleged in another context (Walras to Enrico Barone, October 30, 1895, in 1965, 2, letter 1217, pp. 650–51) that entrepreneurs do not know their production functions, and find out the best combination of inputs for any level of output and the average cost by experimenting with the inputs during the disequilibrium phase of the model. That does not happen in the written pledges model, because there is no hiring of disequilibrium amounts of the inputs.

cost would exceed price and that they would accordingly make losses. They then "abstain completely from producing and retire all the written pledges issued by them for new capital goods and the numeraire good" (ibid, § 257, p. 272). Walras did not make a similar assumption about the behavior of entrepreneurs in consumer-good industries, but it can be presumed to be the same. In framing his statement, Walras was evidently thinking of what happens initially when a parametric change causes an equilibrium situation to be succeeded by disequilibrium. Let it be assumed that there would be losses at the set of prices that existed in the equilibrium and are still being quoted. The set of written pledges ruling in the previous equilibrium is discarded, and all production ceases. During the course of the subsequent equilibrating process, Walras assumed, the entrepreneurs do not issue new pledges (ibid.), so after each price there are none outstanding to be retired. Since there is no desired production, no entrepreneur wants to hire services. That causes the prices of services to fall, which causes the average cost of the product to fall toward its price. Given the situation that Walras created, his readers have to make the ridiculous assumption that the entrepreneurs quote the lower prices of the products despite the fact that they do not issue pledges, that is, without making offers at the successive prices. Remembering that we are assuming for the moment that the model is a functioning system, the reader will recognize that the situation is clearly not like an economy in which there is production in disequilibrium, for in such an economy, actual and expected losses in an industry cause the market supply quantity of its product to be gradually reduced and cause other industries to be affected to a degree or not at all. In contrast, the written pledges model – if it had a pricing process and were a functioning system – would be subject to violent swings of output. Output would fall abruptly to zero in every industry when there are losses in any industry because the set of prices would be a disequilibrium one and there is no production in disequilibrium. If equilibrium were to be reached, the economy in the model would change abruptly from producing nothing to producing at the full employment level.

IV. Equilibrium

Equilibrium prices

In the lessons into which he inserted the barter model of written pledges markets, Walras wrote his account of equilibrating processes almost entirely with reference to the mature market models. The variables in those models, Walras contended, continually tend toward equilibrium (1877b, pp. 251, 254–55, 261; 1889, pp. 234–35, 241–43, 246). There are, however, a few places in which he made similar assertions about the written pledges model. For example, he wrote that if the parameters are unchanged, the successive sets of experimental input prices would converge to the set that equates the supply of each service to its demand (1900, § 207, p. 215; § 251, p. 260). The successive sets of pledged rates of production, he contended, would converge to a set at which ex ante average cost is equal to price in every industry (ibid.). Of course, Walras wanted it to be true that the written pledges model converges to equilibrium as the mature models do. He wanted it to be true that the price of each prospective consumer good and each prospective new capital good would move toward its equilibrium value (1892b, in 1896b, p. 476; 1900, Appendix 1, § 10, pp. 478–79). He wanted it to be true that in equilibrium in the nondurable consumer goods markets, the quantities supplied and demanded of each service would be equal, and the quantities supplied and demanded of each nondurable consumer good would be equal (1877b, p. 264; 1900, § 220, p. 230). He wanted it to be true that in equilibrium in the markets for durable consumer goods and new capital goods, the market quantity demanded of each good at its quoted price would be equal to the market quantity supplied, and that the price and average cost of each kind of good would be equal (1877b, p. 300; 1900, § 260, p. 274). About capital goods properly speaking, Walras postulated that the first condition would be attained by adjustments of the rate of net income of prospective capital goods, and the second by increases or decreases in the amounts of prospective capital goods that entrepreneurs pledge to supply (ibid.). He postulated that "the equilibrium of capital formation will be established first in principle," and he postulated that "it is then established *effectively* by the reciprocal exchange of savings to be accumulated and of new capital goods to be delivered" (1900, § 251, p. 260).

In fact, since the barter model of written pledges markets does not generate market demand functions for consumer goods or capital goods, Walras did not construct a disequilibrium process that could achieve those equilibrium conditions. Since the conditions involve demand functions, they appear in the pages of the *Elements* on the logical level of postulates, but there is no model to which they can be related. They are underivable from forces at work in the barter model and are contradictory to its characteristics. They should be descriptions of equilibrium properties of the written pledges model, but it does not contain the behavior and situations to which they refer. Therefore, Walras's contentions notwithstanding, the variables of the model cannot converge to equilibrium.

The lack of information mechanisms is another factor that invalidates Walras's claim that the written pledges model tends to equate the market supply and demand quantities for each consumer good and capital good respectively. Even if it were to be assumed temporarily that there are pledges to buy so that there are individual demand functions in Walras's model, in order for market excess demand functions to play a role, as distinct from being known only by the theoretician, someone in the model would have to know them and therefore calculate them. That would require an authority, perhaps one in each market, who receives the pledges to buy and to sell, adds up the supply and demand quantities for each commodity, and calculates its market excess demand quantity. The model lacks that feature. In order for supplies and the assumed demands to be functions of all prices, as Walras's equations specify, there would have to be an information collection and dissemination mechanism to enable the traders in each market to learn about prices in other markets.[2] In order for the traders to be able to learn when trade can begin, there would have to be a mechanism to determine when the market excess demands in all markets are zero and to inform the traders of that condition. For example, a central authority could collect the information and give the signal for trade to begin. The model also lacks those mechanisms.

In order to permit a coherent discussion of other features that Walras introduced into the written pledges model, let it be assumed once again that there is an unexplained equilibrating process of price adjustments. The sellers of products and services react to the prices in all markets, and keep issuing new sets of pledges in accordance with the Walrasian pricing procedure. The reader can assume that an equilibrium set of prices is found in the markets for all products and services. At that point in the process, Walras indicated, the pledges made at the equilibrium set of prices are handed by the sellers to their agents. That reformulated written pledges model is still a long way from equilibrium, however, as will now be shown.

Distribution and Fulfillment of Pledges

Consumer goods—no way to distribute or fulfill pledges: Walras stated that after the equilibrium prices have been found, "then the market agents would deliver to the producers the written pledges for services in return for those for products and to the consumers the written pledges for products in return for those for services, and the exchange of services for products and that of services for services would take place" (1900, § 214, p. 224). In a real

---

[2] In his oral pledges model, Walras noted that the prices of securities are published in trade sheets and in the newspapers (ch. 4). He did not make similar provisions about the prices of services and products in the written pledges model, perhaps because they are not publicized in real markets in the same manner as prices of securities and commodities traded on organized exchanges.

organized market, the questions of the amount of a commodity that one participant trades with another and of who trades with whom are settled at the time of the determination of the price or acceptance of the ruling price. In Walras's model, however, as the quotation makes clear, those questions would be settled after the equilibrium prices have been found, if it were possible to settle them. The agents must distribute the pledges. Then the agents leave the scene and the participants call for the fulfillment of the pledges they are holding. That Walras did not investigate these matters was another manifestation of the depletion of his intellectual and physical energy. It is typical of the slipshod construction of his written pledges model that he did not think through and work out distributional and fulfillment matters that are crucial for the functioning of a written pledges model. His lack of attention to the situation may have allowed him to believe that the procedures are so obvious and simple that they do not need to be mentioned. In fact, his brief remark on the distribution and fulfillment of pledges conceals a host of difficulties.

Each producer needs to receive pledges made by service suppliers in the right amounts so that he can present the pledges for fulfillment to their makers, use the services, and thus produce the amount of the product he has pledged to sell. The producers, however, have no way of expressing their demands for services in the marketplace, so the agents do not know the amount of each service each producer wants. Consequently, there is no way the agents can execute the task Walras assigned them of distributing the pledges of services among the producers, and the situation described means that the pledges cannot be distributed or fulfilled and the model is unworkable for that additional reason.

No way to pay incomes: Let it nevertheless be assumed that the service suppliers' pledges are somehow distributed correctly among the producers. The next problem is that Walras did not make the payment of wages, rent, and interest possible in his model. At the price that turns out to be the equilibrium value for any particular commodity, a producer does not make pledges to supply parts of his product to each of his service suppliers. On the contrary, Walras indicated that the producer hands his agent a pledge to supply all his output per time period (ch. 15). That is much more than the quantity that would be required to pay any of his service suppliers. The model has no mechanism to solve that problem.

The reader may wish to provide such a mechanism by assuming that the agent fractionates the producer's pledge of output so that the value the agent gives to those who supply services to that specific producer equals the amount supplied by each individual times the price of the service. The service suppliers could then present the fractional pledges to their employer for fulfillment. That would be a formidable task, complicated by the fact that the agent is in a market for goods, not in a market for services, and yet would have to communicate with each of the suppliers of services.

No way to satisfy consumer demands: Even so, most of the consumer goods received by the service suppliers as remuneration would not satisfy their demands as consumers. It has been noted that Walras indicated that service suppliers can sell services to only a very limited number of producers, and that service suppliers are paid only in the commodities produced by those to whom they sell the services. Therefore, workers would be paid all their consumer-commodity wages in one commodity, and suppliers of other services would receive only a few other kinds of commodities in payment for their services. Furthermore, if Walras's distribution scheme were somehow carried out, the many consumers who do not work in a given industry but who want the consumer good produced by it would not be able to obtain any of it. There are two reasons why this problem cannot be remedied by having the agents divide the producers' pledges among consumers in general. First, the agents have no way of learning consumer demands, and therefore would not know how to fractionate and distribute the producers' pledges to supply consumer goods to the millions of consumers in the model. Second, the producers' output must be paid to the persons who supply them with services.

Walras's belief that services and products can be bartered in a multimarket model with numeraire prices, and Jaffé's endorsement of that notion, would require for their validity that each service supplier offer a part of his services in return for each of the hundreds of different consumer goods that he wants. It would have to be assumed that the commodities are priced, and then that the written pledges are somehow properly distributed. The result would be an absurd situation. For example, let it be assumed that the price of milk established in the market for milk is $1.50 per gallon, and that the price of farm labor is established at $5.00 per hour. The worker who as a consumer wants one gallon of milk would therefore have to work out the relevant ratios and recognize that he must work eighteen minutes for the farmer in order to acquire it. Alternatively, for one hour of labor, he can buy 3⅓ gallons of milk. For other consumer commodities, a worker would have to communicate with hundreds of producers, offering, say ten minutes of his labor to one producer, one minute to another, half an hour to another, thirty seconds to another, and so forth. He would have to work at the different trades for those periods of time and would have to change jobs as his preferences for specific products change.

Walras did not recognize those implications of his barter model, and he surely would not have accepted them as reasonable if they had been drawn to his attention. He never explicitly suggested such a ludicrous procedure, even though it is an implication of his multimarket barter model. On the contrary, he pointed out in a comment made during his mature phase of theorizing that a worker cannot offer his labor to many different producers because he is skilled at only a limited number of tasks. It would be absurd to suppose that a worker has been "apprenticed to two or three trades and changes three or four time a day from one line of work to another" (Walras to Ladislaus von Bortkiewicz, February 27, 1891, in 1965, 2, letter 999, pp. 434–35), and it would be preposterous to suppose that he changes his line of work hundreds of times each year. Similarly, in reality a landowner may rent to several persons, but he does not rent a fraction of his plot of land to each of the dozens of entrepreneurs whose products he wants to acquire. The capitalist rents all the services of a capital good to one entrepreneur during a particular period of time, and cannot possibly rent them simultaneously to many entrepreneurs in return for their varied consumer goods. Furthermore, the services of his particular capital goods that are usable for consumer-good production are in most cases specific to one consumer-good industry or to a limited number of them.

The barter model of written pledges markets would also require producers to divide up their supply so that they try to reach agreements with each individual worker, landlord, and capitalist. The producers do not do that, however. According to Walras, they each write out their total quantity supplied at the quoted price on a single pledge, so there is no way they can reach barter agreements with individual service suppliers. Moreover, the products are supposed to be priced in terms of the numeraire, and are therefore offered in their own markets, not in direct exchange for each of the services. For example, a worker may offer 40 hours of labor per week at a wage of $10 per hour, and a producer may offer 20,000 units of a commodity at a price of $70 per unit. The worker wants many different types of consumer commodities but cannot express those desires because he cannot write pledges to buy commodities. The producer wants a variety of inputs but cannot express those desires because he cannot write pledges to buy services. Clearly, there is no way that the worker's offer and the producer's offer can be related. This shows that Walras did not work out a multimarket barter system, and in fact unwittingly described market processes and outcomes, such as pricing and equilibrium, that are possible only in a monetary economy in which there are individual demands as well as supplies in markets.

No market for consumable services: A final point to be made about consumer commodities in the barter model of written pledges markets is that when Walras mentioned the distribution of written pledges in the passage quoted at the beginning of this section on the distribution and fulfillment of pledges, he introduced a new aspect of the model – namely, the exchange of consumable services among consumers (1900, § 214, p. 224). He neglected to explain that aspect, and left it incomplete regarding both sides of the market. He wrote about written pledges to deliver productive services made by consumers, which are supposed to be transmitted to producers, and he wrote about written pledges to deliver products made by producers, which are supposed to be transmitted to consumers, but he did not anywhere mention written pledges to deliver consumable services and, of course, he did not recognize any such thing as a written pledge to buy consumable services. Thus he did not provide consumers with a process of making pledges to sell such services nor of making pledges to buy them.

Capital goods: Revealing once more his incapacity to undertake the complex task of constructing a complete written pledges model, Walras neglected to mention the distribution of the pledges to produce capital goods or the distribution of the pledges to supply services used in making them. The reader might, however, try to fill out that part of the model by assuming that the written pledges made by capital-goods producers and by suppliers of services to them are distributed in a manner similar to the distribution of written pledges for consumer goods and the services used to make them. If so, the same sort of difficulties would arise as in the distribution of pledges in the consumer-goods market. The would-be capital-goods producers do not express demands for services, so the agents do not know how to distribute the pledges made by would-be suppliers of services intended for capital goods industries. The would-be suppliers of services to capital-goods producers do not make pledges to buy new capital goods, so the agents do not know how to distribute the pledges to produce capital goods among the service suppliers. The discussion could stop at this point.

Let it nevertheless be assumed that the service suppliers' pledges are somehow distributed correctly among the producers. The next problem is that a service supplier can provide services to only a very limited number of capital-goods producers, but he is likely to want a diversified portfolio of several or many kinds of capital goods. In a barter system, however, the service supplier would be paid only with the capital goods he helps to produce, and since his services are specific to a few capital-goods industries, he would be paid in one or a few kinds of capital goods – if that were possible. In fact, it is not, because Walras did not provide a way for the producers to pay their service suppliers. In the peculiar vocational environment of Walras's written pledges model, a service supplier who wants to save – that is, to acquire capital goods – may pledge, for example, one hour of a service per day worth ten numeraire units in the production of capital goods. A producer, however, makes a single pledge to provide an amount of a kind of capital good per time period – for example, one oil tanker per month. That pledge does not provide for the monthly remuneration required by any particular worker, landlord, or capitalist, so Walras's model does not provide a system of making payments.

The reader cannot supplement Walras's model by assuming that the producer's pledge is fractionated by his agent for distribution to his would-be suppliers of services. Apart from the difficulty posed by the fact that the agent is not even in the same market as the service suppliers, the producer's pledge could be fractionated only insofar as the real capital good is divisible. Obviously, the employer cannot split off a piece of an oil tanker to pay a service supplier, nor can the employer pay with shares in the capital good because Walras specified in the barter model that goods are supposed to be traded in kind directly for services.

Primary materials: Entrepreneurs also need to be given a batch of pledges to supply primary materials – raw materials and nondurable inputs such as leather, cloth, and oil – made out by their producers, which the entrepreneurs can then present to the suppliers for fulfillment. Walras did not provide for such pledges. Indeed, he neglected markets for primary materials in constructing the written pledges model. Even in the mature models, he relegated to a footnote a comment that "the price of natural primary materials would be determined like that of productive services" (1892b, p. 60; 1896b, Appendix 1, p. 476, n. 1; 1900, Appendix 1, p. 478, n. 1). He did not eliminate the need to deal with primary materials directly by his argument that the theoretician can logically reduce them to the results of the combination of services if he goes far enough back in his examination of the chain of production (1877b, p. 245; 1900, § 200, pp. 208–9; 1877b, pp. 250–51; 1900, § 205, pp. 213–14), nor by his related belief that the analysis of the pricing of raw materials can be logically reduced to an analysis of the pricing of the services that produce them (1877b, p. 250; 1900, § 205, p. 213), nor by his assuming that there are no stocks of circulating physical capital in the written pledges model (1877b, pp. 224–25; 1900, § 179, pp. 187–88). His assumptions and beliefs do not obviate the facts that producers in reality and in his model have to use primary materials and have to buy some of them from wholesalers. In the *Eléments,* regarding that matter, Walras presented only a model in which the latter acquire raw materials in oral pledges organized commodity markets (1874b, p. 48; 1900, § 41, p. 44). When he decided to transform the *Eléments* by the introduction of written pledges markets, he should therefore have either eliminated the oral pledges markets and constructed written pledges markets for primary materials or explained the relationship between the oral pledges markets and the written pledges markets for those types of commodities, but he did neither.

It was argued by Patinkin (1965, pp. 533–35) that Walras's treatments of tatonnement in exchange with fixed total stocks and in the written pledges model, in which production occurs, were asymmetrical because in the former he did not assume the use of pieces of paper with offers written on them, whereas he did in the latter. Patinkin believed that if they were logically necessary in the latter model, then they were logically necessary in the former. In fact, the correct translation of the word *bons* reveals that the two types of models are not asymmetrical for that reason. If there are pledges to buy and pledges to sell, they may be oral or written. Whether oral or written, in either case they are pledges, no trade or production occurs out of equilibrium, and the pledges are fulfilled when the equilibrium prices are found. Walras had no need to assume that participants write down their offers in the kinds of markets that are in his model of exchange with fixed total stocks – although they could do so with no alteration of the properties of those markets – because they communicate directly by voice and the pledges do not have subsequent uses. If the written pledges model were complete, the pledges would have to be written in order to be used after the price has been determined. In Walras's *Eléments,* there are great differences between the model of exchange of fixed total stocks and the written pledges model, but it cannot be accurately maintained that written pledges are logically necessary in the former. The markets in which the two types of pledges are used are different for other reasons, as has been amply demonstrated.

V. Conclusion

Walras's exposition of the written pledges model indicates that he did not consider its properties in any detail. His sketch is so incomplete that it does not even imply the general outlines of most of the missing features. He did not mention the formidable complications and absurd situations that it entails, and was obviously unaware of them. He apparently believed that to establish an equilibrating system in the model all he needed to do was to state that the markets are organized, that sellers make written pledges, that agents cry prices and distribute pledges, and that services are exchanged for products. In fact, those assumptions do not result in a workable model.

The logical structure of the model is deficient in four major ways. First, Walras's decision not to introduce pledges to buy deprives his model of a way of enabling demands to be expressed. That renders his model unable to allow forces of supply and demand to achieve the equilibrium set of prices. Walras's references to demand and excess demand functions are not descriptions of the behavior of the participants in the written pledges model, do not provide for the behavior to which they should refer, and are inconsistent with its properties. Second, the model lacks an information collection and dissemination system. Third, even if the reader assumes that the equilibrium prices are found, the model could not reach equilibrium because it does not solve the problems of the distribution and fulfillment of pledges nor therefore of the allocation of goods and services. The agents cannot distribute the pledges so as to make the model mimic a real market system. Without pledges to buy and money it is not possible to devise a market clearing mechanism that overcomes the problems presented by the model. Fourth, Walras represented the written pledges model as a general-equilibrium model of a hypothetical economy in which there is no money or inventories of capital goods or consumer nondurable goods (1900, § 274, p. 302). In actuality, it does not include other important economic sectors that cannot justifiably be excluded from even the barter stage of a general-equilibrium model because they are necessary for production to occur, namely, markets for primary materials, old capital goods, and land. Walras also did not provide for the production and sale of consumable services.

If Walras's model were to be judged on the basis of its usefulness or applicability it would obviously be given a failing grade. Nevertheless, since he presented it as the first stage of a model that is supposed to become complete by the addition of money and inventories, the question of usefulness and applicability will be raised in reference to the monetary model. The remainder of this evaluation will therefore be confined to the question of whether Walras was right in his belief that the barter model of the written pledges model illuminates some features of economic behavior. Written pledges seemed to Walras to be a way of solving the problems of reaching equilibrium without disequilibrium transactions and production and all they entail, and he believed that consideration of a hypothetical economy without money sheds light on the real essence of economic exchange activities. In fact, the problems that are solved by the real economy are rendered insoluble in the barter model of written pledges markets. Rather than revealing elements of the structure and functioning of economic reality, the model generates obfuscating and absurd situations that have no counterpart in the real world. Barter and the use of written pledges create more problems than they solve. If the barter model of written pledges reveals anything it is the futility of trying to construct a model of that type and that a model of a multimarket system should be a monetary one. The next task that must be undertaken is the examination of Walras's attempt to construct such a model.

CHAPTER 17

The written pledges markets
in the last comprehensive model

This chapter explains and evaluates Walras's modeling of written pledges markets in his last comprehensive model, concentrating on their characteristics concerning the pricing and determination of the rates of output of goods and services. It is shown that the markets do not have a demand side, that the model has no means to enable the distribution and fulfillment of pledges, and that it is lacking markets for a number of important commodities and money. It is concluded as a consequence that the written pledges markets do not have a pricing process and are not functioning systems. It is also shown that Walras's equations of general equilibrium ostensibly relating to the markets do not have referents in them.

I. Introduction

The term "last comprehensive model" in the opening statement refers to the comprehensive model of markets that Walras constructed during his last phase of theoretical activity. It is comprehensive in the sense that it includes productive services, primary materials, consumer commodities, new capital goods, inventories, and money. The last comprehensive model is the collection of submodels of markets – frequently described simply as models – that Walras mentioned in part VI of the fourth edition of the *Eléments*. He indicated that he believed the submodels are parts of a comprehensive model by describing them as the subjects of a single system of equations.

The equations

Walras presented the equations of his last comprehensive model as being composed of two parts. First, there are the equations he set forth in the *Eléments* in the "Theory of Capital Formation and Credit" (1877b, pp. 285–89; 1889, pp. 274–78; 1900, §§ 245–49, pp. 256–58). He originally developed them in his creative phase, retained them as descriptive of the mature comprehensive model, then presented them, with some changes of order and numbering, as part of the barter model of written pledges, and, finally, presented them as part of his last comprehensive model. Second, there are the terms and equations that Walras introduced in the fourth edition in his consideration of circulating physical capital and money. Thus, he referred to equation systems [1] through [8] presented in his lesson on capital formation (1900, § 275–77, pp. 304–8), added notation for the services of availability of goods and primary materials, and added equation systems he numbered [9] and [10] to describe the supply of money and the equilibrium of the services of money (ibid., § 275, p. 305; § 276, p. 307).[1] It is one of the weaknesses of his exposition that he did not discuss these matters carefully, but partially and elliptically, or by implication.

Replacement of the mature model of the money market: Walras's last comprehensive model could also be called his last monetary model, because it was in that final model, he stated, that he wanted to introduce money. Of course, he had assumed that money is used in models of markets that appear in the fourth edition of the *Eléments* in lessons before the ones in which he presented the last comprehensive model, but those models are part of his mature work, which he neglected to revise or eliminate when he decided to introduce the barter models of written pledges markets and the last comprehensive model. In contrast, in lessons 29 and 30 of the fourth edition, Walras executed a total elimination of his mature model of the money and loan market and replaced it with the last comprehensive model and the associated modeling of circulating physical capital and money. That circumstance and the fact those lessons are a republication of an article that Walras wrote in 1899[2] makes the identification of the work that he did on the last comprehensive model perfectly straightforward, and the defective and fragmentary characteristics of lessons 29 and 30 can unequivocally be ascribed to his last phase of theoretical activity.

All the submodels in the last comprehensive model are monetary. In some of the submodels, however, written pledges are used and in others they are not. The models discussed in this chapter are written pledges models. The submodels of monetary markets in which written pledges are not used are treated in the next chapter. The observation that the "written pledges models" discussed in this chapter are monetary should be emphasized because the same name was used in chapters 15 and 16 to refer to Walras's barter models of written pledges markets.

---

[1] Walras changed the numbers of the equations in the fourth edition, and therefore changed the numbers in the part of the article that he made into lesson 29.

[2] Walras made the article "Equations de la Circulation" (1899) into lessons 29 and 30 of the fourth edition of the *Eléments*. A possible source of confusion for the reader of that article is that Walras neglected to explain that the numbered equation systems to which he referred in it are to be found in the "Theory of Capital Formation and Credit" in the second and third editions of the *Eléments*.

Terminology: The terminology that Walras adopted for commodities in the *Eléments* (1877b, lessons 35–38; 1900, lessons 17–18) is used in this chapter. That terminology is noted elsewhere in this book (introduction; *passim*; ch. 15), but some of it will be reviewed here. The owners of resources will sometimes be called service suppliers and sometimes consumers because they sell some or all of the productive and consumable services yielded by their resources in order to acquire consumer commodities. Henceforward, the word "services" used alone will mean productive services as distinct from consumable services and the services provided by inventories and money. Unless stated otherwise, the terms "new capital goods" and "capital goods" will continue to refer to durable goods that are used to make other commodities for sale in markets. Some of the services used by capital-goods producers are the same as those used by consumer-goods producers; some services are specialized and are used only by one of the two types of producers. Services, like all commodities, are supposed to have their own prices determined in their own markets. Following Walras's practice, producers will often be called entrepreneurs, particularly when suppliers of services – workers, landlords, and capitalists – and suppliers of goods are both being discussed. Walras used the word "market" in the singular to refer to all the particular markets in which either consumer goods or capital goods are priced. When it is desirable to emphasize that each variety of good is priced in its own market, however, the plural word "markets" will be used. Thus, for example, reference will sometimes be made to the capital-goods market and sometimes to capital-goods markets.

Scanty references to written pledges: Another manifestation of the decline of Walras's powers in the last phase of his theorizing was the extreme sketchiness of his treatment of the functions of written pledges in monetary markets. Like his procedure with the barter model of written pledges markets – which was to add a word here and there to passages written about the mature models, and to insert a few paragraphs among them – Walras made only perfunctory references to written pledges. In fact, in the section of the *Eléments* titled "Theory of Circulation and of Money," in which he presented his last comprehensive model directly or by implication, he mentioned written pledges only twice. In neither case did he describe how they are used. The first mention – in a single sentence – occurred on the second page of the treatment of the last comprehensive model (1900, § 273, p. 298). The next mention of them, in part a repetition of the substance of the first, appeared on the sixth page (ibid. § 274, p. 302). Walras followed it with sixty-one pages of discussion of the characteristics of monetary markets, eighteen of which were written during the phase of theoretical activity in which he had conceived of the device of written pledges. On none of those sixty-one pages did he make any mention whatsoever of written pledges. Indeed, he did not mention them subsequently in the *Eléments,* nor, as far as I am aware, in any of his other writings after 1900.

The models of monetary written pledges markets in the last comprehensive model are largely vacuous if Walras's exposition of them is taken to be their complete description. A charitable reader of his work, however, can make them somewhat less vacuous by assuming that Walras tacitly endowed those markets with a number of the features of his barter model of written pledges markets and then added to them the assumption that money is used. To be more than fair, therefore, the presentation of the models will be drawn on constructions and concepts that Walras developed in reference to the barter model of written pledges markets and that have been discussed in the chapters on that topic. Walras can also be supposed to have endowed the monetary written pledges markets with some of the features of his oral pledges markets, so it is necessary to mention those features, even though they have been discussed earlier (chs. 4, 5). Excessive repetition of details and excessive citations of the earlier chapters have been avoided, however. Moreover, contrasts are drawn between the barter model and the monetary model only when doing so serves to illuminate the characteristics of the latter.

Relation of the equations and the models: In addition to the objectives stated, this chapter and chapter 18 address the question of what features of the submodels Walras represented his equations of general equilibrium in his last comprehensive model as belonging to, and the question of whether he provided arrangements that create a functioning monetary model. Walras was fully aware that a set of equations makes no sense unless the mathematical symbols have referents in a model. "It is essential," he declared, "to establish the foundations of economic theory very solidly before erecting on them the mathematical constructions that the foundations are called upon to support" (Walras to Luigi Perozzo, March 18, 1890, in 1965, 2, letter 969, p. 404). To be a functioning system, his remark implies, a general-equilibrium model must contain market institutions, technology, physical structures, procedures, conventions, market rules, government regulations and laws, provisions for the participants to communicate their offers and price suggestions, means whereby information about prices and offers to buy and sell is collected within markets and disseminated among them, means whereby employers and workers come together, ways of making payments of money income, a distributive network that enables consumers and businesses to acquire the goods they want, and many other structural and behavioral features. For the model to function, the theorist must design these features so that they are not contradictory and must fully establish the aspects of the model that are important.

Equations cannot specify or describe those structural and behavioral features and therefore cannot establish them in a model. Equations are meaningless with respect to a model unless it contains features that generate the behavior to which the equations ostensibly refer.[3] To be useful in understanding the workings and states of a model, the mathematical symbols must have referents in the model, and the relationships between the symbols must reflect the forces at work in it. For example, Walras wrote out an equation for the demand for new capital goods. The symbols could have referents in a model only if it contains structural features and procedures that generate and permit expressions of demands for capital goods in marketplaces. The interpretative literature has not answered the question of what market features underlie the equations that appear in Walras's lessons on the last comprehensive model, but has instead discussed his equations on the basis of implicit assumptions about the kind of markets he had in mind. The commentators may have been thinking about how they believe competitive markets in their own economy operate, or perhaps about the modern theory of purely competitive markets, but both of those differ in important respects from Walras's modeling of competitive markets. Certainly the commentators have not had a clear idea of the sort of markets Walras thought the equations of lessons 29 and 30 described, and they would find it very difficult, as I have, to uncover and analyze his conceptions. That is true partially because he conceived of several models of competitive markets, partially because some of his ideas about their structure and behavior were unclear and incomplete, and partially because his last comprehensive model contains logical defects, as this chapter and the next will show.

The purpose of the assumption of written pledges: Walras's reason for introducing written pledges is well-known (see ibid., § 207, pp. 214–15; § 251, pp. 259–60; § 274, p. 302; ch. 15). He wanted to ensure that the equilibrium of the monetary model is the one indicated by the solutions to his equations. He thought that would be achieved by eliminating disequilibrium transactions in the sense of transactions at prices that are not part of a general-equilibrium set, and by eliminating the associated phenomena, such as the use of services in disequilibrium, disequilibrium production, and the payment of disequilibrium incomes. In fact, many other features of a model would be necessary to validate his equations, as will be seen, but it is nevertheless true that Walras had to eliminate disequilibrium transactions in the sense indicated. As he explained, they would cause conditions that are constants in his equations to be transformed into endogenous variables (1900, § 207, pp. 214–15), and if that happened, the equations would not give the true equilibrium values in

---

[3] For a complete exposition of this matter, see Walker 1997.

the model. The use of written pledges eliminates disequilibrium transactions and production because the participants, instead of actually producing and selling commodities at disequilibrium prices, merely state the quantities they are willing to produce and sell at quoted prices. Walras expressed these matters in reference to the last comprehensive model by remarking that it is possible "by means of the hypothesis of *written pledges*" to distinguish clearly the phase "of *preliminary tâtonnements* by which, in principle, equilibrium is established" (1900, § 274, p. 302). In that phase, no economic activity takes place, except, Walras believed, the written pledges process of price determination. Only in a subsequent phase, after the equilibrium prices have been found, he stated, are commodities actually produced and exchanged (ibid.).

There are six types of markets regarding which Walras stated or implied in his last comprehensive model that written pledges are used. They are the input and output markets for consumer goods industries, the input and output markets for capital goods industries, the markets for consumable services, and the market for short-term loans to businesses. They will be considered in turn.

II. Consumer-goods industries

The input markets

Documentation of the use of written pledges to supply services: The justification for stating that the services input side of consumer-goods industries consists of written pledges markets in the last comprehensive model is Walras's statement that "after the preliminary tatonnements made with *written pledges,* the equilibrium once established in principle, the delivery of services will begin immediately and will continue in a determinate manner during the period of time under consideration" (1900, § 272, pp. 298–99). The quotation makes it clear that markets for services in the model are written pledges markets. The statement refers without restriction to the input markets in all industries – that is, both consumer-good and capital-good industries. Walras also evidently included consumable services in that statement because in the same paragraph he went on to mention them in connection with the need of the consumer to hold cash balances in order to acquire them (ibid., p. 299). Thus, he intended that consumable services markets be written pledges markets. This matter is mentioned again later in this chapter.

In Walras's barter model of written pledges markets, pricing is supposed to be accomplished in separate markets, but payment is supposed to be made for consumer goods with the services that are used to make them; the goods and the services are supposed to be exchanged directly for each other. In contrast, the written pledges markets for services in the last comprehensive model are monetary. The justification for that statement is that Walras wrote at the beginning of his lessons on the model that he was considering "productive services . . . no longer *in kind,* but *in money*" (ibid., § 273, p. 299) and that "the payment for these services, evaluated in numeraire, will be made in money" (ibid., § 273, pp. 298–99). Walras thought that his barter model of written pledges markets revealed basic properties of a competitive system, but he introduced money in order to take account of other features to which he believed it gives rise (1889, p. 375; 1900, § 272, p. 297; and see 1874b, p. 171). The functions of money, he specified, are to serve as a numeraire, a medium of exchange, and a store of purchasing power in the sense that it is accumulated for the purpose of making future transactions (1900, § 273, pp. 300–301; § 281, p. 316). In his barter model of written pledges markets, Walras used a numeraire commodity as a standard in terms of which the prices of all commodities are quoted and therefore in terms of which economic values are measured (chs. 15, 16). When he introduced money, he had to indicate its relation to the numeraire. He did so initially by assuming that the numeraire and money are different items (1900, § 275, p. 303), and accordingly he represented prices as being quoted in terms of the numeraire but payments as being made in money. He then assumed, however, that one and the same item is both the numeraire and money (ibid., § 281, p. 316). Thus, in the most fully developed form of the last comprehensive model, prices are quoted in money, payments are made in money, and economic values are measured in money.

Organized competitive markets: The characteristics of the written pledges markets in which money is used are, Walras implied, precisely the same as in the barter model in all respects relating to issuance of pledges and the related activities of the suppliers of commodities and their agents, except that money would be used if trade were to occur. Accordingly, Walras assumed that the monetary input markets are organized and freely competitive. Consumers, in their role as owners of economic resources, offer services to producers by means of writing out on pieces of paper the rates of supply they pledge at each quoted price (ibid., § 207, p. 215). They entrust the pledges to agents (ibid., § 214, p. 244). In the marketplaces, the agents cry the prices and offers that are submitted by the service suppliers, and have the responsibility of trying to find counterparts – that is, agents who will agree on behalf of their clients to purchase the services. The suppliers understand that agreements to sell will be honored only if the price is one at which all traders in all markets have found their counterparts – namely, at the equilibrium price.

It will be recalled that in Walras's oral pledges model and elsewhere in his mature writings on tatonnement processes, he incorporated a market-oriented definition of an individual excess demand function into his discussions of market behavior (ch. 5).[4] Buyers as well as sellers make pledges in that model. For a demander, Walras defined that function as the trader's net demand quantity for a commodity at the quoted price minus the quantity offered for sale to him, at all possible prices at which the difference is non-negative. For a supplier, Walras defined the individual market-oriented excess demand function as the amount demanded of his commodity at the quoted price minus the amount he offers for sale, at all possible prices at which the difference is nonpositive. Of course, whether a market participant is a demander or a supplier depends, given his preferences and economic situation, on the price. Henceforward in this chapter, the term "individual excess demand" refers to the market-oriented variety. In the oral pledges model, the traders have knowledge of their individual excess demand quantities because demanders and suppliers both transmit their pledges to agents, and the latter deal face-to-face with each other. The agents know whether or not they have reached an agreement with a counterpart, and inform their clients as to the situation. If any agents do not reach an agreement, their clients change the price in accordance with the sign of their individual excess demand quantities.

No written pledges to buy services: The Walrasian pricing process that occurs in the oral pledges model cannot, however, take place in the input markets of consumer goods industries in the monetary written pledges model, because there are no pledges to buy commodities in the latter model. The demand term in the definition of an individual excess demand function therefore does not exist in those markets. Although the sellers of services make written pledges to sell them to employers in the consumer-goods industries, employers who want to make consumer goods do not make written pledges to buy the services (1900, § 207, p. 215). Moreover, Walras did not provide the employers with any other means of expressing their demands for inputs. The service suppliers' agents cannot possibly find counterparts because the entrepreneurs do not make pledges to buy services and have no agents in the input markets. Therefore, an entrepreneur does not experience an individual excess demand function for a service and does not know when to raise its

---

[4] In a modern restatement of Walras's definitions relating to sales out of stocks, a self-oriented individual excess demand function is defined as the individual's gross demand quantity for a commodity at each possible price minus the quantity possessed by the individual (1874b, pp. 119–20; 1900, § 118, p. 123). The definition allows the derivation of the net demand and net supply of a trader who wants to add to his stock of a good or to sell some of it. That excess demand function is self-oriented because it does not take account of the offers made to the individual in the way that is about to be described.

price or when to leave it unchanged; and a service supplier does not experience an individual excess demand quantity for his service and does not know when to lower its price or when to leave it unchanged.

It might be speculated that Walras provided for an alternative way for entrepreneurs to express their demands for services through his assumption that they make pledges to supply consumer goods. That speculation is incorrect. An entrepreneur's demands for each of the particular services that are combined to make an output are not expressed by the quantity of the output he offers for sale, and cannot be deduced from a knowledge of that quantity. That obvious fact has been emphasized in relation to Walras's written pledges models in chapter 16. Moreover, entrepreneurs' offers of goods are made in the goods markets in which their pricing is supposed to occur, and those markets are not the same as the markets in which offers of supplies of services are made and in which their pricing is supposed to occur. The model is therefore structurally incomplete in that it does not provide a point of contact between entrepreneurs and service suppliers in a pricing process. To remedy that deficiency, Walras should have assumed that the entrepreneurs make offers to buy services in the markets in which the suppliers of services make offers to sell them.

Equations of demand not part of written pledges model: The situation of the suppliers of any service in Walras's monetary model of written pledges markets is reflected in the state of affairs at the level of the market as a whole for that service. The suppliers of services express their offers through making pledges, so there is a market supply function of each service. There are, however, no individual demand functions for services, so there are no market demand functions for them. Consequently, there are no market excess demand functions for them. Thus, it is also clear from the perspective attained by examining each input market as a whole that there cannot be a pricing process in it and that equilibrium prices of the services that are supposed to be used to make consumer goods do not exist.

It is true that Walras presented equations involving market demand for productive services in his lesson called "Equations of Capital Formation and Credit," and that he stated in the lesson called "Equations of Circulation and of Money" that they were part of his last comprehensive model. Nevertheless, those equations are not part of that model, because it does not contain the behavior symbolized by the equations. Indeed, their implications conflict with the structure of the model and the behavior of the participants in it. The equations could be valid representations of aspects of the model only if, among other features, it contained demanders who express their demands by making written pledges and entrust them to agents in the marketplace and direct them to raise the price when appropriate. On every occasion when

Walras mentioned the structure of the model, however, he assumed that those activities do not take place. The other missing features of the monetary written pledges model are equally crucial. For example, as will be seen, the written pledges cannot be fulfilled, an additional reason why it is not a functioning system and why his equations do not relate to the model.

The output markets

Documentation of the use of written pledges to supply consumer goods: The justification for asserting that the output side of consumer-good industries is written pledges markets in the last comprehensive model is Walras's statement that "after the preliminary tatonnements made with *written pledges,* the equilibrium once established in principle, . . . the delivery of products will also begin immediately and will continue in a determinate manner during the same period" (1900, § 273, pp. 298–99).

Organized competitive markets: Walras made it clear that the written pledges markets for consumer goods in the last comprehensive model are monetary by indicating that each product is supposed to be priced in its own retail market and that "the payment for these products, evaluated in numeraire, will also be made in money at fixed dates" (ibid., § 273, p. 299). Thus, Walras invoked his assumption that written pledges are used in barter output markets, and then added money to them. Like the barter model, the consumer goods markets in the last comprehensive model, even though they are retail markets, are organized and freely competitive. The producers of consumer goods make written pledges to supply amounts of them per time period to consumers (ibid., § 207, p. 215) and transmit the pledges to agents who act on their behalf (ibid., § 214, p. 244).

No written pledges to buy consumer goods: Walras also assumed that consumers do not make pledges to buy the goods, and he did not provide them with any other means of expressing demands for them. Consequently, his monetary written pledges model of consumer goods markets does not generate the demand term of the equation for an individual excess demand function for a consumer good. The model is not properly constructed. A consumer does not have an experience in the marketplace that is necessary for an individual excess demand function to exist for him, so he does not know when to raise the price of the good or when to leave it unchanged. Similarly, a producer does not experience an individual excess demand function, so he does not know when to lower the price of the good or when to leave it unchanged. These considerations are reflected in the state of affairs at the level of the market as a whole. The producers express their offers of supplies through making pledges, so there is a market supply function for each consumer good. Since there are no individual demand functions for the goods, there are no market demand functions for them. Thus, it is also clear from the perspective attained by examining each output market as a whole that there cannot be a pricing process for consumer goods, and equilibrium prices for consumer goods do not exist.

It has been noted in chapter 16 that William Jaffé argued that demands for consumer goods are expressed through the consumers' written pledges of offers of services, stating in one place that their demands are thereby expressed "implicitly" (Jaffé 1967, p. 18 [241]). It should be noted here that Jaffé also persuaded himself to believe that consumers express their demands *explicitly* in Walras's model by issuing written pledges for the amounts of commodities they want to consume: "*Mutatis mutandis* the tickets *issued by buyers of products* as well as *by buyers* and sellers of services are similarly worded" (Jaffé in Walras 1954, p. 528; emphasis added). Jaffé was mistaken in both of his conflicting assertions. The incorrectness of the notion that demands are expressed implicitly by the writing of pledges to sell has been demonstrated in detail elsewhere (ch. 16). It will be repeated here briefly that implicit demands are no guide at all to producers. Producers must know explicitly that there is a demand for their particular product. Such a demand cannot be detected from the homogeneous demand for income that service suppliers express when they offer amounts of services at their quoted prices, a circumstance that is obvious in microeconomic theory and in ordinary everyday experience in the real economy. That truth is made even more evident considering that in Walras's last comprehensive model the consumers do not pay for consumer goods with services. Concerning that model, Jaffé's argument is therefore doubly wrong. Since the markets are monetary, the consumers could signal their demands for goods only by pledging to buy amounts of the goods for certain amounts of money at the quoted price, but, as has been indicated, that is something Walras did not permit them to do. As for Jaffé's assertion that participants in Walras's model make written pledges to buy services and goods, it is simply untrue. This book has documented the fact that Walras assumed that would-be demanders do not issue pledges in written pledges markets. He made that assumption in all the passages in which he described the use of written pledges (1900, § 207, p. 215; § 214, p. 224; § 251, p. 260; §257, p. 272).

Jaffé was not the only source of misconception on the matter of who issues written pledges. Joseph Schumpeter also believed that there are demanders who make written pledges to buy commodities in Walras's model, and he made that mistake independently of Jaffé's translation and commentary on the *Eléments*. Schumpeter – compounding his error by asserting that Walras assumed the use of written pledges in his model of the exchange of fixed total stocks of commodities (the oral pledges model) as well as in a model in which production occurs (Schumpeter 1954, p. 1008) – wrote that Walras's economic actors

decide to give away certain quantities of some commodities and to acquire certain quantities of others at these prices. But as we know they do not actually do so but only note on *bons* what they would '*buy*' or 'sell' at those prices should they persist (ibid., and see p. 1014; emphasis added to "buy").

Similarly, Don Patinkin quoted a passage relating to the barter model, as translated by Jaffé (1954, p. 242), in which Walras refers only to pledges being written by suppliers (1900, § 207, p. 215) and wrote that "there can be no question that this passage describes a process in which entrepreneurs and sellers of productive services merely *note their offers to buy* and sell on 'tickets' " (Patinkin 1965, p. 533; emphasis added). Michio Morishima likewise wrote that Walras's entrepreneurs make written pledges to demand the "inputs they want to . . . employ" (Morishima 1977, p. 55).

I was influenced by Jaffé's writings to make the same mistake, and all the secondary literature on Walras's last comprehensive model has been based on it. I corrected my error, however, in two articles published in 1990 in the *Revue d'economie politique* (see Acknowledgments), and since that time it should not have been perpetuated. Nevertheless, an example, presumably, of the confusion induced by Jaffé's opinion is provided by Tom Kompas's work published in 1992 ostensibly on Walras's model – "presumably" because Kompas used Jaffé's edition of the *Eléments,* and "ostensibly" because Kompas does not really deal with Walras's model. Kompas asserted that "equilibrium is established, in short, through *the issue of 'provisional contracts' or 'pledges,'* for the quantity of goods and services *demanded* and supplied, until price adjustments guarantee a long-run outcome" (Kompas 1992, p. 32; emphasis added). Kompas's exposition of the model must be disregarded because of his attributing to Walras the idea that demanders of goods and services make written pledges.

The market for consumable services

In a lesson preceding the ones on the last comprehensive model, Walras mentioned that consumers exchange consumable services with each other. As has been noted in chapter 16, he did not provide the barter submodel of the exchange of those services with crucial structural elements. Most notably, he did not assume that either buyers or sellers in that submodel make either written or oral pledges. The condition of those services is not satisfactory in Walras's monetary model either, because in it he mentioned markets for them only in the way described above and by repeating his remark that consumers hold cash balances in order to buy consumable services (1900, § 273, p. 300). His remarks justify the presumption that Walras wanted consumer services to be sold in written pledges markets in the last comprehensive model.

Nevertheless, the submodel is not a functioning system because there is no expression of demands for consumable services. To contribute to making it complete, the reader of the *Eléments* would have to provide a feature that cannot be inferred from any of Walras's remarks and that conflicts with his decisions on the structure of both his barter and monetary written pledges models – namely, that consumers also make pledges to buy consumable services. In any event, the reader probably would not want to bother to make the model complete because he would probably balk at Walras's idea that consumers sell services to each other through the instrumentality of agents in organized markets. The reader may prefer to construct other types of models of markets for consumable services that are more reasonable, but, like a complete written pledges model of such markets, they would not be a part of Walras's last comprehensive model that Walras actually constructed.

III. New capital goods

The input markets

Yet another indication of Walras's inability to undertake sustained work on the last comprehensive model is that he failed to write anything specifically about the input markets of capital-goods industries in it. Nevertheless, he implied that he assumed that the input markets for services used in the capital-goods industries in the model are written pledges markets in the passage, already quoted, in which he followed the statement that written pledges are used in the first phase of the model with the statement that services are delivered in its second phase (ibid., § 274, p. 302). He evidently included services used to make capital goods in that statement. Furthermore, some of the broad outlines of how he appears to have conceived of the structure of markets for services that are supposed to be used to make capital goods in the last comprehensive model can be inferred from his treatment of the market for such services in the barter model of written pledges markets. Thus, it can be presumed that as in the barter model, written pledges are made by those who supply services to capital goods producers in the monetary model. Walras also assumed in the barter model that the producers of new capital goods do not make written pledges to buy services, and he did not provide them with any other means of expressing demands for them. He wrote nothing about the monetary model that would lead the reader to suppose it differs in those respects from the barter model.

Walras implied that the markets for the input of services into capital goods industries in the last comprehensive model are monetary. This is evident because he stated with reference to all types of services in that model – and hence implied with reference to those used in capital-goods industries – that after written pledges are used to find equilibrium prices, "the payment for these services . . . will be made in money" (ibid., § 273, pp. 298–99). The use of money in the input markets and in the output markets in the model of new capital-goods industries makes it even more glaringly evident that Walras should have furnished the input markets with a demand side. He could not use the notion that he implicitly employed in his barter model – and that did not make sense even there (ch. 16) – that entrepreneurs' demands for services are expressed by their offers of new capital goods to the service suppliers. The notion did not make sense because in the barter model each commodity is priced in its own market with the use of the numeraire, and because an offer of a type of capital good does not indicate the amounts of the various services needed in its confection. Even if the notion had been sound, Walras could not use it in his last comprehensive model because the producers of the goods cannot offer them as payment for services in that model. They are supposed to pay for the services with money.

Inasmuch as suppliers of services in the last comprehensive model make written pledges to supply them, there are expressions of individual supplies of services used to make capital goods. As a result of the lack of pledges to buy the services, however, there are no expressions of individual demands for them. Consequently, neither service suppliers nor entrepreneurs in capital goods industries have individual excess demand functions in the input markets. Suppliers of a service do not know when to change the price, and would-be buyers of it neither know when to change the price nor have they any means of doing so, inasmuch as they do not make pledges to buy and have no agents. These considerations are reflected in there being market supply functions for the services that should be used to make capital goods in the model, but no market demand functions for them, and therefore no market excess demand functions for them. Thus, it is also clear from the perspective attained by examining each service market as a whole that there cannot be a pricing process in it, and that equilibrium prices of the services that are supposed to be used to make capital goods do not exist in the model.

The output markets

Use of written pledges: The markets for new capital goods in the last comprehensive model are written pledges markets. Walras implied this by his assumption that written pledges are used in markets for products (1900, § 273, pp. 298–99), because in the passage in which he made it, "products" appears to include new durable capital goods. Even clearer on this matter is his statement that the different phases constituted by the processes of pricing, production, and distribution of new durable capital goods can be identified "by means of the assumption of written pledges" (ibid., § 274, p. 302). Walras wrote nothing more about the use of written pledges in that connection. He assumed, however, that written pledges are used in the markets in which new capital goods are offered for sale in his barter model, so the reader who wishes for more details can fill them in for himself, presumably drawing them from the barter model and adapting them to the monetary model. Thus, if the markets for acquiring new capital goods in this monetary written pledges model can be assumed to be like the markets for acquiring new capital goods in the barter model, then they are organized (ch. 16). Also, in the barter model the producers write out pledges indicating how many new capital goods of a given type they will supply per time period at the quoted price, provided that it is a price at which trade is allowed to occur (1900, § 251, p. 260), and the reader can conjecture that the same is done in the monetary model. The producers in the barter model submit the written pledges to agents, who act as their representatives in the marketplace (ibid. § 214, p. 224; ch. 16), and the same can be assumed to happen in the monetary model.

Other properties of the markets: It can be presumed that Walras assumed that the markets for new capital goods are monetary. He did not explicitly state that they are sold for money, but he specified with reference to "products" that "the payment for these products, evaluated in numeraire, will also be made in money" (ibid., § 273, p. 299). Since he did not restrict the meaning of the word "products" in that sentence, he evidently included new capital goods among them. Moreover, as will be seen, he indicated that savers save in money, which obviously implies that they acquire new capital goods by spending money.

Walras was equally vague about the other properties of the markets for new capital goods in his last comprehensive model. He introduced two different procedures by which savers finance the production of new capital goods – namely, by making long-term loans and by purchasing new capital goods, but he furnished few details about either procedure. Instead of developing a model in which both of them operate at the same time, he showed a disposition to pick one of them to the exclusion of the other, and also to vary in his choice of which one he represented as being his exclusive model. His treatment of this matter provides an excellent example of the confusion that results from an unclear and incomplete specification of the structural features of a model. As a consequence, the reader who insists on exegesis is forced to do the work of disentangling and trying to make sense out of Walras's fragmentary comments.

In the submodel in which Walras assumed that the production and purchase of new durable capital goods can be done exclusively through the lending of money for long terms (ibid., p. 300), he described the market as being conducted without written pledges. He nowhere connected his comments about written pledges to the model of long-term loans of money, and did not suggest that they have any applicability to it. Since the model is not a written pledges model, its examination is deferred to the next chapter.

The submodel of the purchase of new capital goods: Walras then abandoned the notion that savers *lend* new capital goods in the form of money, and adopted instead the assumption that they "*buy* new capital goods" (ibid., emphasis added). He appears to have become primarily interested in that submodel, although he lapsed once into mentioning "lending out new capital goods in the form of money" (ibid.), so we will now examine how he conceived of its structure and behavior. As it turns out, he wrote almost nothing about this matter.

Producers of new capital goods make written pledges about the quantities they will supply at the quoted price. Walras did not say so, but it can be inferred from the properties of the barter model that producers give the pledges to their agents. About the demand side of the submodel, Walras indicated that savers plan to accumulate certain amounts of money in cash balances with which to pay for new capital goods (ibid., pp. 299–300; § 278, p. 310). He was thinking of a process in which savers buy the capital goods and rent them out to entrepreneurs, as described in the barter model of written pledges markets, but with money used as the means of payment of the rental fees. It was because he had that process in mind that he did not assume that stock certificates are used in the written pledges model. Clearly, if the savers bought stocks, they would own the firms, so the capital goods would not be rented by entrepreneurs but managed by them on behalf of their owners. In reference to the monetary written pledges model, Walras made no mention of owners delegating to entrepreneurs the function of supervising the use of capital goods. Of course, in a pledges model the would-be savers do not actually save during what Walras intended to be the pricing phase because they do not actually have any incomes, inasmuch as there is no hiring of services or production during that phase.

Unfortunately for the workability of the model, Walras assumed that would-be savers do not make pledges to purchase new capital goods, and he did not provide them with any alternative method of expressing demand functions for them. Consequently, individual demand functions for capital goods do not exist in Walras's model, and would-be savers do not experience individual excess demand functions for those goods. A would-be saver therefore does not know when to bid the price up or when to leave it unchanged;

and, since he has no agent to represent him in the marketplace, he lacks any means of quoting prices. The fact that the producers offer their goods for sale for money makes it even more obvious that Walras should have assumed that the savers make written pledges to buy new capital goods with money, for they cannot pay for them with services.

Furthermore, inasmuch as there are no expressions of demand for new capital goods, a producer does not know how many units of a capital good might be requested from him per time period at the quoted price, nor even whether he should produce the good at all. The producers transmit their pledges to supply the capital goods to their agents, but the latter cannot find counterparts with whom to deal. The producers therefore do not have individual excess demand functions for capital goods, and do not know when to tell their agents to lower the price or when to leave it unchanged. The result of the absence of demand functions is that there is no pricing process in the markets for new capital goods in the last comprehensive model, and would-be savers cannot purchase new capital goods and therefore cannot rent them out.

These considerations are reflected in the state of affairs at the level of the new capital-goods markets as a whole. The producers of the capital goods make written pledges to supply them. It follows that there are individual supply functions for the goods in the model, so there is a market supply function for each of them. In the model, however, there are no individual demand functions for the goods, so there are no market demand functions for new capital goods in it. Consequently, there are no market excess demand functions for them. It is therefore also evident from the perspective attained by examining each capital goods market as a whole that there can be no pricing procedure in it, and that equilibrium prices for new capital goods do not exist in Walras's last comprehensive model. Of course, Walras wrote down equations for the demand and supply of capital goods, but they are equations that he developed in reference to the mature model in which demands are represented in the markets, even if the equations do not indicate the equilibrium values of the variables in that model. The equations do not have any connection to the last comprehensive model. They do not have referents in it, and are indeed contradictory to its properties, and would-be suppliers are unable to act out the behaviors implied by the supply equations.

Contrast of the model of the Bourse and the written pledges model of the market for new capital goods

As a matter totally different from the written pledges models – long before even thinking of them – Walras asserted that the "market for capital goods is the *Bourse*" (1877b, p. 303; 1900, § 270, p. 293), where "the prices of new capital goods are raised and lowered" (1889, p. 287; 1900, § 254, p. 267). It has been shown that by those statements he meant that the market for shares of corporate enterprises is the Bourse and that the prices of the shares are raised and lowered on it. Accordingly, as has been seen, he constructed an oral pledges model in which the shares of corporate enterprises are sold via the instrumentality of stock certificates on a freely competitive organized securities exchange, and in which savers pay money for the certificates (1874b, pp. 49–50; 1889, pp. 67–69; chs. 4 and 5).

There are significant differences between that model and Walras's written pledges model of new capital-goods markets, although the manner of expression of the pledges is not the source of the differences.[5] The first difference is that in Walras's oral pledges model, the pledges are made by both buyers and sellers, whereas in his written pledges model, the pledges are made only by sellers. Thus, in the oral pledges model, both demands and supplies are expressed and the model is complete since there is a pricing process in any particular market. In contrast, the demand side of the monetary written pledges model of new capital goods markets is missing, and there is no pricing process in it. The second difference is that in the oral pledges model, capital goods are acquired indirectly via the purchase of stock certificates, so entrepreneurs are managers hired by the stockholders, whereas in the written pledges model, the new capital goods are priced in their own markets, acquired directly by the savers, and rented out to entrepreneurs – or, rather, those activities would occur if the model were complete.

The oral pledges model of the Bourse and the written pledges models of markets for new capital goods are therefore models of different markets. Walras presented them both in the fourth edition of the *Eléments,* but he did not draw attention to the differences between the two types of models, and indeed seemed oblivious to their differences. He did not even segregate all his references to the models into particular parts of the book, nor did he integrate them. In the midst of discussions of the barter model of written

---

[5] Oral and written pledges are used in some markets. About the manner of submitting pledges to agents, in the French Bourse some are written at the time they are submitted to agents, "but according to the custom the Agents de Change may accept telephone or verbal orders from their clients" (Spray 1964, p. 165), as is the practice in the United States. On the New York Stock Exchange, orders that are made orally before the market opens are registered as written pledges in the order book of the specialist. About the manner of using the pledges in the trading process, whether the pledges made by the owners of the shares and by the owners of purchasing power are oral or written, the amounts pledged and the associated prices are publicized orally by the agents on the floor of the exchange. About agreements that are concluded, the oral pledges made in stock markets are ultimately confirmed by written order slips made out by agents, by written confirmations sent to buyers indicating the terms of the transaction and the amount owed, and by written pledges to deliver stock. In some real markets, however, only written pledges are accepted, as in the U.S. market for new Treasury bills. In some, only oral pledges are used, as in oral auctions.

pledges markets for new capital goods, in which there are no securities, Walras retained passages dating from the first two editions that indicated that the oral pledges model of the Bourse has an important place in his economic theory (1889, p. 287; 1900, § 254, p. 267; 1877b, pp. 303–4; 1889, p. 311; 1900, § 270, pp. 293–94). Walras did not see that he should have modified his model of the Bourse and incorporated it into the last comprehensive model. It is another major defect of the last comprehensive model that it does not have a securities market.

Short-term loans

Walras – in a single sentence – alluded to what appears to be a written pledges market for short-term loans. The evidence, such as it is, is that twenty-five lines after referring in a general way to "the assumption of *written pledges*" (1900, § 274, p. 302), he assumed that "*circulating* capital goods [are] borrowed by the entrepreneurs from the capitalists *in money,* at the prices 1, p_b... p_m..., *for short terms,* that is, until just after the sales" (ibid.) of the commodities they are used to make. Walras did not, however, explicitly state that savers make written pledges to lend the money, nor did he write anything more about the market for short-term loans.

Three phases

Walras assumed that the monetary model of markets in which written pledges are used has three phases. His exposition of this matter has been frequently quoted as though it were an especially constructive part of his modeling of the last comprehensive model. In fact, quite apart from the circumstance that his model does not contain any of the phases to which he referred because he did not provide it with features that would enable it to be a functioning system, his exposition is redundant and flawed, revealing in two additional respects the decline of his analytical powers. Walras had already explained the first two phases just three pages earlier (ibid., § 273, pp. 298–99). Nevertheless, he stated once more that the first phase is one of "*preliminary tatonnements*" (ibid., § 274, p. 302). That is the disequilibrium phase during which prices are supposed to be changed and the equilibrium set is supposed to be found. Then, he repeated, there is "the *static* phase of the effective establishment *ab ovo* of the equilibrium relative to the delivery of productive services and products during the period of time considered, under the specified conditions, without changes in the given conditions of the problem." Third, there is "a *dynamic* phase of continual disturbance of the equilibrium by changes in those given conditions and the continual reestablishment of the equilibrium that is disturbed in that way" (ibid.). Walras went on to assert that "new fixed or circulating capital goods, which will be delivered during the second phase, . . . will not function until the third phase, thus constituting a first change in the given conditions of the problem" (ibid.).

The first problem with Walras's modeling in those sentences is created by his assertion that products, including new fixed and circulating capital goods, are produced and distributed during the second phase. That has been presumed to save his model from a disruptive parametric change before equilibrium is reached (Van Daal 1995). In actuality, if the model were a functioning system, Walras's supposition would not save it. The given conditions of the problem could not be constant in the second phase; it could not be true that the "first change in the given conditions" occurs, as Walras believed, in "the third phase." To say that commodities are produced in the second phase implies that incomes are paid and inventories of the producers are changed in that phase. To say that goods are distributed in the second phase means that the holdings of them by buyers of all types change in that phase. The changes in the holdings of durable capital goods result in a series of new supply functions for their services in the second phase, and that alters the set of equilibrium equations and changes the equilibrium itself, before any other phase is reached. Walras's statements are simply illogical.

The second problem in the modeling is Walras's singular remarks about statics and dynamics. After the equilibrium values of all ex ante variables are found in the model, he wrote, it enters a "static phase" in which goods and services are delivered (1900 § 274, p. 302). By a static phase in this context, Walras meant one in which the conditions he wanted to be parameters are truly constant. Expressing a faulty view of the implications of static versus dynamic equilibrium, Walras contended that "if the society settled up its outstanding debts at the end of the second phase, the *old capital goods,* both *fixed and circulating,* would be paid back by the entrepreneurs to the capitalists *in kind.*" The old durable capital goods would be returned intact to the capitalists, and the nondurable (circulating) capital goods would be replaced with "similar" ones (ibid.). Nondurable capital goods, in Walras's *Eléments,* can be used only once. That is why he wrote that the nondurable capital goods would be replaced by similar ones, not by the original ones. In contrast, he remarked, "if the economy continues in the state of dynamic equilibrium, it is appropriate to assume that the *circulating* capital goods [are] borrowed . . . *in money*" (ibid.). Thus, he believed that in the static phase of his model the short-term loans must be made and repaid in kind, even though he was referring to a state of his monetary model. He indicated he believed that the assumption of borrowing in money is appropriate only for a dynamic situation. In short, he implied that a medium of exchange cannot be used in a static state. His view was obviously a mistake. The goods would be lent and repaid in money in the "static phase" of his monetary model just as in the "dynamic phase," as Walras appears to have recognized in other passages in his lessons on money (for example, ibid., § 273, pp. 299–301). Having expressed those opinions, Walras abandoned any intention he may have had of completing a written pledges model of the market for short-term loans, and did not endow the model with any other structural or behavioral features.

Some other omissions

The written pledges component of the last comprehensive model is incomplete both for the reasons given and because Walras did not provide it with a workable process of the adjustment of output of either consumer goods or new capital goods. He mentioned that "new capital goods, fixed or circulating," are delivered "at prices that are equal to the average cost of production" (1900, § 274, p. 302), but he did not write anything else about the matter. The reader may perhaps infer from that equilibrium condition that Walras intended the disequilibrium adjustment process he wanted to transpire in his written pledges barter model (ch. 16) to be transported mentally by the reader to the monetary model and to be adapted by the reader in whatever ways are necessary. This is another of the many examples of how Walras abdicated the responsibility of undertaking the necessary work of theoretical construction in his last comprehensive model. Unfortunately, his discussion of adjustments of desired disequilibrium rates of output and of the eventual determination of actual rates of output in the barter model does not make sense because there is no pricing process in that model. Similarly, such a process cannot be generated by the structure of Walras's monetary written pledges markets because of the absence of demand functions in them.

Even if the reader adds features that generate demand functions, those markets would still be unworkable because they lack a number of other crucial features. First, they lack the information collection and dissemination mechanisms, discussed in previous chapters, that are necessary to enable the equilibration of a multimarket system. Second, the system of written pledges markets is also incomplete because it does not include some important markets. Walras did not develop a monetary written pledges submodel of the sale of old capital goods. He did not mention that individuals, and incorporated and unincorporated enterprises buy old capital goods and that the ownership of heterogeneous collections of old capital goods is changed by the sale of old securities. Moreover, he did not construct written pledges monetary submodels of the sale of land, the market for long-term loans, securities, or the market for primary materials. Those were serious omissions. Without those markets, a model that is supposed to represent a multimarket monetary economy cannot function, even if it were to be complete in all other respects. Third, the monetary written pledges markets lacks features that would enable the fulfillment of pledges, as will now be shown.

IV. Fulfillment of pledges

Although Walras's monetary written pledges model cannot in fact reach an equilibrium set of prices because it is not a functioning system, he nevertheless assumed that a set of equilibrium prices is found for all commodities and that all participants are informed about that happening. The reader may choose to accept that unsubstantiated postulate as the starting point for a discussion of the remaining aspects of the model that Walras mentioned or implied, in which case the following observations can be made.

It will be recalled that Walras stated that after the equilibrium prices have been found in the barter model of written pledges markets, the agents distribute the pledges and they are fulfilled by the direct exchange of goods and services (1900, § 214, p. 224; ch. 16). Walras neglected to make a similar mention of the distribution or fulfillment of pledges in connection with the monetary written pledges markets. Nevertheless, it is possible he thought that the pledges are distributed by the agents in the monetary model as in the barter model and that a monetary version of their fulfillment occurs. The basis of this speculation is that Walras stated that in the monetary model, written pledges are used during the phase in which the ex ante equilibrium values of all variables are determined, and that actual hiring, production, and distribution of goods occur after the search for equilibrium prices has been completed. The relevant passage can usefully be quoted again:

After the preliminary tatonnements conducted with *written pledges,* once the equilibrium has been established in principle, the delivery of services will begin immediately and will continue in a determinate manner during the period of time under consideration. . . . The delivery of products will similarly commence immediately and will continue in a determinate manner during the same period (ibid., § 273, p. 298–99; and see ibid., § 274, p. 302).

Just as in the barter written pledges model, however, the process of distributing pledges cannot be performed in the monetary model. This results from the lack of pledges to buy, for it prevents the agents from knowing how much of each service is needed by each producer, and from knowing how much of each type of consumer good and capital good is wanted by each consumer. The agents do not know how to distribute the pledges, so they cannot be fulfilled. Even if those problems did not exist in the model, an insurmountable difficulty would be posed by the fact that there would not be a workable distribution system because the pledges to produce goods are made for amounts too large to be given to any single consumer or saver, because many commodities cannot be fractionated, and by other difficulties of the sort delineated in chapter 16.

A contrast can now be made between Walras's mature model of tatonnement in the production of consumer commodities and capital goods and his attempt to devise a different model of tatonnement in his last comprehensive model (1899, p. 103; 1900, §§ 206, 251, 273–74, pp. 214–15, 224, 260, 298). His aim in the mature tatonnement model was to formulate a realistic dynamic process that incorporated disequilibrium production and sales. His aim in his written pledges model was not realism but devising a model that would eliminate disequilibrium production and sales and would thereby have the solutions to his equations as its equilibrium values. As has been shown, his attempt to construct the written pledges model was a failure. The model is incomplete in major respects and therefore does not contain a dynamic process, so he did not construct a second model of tatonnement. There is no process of changing prices in the model.

V. Conclusion

This chapter has examined the written pledges markets in Walras's monetary model with the aim of discovering their structural and behavioral features. The conclusion is that he did not endow these markets with features that would be necessary to make them viable. Walras's notion of a general-equilibrium model of written pledges markets is fatally flawed because it lacks any expressions of demands, lacks written pledges markets for money, for circulating physical capital, and for a number of other important commodities, and lacks an allocation mechanism. Without those features, the consumer and capital goods industries in the model cannot function. The model is not only incomplete, it is hopelessly unrealistic. It was intended by Walras to exclude production, exchange, consumption, and saving until a set of prices has been found at which all excess demand quantities are zero – merely intended to do so, because in fact it is not a functioning system. It is, in short, merely an incomplete sketch.

At the beginning of this chapter it was indicated that a related matter would be examined – determining what foundations Walras may have provided to justify the equations of general equilibrium that he presented as part of his last comprehensive model. The conclusion is that the equations do not describe the behavior of those markets. The equations contain symbols and relationships purporting to represent demand, pricing behavior, and equilibrium, and imply a process of the distribution of commodities, but the market institutions, technology, and procedures do not generate or permit those phenomena, and are indeed contradictory to the structural foundations and the behavior the equations would require for their validation.

It has been noted that Walras claimed that when he introduced written pledges he reconstructed his entire model of general equilibrium on the basis of their use (1900, p. XIII). In fact, the submodels discussed in this chapter are the only ones in the last comprehensive model in connection with which he assumed explicitly or by implication that written pledges are used. This chapter has therefore dealt in its entirety with the written pledges component of the last comprehensive model. It now remains to investigate Walras's treatment of other markets in that model and to provide an overall characterization and evaluation of the model.

Other models and conclusion

CHAPTER 18

The markets for circulating capital and money in the last comprehensive model

This chapter explains and evaluates Walras's treatment of markets for circulating capital and money in his last comprehensive model, and evaluates the model as a whole. It is shown that although he assumed that written pledges are used in the markets for certain commodities to eliminate disequilibrium transactions and production, he also assumed, regarding many of precisely the same commodities, that disequilibrium transactions and production occur in their markets. Moreover, he made the redundant and illogical assumption that there are markets for the services of nondurable goods as well as for the goods themselves. For those and for other reasons, it is concluded that the resulting model is not a functioning system.

I. Introduction

Circulating capital and money included in the last comprehensive model

It was explained in chapter 17 that the term "Walras's last comprehensive model" is used because he represented the various markets he mentioned in lessons 29 and 30 as being parts of a single whole. With reference to the submodels discussed in this chapter, he contended that he had introduced

the rigorous equations of desired money balances and of circulating physical capital into the system of general equilibrium. I have thus completely finished static economics: that is to say, I have completely solved the problem that consists in using as a point of departure given utilities and given quantities possessed of all the species of wealth by a certain number of exchangers, to establish rationally a complete equilibrium of economic society at a given moment (Walras to Hermann Laurent, March 24, 1899, in 1965, *3*, letter 1396, p. 66).

Walras also stated in the *Eléments* that his model of circulating capital completes his system of general equilibrium (1900, § 272, p. 298), and he presented the equations in lessons 29 and 30 as relating to a single comprehensive economic system with fiat money, or a single comprehensive economic system with commodity money, depending on which variety of money he had under consideration (see also ibid., pp. IX–X).

The lessons in which Walras presented his submodels of circulating capital and money reveal in many ways the condition of his state of mind in his last

399

phase of theoretical activity. They convey a strong impression of disorganization and analytical confusion. They are full of poor definitions, illogical constructions, badly arranged statements, lacunae, conflations of separate topics, contradictions, and incomplete treatments. The exposition is atrocious: long but elliptical sentences, rambling discourses, symbols and words crowded together in baffling sequences. Once again, the explanation for that situation was the state of Walras's cerebral and nervous system.

Origin of the material: When he undertook preparation of the fourth edition of the *Eléments,* Walras wrote that "in the course of this preparation" he had found a final problem to solve, that of the *Equations of Circulation*" (Walras to Gustav Maugin, May 6, 1899, in 1965, *3,* letter 1401, p. 71). His health had deteriorated further by the time he took up that problem in a separate paper (1899), and the task of writing it, he complained, "has made me very tired and quite indisposed" (Walras to Gustav Maugin, May 6, 1899, in 1965, *3,* letter 1401, p. 701). He finished it only "with infinite difficulty and fatigue which have made me ill and left me in that condition all summer. I recovered only by means of rest" (Walras to Adrienne Belhache, November 19, 1899, in 1965, *3,* letter 1429, p. 93). At the time that Walras wrote the paper, he had not yet conceived of the device of written pledges, so the paper refers throughout to a model in which there is nothing to prevent disequilibrium transactions and production from occurring – and in which those phenomena do in fact occur. After he had finished the paper, Walras thought of the device of written pledges, and furnished a sketchy two paragraph statement about it in a note he attached to the end of the paper (1899, p. 103).

Insertion of the material into the Eléments: Walras then revised the monetary part of the *Eléments* in 1900 in the sense that he divided the paper into two parts, labeled one of them "lesson 29" and the other "lesson 30," inserted the sentences that are in the note here and there into lesson 29, and added a few passages and equations. He did not mention written pledges in lesson 30 nor imply their use in the submodels of that lesson. Thus, Walras composed the substance and most of the details of his last comprehensive model in the *Eléments* with "infinite difficulty and fatigue," and without having had the device of written pledges in mind. He had expanded somewhat on that device in three paragraphs written in connection with his barter flow model (1900, § 207, p. 215; § 251, p. 260; § 257, p. 272), and he indicated that he wanted to construct a comprehensive model that included nothing but written pledges markets (1900, p. VIII), but by the time he reached the monetary lessons, his capacity to remold them in accordance with a written pledges process was exhausted, and he left much of his last comprehensive model unmodified by that device. To a friend he mentioned inserting the equations of circulation into the *Eléments,* and again described his condition at the time that he was working on his last comprehensive model. His statement is an admission that he had become unable to undertake complex analytical revisions:

I have been ill . . . all summer, unable to take walks, capable only of going to sit down in the groves of trees and to listen to the north wind soughing in the high fir trees and to look at the clouds moving through the blue air. With this regimen one gets away from concrete realities and closes oneself more and more into one's idealistic dream. I have renounced the two things which fatigue and enervate me: the problems of mathematical economics and formulations of contemporary propaganda (Walras to Georges Renard, October 6, 1899, in 1965, *3,* letter 1425, p. 90).

Walras also wrote that he had "almost finished the definitive text of the *Eléments"* (ibid.), but the work took much longer than he had anticipated. In November and December 1899, while he was still working on the revision (Walras to Léon Marie, November 30, 1899, in 1965, *3,* letter 1430, p. 95), he continued to be "prey to a cerebral and nervous crisis which threatens to interrupt my work" (Walras to Léon Marie, December 24, 1899, in 1965, *3,* letter 1434, p. 100).[1] On January 22, 1900, he reported that he had finished the theory of circulation and of money and the entire fourth edition (Walras to Alfred Danbitsh, in 1965, *3,* January 22, 1900, letter 1441, p. 106). In actuality he was unable to do so until April, and by then he was "dead tired" (Walras to Etienne Lorédan Larchy, April 7, 1900, in 1965, *3,* letter 1450, p. 114). Adding to his woes was the illness and death of his wife, which so upset and fatigued him that he was hardly able to correct the last proofs of the *Eléments* (Walras to Charles Gide, August 5, 1900, in 1965, *3,* letter 1458, pp. 123–24). By October, he wrote, he could not "read or write or talk very long without having a crisis of cerebral congestion during the night. In short, my brain, which for a long time has asked for mercy has openly revolted and refuses me its service" (Walras to Louise George Renard, October 27, 1900, in 1965, *3,* letter 1460, p. 125).[2]

---

[1] Sometimes, it is true, he gave a slightly different account: "My nervous fatigue continues to make itself felt by a colic which, when it takes hold of me completely lays me low. Actually, since that does not seem to me to be dangerous, and since after all it is necessary to use one's time well, I occupy myself in my good moments by preparing the fourth and definitive edition of the *Eléments d'économie politique pure,* which is going very well and which is an occupation that is taking a little too much time and is an affair of patience rather than a head-breaker strictly speaking" (Walras to Gustav Maugin, December 31, 1899, in 1965, *3,* letter 1437, p. 102). He contradicted that observation with an overwhelming mass of comments to the opposite effect and with the quality of his work.

[2] Walras's condition continued to deteriorate. "My nerves and my brain are extremely weakened and fatigued. I can no longer write or converse without having a crisis during the night" (Walras to Charles Gide, April 6, 1903, in 1965, *3,* letter 1542, pp. 223–24). Reading, writing, or conversing for even a half an hour, he wrote, caused a nervous crisis, and although his daughter read to him and he dictated letters to her, he explained that "I do not have her read economics, and I do not dictate to her any letters except those that are as short as possible" (Walras to Charles Gide, February 28, 1904, in 1965, *3,* letter 1570, p. 246).

Not written pledges models: This chapter explains and evaluates the submodels of markets for circulating physical capital and money that Walras constructed as parts of his last comprehensive model. These are not written pledges models. The chapter is not directly concerned with Walras's theories about money or his monetary equations,[3] but with his modeling of the structure and behavior of the loan market and of certain markets in which money is used. Consequently, it does not treat such matters as the degree of Walras's adherence to a quantity theory, the differences between his treatment of fiat money and a commodity money, and the relation of his monetary theory to the work of other writers. Those and related topics have been the subject of numerous expositions and interpretations in the secondary literature. The last chapter explained Walras's submodels of the input markets for services and the output markets for consumer goods and capital goods industries, which are written pledges markets. This chapter makes reference to those markets in connection with inventories and money, explains the properties of the remaining markets in the last comprehensive model, examines the character of the model as a whole, and evaluates it.

II. Inventories

New durable capital goods

Walras began his modeling of markets for circulating capital and money with a treatment of types of commodities held in inventories. He first had to take account of new durable capital goods held in the inventories of their producers awaiting sale (1900, § 272, p. 297). Those goods, he thought, could be eliminated from consideration in his model by dealing, not with the new capital goods themselves, but with the services of new capital goods that are used in the production of any commodity (A), and with the service of ready availability they provide to producers of (A) who hold them in inventories (ibid., § 272, pp. 297–98). The latter service is the convenience of having the goods on hand so they can be used at a moment's notice to produce (A). The two types of services are demanded and supplied at their respective prices (ibid., p. 298), Walras asserted, implying that he had disposed of the matter of inventories of new capital goods held by their producers.

In that account, Walras did not do justice to his subject matter in two respects, and his confusions of thought immediately began to manifest themselves. First, he did not explain why new capital goods would be held awaiting sale in a written pledges model. They are not produced in disequilibrium, and so are not held as a result of unintended inventory accumulation.

---

[3] Jan van Daal and Albert Jolinck (1993, pp. 94–106) examine the equations that Walras used in the fourth edition of the *Eléments*.

They would be produced only if their equilibrium price is found and the goods are ordered. In the environment of certainty that Walras assumed for his model (ibid., § 273, p. 300), the future stream of orders would be known to the producers, and the delivery of the goods would be expected as soon as they are produced. Consequently, it is not obvious why inventories of new capital goods would be held in the model. The reader of Walras's account has to supply the reasoning that even if equilibrium and certainty exist, the impossibility of having a perfectly smoothly working process of producing and delivering new capital goods requires that some amount of them be held in inventories. Second, Walras was mistaken when he supposed that the question of the determination of the levels of "new capital goods which producers hold for sale" (ibid., § 272, p. 297) could be eliminated in the way he described. He did not address the issue. Instead, by referring to the services of the new capital goods in the production of (A) he began, obviously unwittingly, to consider a different batch of new capital goods. That batch is owned by a group of entrepreneurs – the producers of (A) – that differs from the group of entrepreneurs – the producers of the capital goods – that holds the inventories that were the initial object of his analysis.

As for the "service of ready availability," or, more briefly, the "service of availability," inasmuch as Walras had thought of it to explain the holdings of inventories, the reader of the *Eléments* expects that Walras would use that concept to explain the inventories of new capital goods held by their producers, for that is the problem he had selected for examination. Instead, once again, he changed the subject to that of the service rendered by inventories of capital goods held by a different group of entrepreneurs – namely, those who buy such goods and hold them for later use to produce (A). The new capital goods their producers hold in inventories are not used by the latter, so the goods do not render them the productive services or the service of availability in the production of (A) that Walras mentioned. The levels of use of productive services that capital goods render to their users affect the size of inventories of such goods that those users hold. But those levels are not sufficient to explain the levels of inventories of capital goods held by their producers, a matter Walras left unexplained. Clearly he became confused about his subject matter, and inadvertently did nothing to eliminate the need for considering the equilibrating process in the holding of new capital goods by their producers or the equilibrium conditions regarding those inventories.

Nondurable goods

Walras then turned to the matter of the holding of inventories of nondurable goods (ibid., §273, p. 299). He gave the name "circulating capital goods" to those items. They circulate in the sense that they are used once – any nondurable item can be used only once because the use of it transforms it into something else – and are then replaced. Walras argued that the reason for holding inventories of nondurables is that they provide the service of the convenience of ready availability (ibid., §275, pp. 302–4). The inventories are of two types.

First, there are nondurable consumer goods held by consumers. Each consumer wants to acquire the amounts of inventories that maximize his utility, in accordance with his utility functions for the inventories' services of ready availability (ibid., §273, p. 299). Walras did not explain why consumers in his model hold stocks of nondurable goods to use for future consumption even though, assuming that equilibrium is reached, they know their future income streams and planned consumption. The reason is clear, as can be shown by a simple example. A consumer keeps some bread in his kitchen because he would not like to leave his house to purchase a slice of bread each time he wants to eat one. Moreover, bread is sold by the loaf, so he has to hold a stock of it until the loaf is consumed.

Second, there are nondurable goods held in inventories by businesses. Walras identified three types of these goods (ibid., §272, p. 297). First is primary materials that businesses have bought and are holding for future use as inputs. These include raw materials and semi-finished goods (1877b, p. 218; 1889, p. 201; 1900, §173, p. 181). Walras did not explain why producers hold inventories of those goods in equilibrium even though they know the size and timing of all future orders for the goods the inputs are used to make. The reader can supply the reasoning, however, that even in a world in which there is certainty on those matters, producers would find it impossible to always purchase each amount of a nondurable input just before it is used. Accidents, natural disasters, and inefficiencies prevent the replacement of the inputs always precisely at the time they are used, whether they are made by the producer who uses them or purchased by him from others. Even if producers greatly reduce inventories, as has been done by automobile manufacturers, they nevertheless hold some inventories of the inputs, draw on them, and replace them either steadily or at intervals. The second type of good is consumer nondurables that their producers hold for future sale. They store them in warehouses and on shelves and on display in sales establishments (1900, §273, p. 229). The goods disappear from the firms' inventories when they are sold, and the firms then produce new goods to replace them. The equilibrium quantities of the inventories are those that result in equality between price and average cost for outputs, and thus depend on the production functions as well as on market conditions (ibid.). The third type of good is primary materials their producers hold for future sale.

Walras classified the first type of good by itself under one heading, and the other two together under another heading. He contended that the two headings can be reduced to a single one – that the three types of nondurables can be combined into one category. To do so, he asserted,

it suffices to assume that the coefficient of production of each product (A) made with primary material (M), a_m, includes both the quantity of the service of ready availability of primary materials held *in the workshop* as inputs and that of primary materials held *on display* for sale. Then the quantity demanded of the service (M) at the price p_m, equal to the existing quantity Q_m, will include the primary materials mentioned in the two headings with which we are concerned (ibid., § 272, pp. 297–98).

There are two difficulties raised by that assertion. First, Walras had stated that he wanted to deal with the holdings of primary materials by their producers. In the foregoing quotation, however, he began to deal instead with the question of the service of availability of other batches of the primary materials – namely, those held by the producers of (A). That explains why they hold inventories of primary materials inputs but not why or at what levels batches of primary materials outputs are held in inventories by their producers. Reference to the former inventories therefore in no way makes it possible to include them along with the latter as though all the goods in question were a single type of phenomenon with one explanation. Second, Walras forgot to carry out his promise to indicate how consumer nondurables held by their producers could be combined into one category along with primary materials, and for that reason also failed to combine the three types of goods into one category. Indeed, he did not write an additional word about consumer nondurables in the section he devoted to classifying the commodities held in inventories. Moreover, in his ensuing investigations he forgot his interest in combining the three types of goods, and proceeded to treat their markets as though he had never contemplated doing so.

Subjects and objectives of the modeling

If Walras had wanted to develop a model of inventories, he would have had to deal not only with inventories of nondurables but also with inventories of durable goods held by their producers and by consumers. He did not develop such a model, and his brief foray into the analysis of inventories persuaded him that he did not need to concern himself with anything but nondurable goods and money. Those items became the subjects of models of markets that occupied his attention in lessons 29 and 30 of the *Eléments*, and accordingly those models are the topics of the next two sections of this chapter.

The basis for those models is that from time to time, the nondurable goods held in inventories are used if they are inputs, or are sold if they are outputs. Consumers and retailers draw on their inventories to replace the goods they buy in markets. Producers hold inventories of outputs, and when they sell them, they must replace them. This means the producers must use up some of the inputs they have in inventories, which in turn means acquiring replacements of them in markets. Furthermore, in Walras's last comprehensive model, nondurable goods are supposed to be purchased with money, so he needed to analyze the determinants of the amounts of money consumers and businesses want to hold to purchase those commodities (ibid., § 273, p. 299). Also, individuals are supposed to provide savings to finance the production and purchase of nondurable and durable capital goods, so Walras had to consider money balances accumulated for making those purposes. His objectives therefore became those of analyzing, first, the adjustments of markets in which purchases are made of nondurable goods held in inventories by consumers and businesses; second, the adjustments of markets in which the financing of the production and purchase of circulating and durable capital goods is arranged; third, the processes by which equilibrium balances of money are determined; and, fourth, the equilibrium conditions in regard to each of the foregoing aspects of his model. His efforts to achieve those objectives will now be examined.

III. Circulating capital goods

Services of availability of nondurables

Walras began the topic of the functioning of the circulating capital-goods markets by considering states of disequilibrium. At this point, he chose to assume that in his model there are markets for the services of availability of nondurables in addition to markets for the nondurables themselves. Here is how he expressed the matter:

> These circulating capital goods (A'), (B')... (M)... yield their services of availability exactly like the fixed capital goods (K), (K'), (K'')... yield their useful services. The prices $p_{a'}, p_{b'},... p_{m'}...$ [of the services of nondurables] are determined like the prices $p_k, p_{k'}, p_{k''}...$ [of the services of durable capital goods] and the prices $p_b... p_m...$ [of the nondurables themselves] like the prices $P_k, P_{k'}, P_{k''}...$ [of durable capital goods] (ibid., § 278, p. 309).

By "determined like the prices . . ." he meant determined by Walrasian pricing (ch. 5), to which he had referred a few sentences earlier (ibid., § 277, p. 308) – that is, he did not mean "determined by the use of written pledges."

Walras believed, without providing a justification or explanation, that his assumption that there are markets for the services of availability of nondurables is necessary in order to introduce circulating capital goods into a "static" model (ibid, p. XIV), by which in that context he meant one that reaches a stable set of equilibrium magnitudes as distinct from one in which there is an equilibrium path of growth. Since Walras wrote down equations for the supply of and demand for the services of availability of nondurables, it appeared to him that all was well on the ground that he had as many equations as unknowns and therefore, he believed, that economically possible solutions exist for the unknowns he had created.

Services of nondurables a nonsensical concept

Generations of writers on Walras have uncritically repeated his remarks about the services of nondurables and his equations relating to them. Nevertheless, they do not make sense. In the real economy, the service of a durable capital good is priced and sold separately from the good, but the service of availability of a nondurable good, just like its want-satisfying services yielded in consumption, cannot be provided separately from the sale of the good. Consequently, there is no market for its service of availability as distinct from the market for the good itself. There is no price of the service as distinct from the price of the good itself. There is, for example, no such thing as a market for the service of availability of gasoline as distinct from the market for gasoline, no such thing as a market for the service of availability of bread as distinct from the market for bread. Indeed, it is not possible for the service of availability of a nondurable good to be sold because the service is not a property of the good when it is for sale in its market. The service is created by the purchaser if he chooses to hold the good in inventory, and the service never exists for that particular item if he chooses to consume the good immediately after sale. The service of availability is renderable to the purchaser by the simple fact of the commodity's being in his possession, and is actually rendered in the moment of its being drawn out of his inventory and used up by him.

The ultimate in absurdity on the topic was committed by Walras when he specified that consumers have "utility or want functions for the services of availability of products *and consumable services*" (1900, § 273, p. 299; emphasis added). In that sentence he was writing about services yielded by services, which makes no sense. Moreover, it is obvious that services cannot be stored; they can be used at any given moment, but they cannot be produced and then held ready to be used so they cannot have a service of availability. The peculiarity of Walras's view of nondurables in the last phase of his theoretical activity was further indicated by his insertion into the 1900 edition of the *Eléments* of the nonsensical statement that the nondurable goods – circulating capital – of businesses are amortized (1900, § 275, p. 303, n. 1).

Thus, when Walras decided to assume that the services of availability of nondurable goods are priced separately from the goods themselves, he created a fictional and nonsensical group of extra markets and prices. Moreover, there was no theoretical reason for him to introduce such markets into his model and no logical way that he could do so. He had already constructed a model for the pricing and production of the nondurable goods qua goods, and it was redundant and contrary to what would be reasonable in his model to construct another one for the pricing and production of the services they render.

In order to be perfectly clear about the construction that Walras tried to make, the comment of a reader of this chapter can be examined. The reader stated that "in principle I do not see why a price for the availability of stocks should not be paid. I may be willing to pay more for items from a store which holds a large and varied stock, getting prompter delivery and wider choice." There is, however, no difference between paying for a good and paying for an available good; the former action means the latter. The willingness of the buyer and the availability of the large and varied stock does not constitute a market for a service of availability of the goods that is different from the market for the goods. Walras contended that there are those two markets in the store, which cannot be true if the goods are nondurables. The price of the goods may indeed reflect their variety and availability in the sense that the reader meant, and the reader may well be willing to pay a premium for goods sold by the store, but the price is nevertheless simply the price of the goods. There is only one price, not two; there is only the market for the nondurable goods in the store, not one for those goods and one for their services. Moreover, as was pointed out the service of availability of a nondurable good is not the availability of a good in the sense of its being stocked by a store. The service of availability cannot be sold. It exists only if the consumer acquires and holds the good.

Tatonnement in markets for services of availability

Nevertheless, in what follows, the nonsensicalness of the notion of markets for the services of availability of nondurables will be overlooked in order to examine Walras's ideas about the properties of those markets in his model. He did not proceed, in the place in which he introduced the topic, to create the markets by assuming structural and behavior features for them. Instead, he asserted (ibid., § 277, p. 308) that the tatonnement in circulating capital goods markets is described and explained by passages (1877b, pp. 258–61; 1889, pp. 243–46; 1900, §§ 215–17, pp. 224–26) dealing with the productive and consumable services of land, personal faculties, and durable capital goods. Having written down equations of supply and demand for the services of availability of circulating capital goods, he was committed to the idea that underlying them must be markets and prices for the services. He therefore specified that the equations "are solved by the raising or lowering of the price in the case of the excess of the quantity demanded [of the service] over the quantity supplied or of the quantity supplied over the quantity demanded, just like for the services (T), (P), (K) . . ." (ibid., § 277, p. 308), thus describing the way the prices take a series of disequilibrium values during the tatonnement process. Walras should not have made that assertion because the passages do not deal with economic tatonnement or with an economic process of any kind, but with a method that a theoretician can use to solve a system of simultaneous equations (ch. 12). Moreover, in his discussion of the services of circulating capital goods in lesson 30 and in the passages in question to which he referred the reader, Walras did not mention written pledges, the latter of which circumstances is explained by the fact that he had written the passages in question more than twenty years before he developed the circulating capital model.

Disequilibrium production

If, however, his discussion of the method for solving the equations were to be interpreted as throwing light on the markets for services in his model, it would have to be concluded that those markets are ones in which disequilibrium production occurs. For example, Walras wrote in one of the sections to which he referred the reader that at one point he "assumed that $D_{a'}$ does not vary, that is to say that the producers of (A) produce always the same quantity of it regardless of the variations of p_t, p_p, p_k ... and consequently regardless of the average cost p_a" (ibid., § 215, p. 225), which is a statement that production and sales occur at disequilibrium prices and when average cost does not equal price. Thus, Walras specified that the supply and demand for the services of availability of nondurables (including primary materials) would be equalized by Walrasian pricing, but he permitted the occurrence of disequilibrium sales in the sense of sales at prices that are not part of a general-equilibrium set. He could not reasonably suppose that the amounts offered of the services of availability are changed except as functions of the changes in the amounts of the goods themselves, and are for that additional reason tied to the production of a service of disequilibrium amounts of the latter, but he did not point out that relationship.

Tatonnement in markets for circulating capital

Walras then took up the question of the structure and behavior of the markets, for nondurable consumer goods and primary materials considered as circulating capital. In examining his approach, it should be remembered that his discussion of the topic appears in lesson 29 of the *Eléments,* which he had opened by making two references to written pledges (1900, § 273, p. 298;

§ 274, p. 302). The reader of that lesson could therefore reasonably expect that he would have had the device of written pledges in the forefront of his mind and that he was going to make the markets for circulating capital goods a part of the written pledges model. Nevertheless, at the precise point at which he began to consider the equilibrating process in their markets he strayed off on a different course. He did not assume that written pledges are used, nor that agents are hired to represent the sellers of circulating physical capital, nor any of the features of a written pledges market.

Instead, he assumed, in total contradiction of everything he wanted to achieve with the device of written pledges, that circulating capital goods are produced in disequilibrium and are acquired at prices that are not part of a general-equilibrium set. During the course of the tatonnement, he specified, the equations of equilibrium relating to the prices and quantities of primary materials and consumer nondurables considered as circulating capital – namely, the goods themselves as distinct from their services, "are solved by increases or decreases of the quantity manufactured [of the goods] in the case of an excess of the price over the average cost or of the average cost over price, just as for new durable capital goods" (ibid.). Walras's last few words in that sentence – to the effect that the markets are like those for new durable capital goods – provide the reader with more detailed information about the features of the model. He reinforced and amplified those words and explained those features by referring (ibid.) the reader to earlier sections of the *Eléments* (ibid., §§ 256–58). What is to be found in those sections? The answer is that they set forth explicitly and repeatedly, and with the exception of two unintegrated sentences about written pledges (ibid., § 257, p. 272), consistently, an equilibrating process conducted through irrevocable transactions at non-general-equilibrium prices and through production at disequilibrium average costs and prices. In section 256, for example, Walras began by stating that capital goods are produced at certain average costs and sold at certain prices, and that "these prices and average costs being generally unequal, the producers of new capital goods will make profits or losses" (1889, p. 289; 1900 § 256, p. 269; and see 1877b, pp. 294–95). The producers therefore change the rates of production and the equilibrating process continues. Profits and losses are made only in disequilibrium transactions and production purely competitive models – that is, only in disequilibrium.

Thus, on the production of nondurables, Walras sketched and implied a model in which businesses buy disequilibrium amounts of inputs of labor, land services, capital-good services, and primary materials, and pay incomes at disequilibrium rates. His account of the equilibrating process also indicates that the prices of producers' and consumers' circulating capital goods are changed in markets in which sales of the goods occur that are disequilibrium ones in relation to a general-equilibrium set. He indicated that the amounts of the nondurable goods produced are changed in the course of the equilibrating process, which implies that the prices at which they and their services are sold are not part of a general-equilibrium set during the adjustment phase.

Contradictory markets for the same commodities

Inasmuch as Walras represented the submodel of the sales of the services of availability of nondurables and the submodel of circulating physical capital as being integral parts of the last comprehensive model, that model contains references both to the written pledges markets examined in chapter 17 and to markets in which disequilibrium production and sales occur. The seriousness of the consequences of Walras's procedure for his last comprehensive model becomes apparent when it is realized that he did not simply add the markets in which disequilibrium production and sales occur to the written pledges markets so as to create a complex model featuring the sale of some commodities in one type of market and the sale of others in the other type. Instead, the markets for the consumer and business circulating capital goods – about which Walras stated that the process of disequilibrium adjustments is one that occurs "by increases or decreases of the quantity produced" in disequilibrium (ibid., § 277, p. 308) – are markets for the very same commodities about which he had indicated a few pages earlier that no disequilibrium transactions or production occur. "By means of the assumption of written pledges," he had explained, it is possible clearly to distinguish the phase of the model during which equilibrium prices are found with no production or sales occurring during that process and the phase in which "the *new capital goods,* both *fixed* and *circulating,* ... will be made available" (ibid., § 274, p. 302).

Indeed, Walras stated explicitly about both consumer nondurables and primary materials that the goods he featured in the markets in his model of consumer commodities are the same items as appear in the markets for circulating capital, writing about "(A), (B), (C), (D)... (M)... being as before the commodities: consumable products, primary materials ... and (A'), (B')... (M)... being *the same* products and primary materials considered as circulating capital goods, that is, as yielding the service of ready availability" (ibid., § 275, pp. 302–3; emphasis added). It is evident that the disequilibrium transactions markets for consumer nondurables described in these paragraphs and the written pledges markets for consumer nondurables described in chapter 17 are markets for exactly the same items. The acquisition of goods to replace inventories by consumers is the acquisition of those same goods for eventual consumption purposes, and the acquisition of a good by a consumer who wants to hold some or all of it for a period of time is done in the same market and at the same price as the acquisition of that type of good by a consumer who uses it all immediately. Similarly, it is evident that the disequilibrium transactions markets for business nondurables and the written pledges markets for business nondurables are markets for exactly the same items. The acquisition of a good by a business to put it into inventory is the acquisition of that same good either to use it in production or to sell it. Walras's postulation within his monetary model of two contradictory market submodels for exactly the same items creates a nonsensical situation.

IV. Money

Types of desired balances

Walras developed a submodel of the holding and adjustment of money balances. Under that heading he presented his treatment of short-term and long-term loans of money and of the equalization of the quantity of money demanded and the supply of it. The first characteristics he specified for the submodel are the types of desired balances. Producers want to hold transactions balances to replenish their inventories of primary materials and manufactured goods held as inputs and outputs, and to purchase productive services (ibid., § 273, pp. 299–301). Consumers want to hold transactions balances of money to purchase consumer goods and consumable services. Consumers also want to accumulate balances of money savings to be used to purchase new capital goods they will rent out, and to lend to finance the production and purchase of new fixed and circulating capital goods by businesses (ibid., pp. 299–300).

Other monetary variables: Walras then provided some additional variables for his model. First, he defined a price of money (p_u), first in the sense of the aggregate desired cash balances in terms of the numeraire (A), divided by the quantity of money. The numerator is the cash balances that consumers want to hold to acquire consumer commodities plus circulating (transactions) balances that businesses want to hold plus the desired money savings of consumers (ibid., § 278, p. 312), so p_u is a measure of the average value or purchasing power of money. Second, he defined its price as its value in terms of itself when it is the numeraire, and that price is, of course, unity (ibid., § 275, p. 303). Walras defined the rate of net income, as in his mature comprehensive model, as the net rate of return on physical capital (ibid., § 281, p. 318), and he defined short-term and long-term market rates of interest on borrowed money (ibid.). Paralleling his treatment of circulating physical capital, he also introduced a phenomenon he had not detected in his previous forty years of studying money – a special market and price ($p_{u'}$) for the service of ready availability of money. Walras believed (ibid., § 275, p. 303) that $p_{u'}$ is different in principle from the rates of interest mentioned above.

He postulated that $p_{u'}$ and p_u are related in the same way as the price of a capital-good service and the price of the good itself. That is, the ratio of $p_{u'}$ to p_u is a rate of return on money, which, in the equilibrium of a fiat money model, is equal to the rate of net income (ibid.).

Markets for loans

As implied by those remarks about rates of interest, Walras assumed in his model that there are markets for short-term and long-term loans, in each of which the financing of the production and purchase of goods is arranged with the use of balances in which are accumulated "the daily sum of savings available for lending in the form of money" (ibid., § 273, p. 300). He expressed a concern with describing the equilibrating process in those markets and the conditions of their equilibrium (ibid., pp. 300–301), but his remarks in the 1900 edition of the *Eléments* about the markets are extremely sketchy. He conceived of two incompatible models of short-term loans. One of them is a written pledges model in which loans are made only in equilibrium. Its brief and incomplete appearance in the *Eléments* was noted in chapter 17. About the other model – which emerges fragmentarily here and there in the monetary lessons and which is not a written pledges model – Walras explained that a series of disequilibrium rates of interest are quoted during the course of the tatonnement of the market (ibid., § 282, p. 319). Since, as has been seen, he also specified that the production and use of circulating physical capital occur in disequilibrium in his monetary model, the loans to finance the production and purchase of that capital must be made when the model is in disequilibrium, and thus must be made in disequilibrium amounts at disequilibrium rates of interest. The consequence of his assuming that the same short-term loans are made simultaneously in two different types of markets is another reason why the last comprehensive model is internally contradictory.

Walras specified very little about his submodel of long-term loans, writing only that "fixed . . . capital [is] *hired out,* not in kind, but *in money,* by means of *credit"* (ibid., § 273, p. 300), that the money is borrowed by entrepreneurs to buy new durable capital goods from their producers, and that each day "a certain fraction of this capital comes due and is paid back by the entrepreneurs-borrowers to the capitalists-lenders" (ibid.). Walras did not assume directly or by implication that the market for long-term loanable funds is one in which savers make written pledges to supply the loans, nor, of course, that entrepreneurs make pledges to borrow them. Walras then considered the equilibrating process for consumers' and businesses' transactions balances and consumers' savings balances, and concomitantly implicitly reconsidered the short-term and long-term loan markets. He treated all those matters together in an undifferentiated way, referring to the locus of the process as "the money market," thus not reserving that term for the market for short-term loans.

Tatonnement for the price of the service of availability of money

Postulating that desired money balances are adjusted by changes in the price of the service of availability of money (ibid., § 278, pp. 310–11), he stated that he was going to take up the "question of arriving at the equality of the quantities supplied and demanded of money by a tatonnement on $p'_{u'}$" (ibid., p. 311).[4] He assumed that the price of the service of availability of money is "cried" (ibid., p. 310). That implies he was thinking of an organized market, because the criers of prices in his various models – the buyers and sellers or their agents – act in that type of market (ch. 4). He did not, however, assume that written pledges are used in the money market, nor does his use of the terminology of "crying the price" imply the use of written pledges, for he used that terminology in the *Eléments* long before thinking of the written pledges procedure (for example, Walras 1877b, p. 229; 1889, p. 212). He asserted that "the price of the service [of availability] of money is established by its being raised or lowered according to whether the desired money balances are greater or smaller than the quantity of money," and that "it is necessary only to continue the general tatonnement to arrive without fail at equilibrium. Now, that is indeed what happens in the [real] money market" (1900; § 278, p. 311).

Redundancy of the price of the service of availability of money

Thus, Walras assumed in several passages that $p_{u'}$ is the only variable in his model on which the levels of desired money balances depend (ibid.), but he was inconsistent on this matter. As has been seen, he elsewhere introduced other equilibrating variables, and also thereby unwittingly emphasized the redundancy of his postulation of a $p_{u'}$. Consumers and businesses in his model also adjust their desired balances of money in reaction to the prices and amounts of goods they want to acquire (ibid., § 275, pp. 304–5), to short- and long-term rates of interest (ibid., § 281, p. 318), and to the rate of net income (ibid., § 282, pp. 318–19).

Walras did not mention a process of changes in rates of interest or desired rates of expenditures and loans in his model with sufficient definiteness to

---

[4] Walras varied between writing this price without a prime ($p_{u'}$) and with one ($p'_{u'}$), the latter indicating an initial disequilibrium value of the price or a new value of it.

permit the assertion that he postulated such a process as an equilibrating mechanism with regard to money balances. By assuming, however, that the sizes of desired money balances are affected by the prices of commodities and by variations in the rate of net income, he implied that consumers spend off excess balances and thereby raise prices, or try to add balances and thereby lower prices, until they want to hold the entire stock of money (ibid., p. 319). That process indicates the occurrence of disequilibrium spending. Moreover, Walras's allegation that his model mimics the equilibrating process in the real money market may lead the reader to reflect that in real economy, the process is one in which disequilibrium transactions occur. Walras was well aware of that, as his many writings on monetary policy attest. If he were to be taken at his word, his remark about the real money market would be interpreted as the assertion that in his model people actually lend and spend money in disequilibrium.

Regardless of what he thought about the real economy, Walras explicitly specified regarding his model, as has been seen, that money is actually spent in disequilibrium to hire inputs in the course of producing circulating capital goods, and that money is spent in disequilibrium in their markets and for their services of availability. He also implied that short-term loans are made to finance the disequilibrium production and disequilibrium purchases of circulating capital goods. Those features of his model imply that its participants attempt to increase or decrease their actual money balances by varying the rates at which they buy goods at disequilibrium prices and by varying the amounts of money they save and lend per time period at disequilibrium rates of interest. If his last comprehensive model were a functioning system that generated such behavior, then equilibrium would be reached, according to Walras, when individuals are content to hold the available stock of money (ibid., § 278, pp. 310–11; § 282, pp. 318–19).

Walras's specification of a price $p_{u'}$ for the service of availability of money does not make sense. It shows in yet another way the deterioration of his analytical abilities in his last phase of theoretical activity. In the real economy, short-term and long-term rates of interest are the prices of borrowing money and the opportunity costs of holding idle money balances. Those rates are therefore also the prices of the service of availability of money held in balances and the prices of whatever other services money balances may provide, and there is no additional market and price $p_{u'}$ for those services. Those rates and the price of money, in the sense of the inverse of the price level, and the related markets were all that Walras's model logically needed on the valuation of money, so $p_{u'}$ is redundant. In the real economy, there are not two markets, for example, for short-term loans, one for money with a price for it and another for the service of availability of money with another price for it. Nor was there any need or logical place for such an additional market and price in Walras's model. In it, the quantities demanded and supplied of loans, and the quantities supplied and demanded of money balances, would have been determinate on the basis of the rates of interest and the purchasing power of money that he identified, if he had also adequately specified the operation of the markets for loans and the spending habits of consumers and businesses. The straightforward and reasonable procedure for him to follow for his type of monetary model would have been to adhere to his mature exposition of the variables and equilibrating mechanism in the market for money and money capital as presented in the second and third editions of the *Eléments* (ch. 11). That was cast in terms of the rate of interest, the supply and demand for loans, and the equalization of the stock of money and the demand for cash balances (1889, p. 381). Walras should have continued to define the equilibrium price of loanable funds and the opportunity cost of holding money in equilibrium as equal to the rate of net income, and he should have defined the day-to-day market prices of loanable funds as simply the rates of interest on loans of short-term and longer-term maturities, as indeed he did in some parts of his confusing exposition of the last comprehensive model (1900, §§ 281–82, pp. 318–19).

V. The last comprehensive model as a whole

Defects of the model

Walras's last comprehensive model includes written pledges markets for labor, land-services, capital-services, retail consumer goods, new durable capital goods, and short-term loans (ch. 17), and it includes markets for circulating capital and money, in which written pledges are not used. There are several observations to be made in evaluation of the structure and behavior of the submodels of written pledges markets. First, pricing cannot take place in them because the participants have no means of expressing demands for commodities or short-term loans (ch. 17). Consequently, the last comprehensive model as a whole cannot converge to an equilibrium set of prices. Second, the markets cannot function because they lack means of intermarket information collection and dissemination. Third, even if the markets were not faulty in the two ways just described, the written pledges could not be fulfilled. The device is fundamentally flawed; it cannot serve in the process of allocating resources and effectuating sales because the pledges are not written in usable amounts. Fourth, to construct the markets, Walras took a giant step away from reality. To assume that written pledges are made in purely competitive markets by landlords, workers, and capitalists to sell productive services and by entrepreneurs to sell consumer goods at retail is a distortion of reality rather than a simplification or an illuminating artifice that captures its essence. Fifth, he took another giant step away from reality by assuming that consumable services are sold by consumers to each other on organized purely competitive exchanges.

As for the submodels in Walras's last comprehensive model in which there are no written pledges, they are deficient in a number of ways. First, the markets and prices for the services of availability of primary materials and nondurable consumer goods are nonsensical. Second, the price posited by Walras for the service of availability of money is redundant. Third, the submodels of markets for circulating capital goods and money are incomplete.

Walras's last comprehensive model is defective for several other major reasons. First, old capital goods and land are present in the model, but it lacks markets for those important commodities. Second, it lacks a securities market. Third, it is inconsistent because it assumes that the same specific items are simultaneously sold in both written pledges markets and in markets in which disequilibrium transactions and disequilibrium production occur. Walras assumed that all consumer goods are produced in written pledges markets and are therefore neither produced in disequilibrium nor sold at disequilibrium prices, but he also assumed that the nondurable goods that enter consumers' inventories – namely, a vast number of consumer goods – are produced in disequilibrium and are sold at disequilibrium prices. He assumed that all productive services are hired in written pledges markets, but also that productive services are hired at disequilibrium prices if they are used to produce primary materials or to produce consumer nondurables that are purchased to replenish inventories. He assumed that there are no disequilibrium incomes or savings when he discussed pledges markets, but also that savings and loans are made at disequilibrium rates of interest. He assumed that written pledges are used to eliminate disequilibrium transactions, but also that consumers and businesses adjust their cash balances to the desired level by making disequilibrium loans and transactions. The resulting composite model is a shambles of contradictory submodels.[5]

Incompatibility of some of the last submodels with the mature submodels

Moreover, early in his career, Walras constructed a monetary model in which oral pledges are used and in which, therefore, no transactions occur at prices

---

[5] A model in which some markets are oral pledges markets and others are disequilibrium transactions markets could be a functioning system if the submodels were properly constructed and do not contradict each other, as is evident from the consideration that the real economy contains both types of markets. Such a model could converge to equilibrium, although the equilibrium values would differ from those of Walras's equations.

at which the market-day demand and supply quantities in any particular market are unequal (chs. 4 and 5), and presented it in the 1900 and 1926 editions of the *Eléments* without remarking on the fact that the model differs from the monetary model of lessons 29 and 30 in those same editions. The oral pledges model of the bond market is unlike the model of long-term loans that makes a fleeting appearance in lessons 29 and 30, for in the latter, disequilibrium loans out of savings are made on any given market day during the adjustment phase that he wanted his model to have. Furthermore, the monetary oral pledges model that deals with goods sold on organized commodity exchanges – notably primary materials – contradicts Walras's monetary submodel of disequilibrium production and disequilibrium sales of them in the last comprehensive model.

As far as I am aware, an unfavorable judgment about the quality of Walras's work on money after his mature phase was made in print by only one other student of his writings – namely Arthur W. Marget. Pointing out that Walras believed (1900, p. IX) that his monetary formulation in the fourth edition of the *Eléments* was superior to his previous efforts, Marget continued with this politely phrased comment:

For myself, however, quite apart from the fact that the successive elaborations have the effect of making Walras' final presentation of the theory of money appear much more complicated than it really is, I must confess to grave doubts as to whether these additional refinements, whatever may be said of them on the score of elegance, do not in fact result in removing still farther from reality the details of Walras' general picture of the mechanism of adjustment of the *"encaisse désirée"* to the "desired" level (Marget 1931, p. 581, n. 29).

Evaluation of the equations

Other scholars, however, have considered the equations ostensibly relating to Walras's last comprehensive model as a difficult puzzle that would teach them the secrets of the real and monetary economic universe, if only they could decipher the message of the cryptic symbols in which his presumed insights are contained. They have concentrated on Walras's equations, erroneously supposing they constitute his model. In actuality, interpretations of equations used in economic studies can be achieved only by finding their meanings in a model in which they have referents, and if there is no such model, the equations are meaningless. We asked at the beginning of the investigation of the last comprehensive model in chapter 17 whether Walras heeded his own injunction to provide the necessary structural and behavioral foundations for his mathematical superstructure. It can now be seen that the answer is that he did not. The mathematical notation and relationships in his equations of general equilibrium do not symbolize phenomena and processes that are in his last comprehensive model, as is evident from the following considerations. The equations present demand functions, but in the submodels of written pledges markets there are no expressions of demand and no demand activities. The equations present equilibrium conditions, but supply cannot equal demand in the written pledges markets of the model.

The solutions to Walras's equations of general equilibrium do not exist in the last comprehensive model nor does any other equilibrium set of values. The equations assume that any particular commodity is priced in only one type of market, but the model contains both disequilibrium transactions and written pledges markets for the same items, so it is not describable by any consistent set of equations. The equations present the holdings of assets as constants during the equilibrating process, but in the model – if it were a functioning system – the holdings would vary as disequilibrium transactions occur. The equations assume that the prices of all commodities and whether or not trade can take place are known to all participants, but in the model there are no institutions, technology, or procedures to generate and disseminate such information. The equations assume that pledges are distributed and fulfilled, but that cannot happen in the model. These problems cannot be identified by studies of Walras's equations. The equations cannot identify the absence of pledges to buy commodities or the problem raised thereby, or the contradictory character of his mixture of submodels, or their incompleteness, or the circumstances that equilibrium does not exist in the monetary model, or that it is neither stable nor unstable because it is not a functioning system.

Irremediable flaws

The last comprehensive model spoiled the *Eléments*. The model is not a functioning system. There is no path of variables in it and it does not have an equilibrium. It is so flawed that it fails to be even a highly abstract analysis of economic behavior. It is inconsistent with the special theories that Walras intended to be realistic treatments of particular aspects of economic behavior, and that the *Eléments* largely depends on for its verisimilitude and explanatory power. It has diverted attention from the important theoretical problems that are posed by disequilibrium production and sales and that were the concern of the mature comprehensive model.

It is evident that the characteristics of the last comprehensive model render it useless in application to real problems or as a guide to how the real economy works. In constructing the model, Walras strayed very far from his ideal, quoted at the beginning of this investigation of his model, of avoiding "that great stumbling block to the application of mathematics to economics – namely, of putting something other than economic reality into the equations" (Walras to Charles E. Wickersheimer, February 11, 1897, in 1965, 2, letter 1297, p. 728).

CHAPTER 19

Conclusion

Walras's great achievement was to develop his mature models of market behavior, in connection with which he constructed or refined many of the building blocks of modern economic theory. He developed a technique of modeling by specifying the parameters, structure and behavior of market models, by designing their equilibrating processes, by identifying their equilibrium conditions, and by studying their comparative static properties. He influenced his contemporaries and he persuaded subsequent generations of economists of the value of the general-equilibrium approach to the study of economics.

I. Contributions to the modeling of markets

When Walras began his investigations in 1868, economics in Europe was hardly a scientific pursuit but rather a mixture of normative prescriptions, classical theories expressed alongside protectionist doctrines, and commercial law. In England, it was in the state exemplified by the work of John Stuart Mill – with much that could be used as a basis for future investigations, but also without a clear view of the relationships of distribution and production, limited by a cost of production theory of value, without consumer demand functions derived from preference functions, and lacking a theory of supply and demand in markets that are related to other markets. The attitude of most of Walras's contemporaries was that since economic behavior involves preferences and the human will, it cannot be modeled, and certainly not described by equations, which were regarded as rigid and deterministic. Walras changed all that, transforming the way that economics was studied on the Continent.

The criticisms made in this book of Walras's barter models of written pledges markets and of his last comprehensive model cannot obscure the greatness of his achievements in his mature comprehensive model, which includes his oral pledges model. His mature models are better than the models of his phase of decline, and are more representative of his thought, inasmuch as he espoused them throughout all but the last year of the long period when he was active as a theoretician. It is a pity that most subsequent general equilibrium theorists constructed versions of the written pledges model and neglected his robust and more realistic mature comprehensive model, for through its development lies the way to a more useful general-equilibrium theory. Walras should have left matters as they were in the second and third editions of the *Eléments,* and thus have given encouragement to efforts to analyze the character and outcomes of the processes of disequilibrium production and sales that are an important feature of economic reality.

Walras's work in his mature phase of the theoretical activity in regard to the modeling of markets can be divided into two interrelated parts. In part one he constructed or refined or adapted to his purposes many of the fundamental building blocks of modern economic theory. It can be seen that in this effort he accomplished an enormous amount of highly creative economic analysis, brilliantly structuring economic reality to bring many of its essential features into clear relief, in nine major original contributions to economic theory. These specific aspects of his work, as distinct from his mature comprehensive model considered as a whole, greatly influenced the development of microeconomic theory. First, he contributed to the development of a theory of demand in which the quantities demanded by the participants in his mature models are functions, in principle, of the prices of all commodities – truly a general-equilibrium approach to the question. Second, he used theoretical concepts and empirical information to construct a vivid and complete model of an organized exchange. Third, he had clear priority in constructing a model of exchange in multiple competitive markets. In that regard, his work was greatly in advance of his predecessors' and was replete with fruitful constructions, theorems and postulates, such as the reciprocal relation of supply and demand, the device of a numeraire, the individual budget equation, Walras's Law, and the laws of change of prices. Fourth, he based his constructions concerning supply on a model of the firm in which he appears to have developed independently the modern idea of a firm's production function, defined a firm's average cost function, expressed the firm's offer of output in functional form, and aggregated the firm's supply functions to obtain the market supply function in a particular industry. Fifth, he was the first to examine the question of the existence of equilibrium in a competitive multimarket system of exchange and production. Sixth, in his work on tatonnement in a disequilibrium production and sales economy, he initiated the study of the problem of the stability of competitive general equilibrium and contributed significantly to its understanding. There is nothing in the literature before Walras's time that is even remotely like his examination of the process of convergence to equilibrium of a competitive multimarket system in which there are disequilibrium production and sales. Seventh, he developed a theory of the entrepreneur, of profits, and of the allocation of resources that became the basis of Continental work on those topics (Pareto, 1896/1897 passim; Pareto 1906/1909, passim; Barone 1896, p. 145; Schumpeter 1911/1926; 1961, p. 76; Schumpeter 1954, p. 893). Eighth, he created a fruitful theory of the market for new capital goods, and achieved an early formulation of the conditions for a Pareto optimum in capital markets. As in a number of his other investigations, his characteristic contribution was not necessarily to be the first to think of the problem of modeling that market but to be the first to structure it thoroughly. Ninth, he developed a detailed model of a loan and money market and of the holding of cash balances that had great originality and has stimulated some valuable research (Marget 1931; Marget 1935; and see Walker 1970, p. 696).

Part two of Walras's contribution was his idea of the general equilibrium of a competitive economic system and his concrete implementation of that idea through working out the interrelationships of its participants and markets. Walras demonstrated that it is possible in principle to describe the functional relationships in a multimarket economy in which complex economic processes occur, thus accomplishing by 1889 far more than any other economist had done in building a model of an economic system as a whole, and more single-handedly than any other economist in the history of the discipline. He thereby provided a substantial beginning for the analysis of the interrelationships of all parts of the economy.

The two parts of Walras's contribution are complementary aspects of a single theoretical whole. Other economists had helped in fashioning the building blocks that he used, but Walras's achievement was not only to develop them but to integrate them into a comprehensive model. To do him complete justice, it is necessary to appreciate the richness of the texture of his work resulting from the many aspects of economic life he analyzed. It is necessary also to appreciate the mathematical structure he devised for the purpose of understanding the interconnections of economic phenomena, despite the defects of that structure stemming from changes in conditions during the equilibrating process of the model.

II. Influence

Walras's work was hardly noticed in France during the twenty-five years after 1874, and as late as 1934 his centennial elicited no conference on his work there. By the 1950s, however, the French attitude toward Walras had changed, as was ultimately symbolized by the creation in 1984 of the Centre Auguste et Léon Walras at the Université Lumière-Lyon 2. With English economists, Walras's experience was also disappointing. His initial cordiality toward William Stanley Jevons, a fellow pioneer in mathematical economics, was dissipated by Jevons's failure to recognize Walras's contributions to the theory of exchange and to the construction of a complete model of a competitive economy. Eventually, Walras, quite unreasonably, came to regard Jevons as a plagiarist of his work (Walras to Maffeo Pantaleoni, August 17, 1889, in 1965, *2*, letter 909, pp. 337–38). Similarly, Walras's relations with Philip H. Wicksteed began well (Wicksteed to Walras, December 1, 1884, in 1965, *2*, letter 619, pp. 16–18) but deteriorated sharply when Wicksteed failed to give credit to those whom Walras considered to be the true originators of the theory of marginal productivity (1965, p. 654, n. 3; 1896b, pp. 490–92). Walras felt neglected by Alfred Marshall, who mentioned him only three times in the briefest of comments in the *Principles of Economics* (Marshall 1890, 1920), and wrote not a word about Walras's development of general-equilibrium models. Walras also came to dislike Francis Edgeworth for criticizing his theories of tatonnement, capital goods, and the entrepreneur (Walras to Charles Gide, November 3, 1889, in 1965, *2*, letter 933, p. 370; Walras to Gide, April 11, 1891, in 1965, *2*, letter 1000, pp. 435–36; Walras to Maffeo Pantaleoni, January 5, 1890, in 1965, *2*, letter 953, pp. 384–386). In general, Walras believed the English had closed their minds to his theories and had become spiteful in their treatment of them (see Walker 1970, pp. 699–70).

The extreme language with which Walras characterized the English was unjustified, because although he had reason for disappointment with their neglect of his general-equilibrium models, Jevons (1879, preface) and Edgeworth (1889a) had recognized valuable elements in his work, and he was the only living economist included in the first edition of R.H. Inglis Palgrave's *Dictionary of Political Economy* (Sanger 1899). The fact is that Walras grew hypersensitive about the motives of his critics, the failure of the majority of economists to recognize the value and priority of his contributions, and the possibility of plagiarism of his ideas during the 1880s and 1890s. There had been two periods in his life, he complained, "one during which I was a madman, and one during which everyone made my discoveries before me" (Walras undated, quoted in Jaffé 1964, p. 93, n. 54).

This account of Walras's disappointments should be balanced by a realization that his scientific labors afforded him, "up to a certain point, pleasures and joys like those that religion provides to the faithful" (Walras to Marie de Sainte Beuve, December 15, 1899, in 1965, *3*, letter 1432, pp. 97–98), and by a recognition of the professional satisfactions that he increasingly experienced in the last two decades of his life. Maffeo Pantaleoni (1889), Enrico Barone (1896), and Vilfredo Pareto (Pareto to Walras, October 15, 1892, in 1965, *2*, letter 1077, p. 508) contributed greatly toward giving Walras's work a secure place in Continental economics, and thus ultimately in economics everywhere. In 1895, Pareto's appointment as Walras's successor to the chair of economics at Lausanne convinced Walras that his doctrines would be perpetuated and developed, and the accessible literary presentations of Walras's ideas in Pareto's books (1896/1897, 1906/1909) began their widespread dissemination.[1] Pareto borrowed most of the ideas of Walras that have been mentioned in this book, using them as the basis for his contributions to the theories of general equilibrium, the monopolistic entrepreneur, capital, and production. Wilhelm Lexis, Ladislaus von Bortkiewicz, and Eugen von Böhm-Bawerk gave Walras's theories serious attention. Knut Wicksell based his theory of price determination squarely on Walras's work (J.G.K. Wicksell to Walras, November 6, 1893, in 1965, 2, letter 1168, p. 596), as did Karl Gustav Cassel (1903, 1918). Walras was given recognition in the United States. In 1892, he was made an honorary member of the American Economic Association, Irving Fisher praised his work (Fisher 1892, p. 45; 1896), and Henry L. Moore became his avowed disciple and explicator (Moore to Walras, May 19, 1909, in 1965, 3, enclosure to letter 1747, p. 413; Moore 1929).

These manifestations of acceptance led Walras to believe he would ultimately triumph, and that enabled him to achieve a mental calmness (Walras to Marie de Sainte Beuve, December 15, 1899, in 1965, 3, letter 1432, pp. 97–98; Walras to Albert Aupetit, May 28, 1901, in 1965, 3, letter 1485, pp. 151–52). "Be assured of my serenity," he wrote to old friends in 1904, "I have not the least doubt about the future of my method and even of my doctrine; but I know that success of this sort does not become clearly apparent until after the death of the author" (Walras to Georges and Louise Renard, June 4, 1904, in 1965, 3, letter 1574, pp. 250–51). A strong indication of what the future would hold for his theories was given by the celebration of his jubilee in 1909 by the University of Lausanne, in the course of which he was honored as the first economist to establish the conditions of general equilibrium, thus founding the School of Lausanne (1965, 3, p. 367; Walker 1996a). His achievements were praised in a statement signed by fifteen leading French scholars, including Charles Gide, Charles Rist, Georges Renard, Alfred Bonnet, Albert Aupetit, and François Simiand (1965, 3, pp. 410–11), and in communications from many others (Moore to Walras, May 19, 1909, in 1965, 3, enclosure to letter 1747, p. 413; Pareto to the Dean of the Faculty of Law of the University of Lausanne, June 6, 1909, in 1965, 3, letter 1755, pp. 420–21; Joseph A. Schumpeter to Walras, June 7, 1909, in 1965, 3, letter 1756, pp. 421–22). It is now clear that his prediction of acceptance of his method of using mathematics to describe economic relationships and of his idea that it is desirable to study general economic equilibrium was accurate (see Weintraub 1983, 1986), and the filiations of many of his special

---

[1] For an account of writers sufficiently influenced by Walras to be considered members of the School of Lausanne, see Walker 1996a.

constructions – as distinct from his mature comprehensive model – have become so numerous and dense as to be an integral and central part of the mainstream of modern economics.

Nevertheless, it is ironic that versions of Walras's last comprehensive model are taken to be his contribution to general-equilibrium analysis. I hope that this book has, on the one hand, shown the inadequacies of that model so extensively and unequivocally that it will no longer occupy attention except as a curiosity, and on the other, that Walras's mature comprehensive model merits being studied. In that latter model, he demonstrated sheer genius and intuitive power in penetrating the veil of the chaos of immediately perceived experience and divining the underlying structure of fundamental economic relationships, their interdependence, and their consequences. Recognition of his true achievement in general-equilibrium modeling is long overdue.

References

Arrow, Kenneth J. 1959. "Towards a Theory of Price Adjustment," in M. Abramovitz, *et al., The Allocation of Economic Resources,* Stanford, 41–51.
— and Frank H. Hahn. 1971. *General Competitive Analysis,* Holden-Day, San Francisco; Oliver & Royd, Edinburgh.
Auspitz, Rudolf and Richard Lieben. 1890. "Correspondance," *Revue d'Economie Politique, 4,* November-December, 599–605.
Barone, Enrico. 1895. "On a Recent Book by Wicksteed," unpublished manuscript, 1895, translated by Donald A. Walker in Jaffé 1983, 182–86.
—. 1896. "Studi sulla distribuzione," *Giornale degli Economisti, 12,* series 2, February, 107–252.
Beaujon, Anthony. 1890. "A propos de la théorie du prix," *Revue d'Economie Politique, 4,* no. 1, January-February, 1–28.
Bertrand, Joseph. 1883a. "Théorie des richesses," *Journal des Savants,* September, 499–508.
—. 1883b. Review of *"Théorie mathématique de la richesse sociale, par Léon Walras professeur d'économie politique à l'académie de Lausanne,* Lausanne, 1883," *Journal des Savants,* September, 504–8.
Bortkiewicz, Ladislaus von. 1890. Review of "Léon Walras. *Eléments d'économie politique pure, ou Théorie de la richesse sociale.* 2ᵉ édition," *Revue d'Economie Politique,* January-February, 4, no. 1, 80–86.
Cassady, R. 1967. *Auctions and Auctioneering,* University of California Press, Berkeley.
Cassel, G. 1903. *Nature and Necessity of Interest,* Macmillan, London.
—. 1918. *Theoretische Socialökonomie,* C.F. Winter, Leipzig; 4th ed. revised, 1927; translated as *Theory of Social Economy,* Harcourt, New York, 1932.
Clark, John Bates. 1899. *The Distribution of Wealth; A Theory of Wages, Interest and Profits,* Macmillan Co., New York; reprint, Kelley and Millman, New York, 1956.
Clower, Robert W. and Axel Leijonhufvud. 1975. "The Coordination of Economic Activities: A Keynesian Perspective," *American Economic Review, 65,* May, 182–88.
Collard, David. 1973. "Léon Walras and the Cambridge Caricature," *Economic Journal, 83,* June, 465–76.
Cournot, A.A. 1838. *Recherches sur les principes mathématiques de la théorie des richesses,* Hachette, Paris.

Edgeworth, Francis Y. 1881. *Mathematical Psychics,* C. Kegan Paul, London; reprint, Augustus M. Kelley, New York, 1961.

—. 1889a. "The Mathematical Theory of Political Economy, *Eléments d'économie Politique Pure.* Par Léon Walras," *Nature, 40,* no. 1036, September 5, 434–36.

—. 1889b. "Points at Which Mathematical Reasoning Is Applicable to Political Economy," address delivered September 12, *Report of the Fifty-ninth Meeting of the British Association for the Advancement of Science Held at Newcastle-upon-Tyne, September,* Murray, London, 1890, 671–96; and in *Nature,* September 19, 1889, *40,* 496–509; and in Edgeworth 1925, *2,* 273–310.

—. 1891. "La Théorie mathématique de l'offre et de la demande et le coût de production," *Revue d'Economie Politique, 5,* no. 1, January, 10–28.

—. 1900. "*The Distribution of Wealth. A Theory of Wages and Interest,* by John Bates Clark," *Economic Journal, 10,* December, 534–37; and in Edgeworth 1925, *3,* 97–101.

—. 1904. "The Theory of Distribution," *Quarterly Journal of Economics, 18,* 159–219; and in Edgeworth 1925, *1,* 13–59.

—. 1907. "Appreciations of Mathematical Theories," *Economic Journal, 17,* June, 221–32; December 1907, 17, 524–31; and in Edgeworth 1925, 2, 321–39.

—. 1909. "On the Use of the Differential Calculus in Economics to Determine Conditions of Maximum Advantage," *Scientia, 7,* 80–103; and in Edgeworth 1925, 2, 367–86.

—. 1911. "Probability," *Encyclopedia Britannica,* 11th ed., *22,* The Encyclopaedia Britannica Co., New York.

—. 1915. "Recent Contributions to Mathematical Economics," *Economic Journal, 25,* March, 36–62; June 1915, 189–203; and in Edgeworth 1925, 2, 451–91.

—. 1925. *Papers Relating to Political Economy,* 3 vols., *3,* Macmillan for the Royal Economic Society, London, 1925; reprint, Burt Franklin, New York, n.d.

Fisher, Franklin M. 1972. "On Price Adjustment without an Auctioneer," *Review of Economic Studies, 39,* 1–15.

Fisher, Irving. 1892. "'Translator's Note' to Léon Walras, Geometrical Theory of the Determination of Prices," *Annals of the American Academy of Political and Social Science, 3,* July, 45–47.

—. 1896. "[Review of] *Eléments d'economie politique pure, Troisième édition. Par Léon Walras,* [and of] *An Essay on the Co-ordination of the Laws of Distribution. By Philip H. Wicksteed...,*" *Yale Review, 5,* no. 1, August, 222–23.

Goodwin, Richard M. 1950. "Static and Dynamic Linear General Equilibrium Models," in *Input-Output Relations; Proceedings of a Conference on InterIndustrial Relations, Held at Driebergen, Holland,* edited by the Netherlands Economic Institute, Leyden, 1953.

—. 1951. "Iteration, Automatic Computers and Economic Dynamics," *Metroeconomica, 3,* 1–7.

Hahn, Frank H. 1987. "Auctioneer," in Eatwell et al. 1987 [see Walker 1987c], *1,* 136–38.

Hicks, J.R. 1934. "Léon Walras," *Econometrica, 2,* October, 338–48.

—. 1946. *Value and Capital,* 2d ed., Oxford University Press, Oxford.

—. 1976. "Some Questions of Time in Economics," in Anthony M. Tang, Fred M. Westfield, and James S. Worley, eds., *Evolution, Welfare, and Time in Economics*; *Essays in Honor of Nicholas Georgescu-Roegen*, D.C. Heath, Lexington, Mass. and Toronto, 135–51.

Hildenbrand, W. and A.P. Kirman. 1988. *Equilibrium Analysis; Variations on Themes by Edgworth and Walras*, North-Holland, Amsterdam.

Isnard, A.N. 1781. *Traité des richesses, contenant l'usage des richesses en général et de leurs valeurs*, Grasset, London and Lausanne.

Jaffé, William. 1935. "Unpublished Papers and Letters of Léon Walras," *Journal of Political Economy, 43*, April, 187–207; and in Jaffé 1983, along with Jaffé's other essays on Walras listed in this bibliography.

—. 1942. "Léon Walras' Theory of Capital Accumulation," in *Studies in Mathematical Economics and Econometrics*, edited by Oskar Lange et al., University of Chicago Press, Chicago, 37–48.

—. 1953. "La théorie de la capitalisation chez Walras dans le cadre de sa théorie de l'équilibre général," *Economie appliquée, 6*, 289–317.

—. 1956. "Léon Walras et sa conception de l'économie politique," *Annales Juridiques, Politiques, Economiques et Sociales*, Faculté de Droit d'Alger, 207–21; translated by Donald A. Walker in Jaffé 1983.

—. 1964. "New Light on an Old Quarrel: Barone's Unpublished Review of Wicksteed's 'Essay on the Coordination of the Laws of Distribution' and Related Documents," *Cahiers Vilfredo Pareto, 3*, 61–102.

—. 1965. "Biography and Economic Analysis," *Western Economic Journal, 3*, Summer, 223–32.

—. 1967. "Walras's Theory of *Tâtonnement*: A Critique of Recent Interpretations," *Journal of Political Economy, 75*, February, 1–19.

—. 1968. "Léon Walras," in *International Encyclopedia of the Social Sciences, 16*, edited by David L. Sills, Macmillan and Free Press, New York; partially reprinted in Jaffé 1983.

—. 1969. "A.N. Isnard, Progenitor of the Walrasian General Equilibrium Model," *History of Political Economy, 1*, Spring, 19–43.

—. 1971. "Reflections on the Importance of Léon Walras," in the P. Hennipman festschrift *Schaarste en Welvaart*, edited by A. Heertje et al., Stenfert Kroese, Amsterdam, 87–107.

—. 1972. "Léon Walras's Role in the 'Marginal Revolution' of the 1870s," *History of Political Economy, 4*, Fall, 379–405.

—. 1974. "Biography, a Genetic Ingredient of Economic Analysis: Answer to a Challenge," paper delivered at the Allied Social Science Associations meetings under the joint auspices of the American Economic Association and the History of Economic Society, San Francisco, December 30, mimeographed, 29 pp.

—. 1975. "Léon Walras, an Economic Advisor *Manqué*," *Economic Journal, 85*, December, 810–23.

—. 1977a. "A Centenarian on a Bicentenarian: Léon Walras's *Eléments* on Adam Smith's *Wealth of Nations*," *Canadian Journal of Economics, 10*, February, 19–33.

430 References

—. 1977b. "The Walras-Poincaré Correspondence on the Cardinal Measurability of Utility," *Canadian Journal of Economics, 10,* May, 300–307.

—. 1977c. "The Birth of Léon Walras's *Eléments*," *History of Political Economy, 9,* Summer, 198–214.

—. 1977d. "The Normative Bias of the Walrasian Model: Walras Versus Gossen," *Quarterly Journal of Economics, 91,* August, 371–87.

—. 1978. Review of *"Walras's Economics: A Pure Theory of Capital and Money,* by Michio Morishima," *Economic Journal, 88,* September, 574–617.

—. 1979. "Academy of Humanities and Social Sciences. Requested self-presentation as newly inducted Fellow of the Royal Society of Canada," in Royal Society of Canada, *Newsletter, 2,* September, 14–15.

—. 1980. "Walras's Economics as Others See It," *Journal of Economic Literature, 18,* June, 528–49.

—. 1981. "Another Look at Léon Walras's Theory of *Tâtonnement*," *History of Political Economy, 13,* Summer, 1981, 313–36.

—. 1983. *William Jaffé's Essays on Walras,* edited by Donald A. Walker, Cambridge University Press, Cambridge.

—. 1984. "The Antecedents and Early Life of Léon Walras," a posthumous publication of William Jaffé's, edited, completed, and in large part translated by Donald A. Walker, *History of Political Economy, 16,* no. 1, Spring, 1–57.

Jevons, William Stanley. 1878. *Primer of Political Economy,* Macmillan, London.

—. 1879. *The Theory of Political Economy,* 2d ed., Macmillan, London.

—. 1957. *The Theory of Political Economy,* 5th ed, Kelley and Millman, New York.

Keynes, John Maynard. 1930. *A Treatise on Money, 1, The Pure Theory of Money,* Macmillan, London.

—. 1934. Letter to J.R. Hicks, December 9, in Hicks 1976.

Kirman, A.P. 1992. "Whom or What Does the Representative Individual Represent?" *Journal of Economic Perspectives, 6,* no. 2, Spring, 117–36.

Kirzner, Israel M. 1979. *Perception, Opportunity and Profit,* University of Chicago Press, Chicago.

Knight, Frank H. 1921. *Risk, Uncertainty and Profit;* reprint, Augustus M. Kelley, New York, 1964.

Kompas, Tom. 1992. *Studies in the History of Long-Run Equilibrium Theory,* Manchester University Press, Manchester and New York.

Kuenne, Robert. 1954. "Walras, Leontief, and the Interdependence of Economic Activities," *Quarterly Journal of Economics, 68,* no. 3, August, 323–54.

—. 1961. "The Walrasian Theory of Money: An Interpretation and a Reconstruction," *Metroeconomica, 13,* August, 94–105.

Lange, Oscar. 1944. *Price Flexibility and Employment,* Principia, Bloomington.

Marget, Arthur W. 1931. "Léon Walras and the 'Cash-Balance Approach' to the Problem of the Value of Money," *Journal of Political Economy, 39,* no. 5, October, 569–600.

—. 1935. "The Monetary Aspects of the Walrasian System," *Journal of Political Economy, 43,* April, 145–86.

Marshall, Alfred. 1879. *The Pure Theory of Foreign Trade, The Pure Theory of*

Domestic Values; reprint, London School of Economics and Political Science, London, 1930.

—. 1890. *Principles of Economics,* Macmillan and Co., London and New York.

—. 1920. *Principles of Economics,* 8th ed., Macmillan Company, New York.

Mester, Lorretta J. 1988. "Going Going Gone: Setting Prices with Auctions," *Business Review,* Federal Reserve Bank of Philadelphia, March/April, 3–13.

Moore, Henry L. 1929. *Synthetic Economics,* Macmillan, New York.

Morishima, Michio. 1977. *Walras' Economics; A Pure Theory of Capital and Money,* Cambridge University Press, Cambridge, London, New York, Melbourne.

—. 1980. "W. Jaffé on Léon Walras: A Comment," *Journal of Economic Literature, 18,* June, 550–58.

Newman, Peter. 1965. *The Theory of Exchange,* Prentice-Hall, Englewood Cliffs, New Jersey.

Ostroy, J.M. 1973. "On the Informational Efficiency of Monetary Exchange," *American Economic Review, 63,* no. 4, September, 597–610.

— and R.M. Starr. 1974. "Money and the Decentralization of Exchange," *Econometrica, 42,* no. 6, November, 1093–1113.

Pantaleoni, Maffeo. 1889. *Principii de economia pura,* Barbèra, Florence.

Pareto, Vilfredo. 1896/1897. *Cours d'économie politique,* F. Rouge, Lausanne; reprint edited by G.H. Bousquet and G. Busino, Librairie Droz, Geneva, 1964.

—. 1906. *Manuale di economia politica,* Società Editrice Libraria, Milan.

—. 1909. *Manuel d'économie politique,* translated from the Italian edition of 1906 by Alfred Bonnet, 2 vols., V. Giard and E. Brière, Paris.

Patinkin, Don. 1956. *Money, Interest, and Prices: An Integration of Monetary and Value Theory,* Row, Peterson, Evanston, Ill.; 2d ed., Harper and Row, New York, 1965.

Piggott, John and John Walley. 1985. *New Developments in Applied General Equilibrium Analysis,* Cambridge University Press, New York.

Poinsot, L. 1803. *Eléments de statique*; 8th ed., Bachelier, Paris, 1842.

Saari, Donald G. 1985. "Iterative Price Mechanisms," *Econometrica, 53,* 1117–31.

Sanger, C. 1899. "Walras, Marie Esprit Léon," in *Dictionary of Political Economy, 3,* edited by R.H. Inglis Palgrave, Macmillan, London.

Say, Jean-Baptiste. 1836. *Cours complet d'économie politique pratique, suivi des Mélanges, Correspondance et Catéchisme d'économie politique,* 3d ed., H. Dumont, Bruxelles.

Schumpeter, Joseph A. 1910. "Marie Esprit Léon Walras," *Zeitschrift für Volkswirtschaft, Sozialpolitik und Verwaltung, 19,* 397–402; and in Schumpeter 1965, 74–79.

—. 1911/1926. *The Theory of Economic Development; An Inquiry into Profits, Capital, Credit, Interest, and the Business Cycle,* translated by Redvers Opie, Oxford University Press, New York, 1961.

—. 1954. *History of Economic Analysis,* Oxford University Press, New York.

—. 1965. *Ten Great Economists, from Marx to Keynes,* Oxford University Press, New York.

Smith, Vernon. 1987. "Auctions," in Eatwell *et al.* 1987, *1,* 138–44.

— and W. Williams Arlington. 1981. "The Boundaries of Competitive Price Theory: Convergence, Expectations and Transactions Cost," Public Choice Society, Meetings, New Orleans, March 13–15, typescript, 32 pp.

—, W. Williams Arlington, Kenneth W. Bratton, and Michael G. Vannoni. 1982. "Competitive Market Institutions: Double Auction vs. Scaled Bid-Offer Auctions," *American Economic Review, 72,* March, 58–77.

Spray, David E., ed. 1964. *The Principal Stock Exchanges of the World; Their Operation, Structure and Development,* International Economic Publishers, Washington, D.C.

Van Daal, Jan. 1995. "Léon Walras's General Economic Equilibrium Models of Capital Formation: Existence of a Solution," delivered at the History of Economics Society meeting at South Bend, June 3, 1995, 22 pp.

Van Daal, and Albert Jolinck. 1993. *The Equilibrium Economics of Léon Walras,* Routledge, London, New York.

Van Daal, Jan and Donald A. Walker. 1990. "The Problem of Aggregation in Walrasian Economic Theory," *History of Political Economy, 22,* no. 3, Fall, 489–505.

Walker, Donald A. 1970. "Léon Walras in the Light of His Correspondence and Related Papers," *Journal of Political Economy, 78,* July-August, 685–701.

—. 1972. "Competitive Theories of Tatonnement," *Kyklos, 25,* 345–63.

—. 1981a. "William Jaffé, 1898–1980," *History of Economics Society Bulletin, 2,* no. 2, Winter, 25–27.

—. 1981b. "William Jaffé, Historian of Economic Thought, 1898–1980," *American Economic Review, 71,* no. 5, December, 1012–19.

—. 1983. "William Jaffé, *Officier de liaison intellectuel,*" in *The Craft of the Historian of Economic Thought,* vol. 1 of *Research in the History of Economic Thought and Methodology,* edited by Warren J. Samuels, JAI Press, Greenwich, 19–39.

—. 1987a. "Walras's Theories of Tatonnement," *Journal of Political Economy, 95,* no. 4, 758–74.

—. 1987b. "Bibliography of the Writings of Léon Walras," *History of Political Economy, 19,* no. 4, 667–702.

—. 1987c. "Léon Walras," in John Eatwell, Murray Milgate, and Peter Newman, eds. *The New Palgrave; A Dictionary of Economics, 4,* Macmillan, London and Basingstoke; Stockton, New York; Maruzen, Tokyo, 852–63.

—. 1991. "[Review of] The Invisible Hand: Economic Equilibrium in the History of Science, by Bruna Ingrao and Giorgio Israel," 1990, *History of Political Economy, 23,* no. 3, Fall, 560–65.

—. 1995a. "[Review of] Auguste et Léon Walras, *Œuvres économiques complètes,*" edited by the members of the Centre Auguste et Léon Walras, *European Journal of the History of Economic Thought, 2,* no. 1, 255–64.

—. 1995b. "The Economic Methodology of Léon Walras," in *The Handbook of Economic Methodology,* edited by John B. Davis, D. Wade Hands, and Uskali Maki, Edward Elgar Publishing, Aldershot.

—. 1996a. "The School of Lausanne," in *Encyclopedia of Keynesian Economics,* edited by Thomas Cate, David Colander, and Geoffrey Harcourt, Edward Elgar Publishing, Aldershot.

—. 1997. *New Directions in General Equilibrium Theorizing,* Edward Elgar Publishing, Aldershot.

Walker, Francis A. 1887. "The Source of Business Profits," *Quarterly Journal of Economics, 1,* April, 265–88.

Walras, Auguste. 1912. Letter to Léon Walras, October 29, 1859, in "Lettres Inédites de et à Léon Walras," in *La Révolution de 1848, 9,* September-October, 298–303.

—. 1990. *Richesse, liberté et société,* edited by Pierre-Henri Goutte and Jean-Michel Servet under the auspices of the Centre Auguste et Léon Walras, in Auguste and Léon Walras, *Œuvres économiques complètes, 1,* Economica, Paris.

Walras, Léon. 1858. *Francis Sauveur,* E. Dentu, Paris.

—. 1860a. "Application des mathématiques à l'économie politique (1ère tentative, 1860)," autograph manuscript, Fonds Walras V 5, 8 p.; summarized in Walras 1965, *1,* 216–17; published in Walras 1993, 329–39.

—. 1860b. *L'Economie politique et la justice; Examen critique et réfutation des doctrines économiques de M.P.-J Proudhon, précédes d'une Introduction à l'étude de la question sociale,* Guillaumin et Cie, Paris.

—. 1860c. "La Bourse et le développement du capital," *La Presse,* December 25 and 26; and in Walras 1987, 111–20.

—. 1861. *Théorie critique de l'impôt, précédée de souvenirs du Congrès de Lausanne,* Guillaumin et Cie, Paris.

—. 1867. "La Bourse et le credit," *Paris guide, par les principaux écrivains et artistes de la France,* deuxième partie, Librairie Internationale, Paris; A. Lacroix, Verboeckhoven et Cie, Bruxelles, Leipzig, et Livourne, 1731–51; and in Walras 1987, 180–200.

—. 1868. *Recherche de l'idéal sociale, Leçons publiques faites à Paris. Première série, 1867–1868, Théorie générale de la société,* Guillaumin et Cie, Paris; and in Walras 1896c, 25–171.

—. 1869–1870. "Application des mathématiques à l'économie politique (2e tentative 1869–1870)," autograph manuscript, Fonds Walras V 5, 47 p.; summarized in Walras 1965, *1,* 216–17; published in Walras 1993, 341–59.

—. 1871. "Discours d'installation en qualité de Professeur ordinaire d'économie politique à l'Académie de Lausanne prononcé dans la séance académique du 20 octobre 1871," *Séances académiques du 23 octobre 1869, du 31 octobre 1870 et du 20 octobre 1871, Discours d'installation,* Imprimerie Siméon Genton, Lausanne, 1872, 69–93.

—. 1874a. *"Principe d'une théorie mathematique de l'echange,"* delivered to the Académie des sciences morales et politiques, meetings of August 16 and 23, 1873, *Séances et travaux de l'Académie des sciences morales et politiques* (Institut de France), *Collection,* new series, 33d year, 101, tome *I,* Paris, Alphonse Picard, January, 97–116; offprint, Imprimerie Ernest Colas, Orléans, 5–24.

—. 1874b. *Eléments d'économie politique pure ou Théorie de la richesse sociale,* 1st part, 1st ed., L. Corbaz, Lausanne; Guillaumin, Paris; H. Georg, Bâle.

—. 1874c. Letter to A.A. Cournot, March 20, in Jaffé 1965, *1,* letter 253, 363–67.

—. 1875. "L'Etat et les chemins de fer," written in 1875, published in *Revue du droit public et de la science politique, 7,* no. 3, May-June, 1897, 417–36; *8,* no. 1, July-August, 1897, 42–58; and in Walras 1898b, 193–232.

—. 1876a. "Equations de l'échange," delivered to the Société vaudoise de sciences naturelles, Lausanne, December 1 and 15, 1875, *Bulletin de la Société Vaudoise des Sciences Naturelles*, 2d série, *14*, no. 76, October, 367–94; and in Walras 1877c; and in Walras 1883, 33–53.

—. 1876b. "Equations de la production," delivered to the Société vaudoise des sciences naturelles, Lausanne, January 19 and February 16, 1876, *Bulletin de la Société Vaudoise des Sciences Naturelles*, *14*, no. 76, October, 395–430.

—. 1877a. "Observation," *Bulletin de la Société Vaudoise des Sciences Naturelles*, March, *14*, 562–64; and in slightly modified form in Walras 1877b, 364–66; and in original form in Walras 1883, 113–15.

—. 1877b. *Eléments d'économie politique pure ou Théorie de la richesse sociale*, 1st ed., 2d part, Imprimerie L. Corbaz, Lausanne; Guillaumin, Paris; H. Georg, Bâle.

—. 1877c. *Théorie mathématique de la richesse sociale. Quatre mémoires lus à l'Académie des sciences morales et politiques, à Paris, et à la Société vaudoise des sciences naturelles, à Lausanne*, Guillaumin, Paris; and in Walras 1883, 33–118.

—. 1879a. "Note préparée pour l'entrevue avec Ferry," in Walras 1965, *1*, 626–29.

—. 1879b. "De la culture et de l'enseignement des sciences morales et politiques," *Bibliothèque Universelle et Revue Suisse*, 84th year, 3d period, *3*, no. 7, July, 5–32; *3*, no. 9, August, 223–51.

—. 1880a. "Théorie mathématique du billet de banque," delivered to the Société Vaudoise des Sciences Naturelles, November 19, 1879, in *Bulletin de la Société Vaudoise des Sciences Naturelles*, 2d série, *16*, no. 80, May, 553–92; and in Walras 1898b, 339–75.

—. 1880b. "La bourse, la spéculation et l'agiotage," *Bibliothèque Universelle et Revue Suisse*, 85th year, 3d period, *5*, March, 452–76; and in Walras 1898b, 401–21.

—. 1880c. "La bourse, la spéculation et l'agiotage," *Bibliothèque Universelle et Revue Suisse*, 85th year, 3d period, *6*, April, 66–94; and in Walras 1898b, 422–45.

—. 1883. *Théorie mathématique de la richesse sociale*, Imprimerie Corbaz, Lausanne; Gillaumin, Paris; Ermanno Loescher, Rome; Duncker & Humblot, Leipzig.

—. 1885. "Un Economiste Inconnu: Hermann-Henri Gossen," *Journal des Economistes*, 4th series, *30*, April-May, 68–90; and in Walras 1896c, 351–74.

—. 1886. *Théorie de la monnaie*, Imprimerie Corbaz, Lausanne; L. Larose & Forcel, Paris; Loescher, Rome; Duncker & Humblot, Leipzig.

—. 1889. *Eléments d'économie politique pure ou Théorie de la richesse sociale*, 2d ed, F. Rouge, Lausanne; Guillaumin, Paris; Duncker & Humblot, Leipzig.

—. 1891a. "De l'échange de plusieurs marchandises entre elles," delivered to the Société des Ingénieurs Civils, Paris, October 17, in *Mémoires et Compte Rendu des Travaux de la Société des Ingénieurs Civils*, 5th series, *44*, January, 1891, 42–49; and in Walras 1896, 463–71; Walras 1926, 465–73.

—. 1891b. Note on entrepreneurs producing equal quantities of products, untitled, undated, probably 1891, in Walras 1965, *2*, 467.

—. 1892a. "Théorie géométrique de la détermination des prix. De l'échange de produits et services entre eux. De l'échange d'épargnes contre capitaux neufs," *Recueil Inaugural de l'Université de Lausanne, Travaux des Facultés*, Imprimerie Ch. Viret-Genton, Lausanne, 169–76.

—. 1892b. "Geometrical Theory of the Determination of Prices," *Annals of the American Academy of Political and Social Science, 3,* 47–65.

—. 1894a. "Le Problème Monétaire," *Gazette de Lausanne,* February 27.

—. 1894b. "La Monnaie de Papier," *Gazette de Lausanne,* December 3.

—. 1894c. Note on Vilfredo Pareto's work prepared for his installation as professor at the University of Lausanne, in Walras 1965, *2,* 624–25.

—. 1895. Enclosure to letter from Léon Walras to Vilfredo Pareto, January 9, in Walras 1965, *2,* 628–32.

—. 1896a. "Théorie de la Propriété," *Revue Socialiste, 23,* no. 138, June, 668–81; and *24,* no. 139, July, 23–25; and in Walras 1896c, 205–39.

—. 1896b. *Eléments d'économie politique pure ou Théorie de la richesse sociale,* 3d ed., F. Rouge, Lausanne; F. Pichon, Paris; Duncker & Humblot, Leipzig.

—. 1896c. *Etudes d'économie sociale (Théorie de la répartition de la richesse sociale),* F. Rouge, Lausanne; F. Pichon, Paris.

—. 1898a. "Esquisse d'une doctrine économique et sociale," *L'Association Catholique,* December 15; and in Walras 1898b, 449–95.

—. 1898b. *Etudes d'économie politique appliquée (Théorie de la production de la richesse social),* F. Rouge, Lausanne; F. Pichon, Paris.

—. 1899. "Equations de la circulation," Bulletin de la Société Vaudoise des Sciences Naturelles, *35,* no. 132, June, 85–103.

—. 1900. *Eléments d'économie politique pure ou Théorie de la richesse sociale,* 4th ed., F. Rouge, Lausanne; F. Pichon, Paris.

—. 1901. Notes for a letter to Albert Aupetit, in Walras 1965, *3,* 158.

—. 1926. *Eléments d'économie politique pure ou Théorie de la richesse sociale,* 5th ed., R. Pichon et R. Durand-Auzias, Paris; F. Rouge, Lausanne.

—. 1954. *Elements of Pure Economics,* translated by William Jaffé from the 5th ed., Irwin, Homewood, Ill.

—. 1965. *Correspondence of Léon Walras and Related Papers,* 3 vols., edited by William Jaffé, North-Holland, Amsterdam.

—. 1987. *Mélanges d'économie politique et sociale,* edited by Claude Hébert and Jean-Pierre Potier under the auspices of the Centre Auguste et Léon Walras, in Auguste and Léon Walras, *Œuvres économiques complètes, 7,* Economica, Paris.

—. 1988. Eléments d'économie politique pure ou Théorie de la richesse sociale, comparative edition, prepared by Claude Mouchot under the auspices of the Centre Auguste et Léon Walras, in Auguste and Léon Walras, *Œuvres économiques complètes, 8,* Economica, Paris.

—. 1993. *Théorie mathématique de la richesse sociale et autres écrits d'économie pure,* edited by Claude Mouchot under the auspices of the Centre Auguste et Léon Walras, in Auguste and Léon Walras, *Œuvres économiques complètes, 11,* Economica, Paris.

Weintraub, E.R. 1983. "On the Existence of a Competitive Equilibrium: 1930–1954, *Journal of the History of Economic Literature, 21(1),* March, 1–39.

Collation of editions of the *Eléments*

This table, which is adapted from William Jaffé's translation of the fifth edition of the *Eléments* (1954, pp. 559–63), enables the reader to find where any section appears in the various editions of the *Eléments*. Italicized section numbers indicate that the parallelism with corresponding sections of the previous edition is found only in the general character of the subject matter. Section numbers in parentheses indicate partial or overlapping parallelism. The sections are found in the lessons enumerated immediately to the right of the first section or group of sections in that lesson. For example, in the fourth and fifth editions, sections 1–5 and 6–9 are in lesson 1.

436

Ed. 4 (1900)[1] and Ed. 5 (1926)		Ed. 2 (1889) and Ed. 3 (1896)[2]		Ed. 1 (1874, 1877)	
Part I[3] §§	Lesson	*Part I*[3] §§	Lesson	*Part I*[3] §§	Lesson
1–5	1	1–5	1	1–5	1
6–9		6–9		6–9	2
10–15	2	10–15	2	10–15	3
16–20		16–20		16–20	4
21–26	3	21–26	3	21–26	5
27–30		27–30		27–30	6
31–34	4	31–34	4	31–34	7
35–39		35–39		35–39	8
Part II		*Part II*[4]		*Part II*[4]	
40–43	5	40–43	5	40–43	9
44–48		44–48		44–48	10
49–55	6	49–55	6	49–55	11
56–61		56–61		56–61	12
62–70	7	62–70	7	62–70	13
71–75	8	71–75	8	71–75	14
76–81		76–81		76–81	15
82		(81)		—	
83–84		82–83		—	
85–91	9	84–90	9	82–88	16
92–98		91–97		89–95	17
99–103	10	98–102	10	96–100	18

Ed. 4 and Ed. 5		Ed. 2 and Ed. 3		Ed. 1	
Part III		—		—	
104–110		103–109		101–107	19
111–114	11	110–113	11	*108–114*	20
115		114		123	21
116		115		—	
117	12	116	12	*116*	
118		117		*117–118, 121*	
119–120		118–119		*119–120*	
121		120		—	
122		—		—	
123		121		122	
124–130	13	122–128	13	124–131	22
131		129		132	23
132		130		115	20
133		131		133	23
134–135		132–133		—	
136–138		134–136		134–136	24
139–144	14	137–142	14	137–142	25
145–150		143–148		143–148	26
151	15	149	15	149–150	
152–154		150–152		151–153	
155		153			
156		154		154	
157–161	16	155–159	16	155–159	27
—		—		160–165	28[5]
162–164		160		—	

Part IV		*Part III*		*Part IV*[6]	
165–169	17	161–165	17	208–212	35
170–177		166–173		213–220	36
178–181	18	174–177	18	221–224	37
182–188		178–184		225–231	38
189–194	19	185–190	19	232–237	39
195–199		191–195		238–242	40
200–206	20	196–202	20	243–249	41
207		203		—	
208		204		250	42
209		205		251–252	
210–212	21	206–208	21	253	
213		209		254	
214–218		210–214		255–259	43
219		215		260–261	
220		216		262	
221–224	22	217–220	22	263–266	44
225–226		221–222		—	
227		223		267	
—		—		*(from Part VI)*	
228–230	23	224–226	23	(353)–355	59
Part V		*Part IV*		*Part V*[7]	
231–235		227–231		268–272	45
236–241		232–237		273–278	46
242–243		238–239		279–280	

Ed. 4 and Ed. 5		Ed. 2 and Ed. 3		Ed. 1	
24	244–245	24	241–242	47	282–283
	246		240		281
	247–250		243–246		284–287
	251		247		—
25	252	25	248	48	288
	253–255		249–251		—
	256		252		289–290
	257		(253)		(291)
	258		(253)–254		(291)
	259		255		—
	—		—	49	292
	260		256		293
26	261–262	26	257–258		—
27	263	27	259		—
	264		260	50	298
	—		261		—
28	265–267		—		—
	268–271		262–265	49	294–297
Part VI[6]		*Part V*[8]		*Part III*[8]	
29	272–277	33	319–323	30	172–178
30	278–282		324–325		—
	283	34	326–331		—
31	284–289	35	332–339		
32	290–297				

Ed. 4 and Ed. 5		Ed. 3		Ed. 2		Ed.1	
§§	Lesson	§§	Lesson	§§	Lesson	§§	Lesson
298–302	33	340–344	36	340–344	36	192–196	33
303		—		—		—	
304		345		345		*197*	
305		—		—		—	
306–311	34	346–351		346–351		198–203	34
312		352		—		—	
313–316		353–356		352–355	37	204–207	29
—		—		356–358		166–168	
—		—		359		170	
—		—		360		169	
—		—		—		171	
—		—		361–362		—	31
—		—		363–365		179–181	
—		—		366		182–183	
—		—		367		184	
—		—		—		185	32
—		—		368	38	186	
—		—		369–371		*187–189*	
—		—		372–374		—	
—		—		375–376		*190–191*	
—		—		377–379		—	

Ed. 4 and Ed. 5 Part VII		Ed. 2 and Ed. 3 (Part IV resumed)		Ed. 1 (Part V resumed)	
§§	Lesson	§§	Lesson	§§	Lesson
317–322	35	266–271	27	299–304	50
323–325	36	272–274	28	305–307	51
326		—		—	
327		(274)–275		(307)–308	
328–329		276–277		309–310	
330–335		278–283	29	311–316	52
336–341	37	284–289	30	317–322	53
342–349	38	290–297	31	323–330	54
350–355	39	298–303		331–336	55
356–362		304–310		337–343	56
363–365	40	311–313	32	334–346	57
366–370		314–318		347–351	58

Ed. 4. and Ed. 5 Part VIII		Ed. 3 Part VI		Ed. 2 Part VI	Ed. 1 Part VI(9)	
§§	Lesson	§§	Lesson	§§	§§	Lesson
371	41	357	37	403	352	59
372		358		404	(352)–(353)	
373–375		359–361		405–407	356–358	60
376–381		362–367		408–413	359–364	61
382–387		368–373		414–419	365–370	
388–393	42	374–379	38	420–425	371–376	62
394		380		426	377	63

	395	42	—	381–383	38	427–429	42	378–380	63
	396–398			—		—		—	
	399			384–385		430–431		381–382	64
	400–401			—		—		—	
	402–404			386–387		432–433		383–384	
	405–406			—		—		—	
	407			388		434		385	
	408			—		—		—	
Appendix I	1–14			1–14		—		—	
Appendix II	1–7			1–7		—		—	
Appendix III	—			1–5		—		—	

(1) The order of the parts, lessons, and sections is exactly the same throughout the fourth and the fifth editions.

(2) Where the order of the parts, lessons, and sections of editions 2 and 3 is the same, the numbers have been combined in a single column. Between the author's "Preface" and the text, the second and third editions contain a mathematical prelude (1889, 1896, pp. 3–21), titled "Des fonctions et de leur représentation géométrique. Théorie mathématique de la chute des corps." This was omitted from subsequent editions.

(3) "Section" in the original is translated as "part" in order to avoid confusion with the numbered subdivisions of the lessons, here called "sections." The title page of Part I of the first three editions is headed "Théorie de la richesse sociale."

(4) In edition 1, the title of Part II reads "Théorie mathématique de l'échange," changed in edition 2 to read "Théorie de l'échange," and finally changed to "Théorie de l'échange de deux merchandises entre elles" in edition 4.

(5) The 28th lesson of edition 1, entitled "Examen critique de la doctrine de M. Cournot sur les changements de valeur, absolus et relatifs," was omitted from all subsequent editions.

(6) In edition 1, the title of Part IV reads "Théorie naturelle de la production et de la consommation de la richesse," changed in edition 2 and subsequent editions for the corresponding part.

(7) In edition 1, the title of Part V reads "Conditions et conséquences du progrès économique," changed in edition 2 (where the corresponding lessons form Part IV) to read "Théorie de la capitalisation et du crédit." In edition 4 and edition 5, the latter title applies to Part V, which comprises only those lessons that correspond to the lessons 45–49 of edition 1 (lessons 23–28 of edition 2). The lessons corresponding to the remainder of Part V of edition 1 were shifted to Part VII in edition 4.

(8) In edition 1, the title of Part III reads "Du numéraire et de la monnaie," changed in edition 2 to read "Théorie de la monnaie" and in edition 4 to read "Théorie de la circulation et de la monnaie" as the title of the corresponding part.

(9) In edition 1, the title of Part VI reads "Effets naturels et nécessaires des divers modes d'organisation de la société." That was changed to "Des tarifs, du monopole et des impôts" in edition 2.

Index